The Participatory Turn

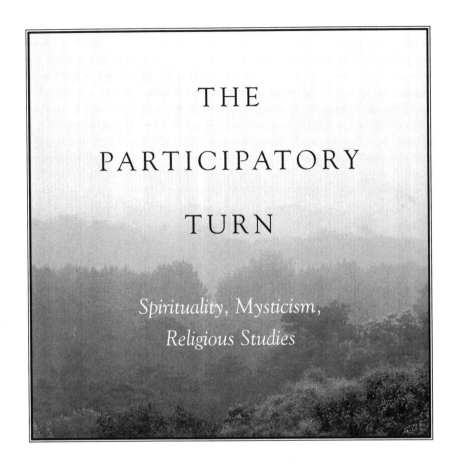

THE

PARTICIPATORY

TURN

*Spirituality, Mysticism,
Religious Studies*

Edited by

JORGE N. FERRER

and

JACOB H. SHERMAN

STATE UNIVERSITY OF NEW YORK PRESS

Cover Photo: Rebecca Searl, *Kiyomizu Temple*, 2007

Published by
STATE UNIVERSITY OF NEW YORK PRESS, ALBANY

© 2008 State University of New York

For information, contact State University of New York Press, Albany, NY
www.sunypress.edu

Production and book design, Laurie Searl
Marketing, Anne M. Valentine

Library of Congress Cataloging-in-Publication Data

The participatory turn : spirituality, mysticism, religious studies / edited by Jorge N. Ferrer and
Jacob H. Sherman.
    p. cm.
  Includes bibliographical references and index.
  ISBN 978-0-7914-7601-7 (hardcover : alk. paper)
  ISBN 978-0-7914-7602-4 (pbk. : alk. paper)
1. Participation. 2. Spirituality. 3. Mysticism. 4. Religion. I. Ferrer, Jorge N. (Jorge Noguera),
1968– II. Sherman, Jacob H.

B105.P35P37 2008
204—dc22

2007052941

10   9   8   7   6   5   4   3   2   1

Contents

Acknowledgments

This volume has been many years in the making and the editors have relied throughout on the generous support of friends and colleagues both near and afar. We are very grateful to our nine contributors for their unflagging patience, enthusiasm, generosity of spirit, and conscientious labor throughout this process. We would also like to thank those who gave us careful feedback on the long introductory chapter: G. William Barnard, Linda Gibler, John Heron, Jeffrey J. Kripal, Beverly Lanzetta, Gregory Mengel, Vicente Merlo, José Antonio Noguera, Rod O'Neal, Richard Tarnas, John Taylor, and the anonymous SUNY Press reviewers. We also want to thank Jane Bunker for her steady support of the project since its very inception. Also at SUNY, we owe a debt of gratitude to Laurie Searl for her efficient production of this book and to Alan V. Hewat for his fantastic editing work.

Jacob would like especially to thank his wife, Karin Holsinger Sherman, for her encouragement. She followed the drama of this project from its conception to its completion with that combination of attention and love that we usually reserve for spiritual practices or consider a mark of sanctity.

Thoroughly revised and containing new materials, Jorge N. Ferrer's chapter, "Spiritual Knowing as Participatory Enaction: An Answer to the Question of Religious Pluralism," draws from sections previously published in chapters 5, 6, and 7 of his *Revisioning Transpersonal Theory: A Participatory Vision of Human Spirituality* (Albany: State University of New York Press, 2002). Some of these materials appeared previously in "Towards a Participatory Vision of Human Spirituality," *ReVision* 24(2), 2001. A few paragraphs included in Ferrer and Sherman's "Introduction: The Participatory Turn in Spirituality, Mysticism, and Religious Studies" are derived from Ferrer's *Revisioning Transpersonal Theory*, and Ferrer's "Embodied Spirituality: Now and Then," *Tikkun* 21 (2006).

INTRODUCTION

The Participatory Turn in Spirituality, Mysticism, and Religious Studies

Jorge N. Ferrer and Jacob H. Sherman

DO WE REALLY need another "turn" in academia and the study of religion? After all, it seems that when one or another turn has been proposed— whether linguistic, interpretive, narrative, pragmatic, or postcolonial—scholars often presented it as a kind of epistemic rupture with the past, a revolutionary paradigmatic shift that would drastically change the way the phenomena studied in their disciplines are to be approached. Whereas claims of epistemic rupture may sound pretentious today, we think that the route of creative scholarship is more like a winding road than a straight highway, and that certain turns are therefore unavoidable if genuine or substantial progress is to be made in any discipline.

Having said this, we do not think of *The Participatory Turn* as a radical break with either the past or the present, but rather as an attempt to name, articulate, and strengthen an emerging academic ethos capable of coherently weaving together a number of the most challenging and robust trends in contemporary Religious Studies. Among these trends and themes we have selected the postcolonial revaluation of emic epistemologies, the postmodern emphasis on embodied and gendered subjectivity, the feminist recovery of the sensuous and the erotic in religious inquiry and experience, the pragmatic emphasis on transformation and antirepresentationalism, the renewed interest in the study of lived spirituality, the resacralization of language, the question of metaphysical truth in religion, and the irreducibility of religious pluralism. If we choose to present our formulation of this growing academic sensibility as a turn, it is only because we believe that, taken together, these trends issue a serious challenge to the currently prevalent cultural-linguistic

1

paradigm in the study of religion. With this in mind, *The Participatory Turn* presents a pluralistic vision of spirituality that accepts the formative role of contextual and linguistic factors in religious phenomena, while simultaneously recognizing the importance, and at times even centrality, of nonlinguistic variables (e.g., somatic, imaginal, energetic, contemplative, and so on) in shaping religious experiences and meanings, and affirming the ontological value and creative impact of spiritual worlds and realities. In other words, we are aiming at a critical, metaphysically thick, and religiously relevant sensibility within the academic study of religion. We believe that this articulation is neither a return to previous epistemological structures nor a drastic rupture from them, but rather reflects the ongoing project of a creative fusion of past, present, and perhaps future horizons that integrates certain traditional religious claims with modern standards of critical inquiry and postmodern epistemological insights about the cocreated nature of human knowledge.

But before introducing the general contours of such a participatory understanding of religious inquiry and experience, it may be important to situate the "participatory turn" in the context of the development of the field of Religious Studies in general, and in relation to the linguistic paradigm in particular. By exploring various challenges to the linguistic turn, we are able see the need to move beyond what Jürgen Habermas calls the "linguistification of the sacred," while at the same time adumbrating the shape of the participatory turn. This rather controversialist approach is intentional. We are not seeking to build a participatory sensibility from the ground up, as if it were one of the great systems of nineteenth-century philosophy, but are instead discovering its contours in the give and take of arguments in the midst of which we (in the field of Religious Studies) already find ourselves. Let us begin then with a brief exposition of the nature and possible limitations of the linguistic paradigm.

THE IMPACT OF THE LINGUISTIC TURN
ON RELIGIOUS STUDIES

One could make the case that twentieth-century Western philosophical thinking—beginning with the work of thinkers as diverse as Bertrand Russell, Martin Heidegger, Ludwig Wittgenstein, or Gottlob Frege—was characterized by an ever-increasing interest in the study of language. The "linguistic turn" in philosophy shifted the focus of inquiry from the inner representations and innate categories of a Cartesian-Kantian subject to the analysis of the elements of language, such as semantics, speech-acts, conditions for a theory of meaning, the relationship between words and world affairs, and so forth.[1] Developing the ideas of the late Wittgenstein, Gilbert Ryle, and others, a growing number of scholars boldly asserted that classical philosophical puzzles were "nothing but" problems of language that could be either resolved or dissolved through a variety of linguistic analyses and reconstructions.[2] In this new philosophical environment, linguistic signs were no longer regarded as mediating factors between the "subjective" representations of a Cartesian ego and the "objective" world, but rather as the primary locus of any plausible cognitive meaning and epistemic justification.[3] In other words, philosophy after the linguistic turn considered *public* language—instead of *private* representations, concepts, or ideas—the true interface between the knowing subject and the world, thereby allegedly overcoming the epistemological skepticism of modern philosophy after Immanuel Kant's critical revolution.[4] As Barbara Fultner points out, after the linguistic turn, the "philosophy of language . . . becomes the 'successor discipline' to epistemology and metaphysics."[5]

Before the linguistic turn, and in the wake of the Enlightenment critique of metaphysics, religious scholars following Friedrich Schleiermacher sought to defend the autonomy and validity of religion by freeing religious experience from its premodern (and at that time dubious) metaphysical anchors.[6] Whether animated by idealist, phenomenological, or comparativist sensibilities, these modernist scholars tended to enthrone a supposedly autonomous, universal, and often disembodied and masculinized Cartesian subjectivity as both the agent and the locus of any genuine and reliable religious inquiry. Several decades of exploration, definition, and reduction of religion in terms of a core religious "human experience" followed, with religion being variously understood as "the feeling of absolute dependence" (Schleiermacher) or the subjective consciousness of "the eternal" (Nygren), "the holy" and "the numinous" (Otto), "the sacred" (Eliade), or "the ultimate concern" (Tillich).[7] Modern Religious Studies were thus shaped by epistemological assumptions and concerns emerging from what Habermas calls "the philosophy of the subject," that is, the philosophy that takes consciousness to be primary in the search for epistemic certainty.[8] As Walter H. Capps aptly puts it, the modern quest for a "first principle" or sui generis element in religion was guided by a "Cartesian temper with a Kantian conceptual framework."[9] This fundamentally modern project in the study of religion was drastically brought to an end by the linguistic turn.

The impact of the linguistic turn on Religious Studies was profound and far-reaching. The linguistic reconstruction of philosophy influenced generations of religious scholars, and the significance of public language over private experience in the study of religion was forcefully asserted from a variety of angles and with different emphases for decades.[10] Methodologically, embracing the linguistic turn in Religious Studies entails abandoning all efforts to assess the epistemic status of private consciousness or suprasensible experiences of the real, the sacred, or the holy. More positively, it involves approaching the study of religion as the examination of both public religious languages and the relationship of such languages to either the sensible world or to other elements of the linguistic framework. Such strategies are employed, for example, in the study of parables and myths, scriptures and canons, doctrines and creeds, rituals and religious behaviors, sacred texts and narratives, religious symbols and metaphors, and so forth. A narrativist understanding of religion, Gavin Flood explains, requires that "rather than subjectivity (belief, cognition, inner states and religious experiences) language and culture, the realm of signs become the locus of inquiry."[11] In the study of mysticism, for example, this paradigm shift is visible in the reframing of its focus from "mystical experience" to "mystical language" (Katz), mystical "meaning events" (Sells), "mystical expressions" (Idel), or in the proposal that mysticism is just "a kind of writing" (Cupitt).[12] Since language was now recognized as not only *expressive* but also *constitutive* of human experience, the ultimate referents of religious discourse were not to be sought in special intuitions or states of consciousness, but in the rich communicative interactions religious practitioners have in an always already linguistically structured world. The postmodern theologian Mark C. Taylor puts it this way: "Far from existing prior to and independent of any inquiry, the very phenomenon of religion is constituted by local discursive practices."[13]

Although the shapes of the linguistic turn in Religious Studies are extremely diverse, it may be helpful to distinguish three major, nonmutually exclusive families of approaches: analytic, interpretive, and postmodern.[14] First, the *analytic* branch of the linguistic turn stems from the influence of a number of Anglo-American thinkers—such as Russell, G. E. Moore, A. J. Ayer, or John L. Austin—who strove to achieve conceptual clarification of obscure philosophical problems through the analysis of language.[15] Whether concerned with formal reconstructions of language or the identification of metaphysical pseudoproblems originated by its ordinary use, many twentieth-century philosophers of religion turned to the tools of analytic philosophy in order to advance, critique, and deepen religious understanding.[16] Among the most important trends in the analytic study of religion, we should mention here the early debates about the verifiability and falsifiability of religious doctrines, the search for the rational foundations of religious beliefs, the theological reinterpretation of Nietzsche's "death of God" as a linguistic affair, the Wittgensteinian account of religions as "language games," the reformed antifoundationalist epistemology in theology, and the understanding of religions as "conceptual frameworks."[17] More recently, analytic philosophy of religion has focused on the epistemology of religious experience and the problem of reference in religious knowledge.[18] Within analytic circles, we can also situate John Hick's pluralistic philosophy of religion and the work of a number of process theologians with analytical dispositions such as David A. Pailin.[19]

Second, the pervasiveness of *interpretive* approaches in contemporary Religious Studies bears witness to the critical influence of the hermeneutic tradition in the twentieth century—especially of the works of Schleiermacher, Heidegger, Paul Ricoeur, and Hans-Georg Gadamer.[20] In contrast to the analytic agendas of linguistic clarification and exploration of the rationality of religious beliefs, a hermeneutic philosophy of religion focuses on the study of religious meanings and symbols, the interpretation of sacred scriptures and revelation, the hermeneutical dimension of translation, scriptural exegesis and (creative) "isogesis," discourse theory in Religious Studies, the relationship between religious experience and its interpretation, and issues raised by the challenges of cross-cultural hermeneutics, among other areas of inquiry.[21] From a hermeneutical standpoint, religious experiences have been framed as "interpretative accounts" (Proudfoot), religious traditions as "textual communities" (Holdrege) or "living hermeneutic processes" (Vroom), and religions as "comprehensive interpretive frameworks" (Lindbeck).[22]

Despite the rich diversity of hermeneutic orientations and sensibilities in the academic study of religion[23]—e.g., phenomenological, comparativist, constructivist, historicist, and so forth—most interpretive writers stress both the contextuality and plurality of religious meanings and worlds.[24] To illustrate the variety of hermeneutic approaches, and with no wish to suggest that the following list is exhaustive or representative, we mention here Mircea Eliade's early plea for a "creative hermeneutics," Elisabeth Schüssler Fiorenzza's development of a "critical feminist hermeneutics," Raimundo Panikkar's proposal of a "diatopical hermeneutics" for interreligious encounters, Sandra M. Schneiders's influential hermeneutic approach to the study of spirituality, David Tracy's interpretive theology, Jeffrey J. Kripal's articulation of a "mystical hermeneutics" or understanding of hermeneutic practice as mystical, and Jeffrey R. Timm's and Donald S. Lopez's revaluations of traditional interpretive approaches.[25]

Third, within the rubric *postmodern* we are locating a number of critical discourses such as those emerging from poststructuralism, Derridean deconstruction, gender studies, postcolonialism, and ethnic studies. Most of these approaches emerged in the late 1970s rather independently and it would be surely a mistake to conflate them, but they all share a commitment to listening to the subjective experience of "the Other" (i.e., the marginal "nonsubjects" of modernity, such as women, ethnic minorities, gays and lesbians, or colonized peoples), as well as to reversing and overcoming traditional hierarchical dualisms such as sacred/profane, God/world, male/female, civilized/primitive, transcendent/immanent, presence/absence, one/many, light/darkness, spirit/body, and so forth. For poststructuralism and deconstruction, we think above all of Thomas Altizer's theology of the "death of God," Jean-Luc Marion's "God without Being," Taylor's deconstructive a/theology, John D. Caputo's Derridean "religion without religion," Don Cupitt's "mysticism of secondariness," and Tomoko Masuzawa's painstaking deconstruction of theories of religion.[26] For the gendering of Religious Studies, one can consult, among other works, Grace Jantzen's, Pamela Sue Anderson's, and Sarah Coakley's feminist critiques of analytic philosophy of religion, Amy Hollywood's and Beverly J. Lanzetta's revisions of the study of mysticism from the perspective of female experience, or the excellent collection of essays on the impact of feminist methods on the study of religion compiled by Arvind Sharma.[27] And for postcolonial studies, we isolate as a representative sample the works of Richard King on Hinduism and mysticism, Donald S. Lopez on Buddhism, David Chidester on indigenous African religions, Michael Taussig on shamanism, and Laura E. Donaldson and Kwok Pui-Lan on the meeting of feminism and postcolonialism.[28] We could also situate here the increasing proliferation of critical analyses that show how foundational categories of the discipline of Religious Studies (such as "religion," "world religions," or "Hinduism") are analytically vacuous or the product of modern European colonial interests and Christian theological agendas—a line of work brilliantly developed by authors such as Jonathan Z. Smith, Talal Asad, Timothy Fitgerald, Daniel Dubuisson, and Masuzawa, among others.[29] Finally, at the interface of postmodern theory and hermeneutics, a growing number of scholars are today providing deconstructions and critical genealogies of diverse religious figures, trends, and schools. This tendency can be illustrated, for example, by reference to the Foucauldian studies of Hugh B. Urban on Tantra, Bernard Faure's critical analyses of Buddhist attitudes toward gender and sexuality, and Kripal's controversial study on the homoerotic nature of Sri Ramakrishna's spirituality.[30]

Despite the significant differences among them, what is common to analytic, interpretive, and postmodern approaches can be explained in terms of their insistence that the study of religion should focus on the examination of the "signs" and "meanings" attached to religious texts, worldviews, and practices.[31] After the linguistic turn, the object of Religious Studies is no longer the elucidation of the origin, nature, or ontological implications of religious experience, but the analysis, interpretation, or critical deconstruction and reconstruction of the textual, the linguistic, and the symbolic. In this light, the shift from a "philosophy of consciousness" to a "philosophy of the sign" in Religious Studies can be seen as advancing the linguistification of the sacred, with which Habermas characterizes the modern era.[32] To "linguistify" the sacred means to subvert its transcendental authority in the Heavens and bring the legitimization of its cognitive and normative claims down to Earth, that is, to the intersubjective space constituted by communicative exchanges among rational human beings. In the disenchanted world of post/modernity, the sacred has been detranscendentalized, relativized, contextualized, and diversified but, most fundamentally, assimilated to linguistic expression. In contemporary religious matters, as Cupitt writes, "language goes all the way down."[33]

BEYOND THE LINGUISTIC TURN

As Thomas Kuhn pointed out, any conceptual revolution both addresses the limitations of the previous paradigm and raises new questions and challenges. Some of these challenges can be answered within the new revolutionary paradigmatic structure, but the effective resolution of other more recalcitrant problems will require surpassing even the new paradigm.[34] There is no reason to believe that the linguistic turn should be an exception. Here we want to isolate a number of increasingly significant themes and trends in both Religious Studies and the academy at large which, taken together, may suggest the need to go beyond the limits of the linguistic paradigm. Specifically, our discussion focuses on the following seven areas: (1) the postcolonial revaluation of emic epistemological frameworks; (2) the postmodern and feminist emphasis on embodiment and sacred immanence; (3) the resacralization of language; (4) the "pragmatic turn" in contemporary philosophy; (5) the renewed interest in the study of lived spirituality; (6) the question of religious truth in postmetaphysical thinking; and (7) the irreducibility of religious pluralism.

The Revaluation of Emic Epistemological Perspectives

Recent developments in postmodern theory, cross-cultural hermeneutics, and postcolonial studies have raised caution among scholars regarding the potential pitfalls and ideological implications of privileging Western epistemological frameworks in the assessment of religious, and especially non-Western, truth claims. First of all, the postmodern critique of the Western scientific/philosophical metanarrative as "onto-theological" suggests that Western epistemologies deserve to be treated today with the same sort of critical suspicion with which modernist scholars previously regarded religion.[35] As Gianni Vattimo points out, "It is (only) because metaphysical meta-narratives have been dissolved that philosophy has rediscovered the plausibility of religion and can consequently approach the religious need of common consciousness independently of the framework of the Enlightenment critique."[36] Secondly, the recognition of a variety of culturally specific criteria that determine what counts as valid knowledge leads many contemporary interpretive writers to regard the long-assumed epistemic superiority of critical rationality simply as one more element in the modern Western narrative, whose ultimately axiomatic status belies its claim to supremacy. In this light, for example, Flood recommends considering scholarly (outsider) and traditional (insider) accounts of religion as legitimate competing narratives, and argues that in this contest neither side can claim epistemological privilege on a priori grounds.[37] Finally, postcolonial studies have exposed and denounced the connection between the supposed cognitive superiority of the West and colonialism, imperialism, and the political domination of non-Western cultures.[38]

Moreover, since no clear asymmetry between Western and non-Western epistemologies can be categorically established, avoiding ethnocentrism requires that we abandon the belief that the currently fashionable Western epistemology should be the preferred framework to assess all cognitive claims.

One of the unifying threads in these criticisms is the recognition of a multiplicity of valid ways of knowing and the consequent challenge to the very idea of universal reason now exposed as being (conveniently) shaped by the assumptions of the Enlightenment project—a challenge issued by feminists decades ago. This awareness animates contemporary postmodern, feminist, and postcolonial critiques of Western epistemology as disembodied, rationalistic, and cognicentric. Taken together, these developments have led many to a revalorization of alternative emic epistemologies and categories in the study of religion. More specifically, it is increasingly claimed that looking at our intellectual concerns against and through the background of non-Western frameworks may not only serve as a wholesome corrective for our inevitable cultural biases, but may also bring fresh perspectives on unsolved problems and debated questions.

In *Orientalism and Religion*, for example, King argues that certain Buddhist and Hindu "constructivist" epistemic viewpoints—such as those of Dignaga, Dharmakirti, Kamasila, and Bhartrhari—effectively challenge Steven T. Katz's assertion that accepting the culturally mediated nature of the contemplative path entails the impossibility of nonconceptual, unmediated mystical experiences.[39] As King explains, these contemplative Asian epistemologists hold that a nonconceptual access to reality may actually require the prior use of conceptual tools.[40] In a similar vein, Robert K. C. Forman points out that the Yogacara Buddhist epistemologist Paramartha, while recognizing the linguistically constituted nature of ordinary experience and knowledge, claims that the goal of meditative practice is precisely to dismantle such constructive mechanisms and lead the practitioner to an unconditioned insight into the nature of reality.[41] Of course, the introduction of these emic frameworks into the contemporary debate about the nature of mysticism does not settle the contested issues. Rather, it simply *but crucially* highlights the fact that Western epistemologies (such as the neo-Kantian one endorsed by Katz) may not be the last arbiters in the assessment of religious knowledge claims, and in particular of those emerging from long-term contemplative practice. As King cautiously states: "My point is not that Western scholars should necessarily accept the emic perspectives over which they are claiming the authority to speak, but rather that they at least entertain the possibility that such perspectives are a legitimate stance to adopt and engage them in constructive debate."[42]

A related development is the proposal to apply emic categories in the study of religion. Consider, for example, Benson Saler's suggestion that scholarship can benefit from the use of folk categories (such as the Hindu *dharma*) as tools of anthropological analysis: "While anthropologists normally devote much attention to native categories in ethnographies of the peoples who utilize them, the time has come, I think, to borrow selectively from such categories and experiment with them as transcultural tools."[43] Donald Rothberg makes a related case in the context of spiritual inquiry:

> To interpret spiritual approaches through categories like "data," "evidence," "verification," "method," "confirmation," and "intersubjectivity" may be to enthrone these categories as somehow the hallmarks of knowledge as such, even if the categories are expanded in meaning from their current western usage. But might not a profound encounter with practices of spiritual inquiry lead to considering carefully the meaning of other comparable categories (e.g. *dhyana*, *vichara*, *theoria*, *gnosis*, or *contemplatio*) and perhaps to developing understandings of inquiry in which such spiritual categories are primary or central when we speak of knowledge? To assume that the categories of current western epistemology are adequate for interpreting spiritual approaches is to prejudge the results of such an encounter, which might well lead to significant changes in these categories.[44]

Expressing a similar sensibility, Peter Ochs writes that Religious Studies will remain colonialist insofar as they "tend to remove 'religious phenomena' from the contexts of their societal embodiments and resituate them within conceptual universes of our own designing."[45] What these and others scholars are persuasively arguing is that importing the language and epistemic categories emerging from Western scientific and philosophical traditions to analyze and account for the validity of knowledge claims from all cultures, ways of knowing, and domains of reality is highly questionable. Most religious and spiritual endeavors, we should stress here, are aimed not so much at describing or explaining human nature and the world, but at engaging and transforming them in creative and participatory ways, and may therefore call for different validity standards than those emerging from the rationalistic study of the natural world.[46]

To add fuel to this fire, an increasing number of Western scholars are today "coming out" as spiritual practitioners, rendering the modern disciplinary divide between Religious Studies and Theology more dubious than ever.[47] The fact that many of these scholars display *both* religious commitments *and* critical perspectives on traditional religious beliefs reinforces the dissolution of strict modernist dichotomies such as insider/outsider, emic/etic, engaged/detached, theological/scholarly, confessional/academic, or caretaker/critic.[48]

Participatory thinkers hold that openness to the potential heuristic value and even validity of alternative epistemic frameworks does not necessarily ensnare us in relativistic dilemmas. In our attempt to rise above the inevitable biases of our perspective, we should not fall into a vulgar relativism incapable of offering grounds for qualitative distinctions or transcultural judgments. This can be avoided, we believe, by evaluating all knowledge claims—etic and emic, insider and outsider, rational and transrational, naturalistic and supernaturalistic—through *validity standards of both dominant and marginal Western and non-Western epistemologies in whatever measure may be appropriate according to the context of the inquiry and the type of knowledge claims.* One of the most vital tasks for those of us who accept this approach is the clarification of the relationship between epistemological frameworks (objectivist, constructivist, hermeneutic, pragmatist, and so on), contexts of inquiry (scientific, religious, artistic, psychological, and so on), and ways of knowing (rational, contemplative, aesthetic, moral, imaginal, somatic, and so on).

In any event, we propose that the dividing line between sound and weak scholarship should not be traced between Western and non-Western epistemologies—or even between naturalistic and supernaturalistic claims—but between approaches that lead to *radically empirical intersubjectively testable outcomes and/or discernible pragmatic consequences* and those which do not. The "and/or" of the previous sentence is fundamental, particularly in the context of religious inquiry. On the one hand, it may be plausible to consider intersubjective consensus a central epistemic standard in the context of what we might call, paraphrasing Kuhn, a single tradition's *"normal" spiritual inquiry,* in which spiritual practice is managed by a prevailing spiritual paradigm and something akin to a correspondence theory of truth is operative (for example, between practitioners' insights and the tradition's mapped "stages of the path"). On the other hand, however, it should be obvious that intersubjective agreement is probably an inappropriate test not only *among traditions* (which bring forth different and often incompatible spiritual insights), but also in periods of *"revolutionary" spiritual inquiry* within one tradition, in which anomalies in relation to accepted doctrines arise and new paradigms of spiritual understanding are developed (for example, it is likely that neither the Buddha's enlightenment nor the claims of the more radical Christian mystics could have been intersubjectively corroborated in their respective times and contexts). In the latter cases, the search for more pragmatic avenues to legitimize spiritual knowledge claims becomes imperative.[49]

The challenge raised by the revaluation of emic epistemologies to the linguistic and social-scientific paradigms in the study of religion should be obvious. In contrast to the textual and/or naturalistic account of religion held by these approaches, many of these emic perspectives regard extralinguistic variables (e.g., supernatural entities, spiritual energies, archetypal principles, etc.) as both constitutive elements and real referents of religious knowledge and experience. As mentioned above, many of these perspectives are not naively ignorant of the linguistically and conceptually mediated nature of human knowledge. And yet, they vigorously defend that ordinary cognitive constructive mechanisms and associated epistemologies are overcome in certain special noetic states, such as those emerging from meditative, visionary, ecstatic, and contemplative practice. Contrary to the hegemonic claims of the linguistic paradigm, then, it is becoming increasingly plausible that epistemological frameworks that take into account a wider—and perhaps *deeper*—engagement with human faculties (not only discursive reason, but also intuition, imagination, somatic knowing, empathic discernment, moral awareness, aesthetic sensibility, meditation, and contemplation) may be critical in the assessment of many religious knowledge claims.

SACRED IMMANENCE AND THE RETURN OF THE SENSUOUS BODY

Postmodern and postcolonial thinkers are neither the first nor the only ones denouncing the ideological and epistemologically dubious nature of the Western metanarrative. Feminists have questioned the professed neutrality and objectivism of Western science and philosophy for decades, showing how androcentric and rationalistic biases make these cognitive enterprises not only one-sided, but also oppressive of women and other marginal populations.[50] In the study of religion, one of the main targets of postmodern and feminist critical analyses are transcendentalist and essentialist accounts of the divine or ultimate reality associated with traditional theologies. Whereas postmodern thinkers consider these views symptomatic of the Western allegiance to an oppressive "metaphysics of presence," feminists see them as products of patriarchal ideologies that tend to deny or, at any rate, undervalue the spiritual dimensions of nature, embodiment, and women. These critical perspectives have inspired the contemporary revival of human faculties and the exploration of facets of reality often overlooked in the modern study of religion, in particular: sacred immanence and the spiritual quality of nature; female experience and feminine ways of knowing; the centrality of the body in religious practice and experience; the role of empathy, the erotic, and emotion in religious knowledge; and the connection between the sexual and the mystical.[51]

In a recent study on radical (postmodern) theologies, for example, Richard Griggs concludes that "[a]ll of them seem to emphasize the immanence of the divine. . . ."[52] This stress on the immanent is tangible, Griggs continues, in Mary Daly's insistence that spiritual liberation lies in fully inhabiting "the Realm of Wild Reality," Taylor's understanding of language as the "divine milieu," Ursula Goodenough's religious naturalism and plea for the worship of nature, David Crosby's consideration of nature as "metaphysically ultimate," Sallie McFague's view of "the world as God's body," or Naomi Goldenberg's thealogy of the immanent Goddess, among other similar proposals. In addition to Taylor's a/theology, which is "in large measure, a critique of the notion of the transcendent God,"[53] sacred immanence is also the mark of a number of postmodern proposals influenced by the writings of Jacques Derrida, such as Caputo's or Cupitt's. Discussing Walter Lowe's work, for example, Caputo asks, "Who is the God who comes after metaphysics? Not a God of infinite distance from earth and flesh, but the infinite freedom to make God immanent, in-the-finite, incarnate."[54]

This affirmation of the immanence of the sacred often comes together with a plea for the resacralization of everyday life, and in particular, of sensuality and the body. In contrast to its previously marginal status, "the body" has become a key hermeneutic category in the study of religion.[55] The last two decades of religious scholarship have produced an astonishing number of studies on perceptions, representations, and uses (and abuses) of the body in religious practice; for example, on embodied spiritual potentials and transformative energies; the essential role of bodily postures and movements in religious experience and ritual practice; the mythical, symbolic, and metaphorical dimensions of the body; and critical appraisals of many historical spiritual practices and understandings as "disembodied."[56] Attuned to the *Zeitgeist*, Kripal gives voice to the new centrality of the body in Religious Studies: "If there is a universal in the history of religions, it is the human body and its physiological shaping of religious practice and experience."[57]

The body has also emerged as a reinvigorated site of knowledge, analysis, and investigation in the anthropology of religion (e.g., Paul Stoller's fascinating participatory research on Songhay sorcery and spirit possession) as well as a fruitful comparative category in cross-cultural studies (e.g., Anne Hunt Overzee's excellent study of body symbolism in Teilhard de Chardin and Rāmānuja).[58] Of related interest are a number of explorations of Eastern views on the body.[59] Showing how Asian views on the body can shed new light on Western perennial questions, for example, Yuasa Yasuo suggests that the unity of the mind/body complex is not a problem to be solved through rational inquiry, but an existential fruit to be achieved through conscious self-cultivation (*shugyo*).[60]

Moving away from the debate about its universal or contextual nature, the contemporary study of mysticism is gradually recentering itself not only on the textual and the historical, but also on the position of the body and its sexual and erotic energies in mystical endeavors. In his innovative analysis of the mystico-erotic experiences of scholars of mysticism, for example, Kripal speaks about the erotic as "a radical dialecticism between human sexuality and the possible ontological ground(s) of mystical experience."[61] For Kripal, the body and its sexual drives can influence and even constitute not only mystical phenomena, but also the very scholarly approaches employed in their study. Even the ancient mystics' ascetic control of sexuality, far from being considered merely repressive, is today reframed as a kind of eroticism capable of transforming desire into religious discourse and discernment.[62] The relationship between embodiment and the mystical has also been analyzed from different feminist angles. Jantzen discusses the political and patriarchal dimensions of the devaluation of the somatic and the erotic in the history of

Christian mysticism, Hollywood explains how corporeal and erotic mystical modes historically associated with women have been denigrated and even pathologized, and Lanzetta offers a meditated consideration of women's bodies as "mystical texts" and sexuality as an area of "women's reclamation of holiness."[63] The trend toward integrating the spiritual into the physical, as well as celebrating the religious significance of sexuality and the immanence of the divine, is also at the heart of the so-called "body theologies" developed in the last two decades. According to James Nelson, "body theology" is not so much a theological reflection on the body but rather "nothing less than our attempts to reflect on body experience as revelatory of God."[64]

This feminist and postmodern turn to embodied subjectivity should not be confused with a return to former decontextualized, apolitical, and "crypto-theological" phenomenological approaches to religion.[65] On the contrary, postmodern feminism replaces a masculinized, discarnate, and supposedly universal and autonomous *Cartesian mental ego* with a gendered, embodied, situated, and participatory *intersubjective self* as the agent engaged in religious pursuits.

Even more relevant for our present concerns, *the body of contemporary scholarship is no longer "dissolving into language."*[66] Listen, for example, to Lisa Isherwood and Elisabeth Stuart's caveat: "What must be guarded against all costs is the disappearance of the real, lived, laughing, suffering, birthing and dying body underneath the philosophical and theological meaning it is called to bear."[67] Furthermore, in contrast to the received view of religious experience and meaning as linguistically determined, as well as received accounts of the body as a kind of objectifiable text, many scholars argue today for a more intricate and reciprocal relationship between language and embodied experience: *Prelinguistic and translinguistic embodied/erotic experience may significantly shape the visionary imagination, spiritual experience, and language of the religious practitioner, the mystic, and even the scholar of religion.*

It is noteworthy that this still minority but increasingly accepted understanding receives support from important trends in modern cognitive science, which strongly challenge the linguistic determination of human experience and thought usually taken for granted after the linguistic turn.[68] In *The Body in the Mind*, Mark Johnson presents compelling evidence from the cognitive sciences suggesting that linguistic metaphors and categories, as well as the very structure of human thinking, emerge from the rich embodied interactions of the human organism with the environment (for example, the concept of "balance" is rooted in our prelinguistic physical sense of being balanced).[69] Interestingly, Johnson adds that this account calls for a recognition of the creative role of imagination as the epistemic bridge between embodied experience and mental conceptualization.[70] As should be obvious, the bodily basis of cognition for which Johnson, George Lakoff, and many others argue raises at least two serious challenges to the linguistic paradigm. First, it questions the linguistic sources of symbolic cognition and meaning defended by interpretive and post-modern thinking, resituating such origins in the imaginal elaboration of embodied experience. And second, it challenges the representational paradigm of cognition embraced by analytic philosophy[71]—a challenge that is central to the pragmatic turn in contemporary philosophy, to which we now turn.

THE PRAGMATIC TURN IN CONTEMPORARY PHILOSOPHY

Among the most important events in contemporary philosophy has been the recovery of American philosophical pragmatism, what William Eggington and Mike Sandbothe call the "pragmatic turn."[72] Dismissed after World War II as an overly optimistic episode in the history of philosophy, the pragmatists have been rediscovered as incisive thinkers who anticipate and, in certain respects, surpass the postmodern problematics we more readily associate with philosophers such as Derrida and Gilles Deleuze. Pragmatists such as Charles Sanders Peirce, William James, and John Dewey are especially attractive today because of their decisive refusal of foundationalism and their rejection of the epistemological paradigm of representation, both of which are central aspects of the participatory turn, as well.

One of pragmatism's chief insights—shared not only by the American originators of the movement but also by subsequent sympathizers such as the late Wittgenstein and Habermas—is that linguistic behaviour is a kind of action and its validity is vouchsafed inasmuch as it achieves desired communicative ends.[73] This pragmatist thesis, rooted in the dual abandonment of foundationalism and representationalism, issues a severe challenge to the linguistic turn for it suggests that language needs to be understood in terms of action, and action puts us in touch with the world of events, of ontology beyond just semantics, of transformation beyond mere interpretation. For the pragmatist, truth is an achievement word. To say that the assertion "that P" is true is rather like saying that a particular strategy proves true; that P is true if it works, in the same way that Odysseus's strategy is true if Troy finally falls.

For the pragmatist, the truth of a proposition, idea, belief, or hunch is not determined by a detached gaze simply surveying and marking the world "as it is," but is rather tested and proved through the fire of action. James repeatedly suggests the following maxim as a guide for pragmatism: "Grant an idea or belief to be true, what concrete difference will its being true make in any one's actual life?" The upshot of James's maxim is the ruin of any lingering philosophical foundationalism that would build systems upon clear, distinct, indubitable ideas. Rather than building upon secure foundations, pragmatist philosophy always begins in the midst of things, colored by sentiments, events, and human needs, a philosophy subject to constant revision and to new demands. Foundationalism, with roots in Locke and Descartes, by contrast, is closely allied to the epistemological strategy of representation. Put simply, representationalism is, as James characterizes it, "the popular notion . . . that a true idea must copy its reality."[74] Representationalist philosophy, what Richard Rorty calls "the mind as the mirror of nature," sets itself the task of discriminating between those ideas that actually represent the world and those ideas that simply pretend to do so. By identifying these privileged representations, the philosopher provides a foundation upon which all beliefs worthy of the honorific "true knowledge" will stand. The representationalist's mirror is a very different thing than the pragmatist's action. As James comments, "[The] great assumption of the intellectualists [foundationalists] is that truth means essentially an inert static relation. When you've got your true idea of anything, there's an end of the matter. You're in possession; you *know*. . . . Epistemologically you are in stable equilibrium."[75] By contrast, James and his fellow pragmatists hold that "[t]he truth of an idea is not a stagnant property inherent in it. Truth *happens* to an idea. It *becomes* true, is *made* true by events. Its verity *is* in fact an event, a process. . . ."[76] From the outset, the pragmatists rejected the foundationalist strategies so characteristic of modern philosophy and so Robert Cummings Neville is right to see them as pioneering "the highroad around modernism."[77]

Antifoundationalism is central to the work of Rorty, the neopragmatist who may be most responsible for the contemporary pragmatic turn. Rorty inherited antifoundationalism from respectable analytic sources that include Wilfrid Sellars's campaign against the "myth of the given," Willard V. O. Quine's critique of the two dogmas of empiricism (analyticity and sense data) and his consequent turn toward holism, and Donald Davidson's overturning of the scheme-content distinction. In Rorty's hands, the critique of foundationalism leads to the abandonment of ontology, a kind of provocative deflationary pragmatism, rooted especially in a particular reading of James and Dewey, which sees knowledge as a toolbox for the democratically oriented transformation of society and reality.[78] Rorty's, however, is not the only viable pragmatism making rounds in the academy. There are also those, such as Christopher Hookway, Ochs, and Frank M. Oppenheim, who in diverse ways contend for a wider, more robust pragmatism. This realist pragmatism, rooted especially in Peirce and the late Josiah Royce, also sees knowledge as properly crafted by human knowers for the transformation of society and the nurturance of "beloved communities," but sees this effective knowledge in realist rather than nominalist terms. Indeed, despite his pragmatist rejection of foundationalism, Peirce considered nominalism to be among the chief specters that his philosophy was designed to exorcise. A pragmatic nonfoundationalist account of knowledge need not evacuate the world of intrinsic intelligibility or worth. In Peirce's thought, nonfoundationalism is an integral part of a complex theory that sees the entire universe as shot through with a real intelligibility and dignity (inherent goodness), intelligibility and dignity that do not need the guarantee of a foundationalist *cogito*. Anti- or nonfoundationalism, it turns out, is capable of multiple iterations—the relativism and nihilism of certain avant-garde antifoundationalists is only one extreme within a spectrum that also affords religious opportunities, a space to value and entertain claims about the sacred, and the possibility that creativity and generosity may in fact be the ultimate, though dubitable, constituents of the universe.

At this point, readers familiar with contemporary neopragmatism may balk. All of this mysticism hardly sits well with the dominant naturalism in neopragmatic philosophy. After all, what has the neopragmatism of Quine, Putnam, and Rorty to do with Religious Studies in general and the participatory turn in particular? Indeed, it is true that the pragmatic turn is often associated with a kind of militant secularism or aggressive atheism, at worst, or an ambivalent tolerance of religious belief, at best, and that contemporary pragmatists such as Rorty and Michael Eldridge have done little to amend this view.[79] However, recent work (particularly that which appeals to the Peirce-Royce axis of "Cambridge pragmatism" as opposed to the James-Dewey axis of "instrumentalist pragmatism") has explored the immense fruitfulness of pragmatist approaches in religion and spirituality.[80] Moreover, as Richard J. Bernstein notes, not only Peirce and Royce, but also James and even Dewey "all repudiated 'aggressive atheism.' In differing ways, each of them took the religious life seriously and made vital contributions to understanding what it means."[81] The more nuanced historiography of American pragmatism emerging today locates its roots in explicitly religious thinkers as diverse as Jonathan Edwards, on the one hand, and Ralph Waldo Emerson, on the other. Although it was once fashionable to drive a wedge between the pragmatists' concern to address religious questions (think of James in the *Varieties*, Peirce's "Neglected Argument," or even Dewey's *Art as Experience*) and their work on pragmatism as such, contemporary historians increasingly recognize the constitutive role that religious questions played in the development and articulation of classical pragmatism.[82] Religious themes were not marginal to the founding generation of pragmatists but central to each philosopher in his own way: James's fascination with individual spiritual experience and the paranormal, Peirce and Royce's interest in community as a spiritual locus, and Dewey's nature-based religious sentiment. The religious fecundity of pragmatism is not only an interesting episode in the history of philosophy but continues today. In the contemporary academy, Cornel West and others call for a renewal of "prophetic pragmatism," a pragmatism deployed in concert with its religious roots for the betterment and correction of societal injustices.[83] Pragmatism plays a similarly aleatory role in providing guidance to the ecumenical dialogical practice of Scriptural Reasoning that seeks to open a critical communicative space for robust relations between Muslims, Jews, and Christians.[84] In the field of Religious Studies proper, diverse pragmatist approaches continue to play an important role in the more philosophical considerations of mysticism.[85]

How, then, do the participatory turn and pragmatism jointly challenge the sufficiency of the linguistic turn? Whereas certain forms of the linguistic turn may also abandon foundationalism, both pragmatists and participatory thinkers go farther in their more radical recognition of the simultaneously interpretive and ontological element in all acts of human knowing. Interpretation does not exhaust being, but invites us into the adventure of ontological transformation and relation. As Sanbothe writes, a focus on transformation (e.g., as a goal of philosophical inquiry) is perhaps the central feature in the pragmatic challenge or "twist" to the linguistic turn:

> The pragmatic twist of the linguistic turn can be understood as transformative. . . . Philosophy is then no longer understood as the methodological analysis of present states of affairs or existing linguistic structures. Instead it is comprehended and carried out as a transformative activity that experimentally works toward changes in common-sense in order to develop new knowledge practices.[86]

This is not an abandonment of the linguistic turn, but a deepening of it. Signs and texts are not only human artifacts, but beings thick with their own creational weight. The pragmatism of Peirce and Royce sees the entire world as an interlocking, relational ("synechistic") sphere of signs. Creatures are not simply sign-bearing or sign-interpreting but signs themselves. The universe is semiotic and, therefore, demands interpretation at every level. As Peirce writes:

> It seems a strange thing, when one comes to ponder over it, that a sign should leave its interpreter to supply a part of its meaning; but the explanation of the phenomenon lies in the fact the entire universe—not merely the universe of existents, but all that wider universe, embracing the universe of existents as a part, the universe which we are all accustomed to refer to as "the truth"—that all this universe is perfused with signs, if it is not composed exclusively of signs.[87]

Neither Peirce nor Royce reduced this pansemiosis to language and by refusing to do so they arguably afforded human language a greater nobility than contemporary linguistifications of reality and the sacred. If there is nothing beyond the text, as Derrida holds, or if we have to keep silence about whatever exceeds our language, as Wittgenstein thinks, then the play of language itself either begins to look vacuous or betokens a linguistic idealism hardly distinguishable from nihilism. However, if semiotics is ontological and thus exceeds the human languages that are its endlessly varying echoes, then language itself is "saved," as Owen Barfield might say.

Rather than conceiving semantics in terms of epistemology and demanding that our languages impossibly represent a wholly nonlinguistic reality, participatory thought considers that Peirce and Royce made the right move by attaching semiotics not primarily to epistemology but to ontology. Communicative acts and semiotic exchanges take place, first and foremost, in the sphere of the real, the ontological, a realm of signifying bodies and events upon which the subtlety of human cognition and language may supervene. Truth expressed in language is not, therefore, of a different order than the truth that simply is the processes of the world. Rather than an internal mirroring of an external realm, our language is an event that can resonate more or less with the events of the world. This allows for theories of truth as relational, endlessly hermeneutic happenings, and even for a nonrepresentationalist correspondence theory that discerns the true in a real ontological proportion between being and intelligibility. Such discernment is not a static intellectualist grasping of the "way things are," but the intuiting through body and mind of an aesthetic fit, a musical harmony, or an occult sympathy between knowing and being. In our epistemic acts, we do not passively register being on an internal screen, but rather participate in the dynamic elevation, transformation, and fulfillment of both the knower and the known through the inauguration of a new relationship.

In accord with the later thought of Peirce and Royce, participatory approaches see the adventure of knowing as ultimately a form of openness to the gifted, unanticipated, and even beguiling disclosures that are mediated to us from ontologically thick events through our own cultural, linguistic, and embodied productions. Truth—even truth about the *mystery* out of which everything arises[88]—is indeed "made" through our actions, inquiries, and processes of validation and, yet, this truth is not thereby simply a secular, nominalist product but rather participates in successive disclosures of a sacred reality.[89] Moreover, our properly human constructions of truth involve us in the dangerous business of affirmation—truth elicits our commitment and investment, which is to say truth-making requires the risk of participation and issues in transformation.[90] We give expression to truth not by representing inwardly an outward reality, but through our creative responses in word and deed to the pressure of a transcendent and immanent mystery and the creation it continually bestows. A pragmatist approach to spiritual questions is not merely analytic or interpretive but is rather self-implicating, critical, and transformative—three characteristics that help push the pragmatic theorist beyond the confines of the linguistic turn.

THE RESACRALIZATION OF LANGUAGE

Going beyond the linguistic turn need not mean leaving language behind, but can rather point us in a direction that accords even greater importance to language—as, for example, when we recognize a self-overcoming or even transcendent drive within language. Indeed, most religious traditions—such as Kabbalah, Hinduism, and Sufism—uphold the sacred nature of their scriptural languages. What this means is that religious tongues are taken as the expression or the embodiment of divine intentions, possessing therefore a different ontic status than secular languages. In these traditions, the idea of revelation is perforce connected to the sacralization of language. Because such texts are taken to participate in the tongues of angels, as it were, they can offer privileged revelations and ultimate truths about the origin, meaning, and purpose of reality. In some cases, these texts are regarded as ontologically primordial—i.e., they are said to have played a central role in the creation of the world and, therefore, to not have been humanly produced.[91] The Vedas and the Torah, for instance, are not traditionally regarded as human artifacts but are instead taken as "multileveled cosmic realities" or "cosmological principles" that mirror or embody the deepest structure of reality and/or the divine.[92] In theosophical Kabbalah, Moshe Idel writes, "language reflects the inner structure of the divine realm, the sefirotic system of divine powers."[93] In this context, textual exegesis naturally becomes a religious imperative of the utmost spiritual and revelatory significance.

Despite the adamant Enlightenment rejection of the cognitive value and authority of religious texts, the sacredness of religious language is gradually resurfacing in the contemporary study of religion. We have already referred to the process of the linguistification of the sacred brought about by modernity and the linguistic turn. As Habermas notes, such lingustification has even reshaped our notions of the divine: "The idea of God is transformed [*aufgehoben*] into a concept of a *Logos* . . . 'God' becomes the name for a communicative structure that forces men, on pain of a loss of their humanity, to go beyond their accidental, empirical nature to encounter one another *indirectly*, that is, across an objective something that they themselves are not."[94] What neither Habermas nor other modern thinkers could have expected, however, is that the transference of religious meanings onto language is leading today to a renewed and perhaps disconcerting revaluation of the sacred dimensions of religious language (and, indeed, of human language per se).[95] The lingustification of the sacred is paving the way for a resacralization of language.

This tendency is evident in discursive sites as diverse as Taylor's understanding of language as the "divine milieu," Cupitt's view of mysticism as "a kind of writing," and Kripal's suggestion that the hermeneutic study of mystical texts constitutes a genuinely mystical path. In his discussion of postmodern theologies, Grigg suggests that the death of God as a transcendental signifier (i.e., a transcendent divine consciousness, ground, or reality) requires that God becomes the Word now embodied in scripture.[96] In other words, much postmodern theology replaces the metaphysical God by a nonsubstantialist divine milieu whose essential dynamism is the free play of language. In this light, the evolution of premodern to modern to postmodern thinking in religion can be seen to have shifted its focus first from God to word and then, shockingly, from word to Word-as-God. The detranscendentalization of religion gives way to the consecration of immanent language.

The postmodern (re-)sacralization of language is not a tidy affair but instead explodes in many directions releasing a series of diverse strategies for overcoming reductionist linguistification. Among the most common of such strategies are the deconstructionist projects of those such as Cupitt and Taylor, who discover a kind of divinity in the sheer unencumbered *différance of* language itself. Such maneuvers restore sacrality to language but arguably do so at a high cost: the nominalism of many deconstructive efforts threatens to cut resacralized languages off from the body, the depths of spiritual experience, the natural world, and mundane human history.

Alternatively, a number of approaches to the postcritical transfiguration of language do not seek to untether language from the natural world, but instead see language as all the more sacred precisely to the degree that they discover it as all the more natural. Early on, thinkers such as Giambattista Vico, Johann Georg Hamann, Johann Herder, and Samuel Taylor Coleridge pioneered an overcoming of modernity through a deepening regard for language as expressive of a profound naturalism. It is not language as a free play alone that deserves to be called sacred, but instead language as constitutive of human thought and inherently expressive of a sacred creation to which humanity and culture likewise belong.

This alternative tradition continues to be an important source for a participatory overcoming of linguistification through a rediscovery of language's most profound springs. Language-wielding humanity stands in what Barfield calls a "directionally creator" relationship to the world. Language does perhaps unleash a kind of divinity, as Cupitt and Taylor recognize, but our creative and even divine linguistic powers are not divorced from a weighty materialism that alone allows our language to ever emerge. In our poetic powers, we do not leave the world behind but create after the manner that nature herself creates. "The world, like Dionysus, is torn to pieces by pure intellect," writes Barfield, "but the Poet is Zeus; he has swallowed the heart of the world; and he can reproduce it in a living body."[97] Participatory approaches to language see human poiesis as a creative manifestation of life or the spirit in the human realm—a swallowing the heart of the world—and they thus radically overcome the modern split between language and ontology. We suggest that it is in the particularities and constraints of nature, culture, and history that language becomes truly revelatory, a stance that affirms the immanence of the mystery without in any way repudiating its transcendence.

THE RENEWED INTEREST IN THE STUDY OF SPIRITUALITY

Any sensitive observer of North American and European culture will have noted the explosion of the use of the word *spirituality* in recent decades. On bookshelves and in the broadcast media, in places of worship and places of learning, in the workplace as well as at vacation destinations there is an unmistakable upsurge in the popularity of spirituality. Although the hackneyed distinction between being "spiritual" and being "religious" is largely specious, the currency of the term *spirituality* does point to an authentic hunger on the part of many for deeply lived religion rather than a simply confessed or routinely performed religiosity. Moreover, this yearning and the cultural phenomena associated with it are not confined to popular culture but have had an effect within academia as well. Indeed, today spirituality is not only a cultural preoccupation, but has emerged as an academic discipline in its own right.

Although the discipline of Spirituality has deep roots, it first solidified into an academic field during the 1990s. During this decade, the discipline established the necessary guild structures for an authentic field of study including societies (e.g., the Society for the Study of Christian Spirituality), journals (e.g., *Spiritus* and its predecessor the *Christian Spirituality Bulletin*, *Mystics Quarterly*, and *Studies in Spirituality*), book series (e.g., the Paulist Press *Classics of Western Spirituality* or the twenty-five volume *World Spirituality: An Encyclopedic History of the Religious Quest*, edited by Ewert Cousins), doctoral programs (e.g., at the Graduate Theological Union in Berkeley), research agendas, a critical methodology, a common terminology, and so forth. Although the field has thus far largely coalesced around the study of Christian spirituality there are signs that this exclusive focus is changing and that a broader field hospitable to differing religious stances is emerging.[98]

The field has largely succeeded in defining itself by delineating its formal and material objects of study. According to Schneiders, the *material object* or the *what* that is studied in the discipline of Christian Spirituality is "lived Christian faith." The *formal object* of study—what Schneiders calls "the particular aspect under which this lived experience of the faith is studied"—is experience:

> Spirituality as a discipline does not seek to deduce from revelation what Christian spirituality must be, or to prescribe theologically its shape, character, or functioning, or even necessarily to promote pastorally its exercise. It seeks to understand it as it actually occurs, as it actually transforms its subject toward fullness of life in Christ, that is, toward self-transcending life-integration within the Christian community of faith.[99]

Arguably, even though it is addressed to Christian Spirituality, Schneiders's programmatic formulation can be adopted for other traditions (with necessary modifications, of course). Thus, for example, Cousins speaks of the study of Global Spirituality as

> a distinct discipline which can be distinguished from other disciplines by the nature of the religious experience on which it reflects. . . . Such a discipline would study spirituality not in one tradition alone, isolated from all

others, but in a comprehensive geographic and historical context in which it would view the spiritual wisdom of each tradition in relation to that of all the others.[100]

Two of the most distinctive methodological features of the emerging discipline of Spirituality are self-implication and transformation and these features raise serious challenges to the hegemony of the linguistic paradigm within Religious Studies. The focus on experience (despite the term's many aporias) already propels the discipline some distance beyond linguistification, for while experience may not be entirely divorceable from language and interpretation, it is always more than just semantics, and more even than epistemology. Experience subverts our established categories and resists capture by our languages. A robust account of experience introduces to our thought an "evental" site, a happening with ontological stakes that cannot be collapsed, a happening that also calls the putative observer into question.[101] In the first issue of the journal *Spiritus*, Mary Frohlich argues for the "self-implicating" character of the study of lived spirituality. Frohlich amends Schneiders's definition in order to contend that, in its formal aspect, Spirituality is not the study of "experience" alone but the study of "the human spirit fully in act." Scholars of spirituality are fascinated by those phenomena that point toward human persons living and acting according to their highest (i.e., spiritual) potential. But, Frohlich says, "We cannot know 'the human spirit in act,' except *as* the human spirit in act. We cannot recognize the constructed expressions that radically engage the human spirit except on the basis of our own radical engagement."[102]

Our own radical engagement, according to Frohlich, involves us participatively in the objects of our study and implicates us in our academic conclusions. Although such self-implication has been traditionally looked at as contaminating inquiry, a number of notable scholars within Religious Studies (from Robert A. Orsi to Kripal) would join hands here with those pioneering the field of Spirituality in recognizing the futility of excising one's own religious journey from scholarly endeavor. As Orsi notes in *Between Heaven and Earth: The Religious Worlds People Make and the Scholars Who Study Them*, academics are necessarily haunted by their own religious histories: "[T]he halls of religious studies departments are thick with ghosts—the minister father, the tongue-speaking mother, the nuns and priests who taught us, the born-again brother. . . ."[103] Such self-implication is inevitable but too rarely acknowledged. As Orsi writes, "If sexual relations in the field is the great taboo subject of anthropology, our own religious histories is the great taboo of religious studies."[104]

Frohlich goes so far as to recommend that attending honestly and critically to our self-implication requires that we return to the language and practice of interiority—not interiority as the kind of private language Wittgen-

stein prohibited, but instead, following Bernard Lonergan, interiority as the
self-attentiveness without which we cannot be present to one another.[105]
Such a vision refuses to reduce spirituality to a private interior affair while
also insisting that some concept of interiority or self-awareness is necessary
for a full account of the human life—public, personal, moral, and relational
life in both its dejection and its exultation. The cultivation of this kind of
self-awareness requires something more than reading or the manipulation
and evaluation of texts. Indeed, argues Frohlich, it requires something akin
to spiritual practice on the part of the scholar. Although we need not jetti-
son the tools and insights offered by the linguistic turn, Frohlich's methodological move takes us fully beyond any linguistic reductionism and back into
the tempestuous, risky, transformative field of lived and embodied relationship to the mystery, to ourselves, and to others. Here, in fact, participatory
thinkers may want to push Spirituality scholars to go a bit farther still. We
welcome the return to a language of interiority but understand, beyond even
Lonergan, that interiority has a paradoxical externality to it. It is not only our
self-awareness that allows us to be present to one another, but also (and
simultaneously) our ecstatic interiority that is the very potential of our
dwelling, as it were, outside of ourselves *in* the consciousness of the other
(and vice versa). Interiority, thus conceived, is not an ethereal subjectivity,
but an ontologically thick ubiquitous reality; it is not a private fortress but the
potentially dangerous site of intimate relationality, exchange, and presence.

To return to interiority without falling into the errors of Enlightenment
representationalism and ontotheology means rescuing a concept of interiority as an event of vulnerable relationality—an event, therefore, of nearly
inevitable transformation. Of course, the importance of transformation has
not gone unnoticed by Spirituality scholars. Indeed, Philip Sheldrake
reflects a disciplinary consensus when he writes that, as self-implicating,
academic spirituality is also self-transforming: "What distinguishes the discipline of Christian spirituality in its fullest sense is that it is not only *infor-
mative* but *transformative*."[106] The artifacts of such a discipline are not just
books, journal articles, conferences, and lectures, but the changing lives of
both professors and their students, scholarly authors and their readers, clerics and religious communities.

Still, a caveat is necessary at this point, for the discipline of Spirituality
is acutely aware that self-implication brings dangers of its own. Therefore,
Spirituality strives to cultivate both the detachment necessary for the *critical*
side of the study of lived religion and the engagement necessary to do justice
to the *lived* side of this equation.[107] In this regard, scholars of spirituality are
very close to advocates of the participatory turn, who likewise argue that a
critical understanding of spirituality, mysticism, and religion can be enhanced
by a certain scholarly vulnerability to the phenomena studied. On the one
hand, because ontologically real religious happenings are not built up around

us but are rather put forth through us, participatory scholars understand that their bodies, souls, and spirits are part of that contested field they are called upon to study. To bracket themselves out of the inquiry (as the "science of religion" partisans would advocate) runs the severe risk of misplaced concreteness, that is, the substitution of an easy academic abstraction for the categorial recalcitrance of lived religion. On the other hand, both Spirituality and the participatory turn recognize that a critical, self-implicating study rebounds upon the spiritual practices and communities of faith thus engaged. Whether or not they share the faith of those they study, scholars are not in an absolutely different ethical, semantic, or religious universe than those they study but in a moral, ontological, and continually rearticulated relationship with the persons, beings, and communities about whom they write.

The Question of Religious Truth in Postmetaphysical Thinking

Perhaps the most universal trope in modern and postmodern approaches to religion is the claim that supposedly metaphysical claims should be more properly understood as statements about language. In the opening essay of a modernist collection on the study of religion, Willi Braun writes: "The 'transcendent' beyond-human beings, such as gods, spirits, ancestors, or whatever else one would name to this class, have their lives not in the some ontic selfhood, but as discursive entities."[108] Similarly, postmodern scholars persistently exploit Derrida's infamous contention that "[t]here is nothing outside the text" in order to discard the extralinguistic cognitive value of religious utterances. Apart from certain confessional or theological works, current academic thinking on religion displays an intense skepticism toward any metaphysical referent or transcendental signifier in religious discourse.[109] Postmetaphysical thinking, in short, deprives religious truth of any ontological significance beyond language.[110]

The implications of this postmetaphysical ethos for our understanding of religious truth are especially evident in Flood's work. According to Flood, religious truth is necessarily discursive because "it is impossible to get behind language and its reference system."[111] Therefore, he continues, religious truths should be valued and assessed in terms of their "intertextual" coherence: "Metaphysical truths proclaimed by a religious tradition . . . can be understood in terms of coherence within given frameworks and their significance within those frameworks."[112] Once freed from its metaphysical weight, that is, the question of religious truth becomes simply one of coherence and representation within each tradition's narrative practices. To support this claim, Flood points out that, since notions such as *nibbana* and *theosis* only have meaning within their respective soteriological frameworks (i.e., Buddhism and Christianity), any attempt to establish their truth value outside these narrative contexts is both futile and misguided. Flood's formulation leads, internally, to a contextualist account of religious truth in terms of linguistic coherence, and externally, to functionalist approaches: from the perspective of the outsider, "it becomes meaningless to ask about the truth of these concepts outside of their cultural function."[113] Here advocates of the participatory turn may want to challenge Flood to go farther. Granting the indisputable holism of religious meanings, we suggest that this holism is not logically inconsistent with the possibility that such meanings *may* possess ontological or metaphysical referents. If we allow for the plausibility of a multiplicity of actual religious worlds capable of referentially anchoring a number of religious meanings, we can coherently affirm both the contextuality *and* the supratextual import of many significant religious notions.

Although the contemporary split between religious language and ontology is generally taken as normative, it is, in fact, unwarranted and even potentially distorting. One of the best accounts of the possible distortions implicit in the postmetaphysical deflation of religious truth claims with which we are familiar is Jeremy Northcote's critique of the widespread scholarly practice of bracketing claims of supernormal causation in the study of religion.[114] Briefly, Northcote argues that the methodological suspension of the validity of supernormal claims (e.g., about metaphysical entities or levels of reality), far from warranting objectivism or scholarly neutrality, may actually constitute a bias against "the possibility that people's thinking and behaviour are indeed based on various supernormal forces." "In this scenario," he adds, "a bracketing approach will falsely attribute mundane sociological explanations to behaviour that is in actuality shaped by supernatural forces."[115] Accordingly, Northcote issues a call for dialogue between Western and alternative perspectives in the appraisal of supernormal claims. The point here is that unless one subscribes ideologically to a materialistic natural metaphysics, it may be prudent, and perhaps heuristically fertile, not to reject a priori the possibility of effective causation from the various supernormal sources described in religious utterances.[116]

The methodological agnosticism problematized by Northcote seems largely rooted in the strong allegiance within Religious Studies to neo-Kantian frameworks that either bracket or deny the existence of supernatural and metaphysical sources of religion. On the one hand, scholars as different as Ninian Smart and Peter Byrne, among others, have forcefully defended for decades that the study of religion should take an agnostic (and supposedly neutral) position regarding the reality of metaphysical or transcendental referents.[117] At the heart of this apparently temperate stance rests the Kantian belief that innate or deeply seated epistemic constraints in human cognition render impossible or illicit any knowledge claim about such metaphysical realities. Though more metaphysically eliminationist than agnostic, Caputo eloquently articulates this intuition: "We cannot, by science, philosophy, or religion, situate ourselves safely in some privileged spot above the mortal fray below having gained the high ground of a Privileged Access to the Way Things Are."[118] On the other hand, many postmodern authors endorse today a "linguistic Kantianism" that often results in the epistemological obliteration of such realities. Giving voice to this view, Taylor states: "Consciousness . . . deals only with signs and never reaches the thing in itself. More precisely, the thing in itself is not an independent entity (be it 'real' or 'ideal') to which all signs refer, but is itself a sign. . . . There is no logos to be revealed, no secret to be uncovered, no truth to be discovered."[119] Nevertheless, to deny that religious phenomena can ever have extralinguistic substance is to make a metaphysical claim, even if a negative one—a claim that arguably undermines the professed postmetaphysical status of these versions of the linguistic paradigm. Neo-Kantian skepticism not only traps many students of religion in a kind of epistemic box hermetically sealed by its critical presuppositions, but also requires the arguably ethnocentric dismissal of the participants' cognitive claims. The ethnocentric core of this skeptical stance becomes apparent in the way it dismisses all ontological and metaphysical claims made by religious practitioners as precritical, ingenuous, dogmatic, or even primitive and superstitious. As Donald Evans once remarked, however, who are the philosophers to decide what mystics can or cannot do?[120]

Clearly, one of the central issues at stake here is whether some kind of personal engagement or even transformation—such as the overcoming of mental pride, the integration of body and mind, the purification of the heart, or the development of contemplative competences—may be required for both the apprehension and the assessment of certain religious truth claims. After all, most contemplative traditions hold that, in order to ascertain their most fundamental truths, practitioners need to develop cognitive competences beyond the structures of linguistic rationality. This question is, of course, at the heart of the conflict between tradition and modernity—and arguably between religion and science—with adherents to the former worldviews claiming such need and proponents of the latter vigorously rejecting it. In the eyes of their respective antagonists, religionists appear epistemologically naïve, elitist, and authoritarian, and the modernists look cognicentric, prejudiced, and even cut off from essential dimensions of their being. Naturally, both camps denounce the rampant dogmatism they sincerely perceive in their opponents' stance.

Whereas we believe that the emphasis on transformation as a primary goal of human inquiry brought about by the pragmatic turn in contemporary philosophy may eventually relax this tension, this issue is profound and real and needs to be faced squarely. We do not claim to have any magical solution to the quandary, but we want to propose that the direction forward calls for a kind of alchemical mixture between intellectual humility and ruthless criticism. Can our mind be humble enough to recognize that its rational structures may not always have the last word in the evaluation of truth claims, and yet maintain and even sharpen its critical look toward oppressive, repressive, and self-deceptive religious dogmas and ideologies? Can the modern mind admit that the epistemic competences fostered by Western education may not be the final or necessarily superior cognitive plateau, and simultaneously denounce authoritarian tendencies possibly emerging from the elitism intrinsic to highly specialized cognitive endeavors such as the contemplative one? In the end, as Kripal reminds us, "Rationalism and reductionism . . . are also state-specific truths (that is, they are specific to highly trained egoic forms of awareness), but their states of mind are more easily reproduced and communicated, at least within our present Western cultures."[121]

Let us have now a closer look at the nature and problems of the neo-Kantianism typical of the contemporary study of religion. Cultural-linguistic approaches usually maintain that religious knowledge is constituted by language, doctrinal beliefs, and soteriological expectations. It is true that religious practitioners generally "discover" the knowledge already cultivated by their traditions, and cultural-linguistic approaches should be credited for recognizing this and having emphasized the contextuality and ensuing diversity of spiritual knowledge claims (even though proponents of these approaches have not always as clearly acknowledged the contextuality of their own analyses). As we have seen, however, from this valid insight these approaches go on to deny or bracket the ontological and metaphysical import of religious truth claims. Although it would probably be unfair to charge *all* contextualist programs with psychologism, subjectivism, or reductionism, it is fair to say, we believe, that they typically operate under the spell of what Karl Popper called the "myth of the framework."[122] Adapted to our present context, this myth suggests the idea that *mystics and religious practitioners are prisoners of their conceptual frameworks and that spiritual knowledge must always be shaped by or screened through them.*

In the study of mysticism, this neo-Kantian stance has been forcibly articulated by Katz: "My view—and it's important that it be understood—is that while such transcendental realities or Reality may well exist, it (or He, She or It) can only be known by us in the way such metaphysical realia become available to us given the sort of beings we are."[123] In other words, metaphysical realities *may* exist, but the only thing we can access is our situated phenomenal awareness of them. Contra mystical claims, no direct knowledge of spiritual realities is therefore possible.[124] One way to challenge the myth of the framework is to show that mystics report insights that their doctrines and beliefs could not have prepared them to "expect" or allowed them to contextually "constitute."[125] Although mysticism does tend to be "conservative" in its reaffirming of previous doctrinal beliefs,[126] neoperennialists are right in noting the emergence of novel and truly "revolutionary" mystical events that cannot be fully explained by ordinary constructive variables or acquired conceptual frameworks. Nevertheless, there is still a more fatal stroke to be given to the myth of the framework. The crucial flaw of the contextualist logic is not the denial that mystics can transcend their conceptual frameworks, *but the very postulation of a dualism of conceptual framework and uninterpreted reality.*

The dualism of framework and reality is not only alive and well in the study of mysticism, but extends throughout the entire discipline of Religious Studies. For instance, both Hick and George Lindbeck have provided influential defenses of religions as interpretative schemes of an ultimately unknowable reality.[127] Likewise, Joseph Runzo's work illustrates how the view of religions as conceptual schemes (which he endorses) places a noumenal spiritual reality out of reach from human consciousness, which then becomes "trapped" in a "merely" phenomenal world. Since all religious truth claims are relative to conceptual frameworks, Runzo argues, religious skepticism can only be avoided by resorting to an exhausted "absolute commitment" to faith.[128] Note also how much the seminal work of Smith perpetuates this dualism. In his often quoted essay, "Map is Not Territory," after rightly critiquing the idea of a pregiven territory (the notorious myth of the given), Smith concludes: "'Map is not territory'—but maps are all we possess."[129] Contrasting Smith with Eliade, Sam Gill writes, "For Smith there is no objective territory. . . . Distinctions in space, time, shape, and body are the human methods of constructing reality, of engaging the world meaningfully. To recognize something as a center or an originating event is not to locate a hierophany . . . but to participate in a mode of human creativity."[130] The setback of Smith's formulation is that it is built on the false dichotomy of "objective" and "constructed," "discovered" and "created." As many of the contributions to this volume show, however, from a participatory perspective the perceived presence of a religious event in the world can be seen as neither a purely objective discovery nor a merely human construction. As is the case with the cocreated nature of a rainbow, an ontologically rich religious event emerges in the world precisely through human perceptual and cognitive participation.

The dualism of framework and reality is widely regarded as implausible, especially in the wake of Davidson's classic essay "On the Very Idea of a Conceptual Scheme."[131] Taking the translatability of languages as a paradigmatic case, Davidson argues that the idea of alternative conceptual frameworks necessarily presupposes a larger common ground that makes these frameworks truly "alternative" and whose existence belies the idea.[132] According to Davidson, the dissolution of this "third dogma of empiricism" (after Quine) not only undermines the existence of conceptual frameworks (and its related self-defeating conceptual relativisms), but also renders the idea of an uninterpreted reality (the myth of the given) unintelligible.[133] Once we give up the dualism of framework and reality, we can, with Davidson, "re-establish *unmediated touch* with the familiar objects whose antics make our sentences true or false."[134] It is crucial to realize that since the overcoming of this dualism implies not only dropping ideas about conceptual frameworks, but also the concept of an uninterpreted reality, these "objects" can no longer be taken to mean the pregiven objects of positivism, empiricism, or naïve realism. On the contrary, giving up this dualism calls us to move beyond objectivism and subjectivism, and thus to redeem our participatory, connected, and direct relationship with reality as the source of our being.[135]

In sum, the legitimacy of the postmetaphysical deflation of religious truth is contingent on the validity of neo-Kantian assumptions and dualisms. On the one hand, this approach requires either the denial of any extralinguistic religious reality or its reification as an inaccessible noumenon about which we must necessarily remain silent. On the other hand, it posits a phenomenal consciousness that is overdetermined by cultural-linguistic variables and constructive cognitive mechanisms. In their various fashions, Kantian epistemological skepticism, phenomenological bracketing, and metaphysical agnosticism all lead to the same practical outcome: the systematic refusal of any possible translinguistic referent for religious truth claims. It seems obvious, then, that the linguistic paradigm in the study of religion led the way out of the Cartesian philosophy of consciousness but not out of the Kantian epistemological pessimism. In lieu of this, we propose that, at least in this fundamental respect, *the linguistic turn has not fully overcome the Cartesian-Kantian paradigm of classical and modern approaches to the study of religion.* But it is worth asking: How genuine a *post*modern and *post*colonial approach can we have so long as we remain bound to Kantianism? In the next section, we consider certain developments in the contemporary discussion about religious pluralism that suggest the need to entertain the ontological bases of the plurality of religious forms while at the same time avoiding the reification of static essences, spiritual hierarchies, or universally paradigmatic metaphysical realities.

The Irreducibility of Religious Pluralism

A few marginal voices notwithstanding, the search for a common core, universal essence, or single metaphysical world behind the multiplicity of religious experiences and cosmologies can be regarded as over.[136] Whether guided by the exclusivist intuitionism of traditionalism or the fideism of theological agendas, the outcome—and too often the intended goal—of such universalist projects was unambiguous: the privileging of one particular spiritual or metaphysical system over all others. Furthermore, modern scholarship shows that inclusivist and even so-called pluralist models of religious diversity also tend to conceal claims for the supremacy of one or another religious tradition, thereby collapsing into the rigid exclusivism of dogmatic stances.[137] In a way, the standard responses to religious diversity—exclusivism, inclusivism, and ecumenical pluralism—can be situated along a continuum ranging from more gross to more subtle forms of "spiritual narcissism," which elevate one's favored tradition or spiritual choice as superior. The religious superiority of one's preferred tradition is normally conceived in terms of its conveying a more complete or accurate picture of a purportedly single religious ultimate or "the way things really are." The dogmatically apologetic nature of these approaches arguably limits their effectiveness to facilitate a genuinely symmetrical, dialogical, and mutually enriching encounter among religious traditions in which deep transformation and even the risk of conversion are real possibilities.

Whereas the search for interreligious parallels continues to be a valid and important scholarly enterprise—especially as guided by the so-called new comparativism[138]—most scholars have wisely given up explaining the differences among religions through open or concealed hierarchical rankings of spiritual insights or traditions. This sensibility is at work in some of the most interesting recent pluralist accounts of religious diversity, such as Mark Heim's "soteriological pluralism" or Stephen Kaplan's proposal of "different paths leading to different summits."[139] Though both authors remain agnostic about the metaphysical status of their proposals, Heim envisions a multiplicity of irreducible religious salvations associated with the various traditions, and Kaplan postulates three independent but equiprimordial religious goals and conceptually possible ultimate realities: theism (in its various forms), monistic nondualism (à la Advaita Vedanta), and process nondualism (exemplified by Yogacara Buddhism).

This combination of radical pluralism and metaphysical agnosticism is a chief feature of the cultural-linguistic solution to the problem of conflicting truth claims in religion. The translation of religious ontologies into culturally mediated discursive artifacts and/or soteriological ends allows scholars to coherently explain interreligious differences as the predictable upshot of the world's various religious beliefs, practices, vocabularies, or language games. As we have seen, this move requires the denial or bracketing of the ontological status of the referents of religious language, which are usually seen as analytically meaningless, hermeneutically obscure, or parasitic upon a despotic metaphysics of presence. After the linguistic turn, the recognition of a genuine plurality of religious goals comes at the cost of either stripping religious ontological claims of any extralinguistic veridicality or denying that we can know such truths even if they exist.[140]

It is interesting to note that the problem of religious pluralism (that is, the exclusivity and incompatibility of religious claims about metaphysical realities) significantly contributes to the modern and postmodern incredulity toward their ontological status. Discussing the need for naturalistic explanations in Religious Studies, J. Samuel Preus writes: "For how can such an enterprise [i.e., the study of religion] proceed without any theory of causes, especially when its primary data, provided by the representatives of specific

religious traditions, are routinely authenticated by references to a divine origin of some sort—especially *when such references function as explanations that
are mutually exclusive?*"[141] Against the background of modernist assumptions
about an objectively singular reality, it is understandable that the presence of
a plurality of mutually exclusive accounts leads to the confident dismissal of
religious explanations. It is as if contemporary scholarship had succumbed to
the Cartesian anxiety behind what W. E. Hocking called the "scandal of plurality," the worry that "if there are so many divergent claims to ultimate truth,
then perhaps none is right."[142] Nevertheless, both the underlying anxiety and
the persuasive force of this intuition fade away if we consider the possibility
of a plurality of culturally mediated but existing religious worlds capable of
anchoring the various religious languages. Once we drop objectivist and universalistic assumptions about a single pregiven spiritual reality or metaphysical ultimate, the multiplicity of religious truth claims stops being a source of
ontological incredulity or metaphysical agnosticism and becomes entirely
natural, perhaps even essential.

In this regard, we should pay special attention to the work of a number
of contemporary scholars who in various ways stress or reclaim the ontological sources and import of religious knowledge while reinforcing pluralistic
and contextualist intuitions. For example, Michael Stoeber's "experiential
constructivism" affirms the culturally mediated nature of religious experiences, and simultaneously maintains that spiritual realities can have a creative impact on the content of religious knowledge, which explains the emergence of novel spiritual insights and mystical heresies.[143] Jess Byron
Hollenback proposes that one of the main effects of many recollective and
meditative practices is the "empowerment" (*enthymesis*) of the mystic's conscious and unconscious thoughts.[144] This process of empowerment transforms
the mystics' imagination into an organ of supranormal perception and knowledge capable of not only obtaining paranormally veridical information, but
also shaping different spiritual landscapes according to the metaphysics,
anthropology, and soteriology of their traditions. It is crucial to stress that
Hollenback is not proposing any type of solipsistic or projective psychologism
whereby mystics merely "create" their spiritual universes by exerting the faculty of their empowered imagination. On the contrary, Hollenback believes
that the empowered imagination can actually transcend the mystic's cultural-
linguistic context and become a source of novel revelations and creative spiritual insights. In the context of Jewish mysticism, Elliot R. Wolfson offers a
thoroughly contextualist and pluralistic *but* ontologically substantial account
of visionary religious imagination. According to Wolfson, the visions of the
Jewish mystic are not entirely constituted by his or her subjective imagination, but actually reflect "ontological realities that have the capacity of being
seen within the imagination of the visionary." This is so because "the imagination is . . . the organ that puts one in contact with spiritual realities that

are perceptible to each individual according to the dominant images of one's religious and cultural affiliation."[145]

The appeal of these highly participatory proposals lies in their being able to offer epistemological bases for a contextually sensitive religious pluralism that overcomes the linguistic deflation of religious ontology or metaphysics. In the context of the dilemmas posed by religious pluralism, one of the many advantages of a participatory account of religious knowing is that it frees religious discourse from the Cartesian-Kantian presuppositions (e.g., about a single pregiven or noumenal ultimate reality) that bind it to reductionistic, exclusivist, or fideistic formulations. Once we do away with the dualism of framework and reality, on the one hand, and recognize the ontologically creative role of spiritual cognition, on the other, the idea of a multiplicity of metaphysical religious worlds becomes not only plausible but perhaps also indispensable. In its most radical version, a participatory perspective does not contend that there are two, three, or any limited quantity of pregiven spiritual ultimates, but rather that *the radical openness, interrelatedness, and creativity of the mystery and/or the cosmos allows for the participatory enaction of an indefinite number of possible self-disclosures of reality and corresponding metaphysical or religious worlds.*[146] These worlds are not statically closed but fundamentally dynamic and open to the continued transformation resulting (at least in part) from the creative impact of human visionary imagination and religious hermeneutical endeavors. Although this may at first sound like a rather "anything goes" approach to religious claims, we hold to the contrary that recognizing a diversity of cocreated religious worlds in fact asks us to be more perspicuous in discerning their differences and merits. Because such worlds are not simply given but involve us as agents and cocreators, we are not off the ethical hook where religion is concerned but instead inevitably make cosmopolitical and moral choices in all our religious actions.

We close this section drawing attention to a potentially significant anomaly within the cultural-linguistic explanation of both religious knowledge and religious pluralism. Modern consciousness research suggests that human beings may be able to access a multiplicity of apparently "given" religious motives and spiritual worlds. The psychiatrist Stanislav Grof, for example, describes how subjects employing different technologies of consciousness modification—such as entheogens or methodical hyperventilation—report having direct experiences of a rich variety of spiritual cosmologies, revelations, and even ultimate principles.[147] What is most striking is that, according to Grof, subjects repeatedly testify to not only having access but also to understanding spiritual insights and cosmologies belonging to specific religious worlds *even without previous exposure to them.* In Grof's own words:

> In nonordinary states of consciousness, visions of various universal symbols
> can play a significant role in experiences of individuals who previously had

no interest in mysticism or were strongly opposed to anything esoteric. These visions tend to convey instant intuitive understanding of the various levels of meaning of these symbols.

As a result of experiences of this kind, subjects can develop accurate understanding of various complex esoteric teachings. In some instances, persons unfamiliar with the Kabbalah had experiences described in the Zohar and Sepher Yetzirah and obtained surprising insights into Kabbalistic symbols. Others were able to describe the meaning and function of intricate mandalas used in the Tibetan Vajrayana and other tantric systems.[148]

Though Grof's research awaits the more systematic replication necessary to achieve superior scientific status, his data suggest the limitations of the contextualist account of religious diversity and, if appropriately corroborated, constitute an empirical refutation of the cultural-linguistic overdetermination of religious knowledge and experience. Let us remember here that, for contextualist theorists such as Katz, religious phenomena are always entirely constructed by doctrinal beliefs, languages, practices, and expectations.[149] As Peter Moore puts it, "[T]he lack of doctrinal presuppositions might prevent the mystic not only from understanding and describing his mystical states but even from experiencing the fullness of these states in the first place."[150] Whether or not Grof's subjects experience "the fullness" of mystical states and attain a complete understanding of traditional spiritual meanings is an open question. But even if this were not the case, the evidence provided by Grof's case studies is sufficient, we believe, to render the cultural-linguistic "strong thesis of mediation" questionable on empirical grounds. Grof's subjects report experiences that should *not* take place if the "strong thesis of mediation" is correct.[151]

This anomaly raises serious challenges to the cultural determination of religious knowledge and the associated linguistic account of religious pluralism. The participatory account of a plurality of historically enacted religious worlds introduced above, however, turns the anomaly constituted by Grof's data into a solved problem that the prevailing cultural-linguistic research tradition cannot explain—a key feature of conceptual advance in understanding according to Larry Laudan's theory of scientific growth.[152]

ॐ

In this section we have seen how the movement away from the essentialism, universalism, and Western colonialism of the classical approaches to religion brought about by the linguistic turn paved the way for the emergence of a plethora of more contextualized, pluralist, and non-Western perspectives. These developments reveal a fundamental paradox at the heart of the linguistic paradigm in the study of religion. On the one hand, linguistic approaches insist on the need to translate religious metaphysical claims into statements about language. On the other hand, many of these approaches stress the centrality of human faculties and perspectives—embodied, erotic, gendered, emic, and so on—that persistently point to extralinguistic sources of meaning and ways of knowing in religious practice and experience.[153] In other words, there is an unresolved tension between the linguistification of the sacred and the emphasis on the nonlinguistic that characterizes important areas of contemporary scholarship on religion. In the next section, we suggest that this tension can be relaxed, and perhaps dissolved, through a more participatory approach to religious phenomena.

THE PARTICIPATORY TURN

Can we take religious experience, spirituality, and mysticism seriously today without reducing them to either cultural-linguistic by-products or simply asserting their validity as a dogmatic fact? In the last section, we identified a number of ways the linguistic turn fails to account for some important issues and developments in the contemporary academic study of religion. As we have already suggested, we believe that an effective exploration of, and possible answer to, these questions calls for another "turn" in Religious Studies—one that incorporates postmodern and pragmatic concerns with the renewed interest in different ways of knowing (embodied, gendered, imaginal, contemplative, and so on), the self-implicating study of spirituality and mystical transformation, and the increasing willingness to consider emic understandings without falling into either uncritical confessional stances or the reductionistic essentialisms and universalisms of most classical approaches. In other words, we want to propose that there is a third way possible, an alternative to both, on the one hand, today's fashionable linguistification of the sacred and, on the other hand, a more conservative precritical fideism.

We are calling this alternative approach the "participatory turn" in the study of religion, spirituality, and mysticism. Briefly, the participatory turn argues for an *enactive* understanding of the sacred, seeking to approach religious phenomena, experiences, and insights as cocreated events.[154] Such events can engage the entire range of human epistemic faculties (e.g., rational, imaginal, somatic, aesthetic, and so forth) with the creative unfolding of reality or the mystery in the enactment—or "bringing forth"—of ontologically rich religious worlds. Put somewhat differently, we suggest that religious and spiritual phenomena are "participatory" in the sense that they can emerge from the interaction of all human attributes and a nondetermined spiritual power or creative dynamism of life.[155] More specifically, we are advancing the admittedly bold hypothesis that religious worlds and phenomena, such as the Kabbalistic four realms, the various Buddhist cosmologies, or Teresa's seven mansions, come into existence out of a process of par-

ticipatory cocreation between human multidimensional cognition and the
generative force of life and/or the spirit.[156]

Our account of participatory knowing as essentially creative, transformative, and performative (versus objective and representational) should not
be confused with a rejection of realism or the endorsement of a mentalist or
idealist worldview. Although the lines of the philosophical divide are often
traced between "representationalist realists" and "antirepresentationalists
constructivists" who tend to reject realism,[157] this generally valid polarization
becomes fallacious if taken to be normative. As Steven Engler shows in an
instructive essay, constructivism, though challenging the correspondence
between linguistic signs and independent facts, is not necessarily antirealist
or relativistic.[158] In Religious Studies, for instance, Katzian constructivism
does not necessarily deny the reality of religious referents or metaphysical
entities, but maintains that, in the case that such entities do exist, we can
only enjoy access to our contextually mediated phenomenal awareness of
them. The adoption of an enactive paradigm of cognition in the study of religion, however, frees us from the myth of the framework and other aporias of
the Kantian two worlds doctrine by holding that human multidimensional
cognition cocreatively participates in the emergence of a number of plausible
enactions of reality. Participatory enaction, in other words, is epistemologically constructivist and metaphysically realist.[159]

This participatory understanding allows a bold affirmation of spiritual
realities without falling into a reified metaphysics of presence, nor into the
naïve essentialisms of dogmatic certainty. On the one hand, a participatory
account of religious worlds overcomes the static and purportedly universal
metaphysical structures of the past because it holds that culturally mediated
human variables have a formative role in their constitution. Whereas the
openness of religious worlds to the ongoing visionary creativity of humankind
entails their necessary dynamism, the contextual and embodied character of
such creative urges requires their plurality. On the other hand, the turn we
are advocating allows the advance of religious inquiry without the danger of
falling into a precritical stance because it draws explicit attention to the constitutive role of human creative participation in all religious phenomena and
truth. We stress, however, that embracing the constitutive role of the human
in religious matters need not bind us with a (quasi-Kantian) epistemic strait-
jacket. Such human participation need not reduce religious and spiritual phenomena to mere products of a culturally or biologically shaped human subjectivity. As Capps explains, religious inquiry after the dawn of modernity has
been conducted with a "Cartesian-Kantian temper" that considers religious
worlds to be either "objective" or noumenal realities that are cognitively
inaccessible (or available only in dubiously "pure" intuitive states) or artifacts
of "subjective" imagination and cultural-linguistic fabrication.[160] Questioning
this Cartesian-Kantian legacy, the participatory turn calls us to move *beyond*

objectivism and subjectivism toward the recognition of the interpretive and therefore largely constituted but nevertheless immediate nature of spiritual and religious knowledge. Speaking about the spiritual dimensions of nature, Richard Tarnas eloquently captures the gist of this post-Kantian formulation:

> This participatory epistemology . . . incorporates the postmodern understanding of knowledge and yet goes beyond it. The interpretive and constructive character of human cognition is fully acknowledged, but the intimate, interpenetrating and all-permeating relationship of nature to the human being and human mind allows the Kantian consequence of epistemological alienation to be entirely overcome. The human spirit does not merely prescribe nature's phenomenal order; rather, the spirit of nature brings forth its own order through the human mind when that mind is employing its full complement of faculties—intellectual, volitional, emotional, sensory, imaginative, aesthetic, epiphanic.[161]

As the essays of this volume illustrate, in the academic study of religion such a participatory understanding can help to dissolve previous antinomies, such as those between contextualist and neoperennialist accounts of mysticism, "cultural-linguistic" and "expressive-emotional" models of religion, scientific and religious epistemologies, or, more generally, modern and traditional worldviews.

MODES OF PARTICIPATION: ARCHAIC, ROMANTIC, AND ENACTIVE

It might be reasonably objected that by championing the importance of the category of participation in the study of religion we are merely returning to Romantic or archaic styles of participatory knowing. We contend, however, that we are not simply "going back" to a participatory mode of thinking, but also modernizing the concept of participation. We are calling for a participatory modernity, even a participatory postmodernity. While we cannot offer here a systematic comparison of pre-Enlightenment and post-Enlightenment modes of participation, it may be important to offer at least some general distinctions between them.[162]

At the beginning of the twentieth century, the French philosopher Lucien Lévy-Bruhl introduced the term *participation mystique* to designate the type of mentality that characterized so-called "primitive" people. In contrast to the logical intelligence of the modern West, Lévy-Bruhl suggested that native mentality can be described in terms of an "affectational participation" based on a prelogical, mystical interconnectedness with others, nature, and things.[163] In his posthumously published *Notebooks* (*Les Carnets*), Lévy-Bruhl relaxed the contrast between logical and participatory mentalities indicating that, instead of being exclusively associated with modern and primitive modes of thinking respectively, both cognitive styles coexisted to some extent in all human beings.[164] For the late Lévy-Bruhl, participation became the universal affective-analogical dimension of the human mind.

Half a century after Lévy-Bruhl's death, the anthropologist of religion Stanley J. Tambiah proposed that these two coexistent modes of thought—which he calls "participation" and "causality"—represent two different "orientations to the world" that are perfectly appropriate in their respective arenas of human inquiry and activity.[165] According to Tambiah, the discourse of causality is proper in science, analytic reasoning, and technical and biomedical sciences, and the discourse of participation in religion, empathic understanding, aesthetics, ritual, and meditation. In a recent reformulation of Tambiah's proposal, Wouter J. Hanegraaf suggests that whereas the human tendency toward participation derives from a feeling-based insight into the nonlocal interconnectedness of all beings, the human tendency to instrumental causality is guided instead by the intuition that all world events are the result of material causation.[166] Hanegraaff also points out that instrumental causality became the privileged mechanism to discern objective truth in the Western world, and that such epistemic supremacy precipitated a counterculture eminently based on participation that can be traced from the Romantics to the contemporary New Age movement.[167]

Indeed, German Romanticism was a richly participatory movement. In their revolt against the Enlightenment's apotheosis of logic and reason, the Romantics affirmed the participatory role of imagination and feeling, intuition and inspiration, volition and spiritual insight, in the elaboration of human knowledge.[168] Romanticism not only rescued the epistemic value of all human attributes, but also forcibly maintained—perhaps most visibly in the writings of Johann Wolfgang Goethe, Friedrich Schelling, and Coleridge—that it is precisely through such multidimensional cognition that human beings can share both effectively and creatively in the ongoing self-understanding and self-perfection of both the spirit and nature.

Despite the strongly pluralistic spirit of many Romantic proposals,[169] classical phenomenologists of religion—from Nathan Söderblom to Rudolf Otto to Friedrich Heider to Gerardus van der Leuw to Eliade—blended the Romantic fascination with religious intuition and feeling with certain universalistic and objectivist assumptions of the Enlightenment project. On the one hand, religious scholars heavily influenced by the Romantics, such as Eliade, developed a view of "the sacred" as a Kantian-like category or universal element embedded in the innermost structure of human consciousness.[170] Though Eliade prudently avoided essentialist or transcendentalist understandings of the sacred and maintained that "hierophanies" emerge from the dialectical relationship between human consciousness and a "constituted given" reality, his research program was firmly guided by the structuralist search for invariant, nonhistorical essences—such as "patterns," "archetypes," or "fundamental religious experiences"—behind the variety of historical religious manifestations.[171] In addition to this structuralist agenda, Eliade's universalistic view of religion, as well as his strong allegiance to what is known today as the "philosophy of consciousness," reveals his commitment to philosophical ideals and paradigms characteristic of the modern episteme.[172] On the other hand, when Van der Leuw, the father of the phenomenology of religion, wrote that the study of religion needs to adopt a participatory subjectivity, he had in mind a kind of "Enlightened" participation in the universal essences of religious forms—essences thought to possess invariant transcultural features that only the phenomenological method could uncover.[173] As Arthur McCalla points out, Romantic phenomenologists regarded "religious experience as an autonomous, irreducible and universal intuition or feeling of the Infinite . . . [and] the various religions of the world as the positive forms in which the essence of religion manifests itself."[174] These assumptions have rightfully raised severe criticisms toward Romantic and neo-Romantic approaches to religion both from postmodern thinkers, who mistrust their essentialist and universalistic motives, and from naturalistic scholars, who are quick to denounce their cryptotheological agendas.[175]

Archaic and Romantic modes of participation share significant features with the participatory turn we are advocating in this volume. Specifically, these participatory proposals not only affirm the import of multidimensional cognition for a richer apprehension of reality, but also eschew the Kantian two worlds doctrine and its associated epistemological skepticism regarding the possibility of direct knowing of reality. Nevertheless, there are also critical differences between the present project and prior participatory formulations. First, whereas archaic participation (as articulated by Lévy-Bruhl) avoids the subject/object divide through a prereflective mystical fusion with the other and the natural world, emerging modes of participation overcome Cartesian dualism self-reflexively by preserving a highly differentiated though permeable individuality or *participatory self* as the agent of religious knowing. Moreover, in contrast to the precritical paradigm of cognition linked to archaic participation, the participatory turn adopts an enactive view of knowledge that allows a critical assessment of religious claims but free from the demand of testing the correspondence between facts and propositions, or between facts and ideas. Secondly, while most types of Romantic religious participation made essentialist and/or structuralist assumptions, the recognition of religious forms as participatory enactions emancipates religious inquiry from not only the dualism of essence and manifestation, but also of "deep" structure and "surface" expression. In other words, whereas the "Enlightened" participatory subjectivity of Romantic phenomenology of religion seeks an intuitive and empathic grasping of the universal, invariant, and, at times, pregiven essences of religious manifestations, enactive participation avoids such modernist (as well as ancient) assumptions, and instead approaches religious forms and worlds as the dynamic sites of genuine plurality and cocreated emergent realities.

The last point deserves further elaboration. From a participatory perspective, the Romantic reduction of all religious manifestations to expressions of a univocal spiritual reality—however transcendentally or phenomenologically conceived—comes at a high price. The conflation of the rich variety of religious manifestations into a limited number of Procrustean phenomenological essences or structures of human consciousness not only undermines the genuine plurality of religious realities, but arguably constrains the scope and possibilities of the role of human creative imagination in their formation. The multiplicity of religious worlds cannot be forced into the reductive molds of being mere reflections of a monochromatic spiritual reality without damaging their autonomy and integrity. The introduction of Enlightenment dogmas into the Romantic fascinations of classic scholars of religion, thus, hindered the complete "liberation of images" with which Barfield evocatively characterizes more creative and self-reflexive forms of participation, forms to which this anthology is devoted.[176]

Participatory Knowing as Creative Multidimensional Cognition

In *The Passion of the Western Mind*, Tarnas explains how both Romantic and Enlightenment sensibilities shaped modern life in a dualistic and ultimately unintegrated manner. Whereas Romantic values continue to guide our appreciation of art, culture, religion, and everyday relationships, the principles of the Enlightenment became paradigmatic in the rational search for valid knowledge.[177] Religious Studies, heir to both Romanticism and the Enlightenment, inherited this Janus-faced disposition. As Flood points out, classical phenomenology of religion was shaped by the "cognitive perspective" of the Enlightenment—i.e., belief in a unitary human nature and the epistemic privilege of reason—and the "affective perspective" of Romanticism—i.e., fascination for the mysterious, as well as an emphasis on feeling, intuition, and aesthetic experience.[178] In a similar vein, Daniel Gold characterizes the modern interpretive study of religion—from Eliade to Clifford Geertz to Dumézil to Wendy Doniger—as a blend of the Romantic empathic allurement for the religious and the Enlightenment cognitive conviction that reason and science should be the preferred means for establishing truth. "Interpretive writers," he tells us, "tend to suffer from an uncomfortable modern dilemma: They *like* religion . . . but they *believe* in science."[179] Though such an ambivalent approach is not free from potential tensions, Gold suggests that what defines the work of the most successful interpretive writers of religion is *precisely* a synthesis of a "soft heart," characterized by empathic imagination and intuition, and a "hard mind" capable of penetrating analysis through the use of the critical intellect.[180]

This synthesis of a Romantic heart and an Enlightenment mind is central to the multidimensional, integrated cognition advanced by the participatory turn in the study of religion. Religious Studies, we suggest, must be neither exclusively guided by a "participatory heart," which feels deeply but lacks critical rigor, nor by a "cognicentric mind," rightfully critical of religious dogma and ideology but out of touch with the person's intuitive powers and the world's mysteries. Multidimensional cognition, however, is not exhausted by a fusion of head and heart. In addition, it needs to incorporate the knowing of the body, the erotic, the imagination, and the mystical. The "gnostic epistemology" outlined by Kripal is an example of a contemporary approach to the study of religion that relies not only on reason and the critical intellect, but also on the symbolic and contemplative, the mystical body and its erotic energies.[181] In this spirit, we propose that a deeper and broader study of religion can emerge from the integration of our Romantic hearts (intuition, feeling, imagination), Enlightened minds (reason and critical inquiry), sensuous bodies (somatic and erotic knowing), and contemplative consciousness (mystical knowing). True, as Gustavo Benavides insists, the linguistic turn needs to be overcome by a return to cognitive considerations, but such cognitivism should not be mentalistically reduced to the causal and naturalistic explanations of the rational intellect.[182] We need to develop, in Stoller's words, a "sensuous scholarship in which writers tack between the analytical and the sensible, in which embodied form as well as disembodied logic constitute scholarly argument."[183]

Incorporating the whole of human attributes into the study of religion is not only personally edifying (e.g., in the sense of fostering postconventional cognitive competences and perhaps human integration), but may also be vital for the attainment of more reliable or comprehensive knowledge about religious phenomena. The potential epistemic significance of multidimensional cognition can be illustrated by reference to the widely transcultural contemplative insight into the existence of a micro-macro homology between human nature, the cosmos, and the divine. Virtually all major religious traditions hold that there is an isomorphism or deep correspondence between the embodied human being, the universe, and the mystery out of which everything arises. In addition to its central role in ancient rituals and cosmogonies, this *cosmotheandric resonance*[184] is captured in the esotericist dictum "as above so below," the Platonic, Christian, Taoist, Islamic, Kabbalistic, and tantric understandings of "the person as microcosm of the macrocosm," or the Biblical view of the human being made of dust and "in the image of God" (*imago Dei*).[185] This account, of course, has tremendous implications for both religious practice and attitudes toward the human body. For the Bauls of Bengal, for example, viewing the body as the microcosm of the universe (*bhanda/brahmanda*) issues in the belief that the divine dwells physically within human embodiment.[186] If there is any truth to the consubstantiality of body and cosmos, or of the body and the divine, then it follows that the more human attributes participate in the study of reality or the mystery, the more complete the ensuing knowledge will be. In our view, this "completion" should not be understood quantitatively but rather in a qualitative sense. In other words, the more human faculties participate in spiritual knowing, the greater the *dynamic congruence* between inquiry approach and studied phenomena and the more grounded in, coherent with, or attuned to the ongoing unfolding of reality and the mystery will the gained knowledge potentially be.

In addition, multidimensional cognition is connected to the participatory emphasis on spiritual creativity. Whereas the mind and consciousness arguably serve as a natural bridge to subtle spiritual forms already enacted in history that display more fixed forms and dynamics (e.g., specific cosmological motifs, archetypal configurations, mystical visions and states, etc.), we propose that attention to the body and its vital energies gives us access to the more generative power of life or the spirit. Against the background of Johnson's cognitive theory regarding the role of the imagination as the link between embodied experience and mental conceptualization, we hypothesize that the energies that "empower" (after Hollenback) the mystic's imagination are thoroughly embodied and quite possibly of erotic nature.[187] Though admittedly speculative, this proposal is in accord with many mystical teachings, such as those regarding the creative role of the primordial *shakti* or *kundalini* in Hindu tantra, the generative power attributed to the chi energy in Taoism, or even the motivation behind *virginae subintroductae* in the early church.[188] If we accept this approach, it becomes plausible to conjecture that the active participation of embodied dimensions in religious inquiry may lead to an increased plurality of creative visionary and existential spiritual developments. Contemporary participatory approaches, we suggest, seek *to enact with body, mind, heart, and consciousness a creative spirituality that lets a thousand spiritual flowers bloom.* As the next section stresses, however, the pluralistic spirit of most contemporary participatory approaches does not entail the uncritical or relativistic endorsement of all past or present religious understandings or forms of life.

TOWARD A PARTICIPATORY CRITICAL THEORY OF RELIGION

The embodied and integrative thrust of the participatory turn is foundational for the development of a participatory critical theory of religion. Briefly, from a participatory standpoint, *the history of religions can be read, in part, as a story of the joys and sorrows of human dissociation.* From ascetically enacted mystical ecstasies to world-denying monistic realizations, and from heart-expanding sexual sublimation to the moral struggles (and failures) of ancient and modern mystics and spiritual teachers, human spirituality has been characterized by an overriding impulse toward a liberation of consciousness that has too often taken place at the cost of the underdevelopment, subordination, or control of essential human attributes such as the body or sexuality. Even contemporary religious leaders and teachers across traditions tend to display an uneven development that arguably reflects this generalized spiritual bias; for example, high level cognitive and spiritual functioning combined with ethically conventional or even dysfunctional interpersonal, emotional, or sexual behavior.[189]

Furthermore, it is likely that many past and present spiritual visions are to some extent the product of dissociated ways of knowing—ways that emerge predominantly from accessing certain forms of transcendent consciousness but in disconnection from more immanent spiritual sources. For example, spiritual visions that hold that body and world are ultimately illusory (or lower, or impure, or a hindrance to spiritual liberation) arguably derive from states of being in which the sense of self mainly or exclusively identifies with subtle energies of consciousness, getting uprooted from the body and immanent spiritual life. From this existential stance, it is understandable, and perhaps inevitable, that both body and world are seen as illusory or defective. In contrast, when our somatic and vital worlds are invited to participate in our spiritual lives, making our sense of identity permeable to not only transcendent awareness but also immanent spiritual energies, then body and world become spiritually significant realities that are recognized as crucial for human and cosmic spiritual fruition. This account does not seek to excoriate past spiritualities, which may have been at times—though by no means always—perfectly legitimate and perhaps even necessary in their particular times and contexts, but merely to highlight the historical rarity of a fully embodied or integrative spirituality. At any rate, we suggest that a reinvigorated participatory study of religion needs to be hermeneutically critical of oppressive, repressive, and dissociative religious beliefs, attitudes, practices, and institutional dynamics.

In *Cosmos and History: The Myth of the Eternal Return*, Eliade makes a compelling case for the "re-enactive" nature of many religious practices and rituals, for example, in their attempt to replicate cosmogonic actions and events.[190] For Eliade, Gill writes, "[r]ather than freedom and creativity, the human modes of engaging reality and meaning are repetition and participation."[191] In other words, essential elements of the participatory engagement promoted by religious traditions were largely "reproductive." Expanding this account, we could say that most religious traditions can be seen as reproductive insofar as their practices aim to not only ritually reenact mythical motives, but also replicate the enlightenment of their founder or attain the state of salvation or freedom described in allegedly revealed scriptures. Although disagreements about the exact nature of such states and the most effective methods to attain them abounded in the historical development of religious practices and ideas—naturally leading to rich creative developments within the traditions—spiritual inquiry was regulated (and arguably constrained) by such predetermined unequivocal goals.

The participatory approaches introduced in this volume, however, over-come the traditional dualism of repetitive participation and creative freedom. Participatory enaction entails a model of spiritual engagement that does not merely reproduce certain tropes according to a given historical a priori, but rather embarks upon the adventure of openness to the novelty and creativity of nature or the spirit. If repetition is involved (and it seems that the condi-tions of finitude may require some repetition), then it is a nonidentical repe-tition, a creative improvisation of themes and inheritances potentially capa-ble of both fidelity to traditions and bold uncharted explorations.[192] Grounded on current moral intuitions and cognitive competences, for instance, a participatory religious inquiry can undertake not only the critical revision and actualization of prior religious forms, but also the cocreation of novel spiritual understandings, practices, and perhaps even expanded states of freedom.

ꝛ

In closing this section, we should stress that we are mindful of the rather sketchy way in which we have introduced the participatory turn. If we have not offered, for example, any generic definition of the concept of *participation*, it is only because the purpose of this anthology is not to advocate for the adoption of any particular participatory framework, but to allow a multiplic-ity of participatory approaches to emerge.[193] In other words, our main inten-tion is not to artificially construct any grand participatory theory of religion, but rather to foster a kind of academic sensibility, so to speak, in the study of religious phenomena. We believe such an approach to be both academically and religiously relevant. In addition to its heuristic potential to open new avenues of inquiry and give birth to novel insights, a critically informed par-ticipatory articulation of spiritual knowing can help relax the abiding tension between Theology and Religious Studies, as well as between their respective methodological standpoints of "engaged participation" and "critical dis-tance." In other words, we want to lay down a path between and across con-fessional and secular styles of scholarship, one that, in Orsi's words, can per-haps enter the space "between heaven and earth."[194] It is now time to introduce the contents of this volume and start exploring the various vistas that walking such a path discloses.

THIS VOLUME

The Participatory Turn is the first in-depth exploration of participatory spiri-tuality in the context of contemporary Religious Studies. The book is divided into two sections. Developing a number of the themes begun in this intro-duction, the chapters of the first section of the anthology offer wider per-spectives and are more theoretical in tone, situating the participatory turn in the context of contemporary philosophy and Religious Studies, and tracing the concept of participation from its inception in Greek philosophy through its permutations, occlusion, and contemporary redeployment. The chapters in the second section of the anthology consist of a series of applications of the participatory approach to the particularities of spirituality and mysticism within various global traditions, both ancient and contemporary. Not only do these chapters explore participation within the context of the major religious traditions, such as Christianity, Hinduism, or Judaism, but certain chapters also address important spiritual and religious perspectives often overlooked in the standard anthologies on mysticism—thus, we are pleased to include chapters dealing with Western esotericism, for example, or with mystical philosophies such as Henri Bergson's intuitive vitalism.

The contributors assembled for the anthology are not only scholars but also religious practitioners of one sort or another, who engage both contemporary academic discussions and spiritual phenomena with equal rigor. Nearly all of them couple the concept of participation with a robust vision of creativity that does justice to the modern discovery of the centrality of cocreative construction in human knowledge and experience, along with a special accent on the involvement of the total human—body, heart, mind, and consciousness—in the emergence of spiritual events. We believe that this creative and integral hermeneutic approach to human spiritual endeavors is one of the outstanding features of the anthology.

This approach leads us to characterize the scholarly style of the present volume as performative rather than merely descriptive. Most innovative proposals about spirituality and mysticism consist in the introduction of an interpretive model or epistemological framework, followed by the theoretical attempt to validate or show the superiority of such framework through the analysis of religious figures, texts, or traditions. By contrast, the present anthology does not attempt to describe or prove the participatory turn so much as it seeks to bring it forth. Although a number of our contributors illustrate how a participatory sensibility can be found in many religious traditions, no attempt is made to advance any kind of unified participatory theory or paradigm. The integral, creative, and relational logic of participation is not imposed upon but rather transpires through the particularities of traditional and emerging religious identities, practices, and communities, as well as through the scholarship that engages such communities.

Such a participatory logic can, moreover, be deployed in many ways, as is evident from the diversity of the contributions to this volume, including the ways that some of us may disagree (perhaps even strongly) amongst ourselves. To reiterate, we in *The Participatory Turn* do not seek to legislate what constitutes a participatory approach to Religious Studies, so much as we intend to adumbrate a participatory sensibility and invite others to explore its value and perhaps engage with us in this manner of pursuing our scholarship.

SUMMARY OF THE CHAPTERS

The first section of the anthology, "Participation and Spirit: Classical and Contemporary Perspectives," consists of a series of essays that seek to give a historical or theoretical context for the use of the term *participation*. In the opening essay of the section, "A Genealogy of Participation," Jacob H. Sherman explains that the concept of participation was once prominent to the point of ubiquity throughout classical, antique, and medieval philosophy, and he argues that the contemporary participatory turn has much to learn from the previous forms of participatory philosophy. In his genealogy, Sherman identifies three previous iterations of participatory thought: the idea of formal participation most regularly associated with Plato, a kind of participation in existence that Sherman finds especially in the thought of Thomas Aquinas, and participation in creativity itself, a mode of participation that Sherman sees as having emerged through certain Baroque and Romantic forms of thought. Sherman's explications intend to show how these three modes of participation (formal, existential, and creative) are of continued relevance to the contemporary participatory turn, situating it in a robust philosophical lineage and providing it with crucial conceptual tools for further developments.

Chapter 2 consists of Sean Kelly's essay "Participation, Complexity, and the Study of Religion." Kelly draws from the work of the French systems thinker Edgar Morin to explore the implications of the paradigm of complexity for the participatory turn in Religious Studies. Although little known in the Anglophone world, Morin is one of France's leading public intellectuals and his work bears directly upon many of the immediate themes of the participatory turn. Kelly begins the essay with a discussion of the distinction between embedded and enactive participation, citing illustrations from the history of religious and philosophical ideas, before turning to Morin for indications of how to honor the complexity of participation, especially as it relates to the question of method in the study of religion. In the remainder of the essay, Kelly argues that the reorganization of knowledge resulting from the knowledge of living self- or "auto-eco-re-organization" has relevance not only for our understanding of the study of religion or spirituality, but for the wider participatory turn advocated in this volume.

In chapter 3, "Spiritual Knowing as Participatory Enaction: An Answer to the Question of Religious Pluralism," Jorge N. Ferrer proposes that spirituality emerges from human cocreative participation in an always dynamic and undetermined mystery, spiritual power, and/or creative energy of life or reality. This understanding of spiritual knowing in terms of participatory enaction not only makes hierarchical rankings of spiritual traditions appear misconceived, but also expands the range of valid spiritual choices that we as individuals can make. Ferrer articulates a participatory account of the nature of spiritual knowing that brings forth a pluralistic understanding of not only spiritual paths, but also spiritual liberations and spiritual ultimates. Illustrating how such participatory understanding can shed new light on the question of religious pluralism, Ferrer explores the implications of his version of the participatory turn for interreligious relations, the problem of conflicting truth claims in religion, the validity of spiritual truths, the nature of spiritual liberation, and the dialectic between universalism and pluralism in Religious Studies.

The second section of the anthology, "Surveying the Traditions: Participatory Engagements," begins with Brian L. Lancaster's articulation of Judaism as offering a strongly participatory world view. In chapter 4, "Engaging with the Mind of God: The Participatory Path of Jewish Mysticism," Lancaster argues that Jewish teachings and practices aim to establish a partnership between human beings and God through which they participate in furthering the goals of creation. In the Jewish mystical tradition, distinctive practices actively deepen this sense of engaging directly with the divine. Lancaster delineates two complementary strands in such engagement: linguistic and theurgical. Through the first strand, mystics enter into an esoteric world of language, in which God is portrayed as creating by means of constructively playing with the Hebrew letters. Mystical texts establish the practices through which the mystic enters into this divine playfulness, thereby encountering the mind of God. The mystic is enjoined to reach a higher state of consciousness, in which emulation of the divine praxis of creation becomes the route par excellence to an intimate encounter with God. The second strand, that of theurgy, establishes the parameters through which the mystic participates in the divine quest to unify His attributes. Lancaster explains how the teachings of Kabbalah—despite the absolute perfection of the ineffable, transcendent divine essence—give rise to a paradoxical tension between the intradivine principles in the process of emanation. Kabbalah asserts that this tension may be resolved only through human agency. From this point of view, Lancaster concludes, Kabbalah may be seen as a set of teachings designed to promote human participation in the very processes of divine manifestation. Exemplifying the revisionary dimension of participatory scholarship, Lancaster brings evidence from modern consciousness studies, transpersonal psychology, and cognitive neuroscience to creatively envision (and catalyze) the future evolution of the Kabbalah.

Chapter 5 consists of Lee Irwin's essay, "Esoteric Paradigms and Participatory Spirituality in the Teachings of Mikhaël Aïvanhov," which explores the theoretical aspects of participatory spirituality as they relate to the religious thinking and transformative spirituality of Mikhaël Aïvanhov (d. 1986), a highly respected Bulgarian-French esotericist. After a discussion of the question of metaphysics in Religious Studies and an introduction to the nature of participatory spiritual inquiry, Irwin explains how Aïvanhov integrates Kabbalah, Yoga, Alchemy, and esoteric Christianity into a developmental paradigm of magical practices based on his own personal transformative process. Irwin argues that Aïvanhov's East-West synthesis and creative spiritual philosophy is a fascinating story of cocreative explorations that result in a highly enactive paradigm consistent with many of the premises of the newly emerging participatory understanding of human spirituality. Central to this paradigm is an emphasis both on the need for personal integration and transformation, and on the formative cognitive role played by human imagination and intuition in spiritual knowing. Irwin explains how this enactive approach to spiritual knowing led Aïvanhov to challenge dogmatic religious teachings and to lay down a truly creative spiritual path centered upon his own spiritual individuation.

In chapter 6, "Wound of Love: Feminine Theosis and Embodied Mysticism in Teresa of Avila," Beverly J. Lanzetta brings together a number of vital participatory insights regarding the centrality of the body, the role of the imagination, and the gendered nature of knowledge in an illuminating and novel reading of Teresa of Avila's mysticism. Lanzetta considers the way that Teresa's life and thought confront us with a boldly integral spirituality based on the inseparable unity of the inner and outer life. As Teresa writes, "For in the active—and seemingly exterior—work the soul is working interiorly. And when the active works rise from this interior root, they become lovely and very fragrant flowers." To an extraordinary degree, Lanzetta maintains, Teresa works out an embodied and participatory mysticism through her struggles to dignify herself as woman and gain a feminine understanding of knowledge, language, spiritual practice, and God. The centrality of gender is evident in Lanzetta's essay. Because knowing the divine is not a timeless disembodied act of representation, but is instead a holistic, socially situated, corporeal, and relational event, Teresa's spiritual growth involves her in a process that is peculiar to her location as a woman in her own society. Lanzetta uncovers what she calls "the dark night of the feminine" in Teresa's spiritual itinerary. In this dark night, Teresa is led by God into the dismantling of repressive cultural stereotypes that would otherwise bar women from the kind of spiritual advance and transformation to which Teresa is called. A participatory reading of Teresa's life unveils the way that the mystical endeavor is not only personal, but also political and cultural, a holistic journey of transformation and liberation.

William C. Chittick's contribution in chapter 7 focuses on the work of Ibn al-'Arabī, known in Sufism as the "Greatest Master," who wrote an unprecedented and unsurpassed exposition of the scriptural, theological, metaphysical, cosmological, and psychological underpinnings of the Islamic tradition. In "Ibn al-'Arabī on Participating in the Mystery," Chittick argues that the work of this Sufi erudite explicates the unlimited range of human participation in the divine infinity with unmatched detail and profundity: Every trace of human life, knowledge, desire, and speech participate in the Mystery's self-disclosure. Human beings alone, among all the participants—

so far as we know—share in the very creativity of the One, for we alone have a say in how the divine attributes and qualities unfold in themselves and the world. Chittick explains that, for Ibn al-'Arabī, human beings are cocreators of our own selves and of the world, for every act we perform and every choice we make shapes the direction in which the Mystery unfolds. Ibn al-'Arabī's teachings about the Mystery might be therefore a model for all who appreciate the breadth and depth of the participatory approach to spirituality and religion.

Chapter 8 consists of Bruno Barnhart's account of the Christ-event as a participatory revolution. In "One Spirit, One Body: Jesus' Participatory Revolution," Barnhart contends, from within the Christian tradition, that the mystery of Christ's incarnation, death, and resurrection inaugurated a new participatory reality within the universe. According to Barnhart, the New Testament writings are everywhere concerned with investigating this new participation understood vertically as the institution of a new divine-human identity and horizontally as the birth of a new communal relationality among human beings. Barnhart proceeds to trace the history of the progressive extinction of participatory consciousness in Western Christianity and points to a contemporary reawakening of the Christian sense of participation, particularly as manifested in the Second Vatican Council. This reawakening, he concludes, may hold the promise of an even wider participatory retrieval—a global, ecumenical, and personal retrieval that may extend beyond Christian theology or practice.

Chapter 9 continues to explore the relationship between various spiritual traditions and the participatory paradigm. In "Participation Comes of Age: Owen Barfield and the Bhagavad Gita," Robert McDermott uses Owen Barfield's understanding of participation to illuminate the way that three early twentieth-century spiritual teachers variously engage the Bhagavad Gita. McDermott argues that Mohandas K. Gandhi, Sri Aurobindo, and Rudolf Steiner all considered the Gita a supremely important text but that none of the three read the Gita as, for example, one of Arjuna's contemporaries might have. Instead, standing at the far end of a sort of participatory evolution, these teachers had to approach the Gita as a self-implicating text that unveils itself diversely to various sorts of participatory sensibilities. McDermott considers the diachronic participatory distance between these three thinkers and the Gita's *sitz im leben*, as well as attending to the important synchronic differences in the ways that Gandhi, Aurobindo, and Steiner each participatively engage the Gita.

In chapter 10, "Pulsating with Life: The Paradoxical Intuitions of Henri Bergson," G. William Barnard directs our attention to the turn-of-the-century French philosopher Henri Bergson as an important source for developing a participatory philosophy of religion. Interest in Bergson has exploded in recent years prompting a number of important engagements with his work, but Barnard's essay is refreshing in that it emphasizes the important spiritual dimension to Bergson's philosophy. Like William James, perhaps his closest philosophical compatriot, Bergson is deep enough to be read in a number of ways. Rather than following Deleuze in retrieving a proto-poststructuralist Bergson, Barnard looks at how the rich spiritual insights that issue from Bergson's analysis of *durée* (lived time) can contribute fruitfully to the discussion on participatory spirituality. Focusing on Bergson's crucial early works *Time and Free Will*, *Matter and Memory*, and *Creative Mind*, chapter 10 outlines Bergson's understanding of the dynamic, interconnected, ever-new nature of consciousness; his attempts to demonstrate how the structure of consciousness is reflected in the world around us; his emphasis on the value of intuitive, embodied knowledge; his investigations into the evolutionary impetus of a conscious cosmic life-force; and his stress on the crucial value of mystical awareness in the development of humanity. Bergson's processive vision of the universe is everywhere self-implicating and transformative, recognizing that the knowledge of both philosopher and mystic requires a participatory relationship, an adventure of becoming for both the knower and the universe that is known.

In chapter 11, "Connecting Inner and Outer Transformation: Toward an Extended Model of Buddhist Practice," Donald Rothberg argues that, in the modern Western world, there are strong tendencies to understand spirituality as primarily subjective and private. In contemporary Buddhist practice, as well as in most other modern traditions and approaches at this time, the "inner" is typically split off from the "outer." Rothberg presents a Buddhist training framework, grounded in traditional practice, which has emerged out of his and others' "socially engaged" efforts to connect inner and outer transformation, identifying a number of guiding principles, each linked with a number of both traditional and potentially novel practices. This framework makes clearer the need for an expanded vision of spiritual practice, the importance of the intermediate "relational" domain as a bridge between the individual and the collective, and the great creative participation invited of us at this time in imagining and enacting awakening in all the parts of our lives. Rothberg's essay illustrates powerfully how a participatory approach that engages dimensions of human life often previously excluded from spiritual practice leads to the exploration of uncharted spiritual territories and the cocreation of innovative spiritual practices and understandings.

NOTES

1. A broad presentation of the nature and early developments of the linguistic turn (the term was coined by Gustav Bergmann) in Anglo-American philosophy can be found in Richard Rorty's edited anthology, *The Linguistic Turn: Essays in Philosophical Method* (Chicago: University of Chicago Press, 1967). See also Michael Dummet's account of the origins of the linguistic turn in Gottlob Frege's logical semantics

(*Origins of Analytic Philosophy* [Cambridge: Harvard University Press, 1996], esp. 4–14). In addition, the expression *linguistic turn* has been associated with Jürgen Habermas's dialogical reconstruction of German philosophy; see Richard J. Bernstein, "Introduction," in Bernstein, ed., *Habermas and Modernity* (Cambridge: The MIT Press, 1985), 14ff, and Cristina Lafont, *The Linguistic Turn in Hermeneutic Philosophy* (Cambridge: The MIT Press, 1999). In the preface to the English edition of her book (ix–xviii), Lafont clarifies the differences between the Anglo-American and German versions of the linguistic turn. On this account, see also Habermas, "Hermeneutic and Analytical Philosophy: Two Complementary Versions of the Linguistic Turn," in *Truth and Justification*, trans. Barbara Fultner (Cambridge: The MIT Press, 2003), 51–81.

2. Rorty, "Introduction: Metaphilosophical Difficulties of Linguistic Philosophy," in *The Linguistic Turn*, 1–39.

3. Habermas, *Postmetaphysical Thinking: Philosophical Essays*, trans. William Mark Hohengarten (Cambridge: The MIT Press, 1992), 7.

4. Furthermore, in contrast to previous understandings of the origins of human subjectivity as either divinely given (i.e., as a feature of the soul) or emerging in relation to the objective world, linguistic philosophy, following the work of George H. Mead and others, situates the birth of selfhood within the structure of language and intersubjective communication (Habermas, "Individuation through Socialization: On George Herbert Mead's Theory of Subjectivity," *Postmetaphysical Thinking*, 149–204). Tim Murphy, for example, tells us that: "Unlike Cartesianism, discourse [theory] sees the subject as located in language, not in consciousness, and so the structure of language determines the nature of subjectivity" ("Discourse," in *Guide to the Study of Religion*, ed. Willi Braun and Russell T. McCutcheon [New York: Cassell, 2000], 402). In his many works, Jacques Derrida also argues for the linguistic origins of self-identity. These accounts, however, are challenged by modern neuroscientific research on the (nonlinguistic) embodied sources of subjective consciousness; see, e.g., Antonio Damasio, *The Feeling of What Happens: Body and Emotion in the Making of Consciousness* (New York: Harcourt, 1999).

5. Fultner, "Do Social Philosophers Need a Theory of Meaning? Social Theory and Semantics after the Pragmatic Turn," in *Pluralism and the Pragmatic Turn: The Transformation of Critical Theory: Essays in Honor of Thomas McCarthy*, ed. William Rehg and James Bohman (Cambridge: The MIT Press, 2001), 148. Cf. Sheila Benhabib: "Whether in analytical philosophy, or in contemporary hermeneutics, or in French poststructuralism, *the paradigm of language has replaced the paradigm of consciousness*. This shift has meant that the focus is no longer on the epistemic subject or on the private contents of its consciousness but on the public, signifying activities of a collection of subjects" (*Situating the Self: Gender, Community and Postmodernism in Contemporary Ethics* [Cambridge: Polity Press, 1992], 208; emphasis in original). The Italian scholar Giorgio Agamben describes this shift as the Copernican revolution of our times: "Thus we finally find ourselves alone with our words; for the first time we are truly alone with language, abandoned without any final foundation. This is the Copernican revolution that the thought of our time inherits from nihilism: we are the first human beings who have become completely conscious of language" (*Potentialities: Collected Essays in Philosophy*, ed. and trans. Daniel Heller-Roazen [Stanford: Stanford

University Press, 1999], 45). See also Rorty's early proposal for a shift from epistemology to hermeneutics in his influential *Philosophy and the Mirror of Nature* (Princeton: Princeton University Press, 1979), 315–56. In contrast to Benhabib, Dummet,
and many others, however, Rorty does not see the philosophy of language as a "first
philosophy" capable of providing epistemic foundations.

   6. See Wayne Proudfoot: "The turn to religious experience was motivated in
large part by an interest in freeing religious doctrine and practice from dependence on
metaphysical beliefs and ecclesiastical institutions and grounding it in human experience. This was the explicit aim of Schleiermacher's *On Religion*, the most influential
statement and defense of the autonomy of religious experience" (*Religious Experience*
[Berkeley: University of California Press, 1985], xii). For Schleiermacher's "turn to the
subject" in the study of religion, see Thomas M. Kelly, *Theology at the Void: The
Retrieval of Experience* (Notre Dame: University of Notre Dame Press, 2002), 11–49.
For critical perspectives of conceptualizing religion and spirituality in terms of inner
experience, see Robert Sharf, "Experience," in *Critical Terms for Religious Studies*, ed.
Mark C. Taylor (Chicago: University of Chicago Press, 1998), 94–116, and Jorge N.
Ferrer, *Revisioning Transpersonal Theory: A Participatory Vision of Human Spirituality*
(Albany: State University of New York Press, 2002), 15–39.

   7. See Jacques Waardenburg, *Classical Approaches to the Study of Religion: Aims,
Methods, and Theories of Research* (New York and Berlin: Walter de Gruyter, 1999
[originally published: The Hague: Mouton, 1973]); Eric J. Sharpe, *Comparative Religion: A History* (La Salle, IL: Open Court, 1986, 2nd edition); Walter H. Cupps, *Religious Studies: The Making of a Discipline* (Minneapolis: Fortress Press, 1995). One does
not need to agree with McCutcheon's political views or naturalistic metaphysics to
appreciate his meticulous deconstruction of the very idea of a sine qua non or sui
generis element in religion in his *Manufacturing Religion: The Discourse of Sui Generis
Religion and the Politics of Nostalgia* (New York: Oxford University Press, 1997).

   8. Habermas, *The Philosophical Discourse of Modernity: Twelve Lectures*, trans.
Frederick G. Lawrence (Cambridge: The MIT Press, 1987), esp. Lecture XI, 294–326.
See also Bernstein, "Introduction," in *Habermas and Modernity*, 11–25.

   9. Capps, *Religious Studies*, 6. Cf. Carl Olson: "The field [Religious Studies] is a
product of Enlightenment thought, and it is especially a combination of Cartesian and
Kantian perspectives" ("Introduction," in Olson, ed., *Theory and Method in the Study of
Religion: A Selection of Critical Readings* [Belmont, CA: Wadsworth/Thompson, 2003],
5). On the Cartesian-Kantian assumptions of the "philosophy of consciousness" underlying classical phenomenological of religion, see Gavin Flood, *Beyond Phenomenology:
Rethinking the Study of Religion* (New York: Cassell, 1999), 9–10. Discussing the modern
conceptualization of mysticism, Grace M. Jantzen denounces the androcentrism of
this approach: "Feminists . . . have demonstrated the extent to which the Carte-
sian/Kantian 'man of reason' is indeed male" (*Power, Gender, and Christian Mysticism*
[New York: Cambridge University Press, 1995], 343–44). On the masculinized character of Cartesian thinking, see also Susan Bordo, *The Flight to Objectivity: Essays on
Cartesianism and Culture* (Albany: State University of New York Press, 1987).

   10. See, for example, George A. Lindbeck, *The Nature of Doctrine: Religion and Theology in a Postliberal Age* (Philadelphia: The Westminster Press, 1984); George Kilcourse,

ed., *The Linguistic Turn in Contemporary Theology* (United States: The Catholic Theological Society of America, 1987); Dan R. Stiver, *The Philosophy of Religious Language: Sign, Symbol, and Story* (Cambridge, MA: Blackwell, 1996); Flood, *Beyond Phenomenology*; John Callaghan, *Thomist Realism and the Linguistic Turn: Towards a More Perfect Form of Existence* (Notre Dame: University of Notre Dame Press, 2003).

11. Flood, ibid., 7. Flood's narrativist metatheory is one of the most clear and cogent linguistic proposals for the study of religion. For a critical review of Flood's work, see Matthew Day, "Anything You Can Do, I Can Do Meta: High Theory and Low Blows in Contemporary Religious Studies," *Religious Studies Review* 27 (2001): 333–36. In a subsequent work, Flood suggests that his narrativist approach can be seen as "a return to the ideal of phenomenology," which replaces the deceptive claim of detached empathy of classical phenomenology with a more socially and historically situated dialogical reading of texts. See *The Ascetic Self: Subjectivity, Memory, Tradition* (Cambridge: Cambridge University Press, 2004), 20ff.

12. Steven T. Katz, ed., *Mysticism and Language* (New York: Oxford University Press, 1992); Michael A. Sells, *Mystical Languages of Unsaying* (Chicago: University of Chicago Press, 1994); Moshe Idel, "Universalization and Integration: Two Conceptions of Mystical Union in Jewish Mysticism," in *Mystical Union in Judaism, Christianity, and Islam: An Ecumenical Dialogue*, ed. Moshe Idel and Bernard McGinn (New York: Continuum, 1996), 25–57; Don Cupitt, *Mysticism after Modernity* (Malden, MA: Blackwell, 1998), 10. Cupitt is paraphrasing here the title of Rorty's famous essay on Derrida, "Philosophy as a Kind of Writing: An Essay on Derrida" [*New Literary History* 10 (1978–79): 141–60], where he suggests that philosophers should abandon their deceptive search for epistemic foundations and objective truth and regard philosophy as a literary genre. For the textual nature of mysticism, see also Macario Ofilada Mina, "The Textuality of Mystical Experiences," *Studies in Spirituality* 11 (2001): 28–46.

13. Taylor, "Introduction," in *Critical Terms for Religious Studies*, 6.

14. Besides linguistic models, the other major paradigm contesting for disciplinary supremacy is the social-scientific study of religion, theoretically developed by such authors as Robert Segal, Donald Wiebe, Ivan Strenski, J. Samuel Preus, or McCutcheon. Though we value the empirical knowledge gained by scientific approaches (see, for example, the ongoing series *Volumes of Research in the Social Scientific Study of Religion: A Research Annual*, published by E. J. Brill, 1989–2002), their allegiance to causal reductionistic explanation, a naturalistic epistemology, and/or methodological agnosticism renders this paradigm philosophically and ideologically suspect. First, to claim that causal reductionism provides the only or the best explanation of religion assumes—in an exhausted positivistic fashion—the superiority of science to account for all human knowledge. It is worth pointing out here that important contemporary trends in complexity theory, nonlinear science, and neuroscience not only postulate diverse forms of downward causation, but also challenge the epistemic superiority of reductionistic explanations. See, for example, Peter Bogh Andersen, Claus Emmeche, Niels Ole Finnemann, and Peder Voechmann Christiansen, *Downward Causation: Minds, Bodies, and Matter* (Aarhus, Denmark: Aarhus University Press, 2000). The nonlinear scientist Alwyn Scott gets to the heart of the matter: "Reductionism is not a conclusion of science but a belief of many scientists" ("Reduc-

tionism Revisited," *Journal of Consciousness Studies* 11 [2004]: 66). Second, the authoritativeness of a naturalistic epistemology is contingent upon the validity of a naturalistic metaphysics arguably based on the same kind of unverifiable normative axioms as the theological approaches naturalistic thinkers critique. And third, methodological agnosticism—or the bracketing of truth claims that are not empirically testable— presupposes the exclusivity of sensory empiricism and the scientific method to establish the epistemic value of all knowledge claims. Moreover, as Timothy Fitgerald points out, methodological agnosticism reinforces the view of religion as sui generis because its methodological stance emerges precisely from its skepticism regarding the existence of, or possibility of knowing, a transcendent referent (e.g., God, "the sacred," etc.) for religious language (*The Ideology of Religious Studies* [New York: Oxford University Press, 2000], 56).

15. See Morton White, *The Age of Analysis* (New York: Mentor Books, 1955) and Morris Weitz, *Twentieth-Century Philosophy: The Analytic Tradition* (New York: Macmillan, 1966).

16. James Harris, *Analytic Philosophy of Religion* (Dordrecht, Netherlands: Kluwer Academic Press, 2002).

17. See, e.g., Antony Flew and Alasdair MacIntyre, *New Essays in Philosophical Theology* (London: Student Christian Movement Press, 1955); Richard Swinburne, *The Existence of God* (Oxford: Clarendon Press, 1979); Michael Peterson, William Hasker, Bruce Reichenbach, and David Basinger, *Reason and Religious Belief: An Introduction to the Philosophy of Religion* (New York: Oxford University Press, 1991); Paul van Buren, *The Secular Meaning of the Gospel* (New York: Macmillan, 1963); D. Z. Phillips, *Faith after Foundationalism* (London: Routledge, 1988) and *Wittgenstein and Religion* (Houndmills, U.K.: St. Martin's Press, 1993); Alvin Plantinga and Nicholas Wolterstorff, eds., *Faith and Rationality: Reason and Belief in God* (Notre Dame: University of Notre Dame Press, 1983); Joseph Runzo, *Reason, Relativism, and God* (New York: St. Martin's Press, 1986). For a thorough critical analysis of the "framework model" in the study of religion, see Terry F. Godlove, *Religion, Interpretation, and the Diversity of Belief: The Framework Model from Kant to Durkheim to Davidson* (Macon, GA: Mercer University Press, 1997).

18. Caroline Frank Davis, *The Evidential Force of Religious Experience* (Oxford: Clarendon Press, 1989); William P. Alston, *Perceiving God: The Epistemology of Religious Experience* (Ithaca: Cornell University Press, 1991); Keith E. Yandell, *The Epistemology of Religious Experience* (New York: Cambridge University Press, 1993).

19. Hick, *An Interpretation of Religion: Human Responses to the Transcendent* (New Haven: Yale University Press, 1992); Pailin, *God and the Process of Reality: Foundations of a Credible Theism* (London: Routledge, 1989).

20. See, e.g., Richard E. Palmer, *Hermeneutics* (Evanston: Northwestern University Press, 1969); Caputo, *Radical Hermeneutics: Repetition, Deconstruction, and the Hermeneutic Project* (Bloomington: Indiana University Press, 1987); David R. Hiley, James F. Bohman, and Richard Shusterman, eds., *The Interpretive Turn: Philosophy, Science, Culture* (Ithaca: Cornell University Press, 1991); and Maurizio Ferraris, *Historia de la Hermenéutica*, trans. Jorge Pérez de Tudela (Madrid: Ediciones Akal, 2000).

21. See, e.g., Waardenburg, *Significados Religiosos: Introducción Sistemática a la Ciencia de las Religiones*, trans. Támara Murillo Llorente (Bilbao, Spain: Desclée De Brouwer, 2001); Philip Sheldrake, "Interpreting Spiritual Texts," in *Spirituality and History: Questions of Method and Interpretation* (New York: Crossroad, 1992); Katz, ed., *Mysticism and Sacred Scripture* (New York: Oxford University Press, 2000); Jorge J. E. Gracia, *How Do We Know What God Means? The Interpretation of Revelation* (New York: Palgrave, 2001); Andrew P. Tuck, *Comparative Philosophy and the Philosophy of Scholarship: On the Western Interpretation of Nagarjuna* (New York: Oxford University Press, 1990); Murphy, "Discourse," in *Guide to the Study of Religion*, 396–408; John Grimes, *Problems and Perspectives in Religious Discourse: Advaita Vedanta Implications* (Albany: State University of New York Press, 1994); Louis Dupré, "Unio Mystica: The State and the Experience," in *Mystical Union in Judaism, Christianity, and Islam*, 3–23; Elliot Deutsch, ed., *Culture and Modernity: East-West Philosophical Perspectives* (Honolulu: University of Hawaii Press, 1991); and Gerald James Larson and Elliot Deutsch, eds., *Interpreting Across Boundaries: New Essays in Comparative Philosophy* (Princeton: Princeton University Press, 1998).

22. Proudfoot, *Religious Experience*; Barbara A. Holdrege, *Veda and Torah: Transcending the Textuality of Scripture* (Albany: State University of New York Press, 1996); Hendrik M. Vroom, *Religions and the Truth: Philosophical Reflections and Perspectives* (Grand Rapids: William B. Eerdmans, 1989); Lindbeck, *The Nature of Doctrine*.

23. As Ursula King once remarked, "There are probably as many different hermeneutics as there are conscious hermeneuticists" ("Historical and Phenomenological Approaches to the Study of Religion," in *Theory and Method in Religious Studies: Contemporary Approaches to the Study of Religion*, ed. Frank Whaling [New York: Mouton de Gruyer, 1995], 120).

24. For various accounts of classical and modern interpretive approaches to the study of religion, see Donald A. Crosby, *Interpretive Theories of Religion* (The Hague: Mouton, 1981); William E. Paden, *Interpreting the Sacred: Ways of Viewing Religion* (Boston: Beacon Press, 1992); King, "Historical and Phenomenological Approaches to the Study of Religion"; and Daniel Gold, *Aesthetics and Analysis in Writing on Religion: Modern Fascinations* (Berkeley: University of California Press, 2003).

25. Eliade, *The Quest: History and Meaning in Religion* (Chicago and London: University of Chicago Press, 1969); Schüssler Fiorenzza, "Method in Women's Studies in Religion: A Critical Feminist Hermeneutics," in *Methodology in Religious Studies: The Interface with Women's Studies*, ed. Arvind Sharma (Albany: State University of New York Press, 2002); Panikkar, *Myth, Faith, and Hermeneutics* (New York: Paulist Press, 1979); Schneiders, "A Hermeneutical Approach to the Study of Christian Spirituality," *Christian Spirituality Bulletin* 2 (1994): 9–14; Tracy, *Plurality and Ambiguity: Hermeneutics, Religion, Hope* (San Francisco: Harper and Row, 1987); Kripal, *Roads of Excess, Palaces of Wisdom: Eroticism and Reflexibility in the Study of Mysticism* (Chicago: University of Chicago Press, 2001); Timm, *Texts in Context: Traditional Hermeneutics in South Asia* (Albany: State University of New York Press, 1992); Lopez, ed., *Buddhist Hermeneutics* (Honolulu: University of Hawaii Press, 1988).

26. See, e.g., Lisa McCullogh and Brian Schroeder, eds., *Thinking through the Death of God: A Critical Companion to Thomas Altizer* (Albany: State University of

New York Press, 2004); Marion, *God Without Being*, trans. Thomas A. Carlson (Chicago: University of Chicago Press, 1991); Taylor, *Erring: A Postmodern A/theology* (Chicago: University of Chicago Press, 1984); Caputo, *On Religion* (New York: Routledge, 2001); Cupitt, *Mysticism after Modernity*; Masuzawa, *In Search of Dreamtime: The Quest for the Origins of Religion* (Chicago: University of Chicago Press, 1993).

27. Jantzen, *Becoming Divine: Towards a Feminist Philosophy of Religion* (Manchester, U.K.: Manchester University Press, 1998); Anderson, *A Feminist Philosophy of Religion* (Oxford: Blackwell, 1998); Coakley, *Powers and Submissions: Spirituality, Philosophy, and Gender* (Oxford: Blackwell, 2002); Hollywood, *Sensible Ecstasy: Mysticism, Sexual Difference, and the Demands of History* (Chicago: University of Chicago Press, 2002); Lanzetta, *Radical Wisdom: A Feminist Mystical Theology* (Minneapolis: Fortress Press, 2005); Sharma, *Methodology in Religious Studies*. For two introductory accounts of the interface between feminism and religion, see Rita Gross, *Feminism and Religion: An Introduction* (Boston: Beacon Press, 1996) and Majella Franzmann, *Women and Religion* (New York: Oxford University Press, 2000).

28. King, *Orientalism and Religion: Postcolonial Theory, India, and "The Mystic East"* (New York: Routledge, 1999); Lopez, ed., *Curators of the Buddha: The Study of Buddhism under Colonialism* (Chicago: University of Chicago Press, 1995); Chidester, *Savage Systems: Colonialism and Comparative Religion in Southern Africa* (Charlottesville: University Press of Virginia, 1996); Taussig, *Shamanism, Colonialism, and the Wild Man: A Study in Terror and Healing* (Chicago: University of Chicago Press, 1987); Donaldson and Pui-Lan, eds., *Postcolonialism, Feminism, and Religious Discourse* (New York: Routledge, 2002).

29. Smith, *Imagining Religion: From Babylon to Jonestown* (Chicago: University of Chicago Press, 1982); Asad, *Genealogies of Religion: Discipline and Reasons of Power in Christianity and Islam* (Baltimore: The John Hopkins University Press, 1993); McCutcheon, *Manufacturing Religion*; Fitgerald, *The Ideology of Religious Studies*; Dubuisson, *The Western Construction of Religion: Myths, Knowledge, and Ideology*, trans. William Sayers (Baltimore: The John Hopkins University Press, 2003); and Masuzawa, *The Invention of World Religions* (Chicago: University of Chicago Press, 2005). For several discussions about the etic nature of the construct "Hinduism," see Gunther-Dietz Sontheimer and Hermann Kulke, eds., *Hinduism Reconsidered* (New Delhi: Manohar, 2001). See also Brian K. Pennington's *Was Hinduism Invented? Britons, Indians, and the Colonial Construction of Religion* (New York: Oxford University Press, 2005) for a nuanced argument regarding the heuristic value of concepts such as "Hinduism" or "religion" so long as we avoid their reification and affirm their multivalent character. For a recent defense of the use of the term *religion*, see Segal, "Classification and Comparison in the Study of Religion: The Work of Jonathan Z. Smith," *Journal of the American Academy of Religion* 73 (2005): 1175–88.

30. Urban, *The Economics of Ecstasy: Tantra, Secrecy, and Power in Colonial Bengal* (New York: Oxford University Press, 2001) and *Tantra: Sex, Secrecy, Politics, and Power in the Study of Religion* (Berkeley: University of California Press, 2003); Faure, *The Red Thread: Buddhist Approaches to Sexuality* (Princeton: Princeton University Press, 1998) and *The Power of Denial: Buddhism, Purity, and Gender* (Princeton:

Princeton University Press, 2003); Kripal, *Kali's Child: The Mystical and the Erotic in the Life and Teachings of Ramakrishna* (Chicago: University of Chicago Press, 1998).

31. This generalized statement is problematic. Whereas an emphasis on language pervades analytical, hermeneutic, and poststructuralist works, it should be obvious that, as we elaborate below, important sections of postcolonial and feminist studies escape linguistic dungeons and pave the way for more embodied and participatory understandings.

32. See Habermas, *The Theory of Communicative Action. Vol. II. Lifeworld and System: A Critique of Functionalist Reason*, trans. McCarthy (Boston: Beacon Press, 1987), 77–111. Also see Eduardo Mendieta, "Introduction," in Habermas, *Religion and Rationality: Essays on Reason, God, and Modernity*, ed. Mendieta (Cambridge: The MIT Press), esp. 11–24.

33. Cupitt, *op. cit.*, 74. In *After God: The Future of Religion*, Cupitt adds: "the supernatural world of religion turn out to have been in various ways a mythical representation of the truly magical world of language" (New York: Basic Books, 1997), 47.

34. Kuhn, *The Structure of Scientific Revolutions*, 2nd ed. (Chicago: University of Chicago Press, 1970).

35. The postmodern account of Western thinking as ontotheological is rooted in the writings of the two prophets of postmodernity: Friedrich Nietzsche and Heidegger. On the one hand, it stems from Nietzsche's equation of the "death of God" with the collapse of the possibility of objective truth, including scientific truth—what is "truth," after all, if there is not a complete and absolute God's eye view of the world? On the other hand, "onto-theology" is most explicitly associated with Heidegger's critique of the Western tradition that confuses the thought of being as such (ontos) with the entitative notion of the highest being (theos) and equates both with rationality (logos). Heidegger famously charges that such ontotheology is not only metaphysically destitute because it is incapable of really thinking being, but also religiously bankrupt because it gives us a God before whom one can "neither dance, nor sing, nor pray." Whereas the Nietzschean course can lead to postmodern forms of nihilism and perspectival relativism (though relativism is not a necessary corollary of perspectivism), the Heideggerian one is the main source of much of today's postmodern constructive theological reflection, which attempts to reimagine God without traditional metaphysical baggage. Two key anthologies on postmetaphysical theology are *The Religious*, ed. Caputo (Malden, MA: Blackwell, 2002), and Mark A. Wrathall, ed., *Religion after Metaphysics* (New York: Cambridge University Press, 2003).

36. Vattimo, "The Trace of the Trace," trans. David Webb, in *Religion*, ed. Derrida and Vattimo (Stanford: Stanford University Press, 1996), 84.

37. Flood, *Beyond Phenomenology*, 139–42. Also see Flood's recent plea for the inclusion of traditions' self-inquiry within the scholarly study of religion: "Reflections on Tradition and Inquiry in the Study of Religion," *Journal of the American Academy of Religion* 74 (2006): 47–58.

38. See, e.g., Asad, *Genealogies of Religion*; King, *Orientalism and Religion*; and Morno Joy, "Postcolonial Reflections: Challenges for Religious Studies," *Method and Theory in the Study of Religion* 13 (2001): 177–95.

39. King, ibid., 175–86.

40. One of the most compelling accounts of the need for an adequate conceptual understanding as the foundation of direct spiritual knowledge can be found in Anne Klein's detailed study of the Gelukba order of Tibetan Buddhism (*Knowledge and Liberation: Tibetan Buddhist Epistemology in Support of Transformative Religious Experience* [Ithaca, NY: Snow Lion Publications, 1986]). Robert K. C. Forman names this mediated path to immediacy "catalytic constructivism"; see his "Introduction: Mysticism, Constructivism, and Forgetting," in *The Problem of Pure Consciousness: Mysticism and Philosophy*, ed. Forman (New York: Oxford University Press, 1990), 10.

41. Forman, "Paramartha and Modern Constructivists on Mysticism: Epistemological Monomorphism versus Duomorphism," *Philosophy East and West* 39 (1989): 393–418.

42. King, 183.

43. Saler, *Conceptualizing Religion: Immanent Anthropologies, Transcendent Natives, and Unbounded Categories*, with a new preface by author (New York: Berghahm Books, 2000), 263 (originally published in Leiden, The Netherlands: E. J. Brill, 1993). For an early argument on the importance of a "mutual modulation" between Western academic and cross-cultural religious categories in the study of religion, see Smith's classic essay, "Sacred Persistence: Toward a Redescription of Canon," in his *Imagining Religion*, 36–52.

Saler's proposal has been harshly criticized by McCutcheon in "'We Are All Stuck Somewhere': Taming Ethnocentrism and Traditional Understandings," in *Critics Not Caretakers: Redescribing the Public Study of Religion* (Albany: State University of New York Press, 2001, 73–83). Using the work of David Couzens Hoy, McCutcheon argues that the study of native religions through Western lenses is inescapable, and that what is truly ethnocentric is to expect that native interests and self-understandings must coincide with our own. Then he goes on to characterize Saler's research program as ethnocentric insofar as it commends the appropriation of native categories for *our* Western goal of transcultural understanding—a goal that may not be shared by the native traditions. McCutcheon's conclusion is that we should continue using exclusively Western categories for our Western purposes, i.e., to seek cross-cultural generalizations—and that we should not regard emic notions as descriptive or analytical tools but merely as data.

Formulated this way, there is no way out of what we might call a self-imposed "ethnocentric double bind": *Either* we use Western categories to describe, analyze, and assess non-Western traditions, *or* we appropriate non-Western categories at the service of our Western research agendas. Though we appreciate McCutcheon's concerns, the problem with this dichotomizing articulation is that it does not exhaust all the possibilities. For example, does the selective use of local categories as methodological tools *necessarily* require that we force them into the molds of our research interests? Can we not entertain, to the contrary, that the very goals of our research programs might be revised in our encounter with non-Western understandings and folk categories? Should not a truly postcolonial scholarship be open to be transformed *at depth* by transcultural methodological interactions? Does the arguably Western origin of a global collaborative inquiry render such endeavors inevitably *ethnocentric* in the pernicious sense of the term? And so forth.

44. Rothberg, "Spiritual Inquiry," in *Transpersonal Knowing: Exploring the Horizon of Consciousness*, ed. Tobin Hart, Peter Nelson, and Kaisa Puhakka (Albany: State University of New York Press, 2000), 175–76.

45. Ochs, "Comparative Religious Traditions," *Journal of the American Academy of Religion* 74 (2006): 126.

46. For a critique of the residual positivism involved in importing empiricist standards to evaluate religious knowledge, see Ferrer's "The Empiricist Colonization of Spirituality," in *Revisioning Transpersonal Theory*, 41–70. Ferrer writes: "In addition to sensory reductionism, positivism holds both that there exists a single method for all valid knowledge (methodological monism), and that the natural sciences represent this methodological ideal for all other sciences (scientism). . . . The problem with positivism, then, is not only the reduction of valid knowledge to sensory evidence, but also . . . the assimilation of all human inquiry (aesthetic, historical, social, spiritual, etc.) to the methods and aims of the natural sciences (experimentation, replication, testing, verification, falsification, etc.)" (57). Of course, the problematic importation of empiricist standards into religious inquiry needs to be sharply distinguished from the entirely valid and crucially important empirical study of religion.

47. José Ignacio Cabezón, "The Discipline and Its Other: The Dialectic of Alterity in the Study of Religion," *Journal of the American Academy of Religion* 74 (2006): 32–34.

48. For the most comprehensive collection of essays on the insider/outsider distinction, see McCutcheon, ed., *The Insider/Outsider Problem in the Study of Religion* (New York: Cassell, 1999), and for a helpful typology of insider/outsider positions based on the participant observer roles of the social sciences, see Kim Knott, "Insider/Outsider Perspectives," in *The Routledge Companion to the Study of Religion*, ed. John Hinnells (New York: Routledge, 2005), 243–58. Our position on this question is germane to Kripal's "methodological nondualism," which intends to "challenge the dichotomy between insider and outsider and not assume *either* that the historian, psychologist, or anthropologist who seem to be outside . . . does not also know and appreciate something of the shimmering truths of which the insider so passionately speaks *or* that the insider, however devoted to an ideal, cannot also see clearly and bravely something of the actual of which the scholar tries to speak" (*Roads of Excess, Palaces of Wisdom*, 323). Cf. McCarthy: "The key to avoiding both a pure 'insider's' or participant's standpoint and a pure 'outsider's' or observer's standpoint is . . . to adopt the perspective of a critical-reflective participant" (in David Couzens Hoy and McCarthy, *Critical Theory* [Cambridge, MA: Blackwell, 1994], 81).

Closely related to the insider/outsider problem is the issue of "participation versus distance" in the study of religion. Here we also find valuable to walk a "middle path" that benefits from the merits of both orientations. In this regard, see Robert Cummings Neville's early proposal to combine the virtues of the dao (i.e., participatory engagement and existential access to religious phenomena) and the daimon (i.e., critical distance and vulnerability to correction) (*The Tao and the Daimon: Segments of a Religious Inquiry* [Albany: State University of New York Press, 1982]). Such a combination, which for Neville shapes a secular or scholarly spirituality, can prevent both the "blindness of uncritical participation" and "the projection of one's methodological, theoretical, and more broadly cultural assumptions onto the religious path being studied" ("Religion and Scholarship," in *Religion in Late Modernity* [Albany: State University of New York Press, 2002], 109). Similarly, in her recent essay "Detachment and Engagement in the Study of 'Lived Experience,'" Ann Taves writes: "I would argue that detached scholarship, like engaged scholarship, allows us to see some things, while obscuring others" (*Spiritus* 3 [2003]: 198). For an illustration of a "critical-participative approach" to the study of ancient sacred texts, see Douglas Burton-Christie, "The Cost of Interpretation: Sacred Texts and Ascetic Practice in Desert Spirituality," *Christian Spirituality Bulletin* 2 (1994): 21–24; and for important discussions of the participatory nature of the study of spirituality, see the essays collected in "Part Two: The Self-Implicating Nature of the Study of Spirituality," in *Minding the Spirit: The Study of Christian Spirituality*, ed. Elisabeth A. Dreyer and Mark S. Burrows (Baltimore: The Johns Hopkins University Press, 2005), 61–151.

49. See Ferrer (this volume), for a suggestion of two pragmatic tests. This discussion raises at least two issues that would require further discussion. The first concerns the possibility of intersubjectively testing deeply experiential or even supernatural claims through a radical empiricist epistemology (after William James) that challenges the scientistic attachment of "empirical validity" to "sensory evidence." After all, contemplatives from the various traditions following similar religious techniques generally reach intersubjective agreement about spiritual insights and realities, even if the falsification of those claims is not possible (on the nonfalsifiability of contemplative claims, see Ferrer, *Revisioning Transpersonal Theory*, 62–65). The second relates to our defense of the cognitive status of religion, which is at odds with contemporary neopragmatist proposals to understand religion as a noncognitive enterprise which, like art, does not require intersubjective agreement in contrast to cognitive endeavors such as science or law. In this regard, see Rorty, "Pragmatism as Romantic Polytheism," in *The Revival of Pragmatism: New Essays on Social Thought, Law, and Culture*, ed. Morris Dickstein (Durham: Duke University Press, 1998).

50. For two recent anthologies on feminism and the study of religion, see Darlene M. Juschka, ed., *Feminism in the Study of Religion: A Reader* (New York: Continuum, 2001), and Sharma, ed., *Methodology in Religious Studies*.

51. See, e.g, Carol Christ, "Toward a Paradigm Shift in the Academy and in Religious Studies," in *The Impact of Feminist Research in the Academy*, ed. Christie Farnham (Bloomington: Indiana University Press, 1987), 53–76; Alice M. Jaggar and Susan R. Bordo, eds., *Gender/Body/Knowledge: Feminist Reconstructions of Being and Knowing* (New Brunswick: Rutgers University Press, 1989); and Gross, *Feminism and Religion*.

52. Richard Griggs, *Gods after God: An Introduction to Contemporary Radical Theologies* (Albany: State University of New York Press, 2006), 128.

53. Taylor, *Erring*, 104.

54. Caputo, "Introduction: Who Comes after the God of Metaphysics?" in *The Religious*, 15. Cf., Aldo Gargani: "Religious transcendence achieves its meaning in the fold of a reflection that reconstructs the immanence of its terms. *Transcendence immanences itself*" ("Religious Experience as Event and Interpretation," in *Religion*, 115; emphasis in original).

Note here that the postmodern avowal of sacred immanence and denial of transcendent spiritual sources retains the very hierarchical relationship between binary oppositions (e.g., immanence/transcendence) that so many of these authors claim to overcome. In deconstruction, let us remember here, the reversal of the hierarchical relationship between binary oppositions is an important but provisional step toward the final (but ever deferred) goal of total emancipation from binary hierarchies. Whereas the rejection of the transcendent is a natural consequence of the attack upon the metaphysics of presence, we suggest that a more consistent move may be to deconstruct the immanence/transcendence polarity *nondualistically*, that is, overcoming their hierarchical relationship without aprioristically obliterating any of the two poles.

55. William R. LaFleur, "Body," in *Critical Terms for Religious Studies*, 36–54. See also Robert C. Fuller's review of a number of recent works stressing the importance of the body in the study of religion: "Faith of the Flesh: Bodily Sources of Spirituality," *Religious Studies Review* 31 (2005): 135–139.

56. See Paula M. Coaley, *Religious Imagination and the Body: A Feminist Analysis* (New York: Oxford University Press, 1994); Jane Marie Law, ed., *Religious Reflections on the Human Body* (Bloomington: Indiana University Press, 1995); Coakley, ed., *Religion and the Body* (New York: Cambridge University Press, 1997); Meredith B. McGuire, "Why Bodies Matter: A Sociological Reflection on Spirituality and Materiality," *Spiritus* 3 (2003): 1–18; and Ferrer, "Embodied Spirituality: Now and Then," *Tikkun* 21 (2006): 41–45, 63–64. See also Lawrence E. Sullivan's review article, "Body Works: Knowledge of the Body in the Study of Religion," *History of Religions* 30 (1990): 86–99.

57. Kripal, *The Serpent's Gift: Gnostic Reflections on the Study of Religion* (Chicago: University of Chicago Press, 2006), 139.

58. Stoller, *Sensuous Scholarship* (Philadelphia: University of Pennsylvania Press, 1997); Hunt Overzee, *The Body Divine: The Symbol of the Body in the Works of Teilhard de Chardin and Rāmānuja* (New York: Cambridge University Press, 1992).

59. See, e.g., Thomas P. Kasulis, Roger T. Ames, and Wimal Dissanayake, eds., *Self as Body in Asian Theory and Practice* (Albany: State University of New York Press, 1993); Geoffrey Samuel, "The Body in Hindu and Buddhist Tantra," *Religion* 19 (1989): 197–210; Kristofer Schipper, *The Taoist Body* (Berkeley: University of California Press, 1994); Holdrege, "Body Connections: Hindu Discourses on the Body and the Study of Religion," *International Journal of Hindu Studies* 2/3 (1998): 341–86; Patrick Olivelle, "Deconstruction of the Body in Indian Asceticism," in *Asceticism*, ed. Vincent L. Wimbush and Richard Valantasis (New York: Oxford University Press, 1995), 188–210.

60. Yasuo, *The Body: Toward an Eastern Mind-Body Theory* (Albany: State University of New York Press, 1987) and *The Body, Self-Cultivation, and Ki-Energy* (Albany: State University of New York Press, 1993). On the existential transformation of the mind-body dualism into its supposedly original oneness, see also Shigenori Nagatomo, *Attunement through the Body* (Albany: State University of New York Press, 1992).

61. Kripal, *Roads of Excess*, 22–23.

62. Virginia Burrus, *The Sex Lives of the Saints: An Erotics of Ancient Hagiography* (Philadelphia: University of Pennsylvania Press, 2004).

63. Jantzen, *Power, Gender, and Christian Mysticism*; Hollywood, *Sensible Ecstasy*; Lanzetta, "Women's Body as Mystical Text," in *Radical Wisdom*, 155–73. See also Dorothee Soelle, "Eroticism," in *The Silent Cry: Mysticism and Resistance* (Minneapolis: Fortress Press, 2001), 113–31.

64. Nelson, *Body Theology* (Louisville: Westminster/John Know Press, 1998), 50. See also Lisa Isherwood and Elisabeth Stuart, *Introducing Body Theology* (Sheffield, U.K.: Pilgrim Press, 1998).

65. Segal, *Explaining and Interpreting Religion* (New York: Peter Lang, 1992); Wiebe, *The Politics of Religious Studies: The Continuing Conflict with Theology in the Academia* (New York: St. Martin's Press, 1999); McCutcheon, *Manufacturing Religion*. For two recent presentations of the phenomenological method that take into account these criticisms, see Douglas Allen, "Phenomenology of Religion," in *The Routledge Companion to the Study of Religion*, 182–207, and Thomas Ryba, "Phenomenology of Religion," in *The Blackwell Companion to the Study of Religion*, ed. Segal (Malden, MA: Blackwell, 2006), 111–21. The dominant tendency today is to regard phenomenological approaches as an element of, or complement to, social-scientific explanation or hermeneutic understanding. The ongoing tension between hermeneutic/phenomenological, naturalistic, and critical approaches to religion is evident in the recent anthology edited by René Gothóni, *How to Do Comparative Religion? Three Ways, Many Goals* (Berlin: Walter de Gruyter, 2005).

66. The expression "dissolving into language" is borrowed from Caroline Walker Bynum's essay, "Why All the Fuss About the Body?: A Medievalist's Perspective," *Critical Inquiry* 22 (1995): 1–33.

67. Isherwood and Stuart, *Introducing Body Theology*, 151.

68. We are developing here an argumentative line advanced by Fuller in "Faith of the Flesh." Interestingly, Johann Georg Hamman, the first and in many ways still the most powerful critic of Kant, foreshadowed not only the modern recognition of the linguistic basis of reason, but also the embodied (and sensuous) foundations of human language and thought. See Garret Green, *Theology, Hermeneutics, and Imagination: The Crisis of Interpretation at the End of Modernity* (New York: Cambridge University Press, 2000), 62ff. See also Terence J. German, *Hamman on Language and Religion* (New York: Oxford University Press, 1981).

69. Johnson, *The Body in the Mind: The Bodily Basis of Meaning, Imagination, and Reason* (Chicago: University of Chicago Press, 1987). See also George Lakoff and Johnson, *Philosophy in the Flesh: The Embodied Mind and Its Challenge to Western Thought* (New York: Basic Books, 1999), for a provoking exploration of the philosophical implications of the notion that human language, thinking, and metaphorical conceptualization are shaped by the body's inner structures and sensory relationships with the world. See also Warren G. Frisina, *The Unity of Knowledge and Action: Toward a Nonrepresentational Theory of Knowledge* (Albany: State University of New York Press, 2002) and the compendium on "body in mind" recently published in *Daedalus*

(Summer 2006), including essays by Damasio, Johnson, Carol Gilligan, and Jerry Fodor, among others.

70. What Johnson perhaps does not realize (understandably since he is a cognitive scientist, not a student of religion) is that his cognitivist account of imagination as an epistemic bridge between the embodied and the mental is strikingly similar to many esoteric and mystical views on the role of the Imagination. For many mystics, the epistemic function of the noetic faculty known as the active Imagination (which is sharply distinguished from "imagination" or merely mental fantasizing) is precisely to raise sensual/perceptual experience to an imaginal level in that isthmus between physical and spiritual realms that Henry Corbin calls *mundus imaginalis*. See Corbin, "*Mundus Imaginalis* or the Imaginary and the Imaginal," in *Swedenborg and Esoteric Islam*, trans. Leonard Fox (West Chester, PA: Swedenborg Foundation, 1995), 1–33, and "A Theory of Visionary Knowledge," in *The Voyage and the Messenger: Iran and Philosophy*, trans. Joseph Rowe (Berkeley: North Atlantic Books, 1998), 117–34. Also see William C. Chittick, *Imaginal Worlds: Ibn al-ʿArabī and the Problem of Religious Diversity* (Albany: State University of New York Press, 1994).

Francisco J. Varela and Natalie Depraz offer a contemporary account of the imagination as being "at the core of life and mind" in "Imagining: Embodiment, Phenomenology, and Transformation," in *Buddhism and Science: Breaking New Ground*, ed. B. Alan Wallace (New York: Columbia University Press, 2003), 196–230. Weaving together threads from modern neuroscience, phenomenology, and Buddhism, Varela and Depraz provide a nonreductive view of human imagination and explore its centrality in promoting human transformation.

71. Note here that both the hermeneutic and postmodern wings of the linguistic turn also challenge the representational paradigm of cognition. For the narrativist challenge, see Flood, *Beyond Phenomenology*, 99–104, and for a general account of postmodern antirepresentationalism, see Pauline M. Rosenau, *Postmodernism and the Social Sciences: Insights, Inroads, and Intrusions* (Princeton: Princeton University Press, 1992), 92–108.

72. Eggington and Sandbothe, eds., *The Pragmatic Turn in Philosophy: Contemporary Engagements between Analytic and Continental Thought* (Albany: State University of New York Press, 2004). See also Dickstein, *The Revival of Pragmatism*.

73. Habermas initially learned his pragmatism from Karl Otto-Appel and the influence of American pragmatists on Habermas's thought has remained strong, as seen, for example, in essays such as "Peirce and Communication" (Habermas, *Postmetaphysical Thinking*, 88–112). For Wittgenstein's pragmatist sympathies, particularly as mediated through Frank Ramsey's *The Foundations of Mathematics*, see *Philosophical Investigations*, trans. G. E. M. Anscombe (New York: Macmillan, 1963).

74. See James, *Pragmatism: A New Name for Some Old Ways of Thinking*, in *William James: Writings 1902–1910*, ed. Bruce Kuklick (New York: The Library of America, 1987), 572–73.

75. Ibid., 573.

76. Ibid., 574.

77. Neville, *The Highroad around Modernism* (Albany: State University of New York Press, 1992).

78. Eggington and Sanbothe use the expression "deflationary pragmatism" to describe the discursive strategy of those neopragmatists who narrow or deflate the concept of pragmatism "in order to distinguish it from the professional self-image of academic philosophy in a marked and even provocative way." See "Introduction," *The Pragmatic Turn in Philosophy*, 1–2.

79. Rorty has, however, begun to explore the possibilities of religious language in a more open way, redirecting his ire not so much at religion in general as at monotheism and clericalism in particular. Rorty's new appeal to religious rhetoric remains reductively humanistic (even Feuerbachian), but at certain times does seem to invite a dialogue with religious practitioners and scholars. For instance, when Rorty defines God as "all the varied sublimities human beings come to see through the eyes that they themselves create," participatory theorists may want to correct Rorty's reductionism (he explicitly forbids God any excess beyond what human beings may see), but may also see in this formula a suggestive insight about cocreativity that is worthy of further exploration. See Rorty, "Pragmatism and Romantic Polytheism," 34.

80. For the distinction between Cambridge pragmatism and Instrumentalist pragmatism (or what is sometimes called Chicago pragmatism), see Oppenheim, *Reverence for the Relations of Life: Re-Imagining Pragmatism via Josiah Royce's Interactions with Peirce, James, and Dewey* (Notre Dame: University of Notre Dame Press, 2005), 48. For a similar distinction, see Kucklick, *A History of Philosophy in America* (Oxford: Oxford University Press, 2001), 95. James himself is too protean to fit neatly, once and for all, into either of these two pragmatisms, some of his writings leaning much more strongly toward Dewey's Instrumentalism than others.

81. Bernstein, "Pragmatism's Common Faith," in *Pragmatism and Religion: Classical Sources and Original Essays*, ed. Stuart Rosenbaum (Chicago: University of Illinois Press, 2003), 129–41.

82. See especially Kuklick, *Churchmen and Philosophers: From Jonathan Edwards to John Dewey* (New Haven: Yale University Press, 1985).

83. See West, *Prophesy Deliverance!: An Afro-American Revolutionary Christianity* (Philadelphia: Westminster Press, 1982), and *The American Evasion of Philosophy: A Genealogy of Pragmatism, Wisconsin Project on American Writers* (Madison: University of Wisconsin Press, 1989).

84. For an introduction to the practice of Scriptural Reasoning see the articles collected in *Modern Theology* 22, no. 3 (2006). Nicholas Adams explores Scriptural Reasoning through a development of Habermas's pragmatics in Nicholas Adams, *Habermas and Theology* (Cambridge: Cambridge University Press, 2006), 234–55.

85. For a variety of different uses of pragmatism in order to approach the phenomena of mysticism and religious experience, see G. William Barnard, *Exploring Unseen Worlds: William James and the Philosophy of Mysticism* (Albany: State University of New York Press, 1997); Nancy K. Frankenberry, ed., *Radical Interpretation in Religion* (Cambridge: Cambridge University Press, 2002); Proudfoot, *Religious Experience*; Sandra B. Rosenthal, "Spirituality and the Spirit of American Pragmatism: Beyond the Theism Atheism Split," in *Pragmatism and Religion*, 229–43; Wainwright, *Reason and the Heart: A Prolegomenon to a Critique of Passional Reason* (Ithaca: Cornell

University Press, 1995); Robert Westbrook, "An Uncommon Faith: Pragmatism and Religious Experience," in *Pragmatism and Religion*, 190–207.

86. Sandbothe, "The Pragmatic Twist," in *The Pragmatic Turn in Philosophy*, 68.

87. Peirce, *Collected Papers of Charles Sanders Peirce*, ed. Charles Hartshorne and Paul Weiss (Cambridge: Harvard University Press, 1931–1958), 5:448n.

88. Our use of the term *mystery* does not entail any kind of essentialist reification of an ontologically given ground of being, as expressions such as "the sacred," "the divine," or "the eternal" often conveyed in classic scholarship in religion. It is also unrelated to Rudolf Otto's account of the human experience of the divine as *mysterium tremendum et fascinans*. In contrast, we deliberately use this conceptually vague, open-ended, and ambiguous term to refer to the nondetermined creative energy or source of reality, the cosmos, life, and consciousness. Thus understood, the term *mystery* obstructs claims or insinuations of dogmatic certainty and associated religious exclusivisms; more positively, it invites an attitude of intellectual and existential humility and receptivity to the Great Unknown that is the fountain of our being.

89. Bracketing the more theological uses of the category "the sacred," we use the term *sacred* as an adjective to refer to the ultimate value, beauty, and arguably inherent "goodness" of reality or the mystery. For a recent discussion of the problems with the use of the category "the sacred" in Religious Studies, see Terence Thomas, "'The Sacred' as a Viable Concept in the Contemporary Study of Religions," in *Religion: Empirical Studies*, ed. Steven J. Sutcliffe (Burlington, VT: Ashgate, 2004), 47–66.

90. On which, see Josiah Royce, John J. McDermott, and Ignas K. Skrupskelis, *The Basic Writings of Josiah Royce* (Chicago,: University of Chicago Press, 1969).

91. See, e.g., Timm, ed., *Texts in Context*.

92. Holdrege, *Veda and Torah*, 5.

93. Idel, *Absorbing Perfections: Kabbalah and Interpretation* (New Haven and London: Yale University Press, 2002), 13.

94. Habermas, *Legitimation Crisis*, trans. Thomas McCarthy (Boston: Beacon Press, 1975), 121.

95. On the divine origins of human language, and in addition to well-known Vedic, Biblical, Platonic, and Kabbalistic formulations, see David Crystal's *Linguistics, Language, and Religion* (New York: Hawthorn Books, 1965).

96. Griggs, *Gods after God*, 31–32. Also see Taylor, "Writing of God," in *Erring*, 97–120.

97. Barfield, *Poetic Diction: A Study in Meaning*, 2nd ed. (Middletown, CT: Wesleyan University Press, 1964), 88.

98. Thus, for example, Judith A. Berling, a scholar of Chinese and Japanese religions, argues that to the two generally accepted constitutive fields of Spirituality (i.e., competence in the history and scriptures of the particular tradition in question), we ought to add Comparative Religions as a third constitutive field. See Berling, "Christian Spirituality: Intrinsically Interdisciplinary," in *Exploring Christian Spirituality: Essays in Honor of Sandra M. Schneiders, I.H.M.*, ed. Bruce H. Lescher and Elizabeth Liebert (Mahwah, NJ: Paulist Press, 2006), 38–41.

99. Schneiders, "The Study of Christian Spirituality: Contours and Dynamics of a Discipline," 5–6.

100. Cousins, "Spirituality in Today's World," in *Religion in Today's World*, ed. Whaling (Edinburgh, U.K.: T and T Clark, 1987), 323–24. Quoted in Ursula King, "Is There a Future for Religious Studies as We Know It? Some Postmodern, Feminist, and Spiritual Challenges," *Journal of the American Academy of Religion* 70 (2002): 380–81.

101. We are borrowing the word *evental* from Peter Hallward, who uses it to translate Alain Badiou's *événementiel*. Badiou's *evental* refers to something characterized by radical irruptive novelty, something that cannot be accounted for by received categories and yet makes universal demands upon those who subject themselves to it. Indeed, Badiou argues that subjects are created through fidelity to such events. Cf. Badiou, *Ethics: An Essay on the Understanding of Evil*, trans. Peter Hallward (London: Verso, 2001); Hallward, *Badiou: A Subject to Truth* (Minneapolis: University of Minnesota Press, 2003).

102. Reprinted in Frohlich, "Spiritual Discipline, Discipline of Spirituality: Revisiting Questions of Definition and Method," in *Minding the Spirit*, 73.

103. Orsi, *Between Heaven and Earth: The Religious Worlds People Make and the Scholars Who Study Them* (Princeton: Princeton University Press, 2005), 14.

104. Ibid.

105. Frohlich, "Spiritual Discipline, Discipline of Spirituality," 70.

106. Sheldrake, "Spirituality and Its Critical Methodology," in *Exploring Christian Spirituality*, 23.

107. Taves, "Detachment and Engagement in the Study of 'Lived Experience.'"

108. Braun, "On Religion," in *Guide to the Study of Religion*, 11.

109. For two recent anthologies exploring the implications of postmetaphysical thought for Religious Studies, see Wrathall, ed., *Religion After Metaphysics*, and Jeffrey Bloechl, ed., *Religious Experience and the End of Metaphysics* (Bloomington: Indiana University Press, 2003). Early discussions appeared in *Religion, Ontotheology, and Deconstruction*, ed. Henry Ruf (New York: Paragon House, 1989).
It may be important to distinguish here between two related but independent meanings of the term *metaphysics*. On the one hand, the notion of metaphysics in Western philosophy is generally based on the distinction between appearance and reality, with a metaphysical statement being one that claims to portray that "Reality" presumably lying behind the realm of appearances (Peter van Inwagen, "The Nature of Metaphysics," in *Contemporary Readings in the Foundations of Metaphysics*, ed. Stephen Laurence and Cynthia Macdonald [Malden, MA: Blackwell, 1998], 12ff). In addition to this use, on the other hand, many religious traditions also speak about "metaphysical worlds" to refer to levels or dimensions of reality existing beyond the sensible world or within the subtle ontological depths of human consciousness. The first usage is the main target of Derrida's attack on the metaphysics of presence. On a strong reading, this critique leads to the a priori denial of the ontological status of any transcendent or metaphysical reality. The weaker reading

simply requires a declaration of metaphysical agnosticism. As we will see in this volume, participatory understandings of religion not only eschew the dualism of appearance and reality, but also endorse modern and postmodern critiques of traditional metaphysics of presence. It is possible, we believe, to consistently drop the mentalist dualism of appearance and reality, and simultaneously entertain the plausibility of a deep and ample multidimensional cosmos in which the sensible world does not exhaust the possibilities of the Real.

110. Perhaps nobody articulates this postmetaphysical *Zeitgeist* more cogently than Habermas in his *Postmetaphysical Thinking*. Though by no means endorsing its metaphysical import, it is noteworthy that even a champion of modernity such as Habermas questions the possibility of a full assimilation of religious meanings into secular language: "Philosophy, even in its postmetaphysical forms, will be able neither to replace nor to repress religion as long as religious language is the bearer of semantic content that is inspiring and even indispensable, for this content eludes (for the time being?) the explanatory force of philosophical language and continues to resist translation into reasoning discourses" (*Postmetaphysical Thinking*, 51). For a discussion of this intriguing sentence, rather anomalous in Habermas's *corpus*, see "A Conversation about God and the World: Interview with Eduardo Mendieta," in *Religion and Rationality*, 162ff.

A perplexing paradox of our times is that we seem to live in a cultural milieu that is as postmetaphysical as it is increasingly postsecular. Vattimo succinctly describes the origins of the contemporary revival of religion: "By now, all of us are used to the fact that disenchantment with the world has generated a radical disenchantment with the very idea of disenchantment. In other words, demythification has finally turned against itself, thereby acknowledging that the ideal of the elimination of myth is myth" ("After Onto-Theology: Philosophy between Science and Religion," in *Religion after Metaphysics*, 30). See also John D. Caputo's "How the Secular World Became Post-Secular," in *On Religion*, 37–66. It is likely that this paradox is the source of the many proposals for a postmetaphysical religion and immanent spiritualities spawning today.

111. Flood, *Beyond Phenomenology*, 15.

112. Ibid., 171.

113. Ibid., 172.

114. Northcote, "Objectivity and the Supernormal: The Limitations of Bracketing Approaches in Providing Neutral Accounts of Supernormal Claims," *Journal of Contemporary Religion* 19 (2004): 85–98.

115. Ibid., 89.

116. Note here how a naturalistically minded scholar such as Strenski chastises McCutcheon for his commitment to a naturalistic metaphysics: "Ironically, and in effect, such assertions of a naturalistic foundation to the study of religion as McCutcheon sees it, in effect, reintroduces [sic] metaphysics into the field" (*Thinking about Religion: An Historical Introduction to Theories of Religion* [Malden, MA: Blackwell, 2006], 339–40). For distinctions between scientific and religious types of naturalism, see the essays by David Ray Griffin and Jerome A. Stone in the sec-

tion "Naturalism: Scientific and Religious," *Zygon: Journal of Religion and Science* 37 (2002): 361–94.

117. Smart, *The Science of Religion and the Sociology of Knowledge: Some Methodological Questions* (Princeton: Princeton University Press, 1973); Byrne, "The Study of Religion: Neutral, Scientific, or Neither"? *Method and Theory in the Study of Religion* 9 (1997): 339–51. As we have seen, Fitgerald argues that Smart's methodological agnosticism hides theological agendas in its implicitly positing a transcendental referent about which scholars need to remain agnostic (*The Ideology of Religious Studies*, 56).

118. Caputo, *On Religion*, 20.

119. Taylor, "Deconstruction: What's the Difference?" *Soundings* 66 (1983): 397, 400. Cf. Cupitt, "The [postmodern] mysticism of secondarieness is mysticism *minus* metaphysics, mysticism *minus* any claim to special or privileged knowledge, and mysticism without any other world than this one" (*Mysticism after Modernity*, 8). It is worth pointing out here that linguistic Kantianism is also surpassed by the pragmatic turn in philosophy. The pragmatization of Kant in contemporary philosophy, however, does not seek or entail the resurrection of metaphysical referents, but rather a detranscendentalization of the conditions for knowledge onto historically originated immanent structures embedded in communicative practices. See Habermas, *Truth and Justification*, 17ff.

120. Evans, "Can Philosophers Limit What Mystics Can Do? A Critique of Steven Katz," *Religious Studies* 25 (1989): 53–60.

121. Kripal, *The Serpent's Gift*, 141–42. The expression "state-specific truths" derives from Charles Tart's original proposal of "state-specific sciences," in "States of Consciousness and State-Specific Sciences," *Science* 176 (1972): 1203–10.

122. Popper, "The Myth of the Framework," in *The Myth of the Framework: In Defense of Science and Rationality*, ed. M. A. Notturno (New York: Routledge, 1994), 33–64.

123. Katz, "On Mysticism," *Journal of the American Academy of Religion* 56 (1988): 754.

124. For several papers challenging the adequacy of Katz's neo-Kantian account of mystical knowledge, see J. William Forgie, "Hyper-Kantianism in Recent Discussions of Mystical Experience," *Religious Studies* 21 (1985): 205–18; Anthony Perovich, "Does the Philosophy of Mysticism Rest on a Mistake?" in *The Problem of Pure Consciousness*, 237–53; James Robertson Price III, "Mysticism, Mediation, and Consciousness: The Innate Capacity in John Ruusbroec," in *The Innate Capacity: Mysticism, Psychology, and Philosophy* (New York: Oxford University Press, 1998), 111–20; Martin T. Adam, "A Post-Kantian Perspective on Recent Debates about Mystical Experience," *Journal of the American Academy of Religion* 70 (2002): 801–17. Of related interest is the essay by Larry Short, "Mysticism, Mediation, and the Non-Linguistic," *Journal of the American Academy of Religion* 63 (1996): 659–75.

Note that perennialist accounts can also be neo-Kantian. In *An Interpretation of Religion*, for example, Hick defends the thesis that the different spiritual ultimates "represent different phenomenal awarenesses of the same noumenal reality" (15). For a critique of Hick's neo-Kantianism, see P. R. Eddy, "Religious Pluralism and the

Divine: Another Look at John Hick's Neo-Kantian Proposal," *Religious Studies* 30 (1994): 467–78. A more recent Kantian-like defense of perennialism is offered by Paul O. Ingram in *Wrestling with the Ox: A Theology of Religious Experience* (New York: Continuum, 1997).

125. Perovich, "Mysticism and the Philosophy of Science," *The Journal of Religion* 65 (1985): 63–82; Forman, "Introduction: Mysticism, Constructivism, and Forgetting," in *The Problem of Pure Consciousness*, 3–49; Michael Stoeber, "Constructivist Epistemologies of Mysticism: A Revision and Critique," *Religious Studies* 28 (1992): 107–16.

126. Katz, "The 'Conservative' Character of Mysticism," in *Mysticism and Religious Traditions*, ed. Katz (New York: Oxford University Press, 1983), 3–60.

127. Hick, *An Interpretation of Religion*; Lindbeck, *The Nature of Doctrine*.

128. Runzo, *Reason, Relativism, and God*.

129. Smith, *Map Is Not Territory: Studies in the History of Religions* (Leiden, Netherlands: Brill, 1978), 309. Cf. Jean Baudrillard: "The territory no longer precedes the map, nor does it survive it. It is nevertheless the map that precedes the territory—*precession of simulacra*—that engenders the territory" (*Simulacra and Simulation*, trans. Sheila Faria Glaser [Ann Arbor: The University of Michigan Press, 1994], 1). Therefore, all we can have access to are our constructions, or, as Nelson Goodman puts it, our "versions" of reality and never reality itself (*Ways of Worldmaking* [Indianapolis: Hackett, 1978]). This postmodern move, however, far from dissolving or transcending the dualism of framework and reality (or map and territory), reinforces it by fatally obliterating one of its poles (reality) and then ontologically inflating the other (frameworks, maps, or versions of reality). The tragic consequence of this move is unequivocal: "The world well lost," as the title of Rorty's classic essay glossed (in *Journal of Philosophy* 69 [1972]: 649–65).

130. Gill, "Territory," in *Critical Terms for Religious Studies*, 305.

131. Davidson, "On the Very Idea of a Conceptual Scheme," in *Inquiries into Truth and Interpretation* (New York: Oxford University Press, 1984), 183–198. In what follows we do not mean to suggest that Davidson himself would have agreed with the participatory argument we are drawing from his classic essay. Nevertheless, we believe that one of the consequences of his dismantling of the scheme-content division is to open the space for such participatory implications.

132. In *Religion, Interpretation, and the Diversity of Belief*, Godlove proposes that once the dualism of scheme and content is deconstructed (after Davidson), we need to give up the idea of religions as conceptual frameworks.

133. For a critique of aspects of Davidson's essay, see Nicholas Rescher's "Conceptual Schemes," in *Midwest Studies in Philosophy. Vol. V. Studies in Epistemology*, ed. P. A. French, T. E. Uehling Jr., and H. Wettstein (Minneapolis: University of Minnesota Press, 1980), 323–45. Although rejecting the myth of the given, Rescher questions that linguistic translatability is an adequate ground for refuting the existence of alternative conceptual schemes. In particular, he suggests that the proper judge of the presence of alternative conceptual schemes is not translatability but interpretability. Rescher's essay is especially helpful in showing how any plausible retention of the idea

of a conceptual scheme needs to let go of both its original Kantian moorings and the notion of a pregiven world. Free from these specters, Rescher continues, potentially different conceptual schemes are no longer seen as alternative or competing a priori interpretations of a ready-made world, but simply diverse a posteriori creative innovations stemming from our empirical inquiries and ontological commitments. Also see Quine, "On the Very Idea of a Third Dogma," in *Theories and Things* (Cambridge: The Belknap Press of Harvard University Press, 1981), 38–42.

134. Davidson, 198; emphasis added.

135. Thinkers as diverse as Bordo, Drew Leder (in *The Absent Body* [Chicago: University of Chicago Press, 1990]), Nagatomo, Varela, and Yasuo suggest that the process of increasing dissociation between mental and somatic worlds that characterized important strains of the modern Western trajectory was an important source of both the postulation and the success of the Cartesian mind-body doctrine. The definitive overcoming of Cartesian dualism, therefore, may not be so much a philosophical but a practical, existential, and transformative task. In a similar spirit, we propose that the Kantian two worlds doctrine (and its associated epistemological skepticism) is parasitic on the estrangement of the human mind from an embodied apprehension of reality. As contemporary cognitive science tells us, "Our sense of what is real begins with and depends crucially upon our bodies. . . . As embodied, imaginative creatures, *we never were separated or divorced from reality in the first place*" (Lakoff and Johnson, *Philosophy in the Flesh*, 17, 93; emphasis in original). If this is correct, then it becomes entirely understandable that the decline of embodied conscious participation in human inquiry, arguably precipitated by the disconnection between mind and body, may have undermined the sense of being in touch with the real, engendering the Kantian mentalist dualism of a merely phenomenal world and an always inaccessible noumenal reality.

136. These "marginal voices" belong to the group of scholars known as traditionalists or perennialists—such as Frithjof Schuon, Seyyed Hossein Nasr, Huston Smith, or James Cutsinger—who in various ways affirm the transcendent or esoteric unity of religions. For two recent accounts of this movement, see the partisan study by Harry Oldmeadow, *Journeys East: 20th Century Western Encounters with Eastern Religious Traditions* (Bloomington, IN: World Wisdom, 2004) and the far superior *Against the Modern World: Traditionalism and the Secret Intellectual History of the Twentieth Century* (New York: Oxford University Press, 2004), by Mark J. Sedgwick. In addition to being textually unwarranted, esotericist universalism has been intersubjectively challenged (refuted?) in the contemporary intermonastic dialogue. Buddhist and Christian monks, for example, acknowledge important differences in both their understandings and their experiences of what their respective traditions consider to be ultimate; see, e.g., Donald W. Mitchell and James Wiseman, eds., *The Gethsemani Encounter: A Dialogue on the Spiritual Life by Buddhist and Christian Monastics* (New York: Continuum, 1997); Susan Walker, ed., *Speaking of Silence: Christians and Buddhists on the Contemplative Path* (New York: Paulist Press, 1987).

The most nuanced defense of a qualified version of the "common core" theory is due to Forman, who presents compelling evidence for the occurrence of a "pure consciousness event" in many, though by no means all, contemplative traditions; see Forman, ed., *The Problem of Pure Consciousness* and *The Innate Capacity*. For two general critiques of traditional and modern varieties of perennialism, see Paul J. Griffiths, *An*

Apology for Apologetics: A Study in the Logic of Interreligious Dialogue (New York: Orbis Books, 1991), 36–39, 46–59; Ferrer, *Revisioning Transpersonal Theory*, 71–111, 135–40.

137. See, for example, the work of Wilhelm Halbfass for neo-Hindu inclusivism (*India and Europe: An Essay in Understanding* [Albany: State University of New York Press, 1988], 403–18); and Gavin D'Costa for Hick's neo-Kantian and the Dalai Lama's Tibetan Buddhist pluralisms (*The Meeting of Religions and the Trinity* [Maryknoll, NY: Orbis Books, 2000], 24–40, 72–95).

138. More self-reflexive and contextually sensitive than prior comparative scholarship, the new post-Eliadean comparativism emphasizes the search for both commonalities and differences, is critical of past theological agendas, and recognizes that cross-cultural patterns may not be necessarily universal. For discussions, see Luther H. Martin, Paden, Marsha E. Hewitt, Wiebe, and E. Thomas Lawson, "The New Comparativism in the Study of Religion: A Symposium," *Method and Theory in the Study of Religion* 8 (1996): 1–49; Kimberly C. Patton and Benjamin C. Ray, eds., *A Magic Still Dwells: Comparative Religion in the Postmodern Age* (Berkeley: The University of California Press, 2000). For a sophisticated recent comparative project, see the three volumes edited by Neville on *The Human Condition, Ultimate Realities,* and *Religious Truth,* all published by State University of New York Press in 2000.

139. Heim, *Salvations: Truth and Difference in Religion* (Maryknoll, NY: Orbis Books, 1995); Kaplan, *Different Paths, Different Summits: A Model for Religious Pluralism* (Lanham, MD: Rowman and Littlefield, 2002).

140. A notable exception to this trend is the metaphysical pluralism advocated by the process theologians John B. Cobb Jr. and Griffin (after Charles Hartshorne). See Cobb, *Transforming Christianity and the World: A Way Beyond Absolutism and Relativism,* ed. Paul F. Knitter (Maryknoll, NY: Orbis, 1999); Griffin, *Reenchantment without Supernaturalism: A Process Philosophy of Religion* (Ithaca and London: Cornell University Press, 2001); Griffin, ed., *Deep Religious Pluralism* (Louisville: Westminster John Knox Press, 2005).

From some participatory standpoints, Cobb-Griffin's dipolar "deep pluralism" is not deep *enough.* In addition to operating within a theistic framework inimical to many traditions, its dipolarity forces all religious ultimates into the arguably Procrustean molds of God's "abstract essence" (unchanging Being) and God's "concrete states" (changing Becoming). Nevertheless, the process-theological challenge to linguistic Kantianism and its postulate that the Divine (at least Its "concrete states") can be influenced by human affairs is harmonious with the cocreative participatory epistemology endorsed in many contributions to this volume.

141. Preus, *Explaining Religion: Criticism and Theory from Bodin to Freud* (New Haven: Yale University Press, 1987), xviii; emphasis in original.

142. Hocking, *The Coming World Civilization* (London: Allen and Unwin, 1956). The wording cited here comes from John James Clarke, *Oriental Enlightenment: The Encounter between Asian and Western Thought* (New York: Routledge, 1997), 134.

143. Stoeber, *Theo-Monistic Mysticism: A Hindu-Christian Comparison* (New York: St. Martin's Press, 1994).

144. Hollenback, *Mysticism: Experience, Response, and Empowerment* (University Park: Pennsylvania State University Press, 1996).

145. Wolfson, *Through a Speculum That Shines: Vision and Imagination in Medieval Jewish Mysticism* (Princeton: Princeton University Press, 1994), 39, 119.

146. Of related interest is the increasing concern with polytheistic religions, which constitute a largely more pluralistic spiritual canvas than the one portrayed by monotheistic faiths. In polytheistic religions, Jordan Paper writes, "[p]eople with differing personalities and experiences meet different deities. Without an enforced monotheistic creed, people are open to an abundance of numinous possibilities;" in *The Deities Are Many: A Polytheistic Theology* (Albany: State University of New York Press, 2005), 13.

147. Grof, *Beyond the Brain: Birth, Death, and Transcendence in Psychotherapy* (Albany: State University of New York Press, 1985), and *The Adventure of Self-Discovery: Dimensions of Consciousness and New Perspectives in Psychotherapy and Inner Exploration* (Albany: State University of New York Press, 1988). Dan Merkur distinguishes twenty-four types of psychedelic unitive states, many of which clearly relate to particular religious traditions, and states that what characterizes the psychedelic state is that it "provides access to all" (*The Ecstatic Imagination: Psychedelic Experiences and the Psychoanalysis of Self-Actualization* [Albany: State University of New York Press, 1988], 155).

148. *The Adventure of Self-Discovery*, 139.

149. For an updated summary of Katz's contextualist views, see Katz, "Diversity and the Study of Mysticism," in *New Approaches to the Study of Religion. Volume 2: Textual, Comparative, Sociological, and Cognitive Approaches*, ed. Peter Antes, Armin W. Geertz, and Randi R. Warne (Berlin: Walter de Gruyter, 2004), 189–210.

150. Moore, "Mystical Experience, Mystical Doctrine, Mystical Technique," in Katz, ed., *Mysticism and Philosophical Analysis* (New York: Oxford University Press, 1978), 112.

151. Of course, the modern mind may be tempted to explain away the phenomena reported by Grof in terms of cryptoamnesia (i.e., the subjects had forgotten their previous exposure to those symbols and the special state of consciousness simply brings these memories to consciousness). In our opinion, however, this explanation needs to be ruled out because Grof's subjects not only can see the form of these religious and mythological symbols, but also gain detailed insight into their deeper esoteric meaning. Furthermore, although the "cryptoamnesia hypothesis" may account for some of the cases reported by Grof (e.g., the self-identification of some Japanese people with the figure of Christ on the Cross), it would be very difficult to explain in these terms reports of subjects accessing detailed knowledge of mythological and religious motifs of barely known cultures such as the Malekulans in New Guinea (*The Adventure of Self-Discovery*, 19–21). In these cases, the possibility of previous intellectual exposure to such detailed information of a barely known culture is remote enough, we believe, to rule out the cryptoamnesia hypothesis as a plausible general explanation of these phenomena. The other alternative is to interpret Grof's data as supporting the existence of something like C. G. Jung's collective unconscious, but in our view such an option is not necessarily incompatible with ontological explanations, for example, if one were to grant a "psychoid" status to metaphysical religious worlds. For an extended discussion, see Ferrer, "The Consciousness Research of

Stanislav Grof and the Study of Mysticism," in *Festschrift for Stanislav Grof*, ed. Richard Tarnas (Albany: State University of New York Press, forthcoming).

152. Larry Laudan, *Progress and Its Problems: Towards a Theory of Scientific Growth* (Berkeley: University of California Press, 1977), 26–31.

153. "The deepest dogma of the linguistic turn in both analytic and Continental hermenutics," writes Richard Shusterman, is the "premise that all understanding and meaningful experience is indeed linguistic" ("Beneath Interpretation," in *The Interpretive Turn*, 117). In this important essay, Shusterman provides a variety of examples of prereflective and nonlinguistic comprehension, such as the way that dancers understand "the sense and rightness of a movement or posture proprioceptively, by feeling it in [their] spine and muscles, without translating it into conceptual linguistic terms" (ibid.). Shusterman distinguishes between "interpretation," which necessarily involves language, and "understanding," which does not require linguistic articulation, and argues that the failure to recognize nonlinguistic sources of meaning stems from the disembodied nature of Western philosophical practice.

154. Our use of the term *enactive* is inspired by Varela, Evan Thompson, and Eleanor Rosch's pioneering articulation of a nonrepresentational paradigm of cognition in *The Embodied Mind: Cognitive Science and Human Experience* (Cambridge: The MIT Press, 1991). Note, however, that Varela et al. understand *enaction* as an embodied action that brings forth a domain of distinctions as the result of the mutual specification of organism and environment, limiting therefore the scope of their proposal to the perceptual cognition of the natural or sensoriomotor world. Our participatory formulation adapts and extends the enactive paradigm to account for the emergence of ontologically real religious realms (or subtle domains of distinctions) cocreated by human multidimensional cognition and the generative force of life or the spirit. For extended discussions of spiritual knowing as enactive, see the essays by Sean Kelly, Ferrer, and Lee Irwin (in this volume). Also see Caputo's *On Religion* (139–40), for a linguistic usage of the term *enactive* as the performance of the *meaning* of God.

155. In their conviction that the participatory turn can reinvigorate the creative partnership between human beings and spirit, many of the contributors to this anthology can be reasonably seen, and perhaps dismissed by some, as religionists. It is important to emphasize, however, that to embrace a participatory understanding of religious knowledge is not *necessarily* linked to confessional, religionist, or supernaturalist premises or standpoints. On the one hand, as many of the contributions to this volume show, participatory approaches often lead to critical assessments and even radical revisions of traditional religious beliefs, practices, and understandings. Most fundamentally, on the other hand, virtually all the same participatory implications for the study of religion can be practically drawn if we were to conceive, or translate, the term *spirit* in a naturalistic fashion as an emergent creative potential of life, nature, or reality. Methodologically, the challenge to be met is to account for a process or dynamism underlying the creative elements of religious visionary imagination that cannot be entirely explicated by appealing to biological or cultural-linguistic factors (at least as narrowly understood by proponents of reductionist approaches). Whether such creative source is a transcendent spirit or immanent life will likely be always a contested issue, but one, we believe, that does not damage the general claims of the participatory turn.

156. See John Heron's *Participatory Spirituality: A Farewell to Authoritarian Religion* (Morrisville, NC: Lulu Press, 2006) for a related account of human spirituality in terms of participatory cocreation with transcendent and immanent spiritual sources. The subtitle of Heron's book intends to convey a "respectful departure" from the authoritarian tendencies he perceives in most past and present religious schools and institutions. A powerful vision of the human, the divine, and the cosmos as participating cocreatively in the unfolding of reality is articulated by Panikkar in *The Cosmotheantric Experience: Emerging Religious Consciousness*, ed. with intro. Scott Eastham (Maryknoll, NY: Orbis, 1993). Also see Philip Hefner's "The Evolution of the Created Co-Creator" for a Christian account of human beings "as participants and co-creators in the ongoing work of God's creative activity" (in *Cosmos as Creation: Theology and Science in Consonance*, ed. Ted Peters [Nashville: Nashville, 1990], 232).

157. See, e.g., Rorty, "A Pragmatist View of Contemporary Analytical Philosophy," in *The Pragmatic Turn in Philosophy*, 131–44.

158. Engler, "Constructionism versus What?" *Religion* 34 (2004): 291–313.

159. In contemporary philosophy, a robust "constructive realist" stance has been eloquently articulated by Joseph Margolis. Though Margolis holds that realist stances are human symbolic constructions (doing away with the disjunction between epistemology and metaphysics), the integrative power of his proposal is undermined by Kantian gestures: "We cannot know the independent world as it is 'absolutely' independent of cognitive conjecture, but we can construct a reasonable sense of what to characterize as the independent-world-as-it-is-known-(and knowable)-to-us" ("Cartesian Realism and the Revival of Pragmatism," in *The Pragmatic Turn in Philosophy*, 238). More attuned to participatory standpoints, Robert Minner offers an account of knowledge as "true construction" that takes human creative pursuits to be participating in divine knowledge and creation; see *Truth in the Making: Creative Knowledge in Theology and Philosophy* (New York: Routledge, 2004).

160. Capps, *Religious Studies*, 2–12.

161. Tarnas, *The Passion of the Western Mind: Understanding the Ideas that Have Shaped Our World View* (New York: Ballantine Books, 1991), 434–35.

162. For other contrasts between premodern, modern, and postmodern modes of participation, see the chapters by Jacob H. Sherman, Kelly, and Robert McDermott (in this volume).

163. Lévy-Bruhl's *How Natives Think*, trans. Lilian A. Clare (London: George Allen and Unwin, 1926); *Primitive Mentality*, trans. Clare (Oxford: Clarendon Press, 1923). For a classic critique of Lévy-Bruhl's participation, see Smith, "I Am a Parrot (Red)," *History of Religion* 11 (1972): 391–413. For a sophisticated discussion of Lévy-Bruhl's participation in the context of the "rationality debate" in the study of religion, see Saler, "Lévy-Bruhl, Participation, and Rationality," in *Rationality and the Study of Religion*, ed. Jeppe S. Jensen and Luther H. Martin. Acta Jutlandica LXXII: 1, Theology Series, 19 (Aahars C., Denmark: AARHUS University Press, 1997), 44–64. See also Segal, "Relativism and Rationality in the Social Sciences: A Review Essay of Lucien Lévy-Bruhl's *How Natives Think*," in *Religion and the Social Sciences: Essays on the Confrontation* (Atlanta: Scholars Press, 1989), 167–80.

164. Lévy-Bruhl, *The Notebooks on Primitive Mentality*, preface by Maurice Leenhardt (Oxford: Basil Blackwell, 1975).

165. Tambiah, *Magic, Science, Religion, and the Scope of Rationality* (Cambridge: Cambridge University Press, 1990), 84–110. Readers should also consult Kasulis's nuanced identification of two different cultural orientations, "intimacy"—i.e., an affective dimension of knowledge characterized by personal objectivity, no sharp distinction between self and other, and psychosomatic integration—and "integrity"—i.e., a cognitive/mental dimension of knowledge characterized by public objectivity, strict differentiation between self and other, and disconnection between the somatic and the psychological. See *Intimacy and Integrity: Philosophy and Cultural Difference* (Honolulu: University of Hawaii Press, 2002).

166. Hanegraaff, "How Magic Survived the Disenchantment of the World?" *Religion* 33 (2003): 357–80.

167. For two well-informed analyses of the New Age movement, see Hanegraaff, *New Age Religion and Western Culture: Esotericism in the Mirror of Secular Thought* (Albany: State University of New York Press, 1998) and Paul Heelas, *The New Age Movement* (Oxford: Blackwell, 1996).

168. M. H. Abrams, *Natural Supernaturalism: Tradition and Revolution in Romantic Literature* (New York: W. W. Norton, 1973); Isaiah Berlin, "The Counter-Enlightenment," in *The Proper Study of Mankind: An Anthology of Essays*, ed. Henry Hardy and Roger Hausheer (New York: Farrar, Straus, and Giroux, 1998), 243–68; Tarnas, *The Passion of the Western Mind*, 366–96.

169. Romantic pluralism received its most powerful and cogent articulation in the hands of Herder. See, e.g., Berlin's inspired essay, "Herder and the Enlightenment," in *The Proper Study of Mankind*, 359–435.

170. In a famous passage, Eliade writes: "It suffices to say that the 'sacred' is an element in the structure of consciousness, not a stage in the history of consciousness" (*The Quest*, i).

In a way, Eliade's view of the sacred owes as much to Otto as it does to Kant. For Otto's influence, see Eliade, *The Sacred and the Profane: The Nature of Religion* (New York: Harcourt Brace Jovanovich, 1959), 8–10. For a contemporary attempt to rethink the sacred within a (non-Eliadean) Kantian framework, see *The Sacred and the Profane: Contemporary Demands on Hermeneutics*, ed. Jeffrey F. Keuss (Burlington, VT: Ashgate, 2003), especially Keuss's "Introduction: The Sacred and the Profane in Hermeneutics after Kant" (1–8).

171. The use of the phenomenological expression "constituted given" to characterize Eliade's view of the sacred comes from Allen's superb *Myth and Religion in Mircea Eliade* (New York: Garland, 1998), 75–76. For an account of Eliade's morphological structuralism, see Norman J. Girardot, "Introduction. Imagining Eliade: A Fondness for Squirrels," in Girardot and Mac Linscott Ricketts, *Imagination and Meaning: The Scholarly and Literary Works of Mircea Eliade* (New York: The Seabury Press, 1982), 3–5. In contrast to Claude Lévi-Strauss's rationalistic structuralism of binary oppositions, Eliade's "Romantic structuralism" incorporates universalistic suppositions of the Enlightenment project into a Goethean imaginal reconstruction of primordial

essences. On the influence of the Romantics on Eliade, see also Rachela Permenter, "Romantic Postmodernism and the Literary Eliade," in *Changing Religious Worlds: The Meaning and End of Mircea Eliade*, ed. Bryan Rennie (Albany: State University of New York Press, 2001), 95–116.

172. In *Reconstructing Eliade: Making Sense of Religion* (Albany: State University of New York Press, 1996), Rennie creatively interprets Eliade as a postmodern constructivist who viewed the sacred phenomenologically (i.e., as the intentional object of the human experience of the sacred) and whose work is therefore basically free from ontological and metaphysical assumptions. On Eliade's putative postmodernism, see Olson's critique of Rennie's thesis in "Mircea Eliade, Postmodernism, and the Problematic Nature of Representational Thinking," *Method and Theory in the Study of Religion* 11 (1999): 357–85; and Rennie's response in *Method and Theory in the Study of Religion* 12 (2000): 416–21. In our view, Allen achieves a fine balance when he suggests that the Eliadean corpus contains *both* modern ontological and metaphysical assumptions (e.g., on the universal structure of the sacred), *and* postmodern themes such as the (admittedly ambiguous) rejection of the myth of the given in religious inquiry and the pioneering of the kind of transformative "creative hermeneutics" that is increasingly in vogue today. In a passage with highly participatory overtones, Allen writes: "Mythic and symbolic structures are 'given,' but as unfinished and 'open'; given to us in such ways that require our active participation as constituting subjects" (*Myth and Religion in Mircea Eliade*, 299–300). Unfortunately, space does not allow us to explore here the parallels and differences between Allen's rendering of Eliade and the participatory turn.

173. See especially the "Epilegomena" to van der Leew's *Religion in Essence and Manifestation: A Study in Phenomenology*, vol. 2 (New York: Harper and Row, 1963), 669–95.

174. McCalla, "Romanticism," in *Guide to the Study of Religion*, 378.

175. See Wiebe's "Phenomenology of Religion as Religio-Cultural Quest: Gerardus van der Leew and the Subversion of the Scientific Study of Religion," in *The Politics of Religious Studies*, 173–90, where he unveils the cryptotheological agenda of the classical phenomenology of religion. According to Wiebe, this agenda is most apparent in the phenomenologist's search—often shaped by Christian categories—for an essence of religion indicative of a single divine reality, ground of being or "the sacred." Cf., Dubuisson: "[T]he diverse essences that these phenomenologists discovered never represented more than the sublimated, disincarnated expressions of an admittedly provincial, northern European [Lutheran] spirituality in search of the absolute and the universal" (*The Western Construction of Religion*, 172). For related critical accounts, see McCutcheon's *Manufacturing Religion* and Fitzgerald's *The Ideology of Religious Studies*. Addressing these criticisms, Allen proposes a softer phenomenology of religion that affirms the "value in uncovering religious essences and structures, but as embodied and contextualized, not as fixed, absolute, ahistorical, eternal truths and meanings" ("Phenomenology of Religion," in *The Routledge Companion to the Study of Religion*, 206).

176. Barfield, *Saving the Appearances: A Study in Idolatry* (London: Faber and Faber, 1957), 132. Neither Lévy-Bruhl nor the Romantics offered systematic discussions of the various degrees of conscious will, creativity, and self-reflexibility available

in participatory knowing. By contrast, though in arguably problematic unilinear evo-lutionary terms, Barfield postulates three different levels of participation: "original" participation (archaic or unconscious *participation mystique*), loss of participation (characteristic of the modern self), and "final" participation (self-reflexive and voli-tional). For a reformulation of Barfield's proposal in the context of indigenous studies, see Jürgen Kremer, "The Dark Night of the Scholar: Reflections on Culture and Ways of Knowing," *ReVision* 14 (1992): 169–78. Also see Peter Reason's use of Barfield's proposal in his presentation of a participatory worldview as framework for participa-tory research methods in the human sciences ("Participation and the Evolution of Consciousness" and "Future Participation," in *Participation in Human Inquiry*, ed. Rea-son [London: SAGE Publications, 1994], 16–39), and McDermott's application of Barfield's participatory scheme to situate and critically engage anthroposophical and neo-Hindu accounts of the Gita (in this volume).

177. Tarnas, "A Divided World View," in *The Passion of the Western Mind*, 434–35.

178. Flood, *Beyond Phenomenology*, 104–105.

179. Gold, *Aesthetics and Analysis in Writing on Religion*, 5.

180. Ibid., 236–38. Highlighting its spiritual and transformative dimensions, Kri-pal suggest that such an integrated academic approach—one that is "capable of forging a tensive mystical-critical practice out of the discipline's dual Romantic/Enlighten-ment heritage"—can be seen as a modern mystical tradition (*The Serpent's Gift*, 108).

181. Ibid., 117–20, 136–42. Following Ludwig Feuerbach's anthropologization of theology, Kripal endorses a "mystical humanism," which, agnostic about the episte-mological status of mystical knowledge claims, "prefer[s] a human referent for these ontic claims" (*Roads of Excess*, 338n71). Clearly, there is a residual Kantianism lurk-ing behind Kripal's metaphysical agnosticism—a Kantian motive claimed to be tran-scended by many of the participatory approaches presented in this volume. Kripal's modernist agnosticism, however, is balanced (problematized?) by his openness to accepting the consubstantiality of human body and cosmos. In this regard, he tells us that "although we must insist on the intrahuman and even biological nature of mys-tical experiences, this does not necessarily mean that such experiential patterns or structures may not actually reflect something about the objective, nonhuman uni-verse" ("Debating the Mystical as the Ethical: An Indological Map," in *Crossing Boundaries: Essays on the Ethical Status of Mysticism*, ed. Barnard and Kripal [New York: Seven Bridges Press, 2002], 57).

182. Benavides, "Postmodern Disseminations and Cognitive Constraints," *Reli-gion* 27 (1997): 129–38. The Enlightenment enthroning of logic and reason clearly shapes the emphasis that modern higher education places on the development of the rational mind and its intellectual powers, with little attention being given to the mat-uration of other dimensions of the person. As many developmental psychologists point out, most individuals in our culture reach their adulthood with a convention-ally mature mental functioning but with poorly or irregularly developed somatic, emo-tional, aesthetic, intuitive, and spiritual intelligences. The greatest tragedy of cogni-centrism, however, is that it generates a vicious circle that justifies itself. Because

modern education does not create spaces for the autonomous maturation of the body, the instincts, and the heart, these worlds cannot participate in an inquiry process unless they are mentally or externally guided. Yet, insofar as they are mentally or externally guided, these human dimensions cannot develop autonomously, and thus the need for their mental or external direction becomes permanently justified. For an extended discussion, see Ferrer, Marina T. Romero, and Ramon V. Albareda, "Integral Transformative Education: A Participatory Proposal," *The Journal of Transformative Education* 3 (2005): 306–30.

183. Stoller, *Sensuous Scholarship*, xv.

184. The term *cosmotheandric* is borrowed from Panikkar's *The Cosmotheandric Experience: Emerging Religious Consciousness*, ed. with intro. Scott Eastham (Maryknoll, NY: Orbis Books, 1993).

185. See, for example, Bruce Lincoln, *Myth, Cosmos, and Society: Indo-European Themes of Creation and Destruction* (Cambridge: Harvard University Press, 1986); Alex Wayman, "The Human Body as Microcosm in India, Greek Cosmology, and Sixteenth-Century Europe," *History of Religions* 22 (1982): 172–90; Antoine Faivre, *Access to Western Esotericism* (Albany: State University of New York Press, 1994); Chittick, "Microcosm, Macrocosm, and Perfect Man," in *Imaginal Worlds: Ibn al-'Arabi and the Problem of Religious Diversity* (Albany: State University of New York Press, 1994), 31–38; Overzee, *The Body Divine*, 112–14, 146–50; Michael Saso, "The Taoist Body and Cosmic Prayer," in *Religion and the Body*, 230–47; Shimon Shokek, *Kabbalah and the Art of Being* (London: Routledge, 2001), 6; Gunnlaugur A. Jónsson, *The Image of God: Genesis 1:26–28 in a Century of Old Testament Research*, trans. Lorraine Svendsen (Lund, Sweden: Almqvist and Wiskell, 1988).

186. June McDaniel, "The Embodiment of God among the Bāuls of Bengal," *Journal of Feminist Studies in Religion* 8 (1992): 27–39.

187. One could argue that human sexuality is an embodiment of the mystery's creative power. In any event, with Origen, we do not reduce the erotic to the sexual, but rather propose that erotic or vital energies may function as both the fountain and the channel for the generative urges of life or the spirit in human embodied reality.

188. The *virginae subintroductae* (also known as the *agapetae*) refers to those women who entered into committed but celibate arrangements (as "sister and brother") with a male partner in the early church for the purpose of "spiritual consolation" (as Jerome, no fan of this arrangement, says). This fascinating episode, which often included sharing the same bed, is cloaked in a great deal of mystery. Some believe that such arrangements were present already in the earliest churches and lie behind Paul's comments in 1Cor. 7:36. By the middle of the third century, the practice was widespread and began to provoke the ire of certain church fathers including Cyprian, Jerome, and John Chrysostom, who felt that such arrangements were too dangerous and gave license to sin. Charles Williams contends that the practice was more than just social but intended to raise and subsequently to sublimate erotic energies in order to make them available for spiritual endeavors and growth. See Williams, *Descent of the Dove: A History of the Holy Spirit in the Church* (Vancouver: Regent College Publishing, 1987), 11.

189. Anthony Storr, *Feet of Clay. Saints, Sinners, and Madmen: A Study of Gurus* (New York: Free Press, 1996); Kripal, "Debating the Mystical as Ethical," in *Crossing Boundaries*, 15–69; Thomas A. Forsthoefel and Cynthia Ann Humes, eds., *Gurus in America* (Albany: State University of New York Press, 2005); Georg Feuerstein, *Holy Madness: Spirituality, Crazy-Wise Teachers, and Enlightenment*, rev. ed. (Prescott, AZ: Hohm Press, 2006).

190. Eliade, *Cosmos and History: The Myth of the Eternal Return*, ed. Robin Winks (New York: Garland Publishers, 1982).

191. Gill, "Territory," in *Critical Terms for Religious Studies*, 302.

192. See, e.g., the essays by Brian L. Lancaster, Lanzetta, Bruno Barnhart, and Rothberg (in this volume).

193. We cannot conclude this introduction to *The Participatory Turn* without mentioning the work of a number of diverse thinkers who have pioneered the recovery of participatory thinking in modern times. We think here of David Abram's ecological phenomenology in *The Spell of the Sensuous: Perception and Language in a More-Than-Human World* (New York: Vintage Books, 1996); Morris Berman's participatory worldview in *The Reenchantment of the World* (Ithaca: Cornell University Press, 1981); Martin Buber's articulation of a participatory relationship with others, the world, and the divine in *I and Thou*, trans. Walter Kaufmann (New York: Simon and Schuster, 1970); Charlene P. E. Burns's participatory Christology in *Divine Becoming: Rethinking Jesus and Incarnation* (Minneapolis: Fortress Press, 2002); Evans's reflections on human openness in terms of participation in life energies in *Spirituality and Human Nature* (Albany: State University of New York Press, 1993); Gadamer's account of understanding in terms of human situated participation in codetermined meanings in *Truth and Method*, trans. Joel Weinsheimer and Donald G. Marshall, 2d rev. ed. (New York: Crossroads, 1990); Heron's proposal of a cooperative participatory spirituality in *Sacred Science: Person-Centred Inquiry into the Spiritual and the Subtle* (Ross-on-Wye, U.K.: PCCS Books, 1998) and *Participatory Spirituality*; Kremer's approach to indigenous studies in *Looking for Dame Yggdrasil* (Red Bluff, CA: Falkenflug Press, 1994); Miner's theological participatory revision of constructivism in *Truth in the Making*; Panikkar's vision of human, divine, and cosmic interrelated participation in *The Cosmotheandric Experience*; Reason's participatory research methods in his edited *Participation in Human Inquiry*; Henryk Skolimowski's and Tarnas's participatory theories of knowledge in *The Participatory Mind: A New Theory of Knowledge and of the Universe* (New York: Penguin Books, 1994) and *The Passion of the Western Mind*, respectively; and Tambiah's anthropology of religion in *Magic, Science, Religion, and the Scope of Rationality*, among others.

See also the two recent monographs on "The Participatory Turn, Part 1 and 2," edited by Gregg Lahood (2007) in *ReVision: A Journal of Consciousness and Transformation* 29 (3–4), which address the implications of the participatory turn for spiritual cartographies, indigenous studies, Native American religion, the anthropology of consciousness, and relational models of spiritual development.

194. Orsi, *Between Heaven and Earth*.

PART I

Participation and Spirit:
Classical and Contemporary Perspectives

ONE

A Genealogy of Participation

Jacob H. Sherman

> Everything may, it seems, be traced back to the Platonic problem
> of participation.
>
> —Gilles Deleuze, *Expressionism in Philosophy*

> Admirable, but, what is this participation about which you speak?
> —the Eleatic Stranger in Plato, *The Sophist*

ONE OF THE appeals of a participatory turn within Theology, Religious Studies, and the Philosophy of Religion, is that the concept of participation already possesses a long and admirable pedigree within these fields. For more than two millennia, Western writers—pagan, Jewish, and Christian, saints, sages, and scholars—have found the concept of participation crucial to the work of elucidating and deepening their respective religious practices, beliefs, and encounters. When, therefore, we employ participation to make sense of inquiries about religion, we are not importing an alien framework but developing and using a concept that emerges immanently from the semantic field of religion itself. But neither is the concept of participation reducible to religious language, as if it were theology pure and simple and nothing else, for participation is also a properly philosophical concept. Participation is, therefore, something of a promiscuous concept able to slide between the discourses of philosophy and theology, and to unsettle the chaste distinction between emic and etic approaches to religion. Thus, for example, we find the first technical use of the term in Plato, who employed participation (*methexis*) as a philosophical concept in order to defend, clarify, and make sense of a world he perceived as everywhere suspended and haunted by transcendence.

In its most general sense, the metaphysical concept of participation refers to a constitutive structure whereby a being or beings share to varying degrees in a positive quality or perfection that they receive from a donating source that alone enjoys the fullness of this quality or perfection. Thus, for Plato, a horse *participates* in the Form of Equinity (Horse as such), and for Aquinas all beings participate in existence, which they receive from God, whom Aquinas names *Esse Ipsum*, Existence Itself. The rich history of the concept gives the idea of participation both depth and breadth, the latter sometimes issuing in apparently equivocal usages. It is not immediately clear, for example, that Lucien Lévy-Bruhl's and Carl Jung's various appeals to *participation mystique*, J. A. Wheeler's physico-cosmological recourse to participation, Paul Tillich's use of the term, Thomistic *participatio*, and Plato's *methexis* really have much in common. At least part of the reason for these seemingly equivocal usages, however, is that a series of previous developments within participatory theory have taken place. Only by understanding some of the concept's history can we make sense of its usage today and develop our participatory thinking in further creative ways. In what follows, I draw attention to the following three significant developments within the concept of participation in the West: formal or essential participation (as exemplified in Plato), existential participation in being per se (as exemplified in Aquinas), and creative participation (a turn that began in the Renaissance continues through the Romantics and is still underway in contemporary theory). Because these three participatory "turns" have taken place over two thousand years and were enacted diachronically, often in complex reliance upon and deviation from one another, I can only rough out a general picture of these developments, a brief genealogy that should nevertheless prove helpful in situating contemporary participatory approaches.

PLATO AND THE FORMAL TURN

The notion of participation (*methexis*) as anything more than merely having a share in something, as one might have a share in treasure or a portion of pie, appears distinctively with Plato, and so we can say that the first participatory turn (from mundane concept to a central philosophic metaphor) owes its genesis to him. However, the problematic to which participation presented a solution preceded Plato and was simply the problem of how to maintain a relationship between two worlds—the divine and the human—that seemed to be growing further apart. As anthropomorphic religious visions fled in the face of developing rationality, the divine (under what Athenian philosophy thought of as Eleatic influence) was increasingly considered something eternal, immutable, and of an entirely different order than the realm of generation. The problem then was not just how to affirm but to think Thales's assertion that "all things are full of gods,"[1] or Heraclitus's version of the same, "all things are full of souls and spirits."[2] Thinking this proved to be a difficult task—Plato will call it the "second journey,"[3] an allusion to that moment on a ship when the wind gives way and progress can only be made by the strenuous effort of rowing—so difficult that we might call it the "hard problem" of the ancient world.[4]

Participation was thus, among other things, an attempt to think the world as divinely saturated. Particulars, Socrates found, were not self-authenticating or self-grounding—they passed away, they deceived, and most explicitly, they were not their own reason for being. Socrates and Plato saw something dangerous in the sheer transience of materialism. Long before Nietzsche, Plato perceived that the absolute deterritorialization of sensual being—i.e., the realm of becoming and generation untethered from any transcendent supplement—could not serve as a foundation for piety and equitable social relations, but instead heralded an amoral politics of the will to power.[5] Socrates and Plato foresaw that without constitutive intelligible reasons to serve as a locus for value, Athenian decadence would only continue and the Good of the City would finally be lost.

What Socrates calls his "second voyage" is his turn from the materialist explanations of his youth to what we today call Platonism, an explanation of the world that relies on a dipolar categorical scheme that sees the world as constituted by the divine realm of Forms, on the one hand, and the manifest realm of becoming-things, on the other. These two realms must be distinguished but by no means divided. For Plato, the one realm becomes the raison d'etre of the other and participation or *methexis* describes this crucial, constitutive relationship of one realm to another. A beautiful rose, Plato suggests, is beautiful by virtue of its participation in Beauty itself; similarly, a good horse is what it is because it participates in both the Good and in the form of Equinity. The embodied and temporal being is not a second-rate version of the Form it participates; it is this Form in embodied and temporal mode. The two realms, Formal and embodied, are not related according to the univocal logic of solid bodies, but neither are they related equivocally, which is to say that the two realms are neither identical nor *entirely* different.[6] Though it may have taken time for Plato to perfect his language, it is clear that by his middle period Plato understands such participation to be analogical in nature.[7] The participated Forms are of an ontologically different but nevertheless related order than the particular beings that participate in them. Thus, in the *Phaedo*, Plato describes the realm of the Forms as immutable,[8] eternal,[9] sensually imperceptible but intellectually apprehensible,[10] divine and incorporeal,[11] and the constitutive cause of being.[12] As the *fons et origo* of beings, there is a real but not univocal relation between the Forms and their participants, a relationship of causality or existential constitution.[13] Statements such as the rose is beautiful are therefore relational, not attributive, statements. A rose is beautiful in virtue of a relationship to Beauty itself, not because beauty is attributed univocally to the Form and to the particular.

Such is the ontological side of Plato's participation. Epistemologically, this participation structure manifests primarily in Plato's doctrine of *anamnesis* or recollection. In both the *Meno* and the *Phaedo*, Socrates argues from his own experience as an interrogator that, when artfully questioned, his interlocutors are able to produce correct answers of their own accord, especially with regard to geometrical problems.[14] His point is that such questioning proves these interlocutors have a depth of knowledge regarding the ideal Forms of things that surpasses their conscious awareness. Socrates argues that such knowledge emerges from a prenatal familiarity with the realm of Forms. Nicholas Sagovsky comments on this teaching in the *Phaedo*:

> The key point about such "remembering" is that it is participatory. When Socrates the master dies, his pupils are not left without recourse. They will not simply recall what he has said to them . . . but, by dint of their participation in the same cosmos of reality, truth, and wisdom, taking Socrates as a guide, they will develop their own philosophical understanding.[15]

The soul is able to discover such entities because it is *like*, though not exactly identical to, a Form itself, "divine, immortal, intelligible, uniform, indissoluble, and ever self-consistent and invariable. . . ."[16]

The crucial issue in Plato begins to appear very different than popular accounts would lead us to believe.[17] Plato's primary concern is not to protect an immutable realm of Formal essences from contamination by the muck of generation, but rather to secure the value of the world of becoming by exposing it to the contagion of the Good.[18] To divide the two realms would be to render both equally superfluous, and so Plato is instead everywhere concerned with the nature of the in-between realm across which daimones shuttle the prayers of mortals to divinities, and convey the blessing of gods and goddesses to the earth. Plato calls this realm the *metaxy* and links it with Eros:

> Interpreting and conveying things from men to gods and things from gods to men, prayers and sacrifices from the other, since being in between [*metaxy*] both, it fills the region between both so that the All [*to pan*] is bound together with itself. Through this realm moves all prophetic art and the art of priests having to do with sacrifices and rituals and spells, and all power of prophecy and enchantment. . . . These divinities [*daimones*] then are many and manifold, and one of them is Eros.[19]

The metaxic realm is the realm of participation and it is the true lynchpin of Plato's cosmos. Reality (*to pan*) is, for Plato, neither the world of noetic being, nor the Heraclitean flux, but a "mixed" world of both realms.[20] It is the metaxy. Perhaps this is why Plato himself never settled on a single word to denote the participation relationship, but employed half a dozen such words. In *Plato's Theory of Ideas*, David Ross proposes making a distinction between these various signifiers. Ross suggests certain words—communion (*koinonia*),

participation (*methexis*), and presencing (*parousia*)—highlight the immanence of Forms in their object, while others—paradigm (*paradeigma*), copy
(*mimesis*), and image (*eikon*)—stress Formal transcendence.[21]

Plato is consistently an advocate to the end of the *metaxy*, the generative
tension that holds reality together in dynamic community.[22] We find our
world and ourselves within this metaxic realm, ecstatically constituted, such
that our depths are discovered only in excess of ourselves. For Plato, then,
insofar as he makes participation central, the good life, the religious life, and
the philosophic life come together in an erotic journey toward the persistent
discovery of beauty in the participatory mediations of the phenomenal world.
In the *Timaeus* account of motion, participation in the Forms is the cause of
generation, even to the extent that movement itself is understood as the
means by which finite beings most properly participate and therefore image
the perfection of the eternal. It is, for Plato, precisely the gap between eternal perfection and creaturely lack (*Penia* and *Poros*) that generates corporeal
motion. The plenitude and splendor of ideal being draws creaturely becom-
ings toward their perfection and sets them moving. For Plato, as for his participatory successors, kinetics is erotics.

This reading of participation in Plato is confirmed by Aristotle's own
reaction to the doctrine of participation. To the degree that Aristotle
rejects Plato's dipolar categorical scheme, he also rejects the concept of
participation.[23] This is often read as if it were evidence of Aristotle's more
positive cosmology, his down-to-earth appreciation for the realm of bodies
and becoming, and his vision of form as always already inherent in matter
(think of all those undergraduate lectures illustrated by Raphael's *School of
Athens*). Close attention however, to the way that Platonism and Aristotelianism are respectively performed in the world (first in their own particular texts, and then in the writings and societies of those they influence) calls this commonplace into question. As Stephen Clark notes, "In
the millennial dispute between Platonists and Aristotelians, it is usually
the Aristotelian who is supposed to treat human beings 'naturalistically. . . .'"[24] But the situation is quite otherwise. It is Plato who considers
the intimacy of the human being's relation to other animals, even to the
point (in the *Statesman*) of thinking of human societies as herds of free
bipeds.[25] Clark continues, "Platonists, not Aristotelians, have usually been
the ones to consider our duties to those not of our species. Platonists, not
Aristotelians, have found corporeal nature sacramental."[26] Religiously,
something similar happens. Whereas Plato's demiurge functions with the
intimacy of a world soul and shows itself to be capable of relationship,
Aristotle's divine is unperturbed to the point of ignorance with regard to
the realm of manifestation—its connection to our world is reduced to a
"relationship" of nonrecursive causality. As the philosopher of religion
Daniel Dombrowski comments:

> Paradoxically, from this emphasis on embodied form [contrary to Plato's dipolar categorical scheme], Aristotle ultimately constructed a more vicious dualism than any ever envisaged by Plato, in that Aristotle's divinities are *completely* self-sufficient entities, unmoved and separated from all change, multiplicity, and embodiment.[27]

In the centuries following Plato and Aristotle, one of the great tasks of philosophy was to bring these two thinkers together, to demonstrate the essential harmony of the Platonic and Aristotelian systems.[28] This project however, accentuated certain tendencies to which the Platonic approach was already susceptible, tendencies that led to a kind of scorn or, at best, mild indifference to the world of particular things.[29] Those whose synthesis of Plato and Aristotle favored the Stagyrite—a contingent whose ranks include most Middle Platonists and the Plotinian strand of Neoplatonism—gave occasional voice to the possibility of a *contemptus mundi* that Plato himself never fully escaped. In opposition to this world-fleeing Platonism, there existed an alternative cosmological Platonism that considered itself the authentic inheritor of Plato's philosophy and religion, a tradition most evident in Iamblichus and Proclus. Where the Plotinian strand largely borrowed theology from Aristotle, Iamblichus's cosmological Platonism wed the theo-cosmology of the *Timaeus* with the theanthropic cosmology of the *Chaldean Oracles* and the *Corpus Hermeticum* (streams already influenced by Semitic faith) and thus sowed the seeds for the last participatory revision we will consider in this chapter. First however, we must consider a prior shift: the existential turn within participation.

THE EXISTENTIAL TURN

If there was a lingering distrust of the world within Platonic philosophy, this partially stems from certain conceptual puzzles that Plato left more or less unexplored. While Platonic participation explains what a being is, it fails to address the basic ontological question of why a being is, or as Leibniz says, "Why is there something rather than nothing?" In order to answer this question a new mode of participation had to be discovered; its reach had to be extended to include the order of existence itself, not merely why something is thus and so but why something is at all. It seems like a simple matter—Chesterton remarked that even a small child is aware that, say, grass primarily is—but the question of being turns out to be notoriously difficult and perhaps, as Chesterton also recognized, only answerable by a kind of religious rather than philosophical insight.[30] It is fitting then, that the existential participatory turn was finally accomplished by Thomas Aquinas who, as Mary Clark states, "was more convinced than Plato that participation helps us to appreciate what is going on in the created universe."[31] Whereas previously, most of the traditions (and indeed, many today) tended to analyze being in terms of essence—i.e., in terms of the what-it-is of a being—Thomas focused on the act of being itself as primary.[32] As he says, "*Ens dicitur ab actu essendi*" (being is spoken or named according to the act of existence).[33]

Thomas frequently employed the Latin *esse* (to be) as a nominal infinitive in order to speak about this primordial act of being. That the act of being might be logically prior to being-some-sort-of-thing is a radical concept for Aquinas—indeed, it is hardly a concept at all, but is rather more like an awareness, or even a clearing, as Heidegger might say.[34] For Aquinas, *Esse* as the act of being is Absolute. "One does not abstract, conceptualize, possess, or grasp the Absolute or the truth," says Mary Clark. "One is awakened by the Absolute, and responds. . . ."[35] We can perhaps gain a clearer understanding of this distinction by considering the way we use the word *is*. On the one hand, we employ the word as a copula in order to distinguish what something is. This is to speak *essentially* or propositionally and poses the kind of questions that Platonic participation was designed to answer. But we also use the same word "is" for the purpose of assertion and, when we do so, we are speaking *existentially* in order to designate a certain "isness," a more primordial presencing than even essence—that is to say, we intend the very act of being itself.

This led Thomas to formulate his famous distinction between essence and existence. This teaching, sometimes referred to as the "real distinction," can only be appreciated within the doctrine of creation.[36] Thomas understood the existence of all creatures to be sheer gift (*donum*) continually received from the generosity of God. Indeed, Thomas insists that this gifted contingency is precisely what creation means. Creation does not describe a transformation as if from one state to another, but rather a radical relationality, a state of dependence upon the divine. "Truly, creation is not a change," says Thomas, "but the very dependence of the creature's act-of-being upon the principle by which it has been set up."[37]

Participation is the way Thomas expresses this dependence. For the most part, Thomas simply presupposes the idea of participation, so self-evident does it seem to his age. While Owen Barfield may overstate the matter when he says that, for Aquinas, *participation* "is not a technical term of philosophy," Barfield is nonetheless right when he notes that in Aquinas "the word *participate* or *participation* occurs almost on every page . . . and [Thomas] is no more concerned to define it than a modern philosopher would be, to define some such common tool of his thought as, say, the word *compare*."[38] Only in his commentary on Boethius's *De Hebdomadibus* does Thomas treat the idea of participation explicitly.[39] He distinguishes therein three types of participation: logical, real, and causal. Logical participation occurs when a logical inferior participates in a logical superior, as for example when species participates in genus. Real participation refers to the way a subject participates in an accident, or a matter in form. Unlike the first type, this involves actual and not simply ideal composition and may therefore be called ontological participation. Finally, Aquinas notes that an effect may participate in its cause. This third type, causal participation, is the kind of participatory relationship that pertains between God and creatures, between *esse ipsum subsistens* and *entia*.[40]

In another text, while trying to better appreciate the nature of angels, Thomas elaborates on the structure of creaturely participation:

> Everything existing after the first being (*ens*), since it is not its *esse* (act-of-being/existence), has *esse* which is received in something by which the *esse* is limited; and thus in every creature the nature of the thing which participates *esse* is one matter, and the participated *esse* is another. And since everything participates in the First Act by likeness insofar as it has *esse*, the participated *esse* in each thing must be related to the nature that participates it as act is related to potency.[41]

This is a remarkably rich text for understanding Thomas's vision. Here again, Thomas draws our attention to the real distinction within creatures between essence and existence. All creatures are, as it were, split—while they have real existence, this existence is not their own but is participated, received as a gratuitous gift. To be created is to be fundamentally ecstatic, to feel the very root of existence as rapturously given from an infinite source not of one's own making.

While Thomas introduces the Aristotelian vocabulary of act and potency (*actus et potentia*) in order to explain such participation, he is in fact enacting a radical reversal of Aristotelian assumptions in his employment of this language. Aristotle could never have conceived of the relationship of the creature to the Creator as a limitation of Infinite Act by potency. For Aristotle, and the Hellenic mind in general, the notion of infinity was distasteful. For Plato and Aristotle, perfection could only be conceived in terms of limit (*peras*). The infinite or unlimited (*apeiron*) appeared threatening to the Greek mind, a penumbral chaos that was generative only when bounded and tamed.[42] This chaos was associated with pure matter (*materia*), a sort of *Tiamat* that required slaying by the immutable, defined *act* that Aristotle and Plato equally equated with form. Every form—no matter how primordial—was understood to be definite, and therefore Aristotle had no difficulty in populating his universe with plurality of ultimates—as many as fifty-five Prime Movers, Norris Clarke, S.J., notes.[43] For Plato and Aristotle, therefore, as earlier for Pythagoras and Parmenides and later for the Stoics, the infinite was always placed on the disagreeable side of the table of opposites. Infinity signaled chaos, evil, and disorder. It was the opposite of form, logos, definition, for as the scholastics maxim says, *omnis definitio est negatio*: every definition is a negation, a limit.

Inklings of an alternative valuation are admittedly found already in Anaximander who conceived the infinite as a kind first principle or divine womb, "neither water nor any of the other so-called elements but some different boundless [*apeiron*] nature from which come into being all the heavens."[44] Accounts of Anixamnder's beliefs on this subject surface in Simplicius, Aristotle, and others, and find a distant echo among the Epicureans, so we can deduce that the concept of a positive infinity was not entirely unknown in the Hellenistic world. Nevertheless, most Hellenes fled from infinity as from an undifferentiated and encroaching substratum. This cultural and philosophical disavowal of infinity was eventually overturned in what amounted to a Neoplatonic revaluation of all values. The revaluation of the infinite was not provoked by the immanent pressures of philosophical reason, as if sheer logic required this discovery, but rather by an encounter with both Semitic faith and the mystery religions that were spreading throughout antiquity. As Clarke notes, the new religions of the East introduced Plotinus to an intuition of divinities marked by ineluctable mystery and power, masters of the limitless heavens newly championed by Syrian astronomy, "above all rational concepts, but with whom the believer could enter into salvific personal union by mystical or other means."[45] The center of activity for these new mystery religions was Alexandria, the home of Plotinus as it had earlier been home to the Jewish philosopher, Philo (the first thinker to use the term *infinite* or *uncircumscibed* [*aperigraphos*] to name God). Plotinus thus effected a revolution by integrating the Platonic concept of participation with the spiritual intuitions of a positive infinity, and the result was his fully articulate doctrine of emanation.

Plotinus's emanative cosmology sees the contraction of form as an isolated mass surrounded on both sides by two infinities; form floats upon the surface of the chaotic illimitation of nonbeing, and gazes heavenward to the infinite pleromatic vaults of the One's ineffable simplicity. As Clarke says, "[Plotinus] becomes the first to apply *apeiron* to signify the trans-formal indetermination of plenitudinous perfection as compared to the limited perfections below it."[46] Plotinus describes his vision:

> The first principle is that which is without form, not that it is lacking form, but that all intelligible forms come from it. That which is produced by that very fact becomes a particular thing and possesses a form proper to it. But who could produce the unproduced? . . . It is infinite. . . . How could anything else measure it?[47]

By wrestling with the concept of a positive infinity, Plotinus adumbrates but never explicitly formulates something akin to Thomas's real distinction between essence and existence and therefore begins to imagine the existential participatory turn. Following in this tradition, someone such as Boethius could assert that every pure form was infinite, and therefore every finite creature had to be understood as a composite of form and subject.[48] Plotinus's emanative vision was inherited by Proclus, who supplemented it with

Iamblichean speculations, and through Proclus's *Elements of Theology* and the *Liber de Causis*, the revaluation of the infinite was felt throughout Western and Eastern thought and religion. It was, in fact, Al-Farabi and Avicenna in the East who, in Plotinus's wake, finally articulated the essence-existence distinction and from whom Aquinas learned of it.[49] Thomas inherited this Neoplatonic structure but amended it, uniting the essence-existence distinction with a new metaphysics of infinite act limited by finite potencies, thereby finding that the ultimate perfection was the "quasi-form" of existence: esse, the infinite act of existence.[50]

Part of Aquinas's genius was the integration of this essence-existence distinction with a revised participatory metaphysics and Christian Trinitarian theology, especially with regard to the doctrine of creation. In the early inquiries of the *Summa Theologiae*, Aquinas argues that all beings are composed of essence and existence save one whose essence perfectly coincides with existence and this being is properly called God.[51] In God alone, essence and existence coincide, and this is precisely what constitutes the difference between Creator and creation, the only dualism Aquinas accepts.

Aquinas's essence-existence distinction preserves the Platonic concept of formal participation, while adding the newly discovered mode of existential participation. On the one hand, each created being is to the extent that it receives (participates) existence from the self-diffusive goodness of God. On the other hand, the essence of a being describes *the manner* it receives its *esse* from its Creator. A creature's essence is a mirror (*speculum*) of exemplars that exist in the divine mind, or, more precisely, in the Word, the second person of the Trinity.[52] These exemplars are not arbitrary but the divine knowledge of the manifold ways that God can be (formally) participated and imaged. In this sense, Thomas's existential vision does not eradicate the idea of essence as happens, for example, in Sartre's existentialism. For Thomas, being and intelligibility are distinct, but as transcendentals they coincide in the divine source in whose bounty all things share. Thomas was convinced that all of the transcendentals—those properties that apply to all reality as such, irrespective of differences in genus and species—were convertible.[53] The convertibility of the transcendentals means that transcendentals are distinguished only in relation to the knowing subject (our *modus cognoscendi*); we abstract these transcendental qualities from the profundity of the real. Every being, therefore, is in some degree one, good, intelligible, active, and beautiful, just by virtue of being. As Clarke notes, "For Aquinas . . . it is *the real itself* that is one, true, good, and beautiful, but seen according to different perspectives and relations."[54] For imaginations accustomed, after Hume, to regard existence itself as simply a brute fact or a surd given, this vision is hard to grasp, but it is essential to St. Thomas's understanding of the participatory cosmos. If we wish to understand Aquinas, we must come to see with Gilson that: "The most marvelous of all the things a being can do is *to be*."[55] As Thomas himself put it,

"The act of being is the most intimate reality in any being, and that which is most profound in all things."[56] As convertible transcendentals, intelligibility and existence are for St. Thomas, indivisibly meaningful and continuous, existing in what Maritain calls a nuptial relationship.[57]

The most persistent misinterpretations of Aquinas err inasmuch as they neglect the dynamic quality of participatory saturation. Some of the most profound thinkers of the twentieth century—from Heidegger to Hartshorne—have mistaken Thomas's vision of substance for an inert, Lockean prison. Nothing could be farther from the truth. No phrase occurs more often in the writings of St. Thomas than the descriptive: *omne agens agit sibi simile* (every agent acts to reproduce something of its likeness). This causal prescription is in many ways the key to Thomas's dynamic participatory understanding of both substances and the divine Mystery that undergirds them. Far from a static form, God is for St. Thomas, the dynamic act of being. As the principle of all participated beings, God overflows, even exteriorizes Godself in the generous diffusion that makes creation possible. As John Milbank and Catherine Pickstock write, "Thomas cites Dionysius's 'daring to say' that God on account of his goodness exists 'as it were outside of himself.' For only this impossible self-exteriorization will explain how there can be something other to God participating in God."[58] This radical activity and relationality is refracted throughout creation; such ecstatic action is part of what it means to be. As Clarke's influential article states, for St. Thomas, "To be is to be substance-in-relation."[59] Beings are dyadically constituted as an inseperable polarity of substantial existence *in* themselves and *for* others. This is no afterthought, for St. Thomas, but the essence of what it means to exist: "Operation is the ultimate perfection of each thing."[60] Again, Thomas reminds us, "Natural things have a natural inclination not only toward their own proper good . . . but also to diffuse their own goodness among others as far as possible . . . to communicate their own goodness to others."[61] Philipp W. Rosemann describes this communicative causality, which is inseparable from a being's substance:

> Causality could be described as the mask through which beings speak to us on the stage of reality: without it, the "play" of reality could not take place; and nevertheless it leaves the "really" real behind the mask unknown—or rather, this "really" real becomes known only mediately . . .[62]

Whitehead and other philosophers have too quickly confused Thomas's notion of substance with later (corrupted) versions as found in Descartes, Locke, and Hume. In so doing, many have been led to believe the notion of substance to be unsalvageable, turning instead to a nonsubstantial metaphysics of pure becoming. Aquinas offers a way beyond both the insular monad of modern thought and the chaosmos of postmodernity. His vision of a being as substantially identical with itself but nonetheless relationally constituted and always already engaged in adventures of change and communication through self-diffusive action may do more justice to both our experience and our intellect than either of the modern and post-modern alternatives. Such communicative action is not impersonal, not exterior, but intimate and relational, a mingling of beings, like the touching of hands or the sharing of breath. "Causality," says Clarke, "is the ecstasy of the agent present by its power *in* its effect."[63]

Participation subverts all competitive dualisms by daring to think this *conspiratio* (shared breath) as the basic movement of creation. The metaphysics of participation envisions a radically relational world without sacrificing difference and distance. It seeks to reconcile the integrity of the Many with the allurement and reality of the One. Thomistic philosophy discovers that participatory relationships are analogically present in the veiled-unveiling of all creatures one to another, and of God to all things. As Rosemann says regarding Thomas's great arcanum of sameness and difference:

> God is not other than his creation in the way in which I am different from you. . . . If God were in any way exterior to his creation, he would be different from it in a creaturely mode; this, in turn, would render his otherness a kind of sameness, and—in the last analysis—reduce transcendence to immanence. . . . [God's] otherness consists precisely in the fact that he does *not* stand in any relationship of negativity with respect to his creatures. God is *supra omnia* not although, but precisely *insofar as* he is *in omnibus et intime*. Transcendence is the superlative mode of immanence.[64]

THE CREATIVE TURN

Formal participation such as we find in Plato addresses the need to account for the intelligibility of beings, while existential participation such as we find in Aquinas provides an accounting for the facticity of beings, but neither of these accountings answers the problem of creative agency. By locating the constitutive causes of a given creature outside of that creature, participatory metaphysics runs the risk of endlessly deferring agency and action to ever higher participatory mediations until finally we are left with hollow creatures, mere puppets or modes of transcendental perfections. This is, of course, neither what Plato nor Aquinas intended, but is nevertheless a possible consequence of their thought. In order to avoid this consequence, a third mode of participation had to be discovered or invented, a mode whereby not only are essence and existence participated, but creativity itself is shared through the series of participatory mediations. This creative turn within participatory thought allows us to see that the doctrine of participation can be articulated in a fully modern idiom, for theories of creative participation both address and develop characteristically modern themes such as art as expression rather than imitation, the human as *homo creator*, the constructive function of language, and the ubiquity of process and history within the cosmos. Because this turn to creative participation is still underway, this section will be a bit longer than the previous two as it will necessarily focus on a broad historical trajectory rather than a single individual who has emerged as a representative or culmination of this turn.

The discovery of participated creativity is largely indebted to our late discovery, as human beings, of our own creative abilities. In contrast to the flippant way that a term such as "creativity" is used today, the ancient world restricted the concept of creativity to the gods alone. When we today find it self-evident that an artist is a creator of sorts, we do so because of a long process whereby human beings appropriated for themselves what was once the province of the divine. This process, however, was not initially as Promethean and hubristic as it sounds, and even, as we will see, had an element of piety about.

A full account of this development would ask us to consider the ambivalent relationship between art and the Platonic tradition, paying special attention to the way that Platonists such as Dio Chrysostom, Philostraus, and Plotinus explore a proto-creative theory of art, one that focuses on contemplation more than on either passive inspiration or simple imitation. There is a quasi-creative activity in their notion of contemplative beholding and subsequent creation, one that parallels the way Plato's Demiurge beheld the Forms in the act of fashioning this universe as recounted in the *Timaeus*. As C. S. Lewis comments, in Dio Chrysostom, Philostraus, and Plotinus, "Art and Nature . . . become rival copies of the same supersensuous original, and there is no reason why Art should not sometimes be the better of the two."[65] The cautious exploration of this proto-creative contemplative moment that occupied Dio Chrysostom, Philostraus, and Plotinus, is radicalized in the more explicitly theurgical strand of Neoplatonism as well as in Hermetic and Patristic traditions. If we had more space we could explore the way that such theurgical Neoplatonists respond to religious pressures—particularly the Alexandrian Helleno-Semitic discovery of a positive infinity within mystery traditions, Judaism, and Christianity—and the way that such religious discoveries issue in a more positive valuation of art and human creativity. These Hermetic and theurgical traditions (e.g., in the *Asclepius*, Iamblichus, and Dionyisus) as well as the proto-creative contemplative theory of art found in Dio Chrysostom, Philostraus, and Plotinus, begin to suggest a new mode of participation, one whereby participation in divine Creativity causes the participant herself to stand (e.g., as artisan, dramatist, theurgist, or political agent) in a new "directionally creator" relation to the world.[66] Nevertheless, none of these traditions went beyond hinting at the artist's likeness to God in this aspect of creativity, of bringing Form forth into the

world of manifestation. Not until the ninth century does John Scotus Eriugena make the theme of *homo creator* central, defining the human being
as essentially both *created* and *creating* (*natura creata* and *natura creans*) and
making the human central to the eschatological re-creation of all things.[67]
In the fourteenth century, by radicalizing Albert the Great's and Thomas
Aquinas's thought, and re-sourcing the likes of Dionysius and Eriguena,
Meister Eckhart defends a theurgical vision of the participatory worldview
that decisively anticipates modern theories of poetic expressivism. In this
regard, Eckhart links the notion of divine exemplarism to his ubiquitous
theme of the birth of Christ in the soul—a Patristic trope Eckhart could
have found even in Origen. Like the proto-creative theory of art we found
above in the contemplative Neoplatonists, Eckhart argues that human
artistry finds its proper object when the imagination rises to contemplate
the Divine Ideas. In Eckhart's understanding, this imaginative work is possible because the imagination participates, through divine illumination, in
God's own thoughts—our thoughts and imagination are echoes of God's
Logos. Unlike his Neoplatonic predecessors, however, Eckhart has an even
more dynamic and generative sense of these archetypal exemplars that the
imagination rises to behold:

> Looking for an artistic exemplar does not mean setting out to create it. It
> means rather the mystical focusing of the attention upon the reality which
> is to be reproduced, to the point of identifying with it. But the ideas subsis-
> tent in God and communicated to men's minds are not Platonic archetypes
> so much as types of activity, forces, operative principles. They are living
> ideas. They do not exist as "standards," but as ideas of actions to be done.
> An actual object emerges from the idea like something growing from it.[68]

Eckhart sees these exemplars as active and generative because his resolute
trinitarianism locates all exemplars not simply in a realm of Forms, but within
the *Logos*, the Second Person of the Trinity who eternally exhales the Spirit
and is begotten by the Father.[69] Every creature is a kind of word expressing the
divine artisanship and echoing in a limited fashion the eternal Word. Going
beyond Aquinas, Eckhart understands the generation of the Son by the
Father as the paradigm of all generation. All beings echo this primal beget-
ting and exist, as it were, through participation in the impossible space
between Father and Son. Our artisanship and action in the world is an
expression of Christ's own birth within our souls.

The subtle but important point to notice here is that by relating image
and archetype, word and referent, to the trinitarian paradigm, Eckhart is led
to reduce the inequity between a simulacrum and its original to almost nil
and to implicate our own making in God's creative process. In the same way
that the Father is not the Son and the Son is not the Father and yet both are
equally God without qualification, so Eckhart is able to write:

> An image, and the thing of which it is an image, are not separate; they are
> not two substances. . . . An image is strictly an emanation, simple, formal, a
> pouring forth of the whole of an essence, pure and naked. . . . A thing's
> image grows out of itself and grows upon itself.[70]

Eckhart's theories ramified throughout the Rhineland tradition and played an
important role in Nicholas of Cusa's remarkable vision of human creativity as
a participation in the divine *explicatio* as also in Tommaso Campanella's *totic-
ipatione* ("total and complete participation"), a term coined as a means of
revising the concept of participation along more thoroughly holistic, expressivist lines.[71] As Umberto Eco writes:

> From these germinal ideas there arose a new vision of the artistic process. If
> we extrapolate them from the psychology of mysticism and the theology of
> the Trinity we can discern something that is not medieval any more, the
> germ of new directions in aesthetics akin to our own world.[72]

There is a protopragmatist logic to this idea of participation in creativity
that begins to adumbrate a vision of human knowing as a relational event,
something more than representation, something that forges truth in the very
act of knowing, a cognition that calls forth novelty on the part of that which
is known. Creation had been the prerogative of the divine alone—for God,
it was understood, to create and to know are one and the same. But now the
human begins to echo this activity. Like the horizon at dusk, the division
between divine and human grows less visible as the logic of participation
complicates the easy distinction between Creator and creature, apparently
merging heaven and earth.

At the dawn of modernity, Benedict de Spinoza made this apparent mingling of divine and human creative agency philosophically explicit by eliding
any real boundary between Creator and creation. As we will see, however,
when Spinoza's pantheism abolishes this boundary it both advances and
threatens to shipwreck the doctrine of participation. This is because participation fundamentally entails a relationship between realms and therefore
requires really distinct if not divisible *relata*. We will conclude this section,
then, by considering the way that Friedrich Schelling sought to rehabilitate
the doctrine of participation in creativity by taking Spinoza's insights and
revising them along the lines of a more complex, nuanced, and postcritical
version of the Renaissance doctrine of participation in creativity.

Spinoza's philosophy can be seen, in one sense, as fundamentally a revision of participatory theories.[73] Spinoza revises the concept of participation in
a thoroughly immanentist fashion by doing away with the transcendence
involved in all earlier participatory theories. By evacuating all forms of transcendence from participation, Spinoza ushers in what is recognized as the era
of modern expressionism.[74] By expressionism, I mean the idea that an agent

is genuinely present within rather than external to its actions. Expressionism or expressivism (I will treat the two terms as functionally equivalent) is often contrasted with emanation. The doctrine of emanation in Plotinus, for example, pictures the many as epiphenomena that proceed from the One but do not remain within the One; like Aristotle's God, Plotinus's One remains unmoved within itself, and the many are thus distinct from this One. Expressionism, by contrast, imagines that an action or artifact genuinely communicates the being of the responsible agent and so the action remains within the agent—the agent issues forth from itself in its action.[75] For emanation, a cause is external to its effect; for expressionism, a cause is immanent to its effect, it indwells the effect, and the effect remains within the cause: "A cause is immanent . . . when its effect is 'immanate' in the cause, rather than emanating from it. What defines an immanent cause is that its effect is in it—in it, of course, as in something else, but still being and remaining in it."[76]

Spinoza is led to this doctrine of expressionism because of his pantheistic doctrine that there can be only one substance. As Spinoza concludes in proposition 14 of the *Ethics*, "*Except God, no substance can be or be conceived.*"[77] If the only substance is God, then God's actions cannot be something different from Godself. Creator and creation, cause and effect, agent and action are not to be conceived as different levels or types of being, but simply as the one being that Spinoza calls God or nature (*Deus sive Natura*) in its many forms. Spinoza thus sees all particular beings of whatever type as the infinitely diverse expressions of a single self-causing energy or substance, the single substance that is God/nature.

Whereas other participatory theorists we have considered understand being (Aquinas's esse) as a spectrum of vast qualitative differences that we can only begin to recognize through the use of analogy, Spinoza holds that being is a univocal concept that admits only quantitative differences and differences in perception. While being may appear to be different, this is only because we see it from different angles, in different lights.[78] All types of being are, in reality, one and the same. Spinoza's single universe is comprised of the one substance (God or nature), but is formally divided into what Spinoza names attributes and modes. God expresses God's one self in infinitely many attributes (such as thought and extension, the only two attributes Spinoza believes humans can know); attributes, in turn, express, produce, or instantiate themselves in specific modes that comprise, for example, the finite creatures we find around us.[79] The crucial point for Spinoza is that the division into attributes and then into modes is not an ontological division but the infinitely diverse manifestations (bodily or mental dispositions) of the one substance. Spinoza writes, "Particular things are nothing but affections of God's attributes, *or* modes by which God's attributes are expressed in a certain and determinate way."[80] These modal expressions follow with geometric, even mechanical necessity from the definition of God/nature. Everything, for Spinoza, is the necessary expression of the impersonal divine substance.

All of this results in a radical revision of the concept of participation. Spinoza still uses the language of participation to convey the relationship between modes, attributes, and God—and in this one can hear echoes of the theurgical and theological traditions discussed above—but Spinoza alters these traditions in a crucial manner so that there is no longer any distance between the modes and substances and that in which they participate. Attributes and modes are the dynamic but necessary expressions of an immanent God, a God who is likewise the result of metaphysical necessity. Spinoza, therefore, finds creativity everywhere; every creature participates in creativity and has the power of expression because every creature is God expressing Godself. Spinoza radicalizes participation by running it through the concepts of immanence and the univocity of being and refusing any doctrine of transcendence.[81] In Spinoza's thought, participation (whether in form, existence, or creativity) is expression pure and simple.[82] Essence and existence (formally distinguishable but substantially identical) are nothing other than the expression of the self-creating intensity that is the one divine substance.[83] God creates Godself in us and in all creatures, but we also create God when we create ourselves moment by moment. In a sense there is only creativity, only this single, dynamic, cosmic autopoiesis.

Spinoza thus articulated an extreme version of the doctrine of participation in creativity by abolishing the distinction between Creator and creation. This radicalized creation's share in creativity but also set up new problems of its own. Spinoza never questions the notion that creativity belongs to God alone; indeed, the only means Spinoza discovered to radicalize creativity was to make everything God. For Spinoza, as much as for classical and scholastic philosophy, nothing other than God can create. But if everything is God, then the notion of participation makes little sense as there is never more than one term, and so there are either no beings to participate or, alternatively, nothing in which to participate. Moreover, how much sense does it make to speak of creativity when everything proceeds with rigid metaphysical and mathematical necessity?

Problems within Spinoza's philosophy were brought to critical light in the "Pantheism Controversy" that shook European culture to its core in the late eighteenth and early nineteenth centuries. The controversy was sparked by Moses Mendelssohn and F. H. Jacobi over the alleged Spinozism of Gotthold Ephraim Lessing. Jacobi alleged that Lessing—a prominent recently deceased father of the German Enlightenment—had confessed his affinity for Spinozism to Jacobi after listening to a recital of Goethe's poem "Prometheus." This was scandalous—one could easily lose an academic post and a career for far less—for Spinoza's fatalism and his pantheism were seen to threaten the bases of morality and faith that preserved the order of the

German republic. But there was something attractive in Spinoza, particularly to those who shared the early-modern frustration with explanatory appeals to transcendence, and to those early Romantics who loved the way Spinoza combined a thoroughgoing naturalism with a mystical sense of oneness and connection to the world. Thus, the controversy raged and, as Frederick Beiser notes, "Almost every notable thinker of the 1790s developed his philosophy as a response to this controversy."[84] Not only Jacobi and Mendelssohn, but Herder, Schlegel, Hegel, Novalis, Hölderlin, and even Kant entered the fray.

Jacobi, however, took the lead. Jacobi argued that Spinoza's naturalism cast its net too wide. He thought that if Enlightenment rationality was true to itself it would end in Spinozism and in fatalism and would thereby destroy its own foundations. Equating rationality with metaphysical necessity, Jacobi argued that when Spinoza subjected everything to the workings of immanent rationality, he left nothing for reason to know and so destroyed knowledge. If everything is rational, then nothing is. Reason will spin its wheels but get nowhere, it will never reach nature or the real, and its pretensions to God are tragic. Jacobi coined the term *nihilism* to describe the vacuity and narcissism of this isolate reason that can only stare at itself. His proposed solution to this dilemma was a *salto mortale*, a leap of faith, head over heels, into the divine. Only such a turn to pure faith, Jacobi argued, can preserve the solidity of the real, and the dignity of freedom, and so give reason a realm within which it can properly work.[85]

Friedrich Schelling, among others, thought Jacobi's diagnosis was apt, but that his constructive suggestions sacrificed too much. Jacobi's turn to pure faith seemed like a move into irrationalism, the immolation of the intellect rather than its redemption. Schelling sought a genuine alternative, a third way beyond Spinoza's fatalism and Jacobi's fideism. Schelling thus proposed an alternative expressivist vision of participation, one that unites immanence and transcendence—not by stages, however, nor by a collapse of the one into the other, but rather through a sort of divine parallax, a vision of "two closely linked perspectives between which no neutral common ground is possible."[86] *Pace* Spinoza, precisely because there is no univocity of common being between the divine and the created, the connection between the two realms can itself be absolute, albeit inscrutable to finite creatures. We cannot hold the divine and created together in a single ontotheological gaze because, for Schelling (as for Eckhart), the eye with which I see God is the eye with which God sees me. Nevertheless, as Schelling understood, this gap does not separate us from the divine but alone allows us to see finitude and material constraints as cooperating with transcendence and spirituality, rather than one needing to negate the other.[87] In effect, Schelling argues that only a genuine transcendence secures rationality and allows it to function at all, but *pace* Jacobi this transcendence cannot simply be irrational. The appeal to transcendence cannot be a leap of faith that negates discursive reason and its material conditions, but must instead be the very transfiguration of reason itself, a transformation that takes us beyond but does not disown reason or materiality. As Schelling writes:

> Philosophy *cannot* just concern itself with the highest things, it must . . . really connect the highest with the lowest. The power of the eagle in flight does not prove itself by the fact that the eagle does not feel *any* pull downwards, but by the fact that it overcomes this pull, indeed makes it into the *means* of its elevation. The tree which strikes its roots deep into the earth can still hope to raise its blossom-laden crown into heaven, but thoughts which separate themselves from nature from the outset are like plants without roots.[88]

Jacobi's *salto* leaves us with a naïve faith in things, a myth of the given. Schelling, to the contrary, wants to recover the solidity and depth of the world through the revelation of things, not a myth of the given but of the gift alive with presence of the giver, the gift continually bestowed, indomitable and gratuitous—the gift that gives us the capacity even to receive, the gift that gives us to ourselves, and gives us the power give in return—the gift, in short, of participation in creativity by which we make ourselves and the world.

Schelling thus brings the metaphysics of participation in creativity to one of its loftiest articulations yet. He argues that the Spinozist theory of expression fails because it determines the Absolute (Schelling's term for the divine) as absolute *object*. The actions of Spinoza's God, you will recall, unfold with mechanistic necessity. Spinoza's God is all manifestation but is barren of agency, and Schelling agrees with Jacobi's assessment that this leads to nihilism and destroys the possibility of meaning. Schelling argues instead that we ought to think of the Absolute as inherently creative and living—not, that is, as object but as subject, not a machine but something more like an organism.

Schelling is determined to think of this in a way that is not philosophically naïve or subject to the Kantian critique, and so he requires a new, complex theory of subjectivity, one that builds upon Kant and Fichte but also incorporates the expressivist insights of Spinoza and others. Kant and Fichte had already argued that the essence of subjectivity was freedom, something entirely lacking in Spinoza's God, and so both Kant and Fichte assigned a constructive or creative power to the subject. But for them, this creative power remained stuck in subjectivity, as it were, resulting in one of two ruptures. For Kant, the ego's constructive power creates the known world, but leaves a non-egoic real world ever unknown and out of reach. Fichte goes even farther: for him, the ego subsumes even Kant's world of the things-in-themselves and thereby collapses the real to the point that nothing properly exists outside of the human ego (the not-I being entirely derivative from the I). At their most extreme, Kant runs the risk of skepticism, and Fichte of solipsism. Schelling, however, argues beyond Kant and Fichte, that subjectivity cannot be restricted to self-consciousness and thus to the human and/or divine ego. The subject can be more than it knows itself to be. This lets Schelling understand the world beyond ourselves—a world that seems recalcitrant and difficult to know, a world that has to be looked at and discovered rather than deduced or made up—this world can also be subject without the risk of it being swallowed by our ego. In this manner, akin to the way Spinoza saw the divine present throughout the world, Schelling's Absolute is able to share its subjectivity prodigally, making teleology, agency, and creativity transcendentals in which all beings participate.[89]

Schelling sees everything, humans and nature alike, as alive and creative through their relationship to a living, creative divinity. This might seem to make Schelling merely one the *Schwärmerei* (religious enthusiasts) of the time. Or, alternatively, it might seem that Schelling is merely inverting the Spinozistic error of pan-objectivity with a pan-subjectivity, and may thereby end in the same nihilism that Jacobi found in Spinoza. Schelling's subjectivity, however, avoids merely inverting Spinoza's position by discovering a complexity of powers within the Absolute Subject itself.[90] This enables Schelling to revise the concept of subjectivity beyond the conventional modern notion of self-presence. By discovering a complexity of powers within subjectivity—indeed, within the Absolute Subject itself—Schelling transforms the notion of subjectivity into a dynamic concept of the self as excessive, the subject as that which does not simply coincide with itself and therefore goes beyond itself. Sometimes Schelling presents this as two powers: a centripetal formative power that gives limit and definition, and a centrifugal, creating power that tends to expand indefinitely.[91] More often, however, and more adequately, Schelling moves beyond this dualism in order to discover a triadicity within the Absolute (which or whom he also calls "God"). The centrifugal and centripetal forces are only able to relate to each other through the prior connection from which they both derive.[92] This third power is the ground of otherness, the union (or non-disunion) of the first two powers. This third power does not resolve nor sublate the tension within Schelling's divine as it would in Hegelian dialectic, but actually preserves this tension by doubling it. Without the third, there could be no tension in the divine at all because there would be no relation between the first two powers; they would go their own endless ways without ever touching each other. The third power doubles the contradiction in the divine by contradicting the disunity of the first two powers thus infinitely preserving the divine's multeity in unity, as Coleridge calls it. If the first power is one of stability and inwardness that only ever collects and re-collects itself, and the second power sails always outward toward the horizon, the third power is like a fold within the divine that brings the trajectory of the first and second powers into a generative tension, introducing life, freedom, and creativity into Schelling's God.

This tension within God, this multiplicity within the divine unity, is the excessiveness of the divine, the God beyond God that is still God: God as creativity, the parallax within the divine itself. This is not a view of God as somehow incomplete, as if God needed or awaited temporal deliverance. It is, rather, the discovery that God's freedom *is* God's own infinite becoming; God completes Godself only by always exceeding Godself. Moreover, there can be no reduction to monism here, for the coinherent mobility of Schelling's God requires that all three powers be coeternal and co-divine; they only exist in relation to each other.

There is a kind of animality to Schelling's God, a sense of becoming, choice, and unpredictability that spills over into Schelling's nontotalizing vision of a creation with its own autopoetic and creative powers.[93] Our inability to reduce Schelling's Absolute to monism, to pacify its contest, coincides with our inability to construct a complete system of rationality, one that forecloses upon agency, freedom, and the novelty of the event that shapes history and the world in unpredictable ways. Schelling writes:

> The ruleless still lies in the ground as if it could break through once again, and nowhere does it appear as though order and form were original but rather as if something initially ruleless had been brought to order. This is the incomprehensible basis of reality in things, the indivisible remainder, that which with the greatest exertion cannot be resolved in the understanding but remains eternally in the ground. Without this preceding darkness there is no reality of the creature; the gloom is its necessary inheritance.[94]

Although our understanding cannot rise to encompass the livingness of God and creation, we can intuit and artistically express this animality through our speaking, our making, our bringing to birth deeds and events. In doing so, we participate in that principle within God that preserves, continues, and intensifies the novelty of the divine life. The principle of externality within God, the third power, thus folds over itself, as it were, creating a membrane that allows a paradoxical outside existence within God.[95] Creation becomes through and in this divine fold.

Schelling explicitly ties this complex vision of God and subjectivity back to the notion of participation. The three powers within God allow Schelling to conceive of multiple participations: participation in existence, in ideality, and in creativity.

> Hence, [everything] partakes in the higher influence of which it is in foremost need, although indirectly all partake in the divine. If the first ground of nature is known in that first potency, by virtue of which the necessary being locked itself up within itself and denied itself externally, and if the spiritual world is known in the second potency which stands opposed to the first potency, then we cannot be in doubt concerning the meaning of the

third potency. It is that universal soul by which the cosmos is ensouled, the soul which through the immediate relationship to the Godhead is now lev-elheaded and in control of itself. It is the eternal link between nature and the spiritual world as well as between the world and God. It is the immediate tool through which alone God is active in nature and the spiritual world.[96]

This soul that is the principle of activity, freedom, and difference within God, becomes the principle of our activity, our freedom, and our difference from each other and from the divine. In our temporal becoming, we participate in the becoming that God eternally and superlatively is. For Schelling, we human beings chiefly do this through the use of our productive imagination, which allows us to intuit the divine infinity and concretize it in a single act.[97] Even in his relatively early works, such as the *System of Transcendental Ideal-ism*, Schelling argues that our access to the Absolute is, therefore, found in the process of creative artistic making, that is, in expressive genius rather than representation. We participate in the Absolute's own creativity and so, through genuine artwork, reveal the infinite within finite forms (in poetry, architecture, sculpture, and so forth). Through his productive imagination, Schelling argues, "Man is not outside God, but in God, and . . . his activity itself belongs to the life of God."[98] In his late philosophy of mythology and revelation, Schelling expands this conception of artwork to include religious revelation and mythopoiesis as activities that are properly our own (i.e., human, cultural, linguistic, etc.) but that also exceed us in the direction of the divine. The mythopoieic imagination does not represent the gods, but participatively expresses them on the canvas of the imagination, the story, the icon, the ritual. Through these actions the divine reveals itself in hiero-glyphic, as it were—a concealed-unconcealing, a participatory expressivism that alone allows the divine entry to our understanding.[99]

CONCLUSION

Let me draw this account to a close by drawing a few conclusions from the preceding genealogy. First, we ought to note that the diversity of participa-tory modes uncovered above accounts for much of the confusion that some-times arises when we defend a participatory turn within Theology, Religious Studies, Philosophy, or some other field. Does the participatory turn mean a *return* to Platonism, to Thomism, or a kind of Romantic expressivism? Not necessarily any one of those, nor in any of those historical forms. The partic-ipatory turn invites us to think differently about our intellectual pursuits by thinking in terms of a noncompetitive logic of intrinsic, constitutive rela-tionality—which is another way of describing the idea of participation that persists through all participatory turns: formal, existential, and creative. If we are interested in retrieving the concept of participation, or understanding those who wish to do so, we will do well to distinguish between these various participatory modalities. Although there is a diachronic order to the participatory turns, it is possible to think one modality without presupposing its predecessor. So, for example, one can think participation existentially and creatively while remaining a nominalist (this is arguably what is going on in Deleuze); or one can think in terms of formal and creative participation, while absconding from existential participation (as Alfred North Whitehead seems to); or, again, one might embrace all three forms of participation (as does Barfield, for example, or Clarke).

Second, beyond simply helping us to schematize and understand various theorists, the advent of the most recent mode of participation, participation in creativity, has consequences for our theories within Theology and Religious Studies. The creative turn within participation lies behind the enactive and expressive language that allows us to go beyond both naïve objectivism with regard to spiritual matters and the Kantian constructivist restriction of spiritual events to a subjective, linguistic sphere. Participatory logic offers a way to think a person's active, shaping contribution to a mystical event without setting this role at odds with some sort of genuine, spiritual encounter. This allows us to more fully envision human soteriological flourishing as simultaneously a *work* and a *gift*. Diverse iterations of this third creative, expressivist participatory impulse recur in thinkers such as Charles Peirce, Maurice Blondel, Henri Bergson, Sergei Bulgakov, Ernst Bloch, as well as a number of contemporary scholars within Religious Studies who have identified themselves with the "participatory turn."[100]

A number of the latter have extended this tradition of thought even yet further, in order to conceive of multiple salvations, if you will, salvations made through human participation in the infinitely creative energies of what they variously identify as the Triune God, the divine, the universe, or the creative Mystery. This results in the most genuine of pluralisms, a soteriology capable of multiple religious ends without collapsing these ends into each other or subordinating them to one single goal. Nirvana becomes a real religious telos, for example, participatively enacted through cooperation with the divine, but so also is the beatific vision as participatory communion with the Triune God. And crucially, these two, and many others, are not equated but need to be morally, politically, and theologically evaluated as different, culturally elicited but ontologically real religious ends.

NOTES

1. Quoted in Plato's *Laws* 899b, and Aristotle's *De Anima*, 405a 19.

2. Reported by Diogenes Laertius, *Lives of the Philosophers*, IX:5–12.

3. The reference to the "second voyage" (*ton deuteron pluon*) comes at the end of a remarkable passage—the first description in a European language of an individual's

mental/intellectual development. Socrates is speaking about the difficulty of thinking *supersensible transcendence*, his metaphor suggesting that the ease of sailing is like the use of the senses while the labor of oars is akin to reasoning. On which, cf. Plato, *Phaedo*, 99c; Giovanni Reale, *Toward a New Interpretation of Plato*, trans. John R. Catan and Richard Davies (Washington, DC: Catholic University of America Press, 1997), 101; and, C. J. Rowe, ed., *Phaedo, Cambridge Greek and Latin Classics* (Cambridge: Cambridge University Press, 1993), 238.

4. Indeed, the hard problem of the ancient world (uniting the two realms) and today's hard problem (the problem of consciousness according to David Chalmers) are continuous. Both struggle to relate an aporetic dualism that nonetheless seems indispensable to thinking. For a provocative essay on the continuity and difference between these two problems, see "Man, Thought, and Nature," in Barfield, *Romanticism Comes of Age* (Middletown, CT: Wesleyan University Press, 1966), 223–40.

5. Cf. Plato, *The Republic*, passim.

6. When Plato himself raises objections to the theory of participation in the *Parmenides*, the problems always stem from characters assuming that the realm of Forms is somehow related in a univocal way to the realm of becoming. This collapses the Forms into a bodily mode and so elides the distinction between Formal and embodied reality. The problems with the theory of participation, it seems, derive not from treating the Forms as transcendent, but precisely in failing to recognize their proper transcendence and thereby subjecting them to the logic of solid bodies.

7. At the very least, certainly in the *Phaedo*, Plato is employing what scholastics will later call the analogy of attribution. So Plato explains, "Each of the Forms exists, and the other things which come to have a share in them are *named after* them" (Phd. 102b2). To understand this naming immediately ends whatever confusion Aristotle, the young Socrates (in the *Parmenides*), and contemporary commentators might have over the "third-man" argument. Supposed cases of self-predication are actually *identity* statements: Beauty is not beautiful, it simply *is* Beauty, just as a pound does not itself weigh a pound but *is* a pound by which other things may be weighed.

8. Phd. 78c (Tredennick). Unless otherwise noted all translations are taken from Plato, *The Collected Dialogues of Plato Including the Letters*, ed. Edith Hamilton and Huntington Cairns (Princeton: Princeton University Press, 1961).

9. *Phd*. 79d (Tredennick).

10. *Phd*. 79a (Tredennick).

11. *Phd*. 80a-b (Tredennick).

12. *Phd*. 100c (Tredennick).

13. Cf. R. E. Allen, "Participation and Predication in Plato's Middle Dialogues," in *Plato I*, ed. Gregory Vlastos (Notre Dame: University of Notre Dame Press, 1978).

14. *Meno* 85d and *Phd*. 75e.

15. Nicholas Sagovsky, *Ecumenism: Christian Origins and the Practice of Communion* (Cambridge: Cambridge University Press, 2000), 59.

16. *Phd*. 80b (Tredennick)

17. In revising Plato, we are doing more than quibbling with classicists, for these are important matters that continue to play a part within the broader concerns of the contemporary academy. For example, Alain Badiou's argument with Deleuze is largely over how to interpret Plato's concept of participation. Badiou argues that Deleuze fails to see that, for Plato, participation invests all beings, even *sensible* beings, with positive value as immanent differentiations of the intelligible. Furthermore, says Badiou, what Deleuze offers in *The Logic of Sense* and *Difference and Repetition* as a reversal of Platonism (overturning the supposed Platonic priority of original over copy) is far closer to the Athenian's vision than the historical misunderstanding Deleuze everywhere attacks. Precisely when he thinks he is demolishing Plato, Deleuze becomes Plato's apostle. Deleuze's vision, Badiou concludes, is "Platonism with a different accent." In his more candid moments, Deleuze admits almost as much. In *The Logic of Sense*, for example, Deleuze asks, "Was it not Plato himself who pointed out the direction for the reversal of Platonism?" (256). Cf. Badiou, *Deleuze: The Clamor of Being*, trans. Louise Burchill (Minneapolis: University of Minnesota Press, 2000), 25–28.

18. Cf. Catherine Pickstock, *After Writing: On the Liturgical Consummation of Philosophy* (Oxford: Blackwell, 1998). Pickstock concentrates her attention on Plato's *Phaedrus*, though one of her students, Simon Oliver, has made a similar argument with regard to the *Timaeus*. Cf. Simon Oliver, *Philosophy, God, and Motion* (London: Routledge, 2005).

19. *Symp.* 202e-203a (Allen).

20. Cf. the story of *gigantomachia* in Plato, *The Sophist*.

21. Ross, *Plato's Theory of Ideas* (Oxford: Oxford University Press, 1951), 228–30. R. G. Collingwood also draws attention to the immanent and transcendent character of these various words. Collingwood concludes that both sets of symbols are necessary, lest one lose sight of either immanence or transcendence: "The arguments of Parmenides are conclusive as against both the immanence-theory and the transcendence-theory taken separately, as one-sided and mutually exclusive theories. They would have no weight against a theory in which immanence and transcendence were regarded as correlatives mutually implying each other." Cf. R. G. Collingwood, *The Idea of Nature* (London: Oxford University Press, 1945), 64.

22. *Symp.* 206b-207a.

23. See Aristotle, *Metaphysics* I, c.6 (987b11–14).

24. Clark, *The Political Animal: Biology, Ethics, and Politics* (London: Routledge, 1999).

25. See *Statesman* 276e.

26. Ibid.

27. See Dombrowski, *A Platonic Philosophy of Religion* (Albany: State University of New York Press, 2005) and Dombrowski, *Analytic Theism, Hartshorne, and the Concept of God* (Albany: State University of New York Press, 1998), 81.

28. For one account of this project see Lloyd Gerson, *Aristotle and Other Platonists* (Ithaca: Cornell University Press, 2005).

29. Only by paying attention to both possibilities within Platonism can we make any historical sense of the fact that Platonists have often been at the forefront of both the ascetic abandonment of the world and the humanistic and Romantic celebrations of art, nature, and society. On these various forms of Platonism cf. M.-D. Chenu, "The Platonisms of the Twelfth Century," in *Nature, Man, and Society in the Twelfth Century: Essays on New Theological Perspectives in the Latin West*, trans. Jeremy Taylor and Lester K. Little (Toronto: University of Toronto Press, 1997), 49–98. Cf. Gregory Shaw, *Theurgy and the Soul: The Neoplatonism of Iamblichus* (University Park: Pennsylvania State University Press, 1995). For an introduction to the role of Platonism within Romanticism, see Beiser, "Früromantik and the Platonic Tradition," in *The Romantic Imperative: The Concept of Early German Romanticism* (Cambridge: Harvard University Press, 2003), 56–72.

30. G. K. Chesterton, *St. Thomas Aquinas: "The Dumb Ox"* (New York: Doubleday, 1933), 138.

31. Mary T. Clark, *An Aquinas Reader* (New York: Fordham University Press, 2000), 23.

32. On this point see especially Etienne Gilson, *Being and Some Philosophers*, 2nd ed. (Toronto: Pontifical Institute of Medieval Studies, 1952).

33. *De Veritate*, q. 1, art. 1, ad 3. All translations of Thomas, unless otherwise indicated, are mine.

34. Indeed, if we were to follow Kant here, we would have to say that *Esse Ipsum* (Being itself) cannot be considered a concept, for every concept requires determinability as an a priori condition (as the law of the excluded middle requires). *Esse*, however, is not like such concepts for it cannot be characterized by one of two opposing predicates. The ontological difference between *Esse* and *essendi* properly places *Esse* beyond opposition and thus beyond determinability, and, therefore, beyond conceptuality. On determinability, see Immanuel Kant, *Critique of Pure Reason*, trans. Paul Guyer and Allen W. Wood (Cambridge: Cambridge University Press, 1998), 553–54, A72–74, B600–02.

35. Clark, *An Aquinas Reader*, 25. The recovery of this sentiment by twentieth-century Thomists is due, in part, to the radical recovery of intuition by Henri Bergson. Jacques Maritain's tempestuous but genuine debt to Bergson is well known. On Gilson's relation to Bergson see Helen James John, S.N.D., *The Thomist Spectrum* (New York: Fordham University Press, 1966), 44.

36. Cf. "The Hidden Key: Creation," in chapter 2 of Josef Pieper, *The Silence of St. Thomas: Three Essays*, trans. John Murray, S.J. and Daniel O'Connor (South Bend: St. Augustine's Press, 1957), 47ff.

37. *Summa contra Gentiles* II, 18.

38. Barfield, *Saving the Appearances: A Study in Idolatry* (Middletown, CT: Wesleyan University Press, 1988), 89.

39. On participation in Thomas's commentary on *De Hebdomadibus*, see especially "Participation and the Problem of the One and the Many," chapter iv in John F. Wippel, *The Metaphysical Thought of Thomas Aquinas: From Finite Being to Uncreated*

Being (Washington, DC: The Catholic University of America Press, 2000), 94–131. See also the first section of Rudi A. te Velde, *Participation and Substantiality in Thomas Aquinas* (New York: E. J. Brill, 1995); L.-B. Geiger, *La participation dans la philosophie de S. Thomas d'Aquin*, 2nd ed. (Paris: J. Vrin, 1953); Cornelio Fabro, *Participation et causalité selon S. Thomas d'Aquin* (Louvain: Publications Universitaires de Louvain, 1961). Fabro presents a shortened version of his work in English in Fabro, "The Intensive Hermeneutics of Thomistic Philosophy: The Notion of Participation," *The Review of Metaphysics* 27 (1974).

40. The first two types are not possible because, in seeking to speak of existence, we are avowedly not speaking ideally but really, and therefore cannot rely on the structure of logical participation. Neither can participation in the act of existence be described in terms of a substance receiving an accident for, without having always already received existence there is no substance to receive an accident, *quod impossibile est!*

41. *Questiones disputatae de spiritualibus creaturis* I.1.

42. In *Sophist* 256e, Plato writes, "In every idea there is a definite amount of being," says Plato, "and an infinity of non-being." Cf. *Philebus* 16c.

43. Clarke, *Explorations in Metaphysics: Being—God—Person* (Notre Dame: University of Notre Dame Press, 1994), 74. My discussion here is heavily indebted to Clarke's seminal essay, reprinted in the aforementioned volume, "The Limitation of Act by Potency in St. Thomas: Aristotelianism or Neoplatonism?"

44. Simplicius, *In Physicorum* 24.13, quoted in Philip Clayton, *The Problem of God in Modern Thought* (Grand Rapids: Wm. B. Eerdmans, 2000), 139.

45. Clarke, *Explorations in Metaphysics: Being—God—Person*, 76.

46. Ibid., 77.

47. *Enneads*, VI, 7, 32.

48. Clarke, *Explorations in Metaphysics: Being—God—Person*, 78.

49. Cf. David Burrell, *Knowing the Unknowable God: Ibn-Sina, Maimonides, Aquinas* (Notre Dame: University of Notre Dame Press, 1986); Kevin Corrigan, "Essence and Existence in the Enneads," in *The Cambridge Companion to Plotinus*, ed. Lloyd P. Gerson (Cambridge: Cambridge University Press, 1996).

50. Clarke, *Explorations in Metaphysics: Being—God—Person*, 79.

51. See, for example, SCG I.22. "In God essence and existence are not different." Properly speaking, of course, one should hesitate to call Aquinas's God a being since God's being, as infinite, is also infinitely different than the beings we know of in creation. To say that God's essence is God's existence is not therefore to say what God is, but rather what God is not. God is not, like creatures, a being whose essence differs from its existence. We can say that God is, but when we do so we are speaking analogically. Being, like all perfections, can only be predicated of God eminently, that is, in the awareness that between God's being—as the cause of our existence—and our being, there exists some analogical resemblance. Thomas is here following in the apophatic path pioneered by Dionysius in his *Divine Names*. On Aquinas's grammati-

cal approach to the ineffability of God, see Burrell, *Aquinas: God and Action* (Notre Dame: Notre Dame University Press, 1973).

52. *Questiones disputates de veritate*, qu. 12, art. 6.

53. This is to be sharply distinguished from the Kantian and post-Kantian use of *transcendental*, which reverses its meaning so that the transcendentals, far from being ontologically ubiquitous, are now conceived as merely epistemologically ubiquitous, derived solely from the constitution of the subject. On the convertability of the transcendentals, see Clarke, *The One and the Many: A Contemporary Thomistic Metaphysics* (Notre Dame: University of Notre Dame Press, 2001), 43.

54. Ibid., 291.

55. Gilson, *The Christian Philosophy of St. Thomas Aquinas*, trans. L. K. Shook, C.S.B (Notre Dame: University of Notre Dame Press, 1956), 83.

56. *S.T.* I, q. 8, ad. 1.

57. As Pickstock and Milbank note, "If Being measures knowledge, knowledge equally measures Being. One might call this 'ideal realism.'" Pickstock and Milbank, *Truth in Aquinas* (London and New York: Routledge, 2001), 8.

58. Cf. Ibid., 37. Thomas dares to so quote Dionysius in S.T. I. q. 2 ad. 1.

59. The essay, "To Be Is to Be Substance-in-Relation" is reprinted in Clarke, *Explorations in Metaphysics: Being—God—Person*, 102–22.

60. S.C.G. III, ch. 113.

61. *S. T.* I, q. 19, art. 2. The translation is from Clarke, *The One and the Many*, 106.

62. Rosemann, *Omne Agens Agit Sibi Simile: A "Repetition" Of Scholastic Metaphysics* (Leuven: Leuven University Press, 1996), 317–18.

63. Clarke, *Explorations in Metaphysics: Being—God—Person*, 198.

64. Rosemann, *Omne Agens Agit Sibi Simile: A "Repetition" Of Scholastic Metaphysics*, 295.

65. Lewis, *English Literature in the Sixteenth Century Excluding Drama*, 320.

66. Barfield, *Saving the Appearances*, 132.

67. See especially Book IV in John Scotus Eriugena, *Periphyseon: The Division of Nature*, trans. John J. O'Meara (Montréal: Bellarmin, 1987). For an introduction to Eriugena's thought, see Deirdre Carabine, *John Scottus Eriugena*, ed. Brian Davies, Great Medieval Thinkers (Oxford: Oxford University Press, 2000), and John J. O'Meara, *Eriugena* (Oxford: Oxford University Press, 1988). For more on his anthropology in particular, see Willemien Otten, *The Anthropology of Johannes Socttus Eriugena* (Leiden: E. J. Brill, 1991).

68. Eco, *Art and Beauty in the Middle Ages*, trans. Hugh Bredin (New Haven: Yale University Press, 1986), 113.

69. On Eckhart's dynamic notion of exemplarism, see Ananda K. Coomaraswamy, "Meister Eckhart's View of Art," in *The Transformation of Nature in Art* (Cambridge: Harvard University Press, 1934).

70. Quoted in Eco, *Art and Beauty in the Middle Ages*, 113.

71. See Bernardino M Bonansea, *Tommaso Campanella: Renaissance Pioneer of Modern Thought* (Washington, DC: Catholic University of America Press, 1969), 147.

72. Eco, *Art and Beauty in the Middle Ages*, 113.

73. Indeed, Deleuze considers participation to be key to understanding Spinoza's work. On which, see Deleuze, *Expressionism in Philosophy: Spinoza*, trans. Martin Joughin (Brooklyn: Zone Books, 1990).

74. On the modernity and postmodernity of Spinoza, see Yirmiyahu Yovel, *Spinoza and Other Heretics: The Adventures of Immanence* (Princeton: Princeton University Press, 1989).

75. Expressivism sees an agent or substance giving *itself* in its gifts, rather than remaining unperturbed and distant despite its emanations. The difference between expressivism and emanation may thus be conceived as the difference between a pragmatist myth of the gift and a representationalist myth of the given.

76. Deleuze, *Expressionism*, 172.

77. Spinoza, *A Spinoza Reader: The Ethics and Other Works*, trans. Edwin Curley (Princeton, N.J.: Princeton University Press, 1994), 93.

78. As such, these differences in perception are formal rather than real differences. It is helpful to consider the similarity between Spinoza's doctrine here and Galileo's distinction between primary and secondary qualities, the former of which alone are real and can be treated quantitatively.

79. On substance "expressing" itself in attributes, see *Ethics* I.10, scholium 1. On only perceiving two attributes, yet knowing that an infinity of such attributes exists, see *Ethics* II.1–2.

80. *Ethics* I.25, cor. in Spinoza, *Spinoza Reader*, 103.

81. "The significance of Spinozism seems to me to be this: it asserts immanence as a principle and frees expression from any subordination to emanative or exemplary causality. . . . And such a result can be obtained only within a perspective of univocity." Deleuze, *Expressionism*, 180.

82. Ibid., 183.

83. This results in a doctrine of pure immanence and univocity that radically undercuts the hard Cartesian distinction between thinking versus extended substances. Rather than bifurcating the universe into these two apparently irreconcilable types of being, Spinoza considers that the order of ideas and the order of things are convertible (cf. *Ethics* II.7). Consequently, he writes, "the thinking substance and the extended substance are one and the same substance, which is now comprehended under this attribute, now under that. So also a mode of extension and the idea of that mode are one and the same thing, but expressed in two ways." See *Ethics* II.7, schol., in Spinoza, *Spinoza Reader*, 119.

84. Beiser, "The Enlightenment and Idealism," in *The Cambridge Companion to German Idealism*, ed. Karl Ameriks (Cambridge: Cambridge University Press, 2000), 26. For a thorough, engaging, and erudite treatment of the pantheism controversy and

its repercussions, see Beiser, *The Fate of Reason: German Philosophy from Kant to Fichte* (Cambridge: Harvard University Press, 1993).

85. We see, then, already in the last decade of the eighteenth century, the problematic of fideism (Jacobi) versus immanent rationalism (Spinoza) that continues in Religious Studies today—in the contest, for example, between perennialist or theologically fideistic confessions and the post-Saussurean lingustification of reality and the sacred (in which meaning itself is perpetually deferred and reality confined by an endless chain of signifiers).

86. See Slavoj Zizek, *The Parallax View* (Cambridge: MIT Press, 2006), 7. Appeal to the idea of the parallax in this context may seem like mystification, but Schelling's concept is illuminating for more than *just* metaphysics. Indeed, the parallax (which is not Schelling's term, but is an apt description of his understanding) uncovers a problem or tension that runs right through many pressing contemporary problems. Zizek, for example, finds the problem of parallax present in, at least, questions of quantum physics, neurobiology, ontological difference, the problem of the Lacanian Real, the tension between desire and drive, the aporias of the unconscious, and what Zizek calls the problem of the vagina (as the icon of the most fetishized sexuality but also the imagined nonsexual ideal of maternity).

87. If the infinite is on the same plane as the finite, it can only be a serial infinity, a bad infinity, one that can never be reached save by annulling finitude altogether, and this is precisely why Spinozism could not succeed in properly valuing finitude and materiality.

88. Schelling, *On the History of Modern Philosophy*, trans. Andrew Bowie (Cambridge: Cambridge University Press, 1994), 173.

89. Schelling thus conceived himself as completing the Spinozist impulse by adding breath and life to Spinoza's system of objects. "The sealed bud can still unfold into a the flower. One might say Spinoza's philosophy . . . is, like Hebrew, a script without vowels, the vowels were only added and made explicit by a later age." Ibid., 69.

90. Fichte already found that subjectivity (Fichte's "I") must posit a "not-I" by which to define itself. Schelling goes further and shows not merely why but how this not-I comes about. Schelling thus introduces a genetic aspect, even a historicity, into his account of the Absolute.

91. In Schelling's "Philosophical Investigations into the Essence of Human Freedom" these forces are problematically conceived as competing personalities within God—one good, one evil—leading Schelling to repeat the error of dualistic Gnostic sects, and Jakob Boehme, a position about which Schelling himself remained uneasy. See Schelling, "Philosophical Investigations into the Essence of Human Freedom and Related Matters," in *Philosophy of German Idealism*, ed. Ernst Behler, *The German Library* (New York: Continuum, 2003). On Schelling's relation to Boehme, see Robert F. Brown, *The Later Philosophy of Schelling: The Influence of Boehme on the Works of 1809–1815* (Cranbury, NJ: Bucknell University Press, 1977).

92. The connection with participatory thought is explicit. For example, in his early commentary on the *Timaeus*, Schelling identifies this third term within the

Absolute as Plato's *koinonon*, a Platonic analogue for *methexis* or participation. See Friedrich Wilhelm Joseph von Schelling, Hartmut Buchner, and Hermann Krings, "*Timaeus*" (1794), *Schellingiana*; Bd. 4 (Stuttgart-Bad Cannstsatt: Frommann-Holzboog, 1994).

93. It is actually here that I find Schelling least adequate, for his vision of God sometimes (not always) threatens to become too voluntaristic, as if the will discordantly trumped the true and the good within the divine. Indeed, there is a line of voluntarism that runs from Schelling through Schopenhauer and to Nietzsche with his concept of the will to power.

94. Schelling, "Philosophical Investigations into the Essence of Human Freedom and Related Matters," 238–39.

95. Schelling's idea of the fold or the "cision" is indebted to the idea of *Zimsum* within Lurianic Kabbalah as the fold within God through which creation is born. For Schelling, it is the third potency that creates the fold thus enabling the birth of a nondivine other as a fourth. Where Plotinus considered two the first number (since One is not properly a number as it lacks multiplicity), Schelling argues that the One is already multiple—that it manifests unity, duality, and triadicity—and therefore that the quaternity is the first number (cf. Schelling, *The Ages of the World. Fragment, from the Handwritten Remains*, 52). Four is therefore the first nondivine principle of otherness (alterity), an alchemical insight that reappears in Russian Sophiology, but also in the likes of Carl Jung, and others. I am grateful to Anthony Baker's dissertation on theology and poiesis for this insight, and a number of other *aperçus* regarding Schelling. See Anthony Baker, "Making Perfect: An Experiment in Theological Ontology" (Charlottesville: University of Virginia, 2004), 153–204.

96. Schelling, *The Ages of the World. Fragment, from the Handwritten Remains*, 37, §252.

97. Schelling describes the productive imagination as that which "waver[s] in the middle between infinity and finitude," Friedrich Schelling, *System of Transcendental Idealism* (1993), 176. The *System* begins with Schelling's defense of *intellectual intuition*, something Kant foreclosed to all but God. This intuition is prereflective and grounds identity elsewhere than either the thinking subject, or the abstract idea of pure consciousness, but in the condition of possibility that allows either of these to emerge. For Kant, all human intuition is either empirical or pure intuition. Pure intuition abstracts from the material to discover the form of appearing as such—space and time are formal or pure intuitions. An intellectual intuition is entirely active and without empirical content; it creates what it perceive and thus, for Kant, only God can have an intellectual intuition. Schelling, however, argues that artistic genius is clearly both active and passive and that, therefore, we must have here at least a human incident of intellectual intuition. See Schelling, *System of Transcendental Idealism*, 223. On Kant, see Kant, *Critique of Pure Reason*, B307.

98. Schelling, "Philosophical Investigations into the Essence of Human Freedom and Related Matters," 222.

99. Schelling writes, "mythology arises just as it is, and in no other sense than that in which it is expressed . . . that is, everything in it is to be understood just as it

is expressed, and not as if one thing were conceived when another is said. Mythology is not allegorical but tautegorical. In it the gods are actually existing beings, whose existence is not something different from their meaning, for they mean only what they are." See Schelling, *Sammtliche Werke* 11:196; quoted in Nicholas Halmi, "Greek Myths, Christian Mysteries, and the Tautegorical Symbol," *Wordsworth Circle* 36, no. 1 (2005): 7. Schelling borrowed the concept of the tautegorical from Coleridge's *Aids to Reflection*, where Coleridge speaks regarding "[t]he base of Symbols and symbolical expressions; the nature of which is always tautegorical (i.e. expressing the same subject but with a difference) in contra-distinction from metaphors and similitudes, that are always allegorical (i.e. expressing a different subject but with a resemblance)." Samuel Taylor Coleridge, *Aids to Reflection*, ed. James Engell and W. Jackson Bate (London: Routledge and Kegan Paul, 1994), 206.

    100. See the essays of this volume.

TWO

Participation, Complexity, and the Study of Religion

Sean Kelly

THIS CHAPTER DRAWS from the work of French systems thinker Edgar Morin to explore certain implications of the paradigm of complexity for the participatory turn in Religious Studies. Following a discussion of the distinction between embedded and enactive participation, with illustrations from the history of religious and philosophical ideas, the paper turns to Morin for indications of how to honor the complexity of participation, both in general and relative to the question of method in the study of religion. The reorganization of knowledge resulting from the awareness of what Morin calls "auto-eco-re-organization" has relevance not only for approaching the study of religion and spirituality, but for the wider participatory turn advocated by the authors of this volume.

EMBEDDED AND ENACTIVE PARTICIPATION: SOME PREMODERN EXAMPLES

Reflecting on the notion of participation, I have found it helpful to distinguish between its *embedded* and its *enactive* inflections. In the most general of terms, the distinction is patterned on the degree to which participation is oriented more toward the world, context, other, or object, on the one hand, or to the person, agent, self, or subject, on the other. The notion of embeddedness—I take the term from Charlene Spretnak[1]—points to what in fact has been a near-universal feature of human experience and belief up until late modern times—namely, the idea that human beings are organically continuous with, and meaningfully integrated within, a living and enchanted cosmos. Militating against the sense of such embeddedness is the modern notion of what Charles Taylor refers to the "disengaged subject," which he traces to the dualistic and mechanistic philosophies of Descartes and Locke, and which became foundational to the dominant scientific paradigm.[2]

A primary source of inspiration for contemporary reflection on the notion of "enaction" is the biocognitive model of Humberto Maturana and Francisco J. Varela, especially as updated in the 1991 book, *The Embodied Mind*, and later adopted and adapted by Jorge N. Ferrer in his *Revisioning Transpersonal Theory*.[3] We will consider elements of this model in greater detail below. By way of anticipation, one could sum up the meaning of "enactive" by saying that all knowing, instead of being a matter of representing independently existing, pregiven objects, involves, as Ferrer puts it, "the bringing forth of a world or domain of distinctions cocreated by the different elements involved in the participatory event."[4] Although Ferrer himself recognizes the "cocreative" presence of both dimensions of participation (self and other, mind and world), the enactive paradigm in cognitive science nevertheless stresses the agency of the living/knowing subject (a stress, however, that has been mitigated by Maturana and Varela's notion of "structural coupling").

The sense of embedded participation is evident in the widespread belief in "correspondences," which is the basis of most systems of magic and of premodern and non-Western medicine, where the nature of particular aspects or features of the human subject is illustrated with reference to their cosmic counterparts. In traditional Western systems, as in Hippocratic or Paracelsian medicine, for instance, we have the link between the heart, gold, and the sun; or in traditional Chinese medicine, the correspondence between the lungs, the element metal, and Autumn. A particularly rich example of embedded participation can be found in the Navajo notion of *nilch'i* or "Holy Wind," which refers "to the whole body of the air or the atmosphere, including . . . the air that swirls within us as we breathe."[5] The wind is thought to leave its traces in the spiral patterns at the ends of our fingers and toes and in the hair on the crown of the head. "These (Winds sticking out of the) whorls at the tips of our toes," according to a Navajo elder, "hold us to the Earth. Those at our fingertips hold us to the Sky."[6]

The root intuition of enaction can be found in the same premodern traditions that manifest the notion of embedded participation. For instance, the Babylonian New Year's festival was no mere celebration or reproduction of a preexisting myth, but a ritual reenactment of the creation of the world, upon whose successful performance the stability of the cosmos (both natural and human or social) depended. Or consider the words that Mountain Lake, a Pueblo elder, shared with C. G. Jung. "We are a people who live on the roof of the world," he said, "we are the sons of Father Sun, and with our religion we daily help our father to go across the sky." Mountain Lake adds:

We do this not only for ourselves, but for the whole world. If we were to cease practicing our religion, in ten years the sun would no longer rise. Then it would be night forever.[7]

We could say that ritual enactment gives expression to the motor/behavioral dimension of enactive participation. But there is also the perceptual/cognitive dimension, which has to do with the more general sense of (en)active "seeing" or "beholding." Again, the premodern world was no stranger to this kind of "seeing," though in the West, at least, we have to wait for Kant before the enactively participatory nature of knowledge is consciously reflected upon. For an especially striking illustration of how the beholding of a spiritual event is tuned to the inner readiness of the beholders, take the situation of the two disciples on the road to Emmaus as described in Luke's Gospel. Despondent, "their heads bowed down" in sorrowful conversation, they are joined by the risen Jesus, but "their eyes were kept from recognizing him" (Luke 24:16). While walking together, the stranger/Jesus reminds them of how the seeming tragedy of Jesus' death is a fulfillment of the prophecies. That evening, after they have invited the stranger to share their food and shelter, they finally recognize him as he breaks and blesses the bread: "And their eyes were opened and they recognized him; and he vanished out of their sight." Whatever else one might say about this intriguing passage (the exegetical possibilities are manifold), it at least points to the manner in which the perception of a spiritual event—or in stronger terms, the cocreated reality of the event itself—depends upon the readiness and active participation of the percipients.

As a second example of the perceptual/cognitive dimension of enactive participation in a religious or spiritual context, I point to the Buddhist notion of "right view" (*samma ditthi*), which in its simplest form can be defined as knowledge of the Four Noble Truths: the universal fact of suffering; its root causes (clinging, hatred, and delusion); that it can cease (nirvana); and the noble eightfold path leading to its cessation. Right View is first among the eight. Here is one of the Buddha's parables on the nature of Right View:

> Just as when a sugar cane seed, a rice grain, or a grape seed is placed in moist soil, whatever nutriment it takes from the soil & the water, all conduces to its sweetness, tastiness, & unalloyed delectability. Why is that? Because the seed is auspicious. In the same way, when a person has right view . . . whatever bodily deeds he undertakes in line with that view, whatever verbal deeds . . . whatever mental deeds he undertakes in line with that view . . . all lead to what is agreeable, pleasing, charming, profitable, & easeful. Why is that? Because the view is auspicious.[8]

Right view, or beholding the world through the gift of the dharma, helps manifest the intrinsic "sweetness, tastiness, & unalloyed delectability" of our true, Buddha nature. Without it, there are only sterile seeds, or ones that yield a bitter taste.

As a final, premodern example of enactive participation, again stressing the perceptual/cognitive dimension, I would mention Plato's theory of vision, which was rejected by Aristotle, whereby the nature or image of the object seen is thought to be the result of the meeting of two "fires" or lights, one of which emanates from the eyes, the other from the visible object. "When the light of day surrounds the stream of vision," we read in the *Timaeus*,

> then like falls upon like, and they coalesce, and one body is formed by nat-ural affinity in the line of vision, wherever the light that falls from within meets with an external object. . . . But when night comes on and the exter-nal and kindred fire departs, then the stream of vision is cut off; for going forth to an unlike element it is changed and extinguished, being no longer of one nature with the surrounding atmosphere which is now deprived of fire: and so the eye no longer sees, and we feel disposed to sleep. . . . And now there is no longer any difficulty in understanding the creation of images in mirrors and all smooth and bright surfaces. For from the communion of the internal and external fires, and again from the union of them and their numerous transformations when they meet in the mirror, all these appear-ances of necessity arise, when the fire from the face coalesces with the fire from the eye on the bright and smooth surface.[9]

Though I have distinguished between two types or inflections of partic-ipation—enactive and embedded—the case of Plato well illustrates the fact that both often go hand in hand, at least prior to the modern period. For instance, while the enactive type is clearly present in Plato—not only in his theory of vision, but in the importance attached to the "care of the soul" (the Platonic equivalent of the Buddhist "Right View") for the ability to achieve the higher vision of the Ideas—Platonic idealism is also participatory in an embedded fashion: all beings *have* their being by virtue of their participation (*methexis, koinonia*) in the Ideas, which alone have *true* being (*to ontos on*). Ritual reenactments, similarly, are never (at least implicitly) separate from a mythic worldview, which in the majority of indigenous and premodern cases, as stated above, represent the human as embedded within a living and enchanted cosmos.

SOME POST-KANTIAN DEVELOPMENTS

I alluded earlier to the notion of the "disengaged subject" as found in the philosophies of Descartes and Locke. It is, however, with Kant that this kind of subject receives its most critical articulation, at least with respect to the problem of participation that we are considering. One could say that, with Kant, the nature of enactive participation is definitively recognized and reflexively thematized. At the same time, however, there is a correlative loss of the sense of embeddedness which had persisted (despite the Cartesian dualism) up until that point. On the one hand, Kant's "second Copernican revolution" establishes the radically participatory nature of the human subject in the process of knowing with the idea of the "transcendental ego" and its associated forms of "intuition"—space and time—and the categories of the understanding—notably, causality and substance. On the other hand, there is a new, unbridgeable gulf between this subject and the unknowable noumena or "things-in-themselves."[10] It was the grand project of Kant's immediate successors—especially Fichte, Schelling, and Hegel—to bridge this gulf while simultaneously preserving the radically participatory nature of the subject.[11] Fichte took the first, decisive move with his notion of the "Absolute Ego," which not only, following Kant, imposes the categories of intelligibility onto the blank screen of nature, but generates the plurality of finite subjects and the totality of nature as the necessary "other" upon which these subjects exercise their endless theoretical and moral "striving." Considering Fichte's move a mere half-measure, however, Schelling and Hegel each in their own way sought to resolve the Kantian split, amplified by Fichte to the utmost extreme, by focusing on the concept of the Absolute or the Whole as a dialectically self-articulating totality (the principle of Absolute "Identity" for Schelling, that of Absolute "Spirit" for Hegel).

Schelling and Hegel in particular were inspired in this post-Kantian project by the example of Goethe, whose life and writings embodied the kind of integral participation in which subject and object, mind and nature, were seen as moments of a dynamically unfolding, organic whole. "A person can know himself, "wrote Goethe, "only insofar as he knows the world, which he perceives only in himself, and himself only in it. Every new object, well investigated, opens up a new organ in one's self."[12] In much more accessible language than that of the younger idealists who looked upon him as their mentor, Goethe sums up the post-Kantian project as follows:

> We ought to be worthy, through the intuition of a continuously creative nature, of mental participation in its productivity. I myself had incessantly pushed, initially unconsciously and from an inner drive, to the primal image [das Urbildliche] and the type [das Typische]. Fortune smiled on this effort and I was able to construct a representation in a natural way; so now nothing more can prevent me from boldly undertaking that "adventure of reason," as the grand old man from Königsberg himself has called it.[13]

While the impact of Goethe and his idealist admirers was considerable—preparing the ground, as Robert Richards demonstrates, for the general reception of the theory of evolution—the organic synthesis of both types of participation that they had variously achieved was eventually eclipsed by the main currents of ninetieth and twentieth-century intellectual history. The "adventure of reason" was not, for the time being at least, to proceed along the lines set out by Goethe, Schelling, and Hegel. Despite the efforts of Wilhelm Dilthey and later phenomenologists and hermeneutical philosophers to safeguard the autonomy of the human sciences (*Geisteswissenschaften*) from colonization by the natural sciences (*Naturwissenschaften*), what one sees is the steady assimilation of the former to the mechanistic, and ultimately materialistic, assumptions of the latter. The field of psychology, for instance, has been dominated by the successive waves of behaviorism, psychoanalysis, and more recently by "neuro-centric" cognitive science.[14]

As a kind of resistance to this colonization, we have the rise of deconstructive postmodernism, which, in one form or another, continues to hold sway in the humanities. In contrast to the often naively realist claims of those working within the confines of the dominant scientific paradigm, deconstructive postmodernism rejects the notion of ontological pregivens—whether natural or spiritual. While all knowledge is seen as being "situated," it does not have a foundation in the non- or more-than-human realms (whether cosmic or metaphysical), and is therefore understood as (re)enacted by the individuals or groups that lay claim to it.

At the risk of oversimplifying matters, we could say that the tendency in the natural sciences has been to stress the side of embeddedness, though in contrast with most premodern expressions of this kind of participation, the cosmos in which the human is embedded is disenchanted and conceived mechanistically. The humanities, for their part, have tended to stress the side of enaction, with, however, an equal tendency toward disenchantment.

THE PARADIGM OF COMPLEXITY

With the hope of opening up possibilities for more fruitful communication between the "two cultures" (the natural and the human sciences) and, in the process, of revisioning the nature of participation, I now turn to the work of Morin. After establishing his reputation as cultural anthropologist and sociologist in 1960s, Morin devoted himself to the ideal and practice of *transdisciplinary* inquiry, taking over from Roland Barthes as the head of the Center for Transdisciplinary Studies (CETSAP), associated with the C.N.R.S. (The National Center for Scientific Research) in Paris. Especially with his multivolume master work, *La Méthode* (from 1977 to the present, with currently six volumes), though in his many other works as well, Morin has sought to articulate what he calls the "paradigm of complexity" as an alternative to the dominant paradigm of simplification or fragmentation, which we see manifested not only in the split between the two cultures, but also among and within the various disciplines on either side of the great divide.

Though especially inspired by a critical appropriation of systems theory and ecology, Morin draws from developments across the disciplinary spectrum, from quantum physics, thermodynamics, and biology to psychology, anthropology, sociology, epistemology, cognitive science, and the philosophy of science, searching for indications of a "new science" (*scienza nuova*) that would allow us "to re-member the mutilated, articulate the disjoined, and think the obscured."[15] The method proper to this new science revolves around the core concept/intuition of *complexity* (from *com-plexere*, "to weave together"), which, writes Morin, "corresponds to the irruption of antagonisms at the heart of organized phenomena, to the irruption of paradoxes or contradictions at the heart of theories." He adds:

> The problem of complex thinking involves the task of holding together, without incoherence, two (or more) ideas which are nonetheless contrary to one another. This is not possible unless we find, a) the meta-point of view that relativizes contradiction, and b) a way to insert into a productive feedback loop antagonistic concepts which thereby also become complementary.[16]

Morin invokes several principles of complex thinking in order to characterize this "productive feedback loop," notably the *dialogic*, *recursivity*, and the *holographic* principles. The dialogic refers to "the symbiotic combination of two or more logics [or explanatory perspectives] which are simultaneously complementary *and* antagonistic."[17] Recursivity describes a process which "produces the effects necessary for its own generation or existence . . . whereby the product or ultimate effect becomes a prime element or first cause."[18] Finally, the holographic principle harbors the insight that "the whole is in the part which is in the whole."[19] All three principles must generally be invoked to honor the complexity of phenomena, though one or the other will often be more in evidence, depending upon the perspective taken.

Take the example of the mind/brain relation: modern brain research, from the pioneering work of Wilder Penfield and early split-brain studies to the influential contemporary research of Antonio Damasio,[20] has left little doubt regarding the degree to which the mind (feelings, emotions, cognition) is dependent upon the brain. The recent revolution in psychopharmacology, especially with the widespread use of selective serotonin reuptake inhibitors (SSRIs) for the treatment of depression, has served greatly to underline this fact. At the same time, however, there is another long tradition, from faith healing and the use of animal magnetism or hypnosis for anesthesia (dating from the mid-nineteenth century) to the birth of psychoneuroimmunology (PNI), the well-documented "relaxation response," and the mysterious placebo effect, which demonstrates that the brain (and more generally, bodily processes) are subject to the influence of the mind (through "belief," intention, visualization, "suggestion," etc.).[21] The antagonistic side of the dialogic in this case can degenerate into dissociation insofar as one is precommitted to a materialist or to an idealist worldview.[22] The challenge is not to dissolve the antagonism in the interest of a too easy complementarity.[23] The holographic principle, similarly, encourages us to see how, while the brain "contains" the mind as one of its functions (the reductive position sees it as a mere epiphenomenon), the brain is also a concept/representation of the mind, the nature of which (along with the nature of nature in general) varies along with the (mental and cultural) perspective from which it is considered. In this instance, the dialogical and holographic principles are taken up in the principle of recursivity as the "productive feedback loop" that weaves together the two terms in relation. "In effect," observes Morin,

> if the brain may be conceived as the instrument of thought, the latter may be conceived as the instrument of the brain. The idea of the brain is effectively the product of a long laboring on the part of the mind; yet the mind is the product of an even longer evolution of the brain. . . . The mind seems to be an efflorescence of the brain; yet the latter appears to us as a representation of the mind. In this way an apparently infernal circle is constituted where each term, equally incapable of explaining either itself or the other to itself, dissolves itself in the other to infinity. . . . It is clear that any conception that is incapable of considering the simultaneously Gordian and paradoxical link in the brain/mind relation is mutilating.[24]

Already in his early work, *The Nature of Nature*, Morin had integrated the pioneering work of Maturana and Varela on autopoietic systems and the biology of cognition, which forms the basis for the enactive approach to cognitive science.[25] This approach, as indicated earlier, is a primary source for what I have called the enactive inflection of the concept of participation. Central to Maturana and Varela's theory is an insistence on the autonomy or "systemic closure" of living beings, whose organizational integrity is maintained in response to, and despite, "perturbations" from the environment. The ongoing self-production or self-maintenance (hence "autopoiesis") of the organism—in metabolism, healing, and the immune response, for instance—involves a conservation of organizational structure (that is, the pattern or network of interactions among the system's constituent elements). The actions or behaviors of the organism that effect this conservation are conceived as fundamentally cognitive, in the sense that they are constrained by something analogous to judgments as what is, or is not, consistent with this conservation. "A cognitive system," writes Maturana (though for myself, at least, with less clarity than could be desired), "is a system whose organization defines a domain of interactions in which it can act with relevance to the maintenance of itself, and the process of cognition is the actual (inductive) acting or behaving in this domain." In short, "Living systems are cognitive systems, and living as a process is a process of cognition."[26]

Though he repeatedly honors the insights of Maturana and Varela, Morin believes that "The idea of *autopoiesis* remains too localized in a school of thinking. It has isolated itself by insisting on the idea of closure, at the very moment when the idea of the openness of living systems was becoming more widespread."[27] For Morin, instead of subordinating openness to closure, or dependence to autonomy,[28] we need to see them as recursively linked. One can see how Morin manages to preserve the essential insight of autopoiesis without the reduction to closure in his meditation on "the recursive loop as that which links openness to closure." "The purely closed circuit," he writes, "is a vicious circle";

> it is the ideal and unreal circle of perpetual motion, banished once and for all from our *physis* by the second principle of thermodynamics. The merely open circle is equally impossible; it is mere sequence and not the feedback loop. It is because it is closed that it is a circle. It is because it is open—i.e., nourished—that it is productive. If one considers the open/closed feedback loop in its profoundly generative nature, one sees that its primary and fundamental production is itself, which is to say that it produces its very being and existence.[29]

Complexifying the notion of autopoiesis or self-organization, Morin integrates the notion of "the recursive loop as that which links openness to closure" with his proposal for the idea of self- or *auto-eco-re-organization*. The relation between *autos* and *oikos* is complex—that is (at least), dialogical, recursive, and holographic. "Every auto-organizational phenomenon," as Morin says, "depends not only on its singular logic or determination [the specificity of the genetic code in an individual cell, for instance], but also on the determinations and logic of its environment. We must therefore strive to link into a dialogical—and therefore complex—discourse, the inner mode of explanation [closure, 'auto-'] with that of the outer [openness, 'eco-']." He adds:

> Living auto-organization necessarily presupposes dependence with regard to the eco-organization of which it is a part, which itself necessarily presupposes the auto-organizations which constitute its biocenose [that is, its biological or ecological community].
>
> The auto-ecological relation is at once one of opposition/distinction and of implication/integration, of alterity and unity.[30]

The relation between *autos* and *oikos* can be seen as paradigmatic for the relation between the enactive (or auto-logical) and the embedded (or eco-logical) inflections of participation. Though arising out of reflection on the complex character of biological organization, or "the life of life," the auto/eco distinction (and therefore also the distinction between enactive and embedded participation) is generalizable, for Morin, to "everything that lives, including society, human being, mind or spirit, ideas, and knowledge."[31] Systems of ideas and beliefs, ideologies, intellectual movements and those of popular culture, can all be seen as so many manifestations of the noosphere (the concept of which Morin adopts from Teilhard de Chardin), which, like the biosphere, is populated by living, and therefore complex auto-eco-re-organizing entities. Noospheric entities, like biological organisms, have their relative autonomy and their particular ecologies, their immune responses and adaptations to environmental challenges.[32] We can consider such entities as "participatory events" (to borrow and to generalize from Ferrer's use of the term, which he applies specifically to religious, spiritual, and transpersonal phenomena), which in a sense is to see them as subjects (and not merely as objects) that are both enactive and embedded—that is, as both relatively autonomous and determining (auto), and as dependent and determined (eco), respectively.

Because "the auto-ecological relation is at once one of opposition/distinction and of implication/integration," it is to be expected that the description and interpretation of participatory events will sometimes stress the enactive, and sometimes the embedded, inflections of participation.[33] Even more, we could say that, depending on the perspective taken, the enactive is embedded and the embedded is enactive. The enactive self-organization of the individual cell, for instance, draws not only from the environment for whatever it cannot produce internally, but also on the generative potential of the genes, through which the cell is embedded in its own line of ancestors, as well as in the life of its species and indeed in the whole of life. Human subjects, for their part, primarily enact or "bring forth" their world by means of language, and language in turn embeds the subject in particular cultures and societies, but, these societies and cultures are themselves self-organizing totalities with their own auto-logic, through which they (co-)enact the life-world in which the individuals participate.

Morin stresses that the revolution in our knowledge of living organization calls for a corresponding reorganization of knowledge. It is in and through such a reorganization of knowledge—what Morin refers to as the "knowing of knowing"—that we can begin to envision a healing of the split between, and even a (complex re-)integration of, the two cultures. The relation between *autos* and *oikos*, along with the more specific example of the brain/mind relation considered above, reveals the possibility of a "meta-point of view" where not only the embedded and the enactive, but also the physical (including the biological) and the human, object and subject, are seen as dialogically, recursively, and holographically related. "The meta-system," Morin writes,

> can only be a retroactive/recursive loop that does not annul, but rather feeds on those contrary movements without which it would not exist and which it integrates into a productive whole. In this way the antagonistic character of the physical and of the anthropo-social points of entry becomes not only that which impedes, but also that which is necessary to, the constitution of the meta-system. . . . It is in and through this loop or circuit that we can establish a twofold theoretical rooting in both "nature" and "culture," in the "object" as well as the "subject."[34]

IMPLICATIONS FOR RELIGIOUS STUDIES

Reflecting the state of the academy in general, the field of Religious Studies exists as a largely fragmented set of disciplinary or methodological approaches to what are often referred to as "religious phenomena." Along with such long established approaches as the sociology, psychology, history, or anthropology of religion, Religious Studies now includes everything from Theology and Biblical Studies to feminist, ecological, sociobiological, cultural, political, LGBT, Queer, and cosmological approaches. This plurality of approaches within Religious Studies is doubtless a function not only of the proliferation of academic disciplines, but also of the complexity of religious phenomena themselves. If Religious Studies is to move in the direction of a coherent field, however, it may need—or at least those of its members who are so inclined may need—to embrace a more explicitly transdisciplinary (meta-)point of view, with respect both to the phenomena under investigation and to existing discipline-bound approaches to these phenomena. Morin's vision of the paradigm of complexity, it seems to me, holds great promise for such an endeavor.

To begin with, we have seen how the principles of complex thinking and the concept of living auto-eco-re-organization with which they are associated can help relink the two cultures. In Religious Studies, this split can be seen in the relative noncommunication between advocates of naturalistic (and often materialistic) explanations of religious phenomena, on the one hand, and those who favor more humanistic approaches, on the other. Examples of naturalistic approaches include Michael Persinger's work on the effects of electromagnetic fields on the temporal lobe,[35] the parallel investigations of Vilayanur Ramachandran and colleagues on the so-called "God spot" or "God module" in the human brain,[36] Richard Strassman's research into DMT as the "Spirit Molecule" (though Strassman himself is not reductive in his interpretations),[37] and Richard Dawkins and Susan Blackmore's theory of memes.[38] Social scientific approaches that rely primarily on quantitative methods, or traditional Freudian psychoanalysis, with its biologistic root assumptions, could also be included on this side of the great divide. On the humanistic side, one would find such approaches as textual analysis, the phenomenology and cultural anthropology of religion, the philosophy of religion, and humanistic, Jungian, and transpersonal psychological approaches to religion.

There have been attempts at coordinating and even integrating these two classes of approaches—I am thinking here of Ninian Smart's multidimensional theory of worldviews (with his inclusion of parallel religious and secular manifestations of experiential, mythic, ritual, doctrinal, ethical, social, material/esthetic, and political/institutional dimensions),[39] or Ian Barbour's work in the area of religion and science, which highlights four possible modes of relationship: conflict, independence, dialogue, and integration (Barbour himself makes the case for dialogue and tentative integration).[40]

At the margins of the academic guild, there is also Ken Wilber's version of an "integral" approach, which seeks to honor and integrate the two cultures as the "right" and "left" sides of a four quadrant model (where the right side represents exterior, and the left side, interior dimensions, while the upper quadrants represent individual dimensions, and the lower, collective).[41] The quadrants are overlaid with a "nested hierarchy" or *holarchy* of levels: matter, life, mind, soul, and spirit (or physiosphere, biosphere, noosphere, and theosphere), with each successive term in the sequence "transcending and including" the one before it. The auto/eco distinction shows up in Wilber's adoption of David Bakan's postulation of agency and communion as fundamental human drives, and also to a certain extent in both axes of the quadrants (where interior and individual might suggest *autos*, and exterior and collective, *oikos*).[42] The strength of Wilber's model is its power of systemic integration—one can easily "see" how disparate and seemingly conflictual elements might fit into a highly structured whole. Wilber calls this way of seeing "vision logic" (also sometimes "network logic"), which in his system corresponds to Morin's complex thinking.

There are significant differences between Wilber and Morin, however. In contrast to Wilber's theory of holarchical integration, Morin's critical appropriation of systems theory involves the recognition that any whole is not only more, but also less, than the sum of the parts.[43] Water (as whole), for instance, possesses the emergent quality of wetness and can (indeed must) be drunk by us to live, but we cannot breathe the oxygen (as part) that has been taken up into its molecular organization. The self-reflexive ego of the adult, similarly, generally must pay for the emergence of conscious mental constructs with a certain loss of sensual vitality and sensitivity to the imaginal. In Jungian terms, the emergence of the ego, and its associated personae, involves the creation of the personal shadow.[44] Though Jung does speak of development as the actualization of wholeness, he stresses the "includes" over the "transcends," and draws attention to the way symbols of wholeness suggest the idea of a coincidence or "weaving together" (*complexere*) of opposites (*coincidentia* or *complexio oppositorum*). This clearly echoes Morin's stress on the dialogical (and recursive) character of complex phenomena and his use of the term *unitas multiplex* and his description of life as "the union of union and disunion."[45]

Wilber does, it is true, point to the notion of Spirit or the nondual Absolute, which he describes in terms largely consistent with Jung and Morin. At the same time, however—and in this way he follows a path already laid by Hegel—he tends to privilege auto-logic (systemic closure) over eco-logic (methodological openness). This same tendency is evident in his treatment of a series of related polarities: mind over nature, or noosphere over biosphere (where the former is said to include the latter, but not the reverse); hierarchy over heterarchy; monotheistic epiphanies over polytheistic (and animistic); the impersonal Absolute over the personal; and so on. Wilber's (auto-)logic is coherent and, to those who share it, convincing. But there is at least one other, antagonistic logic in which the other side of these polarities is favored. Despite the strong resonance between the notions of nature/biosphere and animism/polytheism, all of which easily suggest the eco/embedded side of the logic of participation, not all of the terms on the other side of the polarities should be equated. It should be remembered, moreover, that these terms, or the worldviews associated with them, are also enactive (I shall return to this point in a moment)—and, to the extent that those who hold them do so exclusively, are themselves expressions of an auto-logic. What we have, in other words, is a typically *dialogical* situation which, as you will recall, involves "the symbiotic combination of two or more logics [or explanatory perspectives] which are simultaneously complementary *and* antagonistic."

This privileging of a certain auto-logic leads directly to the thorny issue of the ranking of religious and spiritual traditions. As Ferrer points out, referring specifically to the relationship between impersonal nondual and theistic spirituality, "What at first sight is . . . perplexing about these rankings is that their advocates, apparently operating with analogous criteria (such as encompassing capacity), reach radically opposite conclusions. . . ."[46] For Ferrer, it is not merely that the arguments presented by Wilber and other monistic idealists falter cross-culturally. Ferrer maintains instead that there can in principle be no "necessary, intrinsic, or a priori hierarchical relationship among the various spiritual universes."[47] Instead, he sees the "Truth" to which such universes refer as being "intrinsically indeterminate, malleable, and plural."[48] The reason for this is that these universes are by nature participatory events, which means they are each also relatively autonomous and, at certain points, potentially incommensurable enactions that together constitute the complex ecology of the religious/spiritual phenomenon. As living noospheric (if not theospheric) entities, one can easily imagine that, like all forms of living organization, religious/spiritual universes—and the interpretive schemes associated with these universes—might manifest varying kinds and degrees of hierarchy both within and among themselves. The danger, however, is that of lapsing into a simplified and mutilating understanding of hierarchy.[49] "Conceived in a simplifying manner," writes Morin, "hierarchy is either purely and simply identified with bondage and domination, or it masks this bondage with the rosy colors of integration and functionality. One can therefore see how a mutilated conception of hierarchy can, with respect to anthropo-social problems, support a mutilating sociology and politics." One could just as well add: a mutilating science of religion. Thus, Morin stresses: "It is vitally necessary for us to have a *living*—that is, complex—understanding of hierarchy."[50]

Morin achieves such an understanding, first, by recognizing repression/bondage as the cost exacted for emergence. Hierarchy is both "crushing pyramid" and "rising tree."[51] Second, the complex character of living organization is not exhausted by the notion of hierarchy, or even of holarchy, since "hierarchies depend on that upon which they depend. Even more, we must recognize that, in all living organization, hierarchical organization depends upon non-hierarchical organization." Morin continues:

> Hierarchies only become operationally rich (complex) if there is a certain suppleness and free play between levels, enough autonomy on the part of subjugated elements, and possibilities for decision-making at the base. In fact, organisms, societies, and ecosystems can only auto-produce and auto-reproduce on the basis of relatively autonomous interactions among the individuals/subjects by which they are constituted.
>
> These organisms, societies, and ecosystems require the presence of con-current hierarchies, and even forms of organization that are antagonistic to hierarchy. In short, there must, in all [living] hierarchical organization, be an element of *anarchy*.[52]

In his attempt to honor the complexity of living auto-eco-organization, Morin calls for a "grand bricolage" of the notions not only of hierarchy, het-erarchy, and anarchy, but also the correlative notions of (mono-)centrism, polycentrism, and acentrism.[53] Ranging from single cells to societies of insects and animals, from the human brain to whole ecosystems, Morin shows how now one, now the other, of these correlated terms seems most called for in the description or explanation of the phenomenon at hand. "In fact," Morin concludes, "every time we expand our vision or focus on details, we see that the [complex] combination of centrism/polycentrism/acentrism, and hierar-chy/heterarchy/anarchy . . . describes the fundamental character of living phenomena, and it is only through a monocular vision that some seem only centralized and hierarchical."[54]

Because "we must not conceive of anthropo-social organization in less complex terms than that of biological organization,"[55] I imagine that con-temporary participatory approaches to religion may want to make use of the same "grand bricolage" methodological strategy for dealing with seemingly contradictory or mutually exclusive religious/spiritual universes and their associated truth claims. This strategy would apply not only to the tension between monotheistic, polytheistic, and nontheistic representations of the divine, but also to such clusters of distinctions—both among and within reli-gious traditions—as anthropomorphic (for instance, the exoteric expressions of the Abrahamic religions: God as Father), cosmomorphic (many indige-nous religions: Trickster as Crow), and abstract (many esoteric expressions of religious traditions: use of sacred geometry) and, with respect to temporal frameworks: unidirectional (the Abrahamic traditions) and poly/adirectional (most indigenous and many mystical traditions).

Still, and as we have seen, the method arising out of the paradigm of complexity, whether applied to biological organization or to the organization of anthropo-social, noospheric, or specifically religious and spiritual phenomena, is not only a matter of bricolage, however grand. As auto-eco-re-organizing entities, religious and spiritual phenomena, along with the various disciplinary approaches to the articulation of their nature and significance, call for the full employment of complex thinking. It is not enough, for example—though it is already a big step—to create a cognitive space where monotheistic, polytheistic, and nontheistic traditions can peaceably coexist. Given the *dialogical* nature of complex relations, the goal of the method, or a key measure of its success, is the ability for this space to tolerate explicit antagonism. This antagonism might manifest in the sense of utter incommensurability between two (or more) competing claims—along with, or as variants of, the previous formulations: the belief that the universe has an absolute beginning and end versus the belief in eternally recurring cycles; or the belief in the postmortem survival of a personal soul versus impersonal or nonpersonal views of selfhood and its postmortem fate.

To end this section, I draw attention to a set of related antagonisms, the importance of which Ferrer has highlighted in his treatment of the participatory turn in transpersonal theory—namely, those between absolutism and relativism, universalism and pluralism, and perennialism and contextualism. "The participatory turn," says Ferrer, "can be seen as an attempt to pave a middle way between the Scylla of an authoritarian absolutism and the Charybdis of a self-contradictory and morally pernicious relativism."[56] Ferrer also invokes the idea of a "dialectic between universalism an pluralism" as expressive of the "deepest dynamics of the self-disclosing of Spirit."[57] I would add that such a dialectic—or *dialogic*—is woven together (*com-plexere*) with the associated auto/eco and enactive/embedded distinctions. On the one hand, because absolutism/universalism/perennialism typically manifest the highest degree of systemic closure, they are clear expressions of an auto-logic. Relativism/pluralism/contextualism, by contrast, all suggest openness (to the other) and can therefore be taken as expressions of an eco-logic. While the notion of enaction, as we have seen, derives from Maturana and Varela's biocognitive theory of *auto*poiesis (which is taken up in Morin's concept of *autos*), in the sphere of the human sciences (and in Religious Studies in particular), the notion of enaction is more associated with constructivism and the idea of situatedness, and thus also with Morin's concept of *oikos* and the relativism/pluralism/contextualism side of the polarity under consideration. Here again we see how the embedded, as context (which points to the concept of *oikos*) is also enactive (which points to the concept of *autos*). In other words, both sides of the polarity are not only dialogically, but also recursively, related. Summarizing the complexity of this kind of polarity, Morin writes:

> It is futile to seek to ground knowledge either in Spirit or in the Real. Knowledge [and here we could just as well say *participation*] has no foundation, in the literal sense of the term; but it does have several sources, and is

born from their confluence, from the recursive dynamism of the loop out of which subject and object both emerge. This loop brings into communication the mind and the world [and we could add: *autos* and *oikos*, enactive and embedded], sets each in the other in a dialogical co-production in which each of the terms and moments of the loop participate.[58]

CONCLUSION

In the preceding pages I have tried to show, in however preliminary a fashion, how the participatory turn in Religious Studies calls for the full employment of complex thinking. The initial distinction between enactive and embedded participation, through its encounter with the generative notion of auto-eco-re-organization in the paradigm of complexity, has revealed its complex (dialogical and recursive) character. The paradigmatic character of the relation

also applies, as we have seen, to a series of related binary oppositions which, in the paradigm of simplification, tend to be mutually dissociated. These include:

mind and brain/world
subject and object
culture and nature
hierarchy and heterarchy/anarchy
monocentrism and poly/acentrism
absolutism and relativism
universalism and pluralism
perennialism and contextualism

Because I chose to focus on the question of method, I have had to leave for another occasion a more considered treatment of Morin's understanding of religious myths and doctrines as noospheric entities.[59] Unlike Wilber, Morin never speculates on the existence and nature of a relatively autonomous theosphere and maintains throughout his writings a strong metaphysical agnosticism. Nevertheless, Morin has called for the cultivation of a new, third kind of religion "in the minimal sense"[60] of the term (suggested in one derivation of the word: from *re-ligare*: to join back together)," at the heart of which would be the fact and ideal of "re-liance." The first kind of religion is represented by what are generally called the world religions, which tend to focus on the promise of otherworldly salvation and, though universalist in aspiration, "were and remain a closed form of re-liance that demands faith in an exclusive revelation."[61] Nevertheless, Morin grants that the ideals of love, compassion, and forgiveness that these religions have harbored make of them "a superior type of re-liance of which the children of planet Earth still have need."[62] The second kind of religion, though hostile to the first, was equally universalist in scope and involved a faith in this-worldly salvation (the myth of Reason, of progress and "development"). Modern secular promises of salvation, however—whether from the Left, the Right, or the hollow "Center"—have all have birthed monsters (National Socialism, Stalinism, neoconservative imperialism, the corporate commodification of culture, the mechanization of work, to name a few). The new religion, by contrast,

> would not have promises but roots: roots in our cultures and civilizations, in planetary and human history; roots in life; roots in the stars that have forged the atoms of which we are made; roots in the cosmos where the particles were born and out of which our atoms were made. . . . Such a religion would involve belief, like all religions but, unlike other religions that repress doubt through excessive zeal, it would make room for doubt within itself. It would look out onto the abyss.[63]

In terms of the guiding theme of this volume and the initial distinction with which this chapter began, Morin's stress on cultural, planetary, and indeed cosmic roots as the source of a new sense of re-liance clearly highlights the embedded inflection of the participatory turn. At the same time, however, Morin knows that the cultivation of such re-liance demands the full, conscious and conscientious, engagement of the individual, and is thus equally enactive. Though he obviously sets great store on the mental virtues of an "open rationality,"[64] on the ability to enact the cognitive principles associated with the paradigm of complexity—the recursive loop that (re)links otherwise dissociated polarities is emblematic of this enaction, as is the readiness to tolerate difference, contradiction, and uncertainty—he knows that these virtues call for an equally open heart.

The "religion of re-liance" is the beloved sibling of the paradigm of complexity, and if the ideal of the latter is wisdom, the reality of re-liance is *love*, since "at the highest level of human complexity, re-liance can only take the form of love."[65] This love, whether in the form of simple (or passionate) affection, friendship, forgiveness, or universal fellowship, is what enables one to live with uncertainty and gives the courage to "look out onto the abyss." It is the "prescription for anxiety and the answer to death. . . ."[66] And he adds:

> Love, a resistance to all the cruelties of the world, is born of the re-liance of the world, and it serves to exalt the virtues of this re-liance. . . . Love is the highest potency and superior form, the final avatar, of this re-liance.[67]

Participation as complexity and re-liance, as wisdom and love. Each of these, says Morin, should be linked to the other in the manner of the *yin* and *yang*.[68] He knows in his heart, however, that the greatest of these is love.

NOTES

1. See Spretnak, *The Resurgence of the Real: Body, Nature, and Place in a Hyper-modern World* (Reading, MA: Addison-Wesley, 1997/1999).

2. See Taylor, *Sources of the Self: The Making of the Modern Identity* (Cambridge: Harvard University Press, 1992). This paradigm arguably has deeper sources in an inevitable, if not necessary, phase of the evolution of consciousness where the differentiation of self-reflexive awareness leads to its dissociation from the divine, the cosmos, and itself. See Richard Tarnas, *The Passion of the Western Mind: Understanding the Ideas that Have Shaped Our World View* (New York: Harmony Books, 1991); and Sean Kelly, "Re-visioning the Mandala of Consciousness," in *Ken Wilber in Dialogue: Conversations with Leading Transpersonal Thinkers*, ed. Donald Rothberg and Kelly (Wheaton, IL: Quest Books, 1998), 117–30.

3. See Varela, Evan Thompson, and Eleanor Rosch, *The Embodied Mind: Cognitive Science and Human Experience* (Cambridge: The MIT Press, 1991), and Ferrer, *Revisioning Transpersonal Theory: A Participatory Vision of Human Spirituality* (Albany: State University of New York Press, 2002).

4. Ferrer, 123.

5. Quoted from David Abram, *The Spell of the Sensuous Perception and Language in a More Than Human World* (New York: Vintage Books, 1996), 230.

6. Ibid., 233.

7. Jung, *Memories, Dreams, Reflections* (Glasgow: Collins Fount Paperback, 1961/1982), 280.

8. *Anguttara Nikaya*: http://www.accesstoinsight.org/ptf/dhamma/sacca/sacca4/samma-ditthi/index.html (8/30/06).

9. Plato, *Timaeus*: 45c to 46b. In *The Collected Dialogues of Plato*, ed. Edith Hamilton and Huntington Cairns (Princeton: Princeton University Press, 1982), 1173–74.

10. Something of the nature of the evolution of Western consciousness from antiquity to modernity is evident in the inversion that takes place in the meaning of "noumenal." Whereas for Kant the term refers to the necessarily unknowable "X" behind phenomena, for Plato the term refers to the Ideas, which, through the participatory power of *nous*, is all that truly can be known.

11. As M. H. Abrams points out (*The Mirror and the Lamp: Romantic Theory and the Critical Tradition* [New York: Oxford University Press, 1971]), British Romantic poets and literary theorists were engaged in a parallel exploration of a new, participatory worldview. Apart from Coleridge, who was directly influenced by Kant and Schelling in his philosophical musings, the British Romantic poets seem to have turned instead to the Cambridge Platonists and to Biblical metaphors for an alternative to the dominance of the disengaged subject and its disenchanted, clockwork uni-

verse. Of the Copernican revolution in epistemology, Abrams writes, "If we do not restrict this to Kant's specific doctrine that the mind imposes the forms of time, space, and the categories on the 'sensuous manifold,' but apply it to the general concept that the perceiving mind discovers what it has itself partly made—was effected in England by poets and critics before it manifested itself in academic philosophy. Thus generally defined, the revolution was a revolution by reaction. In their early poetic expositions of the mind fashioning its own experience, for example, Coleridge and Wordsworth do not employ Kant's abstract formulae. They revert, instead, to metaphors of mind which had largely fallen into disuse in the eighteenth century, but had earlier been current in seventeenth-century philosophers outside of, or specifically opposed to, the sensational tradition of Hobbes and Locke" (58). Abrams says that this shift from the dominant representational paradigm to the new (enactive) participatory one can be seen in the way that favored metaphors for the mind themselves shifted from the *mirror* of the representationalist to the *lamp* so beloved by the Romantics.

12. Quoted from Richards, *The Romantic Conception of Life: Science and Philosophy in the Age of Goethe* (Chicago: University of Chicago Press, 2004), 488.

13. Ibid., 480–90.

14. This despite the fact that two of the founders of scientific psychology, G. T. Fechner and William James, were thoroughly transpersonal in orientation, and this long before the "fourth force" (Maslow) of transpersonal psychology made its formal appearance (see Kelly, "The Prodigal Soul: Religious Studies and the Advent of Transpersonal Psychology," in *Religious Studies: Issues, Prospects, and Proposals*, ed. Klaus Klostermaier and Larry Hurtado [Atlanta: Scholars Press, 1991], 429–41; and "Space, Time, and Spirit: The Analogical Imagination and the Evolution of Transpersonal Theory," in *The Journal of Transpersonal Psychology* 34 [2002]: 73–100).

15. Morin, *La Méthode I: La Nature de la Nature* (Paris: Éditions du Seuil, 1977), 23. All of the translations of Morin in this paper are my own.

16. Ibid., 379.

17. Ibid., 80.

18. Ibid., 186.

19. Morin, *La Méthode, III: La Connaissance de la Connaissance* (Paris: Éditions du Seuil, 1986), p, 419.

20. Damasio, *The Feeling of What Happens: Body and Emotion in the Making of Consciousness* (San Diego: Harvest Books, 2000); *Descartes' Error: Emotion, Reason, and the Human Brain* (New York: Penguin Books, 2005).

21. See Ernest L. Rossi, *Psychobiology of Mind-Body Healing: New Concepts of Therapeutic Hypnosis* (New York: Norton, 1993).

22. For a dialogical consideration of the relation between these two perennial philosophical alternatives, see Kelly, "Bohm and Morin: Beyond Materialism and Idealism," in *Idealistic Studies* XXII (1992): 28–38.

23. "There remains," Morin writes, "and there must remain, a mental residue in the most complete and complex description of the brain, as there must remain a cerebral residue in the most complete and complex description of the mind. . . . The two

main approaches—the neuro-cerebral and the 'psy' approach—will, and must, come into contact and communicate with one another, but neither approach will ever be totally integrated or harmonized with the other . . ." (Morin, *La Méthode*, III, 80).

24. Ibid., 74.

25. See Morin, *La Méthode I, passim.*

26. Maturana and Varela, *Autopoiesis and Cognition: The Realization of the Living* (Dordrecht: D. Reidel, 1980), 13.

27. Morin, *La Méthode, II: La Vie de la Vie* (Paris: Éditions du Seuil, 1980), 109.

28. See the description on the back cover of Maturana and Varela's *Autopoiesis and Cognition*: "The authors have constructed a systematic theoretical biology which attempts to define living systems not as objects of observation and description, nor even as interacting systems, but as self-contained unities whose only reference is to themselves."

29. Morin, *La Méthode I: La Nature de la Nature*, 210–11.

30. Morin, *La Méthode, II: La Vie de la Vie*, 66.

31. Ibid., 87.

32. See Morin, *La Méthode, IV: Les Idées* (Paris: Éditions du Seuil, 1991); Kelly, "Integral Ecology and the Paradigm of Complexity," *Futures Journal* (forthcoming).

33. In considering the complexity of the auto-ecological relation, Morin writes: "*Autos* and *Oikos* are clearly distinguished when we consider the particularity of the one and the globality of the other, the auto-centrism of the one and the eco-centrism of the other. However, in one as in the other, and between both, there is a common, fluid, and uncertain zone, and the indistinct character of this zone is evidence of an indistinct unity-in-depth" (*La Méthode, II*, 68).

34. Morin, *La Méthode 1*, 276.

35. Persinger, *Neuropsychological Bases of God Beliefs* (New York: Praeger, 1987).

36. Ramachandran et al., "Neural Basis of Religious Experience," *1997 Society for Neuroscience Conference Abstracts*, 1316. See review article on the "God Spot" at: (http://cas.bellarmine.edu/tietjen/images/new_page_2.htm) (9/2/06).

37. Strassman, *DMT: The Spirit Molecule: A Doctor's Revolutionary Research into the Biology of Near-Death and Mystical Experiences* (Rochester, VT: Park Street Press, 2000).

38. Dawkins, *The Selfish Gene* (New York: Oxford University Press, 1976/2006); Blackmore, *The Meme Machine* (New York: Oxford University Press, 1999).

39. Smart, *Dimensions of the Sacred: An Anatomy of the World's Beliefs* (Berkeley: University of California Press, 1999).

40. Barbour, *Religion and Science: Historical and Contemporary Issues* (New York: HarperSanFrancisco, 1997).

41. Wilber, *Sex, Ecology, Spirituality: The Spirit of Evolution* (Boston: Shambhala, 1995) and *Integral Psychology: Consciousness, Spirit, Psychology, Therapy* (Boston: Shambhala, 2000).

42. Bakan, *The Duality of Human Existence: Isolation and Communion in Western Man* (Boston: Beacon Press, 1966).

43. See Morin, *La Méthode I*, 105–35; and "From the Concept of System to the Paradigm of Complexity," trans. Kelly, in *Journal of Social and Evolutionary Systems* 15 (1992): 371–85.

44. See Kelly, "Re-visioning the Mandala of Consciousness."

45. Morin, *La Méthode, II: La Vie de la Vie*, 371.

46. Ferrer, *Revisioning Transpersonal Theory*, 162.

47. Ibid., 167.

48. Ibid.

49. While Wilber recognizes the existence of what he calls "pathological hierarchies" (*Sex, Ecology, Spirituality*, 22f. and 103f.), Morin sees all hierarchies as presupposing a certain degree of pathology (as we saw above, through the virtualization, suppression, or inhibition of the phenomenal properties of the integrated elements).

50. Morin, *La Méthode, II*, 315.

51. Ibid., 311.

52. Ibid., 314 (emphasis added).

53. "[E]very living being," writes Morin, "is auto-eco-organized, which is to say that a part of its organization comes from ex-centric sources. What this means is that the most centrally organized living being is at the same time polycentric, a-centric, and ex-centric" (ibid., 318).

54. Ibid., 321.

55. Ibid., 324–25.

56. Ferrer, *Revisioning Transpersonal Theory*, 188.

57. Ibid., 191.

58. Morin, *La Méthode, III*, 211.

59. For a brief exposition, see Kelly, "Integral Ecology and the Paradigm of Complexity."

60. Morin, with A. B. Kern, *Homeland Earth: A Manifesto for the New Millennium*, trans. Kelly and Roger Lapointe (Kreskill, NJ: Hampton Press, 1999), 141.

61. Morin, *La Méthode, VI: Éthique* (Paris: Éditions du Seuil, 2004), 34.

62. Ibid.

63. Morin, *Homeland Earth*, 142.

64. See ibid., 123ff.

65. Morin, *La Méthode*, VI, 34.

66. Ibid., 231.

67. Ibid., 34.

68. Ibid., 231.

THREE

Spiritual Knowing as Participatory Enaction

An Answer to the Question of Religious Pluralism

Jorge N. Ferrer

WHEN DAVID B. BARRET, the main editor of the massive *World Christian Encyclopedia*,[1] was asked what he had learned about religious change in the world after several decades of research, he responded with the following: "We have identified nine thousand and nine hundred distinct and separate religions in the world, increasing by two or three religions every day."[2] Although there may be something to celebrate in this spiritual diversity and ongoing innovation, it is also clear that the many conflicting religious visions of reality and human nature are a major cause of the prevailing skepticism toward religious and spiritual truth claims. To the modern mind, the plurality of religious worlds raises a perplexing dilemma: How to account for such important differences when most of these traditions are claiming to depict universal and ultimate truths about existence? Typical responses to this question tend to fall along a continuum between two drastically opposite positions. At one end of the spectrum, materialistic, scientifically minded, and "nonreligionist" scholars downplay or dismiss altogether the cognitive value of religious knowledge claims, regarding religions as cultural fabrications that, like art pieces or culinary dishes, can be extremely diverse and even personally edifying but never the bearers of any "objective" truth whatsoever.[3] At the other end, spiritual practitioners and "religionist" scholars vigorously defend the cognitive value of religion, addressing the problem of religious pluralism by either endorsing the exclusive (or ultimately superior) truth of their preferred tradition or constructing universalist frameworks that at first sight appear to bring order to such religious chaos. Despite their professed inclusivist stance, most universalist visions of human

spirituality tend to distort the essential message of the various religious traditions, hierarchically favoring certain spiritual paths over others and raising serious obstacles for interreligious dialogue, open-ended spiritual inquiry, and
social harmony.[4] In this chapter, I provide a participatory answer to the question of religious pluralism that integrates the modern/postmodern insight into
the constructive element of all human knowledge (including spiritual knowledge) with a defense of the cognitive value of religion that eschews the dogmatic exclusivism involved in the privileging of any particular tradition.

Briefly, I suggest that *human spirituality emerges from cocreative participation in an always dynamic and undetermined mystery, spiritual power, and/or creative energy of life or reality.*[5] Furthermore, I argue that this participatory
understanding not only makes universal hierarchical rankings of religious traditions appear misconceived, but also reestablishes our direct connection
with the source of our being and expands the range of valid spiritual choices
that we as individuals can make. After offering a participatory account of the
nature of spiritual knowing, I provide a pluralistic understanding of not only
spiritual paths, but also spiritual liberations and spiritual ultimates. The
remainder of the essay explores some of the implications of this participatory
turn for a number of issues arising from the question of religious pluralism,
such as the understanding of interreligious relations, the problem of conflicting truth claims in religion, the cross-cultural validity of spiritual truths, the
nature of spiritual liberation, and the dialectic between the One and the
Many—or between universalism and pluralism—in religious inquiry.

Before proceeding farther, however, I should stress that although I
believe that this participatory approach is more sensitive to the spiritual evidence and better honors the diversity of ways in which spiritual awareness
can be expressed, by no means do I claim that it conveys the final truth about
the mystery of being in which we creatively participate. In contrast, my main
intention is to open avenues to rethink and live spirituality and religious
diversity today in a different, and I believe more fruitful, light. Likewise,
although I believe that this approach is advantageous for both interreligious
relations and individual spiritual growth, it should be obvious that its ultimate value is a practical challenge that needs to be appraised by others as
they personally engage it and critically decide whether it fosters their spiritual discernment and blossoming. It is in this spirit of offering, invitation,
inquiry, and perhaps skillful means that I advance the ideas of this chapter.[6]

THE PARTICIPATORY NATURE
OF SPIRITUAL KNOWING

I see spiritual knowing as a participatory action.[7] In the context of this chapter, the term *participatory* has three different but equally important meanings.
First, participatory refers to the fundamental ontological predicament of

human beings in relation to spiritual energies and/or the creative dynamism of life or reality. Human beings are—whether they know it or not—always participating in the self-disclosure of the mystery out of which everything arises. This participatory predicament is not only the ontological foundation of the other forms of participation, but also the epistemic anchor of spiritual knowledge claims. Second, participatory alludes to the fact that spiritual knowing is not objective, neutral, or merely cognitive. On the contrary, spiritual knowing engages us in a participatory, connected, and often passionate activity that can involve not only the opening of the mind, but also of the body, vital energies, the heart, and subtle forms of consciousness. Although spiritual events may only involve certain dimensions of human nature, all of them can potentially come into play in the act of participatory knowing, from somatic transfiguration to the awakening of the heart, from erotic communion to visionary cocreation, and from contemplative knowing to moral insight, to mention only a few. Finally, participatory refers to the epistemic role that human faculties play during most spiritual and transpersonal events. This relation is not one of appropriation, possession, or passive representation of pregiven knowledge or truths, but of communion and cocreative participation.

The last feature of participatory knowing requires further elaboration. Following the groundbreaking work of Francisco J. Varela, Evan Thompson, and Eleanor Rosch, my understanding of spiritual knowing embraces an enactive paradigm of cognition.[8] Spiritual knowing is not a mental representation of pregiven, independent spiritual objects, but an *enaction*, the "bringing forth" of a world or domain of distinctions cocreated by the different elements involved in the participatory event. Some central elements of spiritual participatory events may include individual intentions and dispositions; the creative power of multidimensional human cognition; cultural, religious, and historical horizons; archetypal and subtle energies; and, perhaps crucially, the apparently inexhaustible creativity of a dynamic and undetermined spiritual energy or generative power of life. As I elaborate below, by locating the emergence of spiritual knowing at the interface of human cognition, cultural context, and the creative power of the mystery, this enactive understanding avoids both the modernist reduction of religion to cultural-linguistic artifacts and the religionist dogmatic favoring of a single tradition as superior or paradigmatic. In this chapter, I refer to this account of spiritual knowing in terms of *participatory enaction*—a cocreative process that involves the participation of all levels of the person in the bringing forth of ontologically rich religious worlds.

These features make participatory knowing inherently transformative, at least in the following two senses. First, participation in a spiritual event usually brings forth the transformation of self and, at times, of the world.[9] As the fifteenth-century Christian mystic Catherine of Genoa, for instance, states, "My being is God, not by some simple participation but by a true transformation of my being."[10] Second, a transformation of self is usually necessary to be able to participate in spiritual knowing, and this knowing, in turn, draws forth the self through its transformative process in order to make possible this participation. This is why, as most traditions maintain, one needs to be open to being personally transformed in order to access and fully understand many spiritual knowledge claims. The epistemological significance of such personal transformation cannot be emphasized enough, especially given that the positivist denial of such a requisite is arguably one of the main obstacles for the epistemic legitimization of spirituality in the modern West.[11]

AN OCEAN WITH MANY SHORES

Having outlined my understanding of spiritual knowing, I want now to delineate the contours of a participatory approach to religious diversity that discloses a radical plurality not only of spiritual paths, but also of spiritual liberations and spiritual ultimates. Let us begin our story departing from a classic perennialist account. Perennialism generally postulates a single (or superior) spiritual ultimate that can be directly known through either a transconceptual mystical experience or a metaphysical intuition.[12] This insight, so the story goes, provides an unmediated access to "things as they really are," that is, the ultimate nature of reality and our innermost identity. Central to this view is the idea that once we lift the manifold veils of cultural distortions, doctrinal beliefs, egoic projections, sense of separate existence, and so forth, the doors of perception are unlocked and the true nature of self and reality is revealed to us in a flashing, liberating insight. From a classic perennialist perspective, every spiritual tradition is directed, in practice, to this identical, single vision (even though some spiritual systems are often presumed to be more effective than others in the complete attainment of this goal). Or to use one of the most popular perennialist metaphors, spiritual traditions are like "rivers leading to the same ocean."

Although this metaphor is used by perennialists to imply a cross-cultural spiritual ultimate, I would like to suggest an alternative reading. I propose that most, though by no means all, traditions are directed and can potentially lead to the same ocean, but not the one portrayed on the perennialist canvas. The ocean shared by most traditions does not correspond to a single spiritual referent or to "things as they really are," but, perhaps more humbly, to *the overcoming of narrow self-centeredness* and thus a liberation from corresponding limiting perspectives.

In other words, I believe that most spiritual paths seek a gradual transformation from narrow self-centeredness toward a fuller participation in the mystery of existence.[13] To be sure, this self-centeredness can be variously overcome, for example, through the compassion-raising insight into the interpenetration of all phenomena in Mahayana Buddhism, the knowledge of Brahman in Advaita Vedanta, the continuous feeling of God's loving agapeic presence in Christianity, the cleaving to God in Judaism, or the commitment to visionary service and healing in many forms of shamanism, to name only a few possibilities.[14] In all these cases, however, successful practitioners can experience a liberation from self-imposed suffering, an opening of the heart, and a spontaneous commitment to a compassionate and selfless life.[15] It is in this spirit, I believe, that the Dalai Lama thinks of a common element in religion:

> If we view the world's religions from the widest possible viewpoint, and examine their ultimate goal, we find that all of the major world religions . . . are directed to the achievement of permanent human happiness. They are all directed toward that goal. . . . To this end, the different world's religions teach different doctrines which help transform the person. In this regard, all religions are the same, there is no conflict.[16]

For the sake of brevity, and mindful of the limitations of this metaphor, since most traditions identify the liberation from self-centeredness as pivotal for this transformation, I will call this common element the *ocean of emancipation*.

Furthermore, I concur with perennialism in holding that the entry into the ocean of emancipation may be accompanied, or followed by, a transconceptual disclosure of reality. Due to the radical interpenetration between cognizing self and cognized world, once the self-concept is deconstructed—a common outcome of many contemplative practices[17]—the world may reveal itself to us in ways that transcend both linguistic rationality and mental conceptualization. Nevertheless, and here is where participatory thinking radically departs from perennialism, I maintain that there is *a multiplicity of transconceptual disclosures of reality*. Perennialists erroneously assume that a transconceptual disclosure of reality must be necessarily "one," and, actually, *the* One metaphysically envisioned and pursued in certain traditional spiritual systems. Put somewhat differently, perennialists generally believe that plurality emerges from concepts and interpretations, and that the cessation of conceptual proliferation must then result in a single apprehension of "things as they really are."

But to enter the ocean of emancipation does not inevitably tie us to a particular disclosure of reality, even if this is transconceptual. In contrast, what the mystical evidence suggests is that there are a variety of possible spiritual insights and ultimates (Tao, Brahman, *sunyata*, God, *kaivalyam*, and so forth) whose transconceptual qualities, although sometimes overlapping, are irreducible and often incompatible (personal versus impersonal, impermanent versus eternal, dual versus nondual, etc.). The typical perennialist move to account for this conflicting evidence is to assume that these qualities correspond to different interpretations, perspectives, dimensions, or levels of a single ultimate reality. However, this move is not only unfounded, but also problematic in its covertly positing a pregiven spiritual ultimate that is then, explicitly or implicitly, situated hierarchically over the rest of spiritual ends. I submit that a more fertile way to approach the plurality of spiritual claims is to hold that the various traditions lead to the enactment—or "bringing forth"—of different spiritual worlds, spiritual ultimates, and/or transconceptual disclosures of reality. Although these spiritual ultimates may apparently share some qualities (e.g., nonduality in *Brahmajñana* and *sunyata*), they constitute independent religious aims whose conflation may prove to be a serious mistake (thus, for example, the ontological nonduality of individual self and Brahman affirmed by Advaita Vedanta has little to do with the Mahayana Buddhist nondual insight into *sunyata* as the codependent arising or interpenetration of all phenomena). In terms of our metaphor, then, we could say that *the ocean of emancipation has many shores.*

The idea of different spiritual "shores" receives support from one of the few rigorous cross-cultural comparative studies of meditative paths. After his detailed analysis of Patañjali's *Yogasutras*, Buddhaghosa's *Visudhimagga*, and the Tibetan *Mahamudra*, Daniel P. Brown points out that:

> The conclusions set forth here are nearly the opposite of that of the stereotyped notion of the perennial philosophy according to which many spiritual paths are said to lead to the same end. According to the careful comparison of the traditions we have to conclude the following: there is only one path, but it has several outcomes. There are several kinds of enlightenment, although all free awareness from psychological structure and alleviate suffering.[18]

Whereas neoperennialist scholars such as Brown, Robert K. C. Forman, and others have rightly identified certain parallels across contemplative paths, contextualist scholars of mysticism have correctly emphasized that the enaction of different spiritual insights and ultimates requires specific mystical teachings, trainings, and practices.[19] Or put in traditional terms, particular rafts are needed to arrive at particular spiritual shores: If you want to reach the shore of *nirvana*, you need the raft of the Theravada Buddhist *dharma*, not the one provided by Christian praxis. And if you want to realize the knowledge of Brahman (*Brahmajñana*), you need to follow the Advaitin path of Vedic study and meditation, and not the practice of Tantric Buddhism, devotional Sufi dance, or psychedelic shamanism.[20] And so forth. In this account, the Dalai Lama is straightforward:

> Liberation in which "a mind that understands the sphere of reality annihilates all defilements in the sphere of reality" is a state that only Buddhists can accomplish. This kind of *moksa* or *nirvana* is only explained in the Buddhist scriptures, and is achieved only through Buddhist practice.[21]

What is more, different liberated awarenesses and spiritual ultimates can be encountered not only among different religious traditions, but also within a single tradition itself. Listen once again to the Dalai Lama:

> *Questioner:* So, if one is a follower of Vedanta, and one reaches the state of *satcitananda*, would this not be considered ultimate liberation?

His Holiness: Again, it depends upon how you interpret the words, "ultimate liberation." The moksa which is described in the Buddhist religion is achieved only through the practice of emptiness. And this kind of nirvana or liberation, as I have defined it above, cannot be achieved even by Svatantrika Madhyamikas, by Cittamatras, Sautrantikas or Vaibhasikas. The follower of these schools, *though Buddhists,* do not understand the actual doctrine of emptiness. Because they cannot realize emptiness, or reality, they cannot accomplish the kind of liberation I defined previously.[22]

What the Dalai Lama is suggesting here is that the various spiritual traditions and schools cultivate and achieve different contemplative goals. He is adamant in stressing that adherents to other religions, and even to other Buddhist schools, cannot attain the type of spiritual liberation cultivated by his own. There are alternative understandings and awarenesses of emptiness even among the various Buddhist schools: From the Theravadin *pugdala-sunyata* (emptiness of the person; existence of the aggregates) to the Mahayana *dharma-sunyata* (emptiness of the person and the aggregates) and the Madhyamika *sunyata-sunyata* (emptiness of emptiness). And from Dogen's Buddha-Nature = Impermanence to Nagarjuna's *sunyata* = *pratitya-samutpada* or to Yogachara's, Dzogchen's, and Hua-Yen's more essentialist understandings in terms of Pure Mind, Luminous Presence, or Buddhahood (*Tathagatagarbha*).[23] To lump together these different awarenesses into one single spiritual liberation or referent reachable by all traditions may be profoundly distorting. Each spiritual shore is independent and needs to be reached by its appropriate raft.

By way of concluding this section, I should stress that my defense of many viable spiritual paths and goals does not preclude, of course, the possibility of equivalent or even common elements among them. In other words, although the different mystical traditions enact and disclose different spiritual universes, two or more traditions may share certain elements in their paths and/or goals (e.g., mystical union with a personal God, attention training, purification of the heart, certain ethical guidelines, etc.). In this context, Hendrick M. Vroom's proposal of a "multicentered view of religion" that conceives traditions as displaying a variety of independent but potentially overlapping focal points deserves serious attention.[24] As I see it, this model not only makes the entire search for a "common core" simplistic and misconceived, but also avoids the pitfall of strict incommensurability of spiritual traditions, thus paving the way for different forms of comparative scholarship.[25]

FROM PARTICIPATORY KNOWING
TO SPIRITUAL COCREATION

Although the metaphor of "an ocean with many shores" is helpful in illustrating the variety of spiritual ultimates, it inadequately conveys the enactive and participatory nature of spiritual knowing presented in this chapter. As with all geographical metaphors, one can easily get the mistaken impression that these shores are pregiven, somehow "out there" waiting to be reached or discovered. This view, of course, would automatically catapult us back to a kind of perspectival perennialism, which accounts for the diversity of religious goals in terms of different perspectives or dimensions of the same pregiven ground of being.

A participatory understanding of spiritual knowing should not then be confused with the view that mystics of the various kinds and traditions simply access different dimensions or perspectives of a ready-made single ultimate reality. This view merely admits that this pregiven spiritual referent can be approached from different vantage points. In contrast, the view I am advancing here is that no pregiven ultimate reality exists, and that *different spiritual ultimates can be enacted through intentional or spontaneous cocreative participation in a dynamic and undetermined mystery, spiritual power, and/or generative force of life or reality.*

To be sure, once enacted, spiritual shores become more easily accessible and, in a way, "given" to some extent for individual consciousness to participate in. Once we enter the ocean of emancipation, spiritual forms that have been enacted so far are more readily available and tend more naturally to emerge (from mudras to visionary landscapes, from liberating insights to ecstatic types of consciousness, and so on). But the fact that enacted shores become more available does not mean that they are predetermined, limited in number, organized in a transcultural hierarchical fashion, universally sequential in their unfolding, or that no new shores can be enacted through cocreative participation. Like trails cleared in a dense forest, spiritual pathways traveled by others can be more easily crossed, but this does not mean that we cannot open new trails and encounter new wonders (and new pitfalls) in the seemingly inexhaustible mystery of being.

It is important to clearly distinguish our position not only from perspectival perennialism, but also from spiritual relativism and anarchy. To affirm the creative role of human multidimensional cognition in the shaping of religious worlds does not mean that "anything goes" in religious matters. On the one hand, though the specific limits of future religious forms can never be predetermined (as they will come into being through fusions of horizons between the human, the cosmos, and the mystery that are yet to take place), it is likely that historically enacted religious forms not only guide but also can constrain the visionary and mystical possibilities available at any given moment. In other words, the presence of the past may impose quasi-transcendental pragmatic restrictions upon human religious inquiry. At any rate, though within certain parameters an indefinite number of spiritual enactions may be feasible, we cannot get away with anything we want in our visionary cocreation of spiritual forms and realities.

On the other hand, the threat of spiritual anarchy is short-circuited by the fact that there may be certain identifiable constraints upon the nature of spiritually valid enacted realities. As Varela, Thompson, and Rosch suggest in relation to evolution, the key move "is to switch from a prescriptive logic to a proscriptive one, that is, from the idea that what is not allowed is forbidden to the idea that what is not forbidden is allowed."[26] In our context, we do not have to define the sphere of possible spiritual enactions; we only need to agree on the very few that are unacceptable. A central task for spiritual inquirers and participants in the interreligious dialogue, then, is the isolation of these parameters or restrictive conditions for the enaction of valid spiritual realities. In the context of a participatory worldview, these parameters cannot be considered either purely human constructions or transcendentally given to us, as if they were descending from the Heavens, so to speak. Instead, this search needs to engage human agents—and, perhaps especially, those recognized in their communities as more attuned to the creative power of life or the spirit—in a critical dialogue that honors, affirms, and cultivates the participatory marriage between human epistemic faculties and the mystery's creative urges. Even though the depth of my spiritual discernment is for others to judge, I do feel moved to shift now to a more normative mode of discourse and suggest that it may be more fruitful to envision the nature of these parameters not so much in terms of the specific contents of visionary worlds, but through the discrimination of the ethical values and practical fruits emerging from them. In this regard, it is noteworthy that, although there are important areas of tension (as well as all sorts of fascinating mystical transgressions and antinomianisms), religions have usually been able to find more common ground in their ethical prescriptions than in doctrinal or metaphysical issues.[27]

I should stress right away that I am not suggesting the existence of a "moral perennialism" resting on a supposedly ethical common religious past.[28] By contrast, I propose that any future global ethics will very likely not emerge from our highly diverse and ambiguous moral religious history, but rather from our critical reflection on such history in the context of our present-day moral intuitions. The search for cosmopolitan ethical guidelines, whose particular application must obviously be contextually sensitive, may be vital for the future regulation of interreligious and perhaps other global conflicts. In any event, the regulative role of pragmatic standards not only frees us from falling into spiritual anarchy, but also, as we will see below, paves the way for making qualitative distinctions among spiritual insights and traditions.

Admittedly, to postulate that human intentionality and creativity may influence or even affect the nature and workings of the mystery—understood here as the creative energy or source of reality, life, and consciousness—may sound somewhat heretical, arrogant, or inflated. The claim may look especially presumptuous in the eyes of theistic practitioners who equate the mystery with an omnipotent and entirely self-reliant Creator or God. This is a valid concern, but I should add that it stems from a conventional view of the divine as an isolated and independent entity disconnected from human agency, and that it becomes superfluous in the context of a participatory cosmology. Whenever we understand the relationship between the divine and the human (and the cosmos) as reciprocal and interconnected, we can, humbly but resolutely, reclaim our creative spiritual role in the self-disclosure of the divine.[29]

The idea of a reciprocal relationship between the human and the divine finds precedents in the world mystical literature. Perhaps its most compelling articulation can be found in the writings of ancient Jewish and Kabbalistic theurgical mystics.[30] For the theurgic mystic, human religious practices have a profound impact not only in the outer manifestation of the divine, but also in its very inner dynamics and structure. Through the performance of the commandments (*mizvot*), the cleaving to God (*devekut*), and other mystical practices, the theurgic mystic influences divine activities such as the restoration of the sphere of the *sefirots*, the unification and augmentation of God's powers, and even the transformation of God's own indwelling. As Moshe Idel puts it, the theurgic mystic "becomes a cooperator not only in the maintenance of the universe but also in the maintenance or even formation of some aspects of the Deity."[31]

Furthermore, as both Louis Dupré and Bernard McGinn observe, this understanding is not absent in Christian mysticism.[32] In the writings of the so-called affective mystics (such as Richard of Saint Victor, Teresa of Avila, or Jan van Ruusbroec), for example, we consistently find the claim that the love for God substantially affects divine self-expression and can even transform God himself. In his discussion of Ruusbroec's mysticism, Dupré points out:

> In this blissful union the soul comes to share the dynamics of God's inner life, a life not only of rest and darkness but also of creative activity and light. . . . The contemplative accompanies God's own move from hiddenness to manifestation within the identity of God's own life.[33]

And he adds:

> By its dynamic quality the mystical experience surpasses the mere awareness of an already present, ontological union. The process of loving devotion *realizes* what existed only as potential in the initial stage, thus creating a *new* ontological reality.[34]

Although space does not allow me to document this claim here, I believe that the idea of a spiritual cocreation—"one that many have assumed but few have dared to express"[35]—is also present to some extent in devotional Sufism, Kabbalah, indigenous spiritualities, and in many Indian traditions such as

Shaivism or Vajrayana Buddhism. In any event, my intention here is not to suggest the universality of this notion (which clearly is not the case), but merely to indicate that it has been maintained by a variety of mystics and religious practitioners from different times and traditions.

But, how far are we willing to go in affirming the cocreative role of the human in spiritual matters? To be sure, most scholars may be today ready to allow that particular spiritual states (e.g., the Buddhist *jhanas*, Teresa's mansions, or the various yogi *samadhis*), spiritual visions (e.g., Ezekiel's Divine Chariot, Hildegard's visionary experience of the Trinity, or Black Elk's Great Vision), and spiritual landscapes or cosmologies (e.g., the Buddha lands, the Heavenly Halls of Merkavah mysticism, or the diverse astral domains posited by Western esoteric schools) are largely or entirely constructed. Nevertheless, I suspect that many religious scholars and practitioners may feel more reticent in the case of spiritual entities (such as the Tibetan *daikinis*, the Christian angels, or the various Gods and Goddesses of the Hindu pantheon) and, in particular, in the case of ultimate principles and personae (such as the biblical Yaveh, the Buddhist *sunyata*, or the Hindu Brahman).[36] Would not accepting their cocreated nature undermine not only the claims of most traditions, but also the very ontological autonomy and integrity of the mystery itself? Response: Given the rich variety of incompatible spiritual ultimates and the aporias involved in any conciliatory strategy—whether essentialist, perspectivist, or structuralist—I submit that it is only by promoting the role of human constructive powers to the very heart and summit of each spiritual universe that we can preserve the ultimate unity of the mystery—otherwise we would be facing the arguably equally unsatisfactory alternative of having to either reduce spiritual universes to fabrications of the human imagination or posit an indefinite number of isolated spiritual universes or monads. By conceiving spiritual universes *and* ultimates as the upshot of a process of participatory cocreation between human multidimensional cognition and an undetermined spiritual power, however, we rescue the ultimate unity of the mystery while simultaneously affirming its ontological richness and overcoming the reductionisms of cultural-linguistic, psychological, and/or biologically naturalistic explanations of religion.

THE PARTICIPATORY TURN AND THE
QUESTION OF RELIGIOUS PLURALISM

In this section, I explore some implications of the participatory turn for the question of religious pluralism, in particular regarding the following five interrelated themes: (1) the ranking of spiritual traditions; (2) the problem of conflicting truth claims in religion; (3) the validity of spiritual truths; (4) the nature of spiritual liberation; and (5) the dialectic between universalism and pluralism in religious inquiry.

On Ranking Spiritual Traditions

In order to address the plurality and incompatibility of spiritual cosmologies and ultimates, most religions typically resort to implicit or explicit hierarchical gradations of spiritual traditions. Before problematizing such procedures and proposing an alternative participatory solution, I first offer a few cross-cultural examples of spiritual gradations. As is well known, Christianity often regarded previous pagan religions as incomplete steps toward the final Christian revelation. Likewise, in Islam, the teachings of Jesus and the ancient prophets of Israel are recognized as relatively valid but imperfect versions of the final Truth revealed in the Koran.

The profusion of alternative spiritual gradations in Hinduism is also well known. For example, while Sankara subordinates the belief in a personal, independent God (*Saguna Brahman*) to the nondual monism of Advaita Vedanta, Ramanuja regards the monistic state of becoming Brahman as a stage "on the way to union with [a personal] God" and claimed that the entire system of Advaita Vedanta was resting on wrong assumptions.[37] But there is more: Udayana, from the Nyaya school, arranged the rest of Hindu systems into a sequence of distorted stages of understanding of the final truth embodied in his "ultimate Vedanta," which holds the ultimate reality of the "Lord" (*isvara*). And "Vijñanabhioksu, the leading representative of the revival of classical Samkhya and Yoga in the sixteenth century, states that other systems are contained in the Yoga of Patañjali and Vyasa just as rivers are preserved and absorbed by the ocean."[38] As any scholar of Hinduism well knows, these examples could be multiplied almost endlessly.[39]

In the Buddhist tradition we also find a number of conflicting hierarchies of spiritual insights and schools. As Robert E. Buswell and Robert M. Gimello point out,

> Buddhist schools often sought to associate particular stages along the marga [the path], usually lower ones, with various of their sectarian rivals, while holding the higher stages to correspond to their own doctrinal positions. . . . The purpose of such rankings was not purely interpretive; it often had an implicit polemic thrust.[40]

We have already seen, in the words of the Dalai Lama, how Tibetan Buddhism considers the Theravadin and Yogacarin views of emptiness as preliminary and incomplete. It is important to stress that, for Tibetan Buddhists, their understanding (and practice) of emptiness is not merely different but more refined, accurate, and soteriologically effective.[41] Needless to say, this is not an opinion shared by representatives of other Buddhist schools, who consider their doctrines and methods complete in their own right, and sufficient to elicit the total awakening described by the Buddha. To mention only one other of the many alternative Buddhist hierarchies, Kukai, the founder of the

Japanese Shingon, offered a very exhaustive ranking of Confucian, Taoist, and Buddhist systems culminating in his own school.[42] In Kukai's "ten abodes for the mind" (*jujushin*), Buswell and Gimello explain,

> the fourth abiding mind corresponds to the Hinayanists, who recognize the truth of no-self . . . whereas the sixth relates to the Yogacarins, who generate universal compassion for all. Kukai's path then progresses through stages corresponding to the Sanron (Madhyamika), Tendai (T'ien-t'ai), and Kegon (Hua-yen) systems, culminating in his own Shingon Esoteric school.[43]

Only in the tenth stage, corresponding to the Shingon school, Kukai considers the Buddhist practitioner fully liberated.

Interestingly enough, contemporary discussions of spiritual gradations strikingly mirror some of these ancient debates. For example, whereas Ken Wilber tries to persuade us (à la Sankara) of the more encompassing nature of nonduality when contrasted to dual and theistic traditions, Michael Stoeber's theo-monistic model establishes (à la Ramanuja) a mystical hierarchy where nondual, impersonal, and monistic experiences are subordinated to dual, personal, and theistic ones:[44]

> It is possible in a theistic teleological framework to account for monistic experiences in terms of the nature of theistic experiences, treating these as necessary and authentic experiences in the mystic theology. But the reverse does not hold true in a monistic framework. In a monistic framework theistic experiences are not regarded as necessary to the monistic ideal.[45]

What at first sight is more perplexing about many of these rankings is that their advocates, apparently operating with analogous criteria (such as "holistic capacity"), reach radically opposite conclusions about the relationship between nondual and theistic spirituality. When examined more closely, however, this should not be surprising. The criteria proposed are often vague enough that they can be interpreted to favor one's preferred tradition upon the rest. Take, for example, Wilber's guideline that "a higher level has extra capacities than previous ones." Obviously, what counts as "extra capacities" can be, and actually is, differently assessed by the various authors and traditions according to their doctrinal commitments (e.g., nonduality versus the personal and relational qualities of the divine).

The participatory turn has important ramifications for our understanding of interreligious relations. Most spiritual gradations of traditions stem from the postulation of an ultimate referent or spiritual goal from which the relative, partial, or lower value of all religious systems and insights is assigned. In terms of our metaphor of an ocean with many shores, we could say that, after reaching a previously laid down spiritual shore or enacting a new one, mystics have typically regarded other shores as incomplete, inferior, or simply false. As we have seen, however, there is no agreement whatsoever among mystics or scholars about either the nature of this spiritual ultimate or this hierarchy of spiritual insights. This lack of consensus is not only one of the most puzzling riddles in philosophy of religion, but also an overriding source of the modern incredulity toward religious cognitive claims. What is even more important, the idea of a universal spiritual ultimate for which traditions compete has profoundly affected how people from different creeds engage one another, and, even today, fuels all types of interreligious conflicts, quarrels, and even holy wars.

After the participatory turn, however, these interreligious rankings can be recognized as parasitic upon the Cartesian-Kantian assumption of a universal and pregiven spiritual ultimate relative to which such judgments can be made. To put it another way, these interreligious judgments are intelligible *only* if we first presuppose the existence of a single noumenal or pregiven reality behind the multifarious spiritual experiences and doctrines. Whenever we drop this assumption, however, the very idea of ranking traditions according to a paradigmatic standpoint becomes both fallacious and superfluous. I am not suggesting that spiritual insights and traditions are incommensurable, but merely that it may be seriously misguided to grade them according to any preestablished spiritual hierarchy or traditional religious insight. In the next sections, I suggest some directions where these comparative grounds can be sought.

The Problem of Conflicting Truth Claims in Religion

Closely related to the ranking of traditions is the so-called problem of conflicting truth claims in religion. Roughly, this problem refers to the incompatible ultimate claims religious traditions make about the deepest nature of reality, spirituality, and human identity.[46] Since all religions have been typically imagined to aim at the same spiritual end, the diversity of religious accounts of ultimate reality is not only perplexing and conflicting, but also raises understandable doubts about the cognitive status of religious knowledge claims.

Although with different nuances, the attempts to explain such divergences have typically taken one of the three following routes: dogmatic exclusivism ("my religion is the only true one, the rest are false"), hierarchical inclusivism ("my religion is the most accurate or complete, the rest are lower or partial"), and ecumenical pluralism ("there may be real differences between our religions, but all lead ultimately to the same end").[47] Alternatively, to put it in different terms, cultural-linguistic scholars invoke conceptual frameworks or language games, and perennialists appeal to hierarchical gradations of traditions and/or to esotericist, perspectivist, or structuralist explanations.

After the participatory turn, however, a more satisfactory response to this puzzle naturally emerges. Once we give up Cartesian-Kantian assumptions about a pregiven or noumenal spiritual reality common to all traditions, the so-called problem of conflicting truth claims becomes, for the most part, a pseudoproblem.[48] In other words, the diversity of spiritual claims is a problem *only* when we have previously presupposed that they are referring to a single, ready-made spiritual reality.[49] Nevertheless, if rather than resulting from the access and visionary representation of a pregiven reality, spiritual knowledge is cocreatively enacted, then spiritual truths need no longer be conceived as "conflicting." Divergent truth claims are conflicting *only* if they intend to represent or convey the nature of a single referent with determined features. But if we see such a spiritual referent as malleable, undetermined, and creatively open to a multiplicity of disclosures largely contingent on human religious endeavors, then the reasons for conflict vanish like a mirage. To use a traditional image, in this participatory light, the threatening snake we saw in the dark basement can now be recognized as a peaceful and connecting rope.

In short, by giving up our dependence on Cartesian-Kantian premises in spiritual hermeneutics, religious traditions are released from their predicament of metaphysical competition and a more constructive and fertile interreligious space is naturally engendered. To exorcise the Cartesian-Kantian spell in Religious Studies, that is, leads to affirming the uniqueness and potential integrity of each tradition in its own right, and only from this platform, I believe, can a genuine interreligious dialogue be successfully launched.[50] Once traditions stop thinking of themselves as aprioristically superior or closer to *the* Truth, peoples from diverse belief systems can encounter each other in the spirit of critical dialogue, collaborative inquiry, and mutual transformation.[51]

The diversity of spiritual truths and cosmologies, then, rather than being a source of conflict or even cause for considerate tolerance, can now be reason for wonder and celebration. Wonder in the wake of the inexhaustible creative power of the self-unfolding of being; and celebration in the wake of the recognition of both our participatory role in such unfolding, and the emerging possibilities for mutual enrichment and cross-fertilization out of the encounter of traditions and spiritual perspectives. "This plurality of consensual beliefs," Lee Irwin tells us,

> need not lead to the error that one must choose among alternatives or be lost, must accept the validity of a particular visionary world or suffer the consequences of indecision or despair. There is a creative power in the plurality of visionary worlds, a convergence of forms and ideas of immeasurable depth.[52]

Three points need to be stressed at this point of our discussion. First, in my view, spiritual pluralism does not exist only at a doctrinal level, but at an ontological or metaphysical one. Plurality is not merely an exoteric diversion, but fundamentally engrained in the innermost core of each tradition.

As Raimon Panikkar forcefully puts it, "Pluralism penetrates into the very heart of the ultimate reality."[53] Secondly, there is not a necessary, intrinsic, or a priori hierarchical relationship among the various spiritual universes. There is no final, privileged, or absolutely most encompassing single spiritual viewpoint. No human being can claim access to a God's eye that can judge from above which tradition contains more parcels of a univocal Truth, not because this Truth is noumenally inaccessible, but because it is undetermined, dynamic, malleable, and plural.[54]

Finally, this participatory approach to interreligious relations may lead to a shift from searching for a global spirituality organized around a single ultimate vision to recognizing an already existent spiritual human family that branches out from the same creative root. In other words, traditions may be able to find their longed-for unity not so much in a single spiritual megasystem or global vision, but in their common roots—that is, in that deep bond constituted by the undetermined dimension of the mystery in which all traditions participate in the cocreation of their spiritual insights and cosmologies. Like members of a healthy family, religious people may then stop attempting to impose their particular perception on others and might instead become a supportive and enriching force for the creative "spiritual individuation" of other practitioners, both within and outside their traditions. This mutual empowerment of spiritual creativity may lead to the emergence of not only a rich variety of coherent spiritual perspectives that can potentially be equally grounded in the mystery, but also a human community formed by fully differentiated spiritual individuals. This account would be consistent with a view of the mystery, the cosmos, and/or spirit as moving from a primordial state of undifferentiated unity toward one of infinite differentiation-in-communion.

The Validity of Spiritual Truths

Regarding the thorny issue of the validity of spiritual insights, I should say that the criteria stemming from a participatory account of spiritual knowing can no longer be simply dependent on the picture of reality disclosed, but on the kind of transformation of self, community, and world facilitated by their enaction and expression. That is, once we accept the creative link between human beings and the mystery in spiritual knowing, judgments about how accurately spiritual claims correspond to or represent ultimate reality become nearly meaningless. The goal of most contemplative systems is not merely to describe, represent, mirror, and know, but especially to prescribe, enact, embody, and transform. The gnostic element in contemplative practice is generally subordinated to the transformative end of the contemplative life. To put it in terms of the Buddhist notion of skillful means (*upaya*): "The chief measure of a teaching's truth or value is its efficacy unto religious ends, rather than any correspondence with facts."[55] In other words, the validity of spiritual knowledge does not usually rest in its accurate matching with any pregiven content, but in the quality of selfless awareness disclosed and expressed in perception, thinking, feeling, and action.

I should clarify here that the previous orientation is especially relevant, I believe, when considering qualitative distinctions among religious traditions or types of spiritualities, as well as in the context of a more "creative" spirituality that seeks to enact innovative spiritual paths and goals. Within one tradition, however, as well as in the context of a more "reproductive" spirituality that seeks to reenact already traveled spiritual paths and goals, previously mapped spiritual stages, states, and visions legitimately serve as crucial signposts of progress along the path, and therefore some kind of "correspondence theory of truth" may apply in these cases.

In any event, it cannot be stressed strongly enough that rejecting a pregiven spiritual ultimate referent does not prevent us from making cross-cultural qualitative distinctions in spiritual matters. To be sure, like beautiful porcelains made out of amorphous clay, traditions cannot be qualitatively ranked according to their accuracy in representing some imagined (accessible or inaccessible) original template. However, this does not mean that we cannot discriminate between more evocative, skillful, or sophisticated artifacts. Grounds to decide the comparative and relative value of different spiritual truths can be sought, for example, not in a prearranged hierarchy of spiritual insights or by matching spiritual claims against a ready-made spiritual reality, but by assessing their emancipatory power for self and world, both intra- and interreligiously. By the *emancipatory power* of spiritual truths I mean their capability to free individuals, communities, and cultures from gross and subtle forms of narcissism, egocentrism, and self-centeredness. In very general terms, then, and to start exploring these potential qualitative distinctions, I believe that we can rightfully ask some of the following questions: How much does the cultivation and embodiment of these spiritual truths result in a movement away from self-centeredness? How much do they lead to the emergence of selfless awareness and/or action in the world? How much do they promote the growth and maturation of love and wisdom? To what degree do they deliver the promised fruits? How effective are they in leading their followers to harmony, balance, integration, truthfulness, and justice within themselves, their communities, and toward the world at large? And so forth.

There is another orientation relevant to the making of qualitative distinctions among cross-cultural spiritual insights. Qualitative distinctions can be made among the various enactions by not only judging their emancipatory power, but also discriminating how grounded in or coherent with the fullness of the mystery they are. For example, it is likely that, due to a number of historical and cultural variables, most past and present spiritual visions are to some extent the product of dissociated ways of knowing—ways of knowing that emerge predominantly from the mental access to subtle dimensions of transcendent consciousness, but that are ungrounded and disconnected from vital and immanent spiritual sources. This type of spiritual knowledge, although certainly containing important and genuine insights, is both prey to numerous distortions and, at best, a partial understanding that falsely claims to portray the totality.

Essentially, I see the project of conceptually constructing frameworks to portray a supposedly pregiven reality the hallmark of what we might call "false knowing," that is, the pretension of a proud mind to represent a ready-made reality without the collaboration of other levels of the person (somatic, vital, instinctive, emotional, and so on), which, I believe, are pivotal for the elaboration of more holistic knowledge. By contrast, I propose that an enaction of reality or the mystery is more valid when it is not only a mental/spiritual matter, but a multidimensional process that involves the epistemic power of all levels of the person. It is well known that most spiritual traditions posit the existence of an isomorphism or deep resonance among the human being, the cosmos, and the Mystery out of which everything arises ("as above so below," " the human being as *Imago Dei*," "the embodied person as microcosm of the universe," and so forth).[56] If we accept this view then we can say that the more human dimensions creatively participate in the enaction of spiritual knowledge, the greater will be the dynamic congruence between inquiry approach and studied phenomena and the more coherent with, or attuned to, the ongoing unfolding of reality and the mystery will be our knowledge. The blossoming and epistemic competence of the various human attributes (somatic, vital, sexual, emotional, mental, and so on) may be crucial not only for individual wholeness and interpersonal harmony, but also for the emergence of undistorted and more complete spiritual knowledge.

Therefore, a sharp distinction needs to be drawn between "knowledge that is matched with a pregiven reality" and "knowing that is grounded in, aligned to, or coherent with the mystery." As I see it, the former expression inevitably catapults us back to objectivist and representational epistemologies in which there can exist, at least in theory, one single most accurate representation of reality or the mystery. The latter expressions, in contrast, as well as a more dynamic understanding of truth as "attunement to the unfolding of being," emancipate us from these limitations and open us up to a *potential* multiplicity of spiritual visions that can be firmly grounded in, and equally coherent with, the mystery. This is why there may be, at least in theory, a variety of valid spiritual cosmologies and ultimates that nonetheless can be equally harmonious with the mystery and, in the realm of human affairs, may manifest through a similar ethics of love and commitment to the blooming of life in all its constructive manifestations (human and nonhuman).

Recapitulating our discussion so far, a participatory account of spiritual knowing renders unintelligible the postulation of qualitative distinctions among traditions according to a priori doctrines or hierarchically posited paradigmatic spiritual contents. Rather, these distinctions are to be sought in a variety of markers and practical fruits (existential, cognitive, emotional, interpersonal), perhaps anchored around two basic epistemological orientations, which we might call the *egocentrism test* (i.e., to what extent does a spiritual tradition, path, or practice free its practitioners from gross and subtle forms of narcissism and self-centeredness?) and the *dissociation test* (i.e., to what extent does a spiritual tradition, path, or practice foster the integrated blossoming of all dimensions of the person?).[57] While this approach would render obsolete and inappropriate the ranking of spiritual traditions as wholes according to doctrinal paradigmatic standpoints, it would invite a more nuanced and complex evaluation based on the recognition that traditions, like human beings, are likely to be both "higher" and "lower" in relation to one another, but in *different regards* (e.g., fostering contemplative competences, ecological awareness, mind/body integration, and so forth).[58] It is important then not to understand the ideal of a symmetrical encounter among traditions in terms of a trivializing or relativistic egalitarianism. By contrast, a truly symmetrical encounter can only take place when traditions open themselves to teach and be taught, fertilize and be fertilized, transform and be transformed.

Two important qualifications need to be made about these suggested guidelines. The first relates to the fact that some spiritual paths and liberations may be more adequate for different psychological and cultural dispositions (as well as for the same individual at distinct developmental junctures), but this does not make them *universally* superior or inferior.[59] The well-known four yogas of Hinduism (reflection, devotion, action, and experimentation) come quickly to mind in this regard, as do other spiritual typologies that can be found in both Hinduism and other traditions.[60] The second qualification refers to the complex difficulties inherent in any proposal of cross-cultural criteria for religious truth. It should be obvious, for example, that my emphasis on the overcoming of narcissism and self-centeredness, although arguably central to most spiritual traditions, may not be shared by all. Even more poignantly, most mystical traditions would not rank too highly in terms of the dissociation test; for example, gross or subtle forms of repression, control, or strict regulation of the human body and its vital/sexual energies (versus the promotion of their autonomous maturation, integration, and participation in spiritual knowing) are rather the norm in most past and present contemplative endeavors.[61]

These and other difficulties make it imperative to stress the very tentative and conjectural status of any cross-cultural criteria for spiritual truth. But there is more. I do not think that any resolution of these types of spiritual criteria can be legitimately attained by scholars, religious leaders, or even mystics on a priori grounds. What I am suggesting is that the search for criteria for cross-cultural religious truth is not a logical, rational, or even spiritual problem to be solved by isolated individuals or traditions, but a *practical task* to be accomplished not only in the fire of interreligious dialogue, but also through the critical assessment of actual practices and their fruits.

SPIRITUAL LIBERATION

The thesis of a plurality of spiritual ultimates also has important implications for our understanding of spiritual liberation. Traditionally, spiritual liberation is said to involve two interrelated dimensions: (1) *soteriological-phenomenological*, or the attainment of human fulfillment, salvation, redemption, enlightenment, or happiness, and (2) *epistemological-ontological*, or the knowledge of "things as they really are," ultimate reality, or the divine. Interestingly, according to most traditions, there is a relation of mutual causality or even final identity between these two defining dimensions of spiritual emancipation: To know is to be liberated, and if you are free, you know.

It has been my contention that, although most traditions concur in that liberation implies an overcoming of limiting self-centeredness and associated restricted perspectives, this can be cultivated, embodied, and expressed in a variety of independent ways. Likewise, I also advanced the more radical thesis that this spiritual plurality is not only soteriological or phenomenological, but also epistemological, ontological, and metaphysical. Put simply, there is a multiplicity of spiritual liberations *and* ontologically rich spiritual cosmologies and ultimate principles. The tasks remain, however, to address the tension between this account and the traditional claim that liberation is equivalent to knowing "things as they really are," as well as to explore the implications of our viewpoint for spiritual blossoming.

To begin with, I should admit straight off that this tension is a real one, and that the understanding of spiritual knowing as participatory enaction outlined in this chapter will probably not be acceptable to those who firmly believe in the exclusive or privileged truth of their religions. While respecting the many thoughtful and sensitive individuals who maintain exclusivist or inclusivist stances, I see these pretensions as problematic assumptions that not only cannot be consistently maintained in our pluralistic contemporary world, but also frequently lead to a deadlock in the interfaith dialogue.

The many arguments showing the untenability of religious absolutism are well known and need not be repeated here.[62] To the standard ones, I would like to add that religious exclusivism or absolutism can be seen as inconsistent with the nature of spiritual liberation as maintained by those religious traditions themselves. Most traditions equate spiritual liberation with boundless freedom. But if we rigidly maintain the exclusive Truth of our tradition, are we not binding ourselves to a particular, limited disclosure of reality? And if we tie our very being to a singular, even if transconceptual, disclosure of reality, then, we can rightfully wonder, how truly boundless is our spiritual freedom? Is this freedom truly boundless or rather a subtle form of spiritual bondage? And if so, is this the promised spiritual freedom we are truly longing for?

As I see it, the apparent tension between this participatory account and the mystical claims of metaphysical ultimacy can be relaxed by simultaneously holding that (1) more than one tradition can be potentially correct in maintaining that it leads to a direct insight into "things as they *really* are," and (2) this "really" does not refer to a Cartesian pregiven reality. Despite the deep-seated dispositions of modern Western thought to equate Cartesian objectivity with reality, it is important to realize that when we reject the idea of a pregiven world we do not to say good-bye to reality, but instead pave the way for encountering it in all its complexity, creative dynamism, and mystery. From this perspective, the expression "things as they really are" is misguided only if understood in the context of objectivist and essentialist epistemologies, but not if conceived in terms of participatory enactions of reality free from egocentric distortions and dissociated states of being. After all, what most mystical traditions offer are not so much descriptions of a pregiven ultimate reality to be confirmed or falsified by experiential evidence, but prescriptions of ways of "being-*and*-the-world" to be intentionally cultivated and lived. In the end, mystical traditions aim at transformation, not representation. The descriptive claims of the contemplative traditions primarily apply to the deluded or alienated ordinary human predicament, as well as to the various visions of self and world disclosed throughout the unfolding of each soteriological path. But since there are many possible enactions of more holistic and liberated self and world, it may be more accurate to talk about them not so much in terms of "things as they really are," but of "things as they really *can* be" or, perhaps more normatively, "things as they really *should* be."

In any event, it should be clear that when I say that this "really" refers to an understanding of reality free from the distorting lenses of self-centeredness and dissociated spiritual cognition, I am not limiting contemplative claims to their phenomenological dimension. On the contrary, a participatory epistemology can fully explain, in a way that no Cartesian paradigm can, why most traditions consider these two dimensions of liberation (phenomenological and ontological) radically intertwined. If reality is not merely discovered but enacted through cocreative participation, and if what we bring to our inquiries affects in important ways the disclosure of reality, then the fundamental interrelationship, and even identity, between phenomenology and ontology, between knowledge and liberation, in the spiritual search stops being a conundrum and becomes a natural necessity. If this is the case, there is no conflict whatsoever for a participatory approach to maintain that there may be a plurality of spiritual ultimates disclosing "things as they really are."

A More Relaxed Spiritual Universalism

Although my participatory perspective emphasizes the metaphysical plurality of spiritual worlds, I should stress that I do not believe that either pluralism or universalism per se are spiritually or hermeneutically superior. It is now time, then, to make explicit the kind of spiritual universalism implicit in this account of spiritual knowing as participatory enaction.

There is a way, I believe, in which we can legitimately talk about a shared spiritual power, one reality, one world, or one truth. On the one hand, the discussion about whether there is one world or a multiplicity of different worlds can be seen as ultimately a semantic one, and metaphysically a pseudoproblem. On the other hand, a shared spiritual ground needs to be presupposed in order to make interreligious inquiry and dialogue possible and intelligible. After all, traditions do understand each other and frequently developed and transformed themselves through rich and varied interreligious interactions. The strict incommensurability of traditions needs to be rejected on logical, pragmatic, and historical grounds. Thus, it may be possible to talk about a common spiritual or creative dynamism underlying the plurality of religious insights and ultimates. But let us be clear here, this spiritual universalism does not say that the Tao is God, that emptiness (sunyata) is structurally equivalent to Brahman, or any other such similar, quite empty equations. And neither does it suggest the equally problematic possibility that these spiritual ultimates are different cuts, layers, or snapshots of the same pie. As I see it, the undetermined nature of the mystery cannot be adequately depicted through any univocal positive attribute, such as nondual, dual, impersonal, personal, and so forth.[63] This is why, I believe, so many Western and Eastern mystics chose the so-called via negativa or apophatic language to talk about the divine, and why such nonexperiential language was regarded by most traditions as closer to the divine than any positive statement of its qualities.[64]

A participatory spiritual universalism does not establish any a priori hierarchy of positive attributes of the mystery: Nondual insights are not necessarily higher than dual, nor are dual higher than nondual. Personal enactions are not necessarily higher than impersonal, nor are impersonal higher than personal. And so forth. Since the generative dimension of the mystery is undetermined and dynamic, spiritual qualitative distinctions cannot be made by matching our insights and conceptualizations with any pregiven or fixed features. By contrast, I suggest that qualitative distinctions among spiritual enactions can be made by not only evaluating their emancipatory power for self, relationships, and world, but also discriminating how grounded in or coherent with the ongoing unfolding of the mystery they are. Moreover, because of their unique psychospiritual dispositions, individuals and cultures may emancipate themselves better through different enactions of the mystery, and this not only paves the way for a more constructive and enriching interreligious dialogue, but also opens up the creative range of valid spiritual choices potentially available to us as individuals. In sum, this approach brings forth a more "relaxed" and fertile spiritual universalism that passionately but critically embraces (rather than reduces, conflates, or subordinates) the rich variety of ways in which the creative power of life or the spirit can be cultivated, enacted, and embodied in the world without falling into spiritual anarchies or pernicious relativisms.

The relationship between pluralism and universalism cannot be characterized consistently in a hierarchical fashion, and even less in terms of spiritual evolution. While there may be "higher" and "lower" forms of both universalism and pluralism (i.e., more or less sophisticated, encompassing, explanatory, emancipatory, grounded in the mystery, and so forth), the dialectic between universalism and pluralism, between the One and the Many, displays what may well be the deepest dynamics of the self-disclosing of the mystery. From the rigid universalism of rational consciousness to the pluralistic relativism of some early postmodern approaches, from perennialist universalism to the emerging spiritual pluralism of the interfaith dialogue, the mystery seems to swing from one to the other pole, from the One to the Many and from the Many to the One, endlessly striving to more fully manifest, embody, and embrace love and wisdom in all its forms. Newer and more embracing universalist and pluralistic visions will continue to emerge, but the everlasting dialectical movement between the One and the Many in the self-disclosing of the mystery makes any abstract or absolute hierarchical arrangement between them misleading. If we accept the generative power of the dialectical relationship between the One and the Many, then to reify either of the two poles as the Truth cannot but hinder the natural unfolding of the mystery's creative urges. This is why, although originally offered in a different context, the following remark by Jürgen Habermas seems pertinent here: "The metaphysical priority of unity above plurality and the contextualist priority of pluralism above unity are secret accomplices."[65]

CONCLUSION

In sum, the common ocean to which most spiritual traditions aspire may not be a pregiven spiritual ultimate, but the ocean of emancipation, a radical overcoming of self-centeredness that can be accompanied by a variety of transconceptual disclosures of reality. Some of these disclosures have been already enacted by the world spiritual traditions, while an indeterminate number have not yet emerged and may require a more creative participation, a cocreation with the mystery, if they are to come into being. Although there may be certain pragmatic and normative constraints on their nature, the number of feasible enactions of spiritual worlds and ultimates may be, within these boundaries, virtually limitless. This seemingly overpermissive stance, as well as the affirmation of our creative role in the participatory enaction of spiritual realities, calls for the development of a contextually sensitive but sharply critical evaluative gaze toward spiritual enactions that may not only be deficient in promoting selflessness, but also lead to subtle or gross forms of human dissociation and corresponding partial or distorted pictures of reality.

While I cannot consistently maintain the "objective" superiority of this account over others, I can highlight some of its practical advantages. First, a participatory understanding of spiritual knowing is more generous than other metaperspectives in terms of recognizing the immeasurable creativity of the mystery, contributing therefore to the actual generativity of spiritual unfolding (e.g., allowing, impelling, and catalyzing the mystery's creative urges through human embodied participation). Second, it better honors a diversity of possible equally grounded spiritual enactions than other approaches, affirming, supporting, and legitimizing the largest number of spiritual perspectives on their own terms, while encouraging the critical exploration of more holistic practices and understandings in both existing traditions and emerging forms of spirituality. Third, this participatory account provides a more fertile ground for constructively critical and mutually transformative interreligious encounters, as well as for greater respect and harmony between people holding different religious beliefs. Finally, it has emancipatory consequences for human participation in the self-disclosure of reality, for example, in terms of fostering spiritual individuation and expanding the range of viable options to cultivate, embody, and express the creative power of life or the spirit.

In a participatory cosmos, human multidimensional cognition creatively channels and modulates the self-disclosing of the mystery through the bringing forth of visionary worlds and spiritual realities. These worlds are no longer felt to have an independently objective nature but instead become relational and intersubjective realities that can unfold in a multiplicity of ways, partly depending on the human perspectives and ways of knowing involved in the act of apprehension. Spiritual inquiry then becomes a journey beyond any pregiven goal, an endless exploration and disclosure of the inexhaustible possibilities of an always dynamic and undetermined mystery.

NOTES

1. David B. Barrett, George Thomas Kurian, and Todd M. Johnson, eds., *World Christian Encyclopedia: A Comparative Survey of Churches and Religions in the Modern World*, 2 vols., 2d ed. (New York: Oxford University Press, 2001). The second edition of the encyclopedia offers the most updated and comprehensive map of religious diversity in the entire world with which I am familiar. For a more popular introduction to "the beliefs and practices of more than 200 hundred new religions" (from the

back cover), see Christopher Partridge, ed., *New Religions: A Guide. New Religious Movements, Sects, and Alternative Spiritualities* (New York: Oxford University Press, 2005).

2. Cited in Toby Lester, "Oh Gods! An Explosion of New Religions Will Shake the 21st Century," *The Atlantic Monthly* (February 2002): 28.

3. See, e.g., Richard Rorty, "Pragmatism as Romantic Polytheism," in *The Revival of Pragmatism: New Essays on Social Thought, Law, and Culture*, ed. Morris Dickstein (Durham: Duke University Press, 1998), 21–36. In the Introduction to this volume, we problematize the foundations of the modern skepticism about the cognitive value of religion.

4. See Jorge N. Ferrer, *Revisioning Transpersonal Theory: A Participatory Vision of Human Spirituality* (Albany: State University of New York Press, 2002), and "The Perennial Philosophy Revisited," *The Journal of Transpersonal Psychology* 32 (2000): 7–30.

5. On my nonessentialist understanding of the mystery, see notes 88 and 155 of the Introduction to this volume.

6. Thoroughly updated and containing new materials, this chapter draws from materials published in my book, *Revisioning Transpersonal Theory*. Either through the printed page or via personal communication, I have benefited immensely from the critical feedback of George Adams, G. William Barnard, Michel Bauwens, Sean Esbjörn-Hargens, Robert Fuller, Karen Jaenke, Sean Kelly, Jeffrey J. Kripal, David Lorimer, Bindu Mohanty, Raimon Panikkar, William Parsons, Jacob H. Sherman, Richard Tarnas, Michael Washburn, and, most especially, John Heron, who persistently pushed me to clarify a number of issues previously underdeveloped, as well as made me aware of certain unresolved tensions in my work.

7. Ferrer, *Revisioning Transpersonal Theory*, 115–31, and "Transpersonal Knowledge: A Participatory Approach to Transpersonal Phenomena," in *Transpersonal Knowing: Exploring the Horizon of Consciousness*, ed. Tobin Hart, Peter Nelson, and Kaisa Puhakka (Albany: State University of New York Press, 2000), 213–52.

8. Varela, Thompson, and Rosch, *The Embodied Mind: Cognitive Science and Human Experience* (Cambridge: The MIT Press, 1991). As pointed out in note 154 of the Introduction (this volume), I am extending the scope of the enactive approach beyond its original confinement in the realm of sensoriomotor cognition. For a summary and further refinement of the enactive paradigm, see Thompson, "The Mindful Body: Embodiment and Cognitive Science," in *The Incorporated Self: Interdisciplinary Perspectives of Embodiment*, ed. Michael O'Donovan-Anderson (Lanham, MD: Rowman and Littlefield, 1996), 127–44. For a related enactive approach to human perception of the sensoriomotor world, see Alva Nöe, *Action in Perception* (Cambridge: The MIT Press, 2004). See also Warren Frisina, *The Unity of Knowledge and Action: Toward a Nonrepresentational Theory of Knowledge* (Albany: State University of New York Press, 2002), for a lucid account of both classic and contemporary, Asian and Western, perspectives of the emerging nonrepresentational paradigm of cognition.

9. Elsewhere I propose that the transfiguration of the world typical of many spiritual perceptions should not be understood merely intrasubjectively—as an inner

individual experience—but rather as the emergence in reality of a participatory event in which human individual (multidimensional) cognition creatively participates. See *Revisioning Transpersonal Theory*, 116–20.

10. Cited in Dorothy H. Donnelly, "The Sexual Mystic: Embodied Spirituality," in *The Feminist Mystic and Other Essays on Women and Spirituality*, ed. Mary E. Giles (New York: Crossroad, 1982), 127.

11. See Donald Evans, "Two Dogmas of Skepticism Regarding Spiritual Reality," in his *Spirituality and Human Nature* (Albany: State University of New York Press, 1993), 101–23.

12. See Ferrer, *Revisioning Transpersonal Theory*, 71–111, for a taxonomy of the varieties of perennialism—basic, esotericist, structuralist, perspectivist, and typological—and discussion of their shortcomings.

13. Cf. Donald Evans: "Spirituality consists primarily of a basic transformative process in which we uncover and let go of our narcissism so as to surrender into the Mystery out of which everything continually arises" (*Spirituality and Human Nature* [Albany: State University of New York Press, 1993], 4). Though formulated within a questionable Kantian framework, John Hick also understands spiritual liberation as "the transformation of human existence from self-centeredness to Reality-centeredness" (*An Interpretation of Religion: Human Responses to the Transcendent* [New Haven: Yale University Press, 1992], 14). Similarly, Paul O. Ingram suggests that the "different conceptions of salvation or final liberation share a generic commonality: all, in their own historically and culturally specific way, are concerned with the transformation of human existence from self-centeredness to a new and mutually creative relationship with the relatively inaccessible Sacred" (*Wrestling with the Ox: A Theology of Religious Experience* [New York: Continuum, 1997], 185).

14. Furthermore, this movement away from self-centeredness can be diversely expressed through different existential stances, e.g., monasticism, contemplation, devotional service, selfless action in the world, and so forth. For a survey of some of these expressions in the major religious traditions, see Richard Kieckhefer and George D. Bond, eds., *Sainthood: Its Manifestation in World Religions* (Berkeley: University of California Press, 1988).

15. I should stress here that I am merely suggesting that this liberation from self-centeredness is an *ideal* (or aspiration) shared by virtually all contemplative traditions. Whether such an ideal is ever actualized in practice is an empirical question to be explored through both the historical study of religious communities and biographies, as well as research into the effectiveness of contemporary religious practices in fostering such transformation.

16. H. H. Dalai Lama, *The Bodhgaya Interviews*, ed. José Ignacio Cabezón (Ithaca, NY: Snow Lion, 1988), 12. As Gavin D'Costa suggests in "The Near Triumph of Tibetan Buddhist Pluralist-Exclusivism," however, there is an important tension between the Dalai Lama's spiritual ecumenism and his contention that final or complete liberation can only be achieved through the emptiness practices of his Gelukba school of Tibetan Buddhism (*The Meeting of Religions and the Trinity* [Maryknoll, NY: Orbis Books, 2000], 72–95).

17. The overcoming of self-centeredness should not be confused with the erroneous belief that liberation involves a total transcendence or annihilation of the egoic system or individual personality. As transpersonal psychologists have taken pains to stress, what is overcome in the spiritual path is not the personal identity, but the exclusive and restrictive self-identification with the construct of a separate self. See, for example, Mark Epstein, "The Deconstruction of the Self: Ego and 'Egolessness' in Buddhist Insight Meditation," *The Journal of Transpersonal Psychology* 20 (1988): 61–69.

18. Brown, "The Stages of Meditation in Cross-Cultural Perspective," in *Transformations of Consciousness: Conventional and Contemplative Perspectives on Development*, ed. Ken Wilber, Jack Engler, and Brown (Boston: Shambhala, 1986), 266–67. For a critique, see José Ignacio Cabezón, "Buddhism and Science: On the Nature of the Dialogue," in *Buddhism and Science: Breaking New Ground*, ed. B. Alan Wallace (New York: Columbia University Press, 2003), 53–54.

19. Forman, ed., *The Problem of Pure Consciousness: Mysticism and Philosophy* (New York: Oxford University Press, 1990). For contextualism in the study of mysticism, see Steven T. Katz, "Language, Epistemology, and Mysticism," in *Mysticism and Philosophical Analysis*, ed. Steven T. Katz (New York: Oxford University Press, 1978), 22–74; Robert M. Gimello, "Mysticism in Its Contexts," in *Mysticism and Religious Traditions*, ed. Steven T. Katz (New York: Oxford University Press, 1983), 61–88; John Y. Fenton, "Mystical Experience as a Bridge for Cross-Cultural Philosophy of Religion: A Critique," in *Religious Pluralism and Truth: Essays on Cross-Cultural Philosophy of Religion*, ed. Thomas Dean (Albany: State University of New York Press, 1995), 189–204; and Jess Byron Hollenback, *Mysticism: Experience, Response, and Empowerment* (University Park: Pennsylvania State University Press, 1996).

20. The idea of different spiritual salvations is compellingly articulated in S. Mark Heim's *Salvations: Truth and Difference in Religion* (Maryknoll, NY: Orbis Books, 1995). Heim's work is helpful in revealing the contradictions of other so-called "pluralistic" approaches (such as Hick's or W. C. Smith's), which nonetheless postulate an equivalent end-point for all traditions. A genuine religious pluralism, Heim rightly claims, needs to acknowledge the existence of alternative religious aims, and to put religions on a single scale will not do it: There are "many true religions . . . and each the only way" (219). Although suggesting several possibilities, Heim remains agnostic about the metaphysical vision behind his "more pluralistic hypothesis" (see, e.g., 146) and ultimately slips back to an objectivist account of spiritual truth as universal and pregiven: "Among the various religions," he tells us, "one or several or none may provide the best approximate representation of the character of that cosmos, explaining and ordering these various human possibilities within it" (215). This relapse is also evident when, after comparing the different religious ends to different cities, he writes that "I regard these cities as sites within a single world, whose global mapping has a determinate character" (220). In these statements, it becomes apparent that Heim's "more pluralistic hypothesis" is pluralistic only at a phenomenological or soteriological level (i.e., admitting different human spiritual fulfillments), but not at an ontological or metaphysical one (i.e., at the level of spiritual referents and realities).

21. Dalai Lama, *The Bodhgaya Interviews*, 23.

22. Ibid., 23–24.

23. For discussions stressing the diversity of Buddhist views about the nature of ultimate reality, see John Hopkins, "Ultimate Reality in Tibetan Buddhism," *Buddhist-Christian Studies* 8 (1988): 111–29; Francis H. Cook, "Just This: Buddhist Ultimate Reality," *Buddhist-Christian Studies* 9(1989): 127–42; and Hans Küng, "Response to Francis Cook: Is It Just This? Different Paradigms of Ultimate Reality in Buddhism," *Buddhist-Christian Studies* 9 (1989): 143–52. See also Winston L. King, "Zen as a Vipassana-Type Discipline," in *Asian Religions: History of Religions (1974 Proceedings)*, comp. Harry Partin (Tallahassee: American Academy of Religion, 1974), 62–79, for an analysis of differences between Mahayana and Theravada accounts of *nirvana*, and C. M. Chen, *The Subtle Discrimination Between the Practices of Sunyata in Hinayana, Mahayana, and Vajrayana*, trans. Mr. Jivaka (Kalinpang, India: Mani Press, 1972) for distinctions among Buddhist enactions of emptiness (*sunyata*). Of related interest is the polemical treatise by Sakya Pandita Kunga Gyaltshen, *A Clear Differentiation of the Three Codes: Essential Distinctions among the Individual Liberation, Great Vehicle, and Tantric Systems*, trans. Jared Douglas Rhoton (Albany: State University of New York Press, 2002), where the author highlights the differences between the various Buddhist vows and systems of discipline in order to show the superiority of the Vajrayana lineages for attaining supreme liberation. For a general introduction to some of the controversies among Buddhist schools regarding the substantiality of ultimate reality, see M. R. Chinchore, *Anatta/Anatmata: An Analysis of the Buddhist Anti-Substantialist Crusade* (Delhi: Sri Satguru Publications, 1995).

24. Vroom, *Religions and the Truth: Philosophical Reflections and Perspectives* (Grand Rapids: Eerdmans, 1989), 382–83. For a more detailed exploration of the merits of a multicentered account of interreligious relations, see Frank J. Hoffman, "The Concept of Focal Point in Models for Inter-Religious Understanding," in *Inter-Religious Models and Criteria*, ed. Jürgen Kellenberger (New York: St. Martin's, 1993), 166–84.

25. Roughly, these comparisons can lead to the identification of at least four types of equivalencies: (1) *cognitive*, or common beliefs, doctrines, or ethical guidelines, e.g., belief in reincarnation or the Golden Rule; (2) *functional*, or spiritual doctrines, notions, or practices that, while having different meanings, play an analogous role in two or more religious traditions, e.g, *qi* and soul as mediators between body and spirit in Taoism and Christianity; (3) *homoversal*, or human invariants or universal truths for the human species, e.g., in relation to waking, dreaming, and dreamless sleep states of consciousness; and (4) *ontological*, or overlapping elements in different participatory enactions of ultimate reality, e.g., mystical union with a personal God in Judaism, Christianity, and Islam.

26. Varela, Thompson, and Rosch, *The Embodied Mind*, p 195.

27. A promising starting point can be found in Hans Küng and Karl-Josef Kuschel, eds., *A Global Ethic: The Declaration of the Parliament of the World's Religions* (New York: Continuum, 1993). For a plea for the need of interfaith dialogue in the search for a global ethic, see Küng, *Global Responsibility: In Search for a New World Ethic* (New York: Crossroad, 1991), and for two lucid papers pointing out some of the pitfalls and difficulties involved in the establishment of a global ethic, see Sally King, "It's a Long Way to a Global Ethic: A Response to Leonard Swidler," *Buddhist-Christ-*

ian Studies 15 (1995): 213–19, and Paul F. Knitter, "Pitfalls and Promises for a Global Ethics," *Buddhist-Christian Studies* 15 (1995): 221–29.

28. I am indebted to Kripal, "In the Spirit of Hermes: Reflections on the Work of Jorge N. Ferrer," *Tikkun: Politics, Spirituality, Culture* 18 (2003): 67–70, for kindly challenging the residual "moral perennialism" insinuated in my previous work. For an outstanding collection of essays exploring the ethical status of religion and mysticism, see Barnard and Kripal, eds., *Crossing Boundaries: Essays on the Ethical Status of Mysticism* (New York: Seven Bridges Press, 2002).

29. Perhaps nobody has pursued farther the spiritual implications of the interpenetration of the human, the cosmos, and the mystery than Raimon Panikkar, especially in *The Cosmotheandric Experience: Emerging Religious Consciousness*, ed. with intro. Scott Eastham (Maryknoll, NY: Orbis Books, 1993). See also Jyri Komulainen, *An Emerging Cosmotheandric Religion?: Raimon Panikkar's Pluralistic Theology of Religions* (Leiden: E. J. Brill, 2005).

30. According to Moshe Idel, in Jewish mysticism, "the term *theurgy*, or *theurgical* . . . refer[s] to operations intended to influence the Divinity, mostly in its own inner state or operations, but sometimes also in its relationship to man" (*Kabbalah: New Perspectives* [New Haven: Yale University Press, 1988], 157). Kabbalistic theurgy should be distinguished from the different meanings of this term in Christian and neo-Platonic mysticism, as, for example, in the writings of Dionysius the Areopagite. For accounts of theurgical practices in these traditions, see E. R. Dodds, *The Greeks and the Irrational* (Berkeley: University of California Press, 1951), 283–311, and R. A. Norris, "Theurgy," in *The Encyclopedia of Religion, Vol. 14*, ed. Mircea Eliade (New York: MacMillan, 1987), 481–83. Interestingly, Idel explains how the theurgical aspect of the Kabbalah was lost and transformed into *gnosis* by the Renaissance Christian Kabbalists (260–64), which suggests a shift from a more reciprocal and participatory relationship with a dynamic divinity to a more unilateral and passive knowledge or vision of an immutable and pregiven God. In other words, this is a shift from an "open" divinity to a "closed" one; a transformation of a divine "Thou" into a divine "It" or immutable "He." For a participatory account of Jewish mysticism, see Brian L. Lancaster's essay (this volume).

31. Idel, *Kabbalah*, 181.

32. Dupré, "Unio Mystica: The State and the Experience," in *Mystical Union in Judaism, Christianity, and Islam: An Ecumenical Dialogue*, ed. Idel and McGinn (New York: Continuum, 1996), 3–23; McGinn, "Comments," in *Mystical Union in Judaism, Christianity, and Islam*, 185–93.

33. Dupré, "Unio Mystica," 17.

34. Ibid., 20.

35. Ibid., 22. Dupré is referring here to the idea that human love can transform God himself.

36. If one accepts an afterlife scenario in which personal identity is somehow maintained, it becomes feasible to contemplate the possibility of nonconstructed entities such as deceased saints, *bodhisattvas*, ascended masters, and the like.

37. Although Advaita Vedanta generally considers theism (*saguna Brahman*) as a lower level of understanding, Sankara did not offer a hierarchical gradation of spiritual systems. In contrast to the more inclusivistic projects of Kumarila, Bhartrhari, and most neo-Hindu thinkers, Sankara simply rejects as false, in his *Brahamasutrabhasya* for example, most other systems and philosophies, such as Samkhya, Yoga, and Buddhism. Since these systems are not based on the Vedic revelation, Sankara argues, they are unable to convey any truth whatsoever about the nature of ultimate reality. In this account, see Wilhelm Halbfass, "Vedic Orthodoxy and the Plurality of Religious Traditions," in *Tradition and Reflection: Explorations in Indian Thought* (Albany: State University of New York Press, 1991), 51–85. Ramanuja's words are cited in Robert C. Zaehner, *Hindu and Muslim Mysticism* (1960; reprint, Rockport, MA: Oneworld Publications, 1994), 63. For Ramanuja's attack on Advaita Vedanta, see George Thibaut, trans., *The Vedanta Sutras with the Commentary of Ramanuja. Vol. 48, Sacred Books of the East* (Oxford: Clarendon Press, 1904), 33–37.

38. Halbfass, "Vedic Orthodoxy," 56; Halbfass, *India and Europe: An Essay in Understanding* (Albany: State University of New York Press, 1988), 415.

39. For a critical analysis of spiritual gradations in neo-Hinduism, see Halbfass, "'Inclusivism' and 'Tolerance' in the Encounter between India and the West," in *India and Europe*, 403–18.

40. Buswell and Gimello, "Introduction," in *Paths to Liberation: The Marga and Its Transformations in Buddhist Thought*, ed. Buswell and Gimello (Honolulu: University of Hawaii Press, 1992), 1–36.

41. Cf. Anne Klein: "In Tibet, the four major systems of Buddhist tenets [Vaibhasika, Sautrantika, Cittamara, and Madhyamika] are ranked according to the subtlety with which they identify and rectify the various forms of ignorance considered to prevent liberation and omniscience" (*Knowledge and Liberation: Tibetan Buddhist Epistemology in Support of Transformative Religious Experience* [Ithaca: Snow Lion Publications, 1986], 19). Nevertheless, given the multifarious historical, cultural, and experiential contingencies in the development of these Buddhist schools, insights, and understandings, the suggestion of a continuum of spiritual progress across the Buddhist vehicles appears unwarranted. I am not saying that there cannot be deeper understandings or higher truths in spiritual matters, but to put the various Buddhist vehicles in a continuum of spiritual progress strikes me as an apologetic move spurred by the endorsement of one school over others.

42. See Thomas P. Kasulis, "Truth Words: The Basis of Kukai's Theory of Interpretation," in *Buddhist Hermeneutics*, ed. Donald S. Lopez Jr. (Honolulu: University of Hawaii Press, 1988), 257–72.

43. Buswell and Gimello, "Introduction," 20.

44. Wilber, *Sex. Ecology, Spirituality: The Spirit of Evolution* (Boston: Shambhala, 1995), 279–316; Stoeber, *Theo-Monistic Mysticism: A Hindu-Christian Comparison* (New York: St. Martin's, 1994). There are many precedents to Stoeber's position in Western Religious Studies. To mention two well-known examples, Martin Buber regards the I/Thou relationship with God as spiritually higher than the monistic experience of nonduality (*Between Man and Man* [London: Collins, 1961]), and Zaehner

argues that the monistic ideal is transcended in theistic mysticism, considering Sankara's monistic liberation (*moksa*) a primitive stage in the process of deification (*Mysticism Sacred and Profane: An Inquiry into Some Varieties of Preternatural Experience* [New York: Oxford University Press, 1957]). More recently, Wilber's ranking of nondual mysticism over theism and other contemplative paths has been critiqued and rebutted by Daniel A. Helminiak in *Religion and the Human Sciences* (Albany: State University of New York Press, 1998), 213–92; George Adams, "A Theistic Perspective on Ken Wilber's Transpersonal Psychology," *Journal of Contemporary Religion* 17 (2002): 165–79; and, perhaps most effectively, by Leon Schlamm, "Ken Wilber's Spectrum Model: Identifying Alternative Soteriological Perspectives," *Religion* 31 (2001): 19–39, who uses Andrew Rawlinson's nuanced taxonomy of mystical traditions to show the arbitrariness and doctrinal nature of such rankings. On the shortcomings of Wilber's nondual neoperennialism, see also Ferrer, *Revisioning Transpersonal Theory*, 95–105.

45. Stoeber, *Theo-Monistic Mysticism*, 17–18.

46. See, e.g., W. A. Christian, *Oppositions of Religious Doctrines: A Study in the Logic of Dialogue among Religions* (New York: Herder and Herder, 1972); Paul J. Griffiths, *An Apology for Apologetics: A Study in the Logic of Interreligious Dialogue* (New York: Orbis Books, 1991); and Hick, "On Conflicting Religious Truth-Claims," *Religious Studies* 19 (1983): 485–91.

47. For a concise overview of these three basic models of interreligious relations (exclusivism, inclusivism, and pluralism) in the context of Christian attitudes toward other religions, see D'Costa, *Theology and Religious Pluralism: The Challenge of Other Religions* (New York: Basil Blackwell, 1986). See also Hick and Knitter, eds., *The Myth of Christian Uniqueness* (Maryknoll, NY: Orbis Books, 1987) for a representative defense of ecumenical pluralism and critique of exclusivism and inclusivism, and D'Costa, ed., *Christian Uniqueness Reconsidered: The Myth of a Pluralistic Theology of Religions* (Maryknoll, NY: Orbis Books, 1990) for various critiques of ecumenical pluralism and suggestions of "more" pluralistic attitudes toward interreligious relations. A compelling critique of ecumenical pluralism can also be found in Heim's *Salvations*. For a survey of the varieties of religious pluralism, see Keith E. Yandell, "Some Varieties of Religious Pluralism," in *Inter-Religious Models and Criteria*, 187–211.

48. My discussion of the "problem of conflicting truth claims" is limited to religious *ultimate* claims, that is, about the nature of reality, spiritual ultimates, the divine, and so forth. It should be obvious that religions make other kind of truth claims (e.g., empirical, transempirical, historical, mythical, etc.), which may be not only in real conflict with each other, but also be potentially true or false (e.g., certain supernatural events, reincarnation theories, stories of creation, eschatologies, etc.). For valuable discussions about the assessment of cross-cultural religious truth claims, see Dean, *Religious Pluralism and Truth*, and Vroom, *Religions and the Truth*. Also see Robert Cummings Neville, ed., *Religious Truth. A Volume in the Comparative Religious Ideas Project* (Albany: State University of New York Press, 2001) for an important comparative analysis of the nature of religious truth.

49. Heim suggests the possibility of postulating a plurality of noumenal realities to which the different traditions are geared (*Salvations*, 146). This hypothesis, however,

unnecessarily perpetuates, and even multiplies, the dubious Kantian two worlds doctrine. For a classic critique of Kantian dualism, see G. Schrader, "The Thing in Itself in Kantian Philosophy," in *Kant: A Collection of Critical Essays*, ed. R. D. Wolff (Garden City, NY: Anchor Books, 1967), 172–88.

50. By the "*potential* integrity of each tradition in its own right" I mean to suggest that every spiritual tradition, even those traditionally promulgating arguably dissociative (or unilaterally transcendentalist, disembodied, and/or world-denying) doctrines and practices can be creatively (and legitimately, I would argue) reenvisioned from the perspective of more holistic understandings and embodied ways of knowing. Ian Whicher's reinterpretation of Patanjali's dualistic system of classical yoga—whose aim was the self-identification with a pure consciousness (*purusa*) isolated (*kaivalyam*) from all possible physical or mental contents (*prakrti*)—offers an excellent example of such hermeneutic possibilities. In his own words: "Contrary to the argument presented by many scholars, which associate Patanjali's Yoga exclusively with extreme asceticism, mortification, denial, and the renunciation and abandonment of 'material existence' (*prakrti*) in favor of an elevated and isolated 'spiritual state' (*purusa*) or disembodied state of spiritual liberation, I suggest that Patanjali's Yoga can be seen as a responsible engagement, in various ways, of 'spirit' (*purusa* = Self, pure consciousness) and 'matter' (*prakrti* = the source of psychophysiological being, which includes mind, body, nature), resulting in a highly developed, transformed, and participatory human nature and identity, an integrated and embodied state of liberated selfhood (*jivanmukti*)." "The liberated state of 'aloneness' (*kaivalya*)," he adds, "need not to denote either an ontological superiority of *purusa* or an exclusion of *prakrti*. *Kaivalya* can be positively construed as an integration of both principles. . . ." Though Whicher presents this account in a questionable exegetical fashion (i.e., seeking to ground it on textual evidence), he concludes alluding to the implicit creative (or isogetical) hermeneutic approach inevitably at play in these type of modern reconstructions: "[A]n open ended, morally and epistemologically oriented hermeneutic . . . frees Yoga of the long-standing conception of spiritual isolation, disembodiment, self-denial, and world negation" ("Yoga and Freedom: A Reconsideration of Patanjali's Classical Yoga," *Philosophy East & West* 48 [1998]: 272, 299, 303.). As should be obvious, similar reconstructions are carried out today in the context of many other religious traditions, from Christianity to Buddhism to Hindu tantrism and to Taoism.

51. The idea of "mutual transformation" as the goal of interreligious encounters is forcefully articulated by Frederick J. Streng, "Mutual Transformation: An Answer to a Religious Question," *Buddhist Christian Studies* 13 (1993): 121–26; see also Ingram and Streng, eds., *Buddhist-Christian Dialogue: Mutual Renewal and Transformation* (Honolulu: University of Hawaii Press, 1986). From the perspective of process theology, John B. Cobb Jr. offers an approach to interreligious relations that celebrates the uniqueness of each tradition while urging their openness to positive transformation out of the encounter with others, a stance that he describes as "mutual openness leading to mutual transformation" ("Metaphysical Pluralism," in *The Intercultural Challenge of Raimon Panikkar*, ed. Joseph Prabhu [Maryknoll, NY: Orbis Books, 1996], 55).

52. Irwin, *Visionary Worlds: The Making and Unmaking of Reality* (Albany: State University of New York Press, 1996), 34.

53. Panikkar, "Religious Pluralism: The Metaphysical Challenge," in *Religious Pluralism*, ed. Leroy S. Rouner (Notre Dame: University of Notre Dame Press, 1984), 110. For an excellent *Festschrift* on Panikkar's work, see Prabhu, *The Intercultural Challenge of Raimon Panikkar*.

54. This account of spiritual knowing is consistent, I believe, with William James's pragmatist epistemology and pluralist metaphysics. Although not without tensions and ambiguities, James's work generally rejects the view of a pregiven reality and, contrary to widespread belief, insists on the irreducible diversity of mystical claims. In his late and often ignored essay, "A Pluralistic Mystic," James stresses that "I feel now as if my own pluralism were not without the kind of support which mystical corroboration may confer. Monism can no longer claim to be the only beneficiary of whatever right mysticism may possess to lend *prestige*" (cited in Barnard, *Exploring Unseen Worlds: William James and the Philosophy of Mysticism* [Albany: State University of New York Press, 1997] 31). And he adds: "The monistic notion of oneness, a centred wholeness, ultimate purpose, or climateric result of the world, has wholly given way. Thought evolves no longer a centred whole, a One, but rather a numberless many" (cited in Barnard, *Exploring Unseen Worlds*, 31).

55. Buswell and Gimello, *Paths to Liberation*, 4.

56. For references, see Ferrer and Jacob H. Sherman, "Introduction," note 184 (this volume).

57. It is probably sensible to supplement these orientations with not only a sharp cultural and contextual sensitivity, but also what we might call the *retrospective test*, which alludes to the likely need—at least in certain cases—of allowing the pass of time before assessing the actual fruits of specific spiritual paths and insights. This seems crucial, especially in light of certain dynamics of psychospiritual development, for example, in cases in which—due to either biographical factors or intrinsic features of certain processes of spiritual opening—states or stages of self-inflation or even extreme dissociation may be a necessary step in the path toward a genuinely integrated selflessness. For relevant discussions, see A. H Almaas, *The Point of Existence: Transformations of Narcissism in Self-Realization* (Berkeley: Diamond Books, 1996); Gary Rosenthal, "Inflated by the Spirit," in *Spiritual Choices: The Problem of Recognizing Authentic Paths to Inner Transformation*, ed. Dick Anthony, Bruce Ecker, and Ken Wilber (New York: Paragon House, 1987), 305–23; Michael Washburn, *The Ego and the Dynamic Ground: A Transpersonal Theory of Human Development*, 2d ed. (Albany: State University of New York Press, 1995). I am indebted to Washburn (personal communication) for this important qualification.

58. Cf. Jürgen Habermas: "One society may be superior to another with reference to the level of differentiation of its economic or administrative system, or with reference to technologies and legal institutions. But it does not follow that we are entitled to value this society more highly *as a whole*, as concrete totality, as a form of life" (in *Autonomy and Solidarity: Interviews with Jürgen Habermas*, ed. Peter Dews [London: New Left Books, 1986], 169; emphasis in original). Also see Bernard McGrane's reflections on the "trivialization of the encounter with the Other" resulting from overlooking or denying potential qualitative distinctions in cross-cultural encounters (*Beyond Anthropology: Society and the Other* [New York: Columbia University Press, 1989], 113–29).

59. Cf. Dalai Lama, *The Bodhgaya Interviews*, 38–39. As D'Costa points out, however, the Dalai Lama's psychological rationale for religious pluralism is undermined by his claims for the ultimately exclusive superiority of his own school of Tibetan Buddhism in achieving complete liberation ("The Near Triumph of Tibetan Buddhist Pluralist-Exclusivism").

60. See, for example, C. Beena, *Personality Typologies: A Comparison of Western and Ancient Indian Approaches* (New Delhi: Commonwealth Publishers, 1990); Huston Smith, "Spiritual Personality Types: The Sacred Spectrum," in *In Quest of the Sacred: The Modern World in the Light of Tradition*, ed. Seyyed Hossein Nasr and Katherine O'Brien (Oakton, VA: Foundation for Traditional Studies, 1994), 45–57.

61. For an extended discussion, see Ferrer, "Embodied Spirituality: Now and Then," *Tikkun: Politics, Spirituality, Culture* 21 (2006): 41–45, 63–64. Nevertheless, it may be important to avoid here falling into what Owen Barfield calls a "chronological snobbery" that excoriates past spiritualities as deficient when considered from the perspective of our present standards (cited by C. S. Lewis in *Surprised by Joy: The Shape of My Early Life* [Harvest Books: London, 1966], 205.). It should be clear that many, though by no means all, past dissociative spiritual trends may have been appropriate or perhaps even necessary at different historical and cultural contexts.

62. For example, see Panikkar, "Religious Pluralism," 102–103; James B. Wiggins, *In Praise of Religious Diversity* (New York: Routledge, 1996), 15–20.

63. I should stress here that the denial of pregiven attributes is not equivalent to constructing a positive theory about the mystery, which could then be hierarchically posited as superior to other views. Actually, one of my goals has been precisely to question universalist and objectivist assumptions about the existence of a pregiven spiritual ultimate. To interpret this denial as a self-refuting positive theory is both fallacious and question-begging. In other words, the possible self-contradictory nature of the participatory vision only emerges when it is judged by standards only appropriate in an absolutist or objectivist domain of discourse.

Similarly, my use of the term *undetermined* to qualify the mystery is mostly performative—that is, to evoke the sense of not-knowing and intellectual humility that I find most fruitful and appropriate in approaching the creative power of life and reality that is the source of our being. Rather than affirming negatively (as the term *indeterminate* does), "undetermined" leaves open the possibility of both determinacy and indeterminacy within the mystery (as well as the paradoxical confluence or even identity of these two apparent polar accounts), simply suggesting that the genuinely creative qualities of the mystery cannot be determined a priori, at least until they undergo a process of multidimensional transformation (in body, vital world, heart, and mind) and subsequent manifestation in the light of our consciousness and/or the rich texture of our actions. Once this said, I suggest that the affirmation of *genuine* creativity in the mystery—as well as the affirmation of genuine creativity in the mystery as it unfolds in and through intrapersonal, interpersonal, and transpersonal human enactions—may be more consistent with hypothesizing radical indeterminacy at the core of its generative motor.

64. For two discussions of the problems of using the term *experience* in apophatic mysticism, see Thomas A. Carlson, *Indiscretion: Finitude and the Naming of God*

(Chicago: The University of Chicago Press, 1999) and Denys Turner, *The Darkness of God: Negativity in Christian Mysticism* (New York: Cambridge University Press, 1995). According to Carlson, "the mystical moment can in fact *not* be articulated in terms of categories of what we commonly know and express as experience" (256–257) because "at the very heart of mystical experience there can lie a certain 'nonexperience,' a certain 'impossibility' of experience for the subject of experience" (262). Similarly, for Turner, mystical apophasis is concerned not with an "experience of absence" but with an "absence of experience" (264). Turner´s work is especially helpful in showing the problems of the modern "experientialist" account of mysticism in referring to the message of most Christian medieval mystics. Turner argues that what characterizes most medieval mystics (from Eckhart to the author of *The Cloud of Unknowing* and even to St. John of the Cross) is precisely both a forceful rejection of the "mystical experience" as the means to and location of the union with God, and a severe critique of such distorting "experientialisation" of the mystical path. In contrast to the search for the mystical through the cultivation of special inner experiences, the medieval mind thought of the mystical as "an exoteric dynamic *within* the ordinary, as being the negative dialectic *of* the ordinary" (268). "Experientalism," Turner concludes, "is, in short, the 'positivism' of Christian spirituality. It abhors the experiential vacuum of the apophatic, rushing in to fill it with the plenum of the psychologistic" (259).

65. Habermas, *Postmetaphysical Thinking: Philosophical Essays*, trans. William Mark Hohengarten (Cambridge: The MIT Press, 1992), 116–17.

PART II

Surveying the Traditions:
Participatory Engagements

FOUR

Engaging with the Mind of God

The Participatory Path of Jewish Mysticism

———————————

Brian L. Lancaster

When Moses ascended on high [to receive the Torah], the ministering angels said before the Holy One, blessed be He, "Master of the Universe! What business has one born of woman amongst us?" God answered them: "He has come to receive the Torah." They said to Him, "That secret treasure, which has been hidden by You for 974 generations before the world was created, You desire to give to flesh and blood! Does Scripture not say 'What is man, that You should be mindful of him, and the son of man, that you would visit him? Lord our Master, How excellent is Your name in all the earth; Your glory [the Torah] is set upon the Heavens!' (*Psalm* 8:5, 2)." The Holy One, blessed be He, said to Moses, "Return them an answer!"

—Babylonian Talmud, *Shabbat*

IT IS THE WAY of the Talmud to bring key teachings to life through narrative enactment. In the above, we can almost hear the angels screeching at God: "Are you crazy? Your Torah, this ultimate essence of all that is magical and secret in the Cosmos, you intend to release it into the lowly sphere of humankind? Might we humbly suggest that, at the very least, You need Your head examining?!" The principal teaching comes in God's choice of Moses to answer. Why could God not answer them Himself? No, it is "the man Moses" (to obliquely quote Freud) who must answer. The very essence of the path of

Torah is *participatory*; and there can be no fulfillment of its spiritual challenge without embodying its principles in the everyday life of humans. The answer elaborated by Moses in the *exoteric* reading of the continuation of the above extract stresses the relevance of the words of Torah to life *on earth*; it is a teaching for a way of life through which the physical becomes imbued with the sacred. But there is much more to this seemingly simple Talmudic story, for, at the *esoteric* level, it hints at a teaching that becomes the essence of Kabbalah. God, as it were, seeks a partnership in achieving the aims inherent in the process of creation, a partnership that can be effective only if it includes humankind; the angels cannot fulfill this role. The mystical path within Judaism teaches the methods for engaging with the deepest roots of creation, through which we may achieve the higher states necessary to fulfill our side of the partnership.

A further detail of the Talmudic story is enlightening in this context. God instructs Moses to "hold on to the Throne of Glory" while answering the angels. The Throne of Glory depicts God's immanence; it symbolizes His move to enter into a dynamic relationship with created realms. The image of Moses holding on to that heavenly throne while drawing the Torah down for humankind precisely depicts the unitive role to which the mystic aspires. In pursuing the deepest path of Torah, the kabbalist becomes a bridge between earth and heaven.

This bridge is two-way. The participatory path of Jewish mysticism is symbolized by a traditional motif that holds that the image of the biblical Jacob is engraved on the Throne of Glory.[1] Jacob is both "above"—in heaven—*and* "below"—on earth; indeed it is Jacob that seeds the central kabbalistic tenet that actions in the lower, earthly realm engender parallel enactments in the higher, heavenly realm and, ultimately, in the Godhead. I shall discuss this *theurgic* principle further below, for it is the kernel of the logic of participation as promoted by Jewish mystical teachings. In the daring kabbalistic "myth" that underpins theurgy,[2] God requires human participation in order, as it were, to promote His own wholeness. Jacob is the lynchpin of this myth, for he is the glyph of wholeness, the "perfect being" epitomizing the mystical encounter with God. In the biblical narrative, Jacob's status is confirmed when he prevails against a mysterious adversary in an archetypal "dark night" encounter: "Your name shall no longer be called Jacob, but *Israel*; for as a prince you have power with God and with men, and have prevailed" (*Genesis* 32:28). Linguistically, the name *Israel* alludes not only to princedom but also to the concept of *uprightness* [*with*] *God*. This uprightness implies both integrity and the ability to bridge lower and higher realms.

It is for this reason that, to quote another foundational rabbinic teaching, "Jacob did not die."[3] Jacob lives because "he" is the very principle of unification that lives on through all mystical quests to achieve perfection and harmony in the created order:

Jacob arranged his [twelve] sons around the *Shekhinah*,[4] thereby achieving the perfection of all. . . . Then the sun was gathered together with the moon and the east drew near to the west, as it is written, "he gathered his feet to the bed" (*Genesis* 49:33). The moon was illumined and attained perfection. Certainly, therefore, as we traditionally learn, "Jacob our father did not die." When Jacob saw such perfection as had never been vouchsafed to any other man, he rejoiced and praised The Holy One, blessed be He.[5]

Another tradition surrounding Jacob complements the above, for Jacob is said to have achieved quasi-divine status (and therefore, mythically transcends mortality). The *Midrash* states that Jacob said to God: "You are God in relation to the higher beings and I am god in relation to the lower beings."[6] The interpenetration of higher and lower, the core imperative to kabbalistic participation, becomes crystallized in this portrayal of a divine core within the perfected human.

My goal in this chapter is twofold. Firstly, as should be evident from these opening words, rabbinic and kabbalistic teachings strongly reinforce the "participatory turn" in spirituality. By examining the view of the Divine and the work of creation conveyed in these teachings, I shall uncover the vision that Judaism can bring to the way we understand the meaning of participatory spirituality. Secondly, I shall consider the kabbalistic myth more broadly in the context of contemporary consciousness studies and transpersonal theory. This, in turn, will raise questions about Kabbalah in the twenty-first century. What may be the implications of a participatory approach that transcends the particularities of given traditions? In short, how do we move forward in our understanding of kabbalistic insights in relation to contemporary psychological and scientific knowledge?

PARTNERS IN CREATION

In the beginning—that is, before even the beginning of manifestation as depicted in the biblical creation story—God's partner was the Torah: "I [the Torah][7] was with Him as a confidant, and I was His delight day by day, playing before Him all the time" (*Proverbs* 8:30). The Hebrew for "delight," *sha'ashu'a*, conveys a primal eroticism that initiates the spark of creation.[8] The sixteenth-century kabbalist, Israel Sarug writes:

> He took delight [in Himself] for He is like water or fire that shakes when the wind blows upon it, and it shines like lightening to the eyes, and glistens hither and thither. Thus Ein-Sof[9] shook in Himself and He shone and sparkled from within Himself to Himself, and that shaking is called delight. . . . Know that from this delight there arose the engraving . . . and this engraving is the light, i.e., the Torah that is born from the delight.[10]

The Torah is the core mystery of Judaism. In concrete terms it is a scroll comprising the "Five Books of Moses." Yet, as will be evident from the above, the term plunges into a deeper connotation whereby ontologically it is the primal disclosure of reality, the "world soul." The nonsubstantial nature of this primordial Torah is conveyed in the image of its being composed of fiery letters: it is a Torah of "black fire on white fire." Its six hundred thousand letters are said to comprise the name of God, the primary unfolding of the essence of His Being. The primordial Torah is a resonant mirror of the divine: "The Holy One, blessed be He, is called 'Torah' . . . and Torah is nothing but the Holy One, blessed be He."[11] *Sha'ashu'a* depicts both the autoerotic delight that initially gives rise to this primordial Torah, and the continuing delight that arises through the play between God and His primal creation.

Yet the golden period of this "play" between God and Torah seemingly comes to an end. In its consideration of *sha'ashu'a*, the early kabbalistic work, the *Bahir*, states that: "The Torah said, 'For two thousand years I was delighting in His lap.'"[12] These two thousand years are, symbolically, the period prior to the opening of manifest creation. Does the *sha'ashu'a* cease when there is a further disclosure of reality in God's creation of the *sefirotic* order?[13] If we follow the cryptic allusions so characteristic of kabbalistic writings, we shall find that it does not. The severing of the intimate dialectic between God and Torah is the price God pays, as it were, for His furtherance of creation. From that point onward, the dialectic requires a mediator. Humankind is the goal of creation, and it is, accordingly, humans who are called upon to take responsibility for the continuation of the *sha'ashu'a* that pleasures the divine. We become partners in that creative play that was initially the preserve of God and His Torah alone.

Having stated that the *sha'ashu'a* between God and Torah lasted two thousand years, the *Bahir* goes on to indicate that such delight may reappear intermittently or perhaps "forever," citing two biblical phrases in support: "[For My name's sake, I shall defer my anger, and] for My praise I shall refrain for you" (*Isaiah* 48:9), and "A praise of David; I shall raise You" (*Psalm* 145:1). The first verse takes on a distinctive meaning in kabbalistic tradition on account of etymological links in the Hebrew between the word for "nose" and those in this verse translated as "defer anger" and "refrain." The reference then is to God breathing from His inner merciful nature into creation. The second verse implies the return breath, as it were. God is "raised" by human praise. It is this two-way rapport that kabbalistic teaching emphasizes. The intended meaning of the whole passage in the *Bahir* seems to be that *sha'ashu'a* returns through humans reflecting back to God the impulse He engendered into creation. While the Torah was the primal mirror, humankind becomes the subsequent mirror whereby the divine derives pleasure.

The reciprocity conveyed in the symbolism of God's "breath," whereby His inbreath is mediated via human consciousness, was intimated in the name that God revealed to Moses in the biblical book of *Exodus*. God replies to Moses' question as to the name that he should convey to the Children of Israel, "*Ehyeh asher Ehyeh*" (*Exodus* 3:9), a name perhaps best translated as "I am becoming that which I am becoming." The word *Ehyeh* is repeated, implying a reciprocal "becomingness," as it were. God initiates a process that eventuates in a need for humans to return an impulse in order that the circuit might be completed. In the *Zohar*'s understanding of this name, the repetition implies sexual union:

> The secret of the matter is thus: "*Ehyeh*" includes the totality of all [in potential] since the paths [that will unfold into creation] are as yet hidden and not separated out, being gathered in one place. Therefore is it called [by the single word] "*Ehyeh*," the totality of all—hidden and not revealed. Once the beginning had emerged from it, and the river became impregnated in order that it might produce everything, then it is called "*asher Ehyeh*" . . . to produce and give birth to everything. . . . "*Asher*"[14] refers to joining in pleasure—the supernal union.[15]

To explain: the single word *Ehyeh* implies a nongendered Source that emanates a male principle, referred to as "the beginning," and a female principle, "the river" (also known as the supernal father and mother). The subsequent union between these two reflects the initial oneness of the Source (i.e., "*asher Ehyeh*" reflects "*Ehyeh*") and brings about the further unfolding of creation.

The principle of relationship is present in potential in the nongendered Source, and gives rise not only to this supernal union, but also subsequently to a "lower union" in the emanated structure of creation. In the mythic framework of the *Zohar*, the union of the supernal father and mother generates a "son" who achieves his intended goal when, as "king" of the lower realm of creation (symbolized by the biblical Jacob, as discussed above), he unites with his "queen": "At that moment the son inherits the portion of his father and mother and he delights in that pleasure and luxury. . . . Then blessings are bestowed upon all the worlds and the upper and the lower realms are blessed."[16]

Crucially for my purposes in this chapter, the depiction of the unfolding of creation is not one-way. The lower union is viewed as dependent on human action, implying that we carry responsibilities for the perfecting of that intention that initially sparked an arising of the creative urge in the nongendered Source. In a representative version of this imperative, the *Zohar* asserts that a person should study Torah at night "in order that the holy name should be perfected by him."[17] In the symbolism of the ineffable four-letter name of God (transliterated as Y-H-V-H),[18] the perfection of the name comes about through the union of the final two letters, "V" and "H."

The symbolism in kabbalistic narrative needs considerable unpacking, for there is a danger of dwelling on the pointing finger instead of seeking out the intended meaning. The sexual symbolism involving "higher" and "lower" unions is equally present in the divine name, *Y-H-V-H*. Grammatically, the first letter, "Y," conveys the male form, whilst the second letter, "H," depicts the female. These two are, then, conjoined in the divine name. The letter "V" indicates the son/king and the final "H" is the "lower" feminine, the *Shekhinah*. Unlike the union between the supernal male and female, that between the son/king and his consort is fraught with tension. According to Kabbalah, the higher union is an inevitable consequence of the initial will to create that arose within the nongendered Source; there can be no loss of this union without a catastrophic destruction of the entire created order. The lower union, by comparison, is hindered by a distanced rapport between the two partners. The human role is, then, to bring these two partners together, to promote the union of that which the letters "V" and "H" symbolize in the Godhead. This human role is indicated by a frequently-repeated invocation to be recited privately before prayer and/or ritual observance: "[I engage in this activity] for the sake of the union of The Holy One, blessed be He, with His *Shekhinah*."

As noted above, study of the Torah is considered instrumental in promoting this desired union among the lower emanations in the Godhead. In this context, a second meaning of the Hebrew, *sha'ashu'a*, is instructive. Earlier, I emphasized the erotic connotations of this word in terms of the delight accompanying creative play. The second meaning is "contemplation,"[19] which more overtly relates to Torah study.[20] Indeed, the biblical connotation of the word *know* to mean a sexual encounter ("And Adam knew Eve his wife . . .") prefigures the conjunction of the two meanings. In rabbinic and kabbalistic thought, the complex of "cognition-delight" is transposed to the idea of developing a deep, and ultimately mystical, encounter with the Torah. Given the view of Torah as the primary disclosure of the Real, the central imperative in Judaism—to study the Torah—takes on cosmic proportions. It is as if the shattering of the blissful primordial rapport between God and his Torah might be overcome only when a new rapport is established, this time between man and Torah. The loss of one source of *sha'ashu'a* is replaced by the growth of a second, for, according to Jewish mystical teaching, contemplation of Torah is the necessary path toward realization of the divine essence of mind. The delight to be gained through human contemplation of the Torah is ultimately the mystical rapture of uniting with the Divine (for the Torah is identified with God).[21] Through human involvement in this way with His Torah, God once again experiences delight, this time through human agency.

The participatory implications of the kabbalistic narrative are powerful. From the very inception of that process of creation that the nongendered Source set in motion, there arose an *inevitable* need for relationship, for a partner. *Sha'ashu'a* might be thought of as the erotic rapture of the Source in

Its realization that a source cannot actually be a "source" unless it becomes something other than itself. *Sha'ashu'a* is reawakened when the "other" strives to reunite with its source. Indeed, *otherness* is the crucial second pole in this participatory kabbalistic understanding of creation.

EXILE AND REDEMPTION

The idea of a primordial inception of creation that precedes any manifestation of the biblical "days of creation" is conveyed by the Hebrew term, *tsimtsum*, "contraction." The term itself is associated with the seventeenth-century teacher, Isaac Luria, although the concept is implicit in earlier sources. In order for God to be able to give of Himself—which was the primary impulse behind creation—He had to *contract* His infinite light to create a "vacated space" into which He could pour his creative potential. As a general rule, all creative endeavors require *polarity*, and, in kabbalistic thought, God's act of *tsimtsum* established the archetypal polarity—that between the infinite light and the vacated space—which becomes the germ for all subsequent polarities. At the same time the *tsimtsum* generated the archetypal *paradox*, for the vacated space both is and is not part of God. Ultimately, there is nothing other than God, and yet the whole point of *tsimtsum* was for God to withdraw Himself from part of Himself. In the primordial stirring of creation, the logic of either/or cannot apply, and therefore the seed of all paradox is brought into being.

While polarity and paradox run through the kabbalistic path like the warp and weft of some cosmic tapestry, it is a third condition deriving from *tsimtsum*, *otherness*, that gives the tapestry its foundational image. *Tsimtsum* eventuates in the otherness of God from Himself: the vacated space is devoid of His essential light. And, since the whole of creation unfolds within the vacated space, the whole of creation is understood kabbalistically as being permeated by that foundational sense of loss. A major thrust of kabbalistic practice is directed toward overcoming that sense of loss. The participatory turn—that is, the teaching that we are responsible for resolving God's alienation from Himself—places the existential quest to overcome our own sense of alienation into the context of a cosmic drama. For the Jew, alienation is the partner of exile.

Historically, the idea of exile and redemption is seminal to Jewish experience, for the Jews were sent into exile from their land of Israel and yearned for the redemption that would see them return to their ancestral homeland. This experience of exile and the quest for redemption became one of the most central images in Jewish religious and mystical tradition. Its spiritual focus lies with the *Shekhinah*, the feminine divine presence that is said in rabbinic sources to accompany the Jewish people in their exile. In the kabbalistic formulation of this idea, the *Shekhinah* is in exile from her kingly consort and yearns to be reunited with him. In other words, exile, alienation, and the sense of otherness are the existential conditions that prefigure the kabbalistic myth explored above. The *Shekhinah* is identified as the final "H" in God's name, and she is in exile from her partner, the "V" of the name. As we saw, union within the Godhead is contingent upon human participation, which becomes a critical requirement for bringing the period of the *Shekhinah*'s exile to a close.

In a stunning example of wordplay, the resolution of the tensions deriving from *tsimtsum* is found to lie in God's revelation, the Torah. The wordplay involves the Hebrew root, *galah*, which has two meanings: to "go into exile" and to "reveal." In a simple sense, the human task is to engage with the Torah, which promotes union between the *Shekhinah* and her consort within the godhead, resolving the vicissitudes of exile.

A deeper perspective on this double meaning of *galah* introduces a psychological dimension that underpins the participatory challenge in Kabbalah. This deeper perspective holds that the revelation of Torah *is itself the paradigm of exile*. To understand this notion, we must first grasp the quintessential idea that runs through the whole of Jewish discourse to the effect that "secret" and "higher" meanings are concealed within the outer literary fabric of the Torah. I noted already above a kabbalistic formulation of this idea that holds that the essence of Torah consists simply of the names of God. Obviously, we do not see these names at the level of the surface narrative; they are concealed, and we need the keys of kabbalistic tradition in order to dig sufficiently deeply to uncover them.

In one of the *Zohar*'s formulations of this notion of the inner, concealed mystery within the Torah, the Torah is depicted as a beautiful woman who calls, and sends messages, to her lover. The lover is, of course, the one who would take this path into the inner mysteries of the Torah. By stages, the woman reveals herself to the lover: first she speaks to him through a curtain, then through a fine veil, and, finally, she "reveals herself to him face to face, and speaks of all her concealed mysteries and hidden paths which she had kept hidden in her heart from ancient times."[22]

The deeper perspective on the relationship between "exile" and "revelation" derives from the idea that the inner, or "higher" meaning is "in exile" in the lower garments of the Torah. The beautiful woman—the higher meaning—is, as it were, exiled into the lower world that is the domain of the surface narrative. The princess is trapped, and yearns to be freed. All this is a consequence of *tsimtsum*, for *tsimtsum* is the paradigmatic divine event whereby a higher, transcendent presence is contracted into a "lower" domain. This is expressed in kabbalistic texts by stating that God's infinite presence is contracted into the letters of the Torah, His revelation to humankind. God is effectively *in exile* in the Torah.[23] Indeed, this pattern of the higher contracting into the lower is understood as being recapitulated throughout the created "worlds."[24] Thus, the Hebrew letters of the Torah are understood as revealing a contracted form of the infinite presence of the Source:

> He contracted Himself within the letters of the Torah, by means of which He has created the world . . . and the righteous person, who studies the Torah for its own sake in holiness, draws the Creator downward, blessed be He, within the letters of the Torah as in the moment of the creation.[25]

The study of Torah is not an intellectual pursuit as normally understood: The Talmud holds that one must "cut oneself to pieces for words of Torah," since its words are firmly held only by one "who kills oneself for it." In order to acquire Torah one must "make oneself as a desert."[26] In kabbalistic understanding, we must annul our sense of "I" in order to achieve the state of consciousness that is a prerequisite for the proper contemplation of the Torah—study "for its own sake" with no egotistic aims. This, then, is our *tsimtsum*: to diminish our own selfhood in order to make space for the selfhood of the divine. We are challenged to recapitulate God's actions in order to find the resolution of God's exile. God's revelation—the Torah—itself becomes the antidote to that primary exile of God from Himself that resulted from the originary *tsimtsum*. It is only by going into exile that God can reveal Himself, and it is through human experience of exile that we come to understand the meaning of exile and are able to grasp the depths of the revelation. And, in the completion of this cosmographic narrative of the Ultimate, it is only by becoming conscious of the infinite Being that is confined within the letters of the Torah that we can free the *Shekhinah* from her exile.

Given that the *real* exile[27] is that of God's contraction into the Hebrew letters, then our quest to promote the *Shekhinah*'s release and reunion within the Godhead involves entering into those letters. In the kabbalistic mysticism of language, it is paradoxically the very meaningfulness of words that locks the gates that hold the *Shekhinah* in exile. As letters are grouped into words, phrases, sentences, and narratives, they lose their pristine simplicity and multipotentiality. In a psychological sense, there is a parallel here with the role language plays in structuring our sense of self and perception of the world. Language is a primary system whereby are constructed the schemata, or cognitive structures, that give a sense of order in our worlds. As I have argued elsewhere, the sense of "I" is akin to a magnetic center for these schemata.[28] If a quest to transcendence in some sense means going beyond those rigid schemata, then "contracting" that sense of "I" may be a necessary first step. And the attempt to overturn the habitual ways in which language locks us into the structures that we have erected may be a valuable accompaniment to that step.

The majority of kabbalistic practices relate in one way or another to a vision of language—specifically, the Hebrew language—that sees it as the key to the divine realm. That many of these practices should entail focusing on letters rather than on words reflects the path out of exile, as intimated in this section. We seek the simplest elements of language, in order that we might come closest to the ontological base of *tsimtsum*.

A MYSTICISM OF LANGUAGE

> We have learnt that two thousand years before the creation of the world the Holy One, blessed be He, played around with the twenty-two letters of the Torah and He combined and rotated them and made from all of them one word. He rotated [the word] frontwards and backwards though all twenty-two letters. . . . All this the Holy One, blessed be He, undertook, for He wanted to create the world by means of His word and the epithet of the great name.[29]

This extract is from the tenth-century Shabbetai Donnolo's commentary on the *Sefer Yeszirah*. The *Sefer Yetsirah* is one of the oldest, and most respected, treatises of Jewish mysticism. Donnolo effects an integration between the two meanings of *sha'ashu'a* that I discussed above, namely, "delight" and "contemplation." Indeed, the verbal participle form of *sha'ashu'a* in the extract, translated here by Elliot Wolfson as "played around with," is translated in the same author's later work as "contemplated."[30] We may integrate the two meanings by suggesting that the delight experienced through the Creator's rapport with the Torah prior to manifest creation derives from a contemplative and creative play with the twenty-two letters that make up the Hebrew alphabet.

The context for this view is the central premise of the *Sefer Yetsirah* that creation is achieved through the agency of God permuting the Hebrew letters:

> Twenty-two foundation letters: He placed them in a wheel, like a wall with 231 gates. The wheel revolves forwards and backwards. . . . How? He weighed them and permuted them: *Alef* with them all and all of them with *alef*; *bet* with them all and all of them with *bet*. They continue in cycles and exist in 231 gates. Thus, all that is formed and all that is spoken derive from one Name.[31]

The mechanics of creation as portrayed in the *Sefer Yetsirah* may be likened to the mechanics of the engendering of biological form. The Hebrew letters are akin to the letters of the DNA code, and the exact forms generated depend upon combinations of the letters in the code. Thus, the first letter, *alef* ("A"), combined with the second, *bet* ("B"), produces *av* ("AB"), a word meaning "father." Through God's rotating the wheel for this combination, the category of "father" comes into being, and so on.[32]

The participatory turn is evident in the quest of kabbalists to emulate God's esoteric "letter-working." The language of the *Sefer Yetsirah* is ambiguous: it conveys both a third-person description of what God did ("He placed them in a wheel . . .") and an imperative verbal form ("place them in a wheel . . ."). In other words, the *Sefer Yetsirah* can be read as an instruction manual informing us as to how we engage with the esoteric work of creation. It is worth noting that over successive periods of Jewish mysticism, the text most emphatically *has* been read in this invitational sense. Putting this another way, the *Sefer Yetsirah* is not ambiguous but intentionally conveys *both* verbal forms in order to imply that the path to partnering God in his work of creation entails emulation of His ways.

The paradigmatic success story for this challenge to join with God in creation is the biblical Abraham. The final stanza of most versions of the *Sefer Yetsirah* celebrates his achievement:

> When our father, Abraham, may he rest in peace, looked, saw, understood, probed, engraved and carved, he was successful in creation, as it is written, "And the souls they made in Haran" (*Genesis* 12:5). Immediately, there was revealed to him the Master of all, may His name be blessed forever, and He placed him in his bosom, and kissed him on his head and called him, "Abraham my beloved" (*Isaiah* 41:8).[33]

God's delight in Abraham is clear, as is the notion that the source of the delight is Abraham's success in creation. But, again there are dangers of reading the symbolism too rigidly. The intimate embrace between God and Abraham may appear as some kind of anthropomorphic encounter, as if a father were meting out a pleasing reward following the son's achievement. I read it more as a statement of the intrinsic unfolding of events when this path of kabbalistic work is successfully followed to completion. Abraham emulates God's creative work, and, as an *automatic consequence* of his success, achieves the most intimate relationship with God possible. *Unio Dei* cannot be separated from *Imitatio Dei* in this kabbalistic vision.

There are two key allusions to the nature of this kabbalistic work in the first sentence of the above extract. The first allusion comes with the phrase "engraved and carved," which refers to the mystical techniques for working with Hebrew letters in emulation of God's work of creation. The second is the *Genesis* quote, which alludes to the production of *golems* ("the souls they made . . ."). A *golem* is an artificial hominoid, brought into being through a magical rite. Here is not the place to go into detail on this fascinating, and psychologically important, chapter of Jewish mysticism.[34] For our purposes it is sufficient to note that the ability to make a *golem* is presented as evidence of the consummate mastery of creation. In this rite, the adept integrates the elemental forces of earth and water, fires them by means of the esoteric Hebrew "letter-working," and forms an organismic whole by dint of those letters' higher resonances as portrayed in Jewish and kabbalistic teaching. The goal of the *golem* ritual is best construed as that of achieving a recapitulation of God's own high point in creation, namely, the creation of Adam. The image of some fanciful Frankenstein creation, blown out of proportion by the magic of Hollywood, may blind us to the potential in the *golem* myth to provide a focus for the participatory challenge in our day. A twenty-first-century approach to the *golem* might reflect a deep ecological paradigm at the same time as operationalizing a psychodynamic and spiritual view of the body-mind relationship. The *golem* is, almost uniquely, the one schema that may unite science and the arts, psychology and AI, the spirit body and the meaning of the Temple.[35]

The techniques for working with the letters is expanded earlier in the *Sefer Yetsirah*, where it is stated that "He [God] *engraved* them, *carved* them, *weighed* them, *permuted* them, *combined* them, and *formed* with them all that was formed and all that would be formed in the future."[36] A variety of ways to recapitulate these six actions developed in kabbalistic tradition,[37] with perhaps the most elaborate being found in the ecstatic practices associated with the thirteenth-century Abraham Abulafia. As Moshe Idel has explicated in detail, Abulafia described complex procedures through which deconstruction of language as a normal communicative instrument might eventuate in a mystical state of consciousness.[38]

Scholarly analysis of trends in Jewish mysticism has emphasized a distinction between two dominant approaches. The first, associated especially with the *Zohar* and associated writings, is classed as *theosophic-theurgic*; the second, strongly represented by Abulafia's anomian ways of playing with language, is the *ecstatic-prophetic* Kabbalah.[39] The material I discussed earlier on the mythic understanding of exile and reunification is an expression of the former approach. Thus, Idel uses the term *theurgy* to refer to teachings that hold that activity at a lower level (such as the study of Torah, ritual observance, etc.) influences the higher level of the Godhead (bringing about balance, effecting a beneficial flow to lower levels, etc.). As Isaiah Tishby notes, in the grand scheme of the *Zohar* and the kabbalistic schools that it inspired, "it is this work that is the real purpose of man's life on earth."[40]

The ecstatic mystic, by contrast, seems to be more oriented toward a personalistic type of encounter, which is experienced as a divine influx from a higher realm descending into their own being. At the same time, the ecstatic mystic seeks an ascent experience through which their own soul might unite with the Divine. It is from this perspective that the traditions of ecstatic Kabbalah lend themselves more immediately to psychological analysis. Elsewhere, I have analyzed the techniques of Abulafia in some detail, with particular reference to recent developments in psychology and neuroscience.[41]

Given that the fundamental motivation of the theurgic mystic is to bring about some event within the divine realm that God in some sense desires, the participatory emphasis will be evident. While differing in certain regards, the goals of the other, ecstatic, strand equally fall into a participatory context.

Abulafia, for example, viewed his techniques as restoring the integrity of the divine names, and therefore of the Divine Himself. It should be clear that the participatory paradigm touches the real core of all Jewish mysticism. Indeed, it may be argued that the division between the two kabbalistic approaches is more practical than foundational. Wolfson, for example, argues that the twofold division is misleading and that Kabbalah is more accurately characterized in terms of a core experience of ecstasy that comprises two facets: "reintegration of the soul in the divine, and fusion of the sefirotic potencies into harmonious unity."[42]

Wolfson makes the important point that "it is necessary to reintegrate the theurgic and mystical elements of the religious experience of the kabbalist, for it makes no sense to speak of effecting the nature of God if one is not experiencing God in some immediate and direct sense."[43] I believe that this reintegration is necessary in our day not only for the integrity of the scholarly and historical study of Kabbalah, but also for the renewal of the more individual challenge to find an enriching path of mystical Judaism. An overly theurgic emphasis can lead to an excessively passive and noncreative observance of ritual and Torah study, in the belief that simply "going through the motions" can achieve theurgic goals. On the other hand, when the balance shifts too far from the theurgic such that more ecstatic explorations become dissociated from the traditional myth of exile and redemption, an excessively sentimental attachment to experience can result. To know that one has the potential to "effect the nature of God," and that such a responsibility necessitates "experiencing God in some immediate and direct sense," seems to me to reinforce an appropriate balance between these two extremes. By legitimizing the notion that we are capable of cocreatively participating in the unfolding of the will of the Ultimate, Jorge N. Ferrer's participatory paradigm[44] usefully situates the goals of kabbalistic mysticism in contemporary perspective.

TOWARD A KABBALISTIC PSYCHOLOGY: A TRANSPERSONAL SCIENCE OF THE SACRED

The discipline of transpersonal psychology focuses on depth experiences that include those associated with religion and spirituality, and on analyses of the mind that grant some validity to the transformational value of mysticism. There is little point, however, in simply substituting the terminology of one discipline for the nomenclature of another, unless that substitution offers new ways to integrate and explain the material under consideration. I have argued that transpersonal psychology is able to open up a significant discourse to the extent that it can bring the insights found in spiritual traditions into the arena in which science is attempting to understand consciousness.[45] There is a two-way rapport here: spiritual and mystical insights can advance our understanding of mind, and contemporary psychology can revitalize the way we work with the teachings of the mystics.

There is a specific nexus of interest when it comes to Kabbalah on account of its inherently psychological slant. Two interconnected themes that run through much of the corpus of kabbalistic literature are especially important in opening up this psychological dimension. These themes are the interest in creation and the dynamic between concealing and revealing. Creation is viewed as the unfolding of God's thought,[46] and, on account of the isomorphism that Kabbalah identifies between the human and the Divine, the kabbalistic analysis of creation is implicitly an exploration of human thought. Human creativity recapitulates divine creation, and the concealed fount of our creativity is the meeting ground between the human, and divine, minds. Indeed, a further human-Divine parallel may be drawn when considering the notion of *tsimtsum* that sees the higher insights of the Torah being "exiled" into its lower narrative, as discussed above. The parallel here is with the idea that higher levels of the human mind become clothed in the mundane psychological realm of the "I." Just as the kabbalist seeks to free the higher sparks that are in exile, so the modern seeker may attempt to uncover the higher aspects of mind through psychoanalysis or allied techniques.

Kabbalah views the unfolding of divine thought as a movement from concealed to revealed states, which we may see paralleled by the way in which human thought progresses from preconsciousness to consciousness. But this does not mean that the concealed state is replaced as it becomes revealed; both continue to coexist: "Throughout the entire Torah we find that the revealed co-exists with the concealed. So it is with the world, both this world and the higher world, everything is concealed and revealed."[47] So it is also with thought, in that there are coexistent conscious and unconscious streams of thought.[48] The play between these two streams is enacted in the interactive nature of the brain.

Perceptual systems in the brain comprise *feedforward* and *reentrant* pathways. In brief, the former convey signals deriving from the sensory organs through a hierarchy of progressively more complex analyzers, while the latter modulate these analyses in a "top-down" manner. The modulating influence of the reentrant pathways derives from "higher-order" processing of contextual and other memory-related information. Recent research in neuroscience has established that the reentrant pathway is critical for consciousness; activity in the feedforward system is not conscious. Thus, for example, if the image of a pen were falling on my retina, I would not be conscious of the sensory analyses that yield data about the pen's outline shape, color, etc. (feedforward system); I become conscious of the pen only when the whole object, complete with its meaning, is established (reentrant system). In short, I see a *pen*, that is, an entity that carries meaning by dint of a whole variety of memory images that constellate around its simple "pen-ness" and my relationship to it.[49]

The two concurrent streams of thought—conscious and unconscious—may be conceptualized in terms of the relative activity in the two pathways. To oversimplify: the unconscious stream arises from the feedforward pathway and the multiple associative links to the sensory input that are generated, while the conscious stream depends upon the reentrant pathway and the way it incorporates into perception the immediate sense of "I" as "receiver of impressions." Detaching from "I" in the manner encouraged by mystical practice entails a shift in the relative activity of the two pathways in the direction of an attenuation of the reentrant pathways.

However, my interest here is not primarily in the effects of mystical practice on brain function. I have alluded to these insights from cognitive neuroscience simply to make the key point that the kabbalistic myth discussed earlier sits comfortably with current understanding of the brain. The kabbalistic myth depends upon a logic of interaction whereby a "lower" is in dynamic interplay with a "higher" and is responsible for triggering the beneficial effects that descend from the higher when it is rebalanced. The theurgic principle is summarized in the maxim that "an impulse from below stimulates that above":

> Come and see. Through the impulse from below is awakened an impulse above, and through the impulse from above there is awakened a yet higher impulse, until the impulse reaches the place where the lamp is to be lit and it is lit . . . and all the worlds receive blessing from it.[50]

The highly interactive systems of the brain display some consonance with this pattern. Through *binding* mechanisms, the brain seems to operate to align higher-level processing with the output from low-level processing. And, as we have seen, consciousness is associated not with the higher-level activity itself but rather with its *reentrant* modulation of the lower-level activity. It would appear therefore that there is a "pattern" to the operation of brain systems that corresponds with the macrocosmic pattern identified by Kabbalah.

This system whereby a "lower" triggers a "higher," which gives rise to an influx ("blessing" or, in contemporary terms, "consciousness") back to the lower, seems to me to provide the fundamental logic of participation. I have illustrated the theurgic importance of this perspective as it is known in Kabbalah. That the brain itself displays an analogous logic may provide a scientific window into the teachings of *correspondence* that formed the cornerstone of Renaissance "sacred science." Islamic science, like Kabbalah, conceived of two paths to knowing: observation and revelation. These two interrelate: observing the pattern inhering in the structures of our world (such as the brain) yields a knowledge of the higher pattern to all things, while grasping the higher pattern through study of revelatory wisdom directs our observation to discern the expression of this pattern around us. The additional ingredient that renders such "sacred science" meaningful is the recognition that human consciousness plays the seminal role in the dynamic interplay between lower and higher. As C. G. Jung expressed it, God is mysteriously dependent on human consciousness.[51] Sacred science is not concerned simply with discerning pattern; it is quintessentially a science of human *transformation*. Knowing the Mystery means participating in the Mystery, and such participation necessarily implies inner change. Transpersonal psychology not only studies the psychology of transformation but also explores the links between scientific observation and the spiritual traditions of revealed knowing. I consider that in its emphasis on these pursuits, transpersonal psychology has become the contemporary heir to the older schools of sacred science.

The boundaries that a culture erects ramify throughout its psyche. Another form of correspondence is evident in contemporary shifts in these boundaries. Just as the outward boundaries appear to be softening due to globalization and allied pressures, so the boundaries that have been applied to inner structures are correspondingly under challenge. At the level of the brain, our conception of discrete areas and unidirectional flows of impulses has been shown to be flawed. What were once conceived of as compartmentalized sensory areas are known now to be substantially multisensory.[52] In fact, the very term *sensory* for such areas of the brain appears somewhat inappropriate given the major motor innervations found in them. From a cognitive perspective, perception entails enactive processing and embodiment as much as it depends on sensory analysis.[53] At all levels, boundaries blur and interactivity holds sway.

It is in this context that participation becomes the transpersonal myth for our day. Whether it is the microcosm of the brain, the "mesocosm" of global interactions, or the macrocosm of our link to the Mystery, all is found to cohere in an inclusive frame of engagement. As we have seen, when kabbalists discerned in an earlier age that the inclusive whole was structured through correspondences between "above" and "below," they promoted human participation as the route to effecting the harmony of that whole. I believe we have here a provocative parallel with our day: as the boundaries dissolve and a renewed awakening to the interrelatedness of all things takes hold, a thoroughly modern narrative of human responsibility is gaining momentum. The participatory turn in the study of spirituality forms a key component of that narrative.

CONCLUSION

There is much in the kabbalistic myth—which I have but sketched over these pages—that resonates both with contemporary yearnings toward a more *alive* spiritual path, and with the direction in which psychological science seems to be pointing. As will be evident to anyone who has a grasp of the vicissitudes of Jewish history, the narrative of exile and redemption is powerfully grounded in the exigencies of oppression. Yet the genius of the

Jewish mystical mind peered through historical eventualities into the concealed existential mirroring of God and man. And the spectral image of otherness and distancing that hovers in that mirror seems no longer to be the preserve of a unique people with its distinctive history. When a quest for some form of spiritual meaning to our lives begins to stir in the heart, what lies at its core other than a sense of having somehow lost a primary intimacy with an "other"? And what better way is there for dealing with that potent sense of loss than to identify that it tears at others' hearts in a never-ending hall of mirrors? The pain is not lessened when it is found to be merely an echo of the originary loss of wholeness, as symbolized in *tsimtsum*. But knowing that my aloneness reflects the Mystery that only knew It was alone once It had asserted Its will to become other, and thereby to be expressed, places that aloneness in a more bounded context. And the realization that I, in annulment of this very statement (for "I" is the impostor who incessantly fabricates the semblance of relationships), can participate in the ultimate restitution of balance . . . this realization galvanizes action.

"That was a way of putting it . . . ,"[54] but, contra T. S. Eliot, it is not an emptying humility that gives us a vision of our place in the scheme of things, but a reminder of responsibilities: "You are not obliged to complete the task; but neither are you free to abstain from it."[55]

Knowing, experiencing, and acting form the tripod on which this participatory responsibility stands. For the Jewish mystic, that knowledge of God that derives from contemplation of the Torah is never an abstracted intellection. Knowing God is knowing His name; knowing His name is experiencing both the dynamic polarizations in its constituent letters and the delight, *sha'ashu'a*, in their relationships; experiencing the letters means acting to promote the theurgic goal; and acting in pursuit of the theurgic goal means knowing the ways of Torah and details of *halakhic* observance.[56] If there is one term that epitomizes the kabbalistic quest it is *unification*. Many kabbalistic practices are called unifications on account of their intent to promote unification of the sacred name. At the same time, the psychological connotations of the kabbalistic myth may suggest a more inward form of "unification." Through the tripod of knowing, experiencing, and acting we seek to unify the diverse aspects of self, in order that our disparate inner characters might be brought into integration.

The sense of alienation, of exile, that is abroad in our day is so much larger than that of an ethnic group divorced from its "home." We are alienated from our world, from our climate, from our established roles, from traditions that gave our ancestors a sense of being at home in their lives. The myth of *tsimtsum* and the path to its resolution potentially speaks to us of our responsibilities to the Mystery itself. The "angels" cannot renew that consciousness of the sacred that binds our planet into the unfolding of the Mystery; but with the man Moses holding on to the Throne of Glory, a blessing may still unify heaven and earth.

NOTES

1. Babylonian Talmud, *Hullin* 91b; Midrash, *Genesis Rabbah* 68:12.

2. I am assuming that readers of this book will not identify the term *myth* with something illusory. On the contrary, I use the term to suggest that deep and essential ideas are being conveyed in a form that transcends historical and literal concepts. Compare Paul Ricoeur: "Myth will here be taken to mean what the history of religion now finds in it: not a false explanation by means of images and fables, but a traditional narration that relates to events that happened at the beginning of time and which has the purpose of providing grounds for the ritual actions of men of today and, in a general manner, establishing all the forms of action and thought by which man understands himself in the world" (*The Symbolism of Evil*, trans. Emerson Buchanan [Boston: Beacon Press, 1969], 5).

3. Babylonian Talmud, *Ta'anit* 5b.

4. The *Shekhinah* is the feminine principle in the Godhead. The Hebrew verbal root means "to dwell," giving the connotation that the *Shekhinah* is the divine presence that dwells on earth.

5. The *Zohar* is the principal source text of Kabbalah. It is largely a meditation on the nature of the Godhead and the mystical meanings of the Hebrew Scriptures. Its date of composition is probably the thirteenth century, although it conveys oral teachings that had seemingly been passed on from earlier periods. The extract cited here is from *Zohar* 1:235b. *Sefer ha-Zohar*, ed. Reuven Margolioth (Jerusalem: Mossad ha-Rav Kook, 1978).

6. *Midrash* is the collective term for a rabbinic literary genre that explores diverse meanings in scriptural passages in order to convey homiletic teachings. The extract here is from Midrash, *Bereshit Rabbah* 79:8. This teaching is based on the biblical continuation of the narrative of Jacob's nocturnal wrestling. The following day he encounters his estranged brother, Esau, following which he sets up an altar. The standard translations hold that "he [Jacob] called it [the altar] *El-Elohe Israel*" (Genesis 33:20). This translation is, however, problematic since the verse does not say, "he called *it*," but "he called *to* him [or it]." As the Talmud notes (*Megillah* 18a): "From where do we know that the Holy One, blessed be He, calls Jacob 'god'? Because it says, 'And the God of Israel called him *El* [a Name of God]' (*Genesis* 33:20). Should you suppose that [what the biblical text means is that] Jacob called the altar El, then it should have written, 'And Jacob called it.' Rather, it says, 'He called Jacob El.' And who called him so? The God of Israel."

7. The immediate subject of this passage from the biblical book of *Proverbs* is Wisdom. Throughout kabbalistic literature this wisdom is identified with the Torah.

8. In the passage from the book of *Proverbs* the term is in the plural: *sha'shu'im*. It is unclear what the intent of this plural form may be. Given the context of the primordial stirrings of creation, perhaps the plural form is intended to prefigure the duality that creation brings into being from the primal singularity of the precreative moment. Elliot R. Wolfson conceives of the myth of *sha'ashu'a* "as an articulation of the splintering of the indivisible unity of divine wisdom into the opposite principles

of bestowing and receiving, which are valenced respectively as masculine and feminine" (*Language, Eros, Being: Kabbalistic Hermeneutics and Poetic Imagination* [New York: Fordham University Press, 2005], 279).

The word in the extract from *Proverbs* that I have translated as "confidant" (*amon*) carries additional connotations that are important to the erotic and generative way in which kabbalists view the verse. Thus, the word can mean "nursling" and "artisan."

9. *Ein Sof*, literally "without end," refers to the unknowable infinite essence of God. In kabbalistic symbolism this term refers to the timeless and transcendent Being that is, as it were, the precursor to the divine emanations that constitute the process of creation. Prior to creation (and, of course terms such as "prior" and "precursor" must remain paradoxical in this context) there is only *Ein Sof*; hence the attempt by kabbalists to convey the primordial move to the creative impulse as eventuating in a "shaking" from within the divine core with no connotation of polarity.

10. Cited in Wolfson, *Circle in the Square: Studies in the Use of Gender in Kabbalistic Symbolism* (Albany: State University of New York Press, 1995), 71–72.

11. *Zohar* 2:60a.

12. *Bahir* 4. *The Book Bahir: An Edition Based on the Earliest Manuscripts*, ed. Daniel Abrams (Los Angeles: Cherub Press, 1994).

13. The term *sefirah* (plural *sefirot*) refers to an emanation of God. The central premise of Kabbalah is that the transcendent, unknowable God emanates ten principles, *sefirot*, which find expression in manifest creation. The theosophical path of Kabbalah is largely one of gaining ever deeper knowledge of these principles, as discerned through scriptural revelation and through observation. Not only are the *sefirot* principles of creation but they also form the substructure of human potential. By knowing the inner principles of creation, we come to know ourselves.

14. In their sacred forms, scriptural texts are written in Hebrew without vowels. This gives rise to a distinctive ambiguity of meanings that Midrash and kabbalistic writings exploit. Here, the *Zohar* is exploiting the fact that the Hebrew form, *AShR*, can give rise to two different words depending on the vowels. One word is the relative pronoun "which," the other is a word meaning "happiness" or "bliss." This double meaning bears deeper consideration, since it points to the insight that happiness ultimately depends on relationship (whether that implies objects, another human, or—as would be held by kabbalists—the divine).

15. *Zohar* 3:65b.

16. *Zohar* 3:61b-62a.

17. *Zohar* 2:46a.

18. The name *Y-H-V-H* shares the same verbal root as "*Ehyeh*." While the latter is grammatically a first-person imperfect form, implying "I shall continually unfold being or becomingness," the former is best understood as a third-person amalgam of past, present, and future forms of the verb "to be." From this point of view, the name *Y-H-V-H* depicts the complete pattern in the unfolding of the Creator.

19. Wolfson, *Language, Eros, Being*, 273.

20. For the Jewish mystic, there is no sharp demarcation between scriptural study and the experience of mystical states. The classic mystical texts, such as the *Bahir* and the *Zohar*, engage the reader in a world of mystical transformations of scriptural passages that pulsate with evident experiential connotations: "There is a basic convergence of the interpretative and the revelatory modes; the act of scriptural interpretation is itself an occasion for contemplative study and mystical meditation . . . the vision that generated the text [of the *Zohar*] may be re/visioned through interpretive study" (Wolfson, "Hermeneutics of Light in Medieval Jewish Mysticism," in *The Presence of Light: Divine Radiance and Religious Expereince*, ed. Matthew T. Kapstein [Chicago: The University of Chicago Press], 113).

21. See above, note 11.

22. *Zohar* 2:99a.

23. For a fuller discussion, see Brian L. Lancaster, *The Essence of Kabbalah* (London: Arcturus, 2005), 133–45.

24. This is the understanding of *tsimtsum* as it was formulated within the *Hasidic* movement. According to Rabbi Qalonimus Qalman Epstein, there are "several thousand *tzimtzumim*" (cited in Moshe Idel, *Hasidism: Between Ecstasy and Magic* [Albany: State University of New York Press, 1995], 91.).

Elsewhere I have explored the value of the *tsimtsum* concept for modeling the relationship of consciousness to the brain. The pattern of *tsimtsum* would suggest the possibility that the essence of consciousness is transcendent to the space-time neural structures yet is *contracted* into their domain. See Lancaster, "A Kabbalistic Framework for the Study of Consciousness," in *haHayim keMidrash—Iyunim biPsikhologia Yehudit* (Life as a Midrash: Perspectives in Jewish Psychology), ed. Shahar Arzy, Michal Fachler, and Baruch Kahana (Tel-Aviv: Yedi'ot Aharonot *Lamiskal* Books, 2004), 250–70 (Hebrew).

25. Attributed to the Maggid of Mezeritch, cited in Idel, *Hasidism: Between Ecstasy and Magic*, 93.

26. The extracts are from the Babylonian Talmud, *Berakhot* 63b and *Nedarim* 55a. In typical rabbinic fashion these aphorisms follow from interpretations of scriptural passages. The notion that one must "die" in order to acquire Torah is derived from the juxtaposition in *Numbers* 19:14 of "This is the Torah" and "a person who dies in a tent." The need to make oneself like a desert is derived from *Numbers* 21:18, where a sequence of geographical locations is understood as referring to the stages involved in acquiring Torah. The first two locations are the desert and *Matanah*, a word that literally means "a gift." Hence, "one must make himself as a desert, which is free to all, then the Torah is given to him as a gift."

27. Of course, the word *real* is a hostage to fortune! The historical exile and subjugation of the Jewish people was undoubtedly all too real. However, from the perspective of Jewish mysticism, events in our world happen only as a consequence of happenings in the higher world of the Godhead (just as, in the participatory sense being considered here, our actions have consequences in that higher world). In this sense, the exile of the *Shekhinah* is the *causative* exilic event.

28. Lancaster, "On the Relationship between Cognitive Models and Spiritual Maps: Evidence from Hebrew Language Mysticism," *Journal of Consciousness Studies* 7 (2000): 231–50; Lancaster, *Approaches to Consciousness: The Marriage of Science and Mysticism* (Basingstoke, U.K.: Palgrave Macmillan, 2004).

29. Commentary of Shabbatai Donnolo on *Sefer Yetsirah*, cited in Wolfson, *Through a Speculum that Shines: Vision and Imagination in Medieval Jewish Mysticism* (Princeton: Princeton University Press), 137.

30. Wolfson, *Language, Eros, Being*, 274.

31. *Sefer Yetsirah* 2:4. The 231 gates refer to the logical number of two-letter combinations from a twenty-two letter array. The teaching that God employed the twenty-two letters of the Hebrew alphabet as His agents of creation is found throughout rabbinic literature. Thus, for example, the Talmud states that "Rav Judah said in the name of Rav: Betsalel knew how to combine the letters by which heaven and earth were created" (Babylonian Talmud, *Berakhot* 55a). Betsalel was the artisan who constructed the portable Temple described in the biblical book of *Exodus* chapters 25–40. The implication of the Talmudic statement is that Temple building recapitulates cosmos building, and that therefore a Temple is a microcosm. See Ithamar Gruenwald "A Preliminary Critical Edition of *Sefer Yezira*," *Israel Oriental Studies* 1 (1971): 132–77. For English version, see Aryeh Kaplan, *Sefer Yetzirah: The Book of Creation* (York Beach, ME: Samuel Weiser, 1990).

32. This is not to imply that all two-letter combinations spell a word (which is not the case). Rather, the combinations imply a uniting of specific qualities that brings a product into potential, whether or not a real word is involved.

33. *Sefer Yetsirah* 6:7.

34. Extensive treatments of the history of the golem in Jewish mysticism may be found in Idel, *Golem: Jewish Magical and Mystical Traditions on the Artificial Anthropoid* (Albany: State University of New York Press, 1990); and Gershom Scholem, *On the Kabbalah and its Symbolism*, trans. Ralph Manheim (New York: Schocken Books, 1969). For a more psychological analysis, see Lancaster, "The *Golem* as a Transpersonal Image: 1. A Marker of Cultural Change," *Transpersonal Psychology Review* 1, no. 3 (1997): 5–11, and "The *Golem* as a Transpersonal Image: 2. Psychological Features in the Mediaeval Golem Ritual," *Transpersonal Psychology Review* 1, no. 4 (1997): 23–30.

35. The construction of the *golem* resonates with traditions surrounding the erection of the portable Temple described in the biblical book of *Exodus*. There is an isomorphism between the Temple and man, as pointed out repeatedly in Midrashic and kabbalistic literature, with both of them modeled on the structure of the Godhead as understood in the symbolism of the *sefirot*. I have explored the relevant sources in Lancaster, *The Elements of Judaism* (Shaftesbury, Dorset, and Rockport, MA: Element Books, 1993).

36. *Sefer Yetsirah* 2:2.

37. In a recent work, I indicated how these terms are incorporated in traditional kabbalistic visualization practice as follows:

Preparation for visualisation requires closing or half-closing the eyes. Normally, when we close the eyes we automatically turn the visual sense off inwardly as well. For this kind of a practice, however, we must remain acutely aware of the visual sense even whilst being closed to outward seeing. It is as if we are seeing the screen made by the insides of our eyelids. *Engraving* means outlining the letter in the mind's eye; as the outline is built up, we hold a clear intent to operate with a specific letter. *Carving* entails establishing the letter as a powerful presence in visual consciousness; energy is focused on the letter until it blazes like fire on the inner screen of the mind. The intent behind *weighing* is that of allowing the letter's qualities to impress themselves upon us; a receptive state must be cultivated, in which we might, for example, find meaning in the letter's shape, its constituent parts, its relations with other letters, and so on. This is followed by *permuting* the letter with other letters; maybe, having focused on the letter's constituent lines, other letters using those lines arise in the mind. Letters are then *combined*, enabling them to enter into relationships one with another. The final stage concerns the meaning of those combinations; what kind of a presence is *formed* when those specific letters come together? (*Essence of Kabbalah*, 176–77)

38. Idel, *The Mystical Experience in Abraham Abulafia*, trans. Jonathon Chipman (Albany: State University of New York Press, 1988); Idel, *Language, Torah, and Hermeneutics in Abraham Abulafia*, trans. Menahem Kallus (Albany: State University of New York Press, 1988).

39. Idel, *Kabbalah: New Perspectives* (New Haven: Yale University Press, 1988).

40. Isaiah Tishby, *The Wisdom of the Zohar: An Anthology of Texts*, trans. David Goldstein (Oxford: Oxford University Press, 1949/1989), 736, n120.

41. References given in note 28 above.

42. Wolfson, *Language, Eros, Being*, 209.

43. Wolfson, *Through a Speculum That Shines*, 374.

44. Ferrer, *Revisioning Transpersonal Theory: A Participatory Vision of Human Spirituality* (Albany: State University of New York Press, 2002), and this volume.

45. Lancaster, *Approaches to Consciousness*, 10–19.

46. The Zohar explicitly links the initiatory moment of creation with the arising of thought: "When the most concealed of all concealment sought to be revealed, He made first a single point; and this arose to become *thought*. He sketched within it all the designs, engraved in it all the openings. He engraved within the concealed holy lamp a singular, hidden pattern—Holy of Holies; a deep structure emerging from thought" (*Zohar* 1:2a).

47. *Zohar* 2:230b.

48. There is considerable terminological confusion regarding nonconscious mental content, which I address at some length in my book on *Approaches to Consciousness*. In brief, the term *preconscious* refers to material that is in process of reaching consciousness. In the case of sensory processing, for example, neural activity over the first

100ms or so is preconscious. The notion that there is an ongoing stream of thought that is nonconscious and not in process of becoming conscious is conveyed by the term *unconscious*.

49. For reviews of the role of reentrant neural pathways in relation to consciousness, see Gerald M. Edelman, and Giulio Tononi, "Reentry and the Dynamic Core: Neural Correlates of Conscious Experience," in *Neural Correlates of Consciousness: Empirical and Conceptual Questions*, ed. Thomas Metzinger (Cambridge: MIT Press, 2000); V. A. F. Lamme, "Separate Neural Definitions of Visual Consciousness and Visual Attention: A Case for Phenomenal Awareness," *Neural Networks* 17 (2004): 861–72; V. A. F. Lamme and P. R. Roelfsema, "The Distinct Modes of Vision Offered by Feedforward and Recurrent Processing," *Trends in Neurosciences* 23 (2000): 571–79. See also Lancaster, *Approaches to Consciousness*, 136–41.

50. *Zohar* 1:244a.

51. Jung, *Memories, Dreams, Reflections*, trans. Richard and Clara Winston (London: Fontana, 1963/1967), 371.

52. For a recent analysis of the multisensory nature of sensory cortex, see Asif A. Ghazanfar and Charles E. Schroeder, "Is Neocortex Essentially Multisensory?" *Trends in Cognitive Sciences* 10 (2006): 278–85.

53. For an overview of the enactive basis of perception, see Alva Noë, *Action in Perception* (Cambridge: MIT Press, 2005).

54. Eliot, *Four Quartets* (London: Faber and Faber, 1959 edition), 25.

55. Mishnah, *Pirke Avot* 2: 21.

56. The term *halakhah* refers to the body of Jewish law as it is derived from the core principles laid down in the Torah.

FIVE

Esoteric Paradigms and Participatory Spirituality in the Teachings of Mikhaël Aïvanhov

Lee Irwin

ONE OF THE GREAT problems in the study of spirituality by modern and postmodern scholars is the lack of metaphysical context in theories claiming to identify the sources of spiritual transformation. And yet, for most spiritual practitioners, it is precisely the metaphysics of religious claims that underlies their most significant impact on human life. This lack of metaphysical context has been attributed to the rise of modern scientific rationalism and its incipient dependence on an observable, and often rigid, narrow empiricism.[1] The gist of this narrow empiricism, embedded in the subject/object split, is articulated as a tension between the public, observable phenomenon or "fact," and the private, unobservable datum of "inner perception." By excluding the subjective and private from the discourses of empirical analysis, metaphysical claims by members of various world religions have been marginalized by many academic scholars as myth and fantasy or characterized as mere "folklore" and often dismissed as the detritus of misguided subjectivisms, no longer relevant in a rational, public, measurable, externalized world of observable facts.[2]

When further linked to biological materialism, the Cartesian separation of public reason from private intuition often results in a limiting form of "intellectual Calvinism" by which material facts are presented as the determinative causal variables underlying all religious, spiritual, and transpersonal claims. Those who fail to recognize the truth of this empiricism are condemned to ignorance; "salvation" lies in embracing the materialist belief that all religious causality is reducible to biology, evolutionary psychology, and/or sociocultural conditioning. Causality attributed to nonempirical sources, neither measurable nor scientifically testable, must be relegated to the dust bins of history as quaint misbeliefs held by "folk" believers, whose poor intuitions have led them astray into the murky subterranean depths of the unconscious, social repression, and the denied stirrings of primal needs and desires. In an intellectual climate of humanistic atheism and secular aggrandizement of the empirical fact as the marker of all substantive theory, religious and spiritual claims based on metaphysical intuitions and discernments have suffered a severe displacement from center to margin reflecting the denial of the epistemic import of subjective experience in modern thought.

THE METAPHYSICAL CONTEXT

Postmodern theory also suffers from this miasma of metaphysical denial when its linguistic relativism collapses into a subjective hermeneutic circle in which the authorial "I" cannot see beyond the boundaries of its self-enclosed interpretive horizon. Ironically, the subjective problem is hardly banished and the critical "I" is often eulogized as the only "real" center of interpretive power or meaning. In this secularized hermeneutics, the only authority of the text is the (subjective) interpreter, who seeks to unveil the "chain of texts" and to "rewrite" the text for the reader in response to a limitless context of possible associations leading to all possible texts and all possible meanings, a reading with "no bottom line" and no closure on meaning.[3] This deconstructive attitude, coupled with an arguably strong insensitivity for the meaning of texts for those who do not share those hermeneutic presuppositions, builds a gap not only between the text and the interpreter, but more saliently, between the interpreter and those who may understand the text through alternative metaphysical attitudes. Interpretations of religious texts made into grist for the secular mills of rational or deconstructive analysis often become parodies of their traditional meanings. More significantly, the metaphysical source of the knowledge claimed to underlie or inspire those texts is dismissed as a limiting and confining orthodoxy no longer consistent with modern and postmodern thinking.[4]

All this, of course, is a look at the shadow side of the modern and postmodern condition. There is much good that has come forth from these movements: a greater sense of the factual and the observable in nature, culture, history, and humanity; the value of rational discourse open to self-correction through methodological rigor and testing; the development of a capacity to overcome narrow subjectivism leading to dogmatic exclusivism and intolerance; the practical value of empirical findings to improve the quality of human existence; the formation of communities of discourse whose logic and rules have aided in the articulation of many insightful and creative ideas; a dismantling of ideological forms of authority based on oppressive hierarchical thinking and leading to questionable ethical, political, aesthetic, and moral claims; and a willingness to step beyond the boundaries of traditional religious beliefs, practices, and institutions in a broad search for deeper meaning. These are all necessary steps toward a more integrated and mature realization of human potential in an increasingly global multicultural context.

However, the question of "metaphysical context" remains problematic in both transpersonal theory and the comparative study of religion. The study of religion has been traditionally divided between two general camps: those who claim that the study of religion is best carried out by representing each tradition "on its own terms" (that is, religion from the "insider" point of view— what do members of the traditions believe and practice?); and those who claim that more critical perspectives are necessary in representing religions either drawing on a variety of humanistic approaches or claiming that only quantifiable or empirical data can make the study of religion a true "science" (the strict "outsider" point of view—what believers may or may not believe is not a basis for rational understanding or scientific explanation).[5] Problematically, the "insider" view tends to address metaphysics from within the context of a given tradition—often resulting in the dismissal (exclusivism) or hierarchical arrangement (inclusivism) of other "lower" traditions—and/or stresses a strong "vertical" plane of allegedly perennial or universal truths that transcend any one tradition.[6] The humanistic scholar tends to bracket metaphysical claims (in a modernist fashion) appealing to historical, cultural, psychological, anthropological (and so on) perspectives that often operate on the "horizontal" plane of the comparative datum and use nonreligious theories to interpret or explain religious phenomena. And the "science of religions" tends to dismiss all metaphysical claims as immeasurable and outside its purview of social-scientific analysis. The "insider/outsider problem," then, reflects the tensions between the views of a practitioner and of those of a humanistic or scientific scholar who elaborates nonmetaphysical interpretations and/or explanations of the practitioner's religious claims. Metaphysics in Religious Studies has been confined to theology, the study of mysticism, and/or the comparative philosophy of religion. Even in these contexts, however, metaphysics often becomes either a historical subject delimited by a humanistic theoretical context or an orthodox vehicle for the expression of a particular traditional metaphysics.[7]

Sacred Beingness and Participatory Spirituality

While the humanistic study of religion has constrained metaphysics to a largely comparative or historical context, the subjective emphasis on "individual experience" in transpersonal theory has alternatively delimited metaphysical claims to the realm of the personal and private, thereby undercutting the ontological claims of most religious traditions. The converse problem is found in those theorists who describe the "transpersonal" in an objectivist language that seeks a universalist foundation utterly beyond the subjective in the form of an absolute transcendence that vanquishes the personal to a lower realm of ignorance or egocentric self-concern. Somewhat between these two extremes lies the expanding territory of a "participatory spirituality" based in an ontological position that seeks to reclaim the import of metaphysical context as a valid, indeed irreducible, feature of transpersonal theory.[8] Appropriately positioned "in-between," this emergent paradigm does not deny the value or significance of the affective qualia that both shape and emerge from the transpersonal event, nor does it deny the possibility of a transcendental depth within the context of the transpersonal horizon. Rather, the "event" is an encounter, a disclosure of being, of sacred depths, resulting in a multidimensional and embodied knowing.[9]

The heuristic value of this theory, which emphasizes the interpretive response of the individual to a sacred encounter, opens the way for a less contested valuation of the mystical and metaphysical claims made by various exoteric and esoteric religious practitioners. The participatory model is not based in preconceptions about the validity of (or relationship to) any particular metaphysical view, but seeks to elucidate that view as yet another example of authentic spiritual encounter. A key aspect of the theory lies in the importance given to the spiritual transformative aspects of that encounter and in the subsequent knowledge gained and integrated into the life of the visionary. In this context, the multiple worlds of diverse visionaries are not contested; rather, the unique qualia of an individual vision indicate both the indeterminate depths of its source and the creative power of an individuated interpretation. Interpretations may be contextualized by particular religious and spiritual traditions or they may occur in cultural contexts outside of those traditions (as in art or science). Whatever the context, the participatory model offers a pivotal positive valuation of that context and places its emphasis on the unique worth of each specific case while yet maintaining openness to multiple alternative metaphysical investigations. There is no pregiven closure on the indeterminate depths of being and no attempt to prioritize specific manifestations of those depths in terms of any doctrinal hierarchical relationship among the diverse religious traditions.

The emphasis, as I understand it, falls not on the specific qualia that are felt or sensed by the individual as a result of a transpersonal event, nor on any transcendental absolutes, but on the metaphysical potential opened by the event to the transformation of everyday human existence. This emphasis includes an emancipatory aspect in the sense that such an event can reveal an increasing transparency and correspondence between an authentic spiritual life and an interpenetrating cosmos of cocreative being. In this sense, there is a liberating aspect to all such transpersonal events insofar as they result in a deepening awareness of authentic human spirituality within an emergent sacred cosmos.[10] In other words, focal concern is not placed on the "individual experience" per se, nor on any specific metaphysical valuation, but on a relational, dialogical, and transformative sharing of insights resulting from multiple transpersonal events on a historical and global scale. No particular tradition or esoteric teaching is privileged; there is no paradigmatic vertical ontological criterion other than the relative particularities of individual traditions or schools. What matters is not the subjective experience, nor the absolute radical claims made by any one tradition (or individual) in the name of that experience. Rather, what matters is the contextual nature of the metaphysical claims insofar as those claims reflect an authentic form of spiritual cocreation and coexistence. Such authenticity is not mandated by either the affective aspect or by the expectation of tradition, but arises through a dynamic process of spiritual transformation that results in a visible, reciprocal, and enactive way of life that illustrates the practical value of the transpersonal event.[11] By "enactive," I mean a mode of living and knowing in which the values of the participatory event are integrated creatively into the visions, concerns, and actions of the practitioner. In short, the transpersonal event is a relational opening to or a "participation in" sacred beingness, an ontological potential whose context is best illustrated in the embodied spiritual life of the specific individual and his or her community.

The participatory turn is a turn toward ontological depths and authentic being, toward what I term "sacred beingness"—that is, a deep and indefinable dynamic horizon of transpersonal possibility (or spiritual mystery) that invites a heart-centered and soulful opening of the individual to a genuine metaphysical context that is particular, relative, and cocreative. In this process, what is most significant is not having "transpersonal experiences" but gaining genuine spiritual knowledge and a discernment of the call to actualize that knowledge though an authentic participatory existence.[12] Such a call can take a multitude of forms and be expressed in myriad ways; yet this call is not simply an exploratory call, a mere testing of the transpersonal waters. In a more mature sense, this call increasingly requires embodiment in a particular way of life, in specific practices, and in a deepening knowledge and realization that affirms the spiritual values of a given path. Thus, there can be no "one way" and no "one theory" nor "one epistemology" to account for the multitude and plurality of all spiritual (and nonspiritual) circumstances that result in transpersonal events.[13] Nor can these events be authentically reduced to a single operative paradigm or sweeping explanatory theory in the comparative assessment of all possible metaphysical contexts. No one person can authentically live, and thereby embody, the truths of all possible metaphysical claims. In an increasingly ecumenical era, it is possible to explore multiple paths and traditions but it is impossible to live and "know" those traditions through direct embodiment of the full range and depth of their specific spiritual goals.

Therefore, as "outsiders," even in the most well-educated and informed sense, no comprehensive evaluation of traditions is possible based on simple intellectual investigation or on the application of any one diagnostic theory. Indeed, the theorist who claims otherwise creates an arbitrary closure of metaphysical horizons. The validity of the "insider" view cannot be simply appropriated to serve a theory without denying and even disfiguring the meaning of that view in all its metaphysical richness and complexity.[14]

The embodiment of any knowledge given in the transpersonal event provides a basis for personal spiritual development and a standing ground for articulating a particular spiritual position. However, in a dialogical and pluralistic context, the authenticity of such knowledge is relative to its enactment in real human relations of respect, mutual concern, and appreciation for differences in temperament, culture, gender, tradition, age, and so on. There is no "one interpretive position" that can authentically evaluate all other positions in the global context of world spirituality, even when "personal experience" may seem to legitimize such a position.[15] This is an ontological claim, one consistent with my own transpersonal encounters over the years; these encounters have led me to affirm the multiplicity of spiritual paths as all authentic, possible, and real within the relative context of their metaphysical teachings. In this ontological context, I understand the nature of "sacred beingness" as a transpersonal horizon through which the diversity in human spirituality continues to emerge from narrow self-preoccupation to ever greater resonance with others in the midst of our collective differences. I call the ground of this emergence "sacred" not in an essentialist fashion, but rather to convey the way in which it impinges upon our deepest human potential for meaningful, sustained coexistence within living depths whose existence we can neither fully fathom nor explain.[16] Spiritual differences are made "real" through the embodiment of particular teachings in the lives of committed men and women whose ideals are actualized in everyday life. The transpersonal horizon opening before us is not a singular event but a vast multitude of events, encounters, openings, and "transconceptual disclosures," which, in their diversity and density, reflect the unmediated depths of a sacred beingness (or Mystery) that cannot be fully plumbed by any one strand of tradition or any one theoretical interpretation.[17]

PARTICIPATION AND SPIRITUAL INQUIRY

In this dynamic unfolding of spiritual potential—as in the new religious movements, in emergent cosmological sciences, in the collapse of authorial claims to exclusive truth in any one tradition or science or art—the unveiling of the transpersonal horizon is irreducible to any particular field of study or to any one religious orientation. The dynamics of a given transpersonal event are not isolated from the context of other such events, and yet, in each event there is a qualitative impact that shapes the specific understanding of the individual or community. Thus, the grounding conditions for understanding such events suggest a need to study each person's encounter in the context of his or her community (and place) in order to provide some comparative insights into the specific metaphysical context of a given teaching. The value of the participatory model as a guideline for research into the transpersonal horizon is the freedom it provides for contextual analyses that do not aprioristically eschew the import of metaphysical contexts. If the transpersonal event cannot be authentically reduced to any particular schema of perception or insight, but largely depends on local/metaphysical context and the qualitative impact of the event, then the relevant epistemology must arise out of its immediate context and historical circumstances. Understanding the transpersonal horizon for Buddhist meditation requires the consideration of context, place, school, interpretive frame, criteria for valid and invalid intuitions, and so on. The same can be said in the case of Sufi spirituality, Jewish Kabbalah, neo-pagan mysticism, kundalini arisings, speaking in tongues, mystical nature experiences, mathematical intuitions, artistic inspirations, and the full spectrum of all possible personal and transpersonal human encounters.[18]

Each tradition has to be treated with an attitude of respect that does not seek to place its emergent horizon into a limited theoretical or historical framework. One of the fallacies of any universal scheme of "stages of development" in human spirituality is the possibility of changing modalities of perception and awareness by participants at any "stage." Modalities are not "frozen in time" or "fixed in being" but continue to evolve, develop, and emerge in the context of overall human developmental shifts as communities interact in terms of the specifics of their beliefs and practices. Nor can we assess the content or value of the "other" through an artificial fixation of developmental stages (as in psychoanalysis) as though our understanding of such stages does not itself change or evolve; our understanding of such stages does evolve or, at least, may evolve, as for example in the way that the childhood patterns that Freud observed in late-nineteenth-century Vienna are no longer prevalent today.[19] We can see, therefore, how the issue of respect hinges on the metaphysical principle that the ground of sacred beingness is not a static ground, not a Platonic structure of stable essences, but a dynamic ground of coevolving participants in a communal context of ongoing exploration and dynamic encounter.[20] In such encounters, the horizon of the transpersonal event is irreducible to any particular stage or modality insofar as beings truly do participate at *every level of development* in the embodiment of the transpersonal through many diverse patterns of human maturation. It is not simply an upward journey to light, but an exploration of possibilities in a universe of infinite scope and constant transformation—guided through authentic living and humble embodiment of relative and viable truths.

The indeterminacy of the transpersonal horizon allows for creative deno-
tation, often through the formation of symbolic analogies, metaphors, and
narratives that in turn give focus and shape to the transpersonal search for
that event. This refers to the "quest" aspect of the transpersonal encounter—
to seek an open horizon, to give it form and meaning, based on what is
received and reciprocally shaped in the processes of seeking.[21] As a spiritual
process, the quest is not simply aimed at the realization of a "known" ideal,
traditional essence, or structural goal, but in the most creative sense, the
quest is an ongoing process of removing the veils that cover the beauty and
depths of the human encounter with transpersonal realities.[22] The quest for
knowledge of "sacred beingness" as a creative process may be delineated in
four stages: preparation (a questioning of values and meaning, a motivated
search for better alternatives), incubation (a period of assimilating possibilities), illumination (a creative resolution based often on transpersonal
encounters), and verification (the integration of insights or revelations into
a way of life consistent with the transpersonal knowing resulting from those
encounters).[23] The stage of preparation might be characterized as a learning
and a questioning of fundamental teachings in relationship to the transpersonal aspect (or lack of same) within a tradition. No matter how much the
individual may assimilate (or resist) the teachings or goals of a tradition, or
puzzle over intuitions that do not conform to any particular tradition, incubation represents the next quest stage. It is a period of disciplined practice
and possible experimentation in search of the confirming transpersonal event
(the illumination stage). Verification is bringing the result of the quest into
everyday life through enactment and embodiment that reflects the knowledge gained through the event.

The illumination stage, working through multiple cycles of questioning
and incubation, may or may not confirm a traditional teaching insofar as the
transpersonal event is an open horizon. The transformative nature of the
event, its primary *participatory* quality and character, cocreated in interaction
with a particular metaphysical context, allows for individual and communal
innovation and many creative, emergent forms of embodied spirituality. Multiple transpersonal events may refine and redirect original intuitions and
result in an ongoing process of spiritual development. The transpersonal
event, as a participatory encounter, is not based in either subjective constructivism or objectivist essentialism, but rather reflects a knowingness that
emerges out of a relational opening to the "pleroma" or fullness of sacred
being. The impact of a given experience may well *deconstruct* traditional ideas
or expectations, as well as result in new forms of *unmediated* knowing neither
simply constructed nor simply realized in a traditional sense.[24] The knowing
or gnosis of the illumined stage in the participatory event facilitates a unique
understanding about the assimilation and application of that knowledge in a
lived sense—thus, gnosis results in new wisdom. Significantly, research in

NDEs (near-death experiences) has shown that NDE events often result in an increased sense of self-worth, empathy for others, proactive social behavior, purposefulness, increased aesthetic appreciation and creativity, and heightened paranormal and psychic perception.[25] Because NDEs provide an example of spontaneous transpersonal events that frequently occur outside of a religious context, such research suggests that the simple embodiment of illuminative transpersonal events opens the participant to inherent psychic abilities giving him or her access to shared transpersonal horizons. Such events can enhance our shared sense of meaningfulness and deepen our mutual appreciation for the various cocreative relationships that make up an individual spiritual life.

Another way of framing the participatory aspect of the transpersonal event is to regard participation as not simply confined to the event but as also reflected in the subsequent way of life of the individual, in his or her values, abilities, presence, and ongoing embodiment of the event. In this sense, "illumination" refers to the consequential knowledge manifest in the life of the participant, and not simply to a particular type of "experience" or subjective perception (nor to a dualistic "objectified" content). The shared quality of the event is reflected in the enhanced psychic sensitivity of the participant as a result of participation in an open horizon that affirms the multilayered, multidimensional possibilities within "sacred beingness." The quest for illumination becomes a test of individual capacity for an ongoing participation that may engage imaginative and metaphorical discourse as a strategic means for explicating the full meaning of the transpersonal event.[26]

The role of the imagination in this process is by no means secondary or epistemologically redundant. Imagination as a procreative, visionary aspect of human perception is a means by which the stage of incubation is explored and probed for the substantive, enduring values and meanings inherent to the specific quest of the individual. Through the creative use of the imagination, implicit aspects of the transpersonal event may be symbolized, communicated, and explored. A heart-centered spirituality seeks the realization of transpersonal knowledge through dreams, guiding visions, and creative intuitions that lead the individual toward the actualization of shared spiritual potential. The imaginal realm, for the Sufi the 'alam al-mithal and for certain esoteric streams of Christianity the mundus imaginalis, is that domain of the transpersonal that reflects human intention as a motivating aspiration toward presential witnessing in the mirror of the receptive imagination, through intuitions of what is spiritually possible or yet concealed in the transpersonal horizon.[27] This imaginal aspect is expressed in the creative denotations of the individual in forms consistent with visionary and aesthetic expression as symbolic analogies, metaphors, and storied landscapes reflecting the embodied, multimodal character of the transpersonal event.[28]

THE ESOTERIC TEACHINGS OF MIKHAËL AÏVANHOV

Western esoteric traditions consist of a multitude of influences, historical interactions, individual practitioners, and a wide variety of schools, secret societies,
and various orders conventionally dating from late Renaissance Hermeticism
to the present day. Common themes of interest range from elemental cosmology, astrology, magic, Jewish and Christian Kabbalah, alchemy, and tarot to
esoteric schools and societies such as the Rosicrucians, Masons, and Theosophical occultists, as well as to various magical, psychic, and "New Age"
groups influenced by esotericism.[29] In general, Western esotericism is highly differentiated and cannot be defined in terms of a specific set of doctrines or practices.[30] Sharing a variable set of "family resemblances" based in a hierarchy of
spirits and multidimensional planes of existence with a core relationship
between students and a master, often engaged in magical ritual training and
visualization practices, the various teachers have each developed unique vocabularies, symbol systems, techniques, and ethical guidelines mixed with varying
degrees of Christian esoteric influence (usually marginal to mainstream Christianity). While no specific goal may define all esotericism, in a broad sense,
most esoteric teachers and societies strongly emphasize the transpersonal aspect
of human development and characterize the goal of such development as varying forms of gnosis.[31] Such "higher knowledge" results in the emergence of
human spiritual potential that must then be integrated into a way of life consistent with the ethical and metaphysical teachings of the community.

However, Western esotericism has been marginalized in academic studies of religion primarily because of the individual, developmental, and participatory nature of its many teachers and their schools. Fitting into neither
the linguistic, humanist approach to "canonical texts" interpreted as literary,
historical documents of large-scale sociocultural movements, nor into the
essentialist models of perennialism, nor the "faith-based" (fideist) approach
of religious exclusivist, Western esoteric teachers and schools have been
largely ignored. Many esotericists emphasize developmental growth and personal transformation, open to individual interpretation, and often linked
with imaginative exercises and mythic narrative understood to be largely
symbolic and metaphorical. Such an imaginative, developmental approach
undermines the demythologizing of many constructivists and also throws into
question the "literalist" attitude that would limit spirituality to static models
of transformation for only the rare, exclusive founders, prophets, or the occasional mystic. This esoteric subversion of interpretive orthodoxies may limit
the relevance of Western esotericism within mainstream Religious Studies;
yet, it is these very characteristics of esotericism that open the door for a participatory exploration of its spiritual depths. The participatory model offers a
way of engaging the creative, revelatory aspects of esoteric traditions while
simultaneously honoring the specific metaphysical context of a given teacher.

It also affirms the local, specific context of the participatory encounter without needing to reference that context in terms of any larger "traditional" religion; it is the participatory encounter that matters, not the large-scale dogmas of orthodoxy, religious or scholarly.

A well-known example of a modern esoteric teacher is Mikhaël Aïvanhov (1900–1986), a Bulgarian *Dounovisti* who taught in France for almost fifty years. Aïvanhov epitomizes the creative, multitraditional, integrative approach to esoteric spirituality and his life clearly reveals an ongoing developmental process of personal growth based in multiple participatory encounters. He was born in the mountainous region of Macedonian, in the village of Serbtzi, to a mother famed for her healing abilities (his father died when he was seven). Baptized into the Greek Orthodox church, he was taught to read at a very early age but also had an intense interest in oral traditions, which he learned from his grandmother Astra (also a healer) and other local elders. His skills for storytelling developed quite early and he was able to mix both oral and written sources in developing his later charismatic narrative style.[32] In 1907, after the village was attacked by Greek bandits, Aïvanhov and his mother Dolia moved to the Bulgarian city of Varna on the coast of the Black Sea. It was here, while living in great poverty, that Aïvanhov received his general education. In addition to his institutional education, he also read whatever books he could find in the school library, particularly on the subject of "esoteric sciences." From one of these books, written by an American Yogi (Ramacharaka), he learned Hatha Yoga, breath control, and meditation techniques that he then practiced, as a young adolescent, on a daily basis for many years. From another book, by Louis Jacolliot, he learned visualization techniques that led to the enhancement of his natural psychic abilities. Other early interests focused on music, qualitative differences between colors, and an incipient interest in the physical sciences.[33]

At about the age of sixteen, while meditating during sunrise at the seashore during a daily regime of constant study, meditation, fasting, and breathing exercises, Aïvanhov was unexpectedly bathed in a "nimbus of light" and saw a being immersed in brilliant, luminous colors: "I found myself flooded with light. I was in a state of bliss, of ecstasy so immense and powerful, that I no longer knew where I was. It was a delirious joy, heaven, the universe." Afterward, it was the beauty and power of this event that remained with him as a sign of the nature of divinity. In later life, Aïvanhov described how as a result of this participatory event he felt himself later immersed in "divine fire" and "inundated by an infinite sweetness, peace, and happiness."[34] As a result of these spiritual illuminations, he read intensively, trying to understand more fully the implications of the event. Similar events followed, a drop of fire in his lungs filled his body with sweetness and light, an event he interpreted as a divine baptism by the Christ Spirit. He also had an extremely intense out-of-body event in which he was swept to the "heart of the cosmos" and surrounded by the music of the spheres. He wrote, "The whole world sang, stars, plants, rocks, everything sang . . . and I felt myself expanding until I feared that I would die." He also had a dramatic Kundalini arousal that resulted in a powerful current filling his entire body with a roaring fire that he was forced to subdue through prayer and mental control.[35]

In 1917, in a fragile psychic condition, vulnerable and open to cosmic influences, he fell ill and almost died. In the midst of this "purification through illness," he had a vision of two powerful beings, one dressed in somber black and the other in brilliant white—he was given a choice, either to take the path of power and control over others or to choose a life of service and self-sacrifice. He chose the white path, a choice of service that he marked as a major defining point in his life. It was also at this point that he decided to live a celibate life, a choice he followed until his death. Shortly after his recovery and dedication to the white path, he met Beinsa Douno (1864–1944), who became his spiritual teacher for the next twenty years.[36] Douno, also known as Peter Deunov, was a Bulgarian *uchitelyat*, or "spiritual teacher," who was the founder (1900) of the Fellowship of Light. The White Brothers and Sisters (or *Dounovisti*) movement is believed by his followers to be partly based on the more ancient spiritualist teachings of the Bulgarian Bogomils.[37] After Douno's return from America, where he lived for seven years as a graduate student studying theology and medicine, he became an itinerant teacher and healer and spent prolonged periods of retreat in the mountains. In 1897, Douno received his first spiritual initiation and in 1914, following a second vision of the Christ Spirit, be began teaching a form of Christian esotericism, called the "third testament," and gradually became a renown *uchitelyat*.[38] Douno was an accomplished violinist, a published author (with a PhD), a successful healer, miracle worker, and creator of more than two hundred spiritual songs still sung today. The total collection of his published teachings on esoteric spirituality exceeds one hundred and fifty volumes (taken down in shorthand when he spoke). Douno opened an Esoteric School (Izgrev) in Sofia, the capital of Bulgaria, whose curriculum consisted of spiritual talks (*besedi*, beginning at 5:00 a.m.), a series of special physical movements known as *paneurhythmy*, vegetarianism, song, prayer, and meditation exercises directed toward the sun, which was regarded as a living symbol of the divine world. Master Beinsa summarized his teaching in the following saying: "Purify thoughts, feelings, desires and the body is in a condition for health. Always live and move in love."[39]

In 1917, Douno was expelled from Sofia at the request of the Orthodox Bishop as a result of his "heretical" teachings (he was later excommunicated) and settled in Varna. Aïvanhov soon joined the brotherhood and became a dedicated student of Douno, eventually following him back to Sofia. He received instruction in various esoteric techniques, including out-of-body experiences, induced by Douno; Aïvanhov said, "We would both leave our bodies and he would lead me into the invisible world so I could learn its realities."[40] As a member of the brotherhood at Izgrev, Aïvanhov was also required by Douno to pursue his formal education and eventually acquired a diploma from the University of Sofia. Combining both exoteric and esoteric studies, he also undertook frequent retreats at the brotherhood's summer camps (*bivacut*) in the high mountains. In 1920, while attending a retreat and having climbed high into the mountains, Aïvanhov had a profound opening to spiritual presence within nature. He says, "Everything around me seems to come alive, the stones, trees, grass, became vibrant and luminous as though by magic . . . behind her invisible façade nature conceals realities such as human beings have never dreamed of."[41] His academic studies introduced him to other spiritual traditions such as Buddhism and Kabbalah, and he continued to study mathematics and science; eventually he received graduate diplomas in psychology and education. While the relationship between Aïvanhov and Douno remained formal and somewhat distant (Douno had hundreds of students), in 1937 Aïvanhov was chosen by Douno to carry the teachings of the brotherhood to France.[42]

In France, Brother Mikhaël spent fifty years expanding on and developing the teachings of Beinsa Douno. As a charismatic speaker, never using notes or books, he quickly gathered a small group of interested followers. He eventually formed, with the help of other Bulgarian expatriates and his French enthusiasts, two spiritual centers: Izgrev (1947 in Sèvres, west of Paris) and a second at Bonfin on the Riviera (1953). Having arrived in Paris penniless, he lived very simply for the rest of his life, took no money for his teachings, practiced lifelong celibacy, and exemplified a spiritual path of utmost simplicity and frugality.[43] He also established L'Ecole Divine as a branch of the "invisible college" of the White Brotherhood where he taught a curriculum similar to that followed by Douno. He emphasized establishing a peaceful vision of humanity, based on nonviolence, cooperation, and a pluralistic vision of an ideal brotherhood between all races, creeds, and social and economic levels of society. His teachings centered on "solar religion" with Christ as a supreme symbol of the ideal human being and a model of spiritual accomplishment. In 1959, still known as Brother Mikhaël, he undertook a one-year pilgrimage to India where he met and interacted with many Indian holy men and women and was given the initiatic name Omraam by Neemkaroli Baba. After his return to France from India, notable by a remarkable change in his appearance, he was recognized as an *uchitelyat*, or true spiritual teacher, and from that time forward until his death in 1986 he was known as Master Omraam Mikhaël Aïvanhov.[44]

SPIRITUAL INTUITION

The teachings and spiritual events in the life of Mikhaël Aïvanhov are particularly congruent with a participatory understanding of spirituality. Aïvanhov did not frame the participatory events of his life in terms of "personal experience" but instead referred to them as sources of special *knowledge* (gnosis) that revealed to him the cosmological and metaphysical significance of human life. His teachings, which are highly complex and diverse, extend to more than seventy volumes of recorded talks, ranging over a period of almost fifty years; in all these volumes he only rarely and very briefly speaks of transpersonal events in his life. In fact, he explicitly warns his students against talking about "gifts of the spirit" because such gifts will not be understood by those who lack direct knowledge based on various types of metaphysical or mystical perceptions.[45] Conversely, he speaks at great length about *spiritual knowledge* and its various types, using a template of the human person that is highly esoteric. He states that for a majority of men, the objective, visible, intellectually accessible world is valued above the world of subjective feelings. However, human desires and motivations arise from feelings and intuitions of the heart, and thus any truths that are learned by the intellect must be internalized and felt with the whole body. Only if a truth is lived, fully and completely, can it be understood and actualized in the life of the individual. While the intellect is a significant cognitive faculty, Aïvanhov regards *spiritual intuition* as a higher form of intelligence receptive to subtle perception of a cosmological nature and when attuned to subtle planes of perception, such intuition receives insights far beyond those of the physical senses. Intuition is a revelatory faculty that is "beyond the reach of the intellect" and can be developed "only through meditation, persistent work, and prayer."[46]

Spiritual intuition results in "immediate certitude" of the cosmological depths of human existence; it is a power of cognition beyond that of clairvoyance, clairaudience, and other intermediary, extrasensory perceptual powers. Paranormal perceptions, which can develop as a consequence of participation in transpersonal events, were regarded by Aïvanhov as indications of potential human vulnerability to psychic influences corresponding with the degree of (or lack of) individual spiritual development and maturity.[47] In a developmental sense, the transpersonal event might well stimulate psychic or paranormal perceptions but the deeper ground of such development was realized through the cultivation of spiritual intuitions that resulted in an expansive, cosmological perception open to the ground of sacred beingness, or as Aïvanhov called it, to the Living Spirit. He writes extensively on the "philosophy of Spirit" as symbolized in the sun as a manifestation of the Solar Logos, an extramental reality of spiritual presence working throughout all nature and epitomized in the brilliance of dawn sunlight. The Primordial Fire of creation manifests as visible light, a masculine principle. Through a creative synthesis, visible light (*svetlina*) becomes the carrier of invisible light (*vedelina*), a feminine principle that impacts both the senses and the spiritual intuition. Thus, for Aïvanhov and for Beinsa Douno, the sun is a symbol of the spiritual center of knowledge that is fully transpersonal and yet accessible to psychic perception through spiritual training. When spiritual intuition is developed to the requisite degree, it will open to a perception of *vedelina*, the primordial, invisible light that will then infuse the individual aura with subtle presence. Once this intuitive presence is operative in the individual, he or she will be able to invest thoughts, words, and actions with greater creative potency through the formation of spiritually energized intention. The virtues that best solicit this presence are love, purity, and selflessness; the colors of the spectrum of light reflect these and other spiritual qualities.[48]

Spiritual Identity

Aïvanhov differentiated between "personality," which he saw as a psychic formation based on social, familial, and cultural influences, and "individuality," which he taught as the true basis of authentic spiritual identity. The personality is limited to socially created "stereotyped" responses, attitudes, beliefs, and thoughts. Uncritically accumulated knowledge, based on external learning through memorization and hearsay, can "broaden the mind and point of view, but only on the surface." No matter how much information a person may remember, the deeper character, virtues, and spiritual qualities remain untouched by such information. Authentic spiritual knowledge obligates the seeker to "penetrate the depths and to climb heights" such that it is impossible to remain unchanged in a deep, inner sense.[49]

This change derives from throwing off inherited stereotypes of thought or belief that inhibit the inner transformation that comes through direct participation in transpersonal events. Such knowledge results in an awakening to hidden potential and creates a genuine "individuality" that is differentiated from collective, stereotyped thinking and action. The training involved in the creation of true individuality requires a convergence of "all one's contradictory tendencies" toward "one glorious, beneficial goal, to become a focal point of such intense, powerful light that one is free to send rays of light in every direction, like the sun."[50] The personality resists conformity to this spiritual light because it clings to stereotyped actions and thoughts whereas individuality is nourished though contact with the transpersonal presence and seeks to bring identity into harmony with that presence. The personality must "give in" its impulses and desires to become an authentic individual through a true (alchemical) marriage that is "the goal and aim of all instruction, methods, and exercises offered by an Initiatic School."[51]

For Aïvanhov, true individuality, shaped by transpersonal events, reveals the nature of Self as an awakened, core aspect of identity who, like an engineer guiding a train at night, remains awake and alert while the passengers (in this case the lesser aspects of personality) sleep, dream, or merely gaze passively at the external landscape. The awakened Self is vibrant, a lucid and guiding awareness, which requires the initiate to practice constant vigilance in order to sustain a sense of participation in true self-awareness, even when sleeping at night. He locates the "eternal watcher" in the "center of the forehead between the eyebrows" and when personality and heightened individuality unite, the invisible world opens and allows communication "with the greatest and most marvelous realities" far beyond the normative, stereotyped world of everyday awareness.[52] As an esoteric Christian, Aïvanhov redefines the nature of the Holy Spirit as "not an extraneous entity [but] as the most luminous, powerful, divine peak of man's being." However, and here we have the metaphysical context, "there is only one divine, cosmic Holy Spirit, and each man's higher Self, being divine in nature, receives its spark from this one Spirit." This one Spirit is manifested in the living symbolism of the sun and in its two kinds of light, and when a human being attains sufficient purification, he or she will be united with that higher, invisible light that is already intrinsic to each individual. The Godhead is both the universal cosmic Spirit and the basis of the higher Self of each person who is "but a spark in one great Fire, a drop in the one cosmic ocean."[53]

In defining the higher Self further, Aïvanhov draws on Kabbalah and notes that the Self is not a material nor subtle nor psychic entity, but "belongs to the region known [in Kabbalah] as Ain Soph Aur, the Limitless Light." The personality is constructed of "many changeable, unreliable, contradictory 'selves'" that produce suffering and require constant reparation as a result of their chaotic, expressive actions. The "I" that seeks to coordinate these many lesser selves ("the poet, miser, cook, and liar"), being created as an artifact of socialization and psychological unpredictability based in poorly organized, stereotyped learning, is constantly at the mercy of unintegrated impulses, desires, and habits. Only through the discipline of a motivated effort to know the deeper Self can the individual emerge, like the butterfly from the caterpillar who then dries its wings in the brilliant light of the (spiritual) sun. The butterfly is a esoteric symbol of the reborn soul that has escaped the restrictions of disorganized personality and attained "true resurrection"—not a resurrection of the physical body, but an awakening of the spiritual element within that had been asleep but now "bursts into bloom." Aïvanhov refers to the ego ("the frail screen of self") as a focal point of meditation by which the practitioner may merge with the higher Self. Using the imaginative faculty, the practitioner envisions a flowing current linking the conscious ego and the Self. The expansive nature of Self and the lower ego are two poles of one consciousness that can fuse into one identity through a transpersonal event that opens the horizon of the higher Self to its full cosmic dimensionality. The ego as the "screen of personality" constantly receives the subtle impressions of the higher Self, thus attention must be shifted little by little to those impressions and withdrawn from habitual engagements of personality. As the transformation proceeds, the practitioner will feel "overflowing with light [and] without warning, [will be] thrust upwards into the superconscious and dazzled by the immensity and beauty of the world." Even as one falls back into ordinary life, there must be an intent to cultivate the current of connection, with patience and persistence, until "one fine day, the light will be always with you . . . to know one's Self is to melt into oneness with the Godhead."[54]

Clearly, the metaphysical context here is inseparable from the transpersonal events that were part of Aïvanhov's own development. There is a consistency between these events and the interpretation that suggests something like Jorge N. Ferrer's image of an "ocean with many shores" as an appropriate model for understanding participatory spirituality. Through his own participatory events, and with the help of Beinsa Douno, Aïvanhov was able to interpret transpersonal openings in a way that was consistent with both the qualia of his affective experiences and a metaphysical context grounded in similar such events indigenous to Bulgarian esotericism. The Bulgarian context provided Aïvanhov with a shore upon which he could contextualize spiritual events in his life that gave form and meaning to his personal development. Further, he was sent to another shore (France) where, after learning a second language and culture, he was able to translate his interpretation into the new circumstance without denying the formative import of the transpersonal but also without emphasizing his "spiritual experiences" as a basis for his interpretation. Instead, the basis of the interpretive work was linked to a global vision of a shared brotherhood and sisterhood whose purpose was to cultivate "higher knowledge" that was irreducible to any stage of formative personality. The fusion of the transpersonal with a metaphysical context is the true expressive core of his teachings, which rely very little on his personal experiences and very much on a shared narrative of pilgrimage, quest, and a spiritual epistemology whose goals are to overcome the chaotic, distracting, and polarized consciousness of stereotyped social conditioning for a knowledge that was truly "participatory" in a vaster metaphysical horizon of sacred beingness beyond the merely psychological. In fact, ordinary psychological formation is interpreted as a retardation of spiritual development when it results in only stereotyped thinking, reiterative conventional patterns, and a limited horizon of socially conditioned responses driven by unintegrated (and unrecognized) subpersonality structures.

THE ROLE OF IMAGINATION

Another interesting feature of Aïvanhov's teachings is the importance and role of the imagination as a creative faculty. He describes the imaginative faculty as a generative power similar to that of a pregnant woman who nurtures the incipient potential of sperm into a living being: "Imagination moulds and nurtures the elements it receives, its power is formative." It is inspired thought that provides the seed, while it is the imagination that gives form and content to the initial inspiration. When thoughts and feelings are pure and harmonious, physical and psychic health abound, but disturbed and unhealthy thinking leads directly to psychic impairment. The imagination is an attractive power; it draws into form elements that correspond to indwelling, repeated feelings and thoughts (positive or negative). Therefore, the mind must be disciplined to think wholesome, harmonious, and creative thoughts, ones that apply not simply to the immediate concerns of the personality, but to the good and judicious welfare of all humanity. The initiate is directed to focus his or her thoughts on "heavenly places" and "worlds of beauty" in order to nurture imaginative forms (or images) that reflect "the splendors of heaven itself." The imagination, like a meteorologist's balloon, is sent into the higher atmosphere to gather impressions and information that can then be brought to earth and actualized in daily life. The source of these higher impressions is the deep nature of Self manifested through a creative, visionary power, the imagination, within each person.[55]

One technique for the development of the imaginative capacity is to choose a subject that reflects the highest spiritual ideal and then to concentrate on that ideal vividly but with relaxation. The practitioner should become absorbed in the subject and "simply contemplate and soak up the beauty you have conjured up . . . then, identify with that beauty, moving from concentration to meditation to contemplation." Thus, one should "drink deeply from this beauty, savor it, and find happiness in it." The success of this technique depends, ultimately, on a synthesis of human effort and divine grace, because "only Heaven can give us the light which illumines the imagination." Aïvanhov thus defines "inspiration" as the fusion of human imaginative effort with luminous, divine presence; such presence causes all human faculties to work together in harmony with "the spiritual light received from above." The screen of the imagination thus becomes a medium for a presential witnessing that, like the mirror analogy used in Sufism, can reflect a higher spiritual potential inherent to the imaginal realm. The subtle impressions received by this creative use of the imagination act to facilitate artistic, mystical, and initiatic transformations that correspond to beneficial works of art, spiritual realization, and esoteric teaching. The consequences of such practice will be unique for each person, filtered through the texture of personality, to reflect varying degrees of purity and insight shaped by individual nature and temperament. Thus, inspiration is a relative quality, a communication with higher being, whose manifestations depend on the development, receptivity, and spiritual maturity of the individual.[56]

Aïvanhov spoke often on the importance of harmony and aesthetic balance in living a spiritual life, one that reflected the natural beauty of the world ("living nature") as imbued with a transpersonal (and metaphysical) presence of beauty and vitality. He references such harmony to the transpersonal event of hearing the music of the spheres, a vibratory beauty that per-

meates the world in accordance with "the will of Cosmic Intelligence." It is
his vital awareness of this music that allows him to see "the underlying structure and destination of the universe." He calls this vision of the archetypal
reality "the crowning point of all my research, all my work, all my out-of-body
experiences." He notes that it is the touchstone and criterion that allows him
to understand and recognize the true nature of human life within the greater
cosmos. In knowing this harmony or presence, the whole body vibrates in
unison with its truth; its presence is a source of renewal and enduring health.
It is a heart-centered knowing that attracts many other spiritual qualities to
it, because it is the central harmony that resonates within all living beings.
As an attractor and synthesis of spiritual qualities, it may be symbolized as the
presence of Universal Soul, which he defines as "the currents and forces that
transform and organize everything." The center of initiatic work is to cultivate this harmony in one's life, through disciplined living and loving relationships, to resonate with the harmony that is the whole of creation and the
basis of spiritual well-being. For Aïvanhov, this Hermetic harmony descends
through an esoteric hierarchy from God as Creative Principle and First
Cause, through angels, masters, brother and sister initiates, and other human
beings, to animals, plants, and the stones creating a fully animate nature, a
living cosmos of incomprehensible complexity. However, its immediacy and
its transpersonal quality is a key to human life; its constant and subtle effects
are enhanced and magnified through correct living, mental discipline, and
harmonious relationships.[57]

ESOTERICISM AND PARTICIPATORY SPIRITUALITY

Clearly, Aïvanhov demonstrates a creative, enactive way of life in which the
spiritual principles he teaches are inseparable from both the transpersonal
events in his life and from the emphasis he placed on the need for personal
transformation in the life of the initiate. He records in many places his own
struggles to live according to the ideals he taught and how the challenges in
his life required him to constantly refine his own inner realizations.[58] Participatory knowing is not merely intellectual but, as Ferrer writes, includes the
"emotional and emphatic knowing of the heart, the sensual and somatic
knowing of the body, [and the] visionary and intuitive knowing of the soul."[59]
The basis of Aïvanhov's spiritual vision was actualized through a participatory knowing of Spirit, of sacred beingness, a lived knowing that he then
sought to embody through daily practice, meditation, bodily exercises, music,
art, and further study. His task, given to him by Beinsa Douno, was to enact
and bring forth his vision within the metaphysical context of Bulgarian,
Christian esoteric teachings that he then carried to France. In harmony with
the creative nature of participatory spirituality, however, Aïvanhov went far
beyond the more traditional teachings of Douno as he integrated various

Hindu and Buddhist teachings into his overall views on spiritual life, creating a rich synthesis of Eastern and Western esoteric practices.[60] Furthermore,
his participatory knowing emphasizes the continual need for direct, personal
transformation throughout life. He did not simply teach ideas, but also techniques and practices for emotional, mental, and spiritual development that
induced a continual refinement, embodiment, and manifestation of the realizations of spiritual life.

As lifelong efforts are required to embody spiritual teachings, Aïvanhov
places those teachings into a metaphysical context, not as a supplement to
validate "experience" but as a cosmological basis for all forms of human
development. Self-knowledge for him is inextricably tied to the very nature
of being, which through its embodiment in nature, encompasses and sustains
all life through transformational and transpersonal activities. The challenge
of embodying those activities in consciously attuned service, thought, and
feeling results in a metaphysical resonance, an alignment of soul with deep,
inherent harmonies of nature. What constitutes "personal experience" is only
relevant insofar as it provides a ground for such resonance in the context of
developing an intuitive knowledge whose activity is one of attunement to
higher, transpersonal realities. Like a dancer seeking to express the power and
beauty of music, movement is coordinated with the vibrant sounds and
rhythms that move the individual whose own inner discipline and flexibility
is great enough to express or enact the passion and meaning felt in the music.
The affective qualia of the dancer are secondary to the coordinated expressive movements that reveal the hidden possibilities of the music. In the life
of the initiate, it is the qualitative character and virtuous life that best express
the harmony felt and seen through transpersonal events.

Another characteristic of Aïvanhov's synthesis is the oral and narrative
aspect of his teaching. His constant use of metaphors, stories, and narrative
embellishments enlivens his teaching through its appeal to multisensory perception and a more richly embodied, felt sense of connection with a wide
range of life experiences in contrast to a dry intellectualism whose teachings
rest almost entirely in a realm of abstraction and disembodied thought. As an
expression of enactive cognition, the oral narrative aspect resonates with rich
analogies drawn from daily, embodied life in which imaginative and
metaphorical discourse give a grounded sense of participation in a wide spectrum of human (and nonhuman) relationships. Nature, as a medium of living
presence, brims over in his teachings with a radiance of luminous imagery
that directly impacts the imaginative faculty and thereby stimulates the very
activity he seeks to instill through visualization techniques. His dramatic and
visual analogies give form and substance to mental processes that reflect a
presential witnessing; the mirror of the imagination is polished by his
metaphorical invocation of astral, solar, lunar, and other natural imagery that
abound in his works. His use of symbolic analogies, tied frequently to West-

ern esoteric practices such as those in alchemy, Kabbalah, astrology, and magic, all work to create a vivid resource of images (both Eastern and Western) that help to embody his teachings in visible worlds of form, even though he constantly advises against attachment to those forms.

There is also an emancipatory quality in his teachings as he stresses the import of personal development that, in turn, leads, not to conformity to fixed or dogmatic teachings, but to a generative, creative way of life whose qualitative substance is refined and made subtle through the formation of a true individuality. The very concept of throwing off stereotyped learning for greater spiritual authenticity cuts against any strictly imitative adoption of his teachings and challenges the initiate to find and develop those unique characteristics that, in fact, best reflect an emancipated spiritual life. In terms of a participatory model of spirituality, such an emphasis on becoming a true individual, with less emphasis placed on personal experience, suggests that the "ocean with many shores" is one whose transpersonal horizons can best be known through processes of maturational development that celebrate differences rather than enforcing conformity. Individuation, as a process of spiritual maturity, must inevitably undermine the collective tendency toward simply conformity to cultural (or rational) ideas because the very nature of authentic being is to challenge the static, fixated, and rigidly held attitudes of collective life for a more nuanced, personalized, and individuated expression of mutual growth, interaction, diversity, and complexity. This is exactly the emphasis in the teachings of Aïvanhov.

Another feature of the life of Aïvanhov is the nature of the stages by which he gradually attains his spiritual maturity. In the earlier mention of four stages (preparation, incubation, illumination, and verification), we can see through the lens of his life how these stages are neither sequential, nor linear in relationship to one another. Many transpersonal events occurred to Aïvanhov at a relatively early age, events that can be legitimately characterized as illuminative. And yet during his training with Douno, he raises many questions, has many doubts, and much uncertainty about his own accomplishments while being trained after having had several very profound revelations. Thus, the developmental model must be flexible in describing how the stages may relate, reoccur, and shift according to overall life patterns. There is a psychospiritual point to this observation: human beings in their encounter with transpersonal horizon do not easily, nor even after some difficulties, necessarily comprehend or understand the import of those encounters. Perhaps only after years of effort, reflection, and continual work, do such events begin to clarify and expand into a comprehension that reflects genuine maturity. In this context, "personal experience" does not provide a great enough container for spiritual development because these encounters can take one far beyond the known shore, the conventional or traditional stereotypes, or a particular stage of psychic development, into an expansive horizon of human spiritual potential whose meaning and value can only be known through a lifetime of effort to embody and to understand the contents of those events.

Aïvanhov spent many years in training and many more years as simply a "brother" in the general organization in France before he was recognized as a true teacher. His quest for the full realization of the teachings and goals of a universal brotherhood and sisterhood was a formative structural aspect of his own incubation. Through Douno, he learned the importance of community, loving relations, and consistent discipline and education. This training drew him away from self-fascination with his development and redirected his attention toward larger issues of spiritual concern. As in the participatory model, this movement toward community, social concern, and the global context of spiritual development is consistent with the impact of transpersonal events that point beyond the subjective or personal elements of the event. His East-West synthesis, including his journey to India, shows his willingness to explore spiritual possibilities throughout his life as part of his lifelong quest to realize, as fully as possible, the global implications of human spirituality as revealed to him through transpersonal events. In the context of a quest pattern, the period of incubation was impacted by many such events, and the illuminative knowledge of those events did not rest in a recapitulation of "experience" but in a continuing maturity of spiritual insight and wisdom. This wisdom, in its developmental aspect, is inseparable from both the transpersonal events that inspired him and from the efforts he made over a lifetime to actualize the full implications of those events through an authentic, embodied way of life. Verification was conditional and relative to his own metaphysical perceptions, but the validation was a lifelong process, one realized through a constant testing of his integrity and values as he sought to embody the ideals of his own teachings.

CONCLUSION

The applicability of a participatory model, as a window through which a particular way of life or a teaching is illumined, provides epistemological flexibility in framing the events that constitute the transpersonal aspects of that life or teaching. It does not, however, provide a context for making judgments about that teaching in relationship to implicit doctrinal criteria of which events are more or less authentic, "higher" or "lower." This is exactly as it should be, considering the self-aggrandizement implicit to any such judgments. The value of any transpersonal theory lies, as I see it, in its ability to reveal features of interest implicit to the material under study, not to provide paradigmatic evaluative criteria for the determination of that material's worth or significance. The participatory approach brackets such doctrinal judgments because it recognizes that, in an increasingly globalized and diverse culture, the value of a theory lies not so much in its explanatory power as it does in its capacity to respectfully frame and reframe the way of life and practices of others such that they themselves might find value in the theory. The theory is not a substitute for the context and content that the theory may claim to unpack or open to alien eyes, but it can offer a dialogical view consistent with an ethic of respectful communication and mutual learning.

If some theorists resist this dialogical ethical element, there is little doubt that the value of their theories will remain circumscribed to the boundaries of their own special interests. The ecumenical study of transpersonal phenomena will stultify to the degree that its perspectivism is limited to a monological voice or a closed theory unreceptive to the value and worth of the metaphysical claims made by many of those who are the primary recipients of transpersonal events. The new horizon for transpersonal studies must eventually incorporate insights and understandings from multiple disciplines, including comparative studies in religion as well as theology and mysticism that move beyond reductive "explanatory" models. The emergent paradigms of dialogical interaction, mutual self-development, and cocreative relationships in cultural analysis all contribute to the formation of an ethical concern whose purpose is to foster human understanding across the boundaries of social and historical differences. The truly "postcolonial" mode of analysis is one that is founded on respect for differences that are not undermined by hierarchical thinking or theory building. Metaphysical claims made by those whose lives have been changed and impacted by transpersonal events are exactly one of those differences. Thinking critically about such claims requires theorists both to recognize that such claims are real and valid for the practitioners, and also to frame their theories in respectful and nondismissive ways that create a context for dialogue.

One such theory, the participatory spirituality model, does this admirably with tact and sensitivity. In the esoteric context, it provides a means for examining the formative transpersonal events in the life of an individual, group, or community. It does this by providing a contextual affirmation of metaphysical claims without overvaluing those claims and without making judgments about their explicit significance in relationship to other possibly similar or conflicting claims. The model remains open to the creative aspects of the embodiment of such claims and seeks to elucidate the relationships between the life of the individual (or group) and the way transpersonal events give rise to relevant transpersonal teachings or values. The enactive epistemology of the model allows for an investigation of various forms of knowledge (and practice) as a legitimate basis for the expression of transpersonal truths without violating the integrity of such knowledge by transposing them into a deconstructive framework. The model also allows for comparative and interdisciplinary study without attempting to create hierarchies

among traditions, holding a position of intermediacy between all metaphysical claims, and yet, denying none. Critical thinking is thus directed toward
the operative application of the model and its value in soliciting transformative insight from any transpersonal context, without seeking to justify those
insights at the expense of diminishing the context. It is through such respect
that we can hope to learn from the visionary worlds of others.

NOTES

1. Jorge N. Ferrer, *Revisioning Transpersonal Theory: A Participatory Vision of
Human Spirituality* (Albany: State University of New York Press, 2002), 20–21.

2. See Donald Rothberg, "The Crisis of Modernity and the Emergence of Socially
Engaged Spirituality," *ReVision* 15 (1993): 105–14; Peter Nelson, "Mystical Experience and Radical Deconstruction: Through the Ontological Looking Glass," in
Transpersonal Knowing: Exploring the Horizons of Consciousness, ed. Tobin Hart, Nelson, and Kaisa Puhakka (Albany: State University of New York Press, 2000), 64–66;
and Michael Hays, "The Emergence of a Fourth Force in Psychology: A Convergence
between Psychology and Spirituality," in *Faith in the Millennium*, ed. Stanley Porter
and Michael Hays (Sheffield: Sheffield Academic Press, 2001), 106–22.

3. See Mark Taylor, "Deconstruction: What's the Difference?" *Soundings* 66
(1983): 387–403; Robert Torrance, *The Spiritual Quest: Transcendence in Myth, Religion, and Science* (Berkeley: University of California Press, 1994), 292–94; and Nelson, "Mystical Experience and Radical Deconstruction," 55–84, where he argues for
the desirability of nonclosure on meaning in the interpretation of mystical states.

4. For an overview of the deconstructive problem and the way it undermines science, see John Caputo, *Radical Hermeneutics: Repetition, Deconstruction, and the
Hermeneutic Project* (Bloomington: Indiana University Press, 1987), specifically the
chapter entitled "Toward a Postmetaphysical Rationality."

5. Carl Olsen, ed., *Theory and Method in the Study of Religion* (New York:
Wadsworth Publishing, 2002), passim. For a more nuanced view of the insider/out-
sider problem, see Russell T. McCutcheon, ed., *The Insider/Outsider Problem in the
Study of Religion: A Reader* (New York: Cassell, 1999), and for a review of the problematic aspects of the "inner empiricism" associated with certain humanistic
approaches, see Ferrer, *Revisioning Transpersonal Theory*, 48–51. For articulations of
intermediate "insider/outsider" positions that value both stances and/or seek to overcome the dichotomy, see Kim Knott, "Insider/Outsider Perspectives," in *The Routledge
Companion to the Study of Religion*, ed. John Hinnells (New York: Routledge, 2005),
243–58, and the editors' introduction to this volume.

6. David R. Griffin and Huston Smith, *Primordial Truth and Postmodern Theology*
(Albany: State University of New York Press, 1990). On the relationship between
exclusivism, inclusivism, and pluralism, see Diana Eck, *Encountering God: A Spiritual
Journey from Bozeman to Banaras* (Boston: Beacon Press, 1993), 166–99. For a critique
of the perennialist position in its many variations, see Ferrer, *Revisioning Transpersonal
Theory*, 71–111.

7. The divisions within the study of mysticism also follow the general lines of debate between a secularized "subjective" constructivism and a religionist "objective" perennialism; see Rothberg, "Understanding Mysticism: Transpersonal Theory and the Limits of Contemporary Epistemological Frameworks," *ReVision* 12 (1989): 5–22. For an overview of the philosophy of religion with a neo-Kantian bent, see John Hick, *The Fifth Dimension: An Exploration of the Spiritual Realm* (Boston: Oneworld Publications, 1999).

8. This model was introduced in a single concise article by Ferrer, "Transpersonal Knowledge: A Participatory Approach to Transpersonal Phenomena," in *Transpersonal Knowing*, 213–52; for an updated summary, see his chapter in this volume.

9. Ferrer, "Transpersonal Knowledge," 117–24.

10. Ferrer, *Revisioning Transpersonal Theory*, 129, 174–78; Hays, "The Emergence of a Fourth Force in Psychology," defines spirituality as "beyond cultural concreteness of human expression and action . . . a sense of right relations with the self, the world, and the sacred" (13).

11. Ferrer, *Revisioning Transpersonal Theory*, 151–55.

12. Ferrer, "Transpersonal Knowledge," 234–35; and Ferrer, *Revisioning Transpersonal Theory*, 133ff, where the metaphor of the "ocean with many shores" corresponds to what I am calling "sacred beingness."

13. On religious pluralism, see Raimon Panikkar, "A Self Critical Dialogue," in *The Intercultural Challenge of Raimon Panikkar*, ed. Joseph Prabhu (New York: Orbis Books, 1996), 227–29; and Eck, *Encountering God*, 190–99.

14. In this regard, see Ferrer, "Speak Now or Forever Hold Your Peace: A Review Essay of Ken Wilber's *The Marriage of Sense and Soul: Integrating Science and Religion*," *The Journal of Transpersonal Psychology* 30 (1998): 53–67, where he critically assesses Ken Wilber's work. See also Christian de Quincey, "The Promise of Integralism: A Critical Appreciation of Ken Wilber's *Integral Psychology*," in *Cognitive Maps and Spiritual Models*, ed. Jensine Andersen and Robert Forman (Bowling Green: Imprint Academic, 2000), 177–208; and Sean Kelly, "The Prodigal Soul: Religious Studies and the Advent of Transpersonal Psychology," in *Religious Studies: Issues, Prospects, and Proposals*, ed. Klaus Klostermaier and Larry Hurtado (Atlanta: Scholars Press, 1991), 429–41.

15. Ferrer, *Revisioning Transpersonal Theory*, 144–49, 165–67.

16. See Lee Irwin, *Visionary Worlds: The Making and Unmaking of Reality* (Albany: State University of New York Press, 1996) and *Awakening to Spirit: On Life, Illumination, and Being* (Albany: State University of New York Press, 1999).

17. Ferrer *Revisioning Transpersonal Theory*, 145.

18. Irwin, *Visionary Worlds*, 179–81.

19. See Daniel Merkur, "Transpersonal Psychology: Models of Spiritual Awakening," *Religious Studies Review* 23 (1997): 145.

20. For a good general phenomenological description of the transpersonal encounter, see Jenny Wade, *Changes of Mind: A Holonomic Theory of the Evolution of Consciousness* (Albany: State University of New York Press, 1996), 182–85.

21. Ferrer, *Revisioning Transpersonal Theory*, 126–28, 153.

22. Torrance, *The Spiritual Quest*, 293. Also see Irwin, *The Dream-Seekers: Native American Visionary Traditions of the Great Plains* (Norman: University of Oklahoma Press, 1994), 188–89.

23. The four stages of creativity come from Joseph Wallas (1926) as given by Merkur in "Transpersonal Psychology," 145; I have modified the context and definitions slightly.

24. For more on the weakness of the constructivist position in transpersonal theory, see Rothberg, "Understanding Mysticism," 10–13.

25. Merkur, "Transpersonal Psychology," 144, cites NDE research by Cherie Sutherland (*Reborn in Light*, 1995) and Melvin Morse (*Transformed by the Light*, 1992).

26. See Rothberg, "Spiritual Inquiry," in *Transpersonal Knowing*, where he refers to the quest process as a form of ongoing "spiritual inquiry" (164–66).

27. Zia Khan, "Illuminative Presence," in *Transpersonal Knowing*, 153–54.

28. Irwin, *The Dream-Seekers*, 185ff., 277 n. 9.

29. For an overview of Western esotericism, see Antoine Faivre and Jacob Needleman, eds. *Modern Esoteric Spirituality* (New York: Crossroad, 1992); Wouter Hanegraaff, *New Age Religion and Western Culture: Esotericism in the Mirror of Secular Thought* (Albany: State University of New York Press, 1998); and Arthur Versluis, "What is Esoteric? Methods in the Study of Western Esotericism," *Esoterica* 4 (2002): 1–16, http://www.esoteric.msu.edu/VolumeIV/Methods.htm, accessed May 2006.

30. Faivre, *Modern Esoteric Spirituality*, lists four shared "fundamental characteristics" of esotericism: a complex of cosmological correspondences, living nature, the mediating role of imagination, and "the experience of transmutation" (xv–xx).

31. Faivre, *Access to Western Esotericism* (Albany: State University of New York Press, 1994), defines gnosis as "an integrating knowledge, a grasp of the fundamental relations including the least apparent that exist among various levels of reality" (19) and as "embracing diverse traditions and melding them in a single crucible" (14). Versluis, "What is Esoteric?," writes "the word 'gnosis' refers to direct spiritual insight into the nature of the cosmos and of oneself, and thus may be taken as having both a cosmological and a metaphysical import" (11).

32. Georg Feuerstein, *The Mystery of Light: The Life and Teachings of Omraam Mikhaël Aïvanhov* (Lower Lake, CA: Integral Publishing, 1998), 6–12; Louise Frenette, *Omraam Mikhaël Aïvanhov: A Biography* (Liverpool, U.K.: Suryoma, 1999), 3–14.

33. Feuerstein, *The Mystery of Light*, explains that Ramancharaka was the name taken by William Atkinson, whose book on yoga dates to 1903 (16). See also Frenette, *Mikhaël Aïvanhov*, 33–36, 46–51. At fifteen, Aïvanhov painted all the glass in the windows of his room one color at a time in order to meditate on the psychic qualities induced by each color.

34. Unpublished talk, December 9, 1968, in Feuerstein, *The Mystery of Light*, 16; Frenette, *Mikhaël Aïvanhov*, 54–55.

35. Unpublished talk, 1954, in Frenette, *Mikhaël Aïvanhov*, 60–63; Feuerstein, *The Mystery of Light*, 17–18; Aïvanhov, *Harmony and Health* (France: Prosveta, 1988), 42. For an overview of his Kundalini experience, see Aïvanhov, *Man's Subtle Bodies and Centers: The Aura, the Solar Plexus, the Chakras* (France: Prosveta, 1988).

36. Feuerstein, *The Mystery of Light*, 19–20; Frenette, *Mikhaël Aïvanhov*, 63–67.

37. See David Lorimer, ed., *Prophet for Our Times: The Life and Teaching of Peter Deunov* (Rockport, MA: Element Books, 1991), 4–10; and Beinsa Douno, *The First Day of Love: Texts and Songs*, trans. Atanas Slavov (Bethesda, MD: Sliabhair, 1986), 128. The Bogomil tradition dates from c. 850 CE and is also the imputed origin of the French Cathar movement.

38. Feuerstein, *The Mystery of Light*, 24–27.

39. See Douno, *The First Day of Love*, 133–36; and Lorimer, *Prophet for Our Times*, 16–24, 33. The center outside of Sofia was known as Izgrev ("sunrise") as dawn was considered the most sacred time of each day, with the sunrise to be greeted with prayer, song, and silent contemplation.

40. Feuerstein, *The Mystery of Light*, 27–29, 93ff.; Frenette, *Mikhaël Aïvanhov*, 76–80.

41. Feuerstein, *The Mystery of Light*, 33–34; Frenette, *Mikhaël Aïvanhov*, 96–97.

42. Frenette, *Mikhaël Aïvanhov*, 143–44; after leaving Bulgaria, he never again saw Douno.

43. Feuerstein, *The Mystery of Light*, explains that a modest income came to him after the mid-1970s from the publication of his books (37–48); see also Frenette, *Mikhaël Aïvanhov*, 171–82, 190, 221–29.

44. Feuerstein, *The Mystery of Light*, 50–67; Frenette, *Mikhaël Aïvanhov*, 241–57. Throughout the mid-1970s and 1980s he gave lectures in many countries, including the United States, England, Scotland, and Canada (Québec) where the present largest organization in North America exists; see: http://www.prosveta-usa.com, accessed May 2006.

45. Aïvanhov, *Looking into the Invisible: Intuition, Clairvoyance, Dreams* (France: Prosveta, 1991), 216. His seventy volumes are recorded in French, with thirty-eight volumes presently translated into English in the Izvor collection, and others translated from the Complete Works collection; see: http://www.prosveta.com/ (accessed May 2006), for the full catalogue.

46. Aïvanhov, *Man's Psychic Life: Elements and Structures* (France: Prosveta, 1989), 101–33; *Looking into the Invisible*, 27–35.

47. Aïvanhov, *Looking into the Invisible*, 41–43, 62–63, 211–17.

48. Aïvanhov, *Light is a Living Spirit* (France: Prosveta, 1988), 11–22, 31–33, 57–58, 67–78.

49. Aïvanhov, *Life Force* (France: Prosveta, 1987), 250.

50. Feuerstein, *The Mystery of Light*, 85; Aïvanhov, *The Splendor of Tiphareth: The Yoga of the Sun* (France: Prosveta, 1987), 274.

51. Aïvanhov, *The Key to the Problem of Existence* (France: Prosveta, 1981), 24.

52. Aïvanhov, *Man's Psychic Life*, 191–93.

53. Ibid., 194–97; Feuerstein, *The Mystery of Light*, 119–30.

54. Aïvanhov, *Man's Psychic Life*, 198–205.

55. Aïvanhov, *Creation: Artistic and Spiritual* (France: Prosveta, 1988), 37–48.

56. Ibid., 21–33.

57. Aïvanhov, *Harmony and Health*, 41–45. Aïvanhov uses the metaphor of the body (and person) as a microcosmic aspect of the macrocosm throughout his teachings, usually in the form of layered sheaths corresponding to certain levels of perception; see also Feuerstein, *The Mystery of Light*, 95–99, 105–16.

58. See Aïvanhov, *Harmony and Health*, 65, for one of many examples.

59. Ferrer, *Revisioning Transpersonal Theory*, 121.

60. This synthesis is epitomized in his combination of Christian Alchemy, Jewish Kabbalah, and Hindu Yoga; see Aïvanhov, *The Splendor of Tiphareth*, passim.

Wound of Love

Feminine Theosis and Embodied Mysticism in Teresa of Avila

Beverly J. Lanzetta

OF THE MANY dimensions of medieval mysticism, the writings of Teresa of Avila stand out as testimony to the closeness with which the divine nature is understood and conceived. While other mystical texts are lauded for their erudition, heights of contemplation, or speculative rigor, Teresa's corpus of works is profoundly intimate in its language, interpretation, and intent. This linguistic transparency is felt not only because of the personal nature of her writings, in which she recounts her life, spiritual formation, and monastic founding, but also because the text itself is a performative event. Through her public words we are drawn into her private friendship with God. Reading her text calls us to participate in Teresa's special contribution to spiritual life— her intimal or embodied relationship with God.[1] For her, God is neither outside nor inside, but within every breath she takes and every action she accomplishes. This seamless relationship of intimacy and oneness—which Teresa is given after years of superficial pursuits and agonizing trials—transforms her life and provides the impetus for her bold social and spiritual legacy.

Born in Avila, Spain, on March 28, 1515, Teresa de Ahumada y Cepeda was a descendent of *conversos* (Jews converted to Christianity) on her father's side. Acutely aware of social injustices all her life, Teresa's sensitivity was no doubt related to her family history and to the public confession her paternal grandfather was forced to make in 1485 over his secret practice of Judaism. The early death of her mother—who died in childbirth when

Teresa was thirteen—combined with her mixed ancestry, left an indelible imprint on the young Teresa and sensitized her to the ravages of social injustice and to the suffering of women. Drawn to religious life, Teresa entered the Carmelite Monastery of the Incarnation in 1535, against the wishes of her father. According to her own account, the early years of her profession were marked by severe illnesses and a longing to overcome her attraction to friendship, gossip, and vanity. This situation changed dramatically in 1554 when, during the season of Lent, Teresa experienced a profound transformation before a statue of the wounded Christ. Aware of her own insufficiency and lack of commitment, Teresa was transfixed by a spiritual understanding of how much God suffers for us and how little we do in return. This experience marked a radical turning point in her life and signaled the beginning of what would later become her fame as a spiritual author, mystical theologian, contemplative teacher, and founder of the reformed, or discalced Carmelites.[2]

Her enormous mystical talents and down to earth literary style provide a window onto her profound sense of mutuality with God. While the enormity of her contribution to a participatory spirituality is beyond the scope of this chapter, my explicit concern is to develop a greater appreciation for three critical elements in her thought: Teresa's feminization of the spiritual life, including the deconstructive contemplation she follows toward *theosis*; her development of a distinctive mystical anthropology premised on the purity of the soul and her special concern for female perfection; and her method of mystical self-disclosure—exemplified in the "wound of love"—whereby she discovers a new spiritual lineage and cocreatively participates in the inner life of God.

FEMININE THEOSIS AND THE APOPHASIS OF "WOMAN"

Perhaps more than any other mystic of medieval Europe, Teresa writes with subtlety and boldness about the pains and indignities inflicted on women.[3] Her numerous texts clearly demarcate her awareness of gender issues, and the inferior and often despised place accorded women in sixteenth-century Spain. Adopting a literary style that is at once deeply personal and rigorously cautious of the inquisitional temperament, she develops what Alison Weber has called a "rhetoric of femininity."[4] Not only is she relentless in her pursuit of women's interior suffering, she is quite modern in her keen social analysis of the structural dimensions of violence against women. This combination of profound spiritual gifts and incisive social critique brought Teresa much criticism and personal torment, as her confessors, superiors, and even close monastic friends doubted her veracity, sanity, and underlying motives. Yet, it was precisely her determination to break through the role of a "weak woman" that sets in motion her mystical innovation and becomes the medium for her holistic vision of the divine.

In the lexicon of Christian mysticism, Teresa is usually typed as an affective or spiritual mystic. Despite this primary linguistic affiliation with *via affirmativa*, the substance of her contemplative process—the path she travels toward mystical union and self-dignity—is profoundly apophatic. In her struggle to deconstruct stereotypical gender roles and women's spiritual denigration, Teresa forges a bold path toward women's *theosis*, or deification. Founded on the promise first established in Irenaeus of Lyons' famous phrase, later repeated by St. Athanasius, "God became man so that man might become God" (*De Incarnatione*, 54), *theosis* expresses not only the ontological primacy of the inner self, but also the cooperation between divinity and humanity in building the world. Without explicit reference to this ancient Christian promise, it is quite clear that from the time of Teresa's conversion in 1554 her heart and attention were on women's capacity to achieve not only salvation, but also perfection—divinization.

To accomplish this fervent desire, Teresa is brought into a deepening understanding of her suffering as a woman and a more profound experience of her mutuality with God. Mystically, she undergoes the apophasis of "woman"—that is, of what diminishes and denies the holiness of females—during a twenty-year period in which she confronts and suffers her inability to transcend internalized self-doubt and institutional rejection. As the unsaying of defined female roles, Teresa's apophasis is not only personal and social, it is also mystical. She undergoes the unresolvable dilemma of the tension between her personal wants and desires, social and church demands, and her longing to know God in genuine mutuality and intimacy. This deconstructive process simultaneously contains within it a creative coemergence, which in Teresa is exemplified by her practice of contemplative prayer. What is taken away by society and church, what she is not allowed to know and do, and the gender disparities she suffers culminate for Teresa under the rubric of mental prayer. These two aspects—the contemplative process she forges to displace and transform gendered oppression and her discovery of participatory prayer forms that repeat the theandric cooperation between divinity and humanity—are intricately intertwined.

It is well established that from the twelfth to the sixteenth centuries in medieval Europe, women mystics developed a "new embodied mystical language" in which there was an emphasis on the Eucharist, humanity of Christ, suffering of the soul, goddess figures, and mothering symbols.[5] Yet, beyond the descriptive association between women and embodied mysticism, there are few documented instances of personal gender awareness in the women mystics. Teresa, however, is different in this regard. It is possible to trace her spiritual development and subsequent mystical authority to gender because of her forthrightness about her sufferings and limits as a woman. This fact, however, does not imply a strict feminist or essentialist argument—that because Teresa is a female, and particularly *as female*, she discovers an embodied, participatory spirituality—which would be difficult to support from this historical distance. Rather, it is more precise to indicate that she discovers a new embodied spirituality because she cannot discover it without also affirming her own wholeness as female. The relationship between an intimal, participatory relationship with the divine and the contemplative process that reverses her gendered oppression are intrinsically tied together. It is not possible for Teresa to embody and live out her *theosis* without also healing and accepting her coequality and cocreativity with God. In her life and through her trials, she works out becoming divine, effectively transposing the ancient formula: God *became woman so woman could become God.*

In her struggle to deconstruct stereotypical gender roles and affirm women's spiritual place in sixteenth-century Spain, Teresa pursues what I have elsewhere termed the "dark night of the feminine"—a contemplative process in which God participates in and heals her soul wounds.[6] Using John of the Cross' fourfold typology of the dark night as a conceptual framework, I define Teresa's feminine night an additional stage beyond the passive night of the spirit to highlight her specific soul suffering as a woman.[7] The pain of the feminine night is a breaking away from the misogyny that inhabits her consciousness and conditions her to turn against her self. During this time, Teresa experiences the ancient and historic fracture of her soul and the systematic reviling of the female in the world. In this feminine apophasis, she also suffers the root pain and terrible anguish of stripping away externally imposed limits on her spiritual development.

Having known God primarily through the authority of a male-dominated church, Teresa struggles to reconcile Jesus' loving affirmation of her whole person with the harsh and punishing views directed against her. She recognizes that even Church-sanctioned spiritual directors and prayers mediated by her male confessors do not capture the fullness of her spiritual life or the pain of the purgative contemplation gripping her soul. She confides in her books and letters over and again that a critical element of her and her sisters' spiritual struggles as women is left out. There comes a point on her journey when even classical accounts of the soul can be a hindrance because she assumes that male depictions of the spiritual life are charting the same territory she needs to cross. In *The Book of Her Life*, Teresa recounts how she is continually made to let go of her attachment to the advice, demand, and criticism of male clerics and church officials, in order to claim Jesus'—and her own—loving and sometimes radical advice.

In following the path of feminine apophasis, the role of intimacy becomes a central metaphor in her passage from divine-human suffering to the fullness of female *theosis*. Her identification with Jesus' suffering leads her from mystical union to a deeper, ontological intimacy between the depth of her soul and God. The communion between God and the soul is so total that everything is shared equally and the soul experiences not only its own will, but God's will. For Teresa, mystical intimacy involves identification with God's longing and pathos for humanity, and a bearing of the twofold wounding of Christ's passion. Her soul experiences the afflictions of its most receptive nature, both in terms of the negative wounding sustained from bearing the sin and violence of the world, and the positive touching of Divine Wisdom which opens it to deeper reserves of communion and oneness. Teresa contends these sufferings are felt "in the very deep and intimate part of the soul," and mystically repeat the wounds borne by Jesus.[8]

Yet, the intense suffering over the world's afflictions is connected to the immense exaltation of love God offers to the soul. The inner soul wounding and outer worldly offense exist in reciprocal relationship to the overflowing love between God and the soul. The depth of the soul's ability to bear God's love for the world exists in proportion to the intensity of love's wounding of the soul. In the highest reaches of mystic contemplation, Jesus "begins to commune with the soul in so intimate a friendship," she writes, "that He not only gives it back its own will but gives it His."[9] The communion that takes place between God and the soul in its center teaches Teresa about the closeness God shares with all things and the manner in which she must bear for God the wounding and happiness of the world.

This intimate relationship, therefore, is profoundly mutual. Not only does Teresa participate in God's pathos for creation, God also suffers her wounds. Through a co-mutual bearing of the wound of women's "otherness," in this feminine night Jesus identifies with and assumes her suffering, as she identifies with and bears Jesus' wounds. Christ's suffering compels in Teresa a desire to share in the world's anguishes, to bear for him and for others in an outpouring of solidarity with those who are marginalized, ridiculed, and rejected: "I desire to suffer, Lord, since You suffered," Teresa writes. "Let your will be done in me in every way, and may it not please your majesty that something as precious as your love be given to anyone who serves you only for the sake of consolations."[10] In her meditations on Jesus' suffering on earth and on the cross, Teresa evaluates her actions, and the world's response, in light of his loving passion. She encounters the vulnerability of Jesus' face, body, and wounds, and sheds whatever traces of self-centeredness remain, as her heart is consumed by the fiery flame of sorrow for human arrogance and sin. Yet, this mystical emptiness of self initiates an unreserved responsibility in which she reclaims her dignity as a woman, and articulates a new feminine way of liberation for herself and others.

While imitation of Christ's suffering on the cross is central to Christian spirituality and the soul's healing, Teresa makes an explicit association between her feminine subjectivity and soul wounds, and her intimate sharing in Jesus' suffering. Teresa understands that her denigration as a woman represents God's suffering in her, and that the twofold affliction—human and divine—is profoundly gendered. While Teresa does not explicitly name this passage the "dark night of the feminine," in her writings she is insistent that she encounters an additional, and most crucial and agonizing, aspect of her search for self-subjectivity. As her visions, favors, and experience of God's presence increase, she is subjected to further scrutiny and ridicule by her confessors, inquisitional authorities, townspeople, and even her own monastic community. Beyond the prayer of union described by her, and even beyond the next stage called "raptures," she experiences a "painful prayer . . . a painful experience . . . a deep pain."[11] Associating the wound of love with this final transfiguration of her female "otherness," Teresa depicts her path to feminine *theosis* in terms of a crucifixion between heaven and earth, in which the soul both suffers and is exalted: "Receiving no help from either side, it is as though crucified between heaven and earth . . . the desert and solitude seem to the soul better than all the companionship of the world . . . the body shares only in the pain, and it is the soul alone that both suffers and rejoices on account of the joy and satisfaction the suffering gives . . . it must not be forgotten that this experience of pain comes after all those favors that are written of in this book."[12]

In her negotiation of the soul's journey, Teresa traces her battle with spiritual oppression distinctive to her gender, drawing away from conventional definitions of women's spiritual benefits as well as from traditional women's roles. As she matures in her spiritual life, Teresa confronts a deeper, and more radical fracture that inhabits her consciousness, and struggles to recognize and heal the misogyny that is at the bottom of her self-doubt and worthlessness as a woman. The deconstructive process by which she reverses her inferiority and her internalized self-hatred is the same process whereby she claims her way of perfection and her vision of a continually unfolding divine-human relationship. This feminine night culminates for her in a reality beyond mystical union, and beyond traditional church categories. Here, she is on such intimate terms with God that God now lives in her. There is no division between inner and outer; no tension between active and passive contemplation; but a seamless flow of divinity living within her own person. In Teresa we find not only the path to this dark night, but the aftermath of its effects, as she moves beyond traditional Christian categories and forges her own feminine language and experience.

Her struggles with being a woman are, on a grander scale, the struggle to articulate a fully embodied, fully participatory spirituality that is not tied to sin and salvation but to flourishing and transformation. Without this coequal, co-mutual, and co-intimate participation, Teresa would not have been able to achieve *theosis*, full transparency with the divine. The deconstructive process that leads her from inferiority and self-loathing to mutuality and self-dignity is *necessary* for Teresa to embody and transmit her participatory vision of God. It is through her intimate friendship with Jesus that Teresa is granted an understanding of the cooperation between God and woman in bringing souls to God and building the divinity of the world.

Teresa's feminine apophasis, however, is not founded on classical negative theology. Instead, for her, emptiness of self always exists in dialectical
relationship to intimacy. The tension between the two cannot be dispelled or
resolved. Total surrender of the self, a prerequisite for receiving infused contemplation, is not achieved according to the traditional path of asceticism,
negative theology, or apophatic discourse. Instead, Teresa is drawn to self-sur-
render through the wound of love—discussed in the final section of this
chapter—which enlarges and dilates her soul until she is capable of bearing
divine love as her own. While she describes numerous experiences of compunction, suffering, wretchedness, and sin, she focuses instead on the inner
change brought about by her intense love for God.

An interesting aspect of Teresa's spirituality, and one often overlooked by
her main commentators, is the performative intimacy of her writings, in which
she develops a new mystical grammar that emerges from within its subject and
speaks an embodied vocabulary of the heart. As such, it is a language that per-
forms in the text all of the transitions of apophatic mysticism—emptying of
self, detachment, relinquishing of name and identity. It also overflows with
affectivity: ascribing attributes to God, swimming in the ocean of naming and
feeling, and overwhelmed by visions and locutions. But to leave Teresa there
is to miss her most radical contribution to mystical thought. Teresa, without
benefit of theological training, forges a true innovation in spiritual life epitomized by a participatory event in which her writings perform an integration of
the Mary-Martha story. A central metaphor within Christian spirituality, this
story from the Gospel of Luke has been used over the centuries to teach about
the superiority of the contemplative (Mary) over the active (Martha) spiritual
life. Rather than asserting a distinction, Teresa is explicit that intimacy with
God reproduces the continual interpenetration of active and passive contemplation. It is as if the apophatic moment immediately spills over into a devotional surrender, so that there is a seamless relationship (a Mary-Martha relationship) between contemplative self-emptying and effective cocreation with
God. The inner dynamism of these two poles cannot be resolved or brought to
rest. Teresa does not stop to identify or dwell on these apophatic moments, but
assumes them as foundational to contemplative prayer. It is only when the self
has been made empty—and gives itself away—can it enter into advanced
states of contemplation. All outer works in the fully integrated soul emerge
from the inner stirrings of the spirit. There is no outer work that is not, then,
the fruit of the interior, receptive life. Everything she does is God's work in
her. "Mary and Martha," she teaches, "never fail to work together when the
soul is in this state [mystical marriage]. For in the active—and seemingly exterior—work the soul is working interiorly. And when the active works rise from
this interior root, they become lovely and very fragrant flowers."[13]

She transforms and integrates these two classical paths through a reversal
of her female difference, which brings her into contact with a new feminine

language and understanding. She effects an apophatic transformation of herself as "woman" and "female"—of all that is denied, rejected, and self-loathing—to discover an affirmative language directly from God. She is taught everything she needs to know by God; her language is beyond the "men of letters" and is the speech of God; her wisdom comes from an infused knowing born of having surrendered her socially defined self. In this feminine mystical path, her female body assimilates and transforms reality, thereby giving life to a new spiritual path, marked not by asceticism, but by an affective love and overflowing intimacy between God and soul. On the other side of her "nothingness" as female is an infused, contemplative knowing in which God heals her of self-negation. Teresa writes of anguishes, soul wounds, torments, and crucifixions, but these are not the action of her own will nor the effect of a divine will outside herself. Instead, this is God working in her, leading her to not only claim, but to cocreate her dignity and self-worth.

MYSTICAL ANTHROPOLOGY

Central to the whole of Teresa's life and work is a mystical anthropology premised on the primary and irrevocable bond between God and the human soul, in which we are made to be beloved by God and we are made to long for God. Affirming the transconscious and the suprapersonal beyond traditional notions of the human self, Teresa's journey continually asks: Who is the person when seen from the perspective of God? Premised on a distinctive view of the human person as always one with its divine source, this guiding vision is established in Teresa after many years of struggle, self-doubt, and personal suffering. Most painful was that the monasteries Teresa founded were constantly under scrutiny and her personal integrity was subjected to criticism and ridicule as she labored to withstand the latest inquisitional attack. Her physical sufferings had intensified to the point that she wearily reported: "I have been experiencing now for three months such great noise and weakness in my head that I've found it a hardship even to write concerning necessary business matters."[14]

Yet, in the midst of these disturbing and painful events, Teresa of Avila, under obedience from Fr. Gracian her confessor, began writing her sublime book on prayer, *The Interior Castle*. Toward the end of her life and suffering through some of her greatest trials, Teresa synthesizes her whole mystical corpus on the "magnificent beauty of the soul and its marvelous capacity."[15] On the eve of Trinity Sunday, June 2, 1577, God showed her in a flash of light the whole book she would write and the glorious sensitivity of the soul, made in the image of God. "Today," she writes, "while beseeching our Lord to speak for me because I wasn't able to think of anything to say nor did I know how to begin to carry out this obedience, there came to my mind what I shall now speak about. . . . [I]t is that we consider our soul to be like a castle made entirely out of a diamond or of very clear crystal, in which there are many rooms, just as in heaven there are many dwelling places."[16]

The relationship of the person to the mystical life is exemplified in this masterwork. A thinly disguised autobiographical account of her spiritual journey toward integration, Teresa depicts the soul as a crystalline castle with seven dwelling places or *moradas*, each representing multiple dimensions or levels of consciousness. The entire soul is bathed in the light of God who, dwelling in the center of the soul, honors and cherishes the whole person. Teresa informs us that we are unaware of this always present communion because of the sin, ignorance, and confusion of life in the world. Nonetheless, the soul is a glorious jewel in God's eyes and is never separated from its source. "It should be kept in mind here," she writes, "that the fount, the shining sun that is in the center of the soul, does not lose its beauty and splendor; it is always present in the soul, and nothing can take away its loveliness."[17] The soul in its center is undefiled and indescribably pure; it can never be ultimately tarnished or corrupted. The true self is always one with its divine source.

To explain the mutual sharing of God and the soul, Teresa describes "these mansions as God's very own rooms, another heaven, where God is all in all. Since they are also the saint's dwelling place and the source of her activity, then the divine has become human and the human divine. . . ."[18] While the entire castle is spiritual and divine, the three outer (lower) dwellings or *moradas* represent the activities of the person in relationship to the world and one's intention to grow closer to God. Here, the person practices prayer and virtues, seeks to live a good life, and joins in community with others. Because the outer dwelling places turn toward the world, they are affected by sin and are susceptible to corruption, wounding, and fracture. These lower mansions were the site of Teresa's almost twenty-year struggle to overcome her conflict between the spiritual life and superficial joys, pastimes, and pleasures.[19] The four inner or higher dwellings signal the beginnings of the passive spiritual life—that is, the full receptivity of the soul to God. These interior levels of consciousness are supernatural and remain pure and untouched by sin. At the center of the castle, Christ dwells and it is here, in the seventh mansion, that Teresa experiences exalted mystical intimacies. Sharing in the inner life of God, Teresa's own life becomes the medium of a divine-human self-expression. The progression from lower to higher levels of awareness records Teresa's journey of self-discovery and her numerous spiritual experiences. But, more primary than these effects, the *Interior Castle* focuses on the centering, integrating transformation of Teresa's new life in God. Her life is no longer at the center, as she has been drawn by "His Majesty" toward vulnerability, humility, and annihilation.

Entrance to the castle is through prayer, and the whole of Teresa's mystical anthropology can be subsumed under the rubric of contemplative prayer. While active forms of prayer are the medium of the three outer dwellings and flow out of the person's desire to know God, passive or receptive prayer has its beginnings in God and overflows into human nature, flooding the four interior dwellings with supersensible light. The soul's capacity to withstand the mutuality of divine love—and thus to progress from lower to higher consciousness—is dependent upon a continual self-effacement marked by successive degrees of annihilation and rapture. For Teresa, this mystical process of juxtaposing periods of pain and joy is the method by which God draws her beyond self-effort to surrender, and into full participation in the divine life.

It is possible to read Teresa's notion of contemplative prayer within traditional religious categories, as a spiritual exercise or form of personal communication with God. However, for Teresa, contemplative prayer—her "way of perfection"—is far more complex and comprehensive. It is a whole life hermeneutic, in which all events, actions, knowledge, and being are seen through the lens of a heightened unitive and participatory state of consciousness. Further, far from relegating contemplative prayer to an activity, Teresa uses the phrase *contemplative prayer* as a code to state the unsayable: contemplative prayer is the mystical means of achieving salvation and deification, or *theosis*. It is the royal road to liberation. It is only in fully giving herself to God that she is prepared to receive in God's gifts of love. Wrapped in apophatic language, Teresa emphasizes that self-negation is, in truth, the great favor of love: emptiness is surrender; negation is becoming a host for God; annihilation is the most intimate of intimacies; effacing the self strengths its capability to withstand divine vulnerability, allowing the whole world to flood in.

To understand Teresa's bold stance it is worthwhile to understand what is it about passive contemplation that so attracts Teresa. Why does she single it out as the necessary and superior means to sainthood or salvation? In passive contemplation, Teresa experiences that salvation is mystical and therefore not under the purview of the institutional church or priests. Only in mystical intimacy with God can one find the freedom one seeks. Second, there is a contemplative method of advancing in love of God and drawing closer to authentic being. Teresa emphasizes that through passive or mental prayer a hidden process begins to take place that draws the soul through oppression into freedom from self-interest. It is the prayer of love, of complete and utter surrender to God; it is the path of finally emptying oneself of all attractions and distractions in order to be for and with God. Third, in passive contemplation, the soul is taught everything it needs to know—it is taken by God into God's inner life to know as God knows. When the Church's authorities take everything of meaning away from her—her spiritual books, her right to teach and learn—Jesus grants Teresa a superior knowing not dependent on the world. Through this inner knowing, she learns everything directly through God's presence in her soul. Protected from the language of the schoolmen, a language rooted in a dualistic way of thinking, Teresa mines her transcendent experiences "using feminine eyes, outlook, speech, and writing."[20]

It is significant that so much of her writing and personal struggles revolve around her devotion to and insistence on the power of mental prayer. This was her way of perfection, a path that democratized the spiritual life and put her own liberation outside the priestly caste or church authority. She understood that passive or infused contemplation dissolves the boundaries between the soul and God. It is truly a mutual participation of God in her life and her life in God that revealed to her a better and quicker road to spiritual sanctity. Through surrender of herself, God was compelled to live in her. This new relationship brought her to an intensely dynamic and cocreative manifestation of divinity. In passive prayer, she found her true birthright in becoming divine, neither oppressed nor limited by church authorities and prevailing theological politics.

Further, Teresa, in harmony with centuries of Christian thought, emphasizes that in contemplative prayer the spiritual faculties are stilled, for only then is the soul free to give itself away. She is insistent that in mental or passive prayer, God does all the work. The faculties rest and the soul knows from a place beyond knowing; it surrenders what it cannot ever know for the sake of what is known but cannot ever be said. But, again, Teresa is not left with the usual apophatic "unknowing," or the mystic's experience of "nothingness." Instead, within this designation of the suspension of memory, understanding, and will Teresa uncovers a verdant, flourishing world in which the whole range of participatory events— including enactive or embodied knowing, participatory being, intellective and spiritual visions, locutions, and raptures, *gustos*, and *contentos*—operate.[21] In each of these traditional theological areas, she presents an innovative and unique perspective on the seamless interpenetration of divinity and the soul. While her subsequent commentators were perhaps distracted by her emphasis on visions, locutions, and other extrasensory events, Teresa herself never saw them as anything but participation in divine self-disclosure. In writing divinity through the text of her body and onto the text of the page, Teresa documents and clarifies both the range and the importance of visionary and infused knowledge, types of silent words or locutions from God, the divine center of the soul as the primary interpretive location, and the true self as surrendered and emptied by love. The purpose of all of these interior prayer states, however, is for "the birth always of good works," writes Teresa, "good works."[22]

Teresa's mystical anthropology is neither a preordained state nor an impossible condition, but the continual overflowing of divinity in her own life and work. The foundation of this limitless creativity and mutual friendship is the effacement or negation of the self. The relinquishing of the self is the condition that activates the dissolution of boundaries between the soul and God. Only when the self has surrendered its individual, separate existence is it drawn into God's inner life. The human soul, in Teresa's eyes, is made for intimacy and transparency; this is its true home and greatest achievement. To be truly spiritual, Teresa reminds us, "means becoming the slaves of God."[23]

She also is explicit that women are granted a special place in this mystical anthropology and boldly affirms the superior virtue of women. In her later works, Teresa introduces the theme of the empowerment and dignity of women through highlighting the great perfection and virtue that her nuns were able to achieve. Teresa wants her sisters to achieve spiritual discipleship, as she herself aspires to be an apostle who brings souls to God. Her longing to be a spiritual teacher and a leader of works of mercy and justice ignites her texts; at the same time she is acutely aware of the judgment inflicted on her and her sisters. "Is it not enough, Lord," she writes, "that the world has intimidated us [women] . . . so that we may not do anything worthwhile for You in public or dare speak some truths that we lament over in secret, without Your also failing to hear so just a petition? . . . Since the world's judges are sons of Adam and all of them men, there is no virtue in women that they do not hold suspect."[24]

In *The Book of Her Foundations*, Teresa recounts how, through her monastic communities, she repels the injustice and violence against women and resists the social order by harvesting her mystical knowledge for political purposes. In response to the cultural preference for males, Teresa extolled the virtues of women and the shame of parents who do not realize "the great blessings that can come to them through daughters or of the great sufferings that can come from sons."[25] Teresa describes a number of women who desired to be monastics who were whipped and punished by their families, or who disfigured themselves in order to avoid marriage. In addition to contributing to the renewal of the Carmelite Order and the founding of monasteries for women and for men, Teresa also helped *conversos* by admitting them into her monasteries on the basis of their piety and suitability for the religious life. Constance FitzGerald contends that Teresa's contemplative life led her to envision "a new social order where all were to be equal. In her small communities of contemplative women, Teresa set in motion a reversal of the social and religious order by a spiritual one that would eradicate the highest principles of the established order and undermine the current images of social status. Her fearless struggle to destroy concern for honor and wealth, and therefore uphold the value of the person over money and ancestry, her unswerving struggle for the recognition of women's rights to deep interior prayer and therefore to significant service in the Church at the time of great ecclesial danger and turmoil."[26]

THE WOUND OF LOVE

It is clear from Teresa's testimony that her mystical anthropology culminates in a new ontological reality in which the soul is no longer a separate entity but has become absorbed into or fused with the divine sprit. This new state of being is marked by the reciprocity of love, which instills in the soul a desire to be all and do all for God. Teresa describes this state beyond mystical union, and even beyond the subsequent experience of rapture, flights of fancy, and so forth, as initiated by the wound of love. The wound of love has two effects: to heal and transform the afflictions and sufferings the soul sustains in the world; and to anoint the soul with the transport of love which dilates and magnifies its capacity to receive in divine fullness. Flinging open the door between the soul and God, the wound of love stills the soul's faculties until there is a suspension of thought, memory, and will. Communication now takes place not through the medium of the spiritual senses, but directly through God's own language: locutions, visions, and other intimacies. For Teresa, these communications are not inferior epiphenomena of the spiritual life, but the direct means by which God speaks to its beloved.

The wound of love has a long history in Christian spirituality. Harking back to the Song of Songs 2:5, "Strengthen me with perfumes, surround me with apples, for I am wounded with love," Christian writers such as Origen and Gregory of Nyssa imbue the wound of love with a christological meaning—"Christ the Word is both arrow and sword, wounding the soul from within." The emotional effect of this wounding is compared to love's "bittersweet piercing" and is explained through a variety of metaphors, sensations, "unfulfilled longings."[27] Capturing the emotional intensity of Christ's wounding of the soul, Origen writes: "If there is anyone who has been pierced with the loving spear of his knowledge so that he yearns and longs for me by day and night, can speak of nothing but him, can hear of nothing but him, can think of nothing else, and cannot desire nor long nor hope for anything save him, that soul then truly says, 'I have been wounded by charity.'"[28]

Teresa's many experiences with the wound of love are immortalized in The Book of Her Life, in which she recounts an angel plunging a fiery "golden dart" into the deepest part of her heart.[29] The intensity of pain and excessiveness of bliss that mark the transverberation of her heart are symbolic of the ontological transfiguration she undergoes and the spiritual significance of the wound. She establishes that the wound is not self-activated—"there is clear awareness that the soul did not cause this love"—but is ignited by "a spark from the very great love the Lord has . . . making it burn all over."[30] Since the wound is divinely caused, it cannot be relieved by bodily or mental penances, but by God alone, whose desire it is that the soul dies to the old self. Only in this way can the soul achieve the freedom of co-mutual life in the divine. Teresa is, thus, clear that the wound of love is God's great favor to the soul and not, despite its painful aspects, a trial.

In *The Interior Castle*, Teresa takes up the wound of love, especially in the sixth dwelling place. As a more mature synthesis of her thought, Teresa now situates the wound of love as the necessary precursor to complete integration with God in the seventh *morada*. The suffering is caused by the anguish of her whole being to be drawn not just closer to God, but to be God. It is marked by an intensity of longing and an increasing awareness of the trials she undergoes as a female mystic. She recognizes that the interior and exterior pains she must endure are in many instances the effect of the ignorance of her confessors and their bias against women's sanctity. She labors to reconcile Jesus' loving affirmation and excessive graces with the suspicious rhetoric marshaled against her. Concerned that her spiritual status is inconsistent with her reports of divine favors, her confessors fear that her experiences are from the devil, a fact that causes Teresa to be "deeply tormented and disturbed."[31] These external wounds of love teach her that only God can mend the incisive doubt that grips her soul, and only God can transform her worn and weary heart.

The suffering Teresa feels is not, however, the effect of divine punishment or chastisement. Rather, it is the suffering of love's compunction, the suffering she feels in relationship to her inability to feel worthy of God's love. In the wound of love, redemption and salvation are transposed and bypassed. Teresa recognizes that mystical intimacy overrides theological prescription, because God is the most beneficent reality. The soul is wounded by divine love in order to bring it to the true happiness: God wounds us with love in order that we may receive in and accept God's goodness in us. It is thus that she progresses from the world's wounding into the deeper divine wound in which every trial is, first and foremost, joy. The person, from a mystical perspective, shares in God's life and perceives the world from God's perspective. Certainly, one of the most compelling aspects of Teresa's wisdom is her insistence on the soul's capacity to empathize with, assume, and transform suffering. Just as God bears the world's pain, the fully realized soul participates in the intradivine suffering when God weeps with our weeping. Through the inner eye of love, the soul is given divine vulnerability to bear the wound of love, and divine strength to resist violence and affliction. Finally, the person as the agent of the divine in the world, lifts creation to an embodied, integral understanding of the divinity of the world and the beauty of the soul.

Teresa catalogs a progression of love's wounding. The first effect of the wound is to dilate and expand the soul in order to make it capable of receiving in God's immensity.[32] This wounding is "far different from all that we can acquire of ourselves here below and even from the spiritual delights that were mentioned."[33] The soul knows the wound is something precious and even though the pain is intense, it does not want to be cured of its suffering.

Rather, the action of the divine piercing is so powerful that the soul "dissolves with desire," experiencing a type of surrender without fear of abandonment from God.[34] Experiencing the divine wounds both as an intense suffering and an intense joy in its most intimate depth, the soul feels an overwhelming love as God draws these very depths into its own nature.

> The desire for the Lord increases much more; also, love increases in the measure the soul discovers how much this great God and Lord deserves to be loved. And this desire continues, gradually growing in these years so that it reaches a point of suffering as great as that I shall now speak of. . . . While this soul is going about in this manner, burning up within itself, a blow is felt from elsewhere. . . . Neither is the experience that of a blow; but it causes a sharp wound. And, in my opinion, it isn't felt where earthly sufferings are felt, but in the very deep and intimate part of the soul, where this sudden flash of lightening reduces to dust everything it finds in this earthly nature of ours.[35]

Always concerned that her path is above reproach, Teresa takes great pains to distinguish God's awakening of her soul from any activity from the devil. She notices that only God has the power to join pain with the spiritual delight of the soul. Similarly, God's action leaves the soul in quiet and certitude, fortifying it with great determination to suffer for God. These capacities, she notes, are not within the devil's power to effect. Divine benefits, however, are both more interior and hidden and express special forms of engaged communion between God and the soul. Among these, Teresa mentions an infusion of the senses with a "delightful enkindling" that generates "intense acts of love and praise of our Lord."[36] In addition, the wound of love generates a deeper communion, which Teresa describes in mansions four and five as, respectively, the prayers of quiet and union. But beyond these prayer forms, God draws the soul to betrothal, speaking to its beloved through a variety of locutions (silent words from God), raptures, and intellectual and imaginative visions. Each of these means of communication instill in her a greater understanding of the divine mysteries and a more integral embodiment of her cocreation with God.

In the sixth dwelling place, the wound of love blinds the eyes of the soul and wraps it in a cocoon of unknowing in order to leave "the soul annihilated within itself and with deeper knowledge of God's mercy and grandeur."[37] Through moments of illumination, the soul is taught that there are no closed passages between the lower dwellings and the luminosity of mystical marriage that occurs in the seventh mansion. The soul is now granted an understanding that there is no division, no separation, between the soul and God. Like rain falling into a river or a stream that enters the sea, the soul is inseparably at home, one with its divine source. "Through some secret aspirations," Teresa writes, "the soul understands clearly that it is God who gives life to our soul. These aspirations come very, very often in such a living way that they can in no way be doubted. . . . [W]hen the soul reaches this state in which God grants it this favor, it is sure of its salvation and safe from falling again."[38]

Having reached this height of mystical intimacy, Teresa explains in the seventh mansion that the purpose of the wound of love and the delightful favors is to live like Christ, offering to the world the fruit of good works. The dissolution of the soul into the ocean of divinity effects Teresa's action in the world as her outer works always emerge from this deep inner root. For Teresa, the mutuality and intimacy experienced through the wound of love is more primordial, more fundamental than *unio mystica*, which speaks of joining and uniting. She is quite clear that the reality she wants to convey is beyond union, which implies coming together, making one, and other images of joining two separate entities. No, the new ontological reality she discovers is prior to union; it is the original state, the mothering principle by which and through which coming into manifestation is made possible. It is not the joining together of two separate entities, but the fount and source discovered by way of love. Perhaps in the seventh mansion she realizes the mystical implications of God's suffering on the cross of her womanhood. God cannot create or lead the soul to some reality that has been there all along, but must suffer and wait for human cooperation, until Teresa loves her self with such an intensity of love that she breaks through her inferiority and self-doubt. Then, God's being is manifested in her soul's being, co-liberating God into the world. God is curtailed by her oppression; just as God is freed by her dignity and empowerment. Teresa's description of the soul's journey vacillates in *The Interior Castle* between the sensible idea of a predetermined reality to which the soul is led and a dynamic, interactive reality constantly being cocreated by God and the soul.

Teresa discovers that salvation or spiritual perfection is mystical. That is, all that is longed for, all that requires healing, all that yearns for wholeness is resolved in mystical intimacy with God. Not by austerities, or repression; not by coercion or sacraments; not by liturgy or erudition; but only by making one's whole self a host for God can she achieve feminine *theosis*. Through the wound of love, Teresa's soul is hollowed out and made empty to receive in the realization of her participation in building a sacred community on earth. As God shares all of Teresa's cares, troubles, pains, and triumphs, Teresa shares in God's bountiful gifts and bears God's suffering for the world. Together, they labor to give voice to the voiceless, sanctify life and inspire in others the same desire for truth. The wound signifies both God's absence and presence; God's transcendence and intimate friendship; God's excessive benevolence and assumption of human ignorance.

Teresa learns that the breaking through of the one who gives away all her names, leads to the flowing out of *she* who has been made intimate with her wholly other, God. New language emerges bound in the cloth of the untouched and untainted that is clear and daunting in its light, like Teresa's speculum of divine illumination. This pure presence—a saying that is forever unsaying, an unnaming of the construction "woman"—incites fear and resistance, and is ridiculed, suppressed, even "killed" by those still on the other side of letting go. Having crossed the tremulous river of unknowing and undoing (of all that is claimed, named, and desired), and returned bearing gifts, this new woman, who is no longer "*woman*" has her gifts smashed and broken. They are stillborn, not allowed to come to life. For Marguerite Porete—the ill-fated fourteenth-century Beguine who refused to stop circulating her manuscript, *The Mirror of Simple Souls*—this happens in a stroke. To the fiery burning she is led. The powers that be will destroy the evidence of one so bold, and burn to ash the smoldering embers of a heart enflamed with an apophasis of pure feminine desire.

In Teresa's case, she is scourged by a more lasting and bitter truth, which brings her to a mystical crucifixion between heaven and earth. Her Beloved has a different plan. It is not enough that she bears the gift of mystical marriage—which is, in fact, the gift of her authentic feminine self—she has to become a bride of her whole person, claiming, dignifying, disseminating, and upholding it for others. She cannot go unconscious; she cannot forget the road she traveled or the lessons learned. She cannot deny the power of herself as woman, and must stand testimony and testament to its feminine enduring presence. Her writings inspire the search, for there in her words she gives word to the wordless; she writes outside patriarchy—if not outside religion—finding in her relationship with Jesus an escape from what subjects and diminishes her, and a liberation from confessors and priests, as well as from the denigration of her womanhood. Teresa sustains the wound of love, yielding a continual generosity of spirit: she returns bearing gifts, always bearing gifts.

Teresa's struggle to overcome her inferiority and suppression by the Church, and her intense effort to name and claim her own feminine way released a suppressed or unexpressed realm of consciousness: the feminine incarnational dimension in which co-participation in reality is *the way* of perfection. Her particular struggle as a woman was necessary for its releasement. Through her efforts to be free of gender stereotypes, and gendered limitations in the spiritual life, Teresa embodies the mutuality of love that underpins her mystical apprehension of the person. Having discovered her own feminine *theosis*, Teresa assumes in body and soul the wound of love that pierces the veils between worlds and welcomes her into the "arbor of intimacy."[39]

NOTES

1. From the Latin *intimus* or *intumus*, I employ the word *intimal* to highlight a perspective on reality distinguished by its "within-ness"—its ability to dwell within what

it perceives, touches, or knows. An intimal relationship also implies a cocreative or integral participation in the building of reality.

2. Discalced, from the Spanish *descalzo*, "shoeless," to indicate the wearing of sandals.

3. Several paragraphs in this section have been published before in Beverly Lanzetta, *Radical Wisdom: A Feminist Mystical Theology* (Minneapolis: Fortress Press, 2005). Reprinted here with the kind permission of Fortress Press.

4. See Alison Weber, *Teresa of Avila and the Rhetoric of Femininity* (Princeton: Princeton University Press, 1990) for a thorough analysis of her literary style. A similar theme is developed in Antonio Perez-Romero, *Subversion and Liberation in the Writings of St. Teresa of Avila* (Atlanta: Rodopi, 1996). Also consult Deidre Green, *Gold in the Crucible: Teresa of Avila and the Western Mystical Tradition* (Longmead, U.K.: Element, 1969); Gillian Ahlgren, *Teresa of Avila and the Politics of Sanctity* (Ithaca: Cornell University Press, 1996).

5. Bernard McGinn, "The Language of Inner Experience in Christian Mysticism," in *Minding the Spirit: The Study of Christian Spirituality*, ed. Elizabeth Dreyer and Mark Burrows (Baltimore: The Johns Hopkins University Press, 2005), 143. For further studies on women's embodied mysticism, consult Barbara Newman, *God and the Goddesses: Vision, Poetry, and Belief in the Middle Ages* (Philadelphia: University of Pennsylvania Press, 2003); idem, *Sister of Wisdom: St. Hildegard's Theology of the Feminine* (Berkeley: University of California Press, 1987); McGinn, *The Flowering of Mysticism: Men and Women in the New Mysticism—1200–1350* (New York: Crossroad, 1998); Carolyn Walker Bynum, *Jesus as Mother: Studies in the Spirituality of the High Middle Ages*; Ulrike Wiethaus, ed., *Maps of Flesh and Light: The Religious Experience of Medieval Women Mystics* (Syracuse: Syracuse University Press, 1993).

6. For development of the term "dark night of the feminine" see Beverly Lanzetta, *Radical Wisdom: A Feminist Mystical Theology* (Minneapolis: Fortress Press, 2005); idem, "The Soul of Woman and the Dark Night of the Feminine" paper presented at American Academy of Religion Western Region (WESCOR), UC Davis, March 23, 2003; idem, "Julian and Teresa as Cartographers of the Soul: A Contemplative Feminist Hermeneutic," paper presented at AAR Annual Meeting, Atlanta Georgia, November 25, 2003.

7. John of the Cross inserts the "dark night" as an additional level of soul transformation prior to union, within the threefold purgation, illumination, and union. He conceptualizes the dark night experience according to a fourfold division of active and passive nights of senses, and active and passive nights of the spirit. I insert the dark night of the feminine as an additional dimension of soul healing to highlight that in the history of Christian spirituality, growth in mystical consciousness has been supposedly gender neutral, but, in fact, has ignored gender differences. By placing the night of the feminine beyond John's passive night of the spirit, I intend that there is a further level of mystical transformation that is *both* feminine (in males and females) *and* specific to female bodies.

8. Teresa of Avila, *The Interior Castle, The Collected Works of St. Teresa of Avila*, vols. 1–3, trans. Kieran Kavanaugh and Otilio Rodriguez (Washington, DC: ICS Pub-

lications, 1987), 6.11.2, 422. All citations from Teresa of Avila that follow are from *The Collected Works*.

9. Teresa of Avila, *Way of Perfection*, 32.12, 164.

10. *Book of Her Life*, 11.12, 116. This association between gender and mystical transformation may have been experienced by men, but if men also experience a gendered form of oppression it does not seem to have been commented on in the entire history of male Christian spirituality.

11. Ibid., 20.9, 175.

12. Ibid., 20.15, 179.

13. Teresa of Avila, *Meditation on the Song of Songs*, in *The Collected Works*, vol. 2, 7.3, 257.

14. *Castle*, Prologue, 281.

15. Ibid., 1.1.1, 283.

16. Ibid.

17. Ibid., 1.2.3, 289.

18. Ernest E. Larkin, "St. Teresa of Avila and Prayer," *Studies in Formative Spirituality: Journal of On-going Formation IV*, no. 2 (1983): 404.

19. Teresa of Avila, *The Book of Her Life*, 7:17.

20. Perez-Romero, *Subversion and Liberation in the Writings of St. Teresa of Avila* (Atlanta: Rodopi, 1996), 77.

21. For a thorough analysis of participatory knowing, see the important studies by Jorge N. Ferrer, *Revisioning Transpersonal Theory: A Participatory Vision of Human Spirituality* (Albany: State University of New York Press, 2002); idem, "Transpersonal Knowledge: A Participatory Approach to Transpersonal Phenomena," in *Transpersonal Knowing: Exploring the Horizons of Consciousness*, ed. Tobin Hart, Peter Nelson, and Kaisa Puhakka (Albany: State University of New York Press, 2000), 213–52.

22. Teresa of Avila, *Castle*, 7.4.6, 190.

23. Ibid., 7.4.8, 190.

24. *Way of Perfection*, 3.7, 51.

25. Teresa of Avila, *The Book of Her Foundations*, 20.3,198.

26. Constance FitzGerald, "A Discipleship of Equals: Voices from Traditions—Teresa of Avila and John of the Cross," in *A Discipleship of Equals: Towards a Christian Feminist Spirituality*, ed. Francis A. Eigo (Villanova, PA: Villanova University Press, 1988), 91. See also Carole Slade, "St. Teresa of Avila as a Social Reformer," *Mysticism and Social Transformation*, ed. Janet K. Ruffing (Syracuse: Syracuse University Press, 2001), 91–103.

27. McGinn, "Language of Inner Experience," 138.

28. Ibid.

29. Teresa of Avila, *Life*, 29.13, 252.

30. Ibid., 12.11, 251.

31. Teresa of Avila, *Castle*, 6.1.8, 363.

32. Ibid., 4.2.5–6, 324–25.

33. Ibid., 6.2.2, 367.

34. Ibid., 6.2.4, 368.

35. Ibid., 6.11.1–2, 421–22.

36. Ibid., 6.2.8, 370.

37. Ibid., 6.6.5, 393.

38. Ibid., 7.2.6, 435; 7.2.9, 436.

39. Sharafuddin Maneri, *The Hundred Letters*, trans. Paul Jackson (New York: Paulist Press, 1980), 145.

SEVEN

Ibn al-'Arabī on
Participating in the Mystery

William C. Chittick

JORGE N. FERRER proposes four realms in which a participatory approach to the study of religion and spirituality is more adequate than current methodologies: generosity in recognizing the infinite creativity of the Mystery, respect toward the legitimate diversity of traditions, fertility for interreligious dialogue, and expansion of the emancipatory options of human beings.[1] These in fact are a few of the characteristics of much of premodern Islamic thought, despite the stereotypes so popular in the West. Specifically, they can easily be observed in the writings of Ibn al-'Arabī (d. 1240), who was arguably the single most influential Muslim thinker before the twentieth century.

Ibn al-'Arabī was an enormously prolific author of works that defy easy classification. He was a master of the major branches of Islamic learning— Koran and Koran commentary, Hadith (sayings of the Prophet), jurisprudence (fiqh), Kalam (dogmatic theology), and Sufism in both its practical and its theoretical dimensions. His works integrate and synthesize all these fields, in contrast to the more specialized writings of almost every other important author in Islamic history. If he is commonly called a "Sufi," this is because he made full use of the insights of the "mystics" and was immersed in the practices and realizations of the path to God. It does not mean, however, that he identified himself with the Sufis or that he limited himself to their characteristic approaches. The claim put forth by his followers (and arguably by himself) that he was "the Seal of the Muhammadan Saints" is perhaps less telling than the fact that his tomb in Damascus is still venerated by the common people and frequented by pilgrims from all over the Islamic world, or that he is universally condemned by the so-called "fundamentalists."[2]

To understand Ibn al-'Arabī's teachings in their context, we need to keep in mind that his pertinence to the Islamic tradition and his ability to speak to thoughtful Muslims over the centuries have everything to do with the fact that his writings take the Koran as their constant point of reference. Few authors have been as thoroughly versed in the Koran's own terminology or have taken as much care to recover the meaning of the text as it was understood by the Arabs to whom it was revealed. But he is not a "systematic" thinker. In no way does he try to embrace his subject matter in a comprehensive and hierarchical way. Rather, he writes—as he frequently tells us—under the pressure of divine inspiration, which flows as it wills. This might be how he would explain the fact, attested by any careful reader of his works, that he always surprises. He begins his discussions with the time-honored and well-known (Koran, Hadith), and he ends up by showing that far more is involved than meets the eye. His arguments are always coherent and convincing, even when they fly in the face of conventional logic. If there is any motive that can be ascribed to him, it is that of spiritual teachers everywhere: to open up the soul to the full range of its possibilities.

THE MEANINGS OF *ISLĀM*

A good place to begin investigating the participatory nature of Ibn al-'Arabī's vision and illustrating its seamless fit into the Islamic tradition may be with the word *islām* itself. Typically, it is understood to designate the religion established by Muhammad and the Koran, and its literal meaning is said to be "submission to the will of God." In fact, however, Islam as the name of the religion is not attested unequivocally in the Koran, nor is the "will" of God given special prominence. Rather, its most basic Koranic meaning—"submission" or "surrender"—designates the universal state of everything in the universe. All things are totally controlled by their Creator. The whole cosmos and everything within it participates in the flow of universal being, and nothing has any choice in the matter. As the Koran puts it, "What, do they desire another religion than God's, while to Him has submitted [*islām*] whoso is in the heavens and the earth, willingly or unwillingly?" (3:83). If we replace Ferrer's "participatory" in the following paragraph with *islām*, the basic sense of the word is clearly expressed:

> Participatory also refers to the fundamental ontological predicament of human beings in relation to spiritual energies and realities. Human beings are—whether they know it or not—always participating in the self-disclosure of the Spirit by virtue of their very existence. The participatory predicament is not only the ontological foundation of the other forms of participation, but also the epistemic anchor of spiritual knowledge claims and the moral source of responsible action.[3]

Once we acknowledge that *islām*'s first meaning is ontological, we might then say that all things are submitted to God's "will." In contrast to many Muslim theologians, however, Ibn al-'Arabī sees no reason to highlight will over other divine attributes. Typically, when explaining the submission of all things to God, he begins with the divine attribute of life (*ḥayāt*), then points to knowledge (*'ilm*), desire (*irāda*),[4] and power (*qudra*). God creates things through his power, but he does not exercise his power without first desiring to do so. He cannot desire things without first knowing them, and he cannot know them without being alive.

Notice that Ibn al-'Arabī's discussion of the divine desire is ontological, not moral. When we speak of God's "will," we normally have in view what God "wants" from us, without any suggestion that we are forced to do it. For example, when Muslim theologians read the verse, "Thy Lord has decreed that you worship none but Him" (17:23), they tell us that it means we have the moral obligation to submit our will to that of God. Ibn al-'Arabī, however, says that it refers to the ontological fact that all things worship and serve ('*ibāda*) their Creator by the very act of existing.

In Islamic theology generally God has two sorts of command (*amr*). The first, called the "engendering" (*takwīnī*) command, brings all things into existence and thereby compels them to submit to their Creator. It is mentioned in a number of Koranic verses, such as, "His command, when He desires a thing, is to say to it 'Be!' [*kun*], and it comes to be" (36:82). In respect of this command, all things serve and worship God: "None is there in the heavens and the earth that does not come to the All-merciful as a servant" (19:93). Their service is "essential" (*dhātī*), which is to say that it is part and parcel of what they are. Their being is nothing but the trace of the divine Word, their activity nothing but the impress of the divine Act: "God creates you and what you do" (37:96). Hence, Ibn al-'Arabī tells us, the cosmos, which is defined as "everything other than God" (*mā siwa'llāh*), is the sum total of the divine words articulated within "the Breath of the All-Merciful" (*nafas al-raḥmān*), which is identical with the spirit that God blew into Adam's clay to bring him to life (Koran 15:29).

In sum, *islām* in its broadest Koranic sense means the compulsory submission of all things to the engendering command. There can be no discussion of freedom until we look at a second, narrower meaning of *islām*, which is voluntary submission to the instructions of God as revealed to the prophets. The Koran discusses many prophets, beginning with Adam himself, and calls them and their worthy followers "*muslims*," meaning that they voluntarily submitted to God. The hadith literature tells us that God sent 124,000 prophets, so there is plenty of room for generosity in guessing who they may have been (the Koran mentions only twenty-five or so by name).

Prophetic instructions are contrasted with the engendering command by calling them the "prescriptive" (*taklīfī*) command. They take the form "Perform

the prayers, fast during Ramadan, avoid pork, love your neighbor, do not worship idols!" God prescribes right activity, right speech, and right thought, and
human beings have the freedom to accept or reject his prescriptions. Those
who accept become voluntary *muslims*, whether or not they happen to be followers of Muhammad and the Koran.

As voluntary submission, *islām* has three basic sorts. The first is free
acquiescence to the instructions of the Real; it corresponds roughly to "religion" as a universal phenomenon. It is in reference to this that the Koran
says, "There is no compulsion in religion" (2:256)—it has no meaning without free acceptance. The second sort of voluntary submission is the historical
religion that goes by the name. The third is the practices that are made
incumbent by the Koran and the Prophet for those who choose to follow this
specific revelation. In this last understanding, *islām* is distinguished from
īmān, the realm of faith and understanding, and *iḥsān*, the realm of human
goodness, virtue, and transformation.[5]

THE WAY THINGS ARE

Ibn al-'Arabī's writings deal with all three dimensions of the Islamic tradition—practice, understanding, and transformation—but they stress the second, that is, clarifying the nature of things in order to point the way toward
transformation. It is said that Muhammad used to pray, "Our Lord, show us
things as they are!" Ibn al-'Arabī writes as a guide to the achievement of the
infinitely diverse implications of this vision. He commonly calls those who
achieve it *muḥaqqiq*, "realizer," the active participle of the verbal noun *taḥqīq*,
"realization." So central is this notion to his teachings that his greatest student, Ṣadr al-Dīn Qūnawī, speaks of his master's perspective as *mashrab al-
taḥqīq*, "the standpoint of realization."

The word *taḥqīq* derives from the same root as *ḥaqq*, one of the most important Koranic names of God and a key technical term in several Islamic sciences. *Ḥaqq* means truth, reality, rightness, appropriateness, worthiness. As a
name of God (one that in Persian, for example, is used far more commonly than
Allah), it means Real, True, and Right in the absolute senses. As employed for
other than God, *ḥaqq* designates the truth, reality, rightness, and appropriateness of things, and it is contrasted with *bāṭil*, untruth, unreality, and wrongness.

Taḥqīq means literally "to achieve the *ḥaqq*" or "to put the *ḥaqq* into practice." Like "realization" in English, it has the double sense of understanding
and actualizing. It means to realize and recognize things as true, right, and
appropriate, and to actualize in oneself what is true, right, and worthy. In the
final analysis, self-realization is nothing other than the realization of the Real.

One of the several important scriptural bases for Ibn al-'Arabī's understanding of the word *taḥqīq* is a hadith in which the Prophet explains that
people should always keep the *ḥaqqs* of things in view—their truth, rightness,

appropriateness, and worthiness—and they should respond to these *ḥaqq*s in the right and worthy manner: "Your soul has a *ḥaqq* against you, your Lord has a *ḥaqq* against you, your spouse has a *ḥaqq* against you, your visitor has a *ḥaqq* against you. So, give to each that has a *ḥaqq* its *ḥaqq*." One can translate the word *ḥaqq* here as "right"—and indeed, it is precisely this Arabic word that is used nowadays in discussion of "human rights." But notice that the point of observing rights is not to claim what is due to oneself, but rather to respond rightly, appropriately, and worthily to others. Observing rights is our responsibility—the rights are "against" us, not for us.

In Ibn al-'Arabī's view, the last sentence of this hadith—"Give to each that has a *ḥaqq* its *ḥaqq*"—is both a universal human obligation and the epitome of *taḥqīq*. Realization is to see things as they truly are—that is, it is to see them in respect of their specific *ḥaqq*s—and, simultaneously, it is to act rightfully and worthily. This demands a vision of the Absolute *ḥaqq*—not in itself, but inasmuch as it discloses itself in all things and thereby bestows upon them their "rights." It demands recognizing and observing the *ḥaqq* of our own soul against us, which is our responsibility to ourselves. Our soul or self (*nafs*) is a gift of God, born of the All-Merciful Breath, and it is naturally inclined to serve, worship, and submit to its Lord. Our responsibility toward it is to allow it to realize its own nature." Our Lord's right against us is for us to acknowledge his Lordship and act accordingly, that is, by obeying his prescriptive command. As for spouses, guests, and others, their rights against us are that we act toward them with wisdom and compassion, but these are qualities that do not come easily to us, so again we need the guidance of the prophetic and sagely norms. What exactly all of this entails is precisely the concern of the traditional Islamic sciences, from jurisprudence to Sufism.

THE ONENESS OF THE REAL

Another hadith tells us about the *ḥaqq* of God against us, that is, our responsibility toward him: "God's right against His servants is that they worship God and associate nothing with Him. The servant's right against God is that He not chastise anyone who associates nothing with Him." This saying highlights the importance of the first of the three principles of Islamic faith, that is *tawḥīd*, the assertion of divine unity that is encapsulated in the statement, "(There is) no god but God."[7] The negative counterpart of *tawḥīd* is *shirk*, "associating others with God," which in Koranic terms is the one unrepented human failing that God will never pardon (4:48).

Generally, Muslims have held that the assertion of unity is intuitively understood by anyone of sound mind. The role of the prophets is to "remind" (*dhikr*) those who have forgotten it and to provide guidance for those who remember. Guidance is needed because one cannot reach a happy and harmonious balance with the Real without the Real's initiative. Grace always takes precedence over works. Although we may engage in a quest for the Real, we are prevented from discerning what is rightfully due to it—in itself and in its creaturely manifestations—by its transcendence and omnipresence. We have no way of responding to that which is simultaneously nothing and everything—that is, no specific thing, yet revealed in all things, all God's "signs" (āyāt), which are precisely his creations. This helps explain why the second principle of Islamic faith is "prophecy" (nubuwwa)—not that of Muhammad specifically, but that of all the 124,000 prophets sent by God.

The Koran summarizes God's revelations to the prophets in these words: "And We never sent a messenger before thee save that We revealed to him, saying, 'There is no god but I, so worship/serve Me'" (21:25). A prophetic message, according to this verse, has two basic elements: First is tawḥīd, acknowledging the way things are, beginning with the recognition of the absolute authority of the Real and the compulsory servanthood of all things. Second is voluntary servanthood and worship, that is, observance of the prescriptive command, which delineates appropriate action as instructed by the self-revealing Real. Thus, in the Koranic view of things, tawḥīd is the same for all prophets, but God sent each prophet with "the tongue of his people" (14:4), that is, with "guidance" (hudā), appropriate to the cultural and linguistic context. But the Koran also reminds that God alone is the true guide. Thus, "You [O Muhammad] do not guide whom you want, but God guides whom He wants, and He knows very well those that are guided" (28:56).

THE ROOTS OF MULTIPLICITY

If we attempt to conceptualize all of reality, we can divide it into two realms: God and other than God; or the Real per se and the Real's manifestations; or the Absolute Mystery (al-ghayb al-muṭlaq) and the relatively mysterious.[8] Concerning the Mystery itself, we have no proper response other than to acknowledge our ignorance. Of everything else, we can say, in Ibn al-'Arabī's terms, that it is the self-disclosure (tajallī) of the Mystery.

The term self-disclosure derives from a Koranic passage in which Moses asks God to show himself, and God replies that Moses will not see him. "And when his Lord disclosed Himself to the mountain, He made it crumble to dust, and Moses fell down thunderstruck" (7:143). In Ibn al-'Arabī's interpretation of the divine self-disclosure, the Real in itself remains the absolute Mystery, but it discloses itself always and forever, whether in this familiar world of ours or in any other realm of manifestation. The Mystery is one, so every self-disclosure of the Mystery has its own uniqueness. No two things can ever be the same, and no two moments of any one thing will ever be repeated. This is the meaning of his commonly cited axiom, "There is no repetition in the self-disclosure" (lā takrār fi'l-tajallī).

If all things are unique self-disclosures of the One, each simultaneously reveals and conceals the One. The Koran says, "Wherever you turn, there is the face of God" (2:115), but every face veils every other face, and the faces of God are infinite. As Ibn al-'Arabī sometimes expresses the situation, everything is He/not He (*huwa lā huwa*), that is, Real/not Real. Inasmuch as things disclose God, they are He, but inasmuch as they veil him, they are not He. In all things, the Real is at once manifest and hidden, known and unknown, plain and mysterious.

The Koran tells us, "Everything is perishing but His face" (28:88), and commentators explain that "face" here means the very Essence of the Real. Ibn al-'Arabī agrees, but he also points out that the rules of Arabic grammar would naturally incline us to read the verse to mean "Every thing is perishing except *its* face," that is, the face of the thing, its essence and reality. The fact that the verse is susceptible to two obvious readings follows the divine intention, says Ibn al-'Arabī, for God wants us to understand that the divine face turned toward each thing is identical with the thing's face turned toward God. Thus, each thing in the universe has a "specific face" (*wajh khāṣṣ*), which is its own reality in God's awareness. It is to this face that God says "Be!," and though the face remains with God, its properties and characteristics become manifest as the thing in the world.[9]

The path to self-knowledge leads to the face of the Real, but that face is precisely the realization and actualization of one's own face, one's own true nature, one's own *ḥaqq*. The face of the servant is nothing but the face of the Lord, and each servant is unique, each is a never-repeating self-disclosure of the Real. Inasmuch as all servants are faces, all roads lead to the Real, but inasmuch as each face is specific and unique, each servant achieves a unique actualization of the Real. The Koranic command to seek knowledge is a command to strive to know oneself and one's Lord, for the two knowledges are the same knowledge. "He who knows himself," as the Prophet is famously quoted as saying, "knows his Lord." He who sees his own face sees God's face:

> God possesses relations, faces, and realities ad infinitum. Although they all go back to One Entity, yet the relations are not qualified by existence that finitude should touch them. . . . Nothing is known of the Real save what is given by the specific relation. The relations are infinite, so the creation of the possible things is infinite. Hence creation is constant in this world and the next, and knowledge constantly undergoes new arrival in this world and the next. That is why He commanded [His servants] to seek increase in knowledge.[10]

But the path has no end, for the Real in its very selfhood can never be reached.[11] The object of the search is infinite and the seeker is finite, so the journey goes on forever:

God commanded His Prophet to say, "My Lord, increase me in knowledge [Koran 20:114]. . . . The command was unqualified, so he seeks increase and bestowal in this world and the next. . . . God never ceases creating, within us ad infinitum, so the knowledges extend ad infinitum. . . . The thirst of the seeker of knowledge never ceases. . . . One of the gnostics said, "The soul is an ocean without shore," alluding to infinity. But everything that enters into existence or is qualified by existence is finite. . . . If the objects of knowledge were to be qualified by existence, they would be finite and suffi- ciency could be bestowed. So, you will not know anything of God but what comes to be from Him and comes to exist within you.[12]

REVELATION

Despite the absolute mystery of the Infinite Real in itself, it articulates its own self-disclosure ad infinitum through the never-ending words of the All- Merciful Breath. We perceive these words in three domains: cosmos, soul, and scripture. The last of these is the Real's self-revelation in the language of guidance. It speaks to the uniquely human capacity to reflect upon the world and ourselves and to reorient ourselves appropriately. It addresses us inas- much as we see that we are not yet complete and have a role to play in our own completion. It takes into account the fact that, in a very real sense, we are cocreators of our own selves and of the world, for every act we perform and every choice we make shapes the direction in which the Mystery unfolds. Cocreativity is not a term that one will encounter in Arabic, not least because of the concern to stress that "There is no creator but God." Nonethe- less, Ibn al-'Arabī is not averse to pointing out that human beings do in fact participate in the divine attribute of creativity. He reminds us that the Ara- bic word khalq, "creation," has two basic meanings: to bring what never was into existence, and to give new shape to that which already is. God alone possesses the attribute of saying "Be," so he alone creates in the first sense. But both God and human beings create in the second sense, a point to which the Koran alludes in the verse, "Blessed is God, the best of creators" (23:14).

The role of prophetic revelation is to provide guidance so that people can understand the ḥaqqs of things and exercise their creative powers appro- priately. The outstanding feature of the Koran's own style of guidance is per- haps found in the way it goes about naming the Unnamable. The so-called "ninety-nine most beautiful names of God" permeate the text and provide the fundamental building blocks of Islamic theology. The Mystery discloses itself by calling itself Alive, Knowing, Desiring, Powerful, Speaking, Gener- ous, Just, Merciful, Loving, Forgiving, Vengeful, and so on. In each case the formula of tawḥīd supplies the sense: There is none truly alive but God, none truly knowing but God, none desiring but God, none generous but God, none just but God.

revelation helps us be creative

[handwritten annotation: participation in self-disclosure of the Real is universal, but humans have more influence over how that self-disclosure occurs]

When we understand the divine names in terms of the Mystery's absoluteness, they declare that the Real alone is truth, life, knowledge—all else is illusion, death, ignorance. When we read the names in terms of the Real's infinite self-disclosure, they declare that every trace of life, knowledge, desire, and speech can be nothing but the face of the Real. All without exception participate in the Real's self-disclosure. But human beings alone, among all the participants—so far as we know—share in the very creativity of the One, for they alone have a say in how the divine attributes and qualities unfold in themselves and the world.

Can we then know the Mystery by knowing its names? The answer is always yes and no. We can know it inasmuch as it names itself through the qualities of things and people and discloses itself linguistically and conceptually in the prophetic messages. But its names remain, as Ibn al-'Arabī likes to say, "relations" (*nisab*), not things in themselves. They allow us to orient ourselves rightly and appropriately to the Real, but they do not give access to the Mystery in itself. *[handwritten: the Mystery is fundamentally unknowable]*

Then, of course, there is the whole question of what we mean by "knowing" the Real. Ibn al-'Arabī frequently comes back to the various modalities of understanding and to the difference between mental conceptualization and "cordial" vision, for the heart is the true locus of human selfhood and awareness, the only thing in the universe that can, according to a hadith, embrace God: "Neither My heavens nor My earth embraces Me, but the heart of My believing servant does embrace Me."[13]

In Ibn al-'Arabī's view, real knowledge, real awareness of the way things are, goes back to the Real's presence in every self-disclosure, that is, to the *haqq* of things. The Real is the Alive, the Knowing, the Desiring, the Powerful; the self-disclosures participate in these attributes to the degree of their receptivity. Ibn al-'Arabī quotes the saying of the great Sufi Junayd: "The water takes on the color of the cup." In the last analysis, knowing is an attribute of the Real— "There is none knowing but God." Real knowing, the sort achieved through realization, demands identity with the real knower. Once one finds the specific face of God that is the face of oneself, then one knows. One reaches that state through love, one of the most basic themes of all Sufi teachers. In this sort of discussion Ibn al-'Arabī often cites an authentic hadith that quotes God's words concerning the servant who becomes worthy of his love: "When I love him, I am his hearing through which he hears, his eyesight through which he sees, his hand through which he holds, and his foot through which he walks." Needless to say, God is also his mind and heart through which he knows.

THE ONTOLOGY OF THE HUMAN

One of Ibn al-'Arabī's concerns as an instructor on the path to God is to map out the range of human possibility. Any thorough review of his teachings will alert us to the fact that he provides a vastly complicated exposition of human types that is given overall orientation by the notion of "the perfect human being" (al-insān al-kāmil). Perfection is the ultimate human state, the full realization of the human substance, the furthest goal beyond which none can aspire. But no one should imagine that it is fixed or limiting, nor should one think that there is but one path to its achievement. It is the station embodied by all the prophets, each in his or her own perfect way. And, like anything else, it has degrees—a fact that follows upon the axioms "There is no god but God" and "There is no repetition in the self-disclosure." Absolute perfection is an attribute of the Real alone, and no relative, disclosed perfection can ever be exactly the same as any other.

Ibn al-'Arabī cites a verse that the Koran puts into the mouth of the angels, "None of us there is but has a known station" (37:64). He tells us that this verse applies to everything in the universe, but, in the human case, it does not come into play until after death. All things, in other words, are fixed in their own unique natures and capacities, even if each undergoes constant change as a never-repeating self-disclosure of the Real. But human beings are not yet fixed in their selfhoods, so the Mystery discloses itself within them in unpredictable ways—in contrast to animals and plants, for example, which retain the limitations of their species. The human soul is open-ended, an ocean without shore. As long as people live in this world they possess some degree of freedom in heart, soul, and body, or in awareness, character traits, and activities. As the Prophet put it, the possibility of "repentance" (tawba, literally "turning" toward God) remains until the last breath.

Human beings are essentially mysterious in a way that is not replicated in nonhuman things. God, after all, "created Adam in His own form [ṣūra]"— to cite Muhammad's version of this Biblical saying. Adam and his children are forms of the absolute Mystery; they disclose it in itself, not inasmuch as it has this or that possibility of manifestation. In Koranic terms, Adam was the first prophet and the first perfect human being. God created him to be his vicegerent and taught him all the names (2:30). For Ibn al-'Arabī and others, this means that human beings were given the potential to understand, embrace, and make manifest all the names and qualities of God and things. They can be global self-disclosures of the Mystery, and it is precisely their self-aware participation in the Real's global manifestation that Ibn al-'Arabī calls "realization." It demands recognizing both the Absolute ḥaqq and the relative ḥaqqs of all things. It requires knowing the proper response to the ḥaqqs—that is, the duty and responsibility bestowed upon us by the rights of God and others. And it means that one must act on the basis of the ḥaqqs—this is precisely what ethical and moral activity is all about.

As the all-comprehensive Reality that is the source, sustainer, and destiny of all things, the Mystery is often called al-wujūd, Being, or al-wujūd al-ḥaqq, the Real Being. In the secondary sources, Ibn al-'Arabī is generally described (misleadingly) as the founder of the doctrine of *waḥdat al-wujūd*, "the oneness of Being."[14] The word *wujūd* was central to the vocabulary of the Peripatetic philosophers such as Avicenna, who is famous among other things for his distinction between necessary and possible (or contingent) *wujūd*. The Necessary Being is that which is and cannot not be; the possible is everything else, which may or may not be, given that its existence is utterly dependent upon God's saying "Be!" to it.

Ibn al-'Arabī made use of the Avicennan distinctions, but he also gave prominence to the literal senses of the word *wujūd*, which are to find, perceive, understand, enjoy, and be ecstatic. For him, one of the best ways to gain insight into the Mystery is to conceive of it simply as the One *Wujūd*, that which is truly and uniquely finding, understanding, enjoying. The Mystery is the necessary Being/Consciousness/Bliss, and everything else—all possible, contingent things—are its self-disclosures, limited and confined manifestations of its attributes and qualities. Do they exist, are they conscious, are they blissful? Yes and no, He/not He—yes inasmuch as they are He, no inasmuch as they are not He.

To say that there is only one *wujūd* means that the Mystery alone is truly real and worthy and truly present in all that is. Things have no existence of their own, no self-reality, because *wujūd*—existence, reality—is the exclusive property of the Real. *Wujūd* discloses its own infinity through the beginningless and endless cosmos.[15] Inasmuch as things exist, they can only be its face, but inasmuch as they are what they are in their own specificities, they reveal its possibilities by veiling its infinite light. Things are real enough for practical purposes, just as, in the common analogy, red and blue are truly red and blue, though they are nothing but light.

What distinguishes human beings from other creatures is the fullness of their spectrum. All other things in the universe stand in known stations, which is to say that each is defined by a specific and unique color of Infinite Light. In contrast, human beings, made in the form of the Formless, have no specific color; they are simply light. This is not to deny that every human individual is dominated by specific and changing colors and attributes; it is simply to say that in their fundamental, underlying humanness—in the fact that they are forms of the Real in itself—they are not fixed in their coloration and can strive for colorlessness. They alone among all things can attempt to actualize fullness and totality, "the station of no station," the color of colorlessness, the purity of Being/Consciousness/Bliss.

MODELS OF PERFECTION

Ibn al-'Arabī talks of human perfection in two basic modes: inner and outer, or mysterious and manifest. In respect of inner perfection, all perfect human beings achieve oneness with the Real; all participate in the self-disclosure of

the Real under the aegis of the name Allah, the nonspecific and all-comprehensive name that designates the Mystery both in itself and in the attributes
through which it discloses itself. In respect of the second mode of perfection,
each perfect human being discloses specific divine attributes and character
traits appropriate to the *haqqs* of the historical and social circumstances in
which they find themselves.[16]

This way of looking at perfection can be observed at work in Ibn al-
'Arabī's most famous book, *Fuṣūṣ al-ḥikam*, "The Ringstones of the Wis-
doms."[17] Each of twenty-seven chapters is dedicated to a divine wisdom
embodied in a specific word or logos (*kalima*) of God, in each case identified
with a prophet or perfect man, from Adam down to Muhammad. The wisdom
that is embodied in Adam, to whom the first and longest chapter of the book
is dedicated, is that of the name Allah itself. Here Ibn al-'Arabī investigates
various implications of the fact that human beings were created in the form
of this all-comprehensive name, not in the form of any less inclusive name.
In succeeding chapters, he associates specific divine qualities with other
prophetic figures.

The underlying idea, not completely explicit in the text but clear enough
from his other writings, is that Adam, as the progenitor of the human race
and the father of all the prophets, necessarily represents a plenary disclosure
of Real *Wujūd* itself, with all its concomitant attributes and qualities. As for
the other prophets, each realizes the fullness of the divine form internally but
is governed externally by the implications of a single divine attribute—Noah
by glorification, Ishmael by exaltation, Joseph by light, and so on. As for
Muhammad, he manifests singularity, since, as the last prophet, he represents
the unique example of a human being in whom all of the potentialities
implicit in Adam and made manifest successively in the chain of prophets are
synthesized and actualized in one individual.

So, are some of the 124,000 prophets superior to others? The Koran provides the mythic answer with a set of apparently contradictory verses. From
Ibn al-'Arabī's point of view, some of these verses have in view the inner unity
of human perfection, and others the outer diversity of prophetic function.
Internally, the perfect human beings are one, externally they make manifest
degrees and types of perfection, each of which will have a relative superiority
over others. For example, the Koran commands people to say, "We make no
distinctions among His messengers" (2:285). It also tells us, "We preferred
some of the prophets over others, and We gave David the Psalms" (17:55).

RECEPTIVITY

Ibn al-'Arabī explains the manner in which created things participate in the
self-disclosure of the Real by using the notion of "receptivity" (*qabūl*). Everything in the universe is a "receptacle" (*qābil*) for *wujūd*. Everything, in

Junayd's analogy, is a cup that bestows its color on the water. But, where do the cups come from? The Koran says, "Our only word to a thing, when We desire it, is to say to it 'Be!,' and it comes to be" (16:40). How can God desire a "thing" that does not exist? Ibn al-'Arabī explains that the nonexistence of things is relative to the cosmos, not absolute. The things do not exist in themselves or as objects in the world, but they do exist as concomitants of God's self-awareness, much as our own ideas exist in our minds. Real *Wujūd* transcends all spatial and temporal limitations, for these are simply disclosures of the possibilities and limitations of being-in-the-world. Its consciousness embraces knowledge of all things for all eternity, for each thing in the cosmos, irrespective of time or place, is a possibility of existence contingent upon the Real's own Necessity.

Each "thing" (*shay'*) has a unique "thingness" (*shay'iyya*) known forever to the Real. The specificity of the thing's thingness defines its preparedness (*isti'dād*), the shape and color of its cup, or its capacity to carry the weight of the Real's self-disclosure and to make the divine attributes manifest. Ibn al-'Arabī tells us how this works while explaining why God does not always answer prayers, despite the fact that he says, for example, "Call upon Me, and I will respond to you" (40:60):

> God says, "The giving of thy Lord can never be walled up" [17:20], that is, cannot be withheld. God is saying that He gives constantly, while the loci receive in the measure of the realities of their preparednesses. In the same way, you say that the sun spreads its rays over the existent things. It is not miserly toward anything with its light. The loci receive the light in the measure of their preparednesses. . . . The same thing takes place in the divine self-disclosures. The Self-discloser, in respect of what He is in Himself, is One in Entity, while the forms of the self-disclosures are diverse in keeping with the diversity of the preparednesses of the loci of self-disclosure. The same is the case with the divine gifts. Once you understand this, you will know that God's gift is not withheld, but you want Him to give you something that your preparedness cannot receive, and then you attribute to Him withholding in that which you seek from Him, and you do not turn your attention toward the preparedness. . . . You say, "But—'God is powerful over every thing' [2:20]," and you speak the truth in that. You forget the orderly arrangement of the divine wisdom in the cosmos and what is demanded by the realities of the things.[18]

We seem to be moving in a deterministic direction, but that would be to misread the intention in such explanations. What is being stressed is the reality of the Real, the primacy of the Mystery, the contingent and illusory status of everything else. With all this, there are distinctions to be drawn among the Real's self-disclosures, and choices to be made by beings who possess a certain degree of freedom, however illusory it may be when weighed against the absolute Freedom of the Real. People need always to keep in mind that their own share in the divine gifts has not yet been fixed—our station remains unknown until death. The moral imperative of the message derives precisely from the fluidity of the human situation. Everyone is called upon to act in keeping with the *ḥaqq* of things and to follow the prescriptive command.

Given our unknown stations and the nonrepetition of the self-disclo-sures, our receptivity at this moment is one thing, but our receptivity at the coming moment remains unknown. The only logical course is to accept that the All-Merciful has articulated us within his Breath precisely so that we may partake of Being/Consciousness/Bliss, and that he has also commanded us to exercise our limited freedom in the appropriate way. It is the *ḥaqq* of our souls to be opened up to the fullness of divine mercy, but that *ḥaqq* is "against" us. It is up to us to follow the right path, and that can only happen when we observe the *ḥaqq* of our Lord and follow in the footsteps of his prophets and the perfect human beings.

THE TRANSFORMATIVE JOURNEY

Human life is a journey from the Real to the Real with the Real. This is the perspective of compulsory *islām*. It is made explicit by the doctrine of *tawḥīd*, which says that everything comes from the Mystery, everything is sustained by it moment by moment, and everything returns to it in the end. All are sub-mitted to God "from the origin to the return" (*min al-mabda' ila'l-ma'ād*), as the Muslim philosophers like to phrase it.

Prophecy, the second principle of faith, asserts that human beings have the unique capacity to say "No" to the way things are, for they alone are made in the form of the Formless and stand in no specific station. The Koran alludes to this peculiar human situation in the verse, "Have you not seen how to God bow all who are in the heavens and all who are in the earth, the sun and the moon, the stars and the mountains, the trees and the beasts, and many of mankind?" (22:18). All things bow to the engendering command, but human beings have the option of not bowing to the prescriptive com-mand. This is precisely where the third of Islam's three principles, the "return" to God, comes into play: All things return to their Creator under compulsion, but human freedom allows people to have as say in their own final destination.

Imagery of the path to God is omnipresent in Islamic lore. The revealed law, incumbent on all Muslims, is called *sharī'a*, "the wide road," and the Sufi way is known as *ṭarīqa*, "the narrow path." The path to God is typically described in terms of stations (*maqāmāt*) or waystations (*manāzil*), both of which designate the halting places of a caravan. The number of stages varies in the accounts of the masters—seven, forty, one hundred, three hundred, one thousand and one. The point is that, despite the omnipresence of God's face, we are foundering in ignorance and cannot recover our true human nature without prophetic help and a good deal of dedication and discipline. The goal is transformation, and the very names of the stations bespeak its nature—they designate virtues, character traits, and positive qualities of the soul. Each of them must be actualized and made permanent before the next stage can be reached.

The most famous example of the graduated path to God is provided by 'Aṭṭār's long Persian poem, Manṭiq al-ṭayr, "The Speech of the Birds."[19] The diverse birds that are the human souls need to fly over seven mountains of virtue: seeking, love, self-knowledge, independence, unity, bewilderment, and poverty. The ultimate goal is perfection, which is union with the Real. The penultimate stage, poverty (faqr), refers to the seekers' realization of the way things are, their acknowledgment of the utter emptiness of all things and the illusory nature of their own selves in face of the Real. Like most of the names of the stations, poverty derives from the Koran, specifically the verse, "O people! You are the poor toward God, and God—He is the rich, the praiseworthy" (35:15).

Many masters have summed up the path with a saying of an early Sufi that describes Muhammad's journey: "Two strides and he arrived." With one stride, they tell us, he stepped beyond this world, and with the second stride, he went beyond the realm of the spirit into the presence of the Real. The two-stride model of realization is most famously represented as "annihilation" (fanā') and "subsistence" (baqā'). Both terms derive from the Koranic verse, "Everyone on the face [of the earth] undergoes annihilation, and there subsists the face of thy Lord, Possessor of Majesty and Generous Giving" (55:27). Compared with the omnipresent Mystery, all things are evanescent and illusory. What truly subsists—and what is in fact always and forever present—is the face of God, the self-disclosure of the Real. In order to achieve awakening we need to undergo two simultaneous transformations: the "annihilation" of ignorance, limitation, egocentricity, and narrowness; and the "subsistence" of that which truly is, namely, the specific face of God that is unique to each of us.

Annihilation and subsistence represent one of several pairs of terms that are employed to bring home the nature of the transformative process that carries the soul to its destination. The two are often read as the application of the two halves of the formula of tawḥīd, the negation (nafy, i.e., the words "no god") and the affirmation (ithbāt, the words "but God"). "No god" strips the world, the soul, and all that they contain of any self-reality; "but God" affirms that all reality belongs to the Real alone. All the illusions of ego-centricity—all the ignorance, envy, and greed of the soul—must be negated, and then the face of God will remain, a face that is the fullness of wisdom and compassion and the self-disclosure of Being/Consciousness/Bliss. In still other terms, to undergo annihilation is to see that everything is "not He," and to achieve subsistence is to participate in the realization that all is "He."

THE MERCY OF EXISTENCE

To conclude this brief presentation of Ibn al-'Arabī's participatory vision, let me emphasize his "generosity in recognizing the infinite creativity of the Mystery." What he offers is a vision of the ways thing actually are, and, he tells us, things are this way because of the infinite generosity of the creative Mystery. The overwhelming theme of his writings is the omnipresence of the divine mercy, compassion, and kindness, precisely the point that he is making when he says that the Breath of the All-Merciful is the very substance of manifest reality. He has plenty of scriptural support for this view, such as the verse, "My mercy embraces everything" (7:156) and the hadith, "God's mercy takes precedence over his wrath."

Mercy drives the engendering command, for it bestows the gift of existence on an infinity of creatures that have no claim to it. It is omnipresent, but human freedom allows us to turn away from it. Hence the All-Merciful issues the prescriptive command, which explains how to recognize the faces of mercy in the myriad things and act appropriately and worthily, in keeping with mercy's *ḥaqq*. In a typical passage, Ibn al-'Arabī comments on a hadith in which the Prophet quotes God to the effect that people should think about him in terms of his fundamental nature, which is mercy and generosity:

> "God says, 'I am with My servant's opinion of Me,'" but He does not stop there, because "His mercy takes precedence over His wrath." Hence He said, in order to instruct us, "'So, let his opinion of Me be good'"—as a command. Those who fail to have a good opinion of God have disobeyed God's command and displayed ignorance of what is demanded by the divine generosity [*al-karam al-ilāhī*]. . . . When people have a bad opinion of something, what comes back to them is their own bad opinion, nothing else.[20]

Ibn al-'Arabī's generous appraisal of the divine mercy helps explain his critical response to the type of theological mentality that would confine the "unbelievers" to everlasting torment. As he writes in one of several similar passages:

> How tremendous is God's mercy to His servants! But they are unaware—I even saw a group who dispute concerning the all-embracingness of God's mercy, maintaining that it is confined to a specific faction. They curtailed and constricted what God has made all-embracing. If God were not to have mercy on any of His creatures, He would forbid His mercy to those who say this. But God refuses anything but His mercy's all-inclusiveness.[21]

But again, we should not take Ibn al-'Arabī's position here to the extreme, as if he is negating the reality of wrath or denying the chastisement of hell. All real mercy, after all, is tempered by wisdom and justice, as every mother knows.[22] If God had created us with mercy alone, we would be fixed in glorious stations like the angels, with no means to ascend or to descend.

The fullness of the divine mercy demands the fullness of our own exposure to possibility and choice, and that entails ignorance, forgetfulness, and inclination to do what is ugly and wrong.

In respect of the engendering command and compulsory *islām*, mercy permeates everything, but in respect of the prescriptive command and voluntary *islām*, wrath comes into play to the extent that people willingly fail to employ their divine gifts and freely refuse to make the right choices.[23] And if you say, "Well, why didn't God make us compulsory servants so that we would have a world without evil and always be happy," you are asking to be deprived of your own freedom and denying your own humanity, made in the form of the Formless.

The acknowledgment of the reality of wisdom, justice, and wrath keeps Ibn al-'Arabī far from saying that all is good, all is to be accepted, nothing is to be rejected—a position that sometimes ascribed to him by critics who look only at the affirmation and not the negation in "He/not He." Quite the contrary, Ibn al-'Arabī constantly speaks of the necessity of discernment. To say that everything is embraced by mercy is not to ignore the fact that each thing has its own individual *ḥaqq*—its own truth, rightness, worthiness, and appropriateness—and that, unlike the Absolute *ḥaqq*, each human soul is susceptible to *bāṭil*: illusion, untruth, wrongness, unworthiness. Everything has a right against us, and our responsibility toward it may be to avoid it or even to fight against it.

The standpoint of realization, which demands giving everything its rightful place and seeing things as they really are, helps explain why Ibn al-'Arabī maintains "respect toward the legitimate diversity of traditions." This is, after all, the Koranic position. At the same time, however, the Koran is also critical of those who fail to live up to the prophetic teachings, and Ibn al-'Arabī follows the same pattern. He provides the metaphysics to show that mercy must necessarily disclose itself to all people, but he also names error and shortcoming wherever he finds it.[24]

For the study of religion generally, Ibn al-'Arabī points the way to a balanced view of things, including an acknowledgment of the necessity of discerning between right and wrong. His remarks on the stance one should take toward teachings about the Mystery might be the model for all who appreciate the breadth and depth of the participatory approach:

> He who counsels his own soul should investigate, during his life in this world, all doctrines concerning God. He should learn from whence each possessor of a doctrine affirms his doctrine. Once it has been affirmed for him in terms of the face specific to it, according to which it is correct for him who holds it, then he should support it in the case of him who believes in it. He should not deny it or reject it, for he will reap its fruit on the Day of Resurrection, whatever that belief may be.[25]

NOTES

1. Ferrer, *Revisioning Transpersonal Theory: A Participatory Vision of Human Spirituality* (Albany: State University of New York Press, 2002); for an updated account, see his chapter in this volume.

2. See Michel Chodkiewicz, *The Seal of the Saints* (Cambridge, U.K.: The Islamic Texts Society, 1993). For the best biography of Ibn al-'Arabī, see Claude Addas, *Quest for the Red Sulphur: The Life of Ibn al-'Arabī* (Cambridge, U.K.: The Islamic Texts Society, 1993).

3. Ferrer, *Revisioning Transpersonal Theory*, 121.

4. Many scholars translate the divine attribute of *irāda* as "will" rather than desire, but this distorts the meaning of the word and makes it impossible to translate it consistently, especially since it is used as the generic divine attribute that embraces more narrowly focused attributes such as will or wanting (*mashī'a*) and love (*ḥubb*). On the human level as well, *irāda* is used to point to the spiritual, psychic, and bodily realms, and theologians recognize that it comes to us by way of participation in the divine desire. A good example of the problems with translating the word as "will" can be seen in this famous saying of Abū Yazīd Basṭāmī, a great early saint who knew the Koran by heart and was perfectly aware that *irāda* is a divine attribute. He was asked, "What do you desire?" His reply points to the levels of meaning implicit in the word: "I desire not to desire." In other words, his desire is for his individual, human desire (with all its imperfections) to be effaced in the divine desire. Translating the word as "will" in this saying would sound strange in English and obscure the point.

5. For an analysis of the Islamic tradition as a whole on the basis of these three fundamental dimensions, see Sachiko Murata and William C. Chittick, *The Vision of Islam* (New York: Paragon House, 1994).

6. To the question, "Are there then two of us, one who has rights and one who recognizes them?," the answer is, "Of course, at least two." Any sophisticated autology (Vedanta or Samkhya-Yoga, for example) knows that selfhood is multileveled. Ibn al-'Arabī deals with the issue in great detail and in many different ways; one of his basic schemes describes the human in terms of four basic levels: body (*jism*), soul (*nafs*), and spirit (*rūḥ*), all of which are created; and the uncreated "specific face," about which more will be said shortly.

7. The statement of *tawḥīd* is frequently translated "There is no god but Allah," but this distorts the Koranic view of things by suggesting that the issue is choosing among alternative gods. As understood by Muslim theologians over the centuries, the statement is rather an endlessly applicable methodology for understanding the self-disclosures of the Real and responding to them appropriately. It provides guidance in detaching oneself from illusion and ignorance by recognized both the ultimacy of the Real and its presence in all things. Those who employ the word *Allah* in translating the formula encourage exclusivist readings of the tradition and help preserve one of the deepest misunderstandings of Islam prevalent among non-Muslims, that is, that Muslims worship "another god," which by that very fact must be a false god. The Koran is vociferous in insisting that the God of all the prophets is the same God, the only God there is.

8. Ibn al-'Arabī puts it this way in a famous line of poetry: "I have not perceived the reality of anything—/How can I perceive something in which You are?" Cited in Chittick, *The Self-Disclosure of God: Principles of Ibn al-'Arabī's Cosmology* (Albany: State University of New York Press, 1998).

9. On face, veil, and specific face, see Chittick, *Self-Disclosure*, chapters 3–4.

10. *al-Futūḥāt al-makkiyya* (Cairo: 1911), vol. 2, 671, line 5.

11. One might object that Sufis often speak of "reaching God" or achieving "union with God," so that would clearly be the end of the path. This would be to ignore the numerous disquisitions of Muslim scholars and saints on the subject. To cite but a single example, the most outstanding work of later Islamic philosophy is a massive book known as "The Four Journeys" (*al-Asfār al-arba'a*) by Mullā Ṣadrā (d. 1640). Drawing from a tradition that long predates Ibn al-'Arabī, he explains that the first journey is to God, but three journeys then remain, and these go on forever: the journey in God, from attribute to attribute; the journey from God to the world (like the Buddha who returns with helping hands); and the journey from God to God in the world.

12. *Futūḥāt* 2: 552.12.

13. For a few of the issues that Ibn al-'Arabī develops in addressing knowledge of the Real, see Chittick, *The Sufi Path of Knowledge: Ibn al-'Arabī's Metaphysics of Imagination* (Albany: State University of New York Press, 1989), Part 4.

14. For the reasons why this is misleading, see Chittick, "Rūmī and *Waḥdat al-wujūd*," in *Poetry and Mysticism in Islam: The Heritage of Rūmī*, ed. A. Banani, R. Hovannisian, and G. Sabagh (Cambridge: Cambridge University Press, 1994), 70–111.

15. This does not imply "the eternity of the world," a doctrine for which the Peripatetics were criticized, but rather a much more subtle understanding of what "the world" means. For one of Ibn al-'Arabī's explanations, see Chittick, *Sufi Path*, 84–85.

16. On these two sorts of perfection, see Chittick, *Sufi Path*, chapter 20.

17. The best of the several translations into English is by Caner Dagli, *Ringstones of Wisdom* (Chicago: Kazi, 2004).

18. *Futūḥāt* 1: 287.10.

19. For a poetic, but not especially accurate, translation, see Afkham Darbandi and Dick Davis, *Conference of the Birds* (London: Penguin, 1984). A much more scholarly translation is offered by Peter Avery, *The Speech of the Birds* (London: The Islamic Texts Society, 1998).

20. *Futūḥāt* 2: 474.26.

21. *Futūḥāt* 4: 163.5.

22. One can hardly talk about mercy in Islamic terms without bringing mothers into the picture. Among other things, the very word *raḥma*, "mercy," derives from *raḥim*, "womb." See Murata, *The Tao of Islam: A Sourcebook on Gender Relationships in Islamic Thought* (Albany: State University of New York Press, 1992), chapter 7.

23. Ibn al-'Arabī insists, nonetheless, that wrath itself is the manifestation of mercy, and that hell, despite the real chastisement imposed on its denizens, will turn

sweet in the end, for mercy must have the final say. See Chittick, *Ibn al-'Arabī: Heir to the Prophets* (Oxford: Oneworld, 2005), chapter 9.

24. Mahmoud al-Ghorab reads Ibn al-'Arabī's works from an exclusivist standpoint and is able to find plenty of examples of criticisms of both religions other than Islam and faulty doctrinal positions within Islam ("Muhyiddin Ibn al-'Arabi Amidst Religions [*adyān*] and Schools of Thought [*madhāhib*]," in *Muhyiddin Ibn al-'Arabi: A Commemorative Volume*, ed. S. Hirtensten and M. Tiernan [Shaftesbury, Dorset: Element, 1993], 200–27). Al-Ghorab's study, however, only confirms my point: Ibn al-'Arabī follows the Koran by affirming the universality of mercy and prophetic revelation, but he tempers this by recognizing the omnipresent human phenomena of forgetfulness and willful rebellion, which find their way into all forms of religion. Moreover, his criticisms of other religions are based not on firsthand knowledge, of which he had practically none, but on general Koranic principles, which apply just as well to bad Muslims.

25. *Futūḥāt* 2: 85.11.

EIGHT

One Spirit, One Body

Jesus' Participatory Revolution

———————————

Bruno Barnhart

CHRISTIANITY IS ORIGINALLY—and essentially—a mystery of participation. In the event of Christ, there is made accessible to the human person a new participation in the divine Absolute (God) which becomes the matrix of a new participatory relationship between human persons, as well as between humanity and its natural environment. The dominant modern Western consciousness, on the other hand, is distinguished by its nonparticipatory character: we commonly lack a vital sense of participation in these same three dimensions. Western Christians have, generally, been carried along within the development of this Western consciousness—especially during the last two centuries—so that they have become unaware of the participatory core of their own religious tradition.

The participatory reawakening that is now taking place—and is expressed in this collection of essays—is beginning also within Western Christianity. I write from within the Roman Catholic tradition, in which the Second Vatican Council (1962–1965) has been the great symbolic event marking this participatory turn. The reawakening continues; it is a matter not only of epistemology but of life, and it therefore manifests all the complexity of life. We human beings live continually within a fabric of participations, of which we are only sporadically and minimally conscious.

In this chapter I shall focus upon the sense of participation in Christian tradition, as manifested in the foundational writings of the New Testament, and then in the development of theology, spirituality, and liturgy. "Participation" is not merely a useful category in the field of Religious Studies,[1] but is a reality and an experience central to the Christian tradition. The aim of the present essay is to retrieve this participatory Christian vision, presenting it in a contemporary context. The presentation will unfold in five stages, in the five sections that follow. After briefly reviewing (1) major currents of participatory and nonparticipatory consciousness in the ancient world, we shall look at (2) the "participatory revolution," which is the Christ-event, and then trace (3) the progressive extinction of a participatory consciousness in Western Christianity and move forward to (4) the current participatory reawakening. Finally we shall (5) situate this two-thousand year "participation history" of the Christian and post-Christian West theologically in its larger, global context. The concept of participation is a hermeneutic key that promises to open our common history (both religious and secular) to a new depth of understanding.

Participation distinguishes a mode of consciousness and a way of thinking that has characterized the traditions of "wisdom" or sapiential theology and philosophy. The sense of participation defines the boundary between a "wisdom" consciousness and thought, on the one hand, and modern Western (post-Cartesian) thought on the other hand: between a sapiential and a rational/analytical (i.e., "scientific') mode of knowledge. The New Testament expression of the mystery of Christ is a sapiential literature that challenges not only the objectivism of our dominant modern ways of understanding but also the individualism and subjectivism that is manifested in our sense of "personal experience." The reflective reader will find in this sapiential perspective an implicit challenge to many of the current academic approaches to religious and mystical phenomena—especially to those that attempt to comprehend spiritual realities from within a constricted epistemological framework—whether that of purely subjective experience or that of positive empirical science.

While some readers might prefer a presentation of Christianity starting from the viewpoint of personal spiritual—or even mystical—experience, the choice of a more objective approach corresponds to the central assertion that is being put forward here. Christian spiritual experience is a participation in the "objective" event of Christ, just as Christian theological understanding is a participation in the "objective" mystery of Christ. The event/mystery is prior to the participation and defines the experience and the knowledge. On the other hand, this objective mystery is itself essentially a matter of participation.

THE HISTORICAL BACKGROUND:
PARTICIPATION IN THE ANCIENT WORLD

It is important at the outset to assert the value of a counterpole, a certain "nonparticipation," against any uncritical inclination to see participation as an absolute good. A kind of "nonparticipation" is often a step toward something new—indeed, toward a new participation. We shall continually be dealing with the interaction of these two factors, *newness* and *participation*. In the Bible, the place of an intermediate, apparently nonparticipatory stage in the journey is the *wilderness*. Here we find the biblical Prophets, John the Baptist, and the beginning of the narratives of the people of Israel (in the Exodus) and of the New Testament community. Here, typically, begins a new phase of participation, a participatory revolution.

Primitive peoples are characterized by an intensely participatory consciousness; it is with the development of culture and civilization that the firm rational distinctions and boundaries arise.[2] A crucial turning point in the development of human consciousness arrived during the "Axial Period"[3] of the first millennium BCE, when, in widely separated cultures around the world—in India, China, Persia, Greece, and Israel—a new *personal consciousness* broke free of the matrix of collective consciousness. Karl Jaspers, who originated the term *Axial period*, describes this breakthrough in this way:[4] "What is new about this age, in all three areas of the world, [China, India, and "the West': that is, Israel and Greece] is that man becomes conscious of Being as a whole, of himself and his limitations. . . . He experiences absoluteness in the depths of selfhood and in the lucidity of transcendence."[5] It is reflexive consciousness that distinguishes the Axial breakthrough: "Consciousness became once more conscious of itself, thinking became its own object."[6] In the Axial age were laid the foundations of the present cultures, civilizations, and traditions of the world. "In this age were born the fundamental categories within which we still think today, and the beginnings of the world religions, by which human beings still live, were created. The step into universality was taken in every sense."[7] Within the many different kinds of personal emergence that characterize the Axial time is a single pivotal event.

> It is the *specifically human in man* which, bound to and concealed within the body, fettered by instincts and only dimly aware of himself, longs for liberation and redemption and is able to attain to them already in this world—in soaring toward the idea, in the resignation of ataraxia, in the absorption of meditation, in the knowledge of his self and the world as *atman*, in the experience of *nirvana*, in concord with the *tao*, or in surrender to the will of God. These paths are widely divergent in their conviction and dogma, but common to all of them is man's reaching out beyond himself by growing aware of himself within the whole of Being and the fact that he can tread them only as an individual on his own. . . . What was later called reason and personality was revealed for the first time during the Axial Period.[8]

Cousins points out the decline of participatory consciousness that resulted from this Axial revolution. The earlier primal or tribal consciousness had been intensely participative: both "horizontally" in the human collectivity and "vertically" in a largely undifferentiated relationship with the natural environment.

> Although Axial consciousness brought many benefits, it involved loss as well. It severed the harmony with nature and with the tribe. Axial persons were in possession of their own identity, it is true, but they had lost their organic relation to nature and community. They now ran the risk of being alienated from the matrix of being and life.[9]

As modern Westerners we are heirs to an advanced form of this individualized consciousness—through a long and complex process of evolution. This study will focus upon developments specifically within the Judeo-Christian tradition which I believe have been decisive in the formation of our contemporary Western consciousness.

The Axial Period marked an exodus from an earlier participation in collective consciousness, and sometimes it brought the realization of a more universal, indeed metaphysical participation: as in the Vedanta or in Taoism. In the Greek philosophical tradition, the movement was from an old participative mystique—a mythological common consciousness—to a "nonparticipatory" objective rationality (typified by Socrates), in which the emergent individuality is manifest. But here also, as in the Asian traditions, we find the discovery of a sublime and transcendent participation: in Plato, this is a participation in the divine Ideas, in the Absolute, the Good. The Greek philosophical traditions—particularly through Plato, Aristotle, and Plotinus—will also be a major factor in the evolution of Western consciousness and thought.

The biblical "history of salvation" is bounded at beginning and end by images of total participation: that is, by the unity or reunion of all humanity in a single "person": first in Adam and then, finally, in Christ. The first man, Adam, has the name of Earth: *adamah*. The earth—material creation—is recapitulated in this first man—as it will be later in Christ. God breathes the "spirit of life" into this first human being;[10] Jesus will breathe the divine Spirit into his disciples on the evening of his resurrection.[11]

We continue to find, in the scriptural story of Israel, strong images of collective identity which are typical of tribal societies. The identity of the Israelite is primarily that of his group, his family, tribe, and nation. This group is summed up, "recapitulated," in its head, its patriarch: Abraham, Isaac, Jacob/Israel. This collective identity determines an ethic: the patriarch is absolute lord of his family, and all the power or value is understood to dwell in him. The collective identity is later associated with the kings.[12]

Israel, however, is led in a direction that differs sharply from the religions of the surrounding peoples. Owen Barfield[13] has seen the role of Israel in history as being largely the *elimination of participation*—that is, the elimination of the cosmic participatory myth, ritual, and religion of the nations—particularly of the Canaanites. This takes place through the deconstruction of "idols," of representations of the Divine, and ultimately through the suppression of a consciousness of immanent divinity (or spirit) in nature. Participation in God is to be only through the channels established by God's action: covenant, rituals, sacrifices, priesthood, Levites, sanctuary, and temple—all established by the word of God. And this channeled participation also takes on a new "personal" character through the Prophets' teaching of a religion of faith and love, an interiorized religion of the heart, and the growth of a tradition of the individual's personal relationship with God.

Here we can see the implicit beginning of a further participation in God—participation in God as Person by a personal response and personal relationship with this God. It is as if God is awakening the human individual to his/her identity as person through this relationship which permits no escape and concealment behind the veils of exterior religion—behind ritual, appeasement, self-centered representations of God, behind a mediating priestly class. Each person is to grow in the context of a relationship with this intensely personal God—the arch-Person. The implicit divine participation of the First Testament reaches a peak in the revelation of the divine Name—Yahweh, or "I am"—to Moses.[14] As Barfield points out, a human being cannot utter this divine Name without some degree of implicit appropriation of the divine identity.[15] While, in the course of the history of Israel, participation becomes more and more detached from nature, more and more personalized, a human participation in the divine "identity" itself is quietly intimated beneath the surface of the biblical word: a participation that remains unutterable—and sharply paradoxical in the context of this religion of a uniquely transcendent God. It is in the line of this "undetermined" participation in the divine identity that the unitive revolution of Jesus will take place.

Divine participations, then, are present already in Israel under the First Covenant, and some of the principal participations are explicit. In the biblical writings we find the person of God "projected" into the world through the divine Word and Wisdom, and through the Holy Spirit. Human beings share to some degree in the divine being and life through the Word/Wisdom and Spirit present in the world. Further, the prophets glimpse somewhere in the future another covenant centered in an interior participation in God—a fuller partaking of the divine Spirit—and in a new immediacy of divine knowledge. An astonishing new intimacy with God is promised: "A new heart I will give you, and a new spirit I will put within you; and I will take out of your flesh the heart of stone and give you a heart of flesh. And I will put my spirit within you. . . ."[16]

JESUS' REVOLUTION

The new participation initiated by Jesus Christ is the central subject of the New Testament. Its inauguration is the pivotal event to which the Gospels lead and from which the Acts of the Apostles and the apostolic letters derive. Relevant texts abound. I shall cite a few of the more explicit passages in the Pauline letters and in the Gospel and First Letter of John.

PAUL

Paul's initiatory experience of Christ on the road to Damascus included a revelation of the participation of the Christians (whom Paul had been persecuting) in the person of Christ which became a foundation of his theology. "And he fell to the ground and heard a voice saying to him, 'Saul, Saul, why do you persecute me?' And he said, 'Who are you, Lord?' And he said, 'I am Jesus, whom you are persecuting. . . .'"[17] The center of that theology became the "mystery" of Christ, which Paul would summarize as "Christ in you."[18] For Paul, the mystery involved especially the opening of salvation—or divine participation—to the Gentiles as well as the Jews. Repeatedly he recalls to his Gentile converts the "unrelatedness" out of which they have come.

> [R]emember that you [Gentiles] were at that time separated from Christ, alienated from the commonwealth of Israel, and strangers to the covenants of promise, having no hope and without God in the world. But now in Christ Jesus you who once were far off have been brought near in the blood of Christ. For he is our peace, who has made us both one, and has broken down the dividing wall of hostility, by abolishing in his flesh the law of commandments and ordinances, that he might create in himself one new man in place of the two, so making peace, and might reconcile us both to God in one body through the cross, thereby bringing the hostility to an end.[19]

This participation in Christ is an "incorporation" into him; the believer becomes part of the "body of Christ." The body of Christ includes all the believers; each is a "member" of the body. "So we, though many, are one body in Christ, and individually members one of another. . . ."[20] The *physical realism* with which these texts speak of the new participation in Christ is shocking to a modern reader. "Body of Christ" is not a mere metaphor, but a precise expression of the new participatory reality, though in a way which is beyond our understanding. "For in him the whole fullness of deity dwells bodily, and you have come to fullness of life in him. . . ."[21] This body is at once the body of the risen Christ, the community of believers, and the eucharistic bread. It is the body in which everything—including the individual Christians—is gathered into one. "The cup of blessing which we bless, is it not a participation in the blood of Christ? The bread which we break, is it not a participation in the body of Christ? Because there is one bread, we who are many are one body, for we all partake of the one bread."[22]

One becomes a member of this body through baptismal initiation; in the sacramental rite one participates in the death and resurrection of Jesus.[23] This double participation—in Jesus' death and in his risen life—continues in the existence of the disciples.[24] The body of Christ grows, through the spiritual growth of the believers. "We are to grow up in every way into him who is the head, into Christ. . . ."[25] While Christ is the head,[26] he is also the whole, head and body.[27]

Believers participate both in the one Spirit and in the one Body; the oneness is emphasized again and again, for the mystery is a mystery of unity—of unitive participation. "For just as the body is one and has many members, and all the members of the body, though many, are one body, so it is with Christ. For by one Spirit we were all baptized into one body—Jews or Greeks, slaves or free—and all were made to drink of one Spirit."[28]

The new participation in Christ is the one central and unifying theme of Paul, on which every other assertion depends. He recalls it again and again in writing of various concerns, through his habitual expressions "in Christ," "in him."[29] If, on the one hand, the new participation is a "vertical" union with God and with Christ ("I have been crucified with Christ; it is no longer I who live, but Christ who lives in me"),[30] on the other hand it is a "horizontal" unity of the believers in Christ, which transcends and relativizes all differences between them. "For in Christ Jesus you are all sons of God, through faith. For as many of you as were baptized into Christ have put on Christ. There is neither Jew nor Greek, there is neither slave nor free, there is neither male nor female; for you are all one in Christ Jesus."[31]

The plan of God is to bring all things together in Christ.[32] "A plan for the fullness of time, to unite all things in him, things in heaven and things on earth."[33] "For in him all the fullness of God was pleased to dwell, and through him to reconcile to himself all things, whether on earth or in heaven, making peace by the blood of his cross."[34] The process of recapitulation or ingathering of all things is a new *birth*, which the individual Christian, the church, and the universe undergo together by participation in the divine Energy, the Holy Spirit. "The creation itself will be set free from its bondage to decay and obtain the glorious liberty of the children of God. We know that the whole creation has been groaning in travail together until now; and not only the creation, but we ourselves, who have the first fruits of the Spirit, groan inwardly as we wait for adoption as sons, the redemption of our bodies."[35]

JOHN

The Prologue of John's Gospel, a great theological synthesis in poetic form, begins with the unitive participation of the *Logos*—the divine Word—in God: "In the beginning was the Word, and the Word was with God, and the Word was God."[36] The text proceeds through the event of the new participation of the Word in our human corporeality: "Incarnation": "And the Word

became flesh and dwelt among us. . . ."[37] In its final part the Prologue pro-
claims the believer's participation in God through the Word incarnate: "And
from his fullness have we all received, grace upon grace."[38]

The central theme of John's Gospel is the same as that of Paul—the new
unitive participation in Christ—but it is projected back into the narrative of
Jesus' life. I can mention here only a few of the more evident expressions of
this continual theme. In chapters 4 and 7 of John's Gospel, Jesus promises a
new divine participation through the gift of the Holy Spirit.[39] In the course
of John's narrative, Jesus identifies himself often with the words "I am. . . ."[40]
Sometimes a predicate is appended to the "I am," and the predicated term
denotes a particular mode in which Jesus mediates divine participation to
those who believe in him. "I am the light of the world"; "I am the way, the
truth and the life"; "I am the gate of the sheep"; "I am the true shepherd."
The most extensively developed of these images are the *light* and the *bread of
life*. At the end of his public ministry, Jesus speaks again of participation in
the divine light, recalling the Prologue and his words, "I am the light of the
world. . . . While you have the light, believe in the light, that you may
become sons of light."[41]

Sometimes Jesus uses the words "I am" absolutely, without a predicate;
then it is evident that he is identifying himself with the unutterable divine
Name, Jahweh (or "I AM"). Here the divine participation is expressed without mediation and without determination: Jesus participates fully in the
divine "Identity."[42] It is essential to be aware that, in the New Testament,
what is revealed in Jesus—since he is a human being as well as divine—is to
be understood as given also to those who believe in him. He defends himself
in a surprising way against those who accuse him of blasphemy for claiming
unity with God, in chapter 10 of John's Gospel.[43] When his listeners prepare
to stone him to death "because you, being a man, make yourself God," Jesus
replies, "Is it not written in your law, 'I said, you are gods'? If he called them
gods to whom the word of God came (and scripture cannot be broken), do
you say of him whom the Father consecrated and sent into the world, 'You
are blaspheming,' because I said, 'I am the Son of God'?"[44]

One other person identifies himself with these words, "I am," in John's
Gospel. It is the man born blind (ch. 9), whom Jesus healed by putting clay
in his eyes and sending him to wash in the pool of Siloam. When he has
received his sight, and some of those around him deny that he can be the
same man as the one who was blind, he responds, "I am" (*ego eimi*).[45] The reference to baptismal illumination is clear, and the stunning further implication is an immediate sharing in the divine identity by this new birth in
Christ. In dramatic contrast, two characters in the Johannine narrative
express their nonparticipation in the new divine identity, each in a thrice
repeated denial: John the precursor[46] and Peter the disciple,[47] as he repudiates
his relationship with Jesus.

In John's long supper narrative (ch. 13–17), Jesus speaks to his disciples of the new participation in his being, and thereby in the divine being, which they are about to receive, through a series of images.[48] "In that day you will know that I am in my Father, and you in me, and I in you";[49] "If a man loves me, he will keep my word, and my Father will love him, and we will come to him and make our home with him";[50] "I am the vine, you are the branches. . . . If you abide in me, and my words abide in you, ask whatever you will, and it shall be done for you."[51] After the supper, in his prayer to the Father, Jesus speaks explicitly of the new oneness into which they are about to be initiated. "That they may all be one; even as thou, Father, art in me, and I in thee, that they also may be in us, so that the world may believe that thou hast sent me. The glory which thou hast given me I have given to them, that they may be one even as we are one, I in them and thou in me, that they may become perfectly one . . ."[52]

Among the New Testament writings, none is more continually saturated with the experience of the new divine participation than the First Letter of John. The letter is introduced with a declaration of the new *koinonia*, communion with God and in God, which has been given in Jesus Christ.[53] "The life was made manifest, and we saw it, and testify to it, and proclaim to you the eternal life which was with the Father and was made manifest to us—that which we have seen and heard we proclaim also to you, so that you may have fellowship [*koinonia*] with us; and our fellowship [*koinonia*] is with the Father and with his Son Jesus Christ."[54] The new communion is inseparable from the new participation in the divine life itself. "And this is the testimony, that God gave us eternal life, and this life is in his Son. He who has the Son has life; he who has not the Son of God has not life."[55]

God is participated in as *light*; this light, however, must be embodied in a relational existence among one's fellow human beings.[56] God is participated in as love: this too is not merely a passive but an active participation.[57] The one who believes in Jesus Christ is *begotten* by God, is a *child* of God.[58] The believer *dwells in* ("abides in") God and God in the believer.[59] The *Holy Spirit*, experienced within the believer, verifies the divine participation.[60] The divine *anointing* is a participation that "abides" in the believer, communicating a plenitude of knowledge.[61] This word, "abide" or "dwell" or "remain" (Gk *menein*), is a powerful term for participation both in the Gospel and the First Letter of John.[62]

THE DOUBLE OPENING OF PARTICIPATION

The starting point of this participatory development from Israel to the Christian church was, as we have seen, a rigorously dualistic relationship with God in which, nevertheless, some kind of divine participation was subtly implied. Participation was limited both internally, in the exclusion of a sense of divine immanence, and externally, in the exclusion of all peoples other than the family of Israel. Jesus, through his death and resurrection, opened this circumscribed participation both inwardly and outwardly: that is, by initiating a participation in God that is both immediate (or nondual) and universal. This is obviously a dramatic change, and it confronted the Israel of Jesus' time, especially the religious leaders, as a revolutionary—indeed an unacceptable—proposal. Both the "vertical" or interior and the "horizontal" or exterior movements were shocking to Jewish orthodoxy. Jesus' claim to a unique intimacy with God—indeed, to a participation in the divine identity[63]—was judged blasphemous.[64] The opening of salvation to the Gentiles could be accepted by the first disciples themselves (who were all Jews) only after dramatic demonstrations of divine power.[65]

THE NEW LIFE AS PARTICIPATION

After the revolution of Jesus, the *goal* of life—in contrast to classical spiritual traditions—is not to be understood as the unitive experience or unitive state, a supreme and unmediated participation in the Absolute, as if through a progressive purification or unification by which we transcend the phenomenal world. Rather, this divine union is virtually and substantially given in baptismal initiation as a new divine-human identity. The journey of life has become a progressive realization of this new identity through an existential embodiment, in the following of Christ. Like the Master, one journeys from the gift of self *received* in baptismal initiation to the gift of self *given* in a eucharistic life and death. As one participates in the revolution of Jesus, its form comes to determine the shape of one's own life. This is the form of the cross.[66]

Central to the New Testament and to the revolution of Jesus is the element of *newness*; the fire of newness burns unceasingly within Christian life and activity. In the new participation there must be, finally, a transcending of "system," of any metaphysical paradigm, by this dynamic presence of divine newness.[67] As we shall see, this spirit of newness is active not only in the New Testament and early Christianity; it is somehow present and operative also in the modern secular West. It is a participation in the divine creativity—whether consciously or "anonymously."

The new existence following from the revolution of Jesus is based upon the new participation in God. From a dynamic perspective, this new participation can be seen as *fontality*, a single vital movement that comprehends the traditional "theological virtues" of faith, hope, and love as well as a fourth, world-oriented virtue: creative action. These four actualizations of the divine participation correspond to the "form" of the mystery of Christ—the quaternity of God, Word, Spirit, and Creation:

Hope
Faith + Love
Creative Action

Until now I have said little directly about Christian *spirituality*: that is, about spiritual practice and spiritual experience. As I mentioned in the introductory section, there is a good reason for this. One of the major debilitating trends in Western Christianity has been the separation of "spirituality" from ordinary human life and from theology; or, more broadly, the separation of these three from one another and from liturgical worship during the process of differentiation that has continued through the centuries. Christian spirituality, however, is simply the personal experience and appropriation of that mystery or event of Christ which has been the center of our study. We can, therefore, define spirituality as a personal participation in the (essentially participatory) Christ-mystery. Because of the comprehensiveness of the mystery, this implies a personal participation in the church, its tradition and its life, and in the history of salvation as it embraces all humanity. But first of all it is a participation *in Christ*—in the "body of Christ"—and through Christ, a participation *in God*, in the divine being and life. This latter participation is experienced in two fundamental modes, corresponding to the basic polarity of individual and community. On the personal level, participation in God constitutes the person: it is the ground of the new (yet "original') identity of the baptized person. On the communal level, this participation in God is experienced as the *koinonia* which is constitutive of community or church. In our modern West, as the sense of participation has diminished, both of these modes of unitive experience have nearly disappeared from Christian consciousness and theology.

THE ECLIPSE OF PARTICIPATORY CHRISTIANITY

Christianity is incarnation: the participatory mystery (or event) of Christ is a physical, bodily reality. We can glimpse something of this in the emphasis given by the New Testament writers to the bodily crucifixion and the bodily resurrection of Jesus.[68] "*Caro salutis est cardo*," writes Tertullian early in the third century CE: "The flesh is the hinge of salvation."[69] Participation in the mystery of Christ comes about through the bodily "mysteries" of baptism and eucharist

The mystery, comprehending the three worlds of matter, consciousness (or psyche), and spirit, reaches both above and below the operative level of our human reason. It is particularly difficult of access to the rationality of the modern West, with its flattened epistemology, and to methodologies of the study of religion that exclude the possibility of sacramental mystery. We are dependent, for a theological understanding of the mystery, upon the two objective and "conservative" elements of Christian tradition, which are the scriptural word of God and the liturgy. Scripture and liturgy retain the participatory integrity of the mystery, which is diminished or obscured by every attempt at rational objectification and analysis. While the application of

reason and objective conceptualization to the mystery is necessary and useful—and is found already within the New Testament[70]—it brings with it
invariably the danger of substituting a more accessible rational construction
for the mystery. The history of Christian theology has consisted largely of a
series of progressive rationalizations of the mystery, too often without awareness of this danger.

One can gain an appreciation of the essentially participatory nature of
the mystery of Christ through a study of the doctrinal struggles of the early
centuries, both the Trinitarian and the Christological controversies. The
response of the church's theologians to heterodox formulations of the relation between divinity and humanity in Christ rests upon a double participation: we participate in God because we participate in Christ; in Christ, God
and humanity have become one. The great "heresies" were rejected by the
church because they negated or endangered this human participation in the
divine being and life which was the gift of Christ. Moreover, the central
defense that the church fathers employed against these theological devia-
tions was based directly upon the experience and conviction of this participation. "If God did not become a human person in Christ, then we could not
become God."[71]

Not all of the serious threats to the participatory mystery were clearly
diagnosed and repelled, however. Elements from Greek philosophy and other
sources had been imported into Christian thought from its earliest times,
often with little critical evaluation. Alien philosophical structures that
seemed to make the mystery more understandable to the people of that time
and culture inevitably obscured the simplicity and unity of the mystery, its
essentially participatory character. During the patristic centuries (first
through sixth centuries, approximately) and through the early Middle Ages
to the twelfth century, these were primarily the structures of Platonism and
Neoplatonism. From the twelfth century on, Aristotelian thought began to
predominate, and a new "scholastic" theology—more rational and analytical—began to replace the (biblical and participatory) sapiential theology of
the patristic and medieval monastic traditions. Nominalism from the fourteenth century and Cartesian epistemology from the seventeenth century
onward manifested a swift decline of participatory thought in the West, further diminishing the unitive density of Christian theology.

Each successive division of the Christian Church brought a further hard-
ening of external structures and a further narrowing of perspective, which
made the fragmentation appear more and more irreversible. Religious identity was defined in external "denominational" terms; the simplicity and freedom, the openness and deep assurance of the original experience was lost and
forgotten. We become aware of a circular relationship between consciousness
and ecclesial communion. Division between Christian communities and
eclipse of participatory thought accompany and reinforce one another. Once

the primal unity has been lost, the mystery becomes divided and diminished, the unitive light veiled and inaccessible. Nothing arrests a continuing disintegration and partitioning, permeating every sector of thought and life until, by some grace of history, a sense of the integral mystery begins to dawn once again, and the unity is once again sought in its fullness. This, at least, has been the story of Western Christianity during the past thousand years.

In the centuries following the separation of the Western churches in the sixteenth century, the sense of participation diminished to unprecedented levels in the theology both of the Catholic and of the Protestant communities. This movement was concurrent with the more general intellectual development in the West during these recent centuries. As metaphysics gave way to positive science and as the old matrices of collective consciousness gave place to an individualistic consciousness, a general cultural and social fragmentation took place. The modern Western person is first and foremost an *individual*. In the democratic national state that issues from the Enlightenment (e.g. the United States), the individual is prior to the community, which exists (theoretically, at least) chiefly for the protection of individual rights and the promotion of individual well-being. Participation—political, economic, social, and even religious—is spontaneously conceived as a result of voluntary choice rather than as a preexisting reality; the collectivity is posterior rather than prior to the individual. Modern literature offers a massive testimony to the experience of this radical individualism and of the isolation that it entails.

In this climate, Protestant Christianity underwent an unending series of fissions, and Protestant theology tended to polarize into opposing camps: especially along the axis between "pure faith" and scientific rationality, with fundamentalist conservatism and reductionist historical criticism at the two extremes. The sense of participation is very limited along this axis; at both poles the possibility of unitive depth is negated by a compelling need for literal clarity—whether the massive integrist clarity of unquestioned literal belief or the disintegrative conceptual clarity of a scientific method that dismisses the mystery, which is completely beyond its grasp. Modern rationalist historical criticism gave rise to fundamentalist countermovements; in the long struggle between these two opposing literalisms, the level of theological debate moved farther and farther from the deep sapiential reality of participation.

The post-Reformation Catholic Church and its theology became immobilized in its fortified defensive posture; creative thought was sternly repressed and the New Testament Scriptures themselves came to be valued as a collection of proof-texts to support the preconceived propositions of a militant theology rather than as the embodiment of the living Christ-mystery. Catholic conservatism congealed into an institutional or traditionalist fundamentalism opposed to the biblical fundamentalism of the Protestant churches. Popes of the late nineteenth and early twentieth centuries flailed about with official documents, attempting to repel the tide of "modernist" thought that had begun to seep into the church and stridently denouncing the whole, irresistible forward movement of history and culture that swept around the church on every side.

Let us pause for a closer look at the nonparticipatory Christianity that had evolved in the West by the nineteenth century, specifically in Roman Catholicism. Against the individualism of the Protestant communities, the Roman Church maintained a tight sense of collective identity; this identity, however, was experienced in a context less of communion than of institutional structure and hierarchical authority. One was more likely to think of "the Church" as an invincible sacred structure, or as a clerical authority somewhere above oneself, than as a community in which one participated. One did not, any longer, think of oneself as the Church. Church had become institution and person had become individual. Each of the central elements of Christian faith, in this polarized modern climate of individualism and centralized institutional authority, had become separated from its simple unity with the mystery of Christ and torn from its vital matrix of communion, the primal *koinonia* that is the life of the church.

The New Testament theological term *mystery of Christ* could be defined as "all-comprehending Christ" or simply as "participatory Christ." By the nineteenth century, this participatory quality had been almost completely stripped from the Catholic image of Jesus Christ, and with this the unity of the mystery itself dissolved and Christian faith came to resemble an array of separate, obligatory articles of belief. The foundation stone of Catholic belief, Peter's confession at Caesarea Philippi, "You are the Christ, the Son of the Living God,"[72] continued to be proclaimed firmly by the church authority, but the mystery of Incarnation was limited to Jesus himself (and by extension to the institutional church); its extension to the people was no longer part of the teaching. The Incarnation had become almost nonparticipatory. The dogma of the Trinity had similarly become largely closed to participation; in place of the "economic Trinity" of the church fathers, in which humanity participated in the divine Word and in the Holy Spirit, the first principle of theology was now a divine Trinity closed in upon itself, studied in terms of its reciprocal internal relations.[73] The two basic mysteries of Christian faith had thus been objectified and elevated above the faithful, as if in a reversal of the Christ-event. Redemption, which had been understood by the Eastern Christian theologians of the early centuries participatively, as an incorporation into the "body of Christ,"[74] had since the time of early scholasticism in the twelfth century[75] been conceived primarily in an external, juridical manner, as the reparation—through the sacrifice of Christ, the God-become-man—for the infinite offense against the divine Majesty that was the "original sin" of Adam.

In the early church, baptism was understood theologically as the diviniza-tion of the Christian: that is, as the admission of the baptized person into an immediate participation in the divine being.[76] By the nineteenth century in the West, this central truth of Christianity had virtually been forgotten, and so the simplicity and unity of Christian life had become inaccessible to theol-ogy. Under a reasserted Augustinian doctrine of original sin and the conse-quent depravity of human nature, that human participation in God became inconceivable—while church government was wonderfully facilitated. The essentially participatory sacrament of the eucharist had become attenuated to such an extent that it was thought of only in terms of the sacrifice of Christ and of the communion of the individual with God and Christ. The lateral dimension of *koinonia* had been lost almost completely, and this was reflected perfectly in the style of worship. The priest celebrated the eucharist facing away from the people, in the sacred Latin language which was unintelligible to them; responses were fixed and unvarying, and all spontaneity on the part of the people excluded. The "species" of bread and wine had been reduced to a small wafer that has been jokingly referred to as "a symbol of a symbol." This modern Western reduction of the sacraments of baptism and eucharist makes clearly visible the nadir of participation at which Western Christianity had arrived by the beginning of the twentieth century. Consciousness of the imme-diate participation in God that constitutes the Christian's new birth and new identity, and consciousness of the communal participation in the divine life that is the essence of the church, had both diminished nearly to the vanish-ing point. Spirituality, among Catholics as well as Protestants, had become individualized, subjectivized, and separated from its sacramental ground in baptismal initiation and in the eucharistic body of Christ.

The extinction of a sense of participation in the Roman Catholic Church of the modern age was not only internal but external as well. By the end of the nineteenth century, the church had become isolated from partici-pation in the world around it and in the ever-accelerating European history of its time. Enclosed within a virtual fortress of institution and doctrine since the Reformation, the official church withdrew farther, under the pressure of an unfavorable political and cultural climate, into a sacred ghetto.[77] From this perspective, the contemporary movement of history in the West could be seen only in a negative light, and an Augustinian pessimism colored the offi-cial Catholic view of humanity, its struggles for liberty and its achievements. The church tended fearfully to ally itself with the *ancien régime* against the threatening participatory social movements of popular revolution, of democ-racy and socialism.

At this historical low point of sapiential understanding, both the "Jew-ish" and the "Greek" barriers to participation had been re-erected. "The Sacred'—and the institutional church as its embodiment—had been returned to its pre-Christian elevation above the people, and the mysteries of the faith had been objectified and rationally circumscribed so successfully that their participatory nature—and hence their unity and power—had become largely neutralized. Once again body and community had been largely eliminated from spirituality.

THE REAWAKENING OF
PARTICIPATORY CONSCIOUSNESS

In the midst of the catastrophic events of twentieth-century Europe, a major theological revolution was coming to birth. Among a number of Catholic scholars during the first half of the century, a theological sense of the mystery of Christ—and of the church as mystery of communion—began to reawaken, despite the determined resistance of institutional conservatism. As two world wars and revolutionary cultural changes exposed to radical questioning the foundations of Western civilization, the conventions of Western theology were also challenged and the sources of Christian tradition began to reappear in their luminous unity. A space was opening in which the mystery of Christ could be encountered once again and the essential unity of humanity could be freshly conceived.

Biblical, liturgical, and patristic scholarship converged to bear a common fruit in the documents of the Second Vatican Council (1962–1965) in which the mystery found expression once again with its simplicity and power, its centrality and all-embracing scope. The Council, it can be said, was a participatory revolution in which the Christian community or "People of God" began to become conscious once again of its identity. A theology of collegial government reemerged. The church herself was, after centuries, once again recognized as a mystery which could not be comprehended by a single theological expression, but which unfolded in a series of images: mystery of communion, sacrament of Christ and of God, People of God. . . .[78] The Catholic laity began to recognize themselves once again *as the church*, after for many centuries thinking of the church as an authoritative institution mediating the grace of God to them from above. This was at once an ecclesial experience of the liberation of the person which had been taking place in the revolutionary history of the modern West, and a fresh experience of the liberation experienced by the first Christian community in Jerusalem.

Two passages from principal documents of the Council will illustrate the recovery of a participatory theological sense of Christ and of the church, and of the place of the church in the world and its history.

> Since the Church, in Christ, is in the nature of sacrament—a sign and instrument, that is, of communion with God and of unity among all [human persons]—she here purposes, for the benefit of the faithful and of the whole world, to set forth . . . her own nature and universal mission.[79]

The joy, the hope, the grief and anguish of the [people] of our time, especially of those who are poor or afflicted in any way, are the joy and hope, the grief and anguish of the followers of Christ as well. Nothing that is genuinely human fails to find an echo in their hearts. For theirs is a community composed of [human persons], of [persons] who, united in Christ and guided by the Holy Spirit, press onwards towards the kingdom of the Father and are bearers of a message of salvation for all [human beings]. . . . That is why Christians cherish a feeling of deep solidarity with the human race and its history.[80]

A few audacious spirits within the Catholic intellectual world took the step—hardly imaginable for centuries—of looking at the progress of the modern West in a positive way, indeed as a further unfolding of the event of Christ. Preeminent among them for the breadth and revolutionary boldness of his vision stands Pierre Teilhard de Chardin, who saw Christ at the center of human history and of evolution itself, and developed a participatory vision along the lines sketched by St. Paul but reaching out to the dimensions of the new Western cosmology. At this point we begin to be able to imagine a new Christian theology—or "wisdom"—that, while remaining true to the centrality of the Christ-event, embraces the full magnitude and dynamism of the world and the person that we have come to know in our modern West.

The Future of Christian Wisdom

As I mentioned at the beginning, there is a Christian theology that corresponds to the participative vision of Christianity: it is the tradition of sapiential or wisdom theology. Our attempt to recover a participatory Christian vision is necessarily a journey into sapiential theology. Further, a new phase or mode of participation means implies a *new wisdom*. This is what we see emerging, in very different forms, in such writers as Teilhard de Chardin, Karl Rahner, Thomas Merton, and Bede Griffiths. What is *new* about this "wisdom" is (1) its universality, (2) its distinctly personal character—in contrast to the "pre-personal" nature of much of the classical Christian sapiential theology, (3) its dynamic, historical perspective and, in many instances, (4) a metaphysical depth and simplicity that have been achieved in an interaction with the Asian traditions. The new wisdom, is often characterized as well by (5) an appreciation of *secularity* that is distinctly Western and modern. At the center of its newness, however, is a sense of the *person*: on the one hand, a consciousness of the transcendent depth and autonomy, the freedom and creativity of the individual person in this world, and on the other hand an awareness of the essentially relational and participatory nature of the person, and of the ultimate unity of all humanity. This new sapiential consciousness and thought holds much promise for the study of religious and mystical phenomena, while it challenges the rationalist as well as the purely universalist paradigms of much contemporary academic thought in this area.

Space permits only the briefest confrontation of the participatory sapiential vision which I have proposed with a few of the principal perspectives among contemporary studies of religion and mysticism: (1) linguistic, contextual (or constructivist) treatment of mystical experience,[81] (2) classical Western perennialist views,[82] (3) proposals of "pure consciousness experiences" and "knowledge by identity,"[83] (4) radical pluralism,[84] and (5) the application of the methodologies of positive material science to spiritual experiences and states.[85]

A participatory Christian theology resists the isolation of personal spiritual experience from its context within the person and in the total mystery; experience is regarded as a manifestation of more fundamental entities: the transcendent (or unitive) identity of the person, participating in the objective mystery. Both the rationalist reductionism of a philosophical or linguistic analysis and the perennialist view that reduces a religious tradition to a "universal core" or common denominator are inadequate to the participatory mystery with its transcendent or nondual dimension and its concrete particularity. A dualistic and contracted modern philosophical epistemology (e.g., that of Kant) cannot be conceded the authority to define the limits of possible spiritual knowing. In this participatory view, both an experience of "pure consciousness" and "knowledge by identity" are interpreted as moments of participation in the divine ground of human consciousness. Here—and often—the "transcendental anthropology" of Rahner will be useful.[86] A contemporary sapiential Christian theology will admit a plurality of valid experiences of divinity and paths of spiritual growth, but will retain its principle of a single ultimate divine Principle. The methods of physical science (e.g., experimental procedures, attempts at clear verification or falsification), with their dependence upon the dualistic objectifying mind and sensory data, are inadequate to realities on the level of the inner self (or transcendent subject) which also have their own "particularity," resistant to abstract classification and gradation. It is a participatory, or sapiential consciousness—involving an affirmation of the mystery in faith—which is able to understand these experiences on their own level.

Some contemporary authors propose to integrate an "Eastern" perennialism directly with a Western scientific rationality without considering the historical ground that lies between these two points in our own cultural continuum.[87] In the course of the last millennium of our western history, our epistemological standard has descended from the unitive sapiential to the empirical rational mind. One of the boldest proposals of a new sapiential vision is that this descending history can itself be understood as a participation in the unfolding event of Christ—that is, as a process of incarnation. Between the morning light of contemplation and the evening light of scientific rationality, the great solar arc measures a progressive penetration of divinity into humanity, a transition from passive to active participation. But today we must have the morning light as well!

THE REVOLUTION IN GLOBAL CONTEXT:
TOWARD A THEOLOGICAL INTERPRETATION OF HISTORY

PARTICIPATORY EVENT

In contrast to the teachings of Hindu Vedanta, of Buddhism (though in its "negative" or apophatic language), or of Taoism, as well as the timeless "perennial philosophy," the New Testament discloses not a unitive (participatory) Reality, but a unitive (participatory) *Event*. Presupposing as background a world of imperfect participation, the Christ-event is equivalent to Incarnation: that is, to the union of God and creation in the divine-human person of Christ. This is the basic "new participation" from which every other form of new participation derives.

PERSON

Participation, however, as we have seen, is not the whole story. A second constellation of ideas is required to express the relationship of Christianity to the modern world, particularly the world of the modern West: freedom, agency, and creativity, understood as active and "secular" participations in the event of Christ. These three terms—participation, autonomy, agency (or creativity)—condense within themselves the history of the West in its Christian and secular phases. More simply, we can imagine history working itself out in the interaction of two great principles: participation and autonomy (or creative freedom). The West emerges from a prepersonal phase of participation into a phase of relative personal and collective autonomy and then begins its return—or descent—into participation once again, conforming to the natural, "solar" trajectory of human life. Life unfolds in the dynamic interaction of autonomy (or "identity') and participation. The study of religion in our time must transcend the conventional Western parameters—individualist and subjectivist—if it is to keep pace with the participatory wave-front of history.

The event of Christ can be understood as the revelation and re-creation of the person, both individual and collective. This "new person" exists by immediate participation in the divine Person, and participates also in the incarnational dynamic of the Christ event. The person therefore exists in a participation with all reality which may be called eucharistic. In the one event there is a double movement toward full participatory personhood: from passive to active participation and from "tribal" to universal participation. The double movement can be seen in the teaching of Jesus, then in the revolution that is initiated by his resurrection and the gift of the Holy Spirit; it is evident also in the progressive movement of Western history, and in the development of an individual person. The one event is the awakening of the true Person—in its active freedom, fullness, and universality. A good illustration of the double awakening will be found in Jesus' parable of the Samaritan in the tenth chapter of Luke's Gospel.[88] To the question of the scribe, "Who is my neighbor?" Jesus responds with his story of the alien who steps across the boundaries of religious difference and of hereditary hatred to care for a Jew who has been robbed and beaten. Jesus' response concludes with the words, "Then go and do likewise." It is implicit here both that everyone is already our neighbor and that this common humanity must nevertheless be actualized by an act of personal "fontality." With the divine self-communication that takes place in Christ, a divine authority is breathed into the human person by which we are to override the holiest and most ingrained of differences, affirm the common divine core of the human person and realize one humanity. This is the unfolding of the event of Incarnation in the world.

PARTICULARITY: THE ENDURING CORE

The abstract terms *participation* and *person*, however, do not exhaust the meaning of the Christ event. Judeo-Christian faith is inseparable from a *concrete historical particularity* which is repugnant to more "universalist" philosophies and theories of religion. This concrete core is constituted by a specific divine revelation, by an individual and collective relationship with the personal God of the Bible, and by the biblical "sacred history." For the Christian there is, in addition, the concrete particularity of the event of Incarnation and of the person of Jesus, which is extended in the concreteness and particularity of sacramental participation in baptism and eucharist and in the primordial "sacrament" which is the church itself.[89] These concrete particulars, in their tight coherence, remain as a permanent, intensely participatory "body"—within and around which the developmental energies of freedom and creative fontality expand toward a human totality.

Today, Christians who have avoided the extremes of fundamentalism and rootless relativism thus find themselves mediating in an ambiguous territory between the two poles of particularity and universality. No single law or theological formula resolves the tension—spiritual, intellectual, existential— between the two principles, as their interaction continues to work itself out at the heart of life and history.

THE ROLE OF THE WEST

In the realization of the person, I believe, lies much of the meaning of the singular development of Western civilization. The West occupies a unique position in the "history of salvation," as a people and a culture that has come into being around the unitive core of the Christ-mystery, in a pivotal intermediate position between the historical event of Christ and the realization of a global humanity.[90] The historical realization of the person corresponds to the event of the Incarnation, as manifest within a concrete history.

I believe, then, that there is a constitutive relation between these two unique phenomena in the history of humanity: (1) the event of Christ, and (2) the prominence of the West in world history during the past five hundred years. Let us, for a moment, set aside the conventional division of history into ancient, medieval, and modern, and think of the two millennia of Western history since the time of Christ as a single period, divided into two great phases. Proceeding with this same grand generality, let us provisionally call the first thousand years the age of unity, and the second thousand years the age of autonomy. During the first phase—in which Christianity becomes almost the exclusive religion of the West and the church gradually becomes the central unifying factor in European society—collective consciousness predominates. During the second thousand years, this collective consciousness of Christendom gives way before the emergence of the individual and then before the successive partitions that fragment the Western world, and the emergence of a secular and individualistic modern Western culture.

THE CONCLUSIVE IMAGE: BIRTH OF THE
DIVINE-HUMAN PERSON IN THIS WORLD.

The whole of this two thousand year historical movement can be understood as a progressive unfolding of the event of Christ, understood as "divine birth in this world." In the first phase, *unity* predominates and everything continues to be seen in the "theological" light of faith in God, Christ, and the Church. In the second great phase *differentiation and autonomy* become dominant, and divine potentialities are realized within the human person. As this phase progresses into modernity, one may speak of a *secular incarnation* of the divine gift, a cascading of the grace of new divine birth downward onto the levels of cultural, scientific, technological, and social creativity.[91] In the phase of unity the human person can be imagined as looking back (and eastward) toward the transcendent and undetermined Source, while in the phase of autonomy the person looks forward (and westward) toward its own individuation and realization in this world, and toward a humanization of the material world itself.

At the heart of Christianity is this divine birth, in its successive stages: the birth of the divine Son from the Father, the eternal God, then the birth of Jesus Christ as a human person in this world, then the new birth of the baptized believer in Christ and in God. It is this divine participation which is the source of everything that follows in the "history of salvation" and which—crossing the outer boundary of explicit faith—is the source as well of the self-realization of "Western man." In the course of history, the gift has become separated from its source, the divine participation has been forgotten or denied, and at the same time the Western church and the Western world have passed together into what seems an age of nonparticipation, a Plotinian "land of unlikeness."[92] This disconcerting history, however, is a further unfolding of the one audacious event of divine birth in this world.

GLOBAL BIRTH

As I have suggested, beneath an eclipse of the experience and of the conscious sense of participation there is often proceeding a transition to a new and fuller mode of participation. This, I believe, is true of the desert of nonparticipation through which the Western world has been passing during recent centuries. Beneath the apparent fragmentation there is proceeding an ultimately irreversible movement of the *unification of humanity*. A reversal is taking place, from the prevalent centrifugal dynamic through which we have arrived at our present dominant nonparticipatory consciousness, to a convergent movement toward a global society and a global consciousness.[93] Evidence of this appears in the increasingly numerous efforts at international cooperation and organization of all kinds. A deeper convergence appears in the widening acceptance—gradually approaching a universal consensus—of the dignity and basic rights of the human person, of the imperative of social justice, of the values of human freedom and of political self-determination and democracy. These "Western" or "Enlightenment" ideas originate in the *revelation of the person* which I have identified with the Christ-event.

We are aware today—despite the conflicts that continue to rend humanity—that the world is very quickly becoming *one* world. Humanity begins to be conscious of itself, to reflect and to evaluate as a single—though not yet integral—organism. This has come about through the expansive secular creativity of the West—through the multiplex common "language" which includes commerce, science, technology, and global politics. The unification of humanity is an unfolding of the "secular incarnation" of which I spoke above. From the single event of Christ, and through its unfolding in the secular climate of the modern West, the leading edge of humanity is rapidly moving toward an awareness of the whole person and toward a global consciousness—an awareness both of the one humanity and of the one world, comprehending material nature. That is to say that our consciousness of *participation* is expanding to the full dimensions of the person and of the planet. Although this could not have taken place within the world of Christendom nor within the sphere governed by church authority, I believe that it is a further realization of the event of Incarnation, the event of Christ.[94] The word *freedom* is central to Christian theology,[95] but it is not a "church" word. The new freedom, the agency, the creativity that have emerged into the world through the modern West are participations in the divine energies infused into human nature through the event of Christ, which have had to burst free of the container—the old wineskin—of cultural convention and institutional authority in order to realize themselves. In the one divine Spirit, humanity is coming to birth. Our understanding of religion—and of spiritual experience—must expand to this magnitude, to these dimensions.

NOTES

1. In the course of this chapter I shall occasionally refer to contemporary studies of religion and mysticism, and a brief overview of the relation between this participatory perspective and some of the prevalent theoretical positions in Religious Studies will be found at the end of the fourth section of this chapter, "The Reawakening of Participatory Consciousness."

2. The participatory consciousness of primitive peoples has been studied extensively by Lucien Lévy-Bruhl: among his works available in English translation are *Primitive Mentality* (New York: George Allen and Unwin, 1923) and *Primitives and the Supernatural* (New York: George Allen and Unwin, 1935). See Mircea Eliade et al., eds., *The Encyclopedia of Religion* (New York: Simon and Schuster Macmillan 1995), Vol. 8, 533–34.

3. See Karl Jaspers, *The Origin and Goal of History* (New Haven: Yale University Press, 1953).

4. Ibid., Pt. I, ch.1, "The Axial Period," 1–6.

5. Ibid., 2.

6. Ibid., 2.

7. Ibid., 2.

8. Ibid., 3–4.

9. Ewert Cousins, *Christ of the 21st Century* (Rockport, MA: Element Books, 1992), 6.

10. Genesis 2:7.

11. John 20:21–23. *The Revised Standard Version* translation will be used for biblical texts unless otherwise noted: *The Holy Bible, Containing the Old and New Testaments, Revised Standard Version* (Camden, NJ: Thomas Nelson and Sons, 1957).

12. Cf. Gerhard von Rad, *Old Testament Theology* (London: Oliver and Boyd, 1962), Vol. 1, 344–45.

13. Owen Barfield, *Saving the Appearances: A Study in Idolatry* (New York: Harcourt Brace Jovanovich, 1983), 107–15.

14. Exodus 3:14.

15. *Saving the Appearances*, 113–15.

16. Ezekiel 36:26–27; cf. Jeremiah 31:31–34.

17. Acts of the Apostles 9:4–5.

18. Colossians 1:26–27.

19. Ephesians 2:12–16; cf. Eph 2:11–19.

20. Romans 12:5; cf. Rom 12:3–8.

21. Col 2:9; cf. Col 2:9–11,17.

22. Corinthians 10:16–17.

23. Rom 6:3–5.

24. Cf. 2 Corinthians 4:7–12, Philippians 3:7–11.

25. Eph 4:15.

26. Cf. Eph 5:23.

27. Cf. Eph 4:10–16.

28. 1 Cor 12:12–13; cf. Eph 4:1–6.

29. Cf. Eph 1:3–14.

30. Galatians 2:20.

31. Gal 3:26–28.

32. Cf. Eph 2:13–18.

33. Eph 1:10.

34. Col 1:19–20.

35. Rom 8:21–22.

36. Jn 1:1.

37. Jn1:14.

38. Jn 1:16.

39. Jn 4:14; 7:37–39.

40. A useful summary of the "I am" sayings attributed to Jesus in the Gospels will be found in Raymond E. Brown's *The Gospel According to John* (Garden City: Doubleday, Anchor Bible, vol. 29, 1966), Appendix IV to volume I, 533–38.

41. Jn 8:12; 12:36.

42. See Brown, *The Gospel According to John*, I, 533–37.

43. Cf. Jn 10:31–36.

44. Jn 10:34–36.

45. Jn 9:9.

46. Jn 1:19–21.

47. Jn 18: 17–27.

48. Jn14:20–23;15:1–11

49. Jn 14:20.

50. Jn 14:23.

51. Jn 15:5,7.

52. Jn 17:21–23; cf. 17:11.

53. 1 John 1:1–3.

54. 1 Jn 1:2–3.

55. 1 Jn 5:11–12.

56. 1 Jn 1:5–7.

57. 1 Jn 4:7–16.

58. Cf. 1 Jn 3:1–3; 3:9; 5:1, 4–5.

59. Cf. 1 Jn 2:24; 3:24; 4:12, 15.

60. 1 Jn 3:24; cf. 4:13.

61. Cf. 1 Jn 3:24; 4:12, 15–16.

62. Cf. Jn 6:56; 15:4–7, 9–10; 1 Jn 2:27–28; 3:24; 4:12,15–16.

63. This claim is implicit in Jesus' *I am* sayings.

64. Cf. especially Jn 8:57–59 and 10: 31–36.

65. Cf. Acts 10:1–48; 15:1–21.

66. Cf. Mark 8:34–39; 1 Cor 1:18, 23; 2 Cor 4:8–12; Phil 3:10–11.

67. "God's specific quality in us is the power to break away from the established order of mind and body and create a new future" (Eugen Rosenstock-Huessy).

68. Cf. 1 Cor 1:17–18; 2:2.

69. Tertullian, *De Resurrectione Carnis*, 8.

70. Cf., for example, Paul's Letter to the Romans, chapters 5 through 7.

71. Cf. Irenaeus, *Against the Heresies*, Book V, preface;; Athanasius, *The Incarnation of the Word*, ch. 54; Augustine, Sermo 13 de Tempore, *Patrologia Latina* 39, 1097, *The Liturgy of the Hours* (New York: Catholic, 1975), vol. I, 541.

72. Matthew 16:16.

73. Cf. Catherine Mowry Lacugna, *God For Us: The Trinity and Christian Life* (San Francisco: Harper, 1991).

74. Cf. Eph 2:14–16.

75. While usually attributed to Anselm of Canterbury (1033–1105), this juridical theology of the Redemption was already proposed by Tertullian in the early third century.

76. Cf . 2 Pt 1:3–4.

77. Pope Pius IX, when the former papal states and then Rome were incorporated into the new Italian Kingdom (ca 1860–1870), actually made himself a permanent "prisoner in the Vatican."

78. Cf. Avery Dulles, *Models of the Church* (Garden City: Doubleday, 1974).

79. "Dogmatic Constitution on the Church," n.1, in *Vatican Council II: The Conciliar and Postconciliar Documents*, ed. Austin Flannery (Northport, NY: Costello, 1975), 350. Brackets [ ] indicate modification for inclusive language.

80. "Pastoral Constitution on the Church in the Modern World," n. 1, ibid., 903–904. Brackets [ ] indicate modification for inclusive language.

81. Cf. Steven T. Katz, "Language, Epistemology, and Mysticism," in *Mysticism and Philosophical Analysis*, ed. Katz (Oxford: Oxford University Press, 1978), 22–74; Katz, "Mystical Speech and Mystical Meaning," in *Mysticism and Language*, ed. Katz (Oxford: Oxford University Press, 1992), 3–41.

82. Cf. Aldous Huxley, *The Perennial Philosophy* (New York: Harper and Row, 1945); Rudolf Otto, *Mysticism East and West*, trans. B. Bracey and R. C. Payne (New York: Macmillan, 1932); Evelyn Underhill, *Mysticism* (New York: E. P. Dutton, 1911, reprint New York: Meridian, 1955); Frithjof Schuon, *The Transcendent Unity of Religions*, trans. P. Townsend (New York: Harper, 1975); Huston Smith, *Forgotten Truth: The Primordial Tradition* (New York: Harper and Row, 1976).

83. Cf. Robert K. C. Forman, *Mysticism, Mind, Consciousness* (Albany: State University of New York Press, 1999), ch. 2, 11–30; ch. 7, 109–27.

84. Cf. Katz, "Language, Epistemology, and Mysticism"; Raimundo Panikkar, "Religious Pluralism: The Metaphysical Challenge," in *Religious Pluralism*, ed. L. S. Rouner (Notre Dame: University of Notre Dame Press, 1984), 97–115; Jorge N. Ferrer, *Revisioning Transpersonal Theory: A Participatory Vision of Human Spirituality* (Albany: State University of New York Press, 2002).

85. Cf. C. T. Tart, "Science, States of Consciousness, and Spiritual Experiences: the Need for State-Specific Sciences," in *Transpersonal Psychologies*, ed. Tart (New York: Harper and Row, 1977), 9–58; Ken Wilber, *The Marriage of Sense and Soul: Integrating Science and Religion* (New York: Random House, 1998); Ferrer, *Revisioning Transpersonal Theory*, 42, 51–60 (on Wilber's *Marriage of Sense and Soul*).

86. Cf. Karl Rahner, "Man (Anthropology)," Section III: Theological, in *Sacramentum Mundi* vol. 3 (New York: Herder and Herder, 1969), 365–70, and *Foundations of Christian Faith* (New York: Seabury, 1978), 24–39.

87. Cf. Fritjof Capra, *The Tao of Physics:An Exploration of the Parallels Between Modern Physics and Eastern Mysticism* (Berkeley: Shambhala, 1975); Bede Griffiths, *A New Vision of Reality: Western Science, Eastern Mysticism, and Christian Faith* (Springfield, IL: Templegate, 1989); Wilber, *The Marriage of Sense and Soul*.

88. Luke 10:29–37.

89. This conception of Christ and of the church as the primary sacraments has been revived in the documents of the Second Vatican Council: cf. the text from the Vatican II Constitution on the Church quoted above.

90. Cf. Rahner, "Christianity and the 'New Man,'" *Theological Investigations*, Vol. 5 (London: Darton, Longman, and Todd, 1966), 152–53.

91. This progression corresponds approximately to the movement from the "Ideational" to the "Sensate" culture of Pitirim Sorokin. See his *Social and Cultural Dynamics* (Boston: Porter Sargent, 1957), 20–39.

92. *The regio dissimilitudinis* of Augustine and the medieval spiritual writers; cf. Plotinus, *Enneads*, I.8.13.

93. Teilhard de Chardin identified this historical reversal, and named the convergent movement "socialization" and "planetization." See his *The Future of Man* (New York: Harper and Row, 1964), passim. As we have seen, Cousins identifies this reversal of direction with the dawning of a "second Axial time." See his *Christ of the 21st Century*, 7–10.

94. Cf. Charles Taylor, *A Catholic Modernity?* (Oxford: Oxford University Press, 1999).

95. Cf. Paul's Letter to the Galatians, chapters 4 and 5.

NINE

Participation Comes of Age

Owen Barfield and the Bhagavad Gita

Robert McDermott

There may be times when what is most needed is not so much a new discovery or a new idea as a different "slant"; I mean a comparatively slight readjustment in our way of looking at the things and ideas on which attention is already fixed.

—Owen Barfield, *Saving the Appearances*

THIS CHAPTER makes use of Owen Barfield's understanding of the history of participatory consciousness in order to illumine the way that three early-twentieth-century spiritual teachers variously engaged the Bhagavad Gita. Mohandas K. Gandhi, Sri Aurobindo, and Rudolf Steiner all considered the Gita a supremely important text but none of these three teachers read the Gita as, for example, one of Arjuna's contemporaries might have. Instead, standing at the far end of what Barfield describes as participatory evolution, these teachers had to approach the Gita as a self-implicating text that unveils itself diversely to various participatory sensibilities. Building on Barfield's work, this chapter looks at the diachronic participatory distance between these three thinkers and the Gita's historical setting, as well as attending to the important synchronic differences in the ways that Gandhi, Sri Aurobindo, and Steiner each participatively engage the Gita.

The first half of this chapter summarizes the account of the gradual loss of participation and its possible recovery as described by Owen Barfield (1899–1998), the literary figure, lay philosopher, Coleridge scholar, and anthroposophist. Barfield's major work, *Saving the Appearances: A Study in Idolatry*, argues for the reality and significance of the evolution of consciousness, and particularly for a diachronic shift from original (primal, indigenous) participation to the gradual loss of participation (culminating in certain forms of Enlightenment and post-Enlightenment ways of relating to the world) and, very significantly during the past several centuries of Western thought and culture, to the contemporary possibility of "final" participation (the contours of which can be discerned, albeit imperfectly, in Romanticism and its related movements). The second half of this chapter discusses the ways that three twentieth-century interpreters of the Gita—Gandhi, Sri Aurobindo, and Steiner—struggle with, explain, and engage the revelation that Arjuna received from Krishna. I first consider them one by one and then conclude the chapter with some comparative reflections in light of Barfield's participatory theory of the evolution of consciousness.

OWEN BARFIELD'S THEORY OF PARTICIPATION

Barfield's argument in *Saving the Appearances* builds upon his previous works of sustained scholarship and original thinking. His first book, *History in English Words*, is a masterful analysis of the way that words at one time held a fullness of meaning, both literal and metaphorical, that was gradually lost. This process, which Barfield traces philologically, involved the differentiation of exterior and interior meanings, which were subsequently identified as subjective and objective or literal and metaphorical meanings. This account essentially consists in showing how the world lost its interiors, how concepts lost their multivalence, and the way that the original poetic depth of words collapsed into a merely referential semiosis.

Barfield offers the example of the way we use the word *heart*: originally, the "heart" included both the physical organ and what we now consider its metaphorical associations. In contemporary usage, it is necessary, but difficult, to bridge the literal and metaphorical of a concept such as "heart." At present, we say that the "real" meaning is the organ, the pump in the chest; the metaphorical meaning has become separated from the organ and from the concept that meant both organ and affect. It is as though these have become two separate words such that it takes metaphoric and other forms of imaginative thinking to put these meanings together again. To reunite the physical and metaphoric meanings of heart takes an act of intentionally creative thinking, an imaginative (but not fanciful) act that Barfield calls final participation and which he finds anticipatively present in the Romantic poets (especially Johann Wolfgang von Goethe, William Wordsworth, and Samuel Taylor Coleridge). In *Poetic Diction* (1928), Barfield offers what amounts to a philosophy of poetry, arguing that the essential element in poetic experience is the inducing of a "felt change of consciousness."[1] This felt change is characterized by a distinct wakefulness that serves as a preparation for the kind of extraordinary perception that is final participation, Barfield thus connects our interpretive, poetic, and imaginative capacities to a larger narrative of our participation in the world's own becoming. What Barfield offers throughout his works is an evolutionary vision of transforming participatory sensibilities, an account of the way that the human cocreation of the world has changed over time. Neither subjective nor objective, this change involves both the way that we comport ourselves to the world and also the way the world offers itself to us.

In order to understand Barfield's vision more fully, it will be helpful to consider his account of participation. *Saving the Appearances* focuses primarily on the contemporary loss of participation and the ways this affects modern humanity but it necessarily begins with an account of primal or original participation, the kind of immediate consciousness that humanity has been steadily losing, and in the modern West precipitously, through the entire sweep of history. Influenced by Steiner's philosophy of history (which resembles in important respects the philosophy of history of Georg W. F. Hegel and Friedrich W. J. Schelling), Barfield essentially sees history as a loss of participation and the longing to overcome this loss.[2] It is truer still to say, with Barfield, that this gradual loss of participation is half of history, the devolutionary half; the other half, evolution, is the gradual overcoming, by a series of breakthroughs and contributions, of this loss. Sri Aurobindo, also influenced by Hegel, offers a similar metanarrative: the divine empties itself into time and space, and evolves through diverse civilizations and modes of consciousness. This process leads humanity farther from the divine but, simultaneously, through a series of avatars (divine intercessory beings), overcomes this distance by initiating a new intimacy between humanity and divinity.

In several of his works, Barfield traces the evolution of consciousness, and the loss of original participation. By paying attention to the history of Western languages and supplementing this with the accounts of early-twentieth-century anthropologists, Barfield offers a picture of original (i.e., "early," "primal," or "indigenous") participation. However, as Barfield uses very few examples from outside the Western tradition, it would seem an important test to apply his account of the evolution of consciousness to the axial age of India, specifically the emergence of the Bhagavad Gita from the great Indian epic, the *Mahabharata*, in approximately the sixth century. As India has preserved more thoroughly than the West certain original forms of participation, looking at the Gita offers us special insight into the participatory transformations in which Barfield is interested. The West, of course, has its own original consciousness with which it is partly continuous, but as a rule the West has violently suppressed and replaced each of its successive cultural expressions. The West's commitment to change has been more revolutionary than evolutionary, thus burying much of its memory of original participation, forcing it to look for original consciousness in cultures far removed from its own.

The *Mahabharata*, which includes the events covered in the eighteen chapters of the Bhagavad Gita—particularly the warrior Arjuna in dialogue with Krishna, his charioteer (and not yet revealed as a god) on the firing line of a civil war—can be seen as a mix of primal and historical consciousness, or as a transition from myth to history, rather like the transition from Homer to Sophocles, and progressively to Virgil, Dante, and Joyce. This transition is one from a direct, or easily accessed, relationship to the divine or spirit world, to a consciousness in which both divinity and spirit seem removed and gradually replaced by the reality of the self and the earthly world. This process is characterized by the gradual loss of mythic consciousness and the gradual development of increasingly specific personalities. Even within classical Greek culture, Achilles, Odysseus, Agamemnon, Socrates, Plato, Aristotle, and Alexander can be seen to advance a rather direct line from mythic to historical consciousness, from an immediate relation to the gods and the spiritual world to a dimmer relationship to a spirit world and a more confident relationship to their individual identity and their own thinking.

In original participation, a significant relationship to gods and spirits (e.g., in the afterlife) was neither problematic nor questioned; rather, it was automatic and easily shared. The gods were "here" and "there" in the mind's eye, in the psyche of individuals and communities. A familiar phrase for original participation, "In the beginning," signaled a no-time, or no specific time, an *arche* (an atemporal foundation or original principle), a "time" when the gods were luminously present to humanity. Barfield's point is simply that in the course of several millennia, the accessibility of the gods and spirit beings became less obvious, then not at all obvious, before becoming doubtful, and finally unbelievable. Increasingly in the modern West, God and the world of spirit became realms of the far away, and then the unreachable, before such realms seemed to die entirely. In the West, during the nineteenth and twentieth centuries, a consensus emerged regarding the nonexistence (both past and present) of God, gods, and spirits alike. What had been believed to be the case with respect God and spirits was not so, and never had been so; what had been believed was shown to be an illusion, a projection by humanity in its immaturity (i.e., in its naively conceived original participation).

Devolution of consciousness, characterized by a loss of access to the spirit, is the complement to the evolution of consciousness, ideally characterized by the development of human individuality, love, and freedom. In the modern (and postmodern) West, devolution of consciousness seems almost complete: the gods do seem to be have withdrawn, and truly to have died. Following Lucien Lévy-Bruhl and Emile Durkheim in this regard, Barfield argues that primal consciousness was characterized by a unity of external and internal worlds, by a not-yet separated relationship of inner and outer, psychic and physical, spiritual and material. The separation that would come, a separation that Barfield considered to be at least appropriate and perhaps inevitable, was the terrible loss of gods and spirit beings, and simultaneously a positive gain in independence, objectivity, distance, and individuality. This gain made the modern mind capable of amazing discoveries and creations—and catastrophes.

Advocates of the perennialist, or traditionalist, perspective, such as Frithjof Schuon, René Guénon, Huston Smith, Jacob Needleman, and Seyyed Hossein Nasr resist an evolutionary worldview because they do not see history as progressive.[3] Barfield agrees with these authors that the evolution of consciousness is an evolution of loss, and is therefore a devolution. However, in addition to this agreement, there is also a profound disagreement. According to Barfield, in contrast to the position of the traditionalists, this devolution is simultaneously a progression toward the possibility, and to some extent the realization, of individuality, freedom, and love. Using a developmental simile, we might say that to the extent that the young person withdraws from parental control or influence, he or she will be able to return love freely—and if not free, such love would be less than full. Similarly, it is only when a civilization attains a certain distance from its own commitments that it can reflect on them, and affirm or revise them. Without distance, individuals and cultures can change but cannot make conscious revision. It is crucial to understand that so long as the gods guided humanity, humanity was unable to take the place of the gods in creating new cultural forms. It was by separating from nature, the earth and the cosmos, and gods—and more poignantly, from the goddesses—that the self gained an objective, and then a rational, perspective on all three.

It is by a distance from itself that the self developed the ability to look psychologically at itself. Such distance gives individuals and entire civilizations an opportunity to create new figurations, new paradigms, new ways of seeing and thinking the same sources of a perceived and conceptualized object as were seen in the past but interpreted differently. It is important to grasp that an object, perhaps the Parthenon or Mount Kailash, are really different places as experienced in the past, or in the present. An object perceived in the past contained a fullness of both material and spiritual meanings; this (seemingly) same object as perceived and simultaneously conceptualized by a contemporary Western person no longer presents itself with the same wholeness. Rather, the object appears to us as a divided entity, separated from its concept and able to be rejoined only by an act of imagination.

In *Saving the Appearances*, Barfield tracks the gradual changes of the collective representations that have shaped, by both enabling and limiting, what individuals and groups actually see—not only by the physical act of the eye but by what the mind supplies in the way of meaning, without which whatever would be seen physically would be unintelligible. This is the point of

Barfield's insistence that we do not see, or taste, coffee. "Coffee" is a concept that we provide for the percept,[4] or set of percepts, that "coffee" identifies. In his *History in English Words* Barfield showed that the evolution of consciousness can be observed by many additional concepts that English language speakers have found to express their perceptions. Each new concept, new verb, new split of a word into two or more words, adds to the evolving habit of differentiation and fragmentation that has become characteristic of modern Western consciousness.

Furthermore, these new words advance the separation of inner and outer, mind and world, which were once a unity, the form of consciousness that made possible original participation. Original participation for a modern Western individual is correctly regarded as very difficult and perhaps impossible. More dramatically, nonparticipation might be so characteristic of modern Western consciousness that philosophers and social scientists seem increasingly to regard original participation, or any degree of participation, as not ever having been experienced, or as a false experience. Others think that unitive experience was the case, and occasionally still is, and is called mysticism, i.e., the unity of the self with some larger reality, whether nature, spirit, or divinity.

In *Saving the Appearances*, Barfield gives a splendid example of the separation of concept from its percept characteristic of the loss of participation:

> Anyone who has struggled for a few pages with the Vedas in translation will know that in their language and entanglement of subject and object, of psychology and natural history, of divine and human, of word and thing, is such as to render the thought virtually unintelligible to a modern reader. . . . To take one instance, the word *Namarupa*, or "name-form," takes us back straight away to a stage of consciousness at which that surgical operation . . . whereby the thing is separated from its name, had not yet begun to be performed. In the measure that a man participates his phenomena, in that measure the name is the form, and form is the name.[5]

In *Cratylus*, Plato laments the loss of the natural meaning of words, i.e., the loss of identity of word and thing.[6]

Similarly, dharma, a word that Barfield does not discuss, is an example of a concept that held many meanings at the time of the Upanishads and Bhagavad Gita. One of the foundation terms in the Gita, dharma has no single equivalent in English because it means obligation, place in the world, teaching, and religious practices; in effect, it includes religion, ethics, and social values. Indian thinkers without a knowledge of Sanskrit as well as a modern Western person attempting to understand the Gita must hold in unison the many wide-ranging meanings of this concept. Maya has an equally wide range of meanings: it refers to the gap between the phenomenal world and Brahman but also any entity or event that appears (mistakenly and, in fact, impossibly) to exist or have a meaning unto itself. Barfield's description of primal consciousness functions as a contrasting background to the modern Western consciousness of the past three centuries. As participation was dealt a most deadly blow by the scientific revolution that began in the sixteenth century, Barfield argues that it is the task of humanity at the present time to break through, or transform, scientific thinking by full, final, will- and love-filled thinking. For Barfield, this is the great defining task of contemporary Western culture: to think "scientifically" in a way that reunites mind and world. This reunification is made possible by a thinking that is characterized by affection. Following Goethe, Barfield advocates a "delicate empiricism,"[7] and following Steiner, he advocates a way of thinking and knowing that unites the inner of the self with the inner of the world.[8] The gist of *Saving the Appearances* is to make it clear and consequential that modern Western individuals can attain, and should daily strive for, a consciousness that has a unity similar to original consciousness but made possible by an act of will, infused with affection, and highly individualized.

This entire evolutionary narrative is bound up with a series of controversial and important ontological and epistemological insights. Whereas the dominant narratives of today assume, in Barfield's words, that "whatever the truth may be about the psychological nexus between man and nature, it is an unchanging one and is the same now as it was when men first appeared on earth,"[9] Barfield holds to the contrary that the nexus between humanity and nature has changed decisively with each millennium, and in recent centuries, very nearly with each generation. As he writes:

> This book is being written . . . because it seems to [the author] that certain wide consequences flowing from the hastily expanded sciences of the nineteenth and twentieth centuries, and in particular their physics, have not been sufficiently considered in building up the general twentieth-century picture of the nature of the universe and of the history of the earth and man.[10]

It is possible to grasp Barfield's meaning immediately by considering a rainbow, which is, as he says, "the outcome of the sun, the raindrops and our own vision."[11] Elaborating on this metaphor, he states:

> The practical difference between a dream or hallucination of a rainbow and an actual rainbow is that, although each is a representation or appearance (that is, something that I perceive to be there), the second is a *shared* or collective representation.[12]

Barfield adds:

> It is easy to appreciate that there is no such thing as an unseen rainbow. It is not so easy to grasp that there is no such thing as an unheard noise.[13]

In other words, human thinking contributes not only the union of sun and dew for the cocreation of a rainbow; it is equally necessary for the joining of the right concept to the percept that we know as coffee. This is difficult to articulate because all of the qualities such as color, aroma, and granularity necessary for knowledge of coffee require the same process of joining concept to percept. However unaware of the process by which the rainbow is created, we are all aware that the rainbow has human input. It is more difficult to be aware of human thinking with respect to coffee because we stubbornly believe that it is out there, really there irrespective of my thinking. It is true that the percepts to which I contribute concepts are there but without the concepts that I contribute the percepts would not be named and therefore unknown. Barfield thus advocates a *holistic, self-implicating epistemology* that eschews either empiricist or linguistic reductionism. As Barfield writes: "I do not perceive any *thing* with my sense-organs alone, but with a great part of my whole human being."[14]

This important epistemological point is also important exegetically: what it means in Exodus for Yahweh to speak to Moses or for the bush to burn, or for the Sea of Reeds to part, or the Decalogue to be handed to Moses, or what it means in the Gita for Krishna to speak with Arjuna, depends on the collective representation of that people; its meaning for a contemporary person requires an understanding of that collective representative as well as one's own. But such a double understanding requires an act of imagination, of breaking out of contemporary strictures to arrive at a conscious image of Yahweh, Moses, the burning bush, pharaoh, the Ten Commandments. Because the collective representation of the Book of Exodus is a mix of the mythic and historical, it is difficult to interpret within a contemporary Western collective representation for which mythic and historical consciousness have quite different meanings from the meanings at the time of Exodus. When we turn to interpretations of the Bhagavad Gita it will be important to keep in mind Barfield's fundamental assertion that two processes are necessarily constitutive of thinking, both of which are relevant to the process of interpreting a sacred scripture such as the Bhagavad Gita:

1. "the sense-organs must be related to the particles in such a way as to give rise to sensations";
2. "those sensations must be combined and constructed by the percipient mind into the recognizable and nameable objects we call 'things.'"[15]

One of the "things" to be thought is Krishna, a charioteer who is also collectively represented in the Hindu mind as a god. Clearly, one's own collective representation makes a difference as to how one interprets this complex figure. An interpretation of the Gita according to original participation, and particularly concerning Krishna, would presuppose the ultimate identity of the perceiver and the world, including Arjuna as perceiver in his relationship with Krishna.[16] By enabling Arjuna, the warrior on the battlefield, to experience his identity with Krishna, Krishna in a sense restored Arjuna to an original participation. Yet, this is not quite exact because Arjuna, in his individual representation, lost some of the collective representation of an earlier time when Krishna would have been more immediately and obviously present to him than he is at the start of the Gita when Arjuna has fallen into depression due to the civil war about to begin.

In contrast to original participation, a contemporary Western person whose consciousness is shaped and limited by the Western scientific collective representation would not see a real Krishna behind his representation in the Gita. By contemporary representation, Krishna must be a fictional character, a creation of human imagination (i.e., fantasy, not knowledge of a real image). Such an interpretation would not attempt to reach the real Krishna but instead would "save the appearances," that is, would deal with Krishna "as though" he were real. He is real for the purposes of the story, not ontologically real in time, space, or history. For Barfield, by contrast, the attribution of reality exclusively to material things is epistemologically naïve and spiritually idolatrous. The subtitle of *Saving the Appearances* is "A Study in Idolatry," a study in the loss of participation and the substitution of idols for realities in which humanity in the present seems unable to participate. Humanity creates idols to replace realities it can no longer access and no longer affirm as being real, or as ever having been real.

Because of his subtle attention to the changing contours of both the world and the consciousness within which the world comes to manifestation, Barfield offers us a way of reading the Gita that avoids both the idolatry of literalizing ancient texts and the idolatry of evacuating these texts of any real reference. Instead, Barfield's account suggests that one can participatively engage the Gita in a nonliteral, imaginative but nevertheless real manner. Such an engagement allows the participatory reader entry into an ancient world and the riches of an ancient spiritual vision without the sacrifice of his or her own modernity and autonomy. But what would such a participatory engagement look like? This is the task of the next section.

THE BHAGAVAD GITA IN EVOLVING CONSCIOUSNESS

In the rest of this chapter we will consider three robust, varied yet exemplary participatory interpretations of the Bhagavad Gita. For Gandhi, the Gita teaches nonattachment to the fruits of action. The battle about to be fought, with the bewildered warrior Arjuna on the front line pleading for help from his divine charioteer, is a battle in the human heart, not at all a historical battle. According to Sri Aurobindo, on the other hand, this battle was a historical event, Krishna really did instruct Arjuna to fight, and to do so in accordance with the yogas that Krishna taught and intended for the rest of humanity. When Sri Aurobindo reads the Gita historically (as well as philosophically and spiritually), it is not merely a hermeneutical perspective but also a way of understanding contemporary events. For example, Sri Aurobindo's reading of the Gita convinced him that if Krishna had offered advice to India during World War II, he would have instructed India to join the battle on the side of Britain and against the Axis powers. Steiner offers a still different reading that regards Krishna as a very high spiritual being transmitting the several yogas to humanity as preparation for the great spiritual contributions to be brought subsequently by Buddha and Christ. How does one assess these three very different interpretations?

In the first chapter of the Gita we meet the situation to which the remaining seventeen chapters are the reply:

> O Krishna, I see my own relations here anxious to fight, and my limbs grow weak. . . . I am unable to stand; my mind seems to be whirling. These signs bode evil for us. I do not see that any good can come from killing our relatives in battle. O Krishna, I have no desire for victory, or for a kingdom or pleasures. Of what use is a kingdom or pleasure or even life, if those for whose sake we desire these things—teachers, fathers, sons, grandfathers, uncles, in-laws, grandson, and others with family ties—are engaging in this battle, renouncing their wealth and their lives? Even if they were to kill me I would not want to kill them, not even to become ruler of the three worlds. How much less for the earth alone. (1.28–35)

> Overwhelmed by sorrow, Arjuna spoke these words. And casting away his bow and his arrows, he sat down in his chariot in the middle of the battlefield. (1.47)[17]

Krishna's reply in chapters 2 and 3 favors Gandhi's conviction that the core of the Gita's teaching is *karma-yoga*, action without attachment to the fruits of action: "He who shirks action does not attain freedom" (3.3); "Fulfill all your duties; action is better than inaction" (3.8).

Chapter 4, however, favors Sri Aurobindo's emphasis on the human experience of the divine form and efficacy of Krishna in relation to human conduct:

> You and I have passed through many births, Arjuna. You have forgotten, but I remember them all. / My true being is unborn and changeless. I am the Lord who dwells in every creature. Through the power of my own maya, I manifest in a finite form. / Whenever dharma declines and the purpose of life forgotten, I manifest myself on earth. / I am born in every age to protect the good, to destroy evil, and to re-establish dharma. / He who knows me as his own divine Self breaks through the belief that he is the body and is not reborn as a separate creature. Such a one, Arjuna, is united with me. / Delivered from selfish attachment, fear, and anger, filled with me, surrendering

themselves to me, purified in the fire of my being, many have reached the state of unity in me. / As men approach me, so I receive them. All paths, Arjuna, lead to me. (4.5–11)

These are but a few of the verses that show Krishna's influential and occasionally revealing and inspiring but far from obvious reply to Arjuna. While many of the words and phrases of these texts are ambiguous, it is especially the core revelation of the Gita—Krishna's teaching to Arjuna with reference to the civil war—that is, or certainly ought to be, most confusing and jarring to a contemporary sensibility, whether Indian or Western. There are important respects in which the worldview or *dharma*, implicit in the Gita is incompatible with the contemporary West. While the Gita provides important teachings and practices for a contemporary person, particularly regarding the avatar status of Krishna and the three or four yogas that are stressed in the Gita, even these teachings and practices are revealed in a "soul mood" that is unmistakably old, traditional, mystical, and imaginal, in short, very different from modern Western sensibility.

One way to characterize the context that makes every part of the Gita different from a contemporary mood or mindset would be to say that this consciousness is pre-Greek, i.e., it conveys a worldview that is prior to the kind of thinking that emerged when the efficacy, and then the existence, of the gods came to be questioned. Note the famous critique of the anthropomorphic character of Greek theology by the sixth-century Xenophanes: "If cows could draw, their gods would look like cows." There is no trace of so radical a separation of the divine and human in the Gita. The immediacy and indubitability of Arjuna's world, including the worldview of Krishna, seem to have only now, with Arjuna's great war, come into question: first Arjuna needs guidance, and then he needs a vision, to enable him to understand the nature and extent of the god Krishna and to be able to take Krishna's counsel as his own. The Gita, then, is a transitional, efficacious text, as are all important texts: such texts mediate the transition from one kind of consciousness, and from one paradigmatic insight, to the next. In the case of the Gita, Arjuna, and thereby humanity, is brought from despondency concerning the unhappy unfolding of his own *dharma* and *karma* to another level of consciousness. Depending on one's interpretation, this new *dharma* can be understood metaphorically, as the story of Arjuna's own interior realization, or historically as an injunction to participate in the fratricidal warfare demanded by Arjuna's *dharma*, but to do so with a transformed consciousness

In the Indian consciousness, of which the Gita is a significant but by no means the sole expression of a higher or deeper insight into spiritual reality, profound mystical expressions visited the trained and attentive disciple as though he were listening to music. The refrains poured forth, more like melodies or visions than analytic propositions. Given this easy, if imperfect,

relationship between an individual human being (who is presumably a representative of humanity) and the divine (represented by Krishna, who is at
least a god and perhaps a full manifestation of Brahman, the Hindu conception of the whole of divinity), it is the more remarkable that Arjuna turns to
Krishna in the first chapter to announce that this war, and his part in it, is
not to his liking. He laments that if all of the warriors prepared to kill each
other across the field of battle actually were to do so, the structures (*dharma*)
of society would be destroyed (*adharma*).

Arjuna does not exclaim, in twentieth-century existentialist fashion,
that "God is dead!" He does, however, turn to his charioteer Krishna and
speak in a way that reveals the sudden eruption of *adharma*. He says, in effect,
"This is terrible. It will destroy the whole society. Dharma will not recover
from such a disastrous war." Arjuna pleads with Krishna that if all the leaders
of their society were to kill each other, who would run the government, the
temples, the schools? Shockingly, Krishna tells Arjuna to not worry about
that: those who will be killed are already dead and you should do what you
were born to do, but do it in full and loving consciousness of me.

How could Arjuna become so conscious of Krishna, whom he still knows
as his charioteer and not yet as the god Krishna, that he could kill his cousins
in hand to hand combat and do so with Krishna-inspired equanimity? After
teaching Arjuna the yogas of knowledge (of the divine), action (without
attachment to the fruits of action), love (of Krishna and his creation), and
meditation (so as to withdraw from the influence of the senses), Krishna then
gives to Arjuna a sublime gift, an apparition of his divine form. What does
Arjuna see? If he sees Krishna in a divine manifestation, how is that possible?
It might be the same question to ask what Sri Aurobindo sees in his many and
presumably productive mystical experiences? Sri Aurobindo reportedly saw
Krishna's divine form in the context of the evolution of consciousness. It is
remarkable for a twentieth-century person to see Krishna as a manifestation
of the divine. It is less remarkable for Arjuna, in the time of the Gita, to see
Krishna as divine being. The great achievement of Steiner and Sri
Aurobindo, both writing independently on the Gita in the second decade of
the twentieth century, was to have seen Krishna's experience of Arjuna both
in the light of Arjuna's own historically determined consciousness and also
from their twentieth-century perspectives.

One of the ways that the Gita presupposes a consciousness different from
that of the modern West is the designation of *varna* (caste), or life-work, by
birth. Arjuna is a warrior by the fact that his father was a warrior. To perform
the duties of a warrior, including the unpleasant task of fighting this civil war,
is his *varna*, his caste duty. In the modern West, by contrast, life-work roles
are not determined by birth. In the India of the Gita, one's birth reveals what
one was born to do by virtue of one's previous life and the life of one's parents. That Arjuna could lose track of this essential fact indicates that a new

consciousness, which also brings about a certain amount of chaos, at least temporarily, has arisen. It is surprising, and very revealing of the extent of the emerging change of consciousness, that Krishna should need to remind Arjuna of his *varna*-duty and should need to teach him the discipline to perform it. Because of the emergence of a new *dharma*, Krishna has to teach Arjuna the four yogas—knowledge, action, devotion, and meditation.

The yogas that Krishna teaches to Arjuna in the Gita are theoretically and practically useful for a modern Western person but not without adjustments due to what Steiner, Aurobindo, Barfield, and others see as the evolution of consciousness during the past two and a half millennia. The yoga of spiritual knowledge is simply more difficult for the modern person than it was for Arjuna of the Gita: the spectator knowledge that has dominated Western consciousness since, and because of, the scientific revolution, is characterized by a great distance between the knower, even the spiritual seeker, and the divine, or spirit. It takes a great effort for the modern Western person to travel Arjuna's route to knowledge of Krishna.

How are we to make sense of this epochal change? In the Gita, Krishna teaches Arjuna concerning three gunas, three levels of consciousness: *sattva*, or light; *rajas*, or energy; and *tamas*, or dark and heavy. One way of understanding the evolution of consciousness, particularly the two and a half millennia that separate the present from the consciousness of the Gita, is to say that humanity has devolved from the preponderance of *sattva* and *rajas* to a preponderance of *tamas*. The time characterized by *sattva* (light) would have been much earlier than the Gita, when humanity lived entirely in myth and when divine and spirit beings were immediately accessible in the visible as well as in the invisible world. According to the present mode of consciousness, not only are the gods and spirit not available, the thought that there are such beings, and that they were once accessible, is also inaccessible. In this context, "God is dead" is the report of a *tamasic* consciousness.

The second yoga, *karma-yoga*, the discipline of selfless action, can and should be practiced by contemporary individuals but with a significant revision. According to the Gita, *karma* has already settled the future—those whom Arjuna will kill are already slain. The full meaning of Arjuna's life lies not in his decision whether to kill or to withdraw from battle but rather in his acceptance of necessity. Like the philosophical ideal of the Roman Stoics, wisdom in the Gita consists not in a wise choice but in *amor fati*, love of fate. The only real decision facing Arjuna is whether, with the help of Krishna, he will be able to act—in the most dramatic imaginable way, by killing his cousins and very likely in turn being killed himself—with the loving and knowing consciousness of Krishna. Failing to act yogically, in ignorance and darkness, he will act in the illusion of his own self-sufficiency. According to the Gita's Krishna, it is not the selection of right ends that matters but nonattachment to the ends. As Krishna teaches throughout the

Gita, in a fated world, nonattachment to the fated choice is the only true aim, the only path to liberation.

Krishna also teaches Arjuna the yoga of devotion or love. With this yoga, as with the yogas of knowledge and action, Krishna had a narrower gap to close than would be the case by a god whispering to a contemporary representative of Western humanity. While there are no shortage of mystics at the present time, including some who attest to experiences comparable to Arjuna's experience of Krishna in the middle chapters of the Gita, in general, participation of human consciousness in the consciousness of a divine being has been diminished by several centuries of philosophic and scientific critique, and particularly by a resistance to the possibility of a divine being who is loving, lovable, communicative, and able to be understood. As the West tends to consider a knowing relation between a representative of humanity and a putatively divine being implausible, a loving relationship between these same parties becomes equally suspect.

Sri Aurobindo considers the path of meditation a fourth yoga. In the Gita, as in the writings of Sri Aurobindo and Steiner, and particularly in their interpretations of the Gita, meditation is never separate from the other yogas. Knowledge, action, and love are all intended to be meditative, and meditation is intended to help in their transformation. In the contemporary West, meditation, particularly Hindu and Buddhist practices, tends to have a close relation to action and love but also tend to be separate from knowledge. All of this is only to say that none of the Gita's three or four yogas—neither *bhakti*, nor *karma*, nor *jñana*, nor indeed the path of meditation—make themselves easily available to the contemporary reader. We can only traverse this hermeneutical and chronological distance with great effort, or as Barfield says, with "a goodness of heart and a steady furnace in the will."[18]

GANDHI, SRI AUROBINDO, AND STEINER ON THE GITA

M. K. (MAHATMA) GANDHI

In 1925, Gandhi wrote concerning his devotion to the Gita:

> I find a solace in the Bhagavad Gita that I missed even in the Sermon on the Mount. When disappointment stares me in the face and all alone I see not a ray of hope, I go back to the Bhagavad Gita. I find a verse here and a verse there and I immediately begin to smile in the midst of overwhelming tragedies—and my life has been full of external tragedies. And if they have left no visible, no indelible scar on me, I owe it all to the teachings of the Bhagavad Gita.[19]

The Bhagavad Gita gave Gandhi his deepest and most definite understanding of the inseparability, and perhaps identity, of political, moral, and religious action. Gandhi's fundamental concept, *satyagraha* ("truth-force"), which he practiced and taught for twenty years in South Africa and forty years in India, has as its core *karma-yoga* as taught in the Bhagavad Gita. As *karma-yoga* means nonattachment to the fruits of one's action, *satyagraha* essentially means nonpossession, noncontrol, and nonpleasure seeking, or, in short, nonattachment to the fruits, benefits, and pleasure of one's action.[20]

If *karma-yoga* is the basis of Gandhi's interpretation of the Gita, nonviolence is its fullest expression. There is no doubt about the prominence of *karma-yoga* in the Gita, but it is by no means obvious that the Gita teaches nonviolence in the usual sense of the term (i.e., not inflicting injury). At the end of the Gita, Krishna's sole instruction with respect to the war is that Arjuna should fight. Arjuna's enemies, after all, are in effect already dead. According to Gandhi's interpretation, Krishna instructs Arjuna go and fight against all of his lower impulses, go and fight in such a way that he would not cling to the rewards of his action. He should be equally disposed to his enemy and to himself.

For Gandhi the Gita tells of a battle not on a field of battle, but rather a battle within the human heart, within humanity, between the forces of good and evil. Gandhi taught that the best guarantee of nonviolent consciousness would be to refrain from both violent thinking and from violent action. He does not think, as a pacifist interpreter of the Gita might, that it would be possible to fight when required to do so without a violent emotion or motive, without wanting to harm the enemy. Such seemingly violent but perfectly equanimous action would be like physically—and lovingly—preventing a child from harm or a violent person from committing a violent action. Such a position affirms inner quietude and peaceful consciousness despite action that might appear violent. But Gandhi does not take that position with respect to the Gita; he does not suggest that Krishna tells Arjuna to fight but to do so peacefully, that is, with that total inner calm made possible by a meditative focus on the infinitely and eternally calm Krishna. Instead, Gandhi offers an analogical interpretation: the Gita teaches that the metaphor of the war on the battlefield is like the war in the human heart between positive and negative, higher and lower forces.

Against Gandhi one might argue that Krishna does in fact tell Arjuna to fight, and that he gives reasons why this is the highest teaching. Gandhi, however, would hardly have been swayed by such an argument. Gandhi's interpretation looks past Krishna's instruction to Arjuna to perform his historical, biographical duty, his *dharma* and *karma* in order to discern something that Gandhi considered more essential in the Gita. He was certain that the Gita teaches nonviolence in thought and deed, in motive and physical result, and could not possibly teach violence. Based on the text, this would seem to be a difficult interpretation to sustain. Violence, like slavery and fixed vocational *dharma*, were unquestioned components of classical Indian culture. In rejecting these components, Gandhi essentially ignores them on the way to his own original interpretation. He did not consider it necessary, or particularly productive, to try to ascertain and to consider the teachings of the Gita in their historical setting but instead *creatively reinterpreted* the Gita, all but creating an entirely new text through his novel engagement with the ancient scriptural story.

Gandhi's approach is unapologetically subjective and thus distinctively modern. He says, in effect, this is what this great text means to me, and what it means to me is true because there is no other perspective that could be more true. There is a theory of meaning implicit in all of this. What the Gita means to me is exactly and necessarily what it means—there is no other meaning but what it means to me, or to you, or to anyone—there is no text outside of its interpretation. The revelation of Krishna to Arjuna happens in the personal experience of each interpreter.

Sri Aurobindo

Sri Aurobindo wrote his *Essays on the Gita* from 1914 to 1921, at the beginning of his life in Pondicherry, a section of south India under the colonial rule of France. As Aurovind Ghose, his name before his spiritual experiences led to his being called Sri Aurobindo, he spent 1908 to 1909 in the Alipore Jail, in Calcutta, under charges of sedition against the British Government of India. On the second page of his six hundred-page commentary on the Gita, Sri Aurobindo makes explicit the extent of his subjective interpretation, and the subjective character of all interpretations, of the Gita:

> We hold it therefore of small importance to extract from the Gita its exact metaphysical connotation as it was understood by the men of the time—even if that were accurately possible. That it is not possible, is shown by the divergence of the original commentaries which have been and are still being written upon it; for they all agree in each disagreeing with all of the others, each finds in the Gita its own system of metaphysics and trend of religious thought. Nor will even the most painstaking and disinterested scholarship and the most luminous theories of the historical development of Indian philosophy save us from inevitable error. But what we can do with profit is to seek in the Gita for the actual living truths it contains, apart from their metaphysical form, to extract from it what can help us or the world at large and to put it in the most natural and vital form and expression we can find that will be suitable to the mentality and helpful to the spiritual needs of our present-day humanity. No doubt in this attempt we may mix a good deal of error born of our own individuality and of the ideas in which we live, as did greater men before us, but if we steep ourselves in the spirit of this great Scripture and, above all, if we have tried to live in that spirit, we may be sure of finding in it as much real truth as we are capable of receiving as well

as the spiritual influence and actual help that, personally, we were intended to derive from it. And that is after all what scriptures were written to give; the rest is academical [sic] disputation or theological dogma. Only those Scriptures, religions, philosophies which can be thus constantly renewed, relived, their stuff of permanent truth constantly reshaped and developed in the inner thought and spiritual experience of a developing humanity, continue to be of living importance to mankind. The rest remain as monuments of the past, but have no actual force or vital impulse for the future.[21]

In his *Essays on the Gita* Sri Aurobindo explains some of the ways that each of the yogas can best be understood and practiced in our time. His *Synthesis of Yoga* is a two-volume study of the yogas of knowledge, action, and love plus several hundred pages on *purna yoga* (integral yoga), a discipline to strengthen a commitment to cooperation with the evolution of consciousness understood both as a divine force behind history and human development, and as a goal for humanity to attain. Critics of the evolution of consciousness often hold that it demeans the people and texts of previous times, but in the hands of someone such as Sri Aurobindo or Barfield this is far from the case. Instead, by placing the Gita in an evolutionary context, Sri Aurobindo was able to recognize its historical integrity while at the same time exceeding its teachings according to the demands of his day. Unlike Gandhi, Sri Aurobindo does not conform the Gita to his own teaching, but rather he tries to listen to the words and see the images in the Gita, to affirm what he can of them, and then to move beyond its yogas to his own account of yoga in the transformative context of the evolution of consciousness.

Writing nearly a century ago, Sri Aurobindo makes it very clear that the Gita is an incomplete teaching for contemporary humanity because it does not include—nor could it have included when it was composed—an awareness of the evolution of consciousness and the task of the present age, namely, to work for the transformation of the four levels of the human being: first, the transformation of the body and with it the transformation of the material world of which the body is a part; secondly, the transformation of the vital, or the life-principle, the emotional or feeling life, aesthetics and culture; thirdly, the transformation of the mind, and the realization of higher mental states, including illumined mind, and what he calls Overmind; and then, fourthly, the great achievement for which he and his spiritual collaborator the Mother (née Mira Richard) were reportedly instruments, namely, the descent and spread of the Supermind.

We turn now to Sri Aurobindo's approach to the Gita, the key elements in his interpretation, and the place of the Gita in Sri Aurobindo's Integral Yoga. Sri Aurobindo sees the Gita as a living document, the full meaning of which requires an active participatory or meditative reading. He memorized it and recited it during the year that he spent in the Alipure Jail. It was at that time that he saw the jailers and the prisoners, presumably some of whom were murderers and thieves as well as innocent victims of an unjust and politicized penal system, all equally in the wise and loving grasp of Krishna. At that time in his development as a great spiritual teacher, it seems likely that Sri Aurobindo entered into a deep and intensely individualized relationship to the Krishna of the Gita, and committed himself to Krishna as a spiritual presence and force with the Gita as his outer manifestation. Sri Aurobindo explained his experience of the Overmind as "the descent of Krishna into the physical."[22]

Murderers and jailers, like the two sides of the civil war in which Arjuna was caught by his *dharma* and *karma*, are equally expressions of a divine *lila*, play or drama, of history. Understood within the context of his own teachings and his own reading of the Gita, Sri Aurobindo's spiritual mission placed him in the midst of a grand narrative that perhaps began in previous incarnations and surely included his fourteen years of elementary, high school, and college in England, his years as a radical opponent of the British Government of India, and his year in the Alipure Jail. In this context, all of these experiences themselves became a project of the Krishna of the Gita. Sri Aurobindo's reading of the Gita was far more than simply registering the words on the page or even of offering an interpretation of the text. His entire life became a participatory exegesis of the Bhagavad Gita. After his experience of Krishna and his writing *Essays on the Gita*, it would seem that Sri Aurobindo's entire spiritual endeavor had an Arjuna-Krishna quality, a combination of being on the firing line while at the same time seeing life's battles from a divine perspective.

The key components of Sri Aurobindo's interpretation of the Gita are the yogas—knowledge, action, love, meditation—the reality of Krishna as an avatar, and the task of maximizing *sattva* (light) at the expense of *tamas* (dullness), particularly in relation to the material realm. Sri Aurobindo extends, lifts, and deepens all of these components in the light of the evolution of consciousness. Specifically, he explains the yogas in such a way as to account for a greater degree of individuality than had evolved during the two and a half millennia separating the Gita and his *Essays*. He includes in his treatment of *karma-yoga*, for example, the fact that in the twentieth century a person does not become a warrior by the sole reason of birth but rather has a free, or nearly free, choice as to livelihood. In his treatment of *jñana* (knowledge yoga) and *bhakti* (devotion) he takes account of the fact that Krishna is not the only god affirmed by humanity and, further, that the Hindu spiritual tradition is one of many.[23]

In Sri Aurobindo's total vision and teaching, the Gita is foundational but not final; it is basic but insufficient. The key to Sri Aurobindo's mission, as he himself understood it, is his work on behalf of the spiritual evolution of humanity. This work includes his understanding and teaching but includes as well his spiritual and esoteric battles with antihuman and antievolutionary forces. In these struggles, the Gita was an inspiration for Sri Aurobindo and a text that he recommends to spiritually striving allies, but he insists that the Gita as a text is limited by its time and its consciousness, and needs to be carried forward to a more progressive understanding of the divine-human relationship. It seems plausible to speculate that Sri Aurobindo was alert to Krishna's continuing revelation—through Sri Aurobindo himself and through his collaboration with the Mother as well as through their disciples and, no doubt, legions of spiritual seekers who practice the yogas and struggle on the side of light. The Gita completes itself age to age through the creative engagement of its readers and meditators. Put another way, one could say that, for Sri Aurobindo, the spiritual treasure of the Gita is like a gift that can only be opened through one's deepening relationship to Krishna, the divine presence that inspired the Gita initially.

RUDOLF STEINER

We turn now to Steiner's interpretation of the Gita and in the process summarize his participatory epistemology in relation to the Gita. Given Steiner's emphasis on the evolution of consciousness, we may ask the following questions: What is his approach to the Gita? What are the key elements in his interpretation? And what is the place of the Gita in Steiner's anthroposophy?

Steiner makes two statements concerning the Gita, and particularly concerning the revelation of Krishna, which at first appear to be contradictory. On the one hand, he states that Krishna's teaching of the yogas not only was but is the most advanced teaching concerning the possibilities for the spiritual transformation of the human being. In a later statement, on the other hand, it becomes clear that he considers that Krishna's singularly great contributions were surpassed by the contributions of the Buddha and Christ. He says that the Buddha brought a greater contribution of compassion than Krishna, and that Christ brought himself as a presence and force that transformed humanity and the earth. The key to solving this apparent contradiction lies in the distinction between Krishna's importance for the transformation of the individual and the power of the Buddha and Christ to transform humanity—however insignificant these transformations seem as one observes the affairs of humankind.

The key elements in Steiner's interpretation of the Gita are very similar to the elements in the interpretation of Sri Aurobindo: the yogas, the avatarhood of Krishna, and the struggle on behalf of the evolution of consciousness toward greater light—a light he most regularly interprets in terms of Christ, the Logos, whom he refers to as the Sun Being.[24]

The Gita holds a very important but not central place in Steiner's writings and lectures. It was while he was in a spiritual and esoteric struggle within, or in relation to, the Theosophical Society that Steiner focused rather intensely on Krishna and the Buddha and the spiritual traditions of which he considered them to be the paradigmatic teachers. In 1912, when the complete and final break between the Theosophical Society and what was then forming as the Anthroposophical Society seemed inevitable, Steiner gave two sets of lectures on the Gita: the first, *The Bhagavad Gita and the Epistles of Paul,* which he delivered in December 1912, were the first lectures he delivered to the members of the newly created Anthroposophical Society. In May 1913 he went much deeper into the text itself in a series of nine lectures entitled *The Esoteric Meaning of the Bhagavad Gita.* In the first series he emphasizes the distinctive contribution of Krishna and the Gita as well as the unique and, according to Steiner, greater contribution of Christ. In the second set of lectures in which he went deeper into the text of the Gita, he emphasizes the significance of the samkhya philosophy, the *gunas* (*sattva,* light; *rajas,* energy; *tamas,* dullness), and the transcendent significance of Krishna as avatar.

It would be difficult to find a more appropriate characterization for Steiner's relationship to the Gita than participation. His statements about the teachings of the Gita and their contemporary significance derive directly from his participation in the soul mood of the time, in the reality of Krishna in the spiritual world, the historical fact of Krishna's revelation to Arjuna in the India of sixth century BCE, and the spiritual character of that revelation as expressed, however incompletely, in the words of the Bhagavad Gita. It is clear that Steiner came to his understanding, and deep appreciation, of the Gita by intense participatory esoteric effort; it is also clear that he considers it is necessary for any one who would experience the teachings of the Gita and the reality of Krishna to make a sustained and strenuous effort, under the heading of thinking or love, or a union of the two.

CONCLUSION

This chapter concludes with summaries of the approaches to the Bhagavad Gita by the three interpreters discussed, and some personal reflections on the various participatory modalities of each of these approaches.

It seems fair to say that Gandhi's approach is, by and large, more subjective than participatory—the Gita means what he thinks it should mean for his life work and for the task of the time. In contrasting subjective and participatory, I mean only that participatory affirms a degree of objectivity of a text (or any phenomenon) to be met by the interpreter; subjectivity in this context limits the meaning of the text to the framework of the interpreter with little regard for what the text (or any phenomenon) might mean in its own right. Gandhi's interpretation of the Gita would seem to be an instance of one of the deep, mysterious, and vexatious facts about philosophy and religion, namely the gap between "right view" and "right action." Gandhi's view of the Gita seems at the very least historically mistaken, but his use of the Gita, including his use of his presumably mistaken interpretation, produced manifestly positive results in his own field of battle against the British rule of India and against a wide range of injustices that he opposed first in South Africa and then in India. Many profound, scholarly, and presumably correct interpretations of the Gita by others, including Sri Aurobindo and Steiner, seem to have exercised a less significant effect on the common good than Gandhi's arguably naïve interpretation and use of the Gita. For Gandhi, the most efficacious interpretation would have to be the one that supports what was for him the highest possible truth, the truth of nonviolence.

On this larger topic, the concept and practice of nonviolence, Gandhi is deeply participatory: he was an empiricist, a steady and devoted experimenter, ready to learn from the personal, social, and moral conflicts in which he participated. Within the context of those encounters, Gandhi's focus is not on the Gita as such but rather on the pragmatic use of the Gita, with his unusual interpretation, in the larger cause of nonviolence. It does not seem that Gandhi asked the Gita for its meaning, nor did he ask Krishna. Gandhi's epistemology is a commonsense rationality, a naïve realism, but thoroughly subjectivist, such that the Gita can be taken to mean whatever he, or any one else, thinks it means—provided that it serves the cause of nonviolence. Fortunately for the world, especially for India in the first half of the twentieth century, Gandhi participated brilliantly, generously, and consequently on behalf of peace and justice, perhaps the two most urgent needs during Gandh's lifetime and today.

With respect to the Gita—though not with respect to the cause of nonviolence—Gandhi represents the problem of the loss of participation without a solution, indeed, without even recognizing the problem or the need for a solution. A consistent humanist who was regularly horrified by the conflict among religions, particularly between Hinduism and Islam in India, and justly afraid of religious dogmatism, Gandhi is methodologically sophisticated but epistemologically naïve. Totally pragmatic with respect to a scripture such as the Gita, his was a genius of morality, and particularly the morality of nonviolence. This apparent polarity in his life-work would seem to be due to his attention to human nature and behavior, particularly concerning human injustice—and participation in the causes and solutions of human suffering—combined with his inattention to the competing claims generated endlessly by theology and philosophy. He argues against cruelty and injustice but not against competing claims about God or gods, or the competition among rituals and other religious practices.

Sri Aurobindo interprets the Gita within the framework of the evolution of consciousness but his focus is more metaphysical than epistemological. He is particularly focused on the need to follow the yogas taught in the Gita, and only secondarily on the challenge that faces a modern person who seeks to experience Krishna. Even his extensive writings on *jñana-yoga* ("The Yoga of Divine Knowledge") focus on the nature and function of the Divine, whether as Brahman or as Sat-Chit-Ananda (Being-Consciousness-Bliss), and very little on the problem of knowledge in the present age. He does not so much offer a spiritual epistemology, whether by analysis or argument, as he offers himself as a guide to mystical *noesis*. A likely source of Sri Aurobindo's participatory epistemology was his study of British Hegelian idealists at King's College, Cambridge University, from 1889–1893. These writers clearly support both his explicit ontology and his implicit epistemology, but he scarcely ever cites these philosophers and never quotes them, thus leaving the relationship between his integral philosophy and Hegelian idealism a matter of speculation.

Sri Aurobindo, like Steiner, claims to be an original source; he knows by and from his own experience. Unlike Steiner, Sri Aurobindo does not confront the modern epistemological challenge, the gauntlet laid down first by Hume and then by Kant. Sri Aurobindo simply proceeds to write from his experience oblivious of the maxim of the nineteenth and twentieth century that it is not possible to ignore Kant. Sri Aurobindo develops a metaphysics, including an account of the divine, the human, the earthly, and the relationships among them. He does not, however, confront Hume and Kant directly, and consequently his writings do not help his reader out of, or through, the Kantian foreclosure on certain knowledge. According to the epistemological strictures laid down by Kant, one can affirm the reality and efficacy of a Krishna-like being, and even the mystical vision in the middle chapters of the Gita, but one cannot know this reality and efficacy to be so. By absorbing a Hegelian worldview and using it to render systematic the direct transmission of spiritual truths to the *rsis*, the spiritual teachers at the time of the Upanishads, 1000–500 BCE, Sri Aurobindo presents a synthesis of Upanishadic and Hegelian idealism but without the logical and epistemological justification that Hegel and post-Hegelians have been so at pains to establish.

As he focused on neither the concept of alienation (as explored, for example, in the Hegelian corpus) nor the loss of participation (as traced by Steiner and Barfield), Sri Aurobindo does not offer significant direction to the contemporary Western student of the Gita—and no doubt there are increasing numbers of Indian interpreters in this same situation—whose (explicit or implicit) assumptions are blocked by Humean or Kantian prohibitions. Sri Aurobindo writes as though his readers can simply do what he can: enter into what he refers to as "the core" and "the gist" of the Gita's message and the reality of Krishna as avatar. While he seems to accept something like the loss of participation throughout the evolution of human consciousness, he nevertheless seems entirely optimistic concerning the evolution of humanity to increasingly higher states of consciousness, from the current mental stage (ordinary intellect), to higher mind or illumined mind, to Overmind (the level of consciousness realized by the great spiritual teachers of the past, including particularly the level exhibited in the Gita) and Supermind (reportedly possible since the mid-twentieth century through the agency of Sri Aurobindo and the Mother).

If only by giving instruction to many hundreds of disciples, Sri Aurobindo was made aware of the difficulty, in contrast to his own ease of access, that twentieth-century seekers experience in their attempt to know spiritual realities. It would seem that if anyone knew the Gita from the inside, including its intent and significance, it was Sri Aurobindo, and this participatory intimacy sustained his conviction that Krishna as avatar and the inner meaning of the Gita's teaching, particularly on the yogas, were readily accessible to seekers in the present age. It would be difficult to imagine a text more confident than Sri Aurobindo's *Essays on the Gita*, but at the same time it contains little or no insight as to how the author knows what he knows, either about the Gita or about anything else. This work is thoroughly participatory but not epistemologically critical. As he said quite emphatically, he was not a philosopher; he was a yogi, mystic, a poet, and a spiritual teacher.[25]

As Gandhi developed an interpretation that furthered his case for and practice of nonviolence, Sri Aurobindo developed an interpretation in such a way as to advance the synthesis of yogas at the core of his teaching. In contrast to Gandhi's approach, however, Sri Aurobindo first memorized and then studied the Gita in its original language and meditated on its meaning. Consequently, his approach, unlike Gandhi's, is not merely subjective, but should be considered intersubjective and participatory: Krishna and the Gita are active sources of revelation but they require an active listener, an Arjuna who asks for help and who follows each step from *karma-yoga* to *jñana-yoga* to *bhakti-yoga* to the realization that in the present age these yogas need to take account of the evolution of consciousness. As Sri Aurobindo establishes by precept and example, the Gita requires someone like himself who knows the entire Indian spiritual tradition and the spiritual needs of contemporary humanity.

Sri Aurobindo's work as guru, and perhaps as (co-)avatar, is very different from Gandhi's forty-year commitment to "experiment with truth." Gandhi is neither a poet nor mystic but a moral reformer and activist. With respect to the Gita and virtually every other part of their careers, including the years that they worked in the Indian nationalist movement, Sri Aurobindo and Gandhi missed each other completely. Gandhi's interpretation of the Gita is modest, humanist, entirely nonacademic, and in service of his daily work on behalf of *satyagraha* (truth-force), whereas Sri Aurobindo's approach to the Gita is elegant, brilliant, learned, confident, and vast. Gandhi presents himself as an Arjuna on the firing line fighting

modestly, courageously, and indefatigably against the myriad forces of violence and injustice; Sri Aurobindo presents himself as a Krishna participating in and explaining to a confused humanity the continuing revelation
of divine both in the form of Krishna and in many other manifestations,
both personal and impersonal.

Whereas Sri Aurobindo is rightly understood as a guru and spiritual force,
Steiner is best understood as an initiate, a term he himself uses. Steiner saw
that his initiation involved him in a mission to expose and oppose the dominant Western worldview, one in the grip of materialism and dead thinking.
Steiner's mission was to teach and exemplify a new path of knowledge, one
that would enable a modern Western person to attain with confidence the
kind of knowledge perhaps best called spiritual, the very possibility of which
Kant and the dominant philosophers of the nineteenth and twentieth centuries argue against so decisively. It is appropriate, then, that in his interpretation of the Gita, Steiner is eager to establish that this great text is a true revelation but because of its date and culture of origin it is not, and could not be,
the most important revelation for contemporary Western thought and culture.

Because it is informed by the modern Western scientific and philosophical revolution, Steiner's analysis of the epistemological challenge facing one
who would attempt to know Krishna, or Buddha, or Christ—a saint, an
avatar, bodhisattva, or one's recently deceased beloved—is far more rigorous,
detailed, and challenging than Sri Aurobindo's. He insists that without rigorous self-discipline, essentially in opposition to ordinary thinking, no higher
being will bestow on the seeker what Krishna bestowed on Arjuna. For a typical modern Western person to attain Krishna- or Buddha- or Christ-con-
sciousness, a multidisciplined effort is required. Steiner's anthroposophy, or
spiritual science, is precisely such a multidisciplined effort to reach the spiritual world. As is evident by his characterization of anthroposophy—"a path
of knowledge to lead the spiritual in the human being to the spiritual in the
universe"[26]—it is the very essence of participation. Krishna is precisely one of
the highest and most efficacious links between the spiritual in the human
being and the spiritual in the universe. In Steiner's ecumenical esoteric
research, Buddha and Christ are also sublime links accessible by anyone who
opposes the prevalence of *tamas* by thinking characterized by will and affect.
As the Gita recommends knowledge, action, and love, Steiner recommends
the cultivation of thinking, willing, and feeling, and like the Gita, he also
recommends the mutual strengthening of each by the other two.

Modern Western interpreters of the Gita, and increasingly Indian interpreters influenced by Western ways of thinking, can experience Krishna and
his message intellectually, as an observer, an onlooker, but, unlike Arjuna,
they cannot readily see or hear inside of Krishna's mind where Krishna holds
civilizations and worlds upon worlds. Nor is it easy for an interpreter with typical Western consciousness to experience sufficient depth of Krishna as a

source of knowledge, love, and selfless action. It is precisely because Steiner excelled at knowing, loving, and effective action that he was able to glean from the Gita—and from Krishna, though it is difficult for us to know what that means exactly—its deepest secrets.

To the extent that we take seriously Barfield's description of the evolution of consciousness, and the implications for contemporary thought and culture that follow immediately from it, it is a short step to see that the Bhagavad Gita, and revelatory texts like it—that is, texts with some capacity to reveal spirit and divinity as once known by that sensibility that Barfield calls "original participation," a sensibility that is suppressed or even barred at present—require interpreters to approach its inner secrets with a consciousness that is as direct as it is loving. Such thinking includes the self-consciousness of modern Western thought, but it will also break through the strictures of modern consciousness to the kind of contact with spiritual realities typical of ancient religious traditions and texts. The remarkably different character of what Barfield names original and final participation, and the degrees of loss of participation from original participation to final, provide "the different 'slant,'" the "comparatively slight readjustment in our way of looking at the things and ideas" that will make the difference between the Bhagavad Gita as a set of ideas and practices and the Bhagavad Gita as a revelation of a God or avatar who teaches ways to transform thought, love, and action.

NOTES

I am grateful to the original thinking and writings of my CIIS colleagues, Richard Tarnas, Sean Kelly, Jorge N. Ferrer, and Jacob H. Sherman, on behalf of the development of a participatory epistemology; I am similarly grateful to Rudolf Steiner and an array of thinkers influenced by him—Barfield foremost among them. For a careful reading of this chapter, and suggestions for its improvement, I am grateful to Kathy Ann Woodruff and John Tillyer, and the editors of this volume, Ferrer and Sherman.

1. Barfield, *Poetic Diction: A Study in Meaning* (Middletown, CT: Wesleyan University Press, 1973): "Thus, an introspective analysis of my experience obliges me to say that appreciation of poetry involves a 'felt change of consciousness.' The phrase must be taken with some exactness. Appreciation takes place at the actual moment of change" (52).

2. The first page of Augustine's *Confessions* is a prolegomena for a Christian philosophy and theology of history as well as a Christian anthropology: "Man is one of your creatures, Lord, and his instinct is to praise you. . . . The thought of you stirs him so deeply that he cannot be content unless he praises you, because you made us for yourself and our hearts find no peace until they rest in you." Saint Augustine, *Confessions*, trans., intro. R. S. Pine-Coffin (New York: Penguin Books, 1961), 61.

3. Consider the title of the chapter "Hope, Yes; Progress No," in Huston Smith's *Forgotten Truth: The Primordial Tradition* (New York: Harper and Row, 1976), ch. 6.

4. In *Poetic Diction*, Barfield defines a percept as "that element in my experience, which in no way depends on my own mental activity, present or past—the pure sense-datum" (48).

5. Barfield, *Saving the Appearances: A Study in Idolatry* (New York: Harcourt, Brace, and World, 1965), 105.

6. Plato, *Cratylus* 383b and 385.

7. For Goethe's "delicate empiricism" see Henry Bortoft, *The Wholeness of Nature: Goethe's Way toward a Science of Conscious Participation in Nature* (Great Barrington, MA: Lindisfarne Press, 1996) and David Seamon and Arthur Zajonc, eds. *Goethe's Way of Science: A Phenomenology of Nature* (Albany: State University of New York Press, 1998).

8. See Steiner's characterization of anthroposophy (divine-human feminine wisdom), his esoteric teaching and practice, as "a path of knowledge to lead the spiritual in the human being to the spiritual in the universe," in Steiner, *Anthroposophical Leading Thoughts: Anthroposophy as a Path of Knowledge*, trans. George and Mary Adams (London: Rudolf Steiner Press, 1973), 13; see also Robert McDermott, ed., *The Essential Steiner* (San Francisco: Harper San Francisco, 1984), 415, and McDermott, ed., *The New Essential Steiner* (Great Barrington, MA: Steinerbooks, forthcoming).

9. Barfield, *Saving the Appearances*, 12.

10. Ibid., 17.

11. Ibid., 15.

12. Ibid., 16.

13. Ibid., 22.

14. Ibid., 20.

15. Ibid., 24.

16. Some interpretations of the Gita present Krishna as Arjuna's higher self. See Eliot Deutsch, trans., intro., critical essays, *The Bhagavad Gita* (New York: Holt, Rinehart, and Winston, 1968), 20.

17. *The Bhagavad Gita*, trans., intro. Eknath Easwaran (Tomales, CA: Nilgiri Press, 1985). All passages from the Bhagavad Gita are from this excellent translation by the founder and spiritual guide of Blue Mountain Center for Meditation, Tomalas, California. See his three-volume commentary, *The Bhagavad for Daily Living: The End of Sorrow; Like a Thousand Suns;* and *To Love is to Know Me.*

18. Barfield, *Saving the Appearances*, 161.

19. M. K. Gandhi, *Young India*, 1925.

20. For Gandhi's theory and practice of *satyagraha*, see especially Gandhi, *The Story of My Experiments with Truth*, trans. Mahadev Desai (Boston: Beacon Press, 1957), Part IV, chs. 28–30.

21. Sri Aurobindo, *Essays on the Gita*, Sri Aurobindo Birth Centenary Library: Vol. 13 (Pondicherry, India: Sri Aurobindo Ashram), 4.

22. For Sri Aurobindo's account of his experience of the descent of the Overmind as the descent of Krishna, see K. R. Shrinivas Iyengar, *Sri Aurobindo: A Biography and a History* (Pondicherry, India: Sri Aurobindo International Centre of Education, 1972), 987–90.

23. It should also be acknowledged, however, that for someone who lived in the West for the formative years of his life he was remarkably inattentive to Christ and Christianity, and during his adult years in India he developed no relationship to Buddha or Buddhism.

24. Steiner's approach here reflects what we might call "esoteric ecumenism," an approach that has the advantage of neither dismissing nor facilely equating the diverse religious traditions of humankind. Apropos our present discussion, for example, Steiner reports how the yogas of the Gita were esoterically transmitted to Paul at the time of his experience of Christ while Paul was on his way to Damascus, an unusual but nonetheless suggestive remark. See Steiner's *The Bhagavad Gita and the Epistles of Paul*, in *The Bhagavad Gita and the West*, ed. McDermott (Great Barrington, MA: Steinerbooks, 2007).

25. McDermott, ed., *The Essential Aurobindo* (Great Barrington, MA: Lindisfarne Press, 1987), 23.

26. *The Essential Steiner*, 415. See also *The New Essential Steiner*.

TEN

Pulsating with Life

The Paradoxical Intuitions of Henri Bergson

G. William Barnard

THIS ESSAY ATTEMPTS to demonstrate, in an unavoidably abbreviated and compressed form, how the philosophical perspective of Henri Bergson, a late-nineteenth- and early-twentieth-century French thinker, remains a rich resource, even in the early twenty-first century, in our attempts to articulate the potential value of a "participatory spirituality." While Bergson's work is not without flaws, nor is it uniformly and in all respects supportive of "the participatory turn," nonetheless, I would like to suggest that certain key elements of Bergson's work are not only congruent with the vision of a participatory spirituality, but can also contribute some substantive and worthwhile insights into what new, and perhaps unanticipated, forms this particular spiritual vision might assume in the years to come.

For myself, participatory spirituality is a much needed corrective to the worldview that is so often assumed today by many influential philosophers, social theorists, and scientists, a worldview that tells us that we are nothing more than atomistic cogs in a mindless, uncaring, mechanistic universe. Participatory spirituality, as I see it, proposes a strikingly different vision, a vision of the universe in which each one of us is seen as integrally connected to wider, deeper dimensions of a dynamic, multileveled, and open-ended reality, a reality that is enriched and creatively shaped, moment by moment, by our experiences, choices, and behavior.

In order to accomplish the task of showing how Bergson's work is aligned with, and supportive of, a participatory vision of the universe, I will inevitably present a "spiritual" Bergson—a Bergson that many recent scholars of his work (especially those who are strongly influenced by the thought of the twentieth-century French poststructuralist Gilles Deleuze) might well not recognize nor endorse.[1] However, I would claim that, like William James (Bergson's closest and most influential philosophical ally in America), Bergson is multifaceted enough that it is possible to articulate a wide variety of seemingly mutually exclusive visions of his thought, each of which remains, interestingly, true to certain key aspects of his work. This essay, therefore, intends to highlight aspects of Bergson's thought that have been recently overlooked or ignored, leading, hopefully, to a more nuanced and balanced understanding of Bergson's overall philosophical perspective.

However, it is also my intention to offer something more than a faithful reiteration of Bergson's thought. While I have made every attempt to present his work in a manner that is historically accurate, I have also not shied away from a creative appropriation of his ideas. In many ways, this chapter is perhaps best understood as a type of neo-Bergsonian attempt to offer sound reasons why a participatory spirituality is a persuasive and potentially transformative vision of reality and selfhood. I would argue that this willingness to judiciously adapt Bergson's thought is, ironically, perhaps truer to his perspective than any scholarly attempt to locate Bergson's work solely in the past, as if it were some sort of historical relic. Because Bergson repeatedly emphasizes that the universe itself can be best understood as a ceaseless dynamic flux characterized by a constant (albeit often unrecognized) emergence of genuine novelty, he frequently acknowledges, and in fact emphasizes, that any philosophical vision that hopes to remain viable will itself have to change. Bearing this in mind, I am willing to use Bergson's work for my own, highly individual, ends (without apology and indeed with great gusto) and to make conclusions based on his perspective that he might never have anticipated (or even approved!)—while remaining, I would argue, aligned with and true to what is most importantly "Bergsonian" in his thought.

UNFOLDING DURÉE

Bergson is remembered today, if he is remembered at all, primarily for two crucial Bergsonian concepts that he articulated in his most well-known work, *Creative Evolution*: first, his discussion of intuition, and second, his emphasis on the *élan vital*, the cosmic life force that he argued was the impetus behind all evolutionary development. (Religious Studies scholars might also be aware of Bergson's intriguing proposals on ethics and mysticism found in his last book, *The Two Sources of Morality and Religion*.) At first glance, it might seem that an essay on Bergson and participatory spirituality would primarily emphasize these more overtly "spiritual" topics. However, I am going to take a different, and perhaps unexpected, tack. While a worthwhile essay could (and perhaps should) be written on Bergson's discussion of intuition, the élan vital, and mysticism, I have decided, instead, to focus on the spiritual implications of what I argue is the living, beating heart of Bergson's work: his notion of *durée*.

Bergson's initial exploration of *durée* is found in his doctoral thesis, written at the age of thirty in 1889: *Essai sur les données immédiates de la conscience* (*An Essay on the Immediate Data of Consciousness*, published in English as *Time and Free Will*). As the French title makes clear, this insightful text is Bergson's attempt to peer deeply into what takes place in the moment-to-moment unfolding of our "ordinary" consciousness, an unfolding that he calls "*durée.*"

Bergson argues that any accurate knowledge of consciousness can only emerge as the end result of a rigorous and subtle investigation of what is taking place within our *own* conscious awareness. It is "here," "in the midst of" what is, arguably, the most intimate, undeniable, and vividly felt knowledge that is, arguably, the most intimate, undeniable, and vividly felt knowledge that we possess that we have the possibility of discovering something we might not have anticipated: a reality unlike any other in the world—the ever-changing, ever-new, flux of our own awareness, an awareness not of something that exists separate from us, but rather an awareness that *is* us in our depths, an awareness that persists (while always changing), an awareness that is always present (and always moving). (The use of quotes above is to underscore the fact that, according to Bergson, consciousness is utterly non-spatial in its nature; there is no "here" nor "in the midst of" in consciousness.)

It is important to note that Bergson does not have a naïve or simplistic understanding of the immediacy of our conscious experience. While he consistently maintains that our consciousness is a type of philosophical touchstone, he also argues that this touchstone is not easily accessed due to the fact that it is hidden beneath many layers of deeply engrained psychic habits or predispositions that veil its true nature.[2] Ironically, the immediacy of consciousness only emerges after an arduous inner search, and even then only haltingly and with varying degrees of intensity.

Nonetheless, Bergson insists that even with all the difficulties and limitations that we might face in our quest to know ourselves, even with all of the wrong turns that we might encounter in our introspective endeavors, when we finally make our way into that inner sanctum (or when it presents itself to us as a gift), this intuitive awareness of ourselves is undeniable, non-mediated, and directly evident. As Bergson stresses, once a person has reached this level of awareness "and is acquainted with it in its simple form (which must not be confounded with its conceptual representation)," he or she cannot and will not remain the same; instead, that inner certainty is so powerful and self-evident that the person who has this knowledge will feel "constrained" to change his or her "point of view about reality" so that it aligns with this inner perception.[3]

According to Bergson, if and when we look closely into the nature of our own consciousness, what we will find is an inner life that is ceaselessly chang-ing—an inner world in which one state of consciousness seamlessly flows into the next. However, as Bergson points out, because we tacitly experience everything through language, the prism of our linguistic structure typically fragments our experience, splitting the dynamic flux of our consciousness into what appear to be unchanging, self-contained parts (i.e., "states" of con-sciousness, such as "sadness" or "contentment"). Since words are separate, unchanging units ("contentment," as a word, always stays the same and is always a different word than "sadness"), we tend to assume that as time passes within us one "nugget" of consciousness (e.g., "sadness") is replaced by another "nugget" of consciousness (e.g., "contentment"), almost as if these moments of consciousness were beads of different colors lined up next to each other. This type of tacit spatial symbolism (each bead is solid, separate, mea-surable) makes it extremely difficult to recognize that, in reality, our sensa-tions, thoughts, and feelings are continually in flux, and that while it is pos-sible to distinguish different "shades" to our inner experience, there are, in actuality, no distinct boundaries within it. Within the flux of our conscious-ness, there is nothing static, there are no snapshots cut off from the rest, there is simply the continuous flow of our awareness, each state of consciousness interpenetrating the others—"a spectrum of a thousand shades, with imper-ceptible gradations leading from one shade to another."[4]

The external world, to all outward appearances, seems to consist of a variety of discrete objects, objects that appear to have clear-cut boundaries, objects that seem to be separate from each other in space. However, our inner world, if examined closely, does not have this same structure. Unlike the external world, *durée* manifests as sheer and utter internal multiplicity and diversity, and yet also, paradoxically, as a reality that has no breaks, no gaps, within it. Instead, our consciousness is a seamless continuity, an unin-ter-rupted flow in which, as Ian W. Alexander notes, "each moment is absorbed into the following one, transforming it and being transformed by it, with the consequent transformation of the whole."[5] Consciousness as such is "pure change and heterogeneity," but it is also "the heterogeneity of organic growth."[6] Therefore, *durée* is, as Bergson emphasizes, that which is "ever the same and ever changing."[7] It is always the same in that it is utter continuity, it is always changing in that it is a flux of sheer novelty. It is both, and yet actually neither. No descriptive term, or any clever combination of terms, will ever adequately represent *durée*. Ironically, in order to even come close to an accurate description of our inner world, the only "logical" solution is to resort to paradox and/or to draw upon a series of overlapping metaphors.

To use one of Bergson's favorite metaphorical images, we tend to think of our inner experience as if it were captured on a roll of movie film—essen-tially turning the undivided and unanticipated flux of our consciousness into a linear series of static snapshots, one frozen moment followed by another, each one inevitably leading to the next. In this "cinematographic" perspective, each thought, each memory, each feeling, is tacitly understood to exist separately within us, each having its own discrete identity, each taking up just so much "space" within our psyche, each static snapshot lined up and unrolling, implacably, on the underlying homogenous substance of the film of time.[8] As Bergson points out, our tendency to envision the dynamic flow of our consciousness as static and fragmented, to see it as notes upon a musical score, or as beads threaded together on a string, or as snapshots on a roll of film, may be well suited to the requirements of logic and language, but this "spatialized" mode of understanding deeply distorts the reality of our consciousness. *Durée*, understood and experienced clearly, is literally like nothing else found in the external world, even if we might wish that this were not the case so that we could more easily grasp it.

As Bergson points out, as long as our attention is gripped by the outside world "we have no interest in listening to the uninterrupted humming of life's depths" (CM 176). For the vast majority of us, therefore, it is exceedingly difficult to get back to the real experience of our lived consciousness, a consciousness that flows; in order to do so it is "as if the whole normal direction of consciousness [has] to be reversed" (CM 111). Whereas in actuality our inner world is a "melody where the past enters into the present and forms with it an undivided whole which remains undivided and even indivisible in spite of what is added at every instant," instead, we experience an inner life that is tightly controlled, where every feeling has a label and every idea is carefully weighed and considered (CM 83). Whereas in actuality there is the seamless, dynamic onrush of our awareness in time, instead, we live in a time that is measured and parceled out, split up into seconds, minutes, hours—the efflorescence of ceaseless novelty and inner continuity pulverized into units of sameness, each counted and accounted for.

DURÉE: EVER-NEW

As Milic Capek points out, a crucially important characteristic of *durée* is that it is "forever incomplete . . . in other words, it is a *continuous emergence of novelty*."[9] The flow of our consciousness as time passes—or better yet, as it takes the form of the passage of time—continually takes on completely unexpected and novel shapes. Joseph Solomon underscores this ongoing novelty of *durée* when he says that, for Bergson, "the mind is ever changing by a sort of self-creation, or, more precisely, by active adaptation. It is this that constitutes its freedom. It is making; it is never made."[10] This constant, self-generated, internal change, a change that is rooted in and propelled by memory, also assures the irreversibility of *durée*. As Bergson notes, "We could not live over again a single moment, for we should have to begin by effacing the memory of all that had followed. . . . Thus our personality shoots, grows, and ripens without ceasing. Each of its moments is something new added to what was before."[11]

As much as we might wish to control our inner lives, consciousness of its own accord never remains still, never repeats itself. Even when we are at our most robotic, living a life of habitual reactivity to others, almost sleepwalking through existence, even then our consciousness, under the radar, somehow manages to be genuinely, never-endingly, creative. What is almost miraculous about *durée*, as Bergson notes, is that it is "a reality which is capable of drawing from itself more than it contains, of enriching itself from within, of creating or recreating itself ceaselessly;" it is a reality "which is essentially resistant to measurement because it is never entirely determined, never fully made but always in the process of becoming."[12]

In addition, as Bergson emphasizes, *durée* "is not only something new, but something unforeseeable" (CE 6). As he points out, any pretense of determinism would immediately vanish, if we could only see ourselves immersed in the concrete experience of *durée*, where "the past becomes identical with the present and continuously creates with it—if only by the fact of being added to it—something absolutely new" (CM 185).

Bergson does not deny that our present state of awareness is intimately connected with what happened in the past within us and with what was acting upon us in the past. However, just because our current state of awareness is seamlessly connected with the whole of our prior experience, this in no way implies that our present states of consciousness (or our present actions) are somehow the predictable, automatic outcome of our past. As Bergson points out, every moment of our lives "is a kind of creation" (CE 7). According to Bergson, we each have within us "the feeling . . . of being creators of our intentions, of our decisions, of our acts, and by that, of our habits, our characters, ourselves. Artisans of our life . . . we work continually, with the material furnished us by the past and present, by heredity and opportunity, to mold a figure unique, new, original, as unforeseeable as the form given by the sculptor to the clay" (CM 110).

From a Bergsonian perspective, voluntary actions, to the extent that they are not habitual and rote reactions, are directly experienced within us as free and unanticipated activities. According to Bergson, this creative freedom, which "overflows the body on all sides" (since our consciousness is not spatially limited), which "endures through time," which initiates "unforeseeable and free" actions, which "creates by newly-creating itself," is the true nature of the self.[13] It is this creative power that Bergson is referring to when he uses terms such as "the 'I,' the 'soul,' the 'mind'—mind being precisely a force which can draw from itself more than it contains, yield more than it receives, give more than it has" (ME 39).[14]

As A. A. Luce helpfully indicates, the freedom that we have as conscious beings is not capricious, it does not emerge in an instant out of nowhere.

Instead, our inner freedom carries the "past forward into its present . . . inherited disposition, instinctive impulses, temperament, the idea that guides, the feeling that motivates"—all of these come together to form who we are in our ability to freely choose, freely decide, freely act.[15] For Bergson, who we are, the flow of our *durée*, is not the simple end result of a certain number of past experiences that have been rearranged to produce a fixed and calculable end product. Instead, "real duration is that in which each form flows out of previous forms, while adding to them something new" (CE 362). Our current state of consciousness in its ceaseless emergence is not preordained by mathematically complex but theoretically calculable economic forces; it is not the sum total of our immersion in our particular cultural milieu and institutional structures; it does not arise due to the predetermined mindless interaction of bits of cerebral and neural matter bumping into each other in predictable patterns.[16] Instead, Bergson argues that *durée* is endlessly, naturally, almost unbelievably, creative. Each "moment" of *durée* does not emerge from the past like an automobile coming off of an assembly line, constructed by drawing from and rearranging a previous and finite supply of parts. The reservoir from which all of this incessant newness springs forth is not a bounded, finished, complete whole, in which all of our memories and beliefs and fears and passions and so on are neatly stacked, like some giant inner warehouse. Instead, it is a *virtual* reality—an open-ended, living, unbounded, nonspatial, protoconscious potentiality whose very nature is unimaginable creativity.[17] *Durée*, like an inner cornucopia of consciousness, manages to create, almost magically, genuine newness at each "moment," even while it also remains inextricably connected to the past. (The use of quote marks around the word "moment," although rhetorically awkward, hopefully highlights, and helps to counteract, our tendency to picture the present moment as an atomistic "point" in time.)

A MATTER OF SPIRIT

Beginning in Bergson's second work, *Matter and Memory*, and continuing on in *Creative Evolution* and *The Two Sources of Morality and Religion*, the philosophical presentation of *durée* undergoes a striking, and profound, transformation. What was once simply a lucid analysis of the ongoing, continually changing temporal flux of our individual consciousness becomes, with little warning, the basis for Bergson's assertion that all of existence itself is a densely textured, complex interplay of different levels of consciousness/time. Whereas in *Time and Free Will* Bergson postulates (temporarily?) a type of dualism between the temporal nature of our consciousness and the spatial nature of matter, his perspective on *durée* changes radically in *Matter and Memory*. Beginning with this revolutionary text, and continuing from then on, Bergson argues that the entire cosmos, on every level of existence, is nothing more than various, ever-shifting, rhythms of *durée*. In *Matter and Memory*, therefore, Bergson essentially affirms a type of nondualism, albeit one that is highly unusual and complex—a temporal, dynamic nondualism that, ironically, also strongly affirms the ongoing importance of maintaining a *functional* division between time and space, or between mind and matter.

It is important to stress that Bergson never abandons his initial analysis of the nature of our individual consciousness found in *Time and Free Will*. Instead, he takes that analysis and applies it (with several creative additions) to the entire universe. By doing so, Bergson is able to argue that the cosmos is best understood, not as a highly complex yet inert machine, but rather (in varying degrees) as a pulsating reality that, if examined carefully, looks a lot like our own consciousness. That is, Bergson argues that the physical universe, like our awareness, is fluid, ever-changing, seamless, interconnected, immeasurable, continually moving, interactive, multilayered, ever-new, and inherently creative; that it is best understood as a paradoxical fusion of difference and continuity as well as manyness and oneness; that it is a reality that is inherently and inextricably temporal in nature.

Bergson's perspective in *Matter and Memory* also offers us an intriguing, and radically unique, way of understanding the complex interplay of body and mind, matter and consciousness. Our normal, commonsense understanding of how we come to know the objective world around us is that nonconscious physical stimuli from the external world impact our sense organs and these organs then send signals to our brain via the nervous system. Our brain, receiving these signals, promptly translates them into our conscious perceptions. This understanding of the process of perception leads us to assume that we are, in a sense, taking photographs of the universe, using our sense organs as the camera, and developing a picture of the external world by an elaborate chemical process in the brain. The problem with this commonsense understanding, however, is that there still remains a big chasm between the world of matter and consciousness itself. Our consciousness is nothing like a photograph; it is not an inert physical object like a piece of paper coated with chemicals. Our consciousness appears to operate in ways that are very different from how matter is typically understood to behave, so how can it be the product of purely physical interactions? Bergson's solution in *Matter and Memory* is ingenious, if perhaps difficult at first to grasp.

Bergson begins by positing a universe that is, below the level of appearances, a pulsating, interconnected field of "images." These images, according to Bergson, possess qualities that are similar to both matter and consciousness. Like matter (at least matter as it is currently understood by quantum mechanics), these images are dynamic patterns of energy, vortices of vibrations that radiate outward, contacting and affecting other complexly patterned vortices of energy. Bergson claims that in this universe of images, a transmission of energy/information takes place from image to image, moment to moment, automatically, fully, without hesitation. This measurable, predictable, lawful interaction between images is the basis for the stable, objective world of matter, a world rooted in the dependable, repeatable patterns of cause and effect studied by the natural sciences.

Understood in this way, the universe of images acts identically to the way matter is typically understood to behave (at least by physicists in the twenty-first century). However, the universe of images posited by Bergson is dissimilar to our typical understanding of matter in two ways. First, this universe of images is not inherently divided into a collection of separate objects possessing clear-cut boundaries. The world of separate objects that we normally perceive is not the true nature of matter. Instead, according to Bergson, the physical world, like our consciousness, is an interconnected, dynamic continuum of becoming, in which "numberless vibrations, all linked together in uninterrupted continuity" travel "in every direction like shivers through an immense body."[18]

The second way in which the universe of images posited by Bergson is different than our usual understanding of matter is that we normally think of matter (e.g., a stone) as inert, or non-aware. However, Bergson's universe of images is essentially a type of virtual consciousness. He would argue that consciousness, in a latent form, is already present in the universe of images. The job of the sense organs, nervous system, and the brain (which are themselves images) is not to *create* our conscious perceptions. Instead, perception occurs when our bodies (as well as the bodies of other organisms) receive the pulses of virtually conscious vibrations from the other images of the universe. From this infinitely complex, interpenetrating field of latent consciousness, we then select out and actualize only those pulsations of vibratory information that serve the needs of our particular organism, letting the rest of the information from the universe pass through unimpeded.

According to Bergson, our "pure perceptions" (i.e., the raw data of perception—perceptions minus most of the influence of memory) are a filtrate from the totality of the universal flux of potential consciousness in which we find ourselves. Our pure perceptions are, therefore, the result of a radical truncation, a culling process by which we ignore most of what we might potentially know. As a result, we perceive only the "external crust" or the "superficial skin" of what actually surrounds us (MM 36).

However, while our pure perceptions, in relation to the universe of images, are in this way simply a small part of the greater whole, Bergson claims that they are neither relative, nor illusory. While our pure perceptions may not reveal to us all that there is to know in the world around us, this "raw data" of perception is, nonetheless, not subjective. (As we will see below, the subjectivity of our concrete perceptions comes from the superimposition of memory onto our pure perceptions.) Our pure perceptions, according to Bergson, are not "in our heads"; they are not created by our brains. Instead, this raw data of our perceptions is a part and parcel of the world around us. When we see a tree, we are actually there with that tree as an objective reality in our pure perceptions. Bergson does not shy away from the implications of this unique epistemology. As he puts it, "we are really present in everything we perceive."[19] In reality, therefore, our body is not limited to the small physical organism we typically identify with (although that body always remains the vital center of our world). We also possess a massive body made up of the totality of our conscious perceptions, a body that, in a very real sense, "reaches to the stars" (TS 258).

However, while we might, unknown to us, be part of this huge, quasi-universal body, our smaller body, the "inner and central body" remains vitally important (TS 258). Without our physical body we would have no pure perceptions. Bergson stresses that our senses, nervous system, and brain do not somehow magically change inert material vibrations into consciousness. Instead, acting as a type of dynamic filter, they continually screen out the vast majority of the information we receive from the mass of potential consciousness that surrounds us in order that we might act effectively and flourish as a physical organism.

Bergson goes on to point out that it is crucial for our physical body to play this role. If we were to perceive, and consequently act upon, the world as it exists at its most basic, subatomic vibratory level, if, for example, we no longer saw an oak table as a solid structure of wood, but instead consciously perceived and responded to the flux of almost infinite energetic patterns that underlie the table, we would become incapacitated, lost in the "moving immensity" of what previously had been a motionless, rectangular solid object (CM 69). One of the most basic functions of our physicality is, therefore, to carve out manageable islands of stability in the onrush of universal becoming by choosing to focus only on that level of experience that best serves our needs. In essence, according to Bergson, we create our experience of the world moment by moment through the power of our choices. (Bergson argues that even if these choices happen so rapidly that it may appear that they take place automatically, they are nonetheless still choices, albeit choices that emerge from a subconscious dimension of our being—a dimension that while awash with an ever-changing flux of psychological, cultural, and even biological patterning, still maintains a literally unimaginable level of freedom and creativity).

As Bergson notes, there is a fascinating implication to the understanding that the world that we experience is shaped by the power of our choices. As he puts it,

> [N]othing would prevent other worlds, corresponding to another choice, from existing with [our world], in the same place and the same time: in this way twenty different broadcasting stations throw out simultaneously twenty

different concerts which coexist without any one of them mingling its sounds with the music of another, each one being heard, complete and alone, in the apparatus which has chosen for its reception the wave-length of that particular station. (CM 69–70)

Bergson's fascinating "radio reception" theory that countless different worlds might well concurrently coexist with our own, each of which can be accessed by a corresponding quality of perception, offers us an intriguing potential explanation of the genesis of various forms of paranormal experience. Perhaps the experiences that fill the pages of religious texts and ethnographies (e.g., telepathy, clairvoyance, mediumship, visionary encounters, and so on) are moments when, for a variety of reasons, individuals "change channels" and "tune into" dimensions of reality with which they are already connected subconsciously. Perhaps, as Bergson speculates, these types of experiences arise if and when the "mechanisms" that are "expressly designed to screen" the enormous flood of information we receive from the universe were to stop functioning effectively. If this were to happen, then the "door which they kept shut" would be partially opened, thereby letting in levels of information that would normally be excluded from our more mundane awareness (TS 315).

In many ways, it is understandable that someone who takes for granted a Cartesian separation of mind and matter, as well as a Newtonian fracturing of the universe into a multitude of solid objects "lawfully" interacting in space, would consider most, if not all, narratives of paranormal experiences to be evidence of irrationality, delusion, and/or pathology. However, a Bergsonian perspective offers us an alternative, and perhaps more nuanced, understanding of these phenomena. If Bergson is correct and, under the surface, we are continually connected with the entire universe, if the apparent clear-cut separation between objects is not ontologically real, but instead, is created by the filtering mechanisms of the brain as well as by unconscious deeply engrained patterns of memory and belief (more on this below) then perhaps different spiritual disciplines (e.g., chanting, fasting, meditation, dancing, ritualized ingestion of sacred plants, and so on) simply serve to open up the inner floodgates in a ritually controlled and culturally sanctioned fashion, allowing practitioners to more easily and effectively absorb and integrate the powerful information that is pouring into them from different currents of the pulsating ocean of the ever-changing images that make up the universe as we know it. A Bergsonian understanding of non-ordinary experiences, in fact, allows us to claim that many paranormal phenomena might well be manifestations of a more profound, more inclusive, quality of perception (or, at the very least, a level of perception that is an equally valid and valuable alternative to our more prosaic modes of experience).

However, it cannot be denied that, at least in certain instances, this opening of the inner floodgates might well produce disastrous consequences.

Although Bergson himself does not explicitly address this issue, I would postulate that many forms of mental illness, as well as various types of negative possession states, could well be the result, at least partially, of a premature or overly invasive influx of unwanted "energies" from various strata of the cosmic flux—"energies" that collide, in destructive ways, with a person's immature or distorted psychological structures. However, while a neo-Bergsonian standpoint might well determine that certain types of non-ordinary experiences are potentially destructive or debilitating, this perspective would at least not automatically assume that any and all paranormal experiences are inherently delusional (an assumption that in most cases arises from the tacit metaphysical belief that other dimensions of reality simply do not exist). Instead, this assessment, if it was made, would have to be the end result of applying a complex cluster of pragmatic criteria (e.g., is the person, on the whole, and over the long run, better or worse off as a result of this sort of inner opening?).[20]

When attempting to grasp Bergson's etiology of paranormal phenomena, it is crucial to remember that, for Bergson, while mind and matter may be distinct, they are not ontologically separate. Therefore, Bergson emphasizes that our minds, in a way that is far more pronounced than matter, overlap and interpenetrate each other—and in fact, transcend spatial boundaries altogether. (Bergson argues, quite explicitly, that because consciousness is not spatial in nature that it is incorrect to think that our memories and thoughts are confined within the physical structure of our brain.) This freedom from spatial limitations means that it is not at all clear where, for instance, my mind ends and yours begins (even the need to measure and determine such boundaries itself betrays a deeply rooted spatial orientation). Bergson suggests, therefore, that it is quite possible that our minds are continually blending and overlapping with other minds (perhaps even nonhuman minds) in a reciprocal flow of mental information below the surface of our awareness.

Bergson notes that "if such intercommunication exists, nature will have taken precautions to render it harmless, and most likely certain mechanisms are specially charged with the duty of throwing back, into the unconscious, images so introduced" (ME 97). However, Bergson goes on to suggest that it is possible that certain thoughts, memories, images, or feelings from other minds might occasionally manage, for various reasons, to slip past this mechanism. Extending and applying this Bergsonian insight, I would argue that, if a person consciously nurtures the capacity to open her or himself up to an influx of "spiritual" information emerging from more refined and positive dimensions of nonphysical reality, then this type of mental interpenetration might well be, for instance, another, equally viable, way to understand what is taking place during episodes of telepathic and clairvoyant knowledge, visionary experiences, channeled messages from different spiritual beings, mystical revelations, and so on. (However, it must also be mentioned that if these psychic incursions come unbidden, and if they emerge from denser and more destructive levels of nonphysical reality, and if these psychic energies attack a person who is physically weakened and/or psychologically damaged or traumatized, then this type of invasive psychic infusion might well be one source of the obsessive, persecutory, fearful, and/or hostile thoughts and perceptions that characterize various forms of mental illness and/or negative possession states.)

It is not only the more "spectacular" forms of paranormal experience that can be explained by Bergson's claim that occasionally some of the images (whether "physical" or "mental") that continually flow in and through us manage to slip past our subconscious filters. This theoretical perspective can also account for a variety of seemingly more prosaic levels of intuitive awareness as well, modes of experience that frequently occur within many of us, but which we often choose to ignore or deny. For instance, perhaps our perception that someone is sexually attracted to us is not simply based on subtle bodily cues. Perhaps the sense of danger or wrongness that we pick up from someone is not irrational. Perhaps during those trance-like moments when we are composing a song, or painting a picture, or playing the piano, or writing a story and it seems as if "something or someone else" is working in and through us—perhaps that feeling we have is correct. Perhaps our empathetic feeling of connection with our pets or even wild animals is not a subjective anthropomorphic projection unto another species. Perhaps the subtle awareness of a dearly loved, but deceased, relative watching over and protecting and guiding us is not simply a wish fulfillment rooted in unresolved grief. Perhaps all of these phenomena, instead, are rooted in something real, in the flow of subliminal information that we constantly receive from the wild and mysterious universe that surrounds and interpenetrates us, but which we, for a variety of evolutionary and psychological reasons, typically ignore or choose not to see.

MEMORY AND PERCEPTION

In order to fully understand Bergson's theory of the interaction between matter and consciousness (and its importance for a participatory spirituality), it is crucial to comprehend the role played by memory. Bergson stresses that our concrete, day-to-day experience is not primarily rooted in our pure perceptions. While this aspect of our experience does indeed serve as a type of a nonpersonal, objective touchstone, our pure perceptions by themselves are rather thin—they offer simply a type of schematic outline, or sketch, which in order to be effective, needs to be filled in with a wide range of memories. These memories, according to Bergson, are for the most part not specific memory images of past events (i.e., memory as we normally understand it), but rather are a fluid fund of preconscious, highly distilled, and compressed past experiences, as well as internalizations of cultural and psychological patterns of belief. It is this type of memory, operating beneath the surface of our consciousness, that merges with the raw data of our pure perceptions, and by doing so, shapes these perceptions, giving them order, structure, and meaning. In fact, according to Bergson, this interpretive overlay from memory is so extensive that we end up "constantly creating or reconstructing" our present experience based on the sum total of our past (MM 103).

Bergson's understanding of memory is highly complex and can be difficult to comprehend. There are multiple levels of memory for Bergson—and many of these levels often barely resemble memory as most people typically understand the term. The most fundamental level of memory that Bergson describes is simply the continuity of our consciousness; it is the automatic and ongoing connection of our past to the present. Bergson suggests that this most basic modality of memory, in which the past is automatically carried into the present, is present even at the vibratory level of matter itself. These vibrations are not, according to Bergson, flashes of inert, utterly predetermined energy taking place in a discrete, ceaselessly repeated present. Instead, these vibrations are, even at the atomic and molecular level, bound together by an impersonal substratum of memory, a type of proto-consciousness; they are simply a different degree or "frequency" of *durée*—the duration of matter. It is this type of memory that, according to Bergson, ties together the enormous quantity and range of the vibrations of matter and condenses them into the perceived moments of our consciousness. (For example, drawing upon information from the science of his time, Bergson explains that, if we perceive a pulse of red light for a single second, during that time our consciousness has condensed four hundred billion vibrations of that frequency of light.)

According to Bergson, the universe as a whole consists of a wide spectrum of different levels of *durée*, ranging from the quasi-necessity of the *durée* of matter, through the largely instinctive *durée* of various rudimentary organisms, up to the highly conscious and flexible (if at times habitual) *durée* of human consciousness. Bergson even speculates that it is possible, and is indeed likely, that there exists another level of *durée* (of consciousness) with a "higher degree" of "tension" (or perhaps "attention"?) than our own—a "godlike" level (or levels?) of consciousness that might well be able to condense the entire history of humanity into a very short period of its own duration in the same way that we condense the "history" of the vibrations of matter into the ongoing flux of the perceptions of our conscious experience in any moment (MM 207).

Bergson's description of memory is, however, not always quite so speculative and cosmic in scope. Other levels of memory are also operative within us either in the form of specific recollections of past events (e.g., remembering one's first time riding a bicycle) or in the form of impersonal, bodily-based distillations of past events (e.g., the set of internalized motor skills it takes to ride a bicycle well). According to Bergson, these forms of memory (the vast majority of which operate below the surface of our conscious awareness) are critical to understanding our moment-to-moment experience of life. It is the layering and condensation of these (primarily subconscious) memories that help to create the fullness of our concrete, lived experience by interweaving themselves into each "pure perception" so seamlessly that "we are no longer able to discern what is perception and what is memory" (MM 103). For Bergson, therefore, every moment of our experience is a fusion of perception and memory. Indeed, as he notes, it is only because memory is added to perception that the objective, externalized moments of pure perception (which actually take place "outside of us," among the objects themselves) are converted into experiences that seem to be subjective and internal; that is, it is memory that makes it appear that our experience takes place "inside our heads."

Bergson's emphasis that our ongoing flux of experience is the result of a fusion of pure perceptions and memory might well provide several important contributions to our attempts to articulate the primary features of a participatory spirituality. For example, the dynamic interaction between perception and memory suggests that, up to a point, we are indeed cocreators of our experience of the universe. While Bergson emphasizes our pure perceptions reveal that there are certain tendencies or directions that the material universe insists on taking (regardless of whether we like this stubborn facticity or not), this givenness of the universe does not imply that we, therefore, are simply passive spectators. Instead, in ways that most of us fail to recognize, our memories help us to actively mold the raw data that we receive from the universe into the shapes and forms that we preconsciously or subconsciously expect to see. Therefore, from a Bergsonian perspective, while we all inhabit the *same* universe (even if that universe, ironically, never remains the same), it is safe to say that each of us experiences a very *different* universe—a universe that is (to a degree that is difficult to ascertain) partially shaped by the utterly unique and constantly changing lens of how we *interpret* our world—a lens that comes to us via the "assistance" of our fund of memories.

It is important to stress that how we interpret our world is, itself, partially shaped by the internalization of our psychological background, our physical characteristics, our cultural matrix, our economic status, and so on—that is, by the vast and constantly changing, fund of memories that we each draw upon, below the surface, moment by moment, to shape our experience. However, it is equally crucial to recognize that memory, for Bergson, is a highly refined form of *durée*. As such, Bergson understands memories in a very different way than how they are typically understood. For Bergson, memories are not frozen snapshots of the past tucked away in some cerebral storage chamber. Instead, our memories are interpenetrating fields of consciousness that are inherently creative, fields that while distinct are not separate from one another, fields that can and do combine in unique and unpredictable ways (with varying amounts of freedom) to help create our moment-to-moment experience (including our religious/spiritual experiences). Our memories, as forms of *durée*, are not a coercive, inherited force within us that determines, inexorably, who we are, what we believe, and how we will behave. While we all, arguably, possess numerous deeply embedded, and difficult to change, layers of memory/beliefs within us, there is still hope. Because memory (as opposed to matter) is a deeply "spiritual" form of *durée*, it/we always have a surprising and unpredictable degree of freedom to create new possibilities, new visions, new expectations—that is, to create new worlds of experience for us to inhabit.

However, Bergson never goes so far as to claim that we have some god-like ability to shape our experience of the universe into *whatever* form we choose. While we do possess enormous creative freedom as to how we choose to interpret and understand ourselves and our experience, at certain hard-to-predict points the universe has a very real way of "talking back" to us, of saying—"Yes, you can stretch me this far, but that's just about as far as I can go." Bergson never claims that the universe is utterly plastic and responsive to our internalized beliefs and unconscious thought patterns. We cannot, and will not, experience whatever universe we please. Instead, he maintains that there is a type of "organic organization" in the universe. The universe in-and-through its ceaseless dynamic flux assumes highly specific forms, sounds, smells, and textures. As such, the universe (and our experience of it) is not utterly relative, utterly subjective, but instead, has a level of givenness that cannot, and should not, be ignored.

One final caveat: I would suggest that we may not, in reality, be as limited as we believe in our ability to modify our experience of the world by changing our deeply engrained unconscious belief systems. In fact, I would argue that changing these deeply held unconscious beliefs may even result in our ability to modify the world itself. An orthodox scientific worldview would argue that what happens in the universe is clear cut, that it is determined with mathematical, lawful, and objective certainty, and is utterly unaffected by the subjective beliefs or opinions of anyone. But this claim depends upon a set of metaphysical presuppositions that is radically challenged and undercut by Bergson. Bergson's own "dynamic non-dualism" can go a long way in making sense of a variety of claims frequently made throughout history by a wide variety of religious traditions—that is, claims that mystics and saints possess various "supernatural" abilities, that faith healing is real, that clairvoyant perception is possible, and so on.

SPLITTING UP THE WORLD

In *Matter and Memory*, Bergson encourages us to start to imagine a world in which *durée* is, in Deleuze's words, "the variable essence of things," a world in which the fluidity, mutability, interpenetrability, and creativity of *durée* is found in the world of material objects as well, a world that is less as a collection of static, discrete objects exchanging places in an immutable empty space and more a world in which functional islands of semistability arise out of a highly mutable flux of becoming.[21]

From Bergson's post–*Time and Free Will* perspective, the external world, if understood correctly, is not split up into parts. Rather, in a way that is similar to our consciousness, the material universe is actually an interconnected, flowing, ever-changing, dynamic process. In both our inner and outer worlds, therefore, nothing is static, nothing is immutable. Instead, as Bergson succinctly states, "movement is reality itself" (CM 169).

Bergson points out, however, that as a species we seem to have a deep-seated need to freeze the flux of the world, to create a static tableau in which we, as unchanging subjects, interact with unchanging objects. For practical purposes, it does indeed make sense to believe that we are relatively solid and stable and that we interact with an equally solid, stable world. From the perspective of our day-to-day experience, it seems almost impossible to give anything more than a token nod to Bergson's claim that "there do not exist *things* made, but only things in the making, not *states* that remain fixed, but only states in the process of change" (CM 222). We can be as Bergsonian (or for that matter as Taoist or Buddhist) as we like philosophically, but in our day-to-day experience we certainly do not act as if "things" do not exist. It seems obvious to us that we are surrounded by physical objects with clear-cut boundaries, objects that exist side by side, objects that are separated from one another in space. We all move through the world secure in our tacit conviction that these physical objects (e.g., plates, knives, and spoons) basically remain the same over time (i.e., the silverware may need to be polished, but it remains silverware). Our practical lives, our moment-to-moment activity, indicate that we believe deeply in the reality of separate objects and things.

According to Bergson, however, these "things" only have a functional, not ontological, reality. Underneath it all, existence is a fluid continuity. However, as was pointed out above, human beings seem to have great difficulty tolerating and even surviving in that degree of dynamism and interconnection. We have a deeply rooted biological and psychological need to break the ever-changing wholeness of existence into discrete, apparently static elements (e.g., words and objects) that interact with each other. Our everyday awareness has been systemically distorted by our utilitarian needs and physical desires; any attempt to perceive the world differently goes against millennia of evolutionarily useful tendencies. Even though it may be true that underneath it all both our consciousness and the external world are in actuality an ongoing, interconnected, ceaseless flux (that is to say, they both manifest the qualities of *durée*), this continuity and mutability is hidden from us because of our need to live in a world filled with relatively stable, seemingly separate, objects. Our ordinary lived experience, therefore, while practically useful, is nonetheless philosophically deceptive.

MELODIES OF THE UNIVERSE

One helpful way to penetrate past the perceptual distortions created by our need to live in a world of separate self-contained objects is to "picture" (or, better yet, "hear") the world through one of Bergson's favorite metaphors: a complex, interwoven melody.

Many of us might tend to think of a melody as simply a "juxtaposition of distinct notes"; we, in essence, "listen to the melody through the vision which an orchestra leader would have of it as he watched its score. We picture notes placed next to one another upon an imaginary piece of paper" (CM 174). But if we let go of these spatial and visual images, what do we perceive? If we make the effort, if we listen carefully, it is possible to hear a series of overlapping sounds in which each pulsation is qualitatively unique, and yet is also intrinsically connected to the other pulsations of sound; sounds that have no definite and fixed spatial location; sounds that are both outside and inside us, simultaneously; sounds that have no clear-cut boundaries; sounds that are a continuous, interconnected, yet ever-changing, whole. (Asking "where" the notes of a melody actually *are* can be an illuminating exercise in futility; unlike visually perceived objects in space, sonic realities seem to be nowhere and everywhere. During their time of sounding, are the tones that we hear "in" the body of the instruments or "in" the singer's voice? Are they "in" the air? Are they "in" our ears? Are they all of the above?)

Understanding the world through the metaphor of music also underscores the fact that all of reality (both inner and outer) is intrinsically temporal. A melody cannot, by its very nature, exist without time. A melody cannot just manifest itself in an instant, utterly complete and whole. Instead, it unfolds and appears over time, note by note, phrase by phrase. Listening to a melody takes time, and it has to be experienced *in* time as an organic unity in order for it to be what it is. If it were split into separate, disconnected parts, it would not be the same melody—a melody cannot be reduced to a collection of individual isolated notes. Listening to a melody, each note blends into others—the previous notes linger in our memory to produce a seamless flow of sound—and yet a melody has to change; in fact, it is made of changes, it is, from one perspective, on ongoing flux of continual novelty and diversity.

Imagining the universe as a vast, ongoing musical creation can also help to free us from the tyranny of an Aristotelian "either/or" logic that, either implicitly or explicitly, pressures us to think that oneness cannot coexist with manyness, that change cannot coexist with continuity. "Hearing" the world through the metaphor of music and melody, it becomes easier to grasp how the world might well be such that individuality (whether in persons, things, or events) can and does coexist with some sort of underlying, even if hidden, connection and continuity. For instance, while it is tempting to think of a melody as an aggregate of separate, clearly delineated tones, if we look (or rather, listen) more carefully, what we discover is that each individual tone, while it maintains its uniqueness and distinctness, is not abruptly cut off from the other tones. Instead, each tone, during the time while it physically sounds, infuses and overlaps with the other tones that are concurrently sounding. Furthermore, even after each tone has physically faded, it continues to linger in memory, it continues to persist in the mind—in fact, it is this very persistence in the memory that creates a melodic phrase.[22] Melody, in order to be melody, needs both—the individuality and distinctiveness of particular notes *and* the ongoing continuity and interconnectedness of many notes brought together in the memory. In much the same way as our consciousness is a dynamic continuity of utter diversity, melody is an inseparable fusion of individual tones and the organic, ongoing, gestalt created by memory.

As Capek points out, the metaphor of melody becomes even more intriguing if we cease to think of melody as simply a single melodic phrase and, instead, begin to envision a multileveled polyphonic (and/or polyrhythmic) musical piece in which several relatively independent melodic movements unfold both successively and alongside each other. (Significantly, it does not matter whether the interaction between the movements creates a harmony or dissonance.)[23] For example, let's imagine a piece of music in which a saxophone has one melodic movement, a bass has another, the guitar a third, and we can even add the drums as fourth melodic/rhythmic movement. Even if these various instruments are playing simultaneously, each melodic/rhythmic movement is relatively independent, in that each proceeds "parallel" to the other melodic/rhythmic movements (i.e., the guitar, the sax, the bass, and the drum each have their own parts, even while they are playing together). If we are trained listeners, it is possible to hear each movement separately and distinctly. Yet, at the same time, it is also possible to hear the more inclusive overall musical creation. With this quality of hearing, each movement is enriched and gains a greater significance through its interaction with the other melodic/rhythmic movements. Together, they create a more complex, interesting, dynamic whole, a whole that is composed of relatively independent melodic/rhythmic movements that are organically interconnected and held together in memory. In this world of "co-becoming" or "co-fluidity," ceaseless change and seamless continuity coexist, and sheer diversity lives happily with stable ongoing presence.

In much the same way, perhaps we can imagine a world in which each being or entity (e.g., rabbits, clouds, rivers, spiders, wheat) has its own unique, ever-changing "melody" (or vibratory expression) through time, while simultaneously we could also recognize that each being is not utterly separate, utterly cut off from the other beings. Instead, perhaps we could train ourselves to realize the numerous ways in which each of these various "songs of being" overlaps, interpenetrates, and effects each of the other "songs," creating an almost unimaginably complex, dynamic intermingling of beings within the matrix of a more expansive wholeness.

To fully appreciate Bergson's musical understanding of the cosmos, it is critical that we let go of any latent, quasi-Platonic presupposition that the universe is the rigorously determined instantiation of mathematically precise natural laws (i.e., the "musical score" of nature). Instead, we need to re-vision (or re-hear) the cosmos as a living, unpredictable, ongoing movement of unique and spontaneously improvised vibratory qualities. The improvisational nature of the universe is perhaps most easily grasped if we can let go of a "classical" music metaphor and, instead, begin to think in terms of jazz. A group of polished jazz musicians who have been playing together for a long time will almost never follow, note for note, a predetermined musical score. Instead, as a highly cohesive, interactive group of skilled performers who have learned certain sets of musical skills and who have at their disposal an ever-changing collection of musical patterns, they can create, spontaneously, a new musical experience each time that they play together. Their music isn't utter chaos, nor is it programmed and formulaic. Instead, it is the unplanned, unpredictable, result of listening and responding to each other, as well as listening and responding to their own intuitive musical sense of what is speaking to them in the moment. As such, while there are certain regularities and patterned behavior to be found in jazz music, it is also something that is genuinely new, something that emerges organically from the complex, relational, interconnected interactions of a group of skilled performers, each playing off of the others and yet each also taking the risk to venture into uncharted territory in the service of melodic/rhythmic visions of where the music needs to go.

In a similar way, instead of envisioning the universe as the rigorously formulaic manifestation of some Pythagorean regularity, as the terrestrial echo of the "music of the spheres" obeying the preset "score" given by the Laws of Nature, it might worthwhile to think of all of reality (both inner and outer) as an unimaginably complex jazz performance, in which old standards are frequently performed (making them the "habits" rather than the "laws" of nature), even if, periodically and regularly, something unexpected also occurs, something genuinely new and creative takes place as the result of different individuals and groups responding to and interacting with each other. This jazz-inspired metaphorical way of understanding reality works best if (and here is where the metaphor, like all metaphors, stretches and perhaps breaks) we can imagine that the music is not the end result of a stable group of performers, but rather plays itself—as if the various clusters of melodic movements were each conscious of themselves and the other musical patterns.

"Hearing" the universe as a complex, partially improvised, musical performance helps to underscore the Bergsonian insistence that movement and change itself is what is primary, not stable things or objects that change. In such a world (our world), each note, while having its own inherent integrity, individuality, and uniqueness, also resonates outward, overlapping with and affecting (and being affected by) all of the other notes in the cosmos—creating, therefore, countless overtones and harmonics simply as the result of this interaction. In such a world, certain musical patterns might repeat themselves, again and again, with almost utter regularity (i.e., the "notes" of matter), but other clusters of musical movements would be much more "alive" and would emerge and develop and evolve in and of themselves—creating/composing new and unpredictable musical modes of existence.

In such a world, the decision to "listen" and respond deeply to this ongoing "musical" creation (instead of taking it for granted as some sort of background drone) would itself be a creative act; it would be an opportunity to add our own "song" into the improvisational interplay taking place moment by moment. Any deep immersion into the pulsation of what is occurring in the flux of the moment (e.g., "losing yourself" in music, art, sports, or lovemaking) can often, not surprisingly, become an occasion to experience an upwelling of awe and wonder at the strikingly beautiful patterns that emerge, seemingly effortlessly, one moment to the next. Such moments, when our own previously solid and fixed boundaries become increasingly porous, and our own creative expression becomes freely harmonized and interfused with the countless other songs of life that surround and interpenetrate our own, can also be extremely joyous; they can become moments of true "ecstasy," that is, moments when our previously stable sense of place ("stasis") expands beyond itself ("ec"), and we can experience the inherently limitless and dynamic freedom of our true nature.

A FLOWING IDENTITY

Thinking of reality as a vast, partially improvised, ongoing musical performance also offers a potentially helpful new way to envision the nature of personal identity. As numerous philosophers and psychologists have repeatedly emphasized, it is not at all clear how a person constructs and maintains a stable sense of identity. Given the countless changes that each of us goes through over time, it is almost mystifying why we should feel any solid sense of inner sameness and psychic solidity. On a physical level, our blood constantly flows, our cells never stop metabolizing, and our breath continually comes in and goes out. On a molecular and subatomic level, we are a blur of dynamic movement. Mentally and emotionally, numerous thoughts and feelings ceaselessly arise and subside. The question therefore is: Where are "we" in all of this activity?

Numerous attempts have been made to solve the dilemma of our personal identity, attempts that are, as Eric Matthews points out, typically variations on two themes: (1) essentialism, the conviction that, underneath it all, there is some unchanged essence or core of individual personhood; or (2) convention-alism, the understanding that there really is no inherent personhood to be found and that what we call personal identity is simply a conventional, practical fic-tion created out of cultural and psychological necessity. However, as Matthews goes on to note, "Bergson's view of a person as unified, not by a continuing essence, but by a developing life-*history* seems . . . to offer the possibility" of a viable third alternative, "a view of personal identity which could accommodate the changeability . . . while retaining the idea, so important to us morally and emotionally, that a person remains the same throughout his or her life."[24]

I would argue that Matthews is correct. From a Bergsonian perspective, our experience (of both our "inner" and "outer" world) is characterized by *both* ceaseless change *and* inner continuity. Both aspects of reality need to be acknowledged. The flowing or the passage of life contains within itself both sheer diversity and seamless unity. Our own unique flowings or passages are, in this way, as Bergson stresses, "sufficient in themselves, the flowing not implying a thing which flows and the passage not presupposing any states by which one passes: the *thing* and the *state* are simply snapshots artificially taken of the transition; and this transition, alone experienced naturally, is durée itself" (M 98). What is real is the continual, ongoing flux of *durée*; what is not is our desperate attempt to separate ourselves out from the ceaseless temporal dynamism of life in a futile attempt create an unchanging ego (us) interacting with other separate and equally unchanging egos (them).

From a Bergsonian perspective, if we cease thinking of ourselves as an unchanging "nugget-like" essence that undergoes change on the surface, while underneath remaining the same, if we focus instead on the reality of ceaseless change, then we are not necessarily forced to deny any and all indi-viduality. We can, instead, realize that just as a melody is a combination of both continual change and uninterrupted continuity over time, in the same way, our individuality is, to a certain extent, the ever-changing end result of all of the countless life experiences we have had, held together and unified into a single stream of experience in our memory.

This way of understanding ourselves allows us to acknowledge the very real fact that who we are, on every level, is constantly changing, while also underscoring the equally real fact that we experience an inner continuity and unified identity to our selfhood. With this mode of self-understanding, we can affirm that we are indeed shaped, moment by moment, by each experi-ence we have—by our upbringing, our schooling, our friends, our enemies, our cultural heritage, our economic status, our religious affiliations, and so on. The song of our being is continually changing, moment to moment, as it is (at least partially) formed by the ongoing experiences that enter into our awareness (including, importantly, our mystical and religious experiences). Nonetheless, this vision of selfhood also permits us to maintain that the melodic stream of our identity is not reducible to, or the inevitable and predictable result of, all of our life experiences. Instead, the song of our being (and again, this is where the metaphor stretches to a breaking point) is itself conscious, and as such, responds to and interacts with these various experiences in unique and idiosyncratic ways. It chooses which experiences to highlight and which to mute, and it overlays and infuses each experience with various interpretative frameworks that are themselves continually re-forming in creative, unexpected ways in the hidden recesses of our memory. (As we saw above, for Bergson, our memory is neither a passive receptacle, nor an utterly neutral mechanical "video camera" that simply records what happens. Instead, our memory possesses as a manifestation of consciousness an intrinsic and genuine freedom, a freedom that allows us to take our lives in unanticipated directions in response to the promptings it is constantly receiving from the other melodic movements that surround it.)

What is crucial to emphasize is that our identity, understood in this way, is not only constantly in flux, but it is also intrinsically interactive. Who we are can be found, if anywhere, in the in-between-ness of the ongoing relations that take place between us and the various, equally constantly changing melodies of experience that surround and interpenetrate us. This in-between-ness means that what is outer and what is inner, where "we" begin and end and where the "world" (including the spiritual world) begins and ends is extremely difficult, if not impossible, to discern. And yet, amazingly, we typically act as if we (and everyone else) are solid, bounded, essentially unchanging beings, even while inhabiting a world that is characterized by perpetual flux.

Bergson offers a vivid analogy that can help make sense of how, in all of this constant dynamism, we could ever think that we (and those around us) remain comfortably stable, solid, and clearly delimited. (Bergson's analogy is, by the way, strikingly reminiscent of examples offered by Einstein to help explain certain aspects of relativity theory.) Bergson asks us to imagine two trains moving "at the same speed, in the same direction, on parallel tracks" (CM 169). Seated in each of these two trains, it might well appear, from the perspective of the travelers, that the trains themselves are not moving. In fact, if they wished, travelers on the trains could "hold out their hands to one another through the door and talk to one another" with ease, even if the trains were moving at a high rate of speed (CM 169). Similarly, while all of life may well be in a constant state of motion, nonetheless, when my stream of experience matches the vibratory quality of other streams of experience (including, I would argue, numerous other nonphysical streams of experience—e.g., those beings that go by the name of "ancestors" or "angels" or "spirits" or "gods" or "bodhisattvas"), that is, when my movement or my pattern of energy is in harmony with other similarly vibrating fields, then it may well appear, for all practical purposes, that a stable "subject" is interacting with other equally stable "subjects" or "objects." Nevertheless, while we seem to need to "freeze frame" the living flux of reality in order to exist, by doing so we typically tend to forget that the world is not, in reality, chopped up into a multitude of separate, clear-cut objects. We forget that, underneath it all, fixed immutable boundaries do not exist, and that even if our selfhood does possess a very genuine and important type of cohesiveness and integrity, it also at each moment emerges organically out of its interaction with other resonate modes of existence—modes of existence that themselves are simply complex patterns of ceaseless change, are themselves simply overlapping and interpenetrating melodies of a single cosmic Song.

THE "BOTH/AND" PERSPECTIVE OF BERGSON

The more that I immerse myself in Bergson's musical metaphor of *durée* (and hence, of the cosmos itself), the more that I am impressed with its potential to address some of the major issues raised by a participatory vision of spirituality.

The "both/and" understanding of the self and reality that Bergson advocates can provide a coherent, persuasive vision of a world in which everything and everyone is understood to possess individual integrity, a world in which particularity, difference, uniqueness, and pluralism are central and deeply valued, while it simultaneously affirms that an underlying continuity, interconnection, and unity also exist and are equally crucial. This vision holds that our typical understanding of ourselves (and others) as self-contained, atomistic egos, is both distorted and destructive, leading to self-centered, isolated, narcissistic defensiveness. However, Bergson's vision, simultaneously, challenges the value and validity of a worldview that affirms a static, undifferentiated, monistic, "block" universe—a world in which plurality is denied and which seeks to absorb all differences into an unending Sameness. In a Bergsonian vision, the world and the self (as well as, conceivably, countless other complex and interpenetrating "higher" or "deeper" dimensions of consciousness, i.e., *durée*) are both the same and different, both distinct and united, both many and one.

Such a neo-Bergsonian vision of a participatory spirituality argues that all religious and mystical experiences vary from person to person, and from moment to moment, because nothing is static—especially the deeper, more inclusive, more "spiritual," levels of *durée* that constitute the various dimensions of reality.[25] Each religious and/or mystical experience, according to this perspective, inevitably takes on a unique culturally and psychologically appropriate shape, since it would be formed by the ever-changing pulsations of *durée* that come together (often in subconscious levels of our being) to create our quotidian awareness interacting with the ever-changing pulsations of *durée* that constitute the deeper levels of reality. The differences from one mystical experience to the next are therefore understood as coming from both "direc-tions": either these differences emerge because different strata of the deeper vibratory fields of reality were contacted, or because there were alternations in the vibratory fields that constitute our individual sense of ourselves, or more likely, because both of these alternations took place simultaneously. (In addi-tion, and importantly, in this interactive understanding of the etiology of reli-gious and mystical experiences, it is not always exactly clear where the deeper strata of the self ended and where the other vibratory fields began.)

This vision of the self/reality therefore celebrates the vast multitude of mystical and visionary experiences found in different religious traditions: becoming lost in the nondualistic flashes of *satori*; perceiving the radiant manifestations of Christian and Islamic angels; experiencing the gracious presence of the celestial bodhisattvas of Mahayana Buddhism; hearing the sacred words of the spirits and ancestors of tribal peoples; or having the benef-icent visitation of the Taoist and Hindu gods. Each of these spiritual experi-ences has a legitimate and understandable place within such a worldview.

However, this model of the self and reality also insists that while important, practical, and fascinating differences can be observed from one religious tradi-tion to the next, from one religious person to the next, and from one religious experience to the next, these traditions, people, and experiences are not her-metically sealed off from one another, but rather, overlap and interact with one another. According to this model of the self and reality, there is no such thing as a purely "Hindu" mystical experience or a purely "Jewish" mystical experi-ence. From this perspective, personal and cultural identity are not understood as any sort of static, indivisible essence, but rather, are seen as relatively stable, yet complex, clusters of dynamically interrelated experiences that are open to, and affected by, other clusters of experiences (leading, therefore, to a very deep appreciation of, and respect for, various syncretistic forms of religious life).

As scholars of religious and mystical experience, if we accept this neo-Bergsonian vision, we are asked to take on an exceedingly difficult task: not only do we have to describe and assess the numerous vortices of influences that present within each mystical experience (whether psychological, physi-ological, historical, cultural, linguistic, or economic), we also have to remain open to the very real likelihood that each mystical experience is shaped, in ways that we may never be able to determine, by a wide variety of transcul-tural and transnatural influences as well. This neo-Bergsonian model of the self and reality, therefore, is receptive to, and even encourages, a wide variety of theoretical approaches to mystical experiences, respecting and valuing the countless different ways in which we each choose to explore the unseen worlds that surround and interpenetrate our being.

Furthermore, Bergson's discussion of our human tendency to fear and resist change and our natural inclination to split the world up into fractured, isolated parts that we attempt to manage and control can also give us much-needed insight into some of the central, albeit hidden, causes of many of our most troubling social and psychological problems. For instance (to give only some of the more egregious examples), various forms of religious fanaticism and our troubling historical attraction to totalitarian modes of government clearly have a strong connection to our desire to keep our world the same, to our problematic need to have black and white answers to moral dilemmas, to our intolerance for murky ambiguities, to our yearning for a world in which everything has its systematic, rigidly ordered proper place. Similarly, on a more prosaic level, surely it is not accidental that so many of us work in hermetically sealed offices filled with tidy cubicles, that we design schools with desks bolted to the floor in straight rows, and that we build subdivisions of cookie-cutter houses, carefully separated and isolated from each other by high hedges and manicured lawns. Arguably, all of this behavior (among many more possible examples) is at least in part a sociological/psychological reflection of a visceral, almost instinctual, desire, either to deny or to suppress the ceaseless change that, according to Bergson, characterizes all of life, and/or a reflection of our seemingly insatiable drive to split a flowing, interconnected world into a manageable set of stable, ordered objects.

Obviously, not all habitual behavior is undesirable. Not all need for order is neurotic and destructive. Not all certainty is unwanted. Some momentary places of stability in the flux are not only helpful, but also seem to be congruent with, or reflective of, the dynamic interplay between fluidity and structure that appears to make up the nature of our consciousness and physical reality. Repetition and routine appear to be needed, at least to a certain extent, as long as they do not become too engrained. The desire for clear-cut answers seems to have an important purpose, as long as it does not calcify into a rigid oppositional world of right versus wrong, saved versus damned, us versus them.

Seen from a Bergsonian perspective, it makes perfect sense that, as human beings, we are continually struggling with ways to find some sort of workable middle ground between dogmatic, narrow-minded, self-righteous certainty and a paralyzing, indecisive openness to all perspectives, between atomistic, walled off, fearful isolation from others and a porous, boundaryless dependence upon and merger with others. It makes sense that, as human beings, we need to find some way to simultaneously cultivate creativity, uniqueness, and individuality while also nurturing tradition, heritage, and communal solidarity. From a Bergsonian perspective, it is completely understandable that we would simultaneously be attracted to and disturbed by moments in which we lose our normal sense of ego boundaries (e.g., moments of sexual ecstasy or religious fervor) or that we would work hard to keep our world and our loved ones comfortably regular and secure, becoming anxious (or angry) if they change too quickly or intensely, even while we might also feel trapped or bored if they (and we) remain predictably the same. What is so attractive about a Bergsonian perspective is that it acknowledges and affirms what we already know, but often refuse to acknowledge: that life is rarely black and white, rarely either/or, but instead is a bewildering, frightening, exhilarating, confusing, ever-changing conflux of difference and sameness, oneness and manyness, structure and fluidity. Bergson's philosophy does not offer us any easy answers, but it does offer us at least the hope that we do indeed live in a world that, underneath it all and in a way that we might never fully grasp, makes sense.

NOTES

1. Recent texts on Bergson's work that, to a greater or lesser extent, are influenced by, or responding to, the poststructuralist perspective of Deleuze are: John Mullarkey, *Bergson and Philosophy* (Notre Dame: University of Notre Dame Press, 2000); Keith Ansell Pearson, *Philosophy and the Adventure of the Virtual* (New York: Routledge, 2002); Leonard Lawlor, *The Challenge of Bergsonism* (New York: Continuum, 2003); Elizabeth Grosz, *The Nick of Time* (Durham: Duke University Press, 2004); Suzanne Guerlac, *Thinking in Time* (Ithaca: Cornell University Press, 2006).

2. Milic Capek comes right to the point when he writes: "Without exaggeration, there is hardly anything less immediate, less given, than Bergson's 'immediate data'" (*Bergson and Modern Physics* [Dordrecht, Holland: D. Reidel Publishing Company, 1971], 86).

3. Bergson, *Mélanges* (Paris: Presses Universitaires de France, 1972), 1148. Hereafter cited in the text as (M).

4. Bergson, *The Creative Mind* (New York: Philosophical Library, 1946), 193. Hereafter cited in the text as (CM).

5. Alexander, *Bergson: Philosopher of Reflection* (London: Bowes and Bowes, 1957), 11.

6. Ibid., 22.

7. Bergson, *Time and Free Will* (Mo.: Kessinger Publishing Company, no date given), 101. Hereafter cited in the text as (TFW).

8. Interestingly, in a note in the Introduction of *Creative Mind*, Bergson points out that this analogy (i.e., how the illusion of movement is created on a movie screen by lining up a series of snapshots very close together) is dependent upon an underlying movement in order to create this illusion: "What the cinematograph [movie projector] shows us in movement on the screen is the series of immobile views of the film; it is, of course, understood that what is projected on this screen, over and above these immobile views themselves, is the movement within the projector" (CM 301, note 1).

9. Capek, *Bergson and Modern Physics*, 90.

10. Solomon, *Bergson* (Port Washington, NY: Kennikat Press, 1912), 38.

11. Bergson, *Creative Evolution* (Lantham, MD: University Press of America, 1983), 6. Hereafter cited in the text as (CE).

12. Bergson, "Introduction à la conférence du Pasteur Holland," in *Écrits et Paroles*, II (Paris: Librairie Félix Alcan, 1934), 359. Quoted in Idella J. Gallagher, *Morality in Evolution* (The Hague: Martinus Nijhoff, 1970), 32.

13. Bergson, *Mind-Energy* (New York: Henry Holt, 1920), 39. Hereafter cited in the text as (ME).

14. In later works such as *Creative Evolution*, Bergson does not just limit mind/spirit/consciousness to human beings. Instead, he postulates a vast, universal, spectrum of opposing tendencies—life versus matter, freedom versus determinism, and so on.

15. Luce, *Bergson's Doctrine of Evolution* (New York: Macmillan, 1922), 57.

16. Garrett Barden comments that when we come to realize the creativity of the self, we discover that what lies in the future is not "what is already implied in present knowledge but the invention of the radically new" ("Method in Philosophy," in *The New Bergson*, ed. John Mullarkey [New York: Manchester University Press, 1999], 36). He goes on to note (in the same page) that "the understanding that our future is more than our present . . . allows one to break out of the confining circle variously described by Collingwood, Foucault and Rorty, among others" in that "radical relativism involves a static conception or image of mind in which the mind is conceived as a closed system, the future states of which are contained in its present and consequently calculable in principle"; for Bergson, however, as Barden goes on to add, "the mind is not a closed system."

17. The importance of the virtual in recent philosophical studies of Bergson is highly indebted to the work of Deleuze. See, for instance, Deleuze, *Bergsonism* (New York: Zone Books, 1988).

18. Bergson, *Matter and Memory* (New York: Zone Books, 1991), 208. Hereafter cited in the text as (MM).

19. Bergson, *The Two Sources of Morality and Religion* (Notre Dame: University of Notre Dame Press, 1986), 258. Hereafter cited in the text as (TS).

20. I explore, in much greater detail, some of the issues that arise in any attempt to make a pragmatic assessment of nonordinary states of consciousness in chapter 5 of G. William Barnard, *Exploring Unseen Worlds: William James and the Philosophy of Mysticism* (Albany: State University of New York Press, 1997), 273–357.

21. Deleuze, *Bergsonism*, 34.

22. Capek correctly points out that William James makes much the same observation when James points out that "even a single and 'isolated' tone is not isolated, since it is perceived in the context of antecedent silence" (*Bergson and Modern Physics*, 327).

23. Ibid., 325.

24. Matthews, "Bergson's Concept of a Person," in *The New Bergson*, 133.

25. This perspective is very similar to one that I articulated in chapter 3 of *Exploring Unseen Worlds*, 209–10. The perspectives articulated by James and Bergson are highly compatible, albeit also different in several significant ways.

ELEVEN

Connecting Inner and Outer Transformation

Toward an Expanded Model of Buddhist Practice

Donald Rothberg

> In Zen there are only two things: you sit, and you sweep the garden.
> It doesn't matter how big the garden is.
>
> —Odo Sesso Roshi

WHAT FORMS OF spirituality are "called forth" by our rapidly changing times? While many are content to believe and practice in very traditional ways, and many have little use for religion or spirituality at all (and may be surprised by its modern and postmodern survival), others are deeply drawn to modify traditional spiritual forms and/or to create new forms. Such emerging forms might meet one or more of the following interrelated criteria:

1. They would support and integrate as wisely as possible the main *achievements* of modernity, which can briefly be expressed, following the work of Weber and Habermas, as: the critique of dogmatic religious claims and the related differentiation of the "objective," "intersubjective," and "subjective" worlds (now freed from the hegemony of dogmatic religion); and the ensuing development, respectively, of various forms of rationality, science, and technological innovation (linked with the exploration of the objective world); of democracy and community (in relation to the intersubjective world); and of the autonomous self and modern art (in relation to the subjective world).[1]

2. They would address many of the core *systemic problems* of modernity, such as its lack of integration—the fragmentation of the three worlds of modern

life from each other (e.g., the separation of science and much of the application of technology from intersubjective values and norms, or the separation of the subjective or private world from the two "public" worlds); the uneven development of the three worlds, for example, the lack of a full development of democracy (and the intersubjective domain), for various reasons, linked to capitalism, racism, sexism, etc.; and hyperindividualism, the decline of community, and the dominance of the autonomous rational self over the body, emotions, and spirit.[2]

3. They would also help us to respond with depth to many of the main *global practical concerns* of our times—linked to a large extent with the systemic problems of modernity—such as ecological crisis, particularly global warming; a high level of violent conflict; the increasing gap between rich and poor in the midst of globalization; the imperial ambitions of the militarily powerful, particularly the United States, and the related reactions from nonstate "terrorists"; and the weak state of global government (and the need for further development of global justice and global civil society).

4. They would give us a way to make sense of the diversity of religious and spiritual approaches, and to support "interfaith dialogue" and even the development of innovative religious and spiritual forms.

Such is one way of understanding the visionary horizon of contemporary spirituality, echoed by many who have begun to articulate spiritual responses to the challenges of our times.[3] It suggests that it may take the power and depth of spirituality—at its best, most mature, and most connected across various traditions and approaches—to respond to such challenges. To be sure, expressing such power and depth may appear a tall order, especially for many contemporaries for whom spirituality primarily means simply finding a way to have some peace and good heart in a complex and sometimes overwhelming world.

In this chapter, I want to articulate one way to begin to envision such a more mature, contemporary spirituality, through presenting an integrative framework for contemporary Buddhist practice. I first offer some of my personal background, particularly focusing on efforts to connect inner and outer transformation. Secondly, I give a more historical analysis making sense of some of the longstanding tendencies to separate inner and outer transformative work and of the modern understanding of spirituality as subjective, as well as identifying some of the available resources that help us to connect inner and outer. I then sketch the personal genesis and conceptual outlines of a general integrative spiritual framework, with a particular focus on Buddhist practice, as one way to make such a connection. In the last section, I identify some of the further implications of such a framework for contemporary spiritual practice.

To develop such forms is to express at least two aspects of a *participatory spirituality*, as the term is understood in this volume. First is the contemporary (and ancient) intuition and intention that spirituality be integrative, that spiritual principles and practices might guide the practitioner in all the domains of his or her life, both inner and outer, and in all aspects of his or her being, leading toward a sense of wholeness. This intuition is in tension with some traditional forms, including many derived from early Buddhism, in which certain domains and aspects of life (e.g., political life, much of ordinary work, or marriage, intimate relationships, and sexuality for monastics) are not normally part of the highest spiritual life. Second is the understanding of contemporary spirituality as in part a *creative response* to the particular demands of our times, of our current phase of the evolutionary journey. It is to see our contemporary period as a time of great challenge and transition, calling for widespread participation, cooperation, and dialogue related to developing such a response.

THE CHALLENGES OF CONNECTING THE SPIRITUAL AND THE SOCIAL: A PERSONAL ACCOUNT

By the time I was in my early twenties, I knew that I had two vocations, that I was dedicated to both spiritual and social, inner and outer, transformation. My first initiation, into a life attuned to social transformation, started while growing up in Maryland during the turbulent and revelatory 1960s. I had seen the poverty of African Americans firsthand, in the unpaved roads and dilapidated homes and shacks a mile away from my home. I also became more aware of the social structures and cultural attitudes that supported racism, as well as the details of our often imperial and militaristic foreign policy. In college, I studied politics, philosophy, history, and social theory, participated in many local and national demonstrations, worked in the U.S. Congress, lived in Paris and studied the French student and worker movements, and helped form a campus political group dedicated to social change. My intention to devote my life to helping to develop a more just society felt clear and unwavering.

Yet in my late teen years and early twenties, a second, equally compelling path opened up. I became deeply interested in understanding the deeper roots of injustice, human nature, and human potential, and was particularly drawn first to the study of philosophy and psychology, and then of consciousness, meditation, Western mysticism, and Asian spiritual traditions. I began a daily Buddhist mindfulness meditation practice that has continued to this day, and started attending meditation retreats lasting one to two weeks. These retreats deeply touched my heart and my very motivation for my life, as I contacted the sources both of suffering, fear, and greed, and of peace, understanding, and compassion.

The French writer Albert Camus once said that the life purpose of an individual is "nothing more than to rediscover . . . those one or two images in the presence of which . . . [one's] heart first opened."[4] Yet for me, it has been a major challenge to bring, in Camus' words, the two images—related to the two vocations of spiritual and social transformation—together. It has often seemed as if somehow I had to choose one or the other. To connect the two has been to travel on a long and sometimes lonely journey.

I would go to my social justice buddies and talk about the inner life and meditation. They would often look at me somewhat blankly and either tell me or imply by their sarcastic comments that I was basically being escapist, that I should be more active. Yet while in my meditation circles, I would often wonder why we were not paying more attention to the issues of daily life practice, to our interpersonal relationships, to questions of power and authority in our spiritual communities, to larger social concerns. Sometimes it seemed implied that we were "really living" only when we were on retreat or silently meditating, that the rest of our lives was somehow secondary and superficial. And yet it was not hard to notice that many of my spiritual friends' and even teachers' outer lives and relationships, as well as my own, seemed sometimes rather chaotic, and often without the peace and wisdom experienced in meditation.

HISTORICAL PERSPECTIVES ON THE RELATIONSHIP BETWEEN THE SPIRITUAL AND THE SOCIAL

My experiences of the split between the spiritual and the social, echoed by many reports of similar experiences from friends and colleagues across several generations and continents, suggest that there is likely a pervasive, structural basis for the split. Indeed, as we shall see, many of the core Western ways of categorizing and understanding ourselves and our world over the last few 2,500 years or so, and particularly the last few hundred years, rest on such a split, which has also been prominent in somewhat different ways in the history of Asian traditions, including Buddhism.

However, a split between the spiritual and the social has not always been the case, both globally and in the West. In indigenous cultures on every continent, for example, spirituality has been deeply embedded in all aspects of daily life, in all the core social structures and activities. In the traditions of India and China, there have been mainstream approaches that grounded spiritual life squarely in responsibilities to family and society (even as other approaches, as we shall see later, pointed to the need to leave family and society in order to achieve the greatest spiritual depth). Many of the modern exemplars of a socially engaged spirituality, such as Gandhi or contemporary indigenous resistance movements, draw sustenance from these ancient approaches.

At the dawning of recorded Western history, we also find a unity of the spiritual and the social—in the lives of the Jewish prophets. The prophets proclaimed their messages for some two hundred years, starting in the mid-eighth century BCE, calling for society to realize God's will. They spoke out forcefully against what they saw as the transgression of basic ethical principles, self-centeredness, greed, a lack of compassion for those who were suffering, and moral and spiritual hypocrisy. Their lives and actions deeply informed the life of Jesus and later Christianity, as well as Islam. The "prophetic tradition" has as well greatly influenced modern social and political movements, both secular and religious, including the contemporary work of such figures as Dorothy Day, Martin Luther King Jr., Abraham Joshua Heschel, Michael Lerner, Cornel West, Rosemary Ruether, Gustavo Gutierrez, and Enrique Dussel.

Yet there has also been the perhaps more dominant Western tradition, stemming especially from ancient Greek traditions, of separating the spiritual (or "contemplative") from the political or practical (the activity of *praxis* in the *polis*). This way of understanding the two perspectives has often rested on an opposition between the supposedly timeless, absolute, and other-worldly quality of spirituality (especially in its mystical forms), and the supposedly time-bound, historical, contingent, and this-worldly quality of social and political action.[5]

The opposition between the two goes at least back to the fourth century BCE. At that time, Aristotle systematized a distinction, in the context of Greek society, between "theory" (*theōria*) and "practice" (*praxis*); the latter refers particularly to the life of "political" discussion and decision making. The superior contemplative life of *theōria*, in which we come to know the eternal truths both conceptually and experientially, requires a suspension from the duties and constraints of practical, active life. The philosopher Plotinus, who would provide much of the intellectual framework for later Jewish and Christian mysticism through to the modern period, explained the need for this separation a few centuries later: "The point of action is contemplation. . . . Contemplation is therefore the end of action."[6] For Plotinus, furthermore, the contemplative knows the eternal apart from ordinary human life: "Such is the life of the divinity and of divine and blessed men: detachment from all things here below, scorn of all earthly pleasures, the flight of the lone to the Alone."[7]

This distinction of *theōria* and *praxis* has also been fundamental to the movement of modernity that emerged in the sixteenth and seventeenth centuries, connected with the rise of the sciences, capitalism and industrialism, democracy and individualism, and secularization. We find contemporary secular forms of the distinction between theory and practice in the separation between science and ethics, knowledge and values, objective and subjective, intellectual and activist, contemplation and action. Such polarities deeply structure and influence how we understand spirituality, social action, and their relationship.

With modernity, the split between the spiritual and social has been exacerbated because of the "antireligious" origins of this epoch. One of the basic starting points for the rise of the modern worldview is a fundamental and far-reaching critique of all religion and spirituality. In many ways, such a critique cleared the space so that scientists could study the "objective" world and the political revolutions could focus on democracy and rights, to a large extent without the constraints of religious authorities and dogma, without, for example, theologians and church functionaries serving as the arbiters of knowledge about the external world, the "divine" right of kings, or the identity of church and political rule.

The modern critics of religion have been many and vociferous—their gaze mostly focused on the forms of Christianity that they saw around them in the eighteenth, nineteenth, and early twentieth centuries. Some, like the French Enlightenment philosophers of the eighteenth century, criticized religion as inherently dogmatic and superstitious. Other philosophers and critics, inspired by the sciences, saw religion as irrational and not grounded in evidence. On that basis, they lambasted many religious claims—about the accounts of the Creation or about particular historical events reported in the Bible. Critics such as Freud saw religiosity as an expression of psychological immaturity, while others, such as Nietzsche, saw religion as a sign and cause of weakness of personality and lack of autonomy.

Still others criticized religion as socially oppressive, as linked with centuries of religiously inspired violence and war; a chronic collusion with despots, dictators, and the wealthy; and pernicious views justifying injustice and ignoring or legitimizing the suffering of the many. Another main reason, therefore, for the contemporary split between the spiritual and the social is the fact that many of the modern social justice traditions originated as explicitly antireligious movements. "Ni Dieu ni maitre" ("neither God nor Master") rang the nineteenth-century slogan of the French working-class and anarchist movements.

In the 1840s, Karl Marx articulated his famous analysis of religion as fundamentally escapist, as the "opium of the people." He reversed the primacy of *theōria* in favor of the primacy of *practical reason*, rejecting the contemplative life:

> All social life is essentially *practical*. All the mysteries which lead theory into mysticism find their rational solution in human practice and in the comprehension of this practice. . . . Philosophers [contemplatives in the traditional sense] have only *interpreted* the world . . . the point is to *change* it.[8]

This series of critiques typically led either to the outright rejection of religion and spirituality in the modern world, or to their marginalization as merely *subjective*. There was no or little place for religion in the distinctively *modern public worlds*, whether in the collective quest for objective knowledge about the world grounded in the sciences or in the intersubjective pursuit of democracy and social justice. Religious views, of course, could be expressed.

But there could not be a publicly acceptable *religious* basis for public policies, according to the dominant interpretation of the separation between church and state.

Thus, religious and spiritual pursuits have had increasingly to find a home of sorts outside of the public worlds of science and technology, on the one hand, and social and political action, on the other. They have in this way tended to become primarily "private" and "subjective," even when the vast majority of the population claims religious beliefs, as in the United States. And so most live in the private world during evenings and weekends, while typically living in the public world weekdays from nine to five. To the extent that the modern world holds sway (and it is clearly losing power with the current United States administration), the right to choose and explore faith and religion privately is correlated with their increasing public irrelevance.

In this context, it is not surprising that the revival of spirituality in the modern world should come at first especially through an emphasis on the *subjective* dimensions of spirituality. Kierkegaard, writing in the mid-nineteenth century and providing a beacon for many modern seekers, emphasized the deepening of subjectivity, particularly through reflection, art, and religion. He directed the spiritual aspirant away from the public realms of science, ethics, and public discourse: "Subjectivity," the private world, "becomes the truth. . . . To seek objectivity is to be in error."[9] Authenticity is not possible in the social world: "The public is a monstrous nothing."[10]

Kierkegaard is thus presenting the main *modern* spiritual option. In a way, he accepts Marx's distinction between the spiritual and the social, while reversing his finding as to what is important. Yes, the spiritual and the social are and should be split apart. But, contrary to Marx, the spiritual as private and subjective is the only thing that really matters. Max Weber summarized both the process of secularization and the privatization of spirituality:

> The fate of our times is characterized by rationalization and intellectualization and, above all, by the "disenchantment of the world." Precisely the ultimate and most sublime values have retreated from public life either into the transcendental realm of mystic life or into . . . direct and personal human relations.[11]

Much of the recent Western renewal of spirituality in North America and western Europe has also taken markedly subjective forms, particularly as an intense individual quest toward breakthrough experiences and self-actualization. This has had its roots in a number of different sources, including humanistic and transpersonal psychology, the human potential movement, and psychedelics. Asian traditions have been commonly presented in the West as offering ways of inducing deep subjective experiences.

To be sure, such an interpretation of Asian traditions has some basis in those traditions themselves, where there has sometimes been a marked tension between interpretations of the spiritual life as requiring abandoning society, on the one hand, or as being socially engaged, on the other. Patrick Olivelle writes of the dramatic changes in India in the period around the time of the Buddha (the sixth century BCE), leading to a new emphasis on liberation from the suffering of ordinary human life:

> The religions sharing this world view challenged the society-centered ritual religion of the earlier Vedic period. The result of this confluence of two opposing worlds was a deep and lasting conflict within Indian religions between the value of responsible social engagement within the context of marriage and family and the ascetic withdrawal from society that was seen as the necessary precondition for achieving liberation.[12]

This tension can be found within Buddhism. The Buddha did suggest such a withdrawal, counseling the serious spiritual practitioner to leave the everyday world of family and society, what he sometimes called the "dusty, crowded" world, to become a monk or nun and focus on individual transformation. And yet the Buddha also sometimes expressed concerns about cultivating the conditions for social harmony, and intervened several times to prevent wars. The five ethical precepts given by the Buddha—to refrain from killing, stealing, lying, sexual misconduct, and the harmful use of intoxicants—have often been interpreted as guidelines for society; the great Indian king Asoka (third century BCE) gave edicts based on the precepts, including caring for animals and eliminating the death penalty. The Mahayana ("great vehicle") Buddhist movement, which arose at the time of Jesus, popularized the inspiring figure of the bodhisattva, dedicated to the awakening both of self *and* of others, and grounded in compassion for the suffering of others.

Thus, when Westerners began meditating in larger numbers some thirty-five years ago, they were set up for a kind of conflict. They were primed to approach meditation as a mostly subjective exploration leading to wonderful, life-transforming experiences and understandings. Yet many, including myself, had just come through a highly volatile period of major social turmoil, deep awareness of many social problems, and commitment to social change. We seemed to have to choose between the two. Or we could reject such a choice as a false one, as I did, following the call that many of us were continuing to hear—to integrate inner and outer transformation—increasingly aware of some of the resources, Western, Asian, and indigenous, for such an integration.

DEVELOPING A FRAMEWORK FOR SOCIALLY ENGAGED SPIRITUAL PRACTICE

After I moved to northern California in 1988, I began to find a critical mass of people interested in connecting the spiritual and the social. A number of them participated in the work of the Buddhist Peace Fellowship (BPF), based in Berkeley, a nonprofit membership organization founded in 1978 of some four thousand current members, mostly in North America but also extending into Asia, Australia, and Europe. Within a few years, I began to feel as if I had found a kind of *home* in the extended community of BPF and other socially engaged Buddhists, as well as with those from other traditions and approaches—Jewish, Christian, Islamic, Hindu, pagan, and indigenous—where the spiritual and social were equally welcome, where the core intention was to connect the two.

I became active in BPF and elsewhere, organizing and often teaching at workshops, classes, and summer institutes, as well as beginning to publish articles and training guides. I also began attending some of the annual meetings in Thailand of the International Network of Engaged Buddhists (INEB), founded in 1989, at which I came to know better a number of Asian Buddhists who had long connected the spiritual and social, including the Thai writer and activist Sulak Sivaraksa; the Cambodian spiritual teacher, monk, and activist Mahaghosanada; and many others.

In 1995, I began working as one of two mentors for a new BPF program founded by Diana Winston—the Buddhist Alliance for Social Engagement (BASE) program, inspired especially by the Catholic Worker and the primarily Latin American "base community" movement linked with Catholic liberation theology. We have had more than twenty-five BASE programs in the last twelve years, each bringing together small groups of twelve or fewer people, all of them grounded in spiritual practice and engaged in the world through some kind of social service and/or social change work, either through employment or volunteer work. Some later BASE groups would be organized around a specific focus, forming separate groups for educators, those working in prisons, young people, those doing diversity work, and those working with the homeless—the latter became, of course, Home BASE.

There was one meeting in the first BASE group where I experienced more clearly than before a heightened sense of integration of the spiritual and the social. One evening, one of our group members, who was working part-time at a homeless shelter, reported how that week she had felt the suffering there to be emotionally overwhelming for her. It was too much; she was saturated and could hardly function. In her exploration of this experience with the group, she was able, first of all, to explore her emotions and to look at the personal and psychological dimensions of her responses and reactions, how she had historically related to the suffering of those less well off, how this triggered her own suffering, and how she might work with some of the more personal underlying issues.

As a group that evening, we also, secondly, examined our understandings and practice of the basic Buddhist teachings about the nature of suffering, grounded in the Four Noble Truths proclaimed by the Buddha at the beginning of his teaching career. These teachings point to the possibility both of opening to the pain and suffering of a given situation, and finding ways, through practice, to transform our reactivity in relation to painful occurrences, leading to healing and further freedom.

Thirdly, we brought in some of the social and institutional dimensions of the problem of homelessness: the "deinstitutionalization" of the early 1980s that brought so many persons, including many of the nearly one-third of the homeless who are mentally ill, into the streets; the blaming and even demonization of the homeless in public discourse; and the question of who is responsible for the homeless.

That evening felt to me like a homecoming. I saw that the group was a place where we could look openly at *any* aspect of personal, group, or collective experience when there was an issue or concern, using the resources of psychology, spiritual teachings and practice, and history or social theory. All of these domains or perspectives were welcome; none were off limits. I could also see, furthermore, how these aspects were connected. I did not have to separate out the inner from the outer, the spiritual from the social.

Starting around 2000, my colleagues and I began developing more systematic approaches to integrative spiritual trainings for social engagement. Along with Ann Masai and Jürgen Kremer, I started a two-year interfaith program in "Socially Engaged Spirituality" at Saybrook Graduate School in San Francisco. It was somewhat modeled after the BASE program and combined eight four-day retreats, the study of many of the world's traditions of socially engaged spirituality, on-line work together between retreats, the commitment of each person to ongoing spiritual practice and engagement in the world, and a focus on the group as a microcosm for connecting inner and outer transformation.[13]

I also continued, along with Diana Winston, to clarify the elements of a socially engaged Buddhist training, in writings as well as classes, workshops, and retreats. Grounded in traditional teachings and practice, particularly the traditional Buddhist emphasis on three general aspects of training—ethics, meditation, and wisdom—we articulated over several years a number of *guiding principles* that bridge inner and outer work, eventually developing a (nonexhaustive) list of ten core principles:

1. *Establishing the Conditions for Safety:* Following the basic ethical guidelines, which provide the "container" for all transformative work, inner and outer.[14]
2. *Mindfulness in Action:* Cultivating open, mindful presence in the midst of activities, cutting through our tendencies to be distracted and reactive.
3. *Clarifying Motivation, Setting Intention:* Discriminating between skillful and unskillful intentions and aligning our actions with our deepest values.
4. *Opening to Pain and Suffering, Opening to Compassion:* Learning to be present and nonreactive with pain and suffering, leading to compassionate action.

5. *Taking Care of Myself, I Take Care of the World:* Balancing caring for both self and others.
6. *Not Knowing But Keeping Going:* Remaining open to what is unknown, mysterious, and confusing, listening deeply, and avoiding dogmatic views.
7. *Interbeing:* Cultivating a sense of interdependence of self and other, studying our tendencies to rigidly separate "self" and "other," "us" and "them."
8. *Acting from Equanimity:* Bringing increasing balance, nonreactivity, and understanding to our actions, while avoiding complacency and resignation.
9. *Transforming Anger:* Working skillfully with anger's powerful and sometimes destructive energy, preserving insight into injustice, yet transforming reactivity.
10. *Committed Action, Non-Attachment to Outcome:* Maintaining a deep commitment to compassionate action, freedom, and justice, whatever happens.[15]

We also identified *practices* linked with these principles, and three basic *domains* (which of course could be further subdivided) in which we carry out transformative work: *the individual, the relational, and the collective.* So, for example, we can practice in the *individual* domain, working with the personal, experiential, psychological, and behavioral dimensions of a given situation. We can also look at the *relational* domain, at our interaction in dyads, couples, families, groups, organizations, or communities. Lastly, we can examine our participation in the *collective* domain, in larger social, cultural, political, economic, and ecological, systems, understanding the influence of powerful cultural attitudes as well as institutional policies and structures.

AN INTEGRATED MODEL OF SOCIALLY ENGAGED PRACTICE

We now had a training framework. It was simple and, hopefully, elegant enough that it could be accessible to many people, but also comprehensive and complex enough to lead to considerable creativity and unexpected discoveries and insights. The ten principles could provide powerful lenses through which to understand and transform our experience, each linked with specific practices in each of three domains. We could develop a general map of a training curriculum, which we could read in various ways. We might focus on working with a given principle across domains, or examine a particular domain across multiple principles.

We can notice, furthermore, that a given principle will typically be interpreted somewhat differently, and generate somewhat different practices, in each domain. So we might talk about nonharming, one of the five basic Buddhist ethical guidelines, in terms of how we treat ourselves (the individual domain), how we relate to others interpersonally (the relational domain), and, for example, how we participate as citizens in relation to a government that often harms or kills in our name (the collective domain). We might explore clarifying and setting intentions personally (the individual domain); in a group or organization (the relational domain), for example, through articulating vision and mission statements; or in terms of helping to develop clearer social priorities (the collective domain). We might examine how the process of opening to suffering looks, when we are exploring personal grief (the individual domain), exploring major conflicts—concerning interpersonal issues or power—in a community (the relational domain), or bringing attention to the often hidden suffering of institutionalized racism or poverty through personal witnessing, study, writing, and nonviolent action (the collective domain).

It also became clear that *each of the three domains interpenetrates each of the other domains*. This sense of interpenetrating domains suggests a number of different ways that we might learn, a number of modes of potential spiritual practice. We can talk, for example, about how an *individual* practitioner explores the basic nature of being an *individual* human being. And so in mindfulness meditation (or in some other contemplative practice), we investigate the very nature of bodily sensations, the range and patterns of our emotions and ways of thinking, and general structures of human experience as such. We might of course focus at times on specific practices in one of these areas (somatic, emotional, cognitive, and general) for a sustained period. We can, secondly, also work *individually* with aspects of our *relational* experience, in meditation or reflection, as when we consider patterns of family conditioning, or how we work with conflict in the context of an intimate relationship. Similarly, we can, thirdly, inquire *individually*, by oneself or sometimes in a group, workshop, or retreat, into how we have each internalized *collective* conditioning, as when we contemplate our own racism, sexism, homophobia, or consumerism, in terms of our inner experience and our behavior. Or we might work individually with investigating our reactions and responses to collective events such as violence, war, or ecological crisis, as we are guided to do, for example, in many of Joanna Macy's practices.[16]

In a like manner, we could understand *the practitioner and the field of practice, not just as an individual but as a relational unit* that can focus on the individual, relational, or collective domains. We can work *relationally*, in a dyad, group, or community, for example, while focusing on an *individual*, much as often occurs in psychotherapy or in work with a spiritual teacher or in a group. We can work *relationally* in exploring the *relational* unit itself, whether in looking at group dynamics or interpersonal relationships or in reaching a community-wide decision. Lastly, we can work *relationally* while concerned with *collective* matters, such as when we see how cultural attitudes such as racism or sexism manifest in relational life, or when we consider how we will respond as a group or organization to a collective problem like global warming or a particular governmental policy.

Finally, we can speak of the *collective as practitioner*, although somewhat more tentatively, since this area of practice is less developed. Still, we might interpret South Africa's Truth and Reconciliation Commission (TRC), guided by Desmond Tutu, as exemplifying a *collective* body, representing a nation, which at times worked *individually*. As the TRC invited stories to be told publicly by individuals of some of the apartheid era's horrors, many experienced considerable *individual* healing.[17] We might also interpret the groundbreaking nonviolence of Gandhi, King, and others as developing a kind of *collective* spiritual practice, with social movements as "practitioners," in relation both to more *relational* concerns, perhaps of a given community, and to *collective* issues such as independence (for example, of India from Great Britain), civil rights, or foreign policy. In this latter context, we can think of mass nonviolent training and the ensuing practice of nonviolent demonstrations or civil disobedience as a kind of collective practice oriented to influencing the whole society.[18]

Considering the interpenetration of domains yields a model of nine fields or modes of spiritual practice, shown in Table 11.1:

Domain *Practitioner*	**Individual**	**Relational**	**Collective**
Individual			
Relational			
Collective			

TABLE 11.1. A Matrix of Nine Modes of Spiritual Practice

IMPLICATIONS OF THIS
EXPANDED MODEL OF BUDDHIST PRACTICE

Reflecting on this matrix suggests a number of implications for how we understand spiritual practice in general, how the spiritual and the social become split off, and how we can expand our spiritual practice so that it might take place in all parts of our lives. In the remainder of this chapter, I would like to explore some of these implications.

Our Spiritual Work Is the Same in Any Domain

In this model, our core intention is to transform self and other—and the social space and structures in and through which we appear—in ways suggested by the core principles. We establish the conditions for safety, or learn better to be mindful, or learn to open to pain and suffering, or cultivate equanimity, in each of the interpenetrating domains.

In other words, our spiritual practice is increasingly *seamless*. Wherever we are, the intention is the same. Spiritual practice is everywhere, whether we are on the cushion, at a meeting, or debating foreign policy! The core transformative principles apply in every domain. This understanding can lead to a sense of wholeness and integration in our lives (as well as sometimes to a sense of there being no escape from spiritual practice!).

The fact that we have recourse to the same principles in different parts of our lives also suggests that it may be possible to "transfer" our learning in one domain to that in another domain. What I learn about working with anger individually may be of great benefit to my ability to be skillful with anger in a group or collective setting, both in terms of individual abilities and in terms of my general understanding. What I learn in the latter settings may continue a process of learning about anger that can then inform my practice with my personal anger.

Many Spiritual Approaches Are Based on a
Very Limited Conception of Spiritual Practice

If we look at Table 11.1, it becomes apparent that many wonderful and powerful traditional models of spiritual practice, including many models derived from Buddhism, focus mostly on the upper-left block in the matrix, that of the individual exploring, we might say, the basic nature of existing as a human being and developing further in virtuous individual qualities. This is certainly the case with classical Buddhist mindfulness meditation, even though we can extend mindfulness to any activity, including those of our relational and collective lives, and even though such meditation is often complemented by practices that open the heart (developing in lovingkindness, compassion, joy, and equanimity), in which the individual does transformative work relationally and collectively. Furthermore, in traditional Buddhist monastic practice, there is often also a strong emphasis on the communal dimension of practice (which is often weaker or even absent in the Western secular context).

Such a general form of contemplative practice, which brings us individual awareness of the basics of individual human experience, plays a fundamental role in spiritual life. Yet if such a practice is taken to constitute the *entirety* of our spiritual practice, especially in Western contexts, then we may find ourselves leaving the relational and collective parts of our lives *as such* relatively uninformed by our core spiritual intentions, except insofar as these areas surface in our own individual practice. I may be aware of how *I* am grasping after this aspect of our relationship or afraid in relation to a particular collective situation, but in these cases my practice is confined to my own individual, "inner" response to what is "outer" rather than being explored through a dyadic relational practice or a collective way of responding to a given event.

At the extreme, our community or society becomes a collection of individuals "working on themselves" without any shared relational or collective practices. This can occur because we have (usually only implicitly) assumed that *one of nine* possible forms of spiritual practice (the individual working on the individual) is the only or main or most important form. Those who make this assumption often come, naturally enough, to the conclusion that "all we can do is work on ourselves." They may also claim that society is somehow simply the manifestation of all individuals; we can best contribute to society, if we are interested in that, by doing our own individual spiritual work. The counterpart of this view is held by many secular activists, who believe that the individual is simply a kind of "product" of social conditioning, and that "all we can do is work on society." In both cases, individual spiritual practice and collective social action are separated.

Most of the Possible Modes of Spiritual Practice Are Relatively Unexplored and Undeveloped

In approaches in which spirituality and spiritual maturity have often been limited to the upper-left block, that of the individual working on the individual, it is also no surprise that there are typically few or no forms of spiritual practice associated with the other eight blocks. Those who ask about bringing spiritual intentions to politics, for example, may be told that spiritual practice does not enter that domain; the "map" of spiritual practices does not include participating in political activity as a possible mode of practice.

I encountered this view in 1980, when I met the well-known Korean Zen teacher, Kusan Sunim. I asked him a question about how Buddhist practice had helped in responding to the crisis of martial law and massive political repression occurring at that time in Korea; there had just been a massacre of up to two thousand demonstrators in Kwangju advocating "democracy." He answered (through a translator), "That is politics. We do religion. The two are separate."

Among others, however, there is an ongoing openness to exploring new forms of spiritual practice, as in the widespread interest in connecting psychology and spirituality, in understanding intimate relationships as spiritual practice, or in developing a socially engaged spirituality. Still, this matrix can help clarify why the development of the whole range of modes of practice is important and deserves considerable priority in our times—so that more parts of our lives can be areas of learning and development linked with our deepest aspirations.

The matrix can also help us see why it is important to highlight the *socially* engaged dimension of spirituality. In modern Western societies, as we have seen, it is quite common to deny or ignore the more collective (and even relational) dimensions of spirituality, focusing instead on spirituality as private, subjective, and experiential. Consequently, it is an important step to identify these domains *as locations of spiritual practice*, and this is one reason to use terms such as *socially engaged*. The danger, however, is that these terms themselves implicitly reproduce the very split between the spiritual and the social that is supposedly being remedied. In some contexts, the term *socially engaged* can even encourage or communicate the polarization between the two, suggesting that we are *only* dealing with the social, and not giving attention to the personal. Consequently, in the long run, it may be more accurate to speak of an *integrative* spirituality. Others use the term *integral* with similar intentions, as in the name of the California Institute of Integral Studies or in the development of "integral transformative practices" by George Leonard, Michael Murphy, and others, or in Ken Wilber's "integral" approach.[19]

The work of identifying other forms of spiritual practice, however, is far more than simply a matter of a mapping function. It also frees us to *explore* new territories and even new phenomena that have not been investigated in depth. For example, how might our learning in groups or collectivities manifest these (and other) core spiritual principles? What does mindfulness look like in a transformative group? Is there only the individual mindfulness of each group member or is there an "emergent" group mindfulness? How do we set intentions or work with anger relationally? What does it mean to develop a spiritually grounded ethical approach in terms of our larger ecological and economic systems? Inquiring into the territory opened up by these questions may constitute a significant part of our efforts to express an integrative spirituality.

UNDERSTANDING THE INTERPENETRATION OF DOMAINS
SUGGESTS THE INSEPARABILITY OF THE INDIVIDUAL
AND SOCIAL DIMENSIONS OF SPIRITUAL PRACTICE

An Asian American man tells the story of being at a long Buddhist insight meditation retreat and communicating to his meditation teacher that issues related to racism and ethnicity were surfacing. The teacher responded, "We don't deal with those kinds of issues here. Just pay attention to your individual experience, to the basics of experience."

An African American woman gives a similar account, talking about some of the group dynamics, in a silent retreat, that for her were difficult in the context of her upbringing in the black church. However, after hearing one teacher advise her that such issues were out of place, she found another teacher who was able to integrate her concerns with the more traditional emphases of the retreat.[20]

These examples suggest some of the myriad ways in which ethnicity plays a role in our spiritual lives. We might easily add similar examples having to do with gender, class, and other issues. But if the map of a spiritual path does not leave room for addressing these kinds of issues, are we leaving out important areas, both of suffering and of potential growth and learning?

More broadly, we can ask: What does it mean to focus on individual practice if (to use Buddhist language) part of the greed, hatred, and delusion of the spiritual student is related to his or her internalization of social conditioning—of racism, sexism, privilege, consumerism, national chauvinism, and so on? How does recognition of this interpenetration of domains (which has also only recently been explored in the area of psychotherapy) lead us to shift, if sometimes only in subtle ways, the nature of spiritual practice or the nature of being a spiritual teacher? How do we understand the wounds that each of us carries that call out for attention and possible healing? What kinds of awareness or training in particular should teachers have in being able to be aware of the nature of these wounds and of the ways that we internalize dominant social attitudes?

Having a broader model of the modes of spiritual practice can begin to facilitate an understanding of the problems that occur when this interpenetration of domains is not recognized, when whole domains of possible inquiry and practice are "off the [dominant] map." Such a model can also help us in exploring these challenging questions.

THIS MATRIX CAN BE USED AS A GUIDE FOR OUR OWN INTEGRATIVE SPIRITUAL PRACTICE

For most of us who are active in the world, if we are to approach a seamless spiritual life, we need ways to understand ourselves as developing spiritually in *all* the parts of the our lives. The matrix can be a guide, inviting us to ask a series of questions, whether as an individual, a group, or a larger culture and society: In which of the nine blocks have I (or we) focused the most? Where am I (or we) most developed? Where are my (or our) "gifts" located? Where am I (or we) least developed? What territories have I (or we) least explored? Where is it important for me (or us) to develop? In which areas can I (or we) be of most service to the world? How well do I see the interpenetration of the different domains in my life?

As we more consciously take on the intention to develop spiritually in the different domains, there arises a deeper sense of integration, of the breadth of spiritual practice. We also can begin to discern better where we are *particularly* called to contribute, how we don't "have to do everything" with equal depth, how the most *depth* may occur in the areas of our strongest interests, gifts, and callings. With an integrative understanding, we can feel more connected with others, even if we are not giving so much energy to one or more areas of the matrix; we can see more easily how our own contributions are connected with those of others, leading to less of a sense of isolation.

SMALL TRANSFORMATIVE PRACTICE GROUPS MAY PLAY A SPECIAL ROLE IN HELPING US TO INTEGRATE THE DIFFERENT AREAS OF SPIRITUAL PRACTICE

How do we integrate our practice in these different areas of the matrix? Many will primarily be left to their own devices in finding ways to work transformatively in the more relational and collective areas or perhaps be guided by teachers or mentors who work with this expanded sense of practice.

An important role may be played by small transformative practice groups of between eight and twenty people, similar to the BASE groups described earlier and the "base communities" of Latin America . They may resemble in some ways the more secular activist "affinity groups," women's "consciousness-raising" groups, political councils and collectives, or small town meetings in the American democratic tradition. Such groups, functioning in the "intermediate" relational domain, may be well situated to open up both to the individual and to the collective. Furthermore, such groups may function as a microcosm, and help us bring light to both problems and virtues that may not manifest so clearly in individual practice, where it is possible to "hide out" in ways that are no longer possible in relationships or group settings.

TRANSFORMATIVE WORK IN ONE DOMAIN REVERBERATES IN THE OTHER DOMAINS

Given the interconnection and interpenetration of the domains, we know that when we develop individually, our learning has relational and collective effects. This occurs in several ways. First, a grounding in contemplative practice (such as mindfulness meditation), for example, provides a kind of "laboratory" in which we study in depth the principles and dynamics of transformation, which we can then apply in other domains. Our individual training becomes a kind of reference point which both orients us in the other two domains, and can be influenced by learning in these domains.

Second, our grounding in individual transformation may give us some perspective and faith that support our commitment for the long haul. We may learn more clearly that no transformative practice is wasted, just as the Buddha once said that every moment of mindfulness matters. All transformative moments in any domain matter. All such moments have an effect, often hard to discern.

Third, we know from the lives of the Catholic monk Thomas Merton (1915–1968), living in a Trappist monastery in Kentucky, or the Thai Buddhist monk Buddhadasa (1906–1993), living in a forest monastery near the Malaysian border in the south of Thailand, that relatively solitary meditation can have a great impact on social change. Both spent virtually all of their lives in monasteries, engaged primarily in contemplation and writing, although within communities. Yet their writings touched and guided thousands. Leaders of social movements made pilgrimages to their monasteries, both for renewal and for inspiration and guidance.

Daniel Ellsberg tells the story of meeting the poet, activist, and Zen practitioner Gary Snyder by chance at a bar near the Zen monastery of Ryoanji in Kyoto, Japan, in 1960. Ellsberg was living in Tokyo, working on nuclear weapons policy for the Office of Naval Research, through the Rand Corporation. Snyder was then midway through a nearly ten-year period of Zen practice, staying at or near Zen monasteries for the bulk of the time. Ellsberg had gone to see the Zen garden at Ryoanji because he had read about it in Jack Kerouac's *The Dharma Bums*, in which a lightly fictionalized Snyder was the major figure. The impact and memory of Ellsberg's conversations with Snyder at the bar and the next day at Snyder's cottage, Ellsberg later reported, played a significant role in his decision, some nine years after the meeting, to divulge the *Pentagon Papers*, the secret history of the planning of the Vietnam War. Ellsberg's action was a major contribution to the turn against the war in public opinion in the United States.[21]

Such an awareness of the interpenetration of domains may thus strengthen our faith in the rather mysterious nature of change, whether individual, relational, or collective. It may remind us that change is always possible, that forces are operating in ways not always known to us, even when we may think things stuck or believe change impossible. We have only to remember the recent examples of the end of apartheid in South Africa and the fall of the Soviet Union, happening only a short time after such changes were unimaginable to most.

THE LIMITS OF THIS MODEL

Even as this model can support a broadened sense of spiritual practice, it is important to remember that it nonetheless reflects a major simplification of experience, as do all models. Like any model, this one both reveals and conceals.

"Reality" itself is far more complex. We could easily talk of far more than three domains, particularly subdividing the relational and collective domains into primary relationships, groups, organizations, communities, regional or bioregional organizations, ecosystems, and so on. We could identify more precisely the varied dimensions of individual experience (cognitive, emotional, somatic, sexual, energetic, intuitive, etc.) and chart how these dimensions manifest relationally and collectively. We could focus on the extent to which the domains are organized according to *gender-related constructions*, perhaps talking about how some of the core principles have both "masculine" and "feminine," or "active" and "receptive" expressions.

We might also distinguish how each domain has an *inner and outer* side to it; for example, the "collective" manifests both in cultural ideas and attitudes, and in social structures, while we can look at both individual "inner" experience and "outer" behavior. And we could give more attention to *developmental* dynamics in each of the domains, including how certain practices presuppose certain competences or developmental achievements.

Furthermore, it is helpful to remember that the model itself is not just a simplification but also an *abstraction*, what Weber called an "ideal type." At its best, it can help illuminate experience. But it is also important to reflect that each of the domains and modes of practice interpenetrate and interconnect, so that we never really have one mode of practice, one of the nine blocks, in total isolation. Even the most individual and apparently isolated practice takes place in a community and social context, even for the hermit in isolation for ten years.

CONCLUSION

The fuller development of an integrative spirituality offers both a direct response to the fragmentation of the modern world and a basis for addressing directly the core concerns of our time. Such an expansion of our sense of spiritual practice might also support a movement beyond hyperindividualism, a revitalization of democracy and community, and offer powerful resources helping us to respond to violence and crisis.

In the emphases both on integration and on developing responses to contemporary problems, there are significant "participatory" dimensions, as the term is used in this volume. As we expand our understanding of spiritual practice, we invite, as it were, all dimensions of human life to participate, including those in many cases previously excluded from spiritual life for various reasons. We also invite collaboration and cooperation from others, as we explore relatively uncharted spiritual territories and cocreate innovative spiritual practices and understandings. In a rapidly globalizing world, we can imagine the vitalization of creative participation in this work extending both within and across traditions and approaches, as we all grapple with and attempt to respond to the issues of modernity and postmodernity. As we increasingly find that our concerns and challenges are the same or similar, we may find that bringing love, wisdom, and compassion to all parts of our lives may also lead us to participate in a common work and play, whatever our differences.

NOTES

1. See Donald Rothberg, "The Crisis of Modernity and the Emergence of Socially Engaged Spirituality," *ReVision* 15 (1993): 105–14; Hans Gerth and C. Wright Mills, eds., *From Max Weber* (New York: Oxford University Press, 1946); Habermas, *The Theory of Communicative Action, Vol. 1: Reason and the Rationalization of Society*, trans. Thomas McCarthy (Boston: Beacon Press, 1984).

2. See, for example, Habermas, *The Theory of Communicative Action, Vol. 2: Lifeworld and System: A Critique of Functionalist Reason*, trans. McCarthy (Boston: Beacon Press, 1987); Robert Bellah, Richard Madsen, William Sullivan, Ann Swidler, and Steven Tipton, *Habits of the Heart: Individualism and Commitment in American Life* (New York: Harper and Row, 1985).

3. See Roger Gottlieb, *Joining Hands: Politics and Religion Together for Social Change* (Boulder: Westview, 2002); Michael Lerner, *Spirit Matters* (Charlottesville, VA: Hampton Road Publishing Co., 2000); David Loy, *The Great Awakening: A Buddhist Social Theory* (Boston: Wisdom, 2003); Joanna Macy and Molly Young Brown, *Coming Back to Life: Practices to Reconnect Our Lives, Our World* (Gabriola Island, British Columbia: New Society Publishers, 1998); Rosemary Reuther, *Gaia and God: An Ecofeminist Theology of Earth Healing* (San Francisco: HarperSanFrancisco, 1992); Charlene Spretnak, *States of Grace: The Recovery of Meaning in the Postmodern Age* (San Francisco: HarperSanFrancisco, 1991); Ken Wilber, *Sex, Ecology, Spirituality: The Spirit of Evolution* (Boston: Shambhala, 1995).

4. Quoted in Michael Meade, *Men and the Waters of Life: Initiation and the Tempering of Men* (San Francisco: HarperSanFrancisco, 1993), 10. The passage is from Camus' preface to *L'envers et l'endroit* (1958; reprint, Paris: Gallimard, 1986).

5. Richard Woods, "Mysticism and Social Action: The Mystic's Calling, Development, and Social Activity," *Journal of Consciousness Studies* 3 (1996): 158–71.

6. Elmer O'Brien, ed., *The Essential Plotinus*, 2d ed. (Indianapolis: Hackett, 1981), 167 (Enneads, III, 8: 30, 6).

7. O'Brien, 88 (Enneads VI, 9: 9, 11).

8. Eugene Kamenka, ed., *The Portable Karl Marx* (New York: Penguin Books, 1983), 157–58. These are the eighth and eleventh of the famous "Theses on Feuerbach" written in 1845.

9. Kierkegaard, from *Concluding Unscientific Postscript*, in *A Kierkegaard Anthology*, ed. Robert Bretall (New York: Random House, 1946), 181.

10. Kierkegaard, "The Present Age," in Bretall, 265.

11. Weber, "Science as a Vocation," in Hans Gerth and C. Wright Mills, *From Max Weber: Essays in Sociology* (New York: Oxford University Press, 1946), 155.

12. Olivelle, "Ascetic Withdrawal or Social Engagement," in *Religions of India in Practice*, ed. Donald Lopez (Princeton: Princeton University Press, 1995), 533.

13. See Rothberg, "An Interfaith Training Program in Socially Engaged Spirituality," *Turning Wheel: Journal of the Buddhist Peace Fellowship* (Summer 2006): 36–37, 43.

14. Training in *ethics* traditionally involves, for lay persons, taking five basic ethical precepts as guidelines (rather than as pronouncements by an external authority). These precepts counsel us to refrain, as best we can, from acting in ways in which we harm or kill others (including nonhumans), take that which is not given, speak falsely or harmfully, or abuse sexuality or intoxicants.

15. For a fuller account of these principles, see my book, *The Engaged Spiritual Life: A Buddhist Approach to Transforming Ourselves and the World* (Boston: Beacon Press, 2006). In the writing of that book, I modified somewhat the list of principles that Diana Winston and I had developed from 2001 to 2004 in our teaching. The list outlined in this essay reflects these changes.

16. See Macy and Brown, *Coming Back to Life*.

17. See Rothberg, "Truth, Justice, and Reconciliation in South Africa: A Conversation with Bongani Blessing Finca," *Turning Wheel: Journal of the Buddhist Peace Fellowship* (Fall 2001): 27–31; Antjie Krog, *Country of My Skull: Guilt, Sorrow, and the Limits of Forgiveness in the New South Africa* (New York: Three Rivers Press, 2000).

18. In his early work, especially in *Knowledge and Human Interests* (Boston: Beacon Press, 1971), Habermas also explored analogies between individuals, groups, and societies as "subjects." Following the reception of this text, he has been more circumspect about such analogies, recently writing: "I have been more cautious when using the expression 'emancipation' beyond the area of the biographical development of individual persons, since social collective, group, or communities cannot be imagined as subjects writ large" (*Religion and Rationality: Essays on Reason, God, and Modernity*, ed. Eduardo Mendieta [Cambridge: The MIT Press, 2002], 160).

19. For an overview of integral transformative practices, see Jorge N. Ferrer, "Integral Transformative Practice: A Participatory Perspective," *Journal of Transpersonal Psychology* 35 (2003): 21–42. See also George Leonard and Michael Murphy, *The Life We Are Given* (New York: Putnam, 1995); Murphy, *The Future of the Body* (New York: Jeremy Tarcher/Putnam, 1992), 541–86; and Wilber, "Integral Transformative Practice: In This World or Out of It?" *What is Enlightenment?* 18 (2000): 34–39, 126–27, 130–31.

20. See Sheridan Adams et al., eds., *Making the Invisible Visible: Healing Racism in Our Buddhist Communities*, 2d ed., 2000 (available from Buddhist Peace Fellowship or online at <http://www.spiritrock.org/display.asp?pageid=318&catid=2&scatid=31>).

21. Ellsberg, "The First Two Times We Met," in Jon Halper, *Gary Snyder: Dimensions of a Life* (San Francisco: Sierra Club Books, 1991), 331–39.

Contributors

G. WILLIAM BARNARD is associate professor of Religious Studies at Southern Methodist University. Author of *Exploring Unseen Worlds: William James and the Philosophy of Mysticism* (SUNY Press, 1997) and coeditor (with Jeffrey J. Kripal) of *Crossing Boundaries: Essays on the Ethical Status of Mysticism* (Seven Bridges Press, 2002). Professor Barnard is currently researching the thought of the French philosopher Henri Bergson. He is also a teacher in a school of alternative/ energy healing directed by his wife Sandra: the Full Spectrum Healing Arts School, located in Meadville, PA.

BRUNO BARNHART is a monk at the New Camaldoli Hermitage, Big Sur, California. Since concluding his service as prior of the Big Sur community, Fr. Bruno has been largely occupied with study, teaching, and writing on the Christian sapiential (wisdom) tradition and its rebirth in our time. He is the author of *The Good Wine: Reading John from the Center* (Paulist Press, 1993) and *Second Simplicity: The Inner Shape of Christianity* (Paulist, 1999), editor of *The One Light: Bede Griffiths's Principal Writings* (Templegate, 2001), and coeditor (with Joseph Wong) of *Purity of Heart and Contemplation: A Monastic Dialogue between Christian and Asian Traditions* (Continuum, 2001).

WILLIAM C. CHITTICK is professor of Asian and Asian-American studies in the State University of New York at Stony Brook. He is the author of *The Sufi Path of Love: The Spiritual Teachings of Rumi* (SUNY Press, 1983), *The Sufi Path of Knowledge: Ibn al-'Arabi's Metaphysics of Imagination* (SUNY Press, 1989), and *Imaginal Worlds: Ibn al-'Arabi and the Problem of Religious Diversity* (SUNY Press, 1994), among many other books and scholarly articles.

JORGE N. FERRER is chair of the Department of East-West Psychology at the California Institute of Integral Studies, San Francisco. He is the author of *Revisioning Transpersonal Theory: A Participatory Vision of Human Spirituality*

(SUNY Press, 2002) and editor of a *ReVision* monograph on *New Horizons in Contemporary Spirituality* (Heldreff Publications, 2001). Born in Barcelona, Spain, he received the Fetzer Institute's Presidential Award in 2000 for his seminal work on consciousness studies. Professor Ferrer teaches classes on comparative mysticism, transpersonal studies, and embodied spiritual inquiry.

LEE IRWIN is director of Religious Studies at the College of Charleston, where he teaches in the areas of Native American spirituality, Western esotericism, and contemporary spirituality. He is the author of many articles and five books, including *Visionary Worlds: The Making and Unmaking of Reality* (SUNY Press, 1996) and *Awakening to Spirit: On Life, Illumination, and Being* (SUNY Press, 1999).

SEAN KELLY is professor of Philosophy, Cosmology, and Consciousness at the California Institute of Integral Studies, San Francisco. He is the author of *Individuation and the Absolute: Hegel, Jung, and the Path toward Wholeness* (Paulist Press, 1993), coeditor (with Donald Rothberg) of *Ken Wilber in Dialogue: Conversations with Leading Transpersonal Thinkers* (Quest, 1998), and co-translator of Edgar Morin's *Homeland Earth: A Manifesto for the New Millennium* (Hampton Press, 1999).

BRIAN L. LANCASTER is director of the Consciousness and Transpersonal Psychology Research Unit at Liverpool John Moores University and honorable research fellow in the Centre for Jewish Studies at Manchester University. He has authored several books, including the award-winning *Mind, Brain, and Human Potential* (Element Books, 1991), *The Elements of Judaism* (Element Books, 1993), and *Approaches to Consciousness: The Marriage of Science and Mysticism* (Palgrave, 2004). He has published numerous articles, which have ranged over areas of neuroscience as well as religious mysticism. Dr. Lancaster is currently chair of the Transpersonal Psychology Section of the British Psychological Society. He teaches postgraduate programs in transpersonal psychology both online and by attendance. He is an active member of the UK Jewish community, where he teaches Jewish meditation and Kabbalah.

BEVERLY J. LANZETTA is a professor of Religious Studies who has been a faculty at leading liberal arts institutions over the last fifteen years. Currently a visiting scholar and research associate at the Southwest Institute for Research on Women (University of Arizona, Tucson), she is also a retreat leader, spiritual director, and author of numerous articles and books on mysticism and the spiritual life, such as *The Other Side of Nothingness: Toward a Theology of Radical Openness* (SUNY Press, 2001), *Radical Wisdom: A Feminist Mystical Theology* (Fortress Press, 2005), and *Emerging Heart: Global Spirituality and the Sacred* (Fortress Press, 2007).

ROBERT McDERMOTT is president emeritus and professor of Philosophy and Religion at the California Institute of Integral Studies, San Francisco. He was formerly professor and chair of the Department of Philosophy at Baruch College, CUNY (1970–90) and secretary of the American Academy of Religion. His publications include *Radhakrishnan* (Dutton, 1970), *The Essential Aurobindo* (Lindisfrane Press, 1974), and *The Essential Steiner* (Harper and Row, 1984), as well as essays on comparative philosophy and religion in scholarly journals and anthologies.

DONALD ROTHBERG, a member of the Spirit Rock Center's Teachers Council in Northern California, writes and teaches classes, groups, and retreats on Buddhist meditation, spiritual practice in daily life, epistemology and spirituality, transpersonal studies, and socially engaged Buddhism, in the San Francisco Bay Area and nationally, and directs an eighteen-month interfaith program in Socially Engaged Spirituality for Saybrook Graduate School. A long-time organizer, teacher, and board member for the Buddhist Peace Fellowship, he has practiced Buddhist meditation for more than twenty-five years and has also been significantly influenced by other spiritual traditions, particularly Jewish, Christian, and indigenous. An editor of *ReVision: A Journal of Consciousness and Transformation* for ten years, Donald is the coeditor (with Sean Kelly) of *Ken Wilber in Dialogue: Conversations with Leading Transpersonal Thinkers* (Quest Books, 1998) and author of *The Engaged Spiritual Life: A Buddhist Approach to Transforming Ourselves and the World* (Beacon Press, 2006).

JACOB HOLSINGER SHERMAN is at Emmanuel College, Cambridge, and is completing his PhD in the Faculty of Divinity at the University of Cambridge. He was previously an adjunct faculty member at the California Institute of Integral Studies (CIIS), San Francisco, where he taught courses on Christian spirituality, the history of Western worldviews, and Romantic philosophy.

Index